MINDFULNESS AND PERFORMANCE

Incorporating the theoretical conceptualizations of Jon Kabat-Zinn and Ellen Langer, this volume illustrates how performers from a variety of disciplines – including sport, dance, and music – can use mindfulness to achieve peak performance and improve personal well-being. Leading scholars in the field present cutting-edge research and outline their unique approaches to mindfulness that are supported by both theory and practice. They provide an overview of current mindfulness-based manuals and intervention approaches used around the globe in countries such as the United States, China, and Australia, exploring their effectiveness across cultures. *Mindfulness and Performance* will be a beneficial reference for practitioners, social and sport psychologists, coaches, athletes, teachers, and students.

AMY L. BALTZELL is Clinical Associate Professor of Counseling and Applied Human Development at Boston University, where she directs graduate training in sport psychology. Her publications include *Living in the Sweet Spot: Preparing for Performance in Sport and Life* and *Whose Game Is It, Anyway? A Guide to Helping Your Child Get the Most from Sports, Organized by Age and Stage* (with Richard D. Ginsburg and Stephen Durant).

CURRENT PERSPECTIVES IN SOCIAL AND BEHAVIORAL SCIENCES

Current Perspectives in Social and Behavioral Sciences provides thought-provoking introductions to key topics, invaluable to both the student and scholar. Edited by world-leading academics, each volume contains specially commissioned essays by international contributors that present cutting-edge research on the subject and suggest new paths of inquiry for the reader. This series is designed not only to offer a comprehensive overview of the chosen topics, but to display and provoke lively and controversial debate.

Forthcoming titles:

Genetics, Ethics and Education, edited by Susan Bouregy, Elena L. Grigorenko, Stephen R. Latham, and Mei Tan

Creativity and Reason in Cognitive Development, 2nd edition, edited by James Kaufman and John Baer

Nurturing Creativity in the Classroom, 2nd edition, edited by Ronald A. Beghetto and James C. Kaufman

Teacher Motivation, edited by Helen Watt, Paul Richardson, and Kari Smith

Research and Theory on Workplace Aggression, edited by Nathan A. Bowling and M. Sandy Hershcovis

Culture, Mind, and Brain: Emerging Concepts, Models, and Applications, edited by Laurence J. Kirmayer, Shinobu Kitayama, Carol M. Worthman, and Constance A. Cummings

MINDFULNESS AND PERFORMANCE

EDITED BY

AMY L. BALTZELL

Boston University

CAMBRIDGE
UNIVERSITY PRESS

CAMBRIDGE
UNIVERSITY PRESS

32 Avenue of the Americas, New York, NY 10013–2473, USA

Cambridge University Press is part of the University of Cambridge.

It furthers the University's mission by disseminating knowledge in the pursuit of education, learning, and research at the highest international levels of excellence.

www.cambridge.org
Information on this title: www.cambridge.org/9781107074699

© Cambridge University Press 2016

First published 2016

Printed in the United States of America

A catalog record for this publication is available from the British Library.

Library of Congress Cataloging in Publication Data
Mindfulness and performance / Amy L. Baltzell, editor.
pages cm
Includes bibliographical references and index.
ISBN 978-1-107-07469-9 (Hardback : alk. paper)
1. Mindfulness (Psychology)   2. Performance–Psychological aspects.
3. Meditation–Therapeutic use.   I. Baltzell, Amy, editor.
BF637.M4M567 2016
158.1–dc23   2015027875

ISBN 978-1-107-07469-9 Hardback

*I dedicate this book to my three children,
Shayna Daisy, Luke Henry, and Zoey Violet.*

In the end, just three things matter:
How well we have lived
How well we have loved
How well we have learned to let go
— Jack Kornfield

Contents

Figures

Tables

Contributors

ITAI IVTZAN, PH.D. *University of East London, England*

RONA HART, PH.D. *University of East London, England*

ZELLA E. MOORE, PSY.D. *Manhattan College, U.S.A.*

AMY L. BALTZELL, ED.D. *Boston University, U.S.A.*

SUSAN JACKSON, PH.D *Queensland University of Technology and Body and Mind Flow Consulting, Australia*

SAYYED MOHSEN FATEMI, PH.D. *Harvard University, U.S.A.*

ELIZABETH D. WARD, PH.D. *Harvard University, U.S.A.*

ELLEN J. LANGER, PH.D. *Harvard University, U.S.A.*

FRANK L. GARDNER, PH.D. *Touro College, U.S.A.*

KEITH A. KAUFMAN, PH.D. *The Catholic University, U.S.A.*

CAROL R. GLASS, PH.D. *The Catholic University, U.S.A.*

TIM R. PINEAU, PH.D. *The Catholic University, U.S.A.*

LORI HAASE, PH.D. *University of California, San Diego, U.S.A.*

GÖRAN KENTTÄ, PH.D. *Stockholm University, Sweden*

STEVEN HICKMAN, PSY.D. *University of California, San Diego, U.S.A.*

MARTIN PAULUS, M.D. *Laureate Institute for Brain Research, U.S.A.*

PETER HABERL, ED.D. *United States Olympic Committee, U.S.A.*

GANG-YAN SI, PH.D. *Hong Kong Institute of Education, China*

KAREN LO, ED.M. *Hong Kong, China*

CHUN-QING ZHANG, PH.D. *Hong Kong Institute of Education, China*

JO MITCHELL, PH.D. *AFL Players' Association & The Mind Room, Australia*

CRAIG HASSED, MBBS, FRACGP *Monash University, Australia*

REBECCA SHANGRAW, ED.D. *Boston University, U.S.A.*

VANESSA LOVERME AKHTAR, ED.D. *Kotter International Center for Leaders, U.S.A.*

JESSYCA ARTHUR-CAMESELLE, ED.D. *Western Washington University, U.S.A.*

TREVOR A. COTE, M.A., DOCTORAL STUDENT *Boston University, U.S.A.*

GENE M. MOYLE, D.PSYCH. *Queensland University of Technology, Australia*

PATSY TREMAYNE, PH.D., *University of Western Sydney, Australia*

ASHLEE MORGAN, PH.D. *University of Melbourne, Australia*

TIM PATSTON, PH.D. *Geelong Grammar School* and *University of Melbourne, Australia*

JOE MANNION, M.S. DOCTORAL STUDENT *Pepperdine University, U.S.A.*

MARK ANDERSEN, PH.D. *Halmstad University, Sweden*

JOHN M. MCCARTHY, ED.D. *Boston University, U.S.A.*

LAURA HAYDEN, ED.D. *University Massachusetts, U.S.A.*

BURT GIGES, M.D. *Springfield College, U.S.A.*

GERALD REID, M.A. DOCTORAL STUDENT *Boston University, U.S.A.*

JOSH SUMMERS, LIC. AC. *Boston, U.S.A.*

Preface

I have been a sport psychologist for the past fifteen years – primarily running a graduate training program in sport psychology at Boston University and working with athletes, teams, coaches, and musicians in private practice. I became interested in mindfulness about ten years ago, when I began teaching courses in positive psychology. Gratefully, I had the opportunity to bring Joshua Summers into the classroom to teach my students (and me) about mindfulness and mindfulness mediation. I quickly began to understand that the concept of mindfulness had a depth and offered great potential for helping one to become more fully alive and optimize performance, if the individual could learn to cultivate a mindful approach to living and performance. The challenge, of course, is learning how to cultivate a mindful approach in one's own life and then learning how to bring the approach to others.

Parallel to my teaching, I began to realize that the athletes and musicians who came to me for help were often wrestling with debilitative perform-ance anxiety. I turned to the traditional cognitive behavioral interventions offered by the field of sport psychology. Sometimes these strategies worked for my clients – I would help them create phrases to bring to mind in the predictably most difficult sport moments (being behind in a close game or losing a foot race or boat race by inches and still needing to concentrate on task relevant cues). Or I would help them create imagery scripts of coping with difficulty and, at once, creating an optimal performance experience. Yet, for some athletes, such strategies came up woefully short. And I had nothing to offer but my instincts cultivated from my own experience as an Olympian (rowing) and professional athlete (sailing).

However, I began to realize that it was not just my own experience facing intense anxiety as an elite athlete that was helping me help my clients. I began to realize that what I was doing with them was precisely this: I was helping them learn to cultivate a mindful approach to their competitive performance life. Instead of turning away from fear, I offered my clients strategies and support to tolerate such thoughts, feelings, and physical sensations. I began to see radical change in my clients' internal experience and ability to perform under pressure. I had athletes who would pass out from fear on the field, could not swing a tennis racquet, or were unable to complete a track and field race. With a mindfulness approach, these issues were surprisingly and quickly resolved. At this time, I also began to conduct research on mindfulness in performance. From my own research, I was seeing, firsthand, athletes learning to have a changed relationship to pre-performance anxiety, mistakes on the field, and general debilitative comparisons to others (particularly for the higher-level, elite athlete). As I immersed myself in the mindfulness literature and research, I soon began to realize that we are just at the beginning of this journey of understanding how mindfulness practices help performance (or do not) and how best to cultivate such (beneficial) mindfulness practices.

An edited book on mindfulness and performance became a dream – to bring together top thinkers and practitioners. Through serendipity, good luck, and the courage to ask, we have been given this extraordinary opportunity by Cambridge University Press to compile this volume. I had the courage to create an A-list of contributing authors, and as you can see from the table of contents, they all joined the project. I could not be more grateful and delighted. I see this book as a place for top research-ers, theorists, and top applied practitioners in the field to share their most current thinking within the arena of mindfulness and performance. I consistently experience a deep gratitude to each of you for sharing your ideas and work. The ultimate goal is to bring mindfulness approaches in a wise and productive way to a wide range of performers – from athletes, musicians, and dancers to underserved youth. Although there is still much to be done, this book is an amazing compilation of what we currently know, and together we offer ideas about the next steps in how to best practice mindfulness and what needs further empirical consideration.

With much love and appreciation,
AMY BALTZELL

Acknowledgments

I would like to thank so many people for their support, encouragement, and inspiration. Thank you to all of the chapter authors; you have so generously shared your cutting-edge ideas as researchers and practitioners. I created my A-list of the chapter authors I hoped to secure, and you all agreed. This compilation of chapters is truly extraordinary due to your willingness to join the project and share your expertise from around the world. Thank you to my three children – Shayna Daisy, Luke Henry, and Zoey Violet – for their patience throughout the many early mornings, afternoons, evenings, and weekends when I needed to spend "just a little more time" on this manuscript. Thank you to my many athlete clients who allowed me to share with them a new way of working, of allowing me to support them in cultivating a mindful approach to their own sport and music performance. Thank you, John McCarthy; you have always supported me and encouraged me to follow my heart and do the work that intersects with my skills, passion and aspiration to help others. Thank you to my students at Boston University, who have challenged me and helped me think through these new ideas within the realm of mindfulness and performance. Thank you to my research assistant Trevor Cote; your devoted, tireless, passionate engagement with this manuscript was inspiring and incredibly helpful. Thank you, Dr. Cathy O'Connor, my mentor; you support and challenge me to do the very best that I can, in all instances. And thank you to my best friend Bronwyn Malicoat, who is consistently interested, loving and encouraging in both my best and worst of moments. And, finally, thank you to Cambridge University Press, and in particular David Repetto, for this incredible opportunity.

Introduction to Mindfulness: History and Theoretical Understanding

CHAPTER I

Mindfulness Scholarship and Interventions: A Review

Itai Ivtzan, Rona Hart

In the past three decades, an exponential increase has occurred in the research and theorising on mindfulness, coupled with a growing demand for and application of mindfulness interventions by practitioners, in clinical and nonclinical settings (e.g., Kabat-Zinn, 2009; Langer & Ngnoumen, 2014). Mindfulness is often associated with positive psychology and considered a primary facet of psychological well-being (Brown, Ryan, & Creswell, 2007). At the same time, the research provides consistent evidence attesting to the effectiveness of mindfulness interventions in lessening several physical and psychological conditions (Baer, 2003; Grossman et al., 2004).

The literature on mindfulness has been dominated by the two leading schools of thought: one advanced by Kabat-Zinn and his associates (e.g., Kabat-Zinn, 2003), which draws on Buddhist meditative practices and is often labeled as an Eastern approach to mindfulness, and the other developed by Langer and her colleagues (e.g., Langer 1989), which is and considered a Western approach to mindfulness. We aim, in this chapter, to offer an overview of mindfulness scholarship and interventions by examining both approaches to mindfulness. The chapter discusses the definitions, mechanisms and components of mindfulness, as these are conceptualised by the two approaches. We also briefly review their measurement tools and examine their respective interventions and outcomes.

The chapter opens with a review of Kabat-Zinn's Eastern meditation–based approach, then discusses Langer's Western approach. Both of these sections begin by reviewing scholars' conceptions of mindfulness and then presents a description of the features of mindfulness and their underlying mechanisms, the interventions that each school of thought uses to increase mindfulness, a brief review of their measurement tools, and the evidence regarding their benefits. The closing section discusses the main findings of this review.

The Eastern Meditation–Based Approach to Mindfulness

Definitions and Features

The Buddhist meditative approach to mindfulness was introduced and initially trialled in the West by Kabat-Zinn and his associates in the 1970s. It is considered *therapeutic* in its orientation, since it uses mindfulness meditation practice as a means to alleviate physical and mental conditions. Drawing on Buddhist philosophy, Kabat-Zinn (1994) defines mindfulness as 'paying attention in a particular way: on purpose, in the present moment, and nonjudgmentally' (p. 8). Baer (2003) explains that this entails observing *external* events as well as *internal* experiences as they occur. Kabat-Zinn (2005) describes mindfulness as a 'being' mode and contrasts it with mindlessness, which is he describes as an automatic-pilot 'doing' mode. Wallace (2005) argues that the upshot of this habitual mindless mode is an unregulated mind, where the mind becomes an unreliable mechanism for exploring internal or external experiences. The goal of mindfulness practice is therefore to develop the self-regulatory abilities of a disciplined mind (Kabat-Zinn, 2005).

Kabat-Zinn (1994) draws on the Buddhist concept of mindfulness – *sati* in Pali, which entails awareness, attention and remembering. *Sati* is the key component in insight meditation, which is perceived as a method for noticing how the mind creates suffering. Its aim is to relieve suffering, by improving one's metacognitive awareness and regulatory processes (Wallace, 2005). Shapiro, Carlson and Astin (2006) maintain that mindfulness practice entails three essential components: practitioners' *intention* in mindfulness practice, directing their *attention* to internal or external experiences as they transpire, and the *attitude* that meditators bring to mindfulness practice. Brown and colleagues (2007) maintain that there are six elements that make up the *attention* component: being *present-focused*, having *clarity* as to what one observes, being *nondiscriminatory*, being *flexible*, taking a *value-free stance* towards one's experiences and gaining *stability of attention*. Shapiro, Schwartz and Santerre (2005) unpack the *attitude* component, suggesting that it may contain some or all of the following qualities: *not judging* what is observed; *accepting* one's experiences as they are; being *grateful*; *letting go* of thoughts, feelings or experiences; being *gentle*; *not striving* (not forcing things); being *open-minded*; having *patience* and *trust*; and being *generous, empathetic* and *caring* towards others.

The description offered here of what mindfulness entails may give an impression that this is a cognitive mode that one may experience when meditating. This perception is also promoted by the unclear use of term 'mindfulness' in Kabat-Zinn and his colleagues' work, which is used both to signify a wakeful mindful mode, as well as the means to cultivate it: mindfulness meditation (see, for example, Didonna, 2009; Kabat-Zinn, 2009). This conceptual ambiguity has been noted and critiqued by several authors (Bishop et al., 2004; Brown et al., 2007). However, Kabat-Zinn (2003) clarifies that mindfulness meditation is a training process that is geared to develop meditators' metacognitive and self-regulatory skills and aims to enable practitioners to extend periods of mindfulness in their everyday life. Kabat-Zinn's definition thus suggests that mindfulness entails (1) self-regulation of one's attention, (2) directing one's awareness to internal or external experiences, (3) metacognitive consciousness and (4) adopting an accepting attitude.

Mindfulness Meditation–Based Interventions

Drawing on the complex construct of mindfulness previously described, Kabat-Zinn and his colleagues developed and launched the Mindfulness-Based Stress Reduction (MBSR) program at the University of Massachusetts Medical School in 1979 and have been offering the program ever since (Kabat-Zinn, 1982, 2009). MBSR is a protocolled group-based mindfulness intervention program. It includes eight to ten weekly meetings in which participants are offered mindfulness meditation instruction and practice, yoga exercises, group discussions and individual support. In addition, participants are expected to practice mindfulness meditation at home (forty to sixty minutes per day). Most programs include an intensive mindfulness meditation retreat (for a day or two) (Center for Mindfulness in Medicine, Health Care, and Society, 2014; Kabat-Zinn, 2009).

The program was originally offered as a complementary treatment for patients with chronic pain (Kabat-Zinn, 1982, 1996). Over the years, it has been successfully tested on a range of other conditions and is currently offered as a preventative treatment for people at risk of cancer, heart disease and several chronic illnesses or as a means to relieve the secondary symptoms (such as pain and fatigue) associated with these conditions. It is also offered to patients with a variety of psychological symptoms, such as stress, depression, anxiety, panic, post-traumatic stress disorder (PTSD) and sleep disturbances. Its goal is to reduce physical and psychological ailments through the enhancement of patients' self-regulatory capacities, which are developed through the daily practice of mindfulness meditation (Kabat-Zinn, 1982, 2003).

MBSR was inspired by Buddhist retreats, where participants meditate for hours motionlessly, which often resulted in pain in muscles and joints. Meditators are encouraged not to relieve the ache and instead to direct their attention to the pain and the thoughts, emotions or impulses that arise, while assuming a nonjudgmental attitude towards them. The ability to acknowledge pain with acceptance is believed to relieve the distress that it provokes, since it develops the understanding that the pain sensations, thoughts or emotions are 'just thoughts', and not reality, and thus do not necessitate avoiding them (Baer, 2003; Kabat-Zinn, 1996). Kabat-Zinn (1982) claims that the exposure to pain without catastrophising it can reduce the emotional reactivity prompted by it, thus leading to desensitisation, which in turn eases the pain.

Kabat-Zinn and colleagues (1992) describe a similar procedure that can be applied for the moderation of psychological disorders. They claim that repeated accepting attentiveness to troubling thoughts or emotions, without escaping them, could diminish the emotional reactivity and thereby relieve the symptoms. The assertion of the MBSR approach is that with habitual exercise, patients can become skilful at being less reactive towards their physical or psychological symptoms and more able to experience less adverse patterns of thinking and behaviour (Shapiro et al., 2006).

Since its inception, MBSR has been followed by hundreds of studies that attest to its effectiveness in improving a variety of physical and psychological conditions and in promoting well-being (see the review later in this section). Following these encouraging reports, several versions of MBSR have been developed and trialled to address particular conditions, such as Mindfulness-Based Cancer Recovery (MBCR) (Carlson & Speca, 2010); Mindfulness-Based Therapy for Insomnia (MBT-I) (Ong & Sholtes, 2010); Mindfulness-Based Intervention for People with Diabetes (DiaMind) (van Son et al., 2014); Mindfulness-Based Mind Fitness Training (MMFT) for military personnel (Stanley et al., 2011) and Mindfulness-Based Childbirth and Parenting Education (Duncan & Bardacke, 2010).

Several of these protocolled interventions combine mindfulness with principles of Cognitive Behavioural Therapy. Among these, one of the leading interventions is the Mindfulness-Based Cognitive Therapy (MBCT) for depression (Segal, Williams, & Teasdale, 2002). It was originally designed to prevent relapse in patients with history of depression but has later been trialled successfully with others mental disorders (such as anxiety, PTSD, psychosis and bipolar disorder) (Chiesa & Serretti, 2011).

Its main purpose is to enable participants to develop a metacognitive perspective: to observe their own thoughts, understand the mechanisms by which negative automatic thoughts (NATs) trigger depressive symptoms and be able to severe the connection between NATs and habitual depressive emotional or behavioural responses (Barnhofer et al., 2009). However, unlike the conventional cognitive therapy methodology, which is designed to challenge the contents and the legitimacy of NATs, MBCT trains participants to observe their thoughts and emotions nonjudgmentally and accept them.

Based on the MBCT principles described here, several other interventions have been developed and tested, including Dialectical Behaviour Therapy (DBT) for treating borderline personality disorder (Linehan, 1993); mindfulness-based eating awareness for eating disorders (MB-EAT) (Kristeller & Wolever, 2010); CALM pregnancy for perinatal anxiety (Goodman et al., 2014); Mindfulness-Based Relapse Prevention (MBRP) for substance abuse (Witkiewitz et al., 2014); Mindfulness-Based Tinnitus Stress Reduction (MBTSR) (Gans, O'Sullivan, & Bircheff, 2013); and Acceptance and Commitment Therapy (ACT) (Hayes, Strosahl, & Wilson, 1999), which uses mindfulness interventions to increase psychological flexibility in patients exhibiting various symptoms of psychological distress.[1]

Mechanisms of Mindfulness

The core mechanism of the previously mentioned interventions is mindfulness meditation. Meditation is defined as 'a family of techniques which have in common a conscious attempt to focus attention in a non-analytical way' (Shapiro, 1980, p. 14). The goal of meditation practice is 'the development of deep insight into the nature of mental processes, consciousness, identity, and reality, and the development of optimal states of psychological well-being and consciousness' (Walsh, 1983, p. 19). Olendzki (2009) emphasises that this is a deeper level of perception that is exercised during meditation, a *mode of being*, that meditators aim to bring into their daily lives.

The common meditative techniques can be divided into three main types (Shapiro et al., 2005):

---

[1] ACT does not integrate mindfulness meditation practice, but it is considered a mindfulness intervention since it adheres to mindfulness principles of present-moment consciousness and acceptance.

- *Concentrative meditations:* In concentrative practices, practitioners attempt to control their attention by *focusing* on a single object or idea while ignoring other internal or external stimuli. Awareness is thus focused on the object of meditation, which could be one's breathing, a mantra, a word, a phrase or a sound. The attitude that meditators adopt is nonevaluative. Transcendental meditation and loving-kindness are both considered concentrative practices (Siegel, Germer, & Oldenzki, 2009).

- *Mindfulness meditations:* In mindfulness practices, practitioners attempt to notice whatever predominates their awareness in the moment – internally or externally. They aim to bring an attitude of openness, acceptance and kindness to observed experiences, and avoid evaluating, criticising, altering or attempting to stop these experiences, even when they are taxing (Baer, 2003). Mindfulness meditations are considered mental practices for *opening up* attention, thus, the objective is *not to select* a particular object to focus on, but to notice the shifting experiences (Siegel et al., 2009). Zen meditation is an example of a mindfulness practice. Several authors note, however, that mindfulness meditations include a combination of mindfulness and concentrative techniques, and that concentrative techniques facilitate mindfulness practice (Shapiro, Walsh, & Britton, 2003; Siegel et al., 2009).

- *Contemplative meditations:* These types of meditation involve appealing to a larger spirit (God or a benevolent other) and *asking,* while accepting a state of not knowing. From this responsive position, practitioners may ask questions and bring up unresolved issues. Contemplative meditation practices require some skill in concentration and mindfulness meditations, since it is necessary to have the capacity both to focus and to remain open (Shapiro et al., 2005).

Most meditations involve a dynamic process of monitoring and regulating awareness, where meditators engage their minds (according to the type of meditation they are practicing), and then they are likely to notice that their mind has wandered off. When noting this, meditators aim to come off their train of thoughts gently and return their attention to their key activity, with acceptance and tolerance. This process is repeated when required due to the mind wandering in all types of meditation (Olendzki, 2009). Thus, the essence of the process is not the *content* of consciousness, but the *process* of managing it (Didonna, 2009).

The main mechanisms in mindfulness meditation practice are *decentring,* becoming aware that we are continuously flooded by our river of thoughts; and then *disidentification,* being able to disengage from those thoughts (Kabat-Zinn, 1994; Shapiro et al., 2006). Several authors claim that mindfulness meditation has the capacity to alter our relationship with our thoughts by offering a method through which we can step back from and be less attached to our thoughts, thereby stripping them from the meaning, weight and emotional tone that we ascribe to them, and allowing us to acknowledge and accept them (Chiesa, Anselmi, & Serretti, 2014). Shapiro and colleagues (2006) claim that this change in our perception towards our thoughts is the core mechanism in all mindfulness interventions. They term it *reperceiving* and argue that it is the key to the management of distress, since it quiets the mind and lessens the types of thinking that trigger distress symptoms. Through habitual practice, meditators can strengthen their metacognitive skills, thereby increasing their capacity to direct their awareness at will in their daily lives (Vago, 2014).

The Measurement of Mindfulness

Over the years, several mindfulness questionnaires have been developed in order to assess the degree to which mindfulness meditation practice improves trait or state mindfulness. All of these are self-report measures that have been shown to have robust psychometric characteristics (Baer et al., 2008). The following eight questionnaires measure mindfulness as a disposition, the general inclination to be mindful (or mindless) in everyday life. Though the scales reflect a disposition of mindfulness, mindfulness scores have improved based on mindfulness meditation interventions.

The Freiburg Mindfulness Inventory (FMI)
The FMI is a thirty-item questionnaire designed to measure nonjudgmental, present-focused attentiveness and openness to *negative* experiences (Buchheld, Grossman, & Walach, 2001). It specifically targets experienced meditators. A shorter questionnaire with fourteen items was later developed (Walach et al., 2006) that is considered more suitable for nonmeditators. High scores in both questionnaires were correlated with self-awareness and self-knowledge, lower levels of dissociation and psychological distress among meditators.

The Kentucky Inventory of Mindfulness Skills (KIMS)
The KIMS is drawn from DBT and includes thirty-nine items quantifying four aspects of mindfulness: *observing, describing, acting with awareness and*

nonjudgmental acceptance (Baer, Smith, & Allen, 2004). The authors found significant positive correlations with happiness, gratitude, optimism, satisfaction with life, openness to experience, emotional intelligence, emotional regulation and persistence. Negative correlations were observed with distress scores, stress, anxiety, dissociation, experiential avoidance, alexithymia and depression.

The Cognitive and Affective Mindfulness Scale-Revised (CAMS-R)

The CAMS-R is a twelve-item questionnaire that measures mindfulness as a single factor but can offer subscores for *attention regulation, maintaining focus, awareness* and *accepting* thoughts and feelings (Feldman et al., 2007). Positive correlations were reported between the CAMS-R and measures of well-being (happiness, satisfaction, hope) as well as with emotional regulation, problem analysis and cognitive flexibility. Negative correlations were found with depression, anxiety, rumination, worry, experiential avoidance and thought suppression.

The Philadelphia Mindfulness Scale (PHLMS)

The PHLMS is a twenty-item questionnaire that measures two components of mindfulness: *awareness* and *acceptance* (Cardaciotto et al., 2008). Negative correlations were found between the PHLMS and anxiety, depression and stress.

The Southampton Mindfulness Questionnaire (SMQ)

The SMQ is a sixteen-item clinical inventory that assesses the extent to which respondents mindfully react to *upsetting thoughts and emotions* (Chadwick et al., 2008). It is designed to capture four aspects: *mindful observation, nonaversion, nonjudgmental attitude* and *letting go*. Meditating participants scored higher on the SMQ compared to nonmeditating, and in a clinical trial of MBSR, significant differences were found between pre- and posttests. It was also positively correlated with positive affect.

The Toronto Mindfulness Scale – Trait Version (TMST)

The TMST includes thirteen items and can be scored across two factors: *curiosity* and *decentring* (Davis, Lau, & Cairns, 2009). Participants scored higher after participation in MBSR (Lau et al., 2006).

The Five-Facet Mindfulness Questionnaire (FFMQ)

The FFMQ was developed using items from several existing measures of mindfulness to explore the multifacetted nature of mindfulness (Baer et al.,

2006). The questionnaire has thirty-nine items and includes five sub-scales: *observing, describing, acting with awareness, nonjudging of inner experience* and *nonreactivity to inner experience.* The FFMQ was found to be positively correlated with emotional intelligence and openness to experience, and correlated negatively with thought suppression, alex-ithymia and experiential avoidance. Meditators scored higher compared to nonmeditators. Among meditators, all factors were positively linked with psychological well-being and negatively associated with psycho-logical distress. Scores have also improved following meditation courses (Baer et al., 2006).

In addition to the trait questionnaires reviewed in the preceding, one self-report measure of *state* mindfulness has been developed for meditators.

The Toronto Mindfulness Scale – State Version (TMSS)

The TMSS is similar to the trait version reviewed earlier (with subtle changes to the wording of items and instructions) (Lau et al., 2006). It includes thirteen items and aims to examine the achievement of a mindful state *during* meditation, and thus participants are asked to complete it immediately after a meditation session. Significant correlations were found between the TMSS and self-awareness. Respondents scored higher on TMSS following participation in MBSR, and scores in the decentring factor predicted lower levels of psychological disorders.

The Outcomes of Mindfulness Meditation–Based Interventions

During the past thirty years, extensive research has been conducted to examine the psychological and physiological effects of mindfulness meditation–based therapies (MBTs) (Marchand, 2012; Ospina et al., 2007). Most of these studies assessed the effectiveness of protocolled interventions, particularly MBSR and MBCT, and a few included mind-fulness meditation instruction solely. Several studies examined whether MBTs increase mindfulness scores (however these are measured). Their findings indicated that these interventions indeed led to improvements in trait mindfulness, as well as state mindfulness (Brown & Ryan, 2003; Lau et al., 2006; Shapiro et al., 2011).

Some of the most intriguing research findings on the benefits of MBTs emerged from studies using brain-imaging technology and medical examinations. Several studies found that the electrical activity of the brain is responsive to MBTs, prompting a rise in beta activity (associated with wakefulness) alongside increased alpha and theta waves (both typically generated in a state of relaxation) (Chiesa & Serretti, 2010). A number of studies found growth in grey matter concentration in several areas of the brain following a few weeks (four to eight) of MBTs, thus suggesting that systematic practice in mindfulness meditation can change the constitution and performance of the brain. These areas are associated with consciousness, attention, cognition, self-awareness, self-referential thinking, cognitive monitoring, introspection, memory, sensory and visual processing, regulation of emotional responses and behavioural control (Chiesa & Serretti, 2010). Additionally, several studies reported increases or decreases in activation in these regions *during* meditation, as well as in areas involved in processing emotions, pain and self-awareness (Chiesa, Brambilla, & Serretti, 2010; Marchand, 2012).

Further research has also shown that MBTs induce a state of physical rest, as measured by respiratory and metabolic performance, blood pressure and cortisol secretion (Chiesa et al., 2010; Marchand, 2012; Shapiro et al., 2003, 2005). Several studies that offered MBTs to participants with cancer found that it has strengthened their immune function (Carlson et al., 2003; Witek-Janusek et al., 2008). Other findings revealed that MBTs can improve learning skills: short and long term memory functions, attentiveness, perception, curiosity, concentration, metacognitive awareness, cognitive flexibility, imagination, creativity and inventiveness (Chiesa, Calati, & Serretti, 2011; Ivtzan, Gardner, & Smailova, 2011; Marchand, 2012; Shapiro et al., 2003). As for pain reduction, several clinical trials demonstrated significant declines in subjective pain experience following MBTs (Chiesa & Serretti, 2010; Grossman et al., 2004; Kabat-Zinn et al., 1992). Additionally, MBSR was shown to improve skin condition in patients with psoriasis (Kabat-Zinn, Wheeler, & Light, 1998), and resulted in improved sleep and reduced fatigue in cancer patients (Shapiro et al., 2003).

In relation to psychological disorders, MBTs were tested on clinical as well as nonclinical populations. The findings reveal that MBTs can significantly lower symptoms of psychological distress, including anxiety, panic, worry, stress, depression, dysphoria, suicidal ideation, self-harm behaviours, rumination, neuroticism, anger, cognitive disorganisation, thought suppression, post-traumatic stress disorder and substance abuse (Chiesa, & Serretti, 2009; Keng, Smoski, & Robins, 2011; Ospina et al., 2007). It has also shown to be effective in reducing symptoms of bipolar disorder, social-phobia, psychosis, dissociation, borderline personality disorder and eating disorders (Chadwick, 2014; Kristeller & Wolever, 2010; Linehan et al., 1999; Williams et al., 2008; Zerubavel & Messman-Moore,

2013). Changes in these parameters were correlated with the amount of meditation exercise (Carmody & Baer, 2008, 2009).

Other studies reported on improvements in well-being following MBT participation, including increases in happiness, life satisfaction, psychological well-being, quality of life, positive emotions, hope, sense of coherence, sense of control, autonomy and independence, coping skills, resilience, moral maturity, spirituality, self-actualisation, self-compassion, stress-hardiness, ego-strength, self-esteem, self-acceptance, benevolence, trust, empathy, forgiveness, ability to express emotions, improved social relationships and social adjustment and even increased sense of humour (Brown et al., 2007; Keng et al., 2011; Nyklíček & Kuijpers, 2008; Ospina et al., 2007; Shapiro et al., 2005). Importantly, improved metacognitive awareness (Chiesa et al., 2011; Shapiro et al., 2006) and behavioural or emotional regulation has been registered (Friese, Messner, & Schaffner, 2012; Robins et al., 2012).

Conclusion

The lines of research reviewed here that utilise mindfulness meditation as a key intervention have shown outstanding outcomes: improvements in a range of physical and psychological symptoms, as well as increases in many aspects of well-being. An examination of the mechanisms that operate in mindfulness meditation revealed that it incorporates three metacognitive and self-regulatory processes that work in concert: decentring, disidentification, and reperceiving (Shapiro et al., 2006). Together they enable meditators to monitor their own thoughts and emotions while adopting an accepting attitude towards them. The aim of MBTs is to strengthen meditators' self-regulatory and metacognitive capacities, while its assertion is that the development of these self-regulatory mechanisms can be best achieved and habituated through the regular practice of mindfulness meditation.

The Western Approach to Mindfulness

Langer and her colleagues in the early 1970s introduced the Western mindfulness school of thought. This Western approach to mindfulness investigates mindfulness as a cognitive mode and examines the outcomes of mindfulness and mindlessness as two opposing cognitive states on one's performance, psychological well-being and health (Langer, 1989). Langer conceptualizes mindfulness as an active and effortful mode of conscious

awareness, which entails 'a heightened state of involvement and wakefulness' (Langer & Moldoveanu, 2000, p. 2), in which a person attends to the
present moment and to the events that occur. Carson and Langer (2006)
contend that the purpose of mindfulness is to increase cognitive and
behavioural control in order to facilitate a more meaningful engagement
with one's environment.

Langer contrasts mindfulness with mindlessness, which she describes
as an 'automatic-pilot' cognitive mode in which a person relies on
habitual behavioural scripts to perform routine tasks in an automatic
and superficial manner (Langer, 1992). Although she recognizes that
automatisation can be useful, since it frees our mind to execute higher
levels of cognitive functioning, she argues that running on autopilot
for extended periods can be detrimental to our performance, cognitive
functioning, psychological well-being, physical health and even longevity
(Langer, 1994).

Langer suggests that mindfulness requires more than the absence of
mindlessness, since it involves 'openness to novelty' or 'actively drawing
novel distinctions' (Langer, 2005, p. 214). This necessitates being highly
attentive to *external* stimuli, which can manifest itself in having enhanced
sensitivity to one's environment, by being alert to new information, by
creating new categories to order one's observations or by being able to
assume different perspectives on a subject (Langer & Moldoveanu, 2000).

Langer and her colleagues perceive mindfulness as a cognitive state that
is grounded in a person's disposition (Langer, 1994). In various experimental nonclinical studies, Langer and her coauthors have been able to
induce a *state* of mindfulness through *instructional interventions* (explained
later in this section), which prompt respondents to regulate intentionally
their momentary modes of thinking, thereby switching from mindlessness
to mindfulness. Langer and her coauthors (Langer, 2005; Langer &
Moldoveanu, 2000) contend that by disrupting the cognitive routines
that had been transpiring mindlessly, these interventions can help in
developing heightened levels of mindfulness and in habituating it,
thereby reinforcing the *disposition* of mindfulness.

Langer (2004) operationalizes mindfulness as cognitive disposition that
entails four components (Langer, 2004):

- *Engagement* – awareness of changes taking place in the environment
- *Seeking novelty* – being open to one's environment
- *Novelty producing* – constructing new meanings
- *Flexibility* – adopting multiple perspectives

Dhiman (2012) suggests that the type of mindful mode described here facilitates the experience of flow (Csikszentmihalyi, 1990). Flow is a state of functioning, where a person experiences full immersion in the activity that he or she is doing, an activity that is intrinsically rewarding for the enjoyment of engaging in moment-to-moment experience of the activity itself. Flow often characterizes, or is closely aligned with, the state of peak performance and creativity (Nakamura & Csikszentmihalyi, 2005).

In line with this conception, much of Langer's (1989, 2006) work links between mindfulness with creativity and suggests that mindfulness promotes creativity while mindlessness inhibits it. Creativity is defined as 'the ability to transcend traditional ways of thinking by generating ideas, methods and forms that are meaningful and new to others' (Levy & Langer, 1999, p. 45). Langer (2006) claims that mindfulness and creativity are strongly associated, since the key component of mindfulness is an openness to new ideas, which awakens the cognitive processes that are necessary for creativity (such as curiosity, insight, analogical reasoning, remote associations, ideational productivity, divergent and convergent thinking, flexibility or critical thinking). Langer's definition thus suggests that mindfulness entails (1) self-regulation of one's consciousness (which is described as self-exerting control to override prepotent response [Vohs & Baumeister, 2011]), (2) directing one's attention to external stimuli and (3) engaging with it cognitively in a creative way.

Brief Langerian Mindfulness Interventions

Several studies have tested what has been termed as 'brief mindfulness interventions' (Keng et al., 2011). These studies aim to interrupt mindless, automated habitual cognitive states by prompting mindful states of awareness through a variety of stimuli that are designed to evoke deliberate self-regulation of attention. Most of Langer's work can be associated with this line of scholarly work (Langer, 1993, 1997, 2000).

In most of these studies, Langer and her associates stimulated a *state* of mindfulness, through instructions that compel participants to be more mindful and attend carefully to the task at hand. For example, in Anglin, Pirson, and Langer's (2008) study of mindfulness in math education, participants were given conditional instructions and asked to look closely at the information given to them and to explore different possibilities and perspectives. Similar interventions were used in other studies, most of which took place in laboratory settings (controlled or noncontrolled) and with nonclinical populations (Crum & Langer, 2007; Langer, 1994, 1997, 2000; Langer et al. 1989).

Mechanisms operating in brief Langerian mindfulness interventions
Langer and her coauthors do not explore the cognitive mechanisms that underlie these interventions. However, in a recent publication (Hart, Ivtzan, & Hart, 2013), we have attempted to apply Kahneman's (2011) dual information-processing model to explain how mindfulness and mindless cognitive modes operate. Kahneman maintains that there are two cognitive modes of information processing that operate simultaneously. System 1 (S1) produces a mindless mode of awareness and is experiential, automatic, effortless, intuitive, unconscious, energy-efficient and faster mode of processing. System 2 (S2) generates a mindful mode of awareness and is therefore deliberate, consciously effortful, energy-consuming and a relatively slow mode of cognitive functioning.

Kahneman (2011) explains that the activation of a mindful mode of awareness (S2) necessitates regulation of one's attention, while the operation of the mindless mode (S1) can be seen as a cognitive mode where one's consciousness is underregulated (Baumeister & Heatherton, 1996). Kahneman (2011) also notes that while cognitive reasoning is at the core of mindful processes, emotions are the main driver of mindless processes.

Since the resources available to perform effortful self-regulatory processes are limited and prone to depletion (Muraven & Baumeister, 2000), Kahneman (2011) assesses that a large proportion of people's information processing is conducted by S1, resulting in what Langer (1997) describes as a mindless and automatic mode of functioning. S2, Kahneman argues, is prompted into action (thereby producing a mindful state of awareness), when people face situations or information that S1 cannot handle. This can explain how mindfulness is triggered through the brief mindfulness interventions described previously: the carefully worded instructions presented to participants seem to trigger self-regulation of one's attention, thereby activating S2. Kahneman's (2011) model is thus consistent with the notion that self-regulation of attention is a key process in such brief mindfulness interventions.

Based on Masicampo and Baumeister's (2007) work on self-regulation, it can be argued that self-regulatory processes mediate the positive association found between mindfulness and well-being. Studies on a variety of self-regulatory processes (control of one's thoughts, emotions, attention or behaviour) strongly support the claim that self-regulatory capacities are positively associated with well-being (Baumeister & Vohs, 2003).

Langerian Mindfulness Scales

Two trait mindfulness scales have been developed by Langer and her colleagues over the years: the Langer's Mindfulness/Mindlessness Scale (LMS; Langer, 2004) and the Langer Sociocognitive Mindfulness Scale (LMS14; Pirson et al., 2012). Both inventories include four subscales (novelty seeking, engagement, novelty producing and flexibility). The original scale includes twenty-one items, while the newer scale has fourteen items. A positive association was found between LMS scores and the aptitude to perceive events from multiple points of view, openness to experience and creativity (Langer, 2004). Pirson and colleagues (2012) report that the LMS14 was found to be positively correlated with psychological well-being, satisfaction with life, self-esteem, positive relationships, positive affect, humor, creativity, engagement at work and physical health. It was also negatively correlated with the need for structure, neuroticism, negative affect, depression and pain.

In addition to the questionnaires developed by Langer and her colleagues, two other questionnaires have frequently been used in brief mindfulness interventions: the Trait Mindful Attention and Awareness Scale (MAAS) and a similar scale measuring states of mindfulness, the state MASS (Brown & Ryan, 2003).

The Mindful Attention Awareness Scale (MAAS), trait version

The MAAS includes fifteen items and evaluates the general disposition to be *mindless and on auto-pilot mode* and thus defines mindfulness as the *absence of mindlessness* (Carlson & Brown, 2005). The developers report positive correlations with well-being, satisfaction in life, joy, pleasant affect, emotional intelligence, self-esteem, sense of autonomy, competence, gratitude, hope, optimism, vitality and openness to experience, and negative relationships with rumination, depression, stress, anxiety and social anxiety.

The Mindful Attention Awareness Scale (MAAS)

The state MAAS was used to quantify a state of mindfulness among participants who carried pagers for a few weeks (Brown & Ryan, 2003). When paged, participants were requested to respond to a five-item inventory and assess the extent to which they were mindfully attending (or behaving automatically) to the activity they were doing. As might be expected, MAAS state mindfulness scores are significantly correlated with MAAS trait mindfulness scores. Scores also predicted positive emotions (Baer, Walsh, & Lykins, 2009).

The Outcomes of Brief Mindfulness Interventions

Many of the intervention studies of Langer and her colleagues have been conducted in nonclinical settings and were geared to assess the impact of brief mindfulness interventions on various aspects of performance and well-being. However, several other scholars have trialled brief mindfulness interventions in clinical settings and reported on impressive results.

In her studies, Langer and her associates consistently found that the brief mindfulness interventions had beneficial outcomes, mainly in improving *trait mindfulness* (Burpee & Langer, 2005; Djikic, Langer, & Fulton-Stapleton, 2008; Langer, 2004), cognitive performance (Anglin et al., 2008), learning skills (attention, memory and ability to concentrate) and problem-solving skills (Langer, 1993, 1997, 2000). As noted, creativity is a central construct in Langer's work, and accordingly in several studies Langer and her coauthors reported on improvement in creativity following mindfulness interventions (Langer, Heffernan, & Kiester, 1988; Pirson et al., 2012).

Langer's (1989) model not only associates mindfulness with improved cognitive performance, but compellingly argues that mindfulness is positively correlated with psychological well-being and health measures. In several studies, the authors found that mindfulness had beneficial outcomes in terms of improved self-acceptance (Carson & Langer, 2006), improved relationships and relational satisfaction (Burpee & Langer, 2005), decreased burnout (Langer, 1994; Langer et al., 1988) and reduced stress (Langer, Janis, & Wolfer, 1975). However, it is worth noting that in these studies, *state* mindfulness was not measured, making it difficult to assess the characteristics or components of the cognitive state that was triggered. In some studies (Burpee & Langer, 2005; Djikic et al., 2008), trait mindfulness was measured, and correlational findings have demonstrated a positive relationship between trait mindfulness and well-being; however, the effects of the interventions in terms of changes in trait mindfulness were not measured.

Several studies that tested the effectiveness of similar types of brief interventions found that instruction-induced mindfulness interventions lowered psychological distress symptoms ranging from rumination to depression in healthy participants as well as in clinical patients (Broderick, 2005; Huffziger & Kuehner, 2009) and improved *emotional regulation* (Arch & Craske, 2006; Campbell-Sills et al. 2006). They also reported on improvements in health conditions (Alexander, Druker, & Langer,

1990; Delizonna, Ryan, & Langer, 2009; Langer et al., 1984, 2010). In a study of smoking cessation, smokers given mindfulness-evoking instructions demonstrated significant reduction in smoking behaviours in the following days (Bowen & Marlatt, 2009).

Conclusion

The studies reviewed here induced mindful states of consciousness mostly through brief instructional interventions and have shown remarkable results: improvements in a variety of cognitive functions, well-being and health measures, as well as reductions in psychological distress symptoms. To explore the cognitive mechanisms that operate in these interventions, we drew on Kahneman's dual information-processing system model and on Baumeister's work on self-regulation, which provide an explanation as to how these interventions activate states of mindfulness, and how mindfulness promotes psychological well-being through the enhancement of self-regulatory capacities.

Discussion and Conclusion

This chapter began with the observation that mindfulness scholarship is divided into Western and Eastern schools of thought, which have been running in parallel lines for more than thirty years. Both of these schools have seen a surge of publication and public interest in recent years, alongside significant development and application of mindfulness interventions in clinical and nonclinical settings. As the evidence attesting to the effectiveness of mindfulness interventions spill out from the academia to the media and to the public, mindfulness practice has become the latest quick-fix self-help fashion buzzword, with hundreds of books, CDs, websites and workshops offering it as a shortcut to the alleviation of distress and for attaining Nirvana. In view of the surge in public interest, this chapter aimed to offer an overview of both strands of research by exploring four aspects of each school of thought: their definitions and components of mindfulness, their interventions, their measurement tools and the evidence regarding the effectiveness of their interventions.

The review of Langer's and Kabat-Zinn's work suggests that there are three aspects of their conceptions that show some degree of convergence: their definitions and the type of outcomes they generate. Importantly, self-regulation is considered to be a key mechanism involved in both types of mindfulness interventions. However, the two schools of thought seem to differ along several key aspects: the philosophies upon which they draw, their components of mindfulness, their measurement tools, their target clientele, their respective settings and goals, the interventions they employ to promote mindfulness and the qualities of mindfulness evoked by the interventions. Furthermore, they vary in the scope and comprehensiveness of their constructions, with Kabat-Zinn's model presenting more detail and breadth compared to Langer's.

The definitions of mindfulness reviewed here, along with the examination of the components of mindfulness and the analysis of the mechanisms that underlie mindfulness interventions, suggest that the different strands of research may be exploring different cognitive modes. The Western approach describes mindfulness as an effortful attentive-creative mode of awareness, where one engages closely with an external experience or environment. The Eastern approach, on the other hand, depicts mindfulness as a metacognitive mode, in which one attends to internal or external experiences in a manner that paradoxically involves an intimate engagement with the experience, and at the same time an ability to *disidentify* oneself from the cognitions and emotions that the experience provokes.

In line with this assertion, the review of the interventions utilised by the two research teams reveals that there are significant differences between Kabat-Zinn's meditation-based clinical interventions and Langer's nonclinical brief mindfulness interventions. These pertain not only to their goals and their target population, but also to the fact that the brief interventions are designed to trigger a *mindful state*, while the habitual meditation practice is designed to develop *trait mindfulness*. Despite these differences, the literature is explicit in asserting that mindfulness and its cultivation, however it is defined, induced, measured or cultivated, can elevate positive psychological aspects of well-being and improve functioning in healthy people, as well as lessen a range of physical and psychological disorders in clinical patients. Importantly, self-regulatory processes are central to both types of interventions and seem to mediate the impact of mindfulness interventions on well-being.

REFERENCES

Alexander, C. N., Druker, S. M., and Langer, E. J. (1990). Major issues in the exploration of adult growth. In C. N. Alexander and E. J. Langer (Eds.), *Higher stages of human development: Perspectives on adult growth* (pp. 3–32). New York, NY: Oxford University Press.

Anglin, L. P., Pirson, M., and Langer, E. J. (2008) Mindful learning: A moderator of gender differences in mathematics performance. *Journal of Adult Development*, 15, 132–139. doi: 10.1007/s10804-008-9043-x

Arch, J. J., and Craske, M. G. (2006). Mechanisms of mindfulness: Emotion regulation following a focused breathing induction. *Behavior Research and Therapy*, 44(12), 1849–1858. doi: 10.1016/j.brat.2005.12.007

Baer, R. A. (2003). Mindfulness training as a clinical intervention: A conceptual and empirical review. *Clinical Psychology: Science and Practice*, 10(2), 125–143. doi: 10.1093/clipsy.bpg015

Baer, R. A., Smith, G. T., and Allen, K. B. (2004). Assessment of mindfulness by self-report: The Kentucky Inventory of Mindfulness Skills. *Assessment*, 11(3), 191–206. doi: 10.1177/1073191104268029

Baer, R. A., Smith, G. T., Hopkins, J., Krietemeyer, J., and Toney, L. (2006). Using self-report assessment methods to explore facets of mindfulness. *Assessment*, 13(1), 27–45. doi: 10.1177/1073191105283504

Baer, R. A., Smith, G. T., Lykins, E., Button, D., Krietemeyer, J., Sauer, S., . . . Williams, J. M. G. (2008). Construct validity of the five facet mindfulness questionnaire in meditating and nonmeditating samples. *Assessment*, 15(3), 329–342. doi: 10.1177/1073191107313003

Baer, R. A., Walsh, E., and Lykins, E. L. B. (2009). Assessment of mindfulness. In F. Didonna (Ed.), *Clinical handbook of mindfulness* (pp. 153–168). New York, NY: Springer.

Barnhofer, T., Crane, C., Hargus, E., Amarasinghe, M., Winder, R., and Williams, J. M. G. (2009). Mindfulness-based cognitive therapy as a treatment for chronic depression: A preliminary study. *Behaviour Research and Therapy*, 47(5), 366–373. doi: 10.1016.j. brat.2009.01.019

Baumeister, R. F., and Heatherton, T. F. (1996). Self-regulation failure: An overview. *Psychological Inquiry*, 7(1), 1–15. doi: 10.1207/s15327965pli0701_1

Baumeister, R. F., and Vohs, K. D. (2003). Self-regulation and the executive functioning of the self. In M. R. Leary and J. P. Tangney (Eds.), *Handbook of self and identity* (pp. 197–217). New York, NY: Guilford Press.

Bishop, S. R., Lau, M., Shapiro, S., Carlson, L., Anderson, N. D., Carmody, J., and Devins, G. (2004). Mindfulness: A proposed operational definition. *Clinical Psychology: Science and Practice*, 11(3), 230–241. doi: 10.1093/clipsy. bph077

Bowen, S., and Marlatt, A. (2009). Surfing the urge: Brief mindfulness-based intervention for college student smokers. *Psychology of Addictive Behaviors*, 23(4), 666–671. doi: 10. 1037/a0017127

Broderick, P. C. (2005). Mindfulness and coping with dysphoric mood: Contrasts with rumination and distraction. *Cognitive Therapy and Research*, 29(5), 501–510. doi: 10. 1007/s10608-005-3888-0

Brown, K. W., and Ryan, R. M. (2003). The benefits of being present: Mindfulness and its role in psychological well-being. *Journal of Personality and Social Psychology*, 84(4), 822–848. doi: 10.1037/0022-3514.84.4.822

Brown, K. W., Ryan, R. M., and Creswell, J. D. (2007). Mindfulness: Theoretical foundations and evidence for salutary effects. *Psychological Inquiry*, 18(4), 211–237. doi: 10.1080 /10478400701598298

Buchheld, N., Grossman, P., and Walach, H. (2001). Measuring mindfulness in insight meditation (Vipassana) and meditation-based psychotherapy: The development of the Freiburg Mindfulness Inventory (FMI). *Journal for Meditation and Meditation Research*, 1(1), 11–34.

Burpee, L., and Langer, E. J. (2005). Mindfulness and marital satisfaction. *Journal of Adult Development*, 12(1), 43–51. doi: 10.1007/s10804-005-1281-6

Campbell-Sills, L., Barlow, D. H., Brown, T. A., and Hofmann, S. G. (2006). Effects of suppression and acceptance on emotional responses of individuals with anxiety and mood disorders. *Behaviour Research and Therapy*, 44(9), 1251–1263. doi: 10.1016/j. brat.2005.10.001

Cardaciotto, L., Herbert, J. D., Forman, E. M., Moitra, E., and Farrow, V. (2008). The assessment of present-moment awareness and acceptance: The Philadelphia Mindfulness Scale. *Assessment*, 15(2), 204–223. doi: 10.1177/1073191107311467

Carlson, L. E., and Brown, K. W. (2005). Validation of the Mindful Attention Awareness Scale in a cancer population. *Journal of Psychosomatic Research*, 58(1), 29–33. doi: 10.1016/j.jpsychores.2004.04.366

Carlson, L. E., and Speca, M. (2010). *Mindfulness-based cancer recovery*. Oakland, CA: Harbinger.

Carlson, L. E., Speca, M., Patel, K., and Goodey, E. (2003). Mindfulness-based stress-reduction in relation to quality of life, mood, symptoms of stress, and immune parameters in breast and prostate cancer outpatients. *Psychosomatic Medicine*, 65, 571–581. doi: 10.1097/01.PSY.0000074003.35911.41

Carmody, J., and Baer, R. A. (2008). Relationships between mindfulness practice and levels of mindfulness, medical and psychological symptoms and well-being in a mindfulness-based stress reduction program. *Journal of Behavioral Medicine*, 31(1), 23–33. doi: 10.1007/s10865-007-9130-7

(2009). How long does a mindfulness-based stress reduction program need to be? A review of class contact hours and effect sizes for psychological distress. *Journal of Clinical Psychology*, 65(6), 627–638. doi: 10.1002/jclp.20555

Carson, S. H., and Langer, E. J. (2006). Mindfulness and self-acceptance. *Journal of Rational-Emotive and Cognitive-Behavior Therapy*, 24(1), 29–43. doi: 10.1007/s10942-006-0022-5

Center for Mindfulness in Medicine, Health Care, and Society (2014). *Stress Reduction Program*. Retrieved from www.umassmed.edu/uploadedFiles/cfm2/SRP_for_desktop_printing.pdf.

Chadwick, P. (2014). Mindfulness for psychosis. *British Journal of Psychiatry*, 204, 333–334.

Chadwick, P., Hember, M., Symes, J., Peters, E., Kuipers, E., and Dagnan, D. (2008). Responding mindfully to unpleasant thoughts and images: Reliability and validity of the Southampton Mindfulness Questionnaire

(SMQ). *British Journal of Clinical Psychology*, 47(4), 451–455. doi: 10.1348/014466508X314891

Chiesa, A., Anselmi, R., and Serretti, A. (2014). Psychological mechanisms of mindfulness-based interventions: What do we know? *Holistic Nursing Practice*, 28(2), 124–148. doi: 10.1097/HNP.0000000000000017

Chiesa, A., Brambilla, P., and Serretti, A. (2010). Functional neural correlates of mindfulness meditations in comparison with psychotherapy, pharmacotherapy and placebo effect. Is there a link? *Acta Neuropsychiatrica*, 22 (3), 104–117. doi: 10.1111/j.1601-5215.20 10.00460.x

Chiesa, A., Calati, R., and Serretti, A. (2011). Does mindfulness training improve cognitive abilities? A systematic review of neuropsychological findings. *Clinical Psychology Review*, 31(3), 449–464. doi: 10.1016/j.cpr.2010.11.003

Chiesa, A., and Serretti, A. (2009). Mindfulness-based stress reduction for stress management in healthy people: A review and meta-analysis. *Journal of Alternative and Complementary Medicine*, 15(5), 593–600. doi:10.1089/acm.2008.0495

(2010). A systematic review of neurobiological and clinical features of mindfulness meditations. *Psychological Medicine*, 40(8), 1239–1252. doi:10.1007/S0033291709991747

(2011). Mindfulness based cognitive therapy for psychiatric disorders: A systematic review and meta-analysis. *Psychiatry research*, 187(3), 441–453. doi: 10.1016/j.psychres.2010.08.011

Crum, A. J., and Langer, E. J. (2007). Mind-set matters: Exercise and the placebo effect. *Psychological Science*, 18(2), 165–171. doi: 10.1111/j.1467-9280.2007.01867.x

Csikszentmihalyi, M. (1990). *Flow: The psychology of optimal experience*. New York, NY: Harper and Row.

Davis, K. M., Lau, M. A., and Cairns, D. R. (2009). Development and preliminary validation of a trait version of the Toronto Mindfulness Scale. *Journal of Cognitive Psychotherapy*, 23(3), 185–197. doi:10.1891/0889-8391.23.3.185

Delizonna, L. L., Ryan P. W., and Langer, E. J. (2009). The effect of mindfulness on heart rate control. *Journal of Adult Development*, 16(2), 61–65. doi: 10.1007/s10804-009-950-6

Dhiman, S. (2012). Mindfulness and the art of living creatively: Cultivating a creative life by minding our mind. *Journal of Social Change*, 4(1), 24–33. doi: 10.5590/JOSC.2012. 04.1.03

Didonna, F. (2009). Introduction: Where new and old paths to dealing with suffering meet. In F. Didonna (Ed.), *Clinical handbook of mindfulness* (pp. 1–17). New York, NY: Springer.

Djikic, M., Langer, E. J., and Fulton-Stapleton, S. (2008). Reducing stereotyping through mindfulness: Effects on automatic stereotype-activated behaviors. *Journal of Adult Development*, 15(2), 106–111. doi: 10.1007/s10804-008-9040-0

Duncan, L. G., and Bardacke, N. (2010). Mindfulness-based childbirth and parenting education: Promoting family mindfulness during the perinatal period. *Journal of Child and Family Studies*, 19(2), 190–202. doi: 10.1007/s10826-009-9313-7

Feldman, G., Hayes, A., Kumar, S., Greeson, J., and Laurenceau, J. P. (2007). Mindfulness and emotion regulation: The development and initial validation of the Cognitive and Affective Mindfulness Scale-Revised (CAMS-R). *Journal of Psychopathology and Behavioral Assessment*, 29, 177–190. doi: 10.1007/s10862-006-9035-8

Friese, M. Messner, C., and Schaffner, Y. (2012). Mindfulness meditation counteracts self-control depletion. *Consciousness and Cognition*, 21(2), 1016–1022. doi: 10.1016/j. concog.2012.01.008

Gans, J. J., O'Sullivan, P., and Bircheff, V. (2013). Mindfulness based tinnitus stress reduction pilot study. *Mindfulness*, 5(3), 1–12. doi: 10.1007/s12671-012-0184-4

Goodman, J. H., Guarino, A., Chenausky, K., Klein, L., Prager, J., Petersen, R., Forget, A., and Freeman, M. (2014). CALM pregnancy: Results of a pilot study of mindfulness-based cognitive therapy for perinatal anxiety. *Archives of Women's Mental Health*, 17(5), 373–387. doi: 10.1007/s00737-013-0402-7

Grossman, P., Niemann, L., Schmidt, S., and Walach H. (2004). Mindfulness-based stress reduction and health benefits: A meta-analysis. *Journal of Psychosomatic Research*, 57(1), 35–43. doi: 10.1016/S0022-3999(03)00573-7

Hart, R., Ivtzan, I., and Hart, D. (2013). Mind the gap in mindfulness research: A comparative account of the leading schools of thought. *Review of General Psychology*, 17(4), 453–466. doi: 10.1037/a0035212

Hayes, S. C., Strosahl, K., and Wilson, K. G. (1999). *Acceptance and commitment therapy: An experiential approach to behaviour change*. New York, NY: Guilford Press.

Huffziger, S., and Kuehner, C. (2009). Rumination, distraction, and mindful self-focus in depressed patients. *Behaviour Research and Therapy*, 47(3), 224–230. doi: 10.1016/j. brat.2008.12.005

Ie, A., Ngnoumen, C. T., and Langer, E. J. (2014). *The Wiley Blackwell handbook of mindfulness*. Chichester, UK: John Wiley & Sons.

Ivtzan, I., Gardner, H. E., and Smailova, Z. (2011). Mindfulness meditation and curiosity: The contributing factors to well-being and the process of closing the self-discrepancy gap. *International Journal of Wellbeing*, 1(3), 316–326. doi: 10.1016/S0022-3999(03)0057 3-7

Kabat-Zinn, J. (1982). An outpatient program in behavioral medicine for chronic pain patients based on the practice of mindfulness meditation: Theoretical considerations and preliminary results. *General Hospital Psychiatry*, 4(1), 33–47. doi: 10.1016/0163-8343(82)90026-3

(1994). *Full catastrophe living: Using the wisdom of your body and mind to face stress, pain, and illness*. New York, NY: Delacorte.

(1996). Mindfulness meditation: What it is, what it isn't, and its role in health care and medicine. In Y. Haruki, Y. Ishii and M. Suzuki (Eds.), *Comparative and psychological study on meditation* (pp. 161–170). Delft, Netherlands: Eburon.

(2003). Mindfulness-based interventions in context: Past, present, and future. *Clinical Psychology: Science and Practice*, 10(2), 144–156. doi: 10.1093/clipsy. bpg 016

(2005). *Coming to our senses*. London, UK: Piatkus.

(2009). Forward. In F. Dinonna (Ed.), *Clinical handbook of mindfulness* (pp. xxv–xxxiii). New York, NY: Springer.

Kabat-Zinn, J., Massion, A. O., Kristeller, J., Peterson, L. G., Fletcher, K., Pbert, L., . . . Santorelli, S. F. (1992). Effectiveness of a meditation-based stress reduction program in the treatment of anxiety disorders. *American Journal of Psychiatry*, 149, 936–943.

Kabat-Zinn, J., Wheeler, E., and Light, T. (1998). Influence of a mindfulness meditation based stress reduction intervention on rates on skin clearing in patients. *Psychosomatic Medicine*, 60(5), 625–632.

Kahneman, D. (2011). *Thinking fast and slow*. New York, NY: Farrar, Straus and Giroux.

Keng, S. L., Smoski, M. J., and Robins, C. J. (2011). Effects of mindfulness on psychological health: A review of empirical studies. *Clinical Psychology Review*, 31(6), 1041–1056. doi: 10.1016/j.cpr.2011.04.006

Kristeller, J. L., and Wolever, R. Q. (2010). Mindfulness-based eating awareness training for treating binge eating disorder: The conceptual foundation. *Eating Disorders*, 19(1), 49–61. doi: 10.1080/10640266.2011.533605

Langer, E. J. (1989). *Mindfulness*. Cambridge, MA: Da Capo Press.

(1992). Matters of mind: Mindfulness/mindlessness in perspective. *Consciousness and Cognition*, 1(3), 289–305. doi: 10.1016/1053-8100(92)90066-J

(1993). A mindful education. *Educational Psychologist*, 28(1), 43–50. doi: 10. 1207/s15326985ep2801_4

(1994). Mindfulness and work. In C. Whitmyer (Ed.), *Mindfulness and meaningful work: Explorations in right livelihood* (pp. 223–230). Berkeley, CA: Paralax Press.

(1997). *The power of mindful learning*. Cambridge, MA: De Capo Press.

(2000). Mindful learning. *Current Directions in Psychological Science*, 9(6), 220–223. doi:10.1111/1467-8721.00099

(2004). *Langer mindfulness scale user guide and technical manual*. Worthington, OH: IDS.

Langer, E. J. (2005). Well-being: Mindfulness versus positive evaluation. In C. R. Snyder and S. J. Lopez (Eds.), *Handbook of positive psychology* (pp. 214–230). New York, NY: Oxford University Press.

(2006). *On becoming an artist: Reinventing yourself through mindful creativity*. New York, NY: Ballantine.

Langer, E. J., Beck, P., Janoff-Bulman, R., and Timko, C. (1984). An exploration of relationships among mindfulness, longevity, and senility. *Academic Psychology Bulletin*, 6(2), 211–226.

Langer, E. J., Djikic, M., Pirson, M., Madenci, A., and Donohue, R. (2010). Believing is seeing: Using mindlessness (mindfully) to improve visual acuity. *Psychological Science*, 21(5), 661–666. doi: 10.1177/0956797610366543

Langer, E. J., Hatem, M., Joss, J., and Howell, M. (1989). Conditional teaching and mindful learning: The role of uncertainty in education. *Creativity Research Journal*, 2(3), 139–150. doi: 10.1080/10400418909534311

Langer, E. J., Heffernan, D., and Kiester, M. (1988). *Reducing burnout in an institutional setting: An experimental investigation.* Cambridge, MA: Harvard University Press.

Langer, E. J., Janis, I., and Wolfer, J. (1975). Reduction of psychological stress in surgical patients. *Journal of Experimental Social Psychology*, 11(2), 155–165. doi: 10.1016/S0 022-1031(75)80018-7

Langer, E. J., and Moldoveanu, M. (2000). The construct of mindfulness. *Journal of Social Issues*, 56(1), 1–9. doi: 10.1111/0022-4537.00148

Lau, M. A., Bishop, S. R., Segal, Z. V., Buis, T., Anderson, N. D., Carlson, L., and Carmody, J. (2006). The Toronto Mindfulness Scale: Development and validation. *Journal of Clinical Psychology*, 62(12), 1445–1467. doi: 10.1002/jclp.20326

Levy, B., and Langer, E. J. (1999). Aging. In M. A. Runco and S. R. Pritzker (Eds.), *Encyclopaedia of creativity* (Vol. I, pp. 45–52). San Diego, CA: Academic Press.

Linehan, M. (1993). *Cognitive-behavioral therapy of borderline personality disorder.* New York, NY: Guilford Press.

Linehan, M. M., Schmidt, H., III, Dimeff, L. A., Craft, J. C., Kanter, J., and Comtois, K. A. (1999). Dialectical behavior therapy for patients with borderline personality disorder and drug dependence. *American Journal of Addiction*, 8(4), 279–292. doi: 10.1080/10 5504999305686

Marchand, W. R. (2012). MBSR, mindfulness-based cognitive therapy, and Zen meditation for depression, anxiety, pain, and psychological distress. *Journal of Psychiatric Practice*, 18(4), 233–252. doi: 10.1097/01.pra.0000416014.53215.86

Masicampo, E. J., and Baumeister, R. F. (2007). Relating mindfulness and self-regulatory processes, *Psychological Inquiry*, 18(4), 255–258. doi: 10.1080/10478400701598363

Muraven, M. R., and Baumeister, R. F. (2000). Self-regulation and depletion of limited resources: Does self-control resemble a muscle? *Psychological Bulletin*, 126(2), 247–259. doi: 10.1037/0033-2909.126.2.247

Nakamura, J., and Csikszentmihalyi, M. (2005). The concept of flow. In C. R. Snyder and S. J. Lopez (Eds.), *Handbook of positive psychology* (pp. 89–105). Oxford, UK: Oxford University Press.

Nyklíček, I., and Kuijpers, K. F. (2008). Effects of mindfulness-based stress reduction intervention on psychological well-being and quality of life: Is increased mindfulness indeed the mechanism? *Annals of Behavioral Medicine*, 35(3), 331–340. doi: 10.1007/ s12160-008-9030-2

Olendzki, A. (2009). Mindfulness and meditation. In F. Didonna (Ed.), *Clinical handbook of mindfulness* (pp. 37–44). New York, NY: Springer.

Ong, J., and Sholtes, D. (2010). A mindfulness-based approach to the treatment of insomnia. *Journal of Clinical Psychology*, 66(11), 1175–1184. doi: 10.1002/jclp.20736

Ospina, M. B., Bond, K., Karkhaneh, M., Tjosvold, L., Vandermeer, B., Liang, Y., and Klassen, T. P. (2007). *Meditation practices for health: State of the research* (Publication No. 07-E010). Retrieved from Agency for Healthcare Research and Quality website: http://archive.ahrq.gov/downloads/downloads/pubs/evidence/pdf/meditation/medit.pdf

Pirson, M., Langer, E. J., Bodner, T., and Zilcha, S. (2012, October). The development and validation of the Langer Mindfulness Scale – enabling a socio-cognitive perspective of mindfulness in organizational contexts. Fordham University Schools of Business Research Paper. Retrieved from http://papers.ssrn.com/sol3/papers.cfm?abstract_id= 2158921

Robins, C. J., Keng, S. L. Ekblad, A. G., and Brantley, J. G. (2012). Effects of mindfulness-based stress reduction on emotional experience and expression: A randomized controlled trial. *Journal of Clinical Psychology*, 68(1), 117–131. doi: 10.1002/jclp. 20857

Segal, Z. V., Williams, M. G., and Teasdale, J. D. (2002). *Mindfulness-based cognitive therapy for depression: A new approach to preventing relapse*. New York, NY: Guilford Press.

Shapiro, D. H. (1980). *Meditation: Self-regulation strategy and altered state of consciousness*. New York, NY: Aldine.

Shapiro, S. L., Bootzin, R. R., Figueredo, A. J., Lopez, A. M., and Schwartz, G. E. (2003). The efficacy of mindfulness-based stress reduction in the treatment of sleep disturbance in women with breast cancer: An exploratory study. *Journal of Psychosomatic Research*, 54(1), 85–91. doi: 10.1016/S0022-3999(02) 00546-9

Shapiro, S. L., Brown, K. W., Thoresen, C., and Plante, T. G. (2011). The moderation of mindfulness-based stress reduction effects by trait mindfulness: Results from a randomized controlled trial. *Journal of Clinical Psychology*, 67(3), 267–277. doi: 10.1002/jclp.20761

Shapiro, S. L., Carlson, L. E., and Astin, J. A. (2006). Mechanisms of mindfulness. *Journal of Clinical Psychology*, 62(3), 373– 386. doi: 10.1002/jclp.20237

Shapiro, S. L., Oman, D., Thoresen, C. E., Plante, T. G., and Flinders, T. (2008). Cultivating mindfulness: Effects on well-being. *Journal of Clinical Psychology*, 64(7), 840–862. doi: 10.1002/jclp.20491

Shapiro, S. L., Schwartz, G. R., and Santerre, C. (2005). Meditation and positive psychology. In C. R. Snyder. and S. J. Lopez (Eds.), *Handbook of positive psychology* (pp. 632–645). Oxford, UK: Oxford University Press.

Shapiro, S. L., Walsh, R., and Britton, W. B. (2003). An analysis of recent meditation research and suggestions for future directions. *Journal of Meditation and Meditation Research*, 3, 69–90.

Siegel, R. D., Germer, C. K., and Olendzki, A. (2009). Mindfulness: What is it? Where does it come from? In F. Didonna (Ed.), *Clinical handbook of mindfulness* (pp. 17–36). New York, NY: Springer.

Stanley, E. A., Schaldach, J. M., Kiyonaga, A., and Jha, A. P. (2011). Mindfulness-based mind fitness training: A case study of a high-stress predeployment military cohort. *Cognitive and Behavioral Practice*, 18(4), 566–576. doi: 10.1016.j.cbpra.2010.08.002

Vago, D. R. (2014). Mapping modalities of self-awareness in mindfulness practice: A potential mechanism for clarifying habits of mind. *Annals of the New York Academy of Sciences*, 1307, 28–42.

Van Son, J., Nyklíček, I., Pop, V. J., Blonk, M. C., Erdtsieck, R. J., and Pouwer, F. (2014). Mindfulness-based cognitive therapy for people with diabetes and emotional problems. *Journal of Psychosomatic Research*, 77, 81–84.

Vohs, K. D., and Baumeister, R. F. (2011). *Handbook of self-regulation: Research, theory and applications*. New York, NY: Guilford Press.

Walach, H., Buchheld, N., Buttenmuller, V., Kleinknecht, N., and Schmidt, S. (2006). Measuring mindfulness – the Freiburg Mindfulness Inventory (FMI). *Personality and Individual Differences*, 40(8), 1543–1555. doi: 10.1016/j.paid.2005.11.025

Wallace, B. A. (2005). *Balancing the mind*. Ithaca, NY: Snow Lion.

Walsh, R. N. (1983). Meditation practice and research. *Journal of Humanistic Psychology*, 23(1), 18–50. doi: 10.1177/0022167883231004

Williams, J. M. G., Alatiq, Y., Crane, C., Barnhofer, T., Fennell, M. J. V., Duggan, D. S., and Goodwin, G. M. (2008). Mindfulness-based cognitive therapy (MBCT) in bipolar disorder: Preliminary evaluation of immediate effects on between-episode functioning. *Journal of Affective Disorders*, 107, 275–279. doi: 10.1016/j.jad.2007.08. 022

Witek-Janusek, L., Albuquerque, K., Rambo Chroniak, K., Chroniak, C., Durazo-Arvizu, R., and Mathews, H. L. (2008). Effect of mindfulness-based stress reduction on immune function, quality of life and coping in women newly diagnosed with early stage breast cancer. *Brain, Behavior, and Immunity*, 22(6), 969–981. doi: 10.1016/j.bbi.2008.01. 012

Witkiewitz, K., Bowen, S., Harrop, E. N., Douglas, H., Enkema, M., and Sedgwick, C. (2014). Mindfulness-based treatment to prevent addictive behavior relapse: Theoretical models and hypothesized mechanisms of change. *Substance Use and Misuse*, 49(5), 513–524. doi:10.3109/10826084.2014.891845

Zerubavel, N., and Messman-Moore, T. L. (2013). Staying present: Incorporating mindfulness into therapy for dissociation. *Mindfulness*, 1–12. doi: 10.1007/s1267-013-0261-3

CHAPTER 2

Mindfulness, Emotion Regulation, and Performance

Zella E. Moore

The publication of this text and the fact that you are reading it at this very moment are clear indicators of a great achievement – mindfulness theory and associated interventions have made a mark on the field of sport psychology and have changed the way many sport psychologists worldwide think about their athletes' performance and overall well-being! Yet although mindfulness has garnered increasing attention within sport psychology since the early 2000s, important and related concepts such as emotion regulation haven't quite received the attention within sport psychology that they deserve. Mindfulness and emotion regulation are inextricably connected, and as such, greater efforts to incorporate these scientific advancements into sport psychology research and practice are warranted. To this end, the present chapter considers athletic performance enhancement from the perspective of mindfulness *and* emotion regulation in order to further this line of inquiry and promote increased discussion of these theoretically linked constructs.

Mindfulness- and acceptance-based interventions for performance enhancement, represented first and most notably by the Mindfulness-Acceptance-Commitment (MAC) approach (Gardner & Moore, 2004, 2007, 2012; Moore & Gardner, 2001), have garnered increasingly supportive empirical data for their efficacy (Gardner & Moore, 2012). These intervention approaches work via substantially different mechanisms of change than more traditional change-based models of performance enhancement (Gardner & Moore, 2012; Moore, 2009), essentially by decreasing reactivity to internal experiences such as cognitions and emotions through greater acceptance/tolerance of these states, coupled with enhanced moment-to-moment awareness (i.e., task-relevant focus of attention) and enhanced activation of behaviors toward one's goals and values.

Contemporary developments in the emotion sciences, specifically regarding the processes underlying the regulation of emotion, illuminate ways to better understand mindfulness/acceptance-based interventions.

Yet in order to coherently connect the theoretically linked constructs of mindfulness and emotion regulation, it is useful to reflect first on the nature and function of emotion. In turn, this allows us to better understand the purpose and processes of emotion regulation.

The Nature and Function of Emotion

From an evolutionary perspective, emotions can help human beings adapt to the daily challenges they face by preparing us to respond both physiologically and behaviorally to direct and indirect situations, facilitating in the decision-making process, and effectively navigating numerous interpersonal challenges (Gross & Thompson, 2007). As presently conceived, emotion consists of three basic components (Barlow et al., 2011). The first component is physiological, resulting in a subjective "feeling" state. The second component is cognitive, consisting of the multitude of thoughts and images that accompany specific emotions. Together, these two components comprise the *experience* of emotion. Lastly, the third component is a behavioral action tendency, echoing the athlete's (or any person's) learned behavioral responses to the aforementioned experience of emotion. This third piece comprises the *expression* of emotion. So, emotion can be described as a multicomponent process consisting of both the experience and expression of a specific emotional state, whether anxiety, sadness, anger, or another emotion.

Of course, while different emotions have differing subjective and personally derived levels of positive or negative valence for the individual, distinguishing whether a particular emotion is adaptive or maladaptive is ultimately based on *context*. That is, the determination of "adaptive" or "maladaptive" is based on whether it promotes or impedes functional goal-directed action, For instance, a maladaptive emotional response is illustrated by the athlete who becomes angry at a call and pushes the referee, and an adaptive emotional response is present when that athlete is able to be in the presence of that anger and yet continue to focus on the task at hand. If one is driven to behave in a manner that includes avoidance and escape from the experience of emotion, then there is a high degree of probability that the emotion itself will be seen as maladaptive in the pursuit of one's goals and values, whereas if one's response is to confront and deal with the situation associated with the emotion, the emotion would likely be regarded as relatively adaptive in the pursuit of one's goals and values. Essentially, then, understanding this concept necessitates careful attention to whether the individual's emotion leads to (a) goal/values-directed behavioral choices or (b) behavior aimed at avoiding or escaping from the experience of the emotion. This important process is called *emotion regulation.*

Emotion Regulation

Emotion regulation can be defined as the "internal and external processes responsible for experiencing, expressing, and modulating one's emotions in the service of goal achievement" (Moore & Gardner, 2011, p. 249; Thompson, 1994). Emotion regulation processes come in multiple types and forms – they can be either automatic or effortful (Gross & Thompson, 2007), and they consist of skills and strategies through which we monitor, evaluate, experience, express, and tolerate or modulate emotional reactions. Importantly, while emotion regulation sometimes entails modulating the intensity or frequency of an emotional state, it also involves the highly adaptive capacity to generate, sustain, and tolerate emotions when necessary and appropriate for situational adaptation (Calkins & Hill, 2007). Of course, this is not simply in reference to what are commonly (yet problematically) referred to as "negative" emotions (e.g., anger, anxiety). Emotion regulation processes are involved with "negative" emotions (e.g., anger, anxiety) and "positive" emotions (e.g., happiness), as well (Gross & Thompson, 2007). In its most basic sense:

> Adaptive emotion regulation constitutes an array of processes that can allow athletes to respond adaptively to the demands of their environment.

In order to respond adaptively to one's environment, it is necessary to have the skills necessary to appropriately experience, tolerate, and express emotions while simultaneously functioning in a goal/values-directed manner. To this end, emotion regulation involves a range of active cognitive and behavioral processes. As described by Gross and Thompson (2007), emotion regulation strategies can be broken down into two primary categories: (a) antecedent-focused strategies, which occur before an emotion has been elicited and (b) response-focused strategies, which occur after the onset of an emotion.

Antecedent-Focused Strategies

Antecedent-focused emotion regulation strategies occur before an emotion is generated and aim to modulate (or possibly even completely prevent/

eliminate) an emotional experience that might be forthcoming (Gross & Thompson, 2007). Some particular antecedent-focused strategies include:

- Situation selection: This strategy involves engaging in behaviors that allow the individual to avoid situations that are likely to result in the experience of undesired emotions.
- Situation modification: This strategy seeks to modify a stimulus or situation that is eliciting a personally undesired emotional experience, thereby limiting its emotional impact.
- Attentional deployment: This strategy intends to control attentional processes such as worry, rumination, and distraction in order to up- or down-regulate emotional responses.
- Cognitive modification: This strategy seeks to change the meaning of cognitive content, or the frequency of cognitions that surround a particular situation, thereby resulting in a modification of the emotional response. Common cognitive modification efforts include the reappraisal of meaning, and the suppression (e.g., elimination, reduction) of thoughts associated with a situation.

Response-Focused Strategy

As can be noted from the preceding discussion, the multitude of antecedent-focused strategies are directed toward controlling and/or avoiding the triggering of emotional experiences. By contrast, the literature suggests that there is one response-focused emotion regulation strategy, which is implemented *following* the generation of an emotional experience (Gross & Thompson, 2007). Since in this case the emotion has already been triggered, a response-focused strategy aims either (a) to reduce the experience and/or expression of the emotion or (b) to allow the individual to tolerate the experience and/or expression of the emotion. Specifically, this type of strategy, directly referred to as *response modulation*, seeks to influence one's tendencies toward particular intensity and duration of emotional experience and expression. This general strategy occurs following the onset of an emotional experience, and its purpose is to help the individual function adaptively with whatever emotion is experienced.

It is important to note that emotion regulation strategies are not inherently adaptive or maladaptive. Actually, everyone engages in these strategies on a regular basis as we traverse through life's multitude of opportunities and obstacles (Gross & Thompson, 2007). Yet, emotion regulation strategies can indeed become maladaptive, especially when we overuse a particular strategy to the exclusion of others and when we *excessively* use them to heavily control, minimize, or even eliminate the experience of particular emotions. Using emotion regulation strategies in a strict effort to obstruct the experience of emotions (especially those we don't like!) can keep us from pursuing important personal values and goals – and in fact, optimal functioning necessitates pursuing goals and values *even* when in the presence of the full range of emotions and cognitions (Aldoa, Nolen-Hocksema, & Schwiezer, 2010; Barlow et al., 2011). A tidal wave of recent evidence clearly indicates that disproportionate engagement in emotion regulation strategies in order to markedly and unrealistically control, minimize, or eliminate one's emotional experience is a core transdiagnostic process for an extensive range of psychopathological syndromes, including anxiety disorders, depressive disorders, post-traumatic stress disorder (PTSD), anger-related difficulties, eating pathologies, and borderline personality disorder, to name but a few (Aldoa et al., 2010; Barlow et al., 2011; Hayes et al., 1996; Kashdan et al., 2006).

Mindfulness and Emotion Regulation

While this text is not short on slightly varied definitions of mindfulness, core definitions of mindfulness include full awareness of present-moment experience and involve deliberately allocating sustained attention to enduring physical, cognitive, and emotional experiences, without judging any aspect of these experiences as good/bad or right/wrong (Gardner, Moore, & Marks, 2014; Kabat-Zinn, 1994). Mindfulness training, which can be seen as a form of mental training (indeed, cognitive neuroscience literature refers to mindfulness training as a specific form of mental training), aims to increase one's moment-to-moment awareness and attention and, importantly, rejects the need to change or modify one's internal experiences, such as emotions and cognitions. As has now long been described in the sport psychology literature (see Gardner & Moore, 2012, for a review), mindfulness training through meditative practices emphasizes exactly this expansion and enhancement of present-moment nonjudging awareness and attention to one's immediate experience. The question still remains, however, what if any is the association between mindfulness and emotion regulation? In answering this question, we can begin with some basic empirical data.

Mindfulness training has been consistently shown to promote self-regulated attention and emotion regulation (Kabat-Zinn, 1994; Marks, 2008). In fact, research has uncovered a significant correlation between levels of mindfulness and self-report scores on the Difficulties in Emotion Regulation Scale (DERS; Gratz & Roemer, 2004), demonstrating that higher scores on mindfulness reflect fewer difficulties with emotion regulation. Likewise, Feldman and colleagues (2007) discovered significant correlations between mindfulness and the utilization of *adaptive* emotion regulation strategies. Since studies have clearly suggested a strong relationship between mindfulness and adaptive emotion regulation, an important question, then, concerns the nature of that relationship and its specific relationship to sport performance.

It has been suggested that nonjudgmental awareness, a central component of mindfulness, may enable a healthy engagement with emotional states (Hayes & Feldman, 2004), which can subsequently allow for a genuine experience and expression of emotional content (Bridges, Denham, & Ganiban, 2004) without emotional underengagement (e.g., experiential avoidance and/or thought suppression; Hayes et al., 1996; Wegner, 1994) or emotional overengagement (e.g., worry and/or rumination; Borkovec, 1994; Nolen-Hoeksema, 1998). In essence, nonjudging emotional awareness may thus lead to positive outcomes by changing the *relationship* someone has with his or her emotional experiences (Ivanovski & Malhi, 2007; Kabat-Zinn, 1990). Here, I am speaking of changing the *meaning* of specific emotions and in turn the behavioral response tendencies associated with those same emotions. Seen from another angle, it could be stated that experiencing emotions differently requires less working memory (i.e., attentional resources), and thus greater attention can be focused on task-relevant stimuli and goal-directed behavior, an outcome with obvious sport performance consequences. In other words, the less attentional effort one needs to utilize on one's feelings (i.e., feeling less, feeling more, feeling differently), the more attention can be allocated to the task at hand.

Mindfulness is fully inconsistent with any form of emotional control or emotional suppression, and instead emphasizes enhancing *awareness* of and fully *accepting* the full range of emotional (and cognitive) experiences, regardless of perceived valence (e.g., negative, positive), intensity, duration, or perceived utility. Thus, mindfulness cannot correctly be intended or implemented to help someone think "better," more "positively," or more "successfully," and any such efforts are completely inconsistent with mindfulness goals and procedures.

Some authors have suggested that mindfulness reflects a response-focused approach to emotion regulation, which I described earlier as a strategy that is used after the generation of a specific emotion. For example, Hofmann and Asmundson (2008) suggested that while traditional cognitive interventions attempt to modify the content of emotional and cognitive events (which is thus highly antecedent-focused), mindfulness- and acceptance-based models seek to modify the individual's *relationship* with these internal events and, as such, represent a response-focused strategy. Therein, the relationship is modified by developing the capacity to accept or tolerate emotions and cognitions, rather than reflexively acting upon these transient internal events. I suggest that while mindfulness can certainly be utilized as a response-focused strategy, it can also readily function as an antecedent strategy due to its emphasis on full awareness of one's experience, both internal (cognitions, emotions) and external (life events). As such, there is no need to engage in behaviors that seek to avoid situations, alter situations, or modify our cognitive processes, which are most typically seen as antecedent-focused strategies.

Mindfulness- and Acceptance-Based Models

As I have just discussed the nature of varying emotion regulation strategies, including differences between how mindfulness- and acceptance-based models view cognition apart from more traditional models, at this juncture of the chapter, it should be reemphasized that the development of mindfulness is fundamentally different from cognitive reappraisal, with which sport psychologists are quite familiar. Although reappraisal has garnered empirical support within the clinical literature as an adaptive, cognitively oriented emotion regulation strategy, reappraisal can also promote experiential avoidance when its use is driven by an unwillingness to experience or remain in the presence of a specific emotion or cognition. Indeed, "reappraisal" refers to the specific process of cognitively reevaluating specific situations (usually related to the likelihood and/or consequences of a particular event) in order to prevent or modify the generation of distressing emotions. This reappraisal is typically intended to occur either before or early in the emotion-generative process.

Importantly, cognitive reappraisal and mindfulness are fundamentally opposed, in part because cognitive reappraisal (a) views cognitions and emotions as possessing some definitive elements of "good" and "bad," and "right" and "wrong" and (b) directly promotes controlling or modifying these internal events in some way. Traditional change-based forms of cognitive behavioral therapy (CBT) do attempt to provide the perspective that cognitions are simply appraisals or hypotheses rather than facts and instead directly endorses efforts to change these appraisals in order to reflect greater accuracy, logic, and "psychologically beneficial" depictions of reality. From the traditional CBT perspective, cognitions and appraisals perceived as unpleasant should be acted upon or modified so that they are more acceptable and less distressing to the individual. Conversely, mindfulness theory maintains that all mental phenomena (cognitive and emotional) are simply internal events that inevitably come and go in the human experience, and thus do not need to be acted upon in any way. The capacity to simply notice these internal events and allow them to ebb and flow is steadily developed through meditative training, and subsequently behaviors can be chosen based on values and goals. This is consistent with the concept of *decentering*, which is the ability to observe one's thoughts and feelings and regard them as transient, object- ive events of the mind. They do not necessarily reflect truth or reality, and they do not necessitate automatic action.

Another important but often neglected distinction between mindful- ness- and acceptance-based models and traditional change-based cognitive behavioral models (including the unsubstantiated coping skills model long utilized in sport psychology) concerns the assumed relationship between cognitions and emotions. A fundamental "truism" of cognitive- based interventions has historically been that cognitions trigger, or directly lead to, emotional reactions and subsequent behaviors (Beck et al., 1979; Ellis, 1976). This linear assumption implies that cognitions and emotions can be meaningfully separated. Yet, to date there is no direct or compelling evidence for this in the vast cognitive psychology literature.

In contrast, mindfulness interventions make no such distinction, and in fact, the Buddhist literature from which Western mindfulness interventions have evolved contains no word for "emotion" as separate from cognitive processes (Ekman et al., 2005). Further, Buddhist litera- ture has suggested that emotions represent mental states encompassing both cognitive appraisal and a strong affective component (Goleman, 1995), a perspective that is consistent with contemporary views on emotion (Ledoux, 1996). To further illustrate this point, contemporary neurocognitive findings have shown that the "emotional centers" in the brain are also directly involved in aspects of cognitive processing (Davidson & Irwin, 1999). Indeed, it has been proposed that infor- mation processing transpires in a hierarchically fashion across cognitive, emotional, and physiological systems, and these systems appear to be functionally interdependent and inextricably connected (Damasio, 1999; LeDoux, 1996).

Emotion Regulation, Mindfulness, and Sport Performance

So where does all of this important information take us today? As readers of this text are surely aware, there have been two primary models of psychosocial intervention for the enhancement of athletic performance. The first model is the traditional model known as psychological skills training (PST), and the second model, more contemporary in nature, is the more recent mindfulness- and acceptance-based model of performance enhancement. Although the traditional PST model was the dominant approach in sport psychology for nearly forty years, the model has suffered from a lack of substantiated and consistent overarching theory by which to understand its potential relationship to athletic performance (Gardner, 2009) and has struggled mightily on empirical grounds. Conversely, mindfulness- and acceptance-based models have directly and successfully identified (and are empirically testing) proposed mechanisms of change for their associated techniques (Gardner & Moore, 2007; Goodman et al., 2014; Gross et al., 2015). The purpose of this chapter is not to identify once again the theoretical and empirical discrepancies between these two dominant models. Rather, my intent herein is to suggest that we may be able to deepen our understanding of performance enhancement by integrating scientific findings associated with emotion regulation and emotion regulatory strategies. So, what follows is a more in-depth discussion of each emotion regulation strategy that I previously defined in brief, and further, a focus on both adaptive and maladaptive ways that each strategy is often applied in the context of athletic performance.

Situation Selection

As previously noted, situation selection is an antecedent-focused emotion regulation strategy, which means that it is a strategy that is implemented prior to the generation of emotion with the intent of modulating, preventing, or eliminating an emotional experience that might possibly be forthcoming. With the use of the situation selection emotion regulation strategy, the athlete determines whether to enter into a situation that may stimulate a particular emotional response. Within athletics, the adaptive utilization of situation selection could be seen, for instance, in circumstances in which an athlete avoids social situations that might be either tempting (i.e., a late-night party just before a big game) or challenging/frustrating (i.e., social activities that include reporters, overzealous fans, and/or photographers). In the preceding examples, the situation selection emotion regulation strategy allows the athlete to eliminate a possibly troubling situation. Likewise, situation selection is involved when the athlete purposely engages in calm, pre-performance activities instead of more frenetic, distracting, and stressful situations.

There is no doubt that this emotion regulation strategy can certainly be adaptive. Yet, consider that an *excessive* or *maladaptive* use of situation selection could indeed be problematic. Some examples of the maladaptive/ excessive use of situation selection would be the athlete who repeatedly skips injury rehabilitation in order to avoid physical discomfort or pain; the athlete who avoids off-season training because she finds it uncomfortable to face difficult tasks; and the athlete who reports days late to training camp because he didn't want to "feel anxious" on his first day. While all athletes and nonathletes alike often engage in adaptive situation selection in order to avoid a particularly aggravating or noxious situation, negative consequences can ensue when athletes overuse this strategy or use it to avoid negative internal processes rather than using it for the promotion of their goals and personal values. Whether avoiding necessary training or rehabilitation due to its discomfort, or avoiding contemplation of future career options because it triggers anxiety, what distinguishes adaptive from maladaptive uses of situation selection is whether the pursuit is geared toward the avoidance of emotions (maladaptive emotion regulation) or is in the service of goals and values (adaptive emotion regulation).

Based on the mindfulness- and acceptance-based theoretical perspective, effective interventions would likely focus on exposure-based strategies that actually *promote* the experience of the previously avoided emotion. If implemented in a strategically sound manner, such strategies would serve to improve distress tolerance and foster behaviorally activated commitment to values-driven behavior, thereby loosening the athlete's adherence to emotion-driven avoidant behavior, which is at the heart of the excessive use of situation selection. In this regard, mindfulness- and acceptance-based strategies actually encourage the athlete to experience (and thus learn to tolerate) the emotion (or cognition) that he or she is avoiding and make no effort whatsoever to reduce those feelings or in any way try to bypass the emotion. In fact, mindfulness meditative techniques can be thought of as a general form of exposure. While typical exposure techniques often seek to modify emotional reactions to specific cues or situations (especially in the treatment of anxiety disorders), mindfulness may be considered to be an exposure to one's own internal experiences (cognitions and emotions) and not overt situations. Thus, rather than changing one's response to an external situation, the intent is to change one's relationship with personal internal experiences – in essence, to become more comfortable with, accepting of, and tolerant of cognitions, emotions, and physiological sensations, whatever they may be.

Situation Modification

When using this particular antecedent-focused emotion regulation strategy, after entering into a situation, a person would make some effort to change the situation in some way in order to negate its emotional impact. For example, a coach may use humor to reduce negative affect during a tense plane ride home after a tough loss, or an athlete may change the topic of a conversation to derail a discussion that she does not want to have. As with any emotion regulation strategy, adaptive and maladaptive uses may occur, and maladaptive uses can lead to detrimental effects. For instance, superstitious behavior is a form of situation modification that is notably common among competitive athletes and athletic organizations. At more normative levels, superstitions function as a form of safety behaviors, and in such cases can effectively and temporarily reduce anxiety and take the edge off. On the other hand, there are certainly occasions in which superstitious behaviors become maladaptive, such as when the athlete begins regarding (albeit irrationally) either positive outcomes and/ or the absence of negative consequences as partly or completely the result of the superstitious behavior (i.e., the superstitious behavior becomes negatively reinforced) rather than a reflection of skill acquisition, execution, or context.

To provide a less extreme example of the maladaptive use of situation modification, let's revisit the earlier example that I used to illustrate an adaptive utilization of situation modification, which was the use of humor to reduce negative affect among team members. While the use of humor in that version of the example was fairly adaptive, it would be maladaptive if an athlete used humor and/or chattiness in a tense pre-performance situation in order to reduce perceived tension in the locker room *if* in turn such humor or chattiness interfered with the concentration and pre-performance preparation of teammates (who may or may not be experiencing the tension as intolerable).

Importantly, occasional use of the situation modification emotion regulation strategy would not be particularly problematic at all. Instead, maladaptive utilization would be determined by (a) the overuse of this strategy and/or (b) whether the primary intent is to excessively avoid or escape from uncomfortable emotional states. One example of situation modification that has long been used in sport psychology is precompetitive routines, a form of traditional behavioral stimulus control adapted for use in the sport milieu. When *appropriately targeted* to right the athlete-client, use of precompetitive routines may reduce extraneous emotion-eliciting stimuli and promote concentration toward competitive tasks by trimming the available stimuli that may elicit distracting internal reactions. Yet importantly, sport psychologists who choose to employ precompetitive routines should *not* view it as a catch-all technique that is likely to be effective with everyone. If practitioners do in fact decide to employ situation modification in the form of precompetitive routines, they should see this strategy as a rational and theoretically appropriate technique only *if* and *when* the athlete's performance needs or concerns center around the overuse or intended use of maladaptive situation modification behaviors.

Of course, in addition to stimulus control–based procedures such as precompetitive routines, sport psychologists can incorporate mindfulness training exercises that encourage a nonjudging acceptance of (and subsequent decentering from) internal experiences. The exceptional result of this acceptance and decentering is greater tolerance of and/or comfort with the experience of emotion, which subsequently reduces the need to modify situations in order to minimize, avoid, or escape from associated emotional experiences (Gardner & Moore, 2007; Kabat-Zinn, 1990).

Attentional Deployment

While the previously described antecedent-focused emotion regulation strategies seek to alter the person–environment interaction, the attentional deployment strategy does not. Rather, the athlete uses this emotion regulation strategy to *redirect attention* within a particular situation with the purpose of influencing the emotional experience. Adaptive use of attentional deployment may be seen among competitive athletes in efforts made to redirect attention *away from* task-irrelevant and/or highly distracting stimuli in the environment (e.g., travel issues, arrangements for family attendance at games, paparazzi issues, social media presence) and *toward* task-relevant stimuli (e.g., personal game preparation, competitive strategies). Deep-breathing relaxation techniques (for the purpose of arousal control) may also be an example of an attentional deployment strategy if they are implemented *before* heightened arousal begins and are used to redirect attention away from ruminative thoughts (i.e., worry) and onto the individual's bodily processes (i.e., breathing).

Now, I should state that:

> It is not uncommon for sport psychologists to incorrectly assume that mindfulness and relaxation are the same or are efforts toward the same goal.

Such a misconception is absolutely untrue, and the distinction needs to be made so that readers do not confuse the two. One of the central differences between mindfulness training and deep-breathing–based relaxation exercises is, in fact, the goal itself. In relaxation exercises, the goal is to lower arousal levels, which can have a place with athletes who experience extreme and maladaptive precompetitive arousal. On the other hand, mindfulness exercises make absolutely no attempt to enhance relaxation or lower arousal. In fact, this would be counter to the basic premise of mindfulness, which is that there is no good/bad, right/wrong cognition, emotion, or physical sensation. Rather, mindfulness training seeks to develop an openness and acceptance of all internal states as normal and transient, and these states should not be the focus of our efforts.

Although attentional deployment can at times be adaptive, there are also a number of problematic attentional deployment strategies, such as worry, rumination, and efforts to redirect attention via distraction. In particular, notable clinical researcher Steve Hayes and his colleagues have described maladaptive attentional deployment strategies such as worry and rumination as "avoidant concentration" (Hayes, Strosahl, & Wilson, 2011). Using these maladaptive efforts at emotion regulation, athletes often excessively replay and analyze historical events and mentally rehearse or plan future events based on the faulty assumption that such cognitive efforts will prevent or minimize a reoccurrence of "negative" emotions. Ultimately, such strategies draw attention away from the present moment (which is certainly where an athlete needs to be) and places attention onto past events or future possibilities.

Although seemingly counterintuitive, research findings consistently demonstrate that both worry and rumination are negatively reinforced (because they allow for the removal or avoidance of aversive emotions) (a) in their successful attempts to avoid the present and (b) in their ability to dampen the full experience of emotion. In essence, cognitive activity is decidedly high during periods of rumination and worry aimed at replaying historical events and planning or rehearsing future events, and this is accompanied by real and often subtle reductions in uncomfortable physiological arousal and emotional distress (Borkovec, 1994; Borkovec & Hu,

1990; Gardner & Moore, 2006). The emotion-avoidant function of worry and rumination is strongly correlated with numerous negative effects, including some particularly relevant to athletes, such as impaired decision making (Butler & Gross, 2004). Likewise, rumination and worry are highly associated with other forms of cognitive avoidance often seen in athletes, such as maladaptive perfectionism (Santanello & Gardner, 2007).

While worry and rumination are profound in their association with an array of negative outcomes and therefore gain extensive research attention in the clinical milieu, another highly common form of attentional deployment is *distraction*. The readers of this text who are sport psychologists are surely no strangers to witnessing the deleterious effects of distraction among their athletes. Distraction strategies are geared toward the refocusing of one's attention onto aspects of a situation that are not emotionally provocative. For instance, classic PST-oriented imagery scripts could be viewed as adaptive attentional deployment strategies, even though imagery has not demonstrated efficacy in actually enhancing competitive performance. Such imagery scripts often seek to circumvent the affective aspects of a particular situation by instead directing the athlete toward functional performance-relevant behaviors. This can subsequently alter the affect-eliciting components of an event. Likewise, relaxation exercises (not to be confused with *mindfulness*) can be utilized as a distraction-based attentional deployment strategy.

However, allow me to emphasize once again that the primary distinction between what makes this or any other emotion regulation strategy adaptive or maladaptive is the ultimate purpose. If the purpose is primarily to modulate internal experiences in order to respond mentally and physically to the task-related demands inherent in competitive athletics, then one could suggest that the strategy is being used in an adaptive manner. However, if the primary purpose is the avoidance or escape from uncomfortable internal experiences, then the likelihood is that the strategy is maladaptive.

The challenge is that some athletes (and sport psychologists, for that matter) believe that optimal performance can come only in the relative absence of strong emotion.

The reality is that optimal competitive performance often occurs with strong and uncomfortable (sometimes incorrectly judged to be "negative") internal experiences, and any suggestion that optimal performance requires the absence of such experiences is simply wrong and flies in the face of both empirical and anecdotal evidence.

Mindfulness- and acceptance-based interventions are once again more likely to utilize mindfulness-based strategies, not to redeploy attention away from emotion-generating stimuli, but in fact to enhance task-relevant attention *while* experiencing emotion. As we have previously described, "mindfulness exercises pursue effortless and *automatic* self-regulation of attention for the purpose of maintaining awareness of one's immediate experience. There is no effort to attend to internal or external stimuli pre-defined as 'good' or 'bad,' but rather, the effort is to promote the idea that one will inevitably experience a wide variety of naturally occurring experiences. . .," along with the capacity to refocus one's attention onto in-the-moment task-relevant stimuli (Moore & Gardner, 2011, p. 254). So, if a sport psychologist theoretically comprehends, effectively describes, and accurately trains an athlete in mindfulness-based skills (I have to admit that we aren't always certain that this is done correctly), mindfulness stimulates an enhanced awareness of both internal and external experiences. Further, when training mindfulness within the context of acceptance (i.e., experiences of many types are likely to come and go and need not be judged or controlled), mindfulness allows for enhanced attention to, and ongoing awareness of, present-moment stimuli and contingencies, and this result is capable of generating high and sustainable levels of performance (Bernier et al., 2009; Csikszentmihalyi, 1990; Gardner & Moore, 2007, 2010; Gross et al., 2015; Schwanhausser, 2009). This approach, therefore, is in many respects the complete opposite of controlled attentional deployment, as previously described.

Cognitive Modification

Cognitive modification is the final antecedent-focused emotion regulation strategy, and through this strategy, the athlete seeks to in some way reduce, eliminate, or otherwise change a potential emotional response by altering either the meaning or the frequency of his or her thoughts about a given situation. This should be a very familiar strategy to those practicing sport psychology, as it entails altering how the athlete thinks about and appraises an impending event. On one hand, empirical findings indicate that *antecedent reappraisal*, which is the reframing or modification of the individual's thoughts about an upcoming event, can positively impact the person's emotional experience associated with confronting the event (Gross & John, 2003). For instance, consider the athlete who reframes a stressful upcoming competitive performance to see it as challenging, exciting, and enjoyable. By doing this, reappraisal can have some clear benefits. Yet, many athletes (and people in general, for that matter) engage in a maladaptive form of cognitive modification known as cognitive *suppression*, which involves direct and indirect efforts to control one's thoughts – not by a reconsideration of the logic and accuracy of thought content, but rather by control-based tactics such as rote language substitution (such as inserting positive self-talk); attempts to obstruct thoughts (such as "thought stopping" techniques); and resisting cognitive content (such as thinking, "I can't let myself think this way!" and, "Thinking these things will screw me up!").

Contrary to the aforementioned benefits of cognitive reappraisal that are possible when it is implemented appropriately, *cognitive suppression* frequently culminates in a variety of noxious consequences, such as decreases in general psychological well-being and actual *increases* in both the frequency and intensity of negative thoughts and images (Gardner & Moore, 2007), particularly when used excessively or incorrectly (as noted previously). So, while this may be surprising to sport psychologists long-committed to the use of traditional PST procedures, consider that promoting the utilization of PST-oriented "self-talk" procedures in a rote, language replacement–oriented fashion (as is commonly done in sport psychology practice) is actually promoting and reinforcing the use of a maladaptive emotion regulation strategy that may very well lead to unanticipated negative personal and performance outcomes. Indeed, this fits perfectly with what we have seen in the forty-plus years of study of PST-oriented self-talk procedures with athletic clientele. Comprehensive qualitative reviews of the sport psychology literature have discovered that PST-oriented self-talk strategies have led to mixed and at times even negative results in research investigations, thus signifying that use of this procedure, in its common form, should be reconsidered (Gardner & Moore, 2006, 2007; Moore, 2003). Herein viewing self-talk procedures from the perspective of emotion regulation may suggest a theoretical explanation for these less-than-robust empirical findings. Based upon the extant literature, I suggest that although the use of appropriate precompetition antecedent reappraisal strategies may at times help athletes in some ideographically determined specific situations, the use of rote corrective self-talk procedures should be avoided in professional practice – and it *certainly* should never be mixed with any efforts at mindfulness and acceptance training, which maintains an antithetical theoretical foundation.

Borkovec, T. D. (1994). The nature, functions, and origins of worry. In G. C. I. Davey and F. Tallis (Eds.), *Worrying: Perspectives, theory, assessment and treatment* (pp. 5–33). New York, NY: John Wiley & Sons.

Borkovec, T. D., and Hu, S. (1990). The effects of worry on cardiovascular response to phobic imagery. *Behaviour Research and Therapy* 28, 69–73. doi:10.1016/0005-7967(90)90056-O

Bridges, L. J., Denham, S. A., and Ganiban, J. M. (2004). Definitional issues in emotion regulation research. *Child Development*, 75(2), 340–345. doi: 10.1111/j.1467-8624.2004.00675.x

Butler, E. A., and Gross, J. J. (2004). Hiding feelings in social contexts: Out of sight is not out of mind. In P. Philippot and R. S. Feldman (Eds.), *The regulation of emotion* (pp. 101–120). Mahwah, NJ: Erlbaum.

Calkins, S. D., and Hill, A. (2007). Caregiver influences on emerging emotion regulation: Biological and environmental transactions in early development. In J. J. Gross (Ed.), *Handbook of emotion regulation* (pp. 229–248). New York, NY: Guilford Press.

Csikszentmihalyi, M. (1990). *Flow: The psychology of optimal experience*. New York, NY: Harper & Row.

Damasio, A. (1999). *The feeling of what happens*. New York, NY: Harcourt, Brace.

Davidson, R. J., and Irwin, W. (1999). The functional neuroanatomy of emotion and affective style. *Trends in Cognitive Science*, 3(1), 11–21. doi:10.1016/S1364-6613(98)01265-0

Ekman, P., Davidson, R. J., Ricard, M., and Wallace, A. B. (2005). Buddhist and psychological perspectives on emotions and well-being. *Current Directions in Psychological Science*, 14(2), 59–63. doi: 10.1111/j.0963-7214.2005.00335.x

Ellis, A. (1976). RET abolishes most of the human ego. *Psychotherapy: Theory, Research and Practice*, 13, 343.

Fairholme, C. P., Boisseau, C. L., Ellard, K. K., Ehrenreich, J. T., and Barlow, D. H. (2010). Emotions, emotion regulation, and psychological treatment: A unified perspective. In A. M. Kring and D. M. Sloan (Eds.), *Emotion regulation and psychopathology*. New York, NY: Guilford Press.

Feldman, G., Hayes, A., Kumar, S., Greeson, J., and Laurenceau, J. P. (2007). Mindfulness and emotion regulation: The development and initial validation of the Cognitive and Affective Mindfulness Scale-Revised (CAMS-R). *Journal of Psychopathology and Behavioral Assessment*, 29(3), 177–190. doi: 10.1007/s10862-006-9035-8

Gardner, F. L. (2009). Efficacy, mechanisms of change, and the scientific development of sport psychology. *Journal of Clinical Sport Psychology*, 3(2), 139–155.

Gardner, F. L., and Moore, Z. E. (2004). A mindfulness-acceptance-commitment (MAC) based approach to athletic performance enhancement: Theoretical considerations. *Behavior Therapy*, 35, 707–723. doi:10.1016/S0005-7894(04)80016-9

(2006). *Clinical sport psychology*. Champagne, IL: Human Kinetics.

(2007). *The psychology of human performance: The mindfulness-acceptance-commitment approach.* New York, NY: Springer.

(2010). Acceptance-based behavioral therapies and sport. In S. Hanrahan, and M. Andersen (Eds.), *Handbook of applied sport psychology* (pp. 186–193). New York, NY: Routledge.

(2012). Mindfulness and acceptance models in sport psychology: A decade of basic and applied scientific advancements. *Canadian Psychology*, 53(4), 309–318. doi: 10.1037/a0030220

Gardner, F. L., Moore, Z. E., and Marks, D. R. (2014). Rectifying misconceptions: A comprehensive response to "Some concerns about the psychological implications of mindfulness: A critical analysis." *Journal of Rational-Emotive and Cognitive Behavior Therapy*, 32(4), 325–344. doi: 10.1007/s10942-014-0196-1

Goleman, D. (1995). *Emotional intelligence.* New York, NY: Bantam.

Goodman, F. R., Kashdan, T. B., Mallard, T. T., and Schumann, M. (2014). A brief mindfulness and yoga intervention with an entire NCAA Division I athletic team: An initial investigation. *Psychology of Consciousness: Theory, Research, and Practice*, 1, 339–348. doi: 10.1037/cns0000022

Gratz, K. L., and Roemer, L. (2004). Multidimensional assessment of emotion regulation and dysregulation: Development, factor structure, and initial validation of the Difficulties in Emotion Regulation Scale. *Journal of Psychopathology and Behavioral Assessment*, 26(1), 41–54. doi: 10.1023/B: JOBA.0000007455.08539.94

Gross, M., Gardner, F. L., and Moore, Z. E. (2012, November). *Using the mindfulness-acceptance-commitment (MAC) approach with high school student-athletes: An investigation of its effectiveness as a prevention program.* Paper presented at the annual convention of the Association for Behavioral and Cognitive Therapies, National Harbor, Maryland.

Gross, J. J., and John, O. P. (2003). Individual differences in two emotion regulation processes: Implications for affect, relationships, and well-being. *Journal of Personality and Social Psychology*, 85, 348–362. doi: 10.1037/0022-3514.85.2.348

Gross, M., Moore, Z. E., Gardner, F. L., and Marks, D. R. (2015). *Empirical examination of the mindfulness-acceptance-commitment (MAC) approach for the mentalhealth and sport performance of student athletes.* Manuscript submitted for publication.

Gross, J. J., and Thompson, R. A. (2007). Emotion regulation: Conceptual foundations. In J. J. Gross (Ed.), *Handbook of emotion regulation* (pp. 3–25). New York, NY: Guilford Press.

Hayes, A. M., and Feldman, G. (2004). Clarifying the construct of mindfulness in the context of emotion regulation and the process of change in therapy. *Clinical Psychology: Science and Practice*, 11(3), 255–262. doi: 10.1093/clipsy.bph080

Hayes, S. C., Luoma, J., Bond, F., Masuda, A., and Lillis, J. (2006). Acceptance and Commitment Therapy: Model, processes, and outcomes. *Behaviour Research and Therapy*, 44, 1–25. doi: 10.1016/j.brat.2005.06.006

Hayes, S. C., Strosahl, K. D., and Wilson, K. G. (2011). *Acceptance and commitment therapy: The process and practice of mindful change.* New York, NY: Guilford Press.

Hayes, S. C., Wilson, K. W., Gifford, E. V., Follette, V. M., and Strosahl, K. (1996). Experiential avoidance and behavioral disorders: A functional dimensional approach to diagnosis and treatment. *Journal of Consulting and Clinical Psychology*, 64(6), 1152–1168. doi: 10.1037/0022-006X.64.6.1152

Hofmann, S. G., and Asmundson, G. J. G. (2008). Acceptance and mindfulness-based therapy: New wave or old hat? *Clinical Psychology Review*, 28(1), 1–16. doi:10.1016/j.cpr.2007.09.003

Ivanovski, B., and Malhi, G. S. (2007). The psychological and neurophysiological concomitants of mindfulness forms of meditation. *Acta Neuropsychiatrica*, 19(2), 76–91. doi: 10.1111/j.1601-5215.2007.00175.x

Kabat-Zinn, J. (1990). *Full catastrophe living: Using the wisdom of your mind and body to face stress, pain, and illness.* New York, NY: Delacorte.

   (1994). *Wherever you go, there you are: Mindfulness in everyday life.* New York, NY: Hyperion.

Kashdan, T. B., Barrios, V., Forsyth, J. P., and Steger, M. F. (2006). Experiential avoidance as a generalized psychological vulnerability: Comparisons with coping and emotion regulation strategies. *Behaviour Research and Therapy*, 44, 1301–1320. doi:10.1016/j.brat.2005.10.003

LeDoux, J. (1996). *The emotional brain.* New York, NY: Simon and Schuster.

Marks, D. R. (2008). The Buddha's extra scoop: Neural correlates of mindfulness and clinical sport psychology. *Journal of Clinical Sport Psychology*, 2, 216–241.

Mennin, D. S., Heimberg, R. G., Turk, C. L., and Fresco, D. M. (2002). Applying an emotion regulation framework to integrative approaches to generalized anxiety disorder. *Clinical Psychology: Science and Practice*, 9(1), 85–90. doi: 10.1093/clipsy.9.1.85

Moore, Z. E. (2003). Toward the development of an evidence based practice of sport psychology: A structured qualitative study of performance enhancement interventions (Doctoral dissertation, La Salle University). *Dissertation Abstracts International-B*, 64 (10), 5227 (UMI No. 3108295).

   (2009). Theoretical and empirical developments of the mindfulness-acceptance-commitment (MAC) approach to performance enhancement. *Journal of Clinical Sport Psychology*, 3(4), 291–302.

Moore, Z., and Gardner, F. (2001, October). *Taking applied sport psychology from research to practice: Integrating empirically supported interventions into a self-regulatory model of athletic performance.* Symposium presented at the annual conference of the Association for the Advancement of Applied Sport Psychology, Orlando, FL.

Moore, Z. E., and Gardner, F. L. (2011). Understanding models of performance enhancement from the perspective of emotion regulation. *Athletic Insight*, 3(3), 247–260.

Nolen-Hoeksema, S. (1998). The other end of the continuum: The costs of rumination. *Psychological Inquiry*, 9, 216–219. doi: 10.1207/s15327965pli0903_5

Santanello, A., and Gardner, F. L. (2007). The role of experiential avoidance in the relationship between maladaptive perfectionism and worry. *Cognitive Therapy and Research*, 31, 319–332. doi: 10.1007/s10608-006-9000-6

Schwanhausser, L. (2009). Application of the mindfulness-acceptance-commitment (MAC) protocol with an adolescent springboard diver: The case of Steve. *Journal of Clinical Sport Psychology*, 3, 377–395.

Thompson, R. A. (1994). Emotion regulation: A theme in search of definition. *Monographs of the Society for Research in Child Development*, 59, 25–52. doi: 10.1111/j.1540-5834.1994.tb01276.x

Wegner, D. M. (1994). Ironic processes of mental control. *Psychological Review*, 101(1), 34–52. doi: 10.1037/0033-295X.101.1.34

CHAPTER 3

Self-Compassion, Distress Tolerance, and Mindfulness in Performance

Amy L. Baltzell

The focus of this chapter addresses both theoretical and applied considerations of how to help athletes deescalate from performance triggered emotionally reactivity through self-compassion. Researchers and practitioners bringing mindfulness to the performance realm are offering new pathways to cultivate mind states that support enhanced performance. Yet, for some athletes, being asked to *accept aversive thoughts* or *just focus on novel stimuli* is not enough. Some performers who suffer from intense negative emotions as a result of fear or harsh self-criticism, particularly resulting from high-pressure performance expectations, may need more than current mindfulness interventions in sport. Some athletes require more support coping with debilitating thoughts and emotions beyond practitioners guiding athletes to tolerate their feelings (such as terror) and refocus on the task at hand. Zella Moore (in Chapter 2) offers a persuasive theoretical and conceptual argument for the place of emotion regulation in the mindfulness and performance arena. The ultimate goal is to help performers be more empowered to emotionally regulate appropriately in the face of intensive anxiety or fear with the goal of optimal performance.

The quality of the internal experience of the athlete must be given more attention as we consider how to create mindfulness interventions such that athletes are willing to accept and, at worst, tolerate what emerges internally while engaged in the world of competition and high-demand performance. We need to offer athletes more than simply prompting them toward raw acceptance and exploration of what is occurring moment to moment; athletes who are suffering need more guidance than simply to hold an openness and curiosity to moment-to-moment internal and external experience, when such moments are at times extremely difficult to tolerate (e.g., performance anxiety). I contend that helping performers with emotional tolerance via practices of self-compassion is a pathway to support athletes becoming more mindful and fully engaged in moment-to-moment experience and ultimately perform better.

As a practicing sport psychologist, I have witnessed myriad stories of elite athletes and musicians who become unable to function in their performance realm due to overwhelming thoughts and emotions. Many of these said performers had first seen psychologists, psychiatrists, and/or medical doctors for help (for psychological and somatic symptoms, respectively) – and to no avail. In this chapter, I will present the ancient idea of compassion and how introducing compassion to the self (self-compassion) offers performers pathways to overcome the seemingly impossible – for high-level performers to face their aversive thoughts and emotions with authentic self-kindness such that they can fully refocus on task-relevant cues. In this chapter, I will discuss distress tolerance and self-compassion and offer specific interventions that can be integrated with a mindful approach to help performers ultimately tolerate aversive subjective internal experience such that they can optimally perform.

Compassion and Mindfulness

Compassion is an intended aspect of mindfulness that often gets lost in the more secular application of mindfulness practices. Jon Kabat-Zinn (2003) emphasizes the importance of both what we *think* and how we *feel* in connection to mindfulness. He writes (2003) that "the word for mind and heart are the same in Asian languages; thus 'mindfulness' includes an affectionate, compassionate quality within the attending, a sense of openhearted, friendly presences and interest" (Kabat-Zinn, 2003, p. 145). Ronald Siegel (2010), a leader in teaching mindfulness meditation, directly notes, when considering suffering, that the ability to accept (or tolerate) internal difficulty "adds warmth, friendliness and compassion" to one's experience (p. 32).

Yet the idea of kindness and self-compassion is often not part of the conversation when considering mindfulness in sport. Without direct instruction about how to cultivate self-compassion, the idea of kindness to self in difficult moments in sport and performance will not be brought to bear. In fact, the sport realm spurns such notions of self-kindness and gentleness with self. Sport is about mental toughness and grit, and in most traditional sport psychology circles, the idea of encouraging self-compassion would either not be understood or not considered a viable pathway to contending with emotional difficulty. Anecdotally I recall a Division I coach of a full scholarship team note that "There is no room for emotion in sport!" suggesting that her athletes should function above emotion and be professional; they should either not experience or, at worst if felt, not succumb to sport-related negative thoughts or feelings

However, imagine an athlete who is going into a competition that will determine whether or not she will make the Olympic team, a professional baseball player who is going to pitch a game with the decision makers watching determining who will get bumped up to the majors, or a musician preparing for an audition that will select one musician from five hundred for a full-time seat on one of the best orchestras in the country. There are myriad examples in sport and other performance realms in which the performer's position is threatened and that the outcome of one event could mean lifetime achievement or failure. Such instances can evoke debilitating thoughts and emotions. There are less intense moments as well, such as simply missing a shot or going into daily practice with a coach who tends to be harsh and belittling, that for some athletes and performers can evoke debilitating emotional responses that aversely impacts the ability to swim, run, throw, jump, create music, or dance.

For some performers, such aversive thoughts and emotions can snowball into suboptimal performance or *choking*. Hill and colleagues (2009) define choking as "a process whereby the individual perceives their resources are insufficient to meet the demands of the situation, and concludes with a significant drop in performance – a choke" (p. 206). Hill and colleagues (2009), in their study of golfers, offer traditional sport psychology interventions that they note are efficacious in helping athletes cope with choking situations, including the setting of process goals, cognitive restructuring, and imagery. Certainly traditional mental skills training works, sometimes, as a tool to help performers face potentially debilitative performance anxiety.

Such prompts are asking performers to shift their attention away from their anxiety and toward performance relevant cues. Athletes and performers are essentially being asked, implicitly, to accept the anxiety and simply focus on the task at hand to optimize performance. (See Chapter 2 for a full consideration of ways athletes are taught to ignore aversive thoughts). At best, the performer, when faced with thoughts of fear, self-doubt, and harsh self-criticism, is able to do what he or she is told and move on and focus on the next play (e.g., "Hey, don't worry about it – just get the next ball!"). Yet, anecdotally, we know that *some* athletes, at times, are unable to accept the aversive internal emotions. What is it that gets in the way of performers not being able to shift their attention and *just* focus on the next play?

Steven Hayes (2004), who created Acceptance Commitment Therapy (ACT), offers a clear theoretical explanation of what can go awry, internally, when harsh, negative thoughts emerge (e.g., the world champion thinking, "I can never win this one," or the twenty-year veteran violinist thinking at an orchestra audition, "I am just not good enough"). When one's thinking process is maladaptive, Hayes contends, the individual tends to experience either *cognitive fusion*, in which the individual reacts as if his thoughts are literally true (e.g., the basketball star doesn't believe his shot can go in, so he stops taking shots), or *experiential avoidance*, "the attempt to escape or avoid private events" (Hayes, 2004, p. 650), such that the thoughts are so repugnant that the performer might opt to skip practice or simply not try and go through the motions. Hayes contends, in concert with Buddhist philosophy, that one's thoughts are not the problem: the problem is how we respond to them. Hayes (2004) notes, it is "the tendency to take these [internal] experiences literally and then to fight against them that is viewed as harmful" (p. 651).

Performance dukkha is born when such unintentional, harsh thoughts go through the mind, and the performer reacts as if his or her thoughts are literally true. Performance dukkha is, then, defined as psychic pain and internal performance distraction that emerges as a function of the performer overengaging with or trying to avoid performance-related, aversive, internal experience (Baltzell, in press). As a practicing sport psychologist, I have worked with athletes who can no longer swim, row, throw a ball, run, or jump. The performance dukkha is so debilitating that the thoughts and feelings sometimes somaticize such that the performers can literally no longer physically function within the sport context (e.g., the runner stops running; the soccer players faints from the emotional pressure). Though these athletes may represent an extreme, they also reflect the issue of performers' unproductive response to performance anxiety, harsh self-talk, or loss of confidence that is quite common across levels and types of performance realms that if left unchecked might lead to consistently subpar performance.

For decades, the main prompt has been to urge athletes to be *mentally tough* and simply focus on the task at hand. Even Mihaly Csikszentmihalyi (1999), thought leader in sport and positive psychology and author of the concept of *flow*, whose focus has been on happiness, creativity, and engagement, emphasizes the need to refocus on the task at hand when experiencing aversive internal subjective experience. In his seminal text, *Finding Flow* (Csikszentmihalyi, 1997), he states, "It is better to look suffering straight in the eye, acknowledge and respect its presence, and then get busy as soon as possible focusing on things we choose to focus on" (p. 128). This sentiment is shared by the mindfulness movement in performance: we need to urge performers to learn to accept unhelpful thoughts, emotions, and body sensations, and through commitment to personal values and goals refocus on the task at hand (e.g., Chapter 7; Gardner & Moore, 2007). And such an approach is quite wise much of the time.

Yet even the best athletes sometimes do not accept aversive internal experience and refocus on the task at hand consistently. Almost twenty years hence, world-respected social psychologist Albert Bandura (1997), summarizes the debilitating effect that can occur from harshness to self within the sport realm:

> Elite athletes drive themselves to success through stringent self-standards. To the extent that they tie their self-evaluation to standards of athletic excellence, they can be cruelest to themselves when the performance falls short in crucial situations. They dwell on their failures rather than savor their successes. . . . Because of the intense pressure of athletic competitiveness, development of efficacy in self-management of thought processes is vital to success (p. 391).

Yet, we are missing a step. What can empower the athlete to refocus on the task at hand when bombarded by fear, anxiety, or self-doubt?

Csikszentmihalyi (1997) offers a potential solution. He notes that keeping a *mindful*, steady response to such challenge in the face of aversive subjective experience is requisite, "To deny, repress, or misinterpret such events is no solution either, because the information will keep smoldering in the recesses of the mind" (p. 128). Csikszentmihalyi's statement truly is a call for a mindful approach – one that is not blocking the fear or collapsing into the fear, but instead the performer facing and tolerating that which is most difficult. Yet, facing the negative thoughts and feelings can create distress, so the athlete or performer must learn to tolerate such performance dukkha.

Distress Tolerance

How athletes or other performers handle debilitative emotions and thoughts is predictive of performance. Specifically, their ability to tolerate emotional distress is often fundamental to their retaining or regaining requisite attention on the task at hand, particularly in high-pressure performance situations. *Distress tolerance* is the term used in the clinical psychology research to encapsulate the concept of how an individual withstands aversive internal psychological states (Zvolensky et al., 2011). The literature focuses on the "(a) the *perceived capacity* to withstand negative emotional and/or aversive states (physical discomfort) and (b) the *behavioral act* of withstanding distressing internal states elicited by some type of stressor" (Leyro, Zvolensky, & Bernstein, 2010, p. 578; emphasis added). Paul Gilbert (2009a), who coined the term Compassion Focused Therapy (CFT), defines distress tolerance as "being able to contain, stay with and tolerate complex and high levels of emotion, rather than avoid, fearfully divert from, close down, contradict, invalidate or deny them" (p. 203). (I will address CFT and ways to cultivate compassion to strengthen distress tolerance later in the chapter.)

Tolerating or withstanding aversive psychological states, often in terms of anxiety or physical pain, is just what many athletes are called to do. Unfortunately, most athletes and high-level performers are bereft of education and training about how to best endure such states – even within most performance-based mindfulness training interventions. I have found as a practicing sport psychologist that *distress tolerance* is precisely what many high-level performers need, particularly athletes susceptible to performance anxiety.

Simons and Gaher (2005) offer four dimensions of distress tolerance that map well onto the experience of a high-level performer who experiences performance-related distress. Such emotional and cognitive distress emerges both when the individual is both anticipating (e.g., in sport, fear of losing a race or a game) and experiencing negative emotions (e.g., in sport, embarrassment or frustration resulting from missing a shot or not blocking a ball). Under Simons and Gaher's (2005) four dimensions of distress tolerance, with high distress tolerance the individual has the ability to:

1. *Tolerate negative emotions,* such as being distressed or upset.
2. *Accept emotional distress.*
3. *Accept negative emotions as part of the emotion regulation process* (and lower the need to avoid negative emotions).
4. *Mitigate the amount of attention absorbed by the negative emotions.* If distress tolerance is low, "attention is *absorbed* by the presence of the distressing emotions and their functioning is significantly disrupted by the experience of negative emotions" (Simons & Gaher, 2005, p. 83; emphasis added).

When performers are mentally caught up in unrelenting psychological distress, they tend to place undue focus on such experience, which in turn thwarts performance. Theoretically, with high levels of distress tolerance, performers are empowered to tolerate and even normalize such negative emotions and aversive somatic experience (Leyro et al., 2010).

As a sport psychologist, I have witnessed a range of elite athletes literally stop competing in an effort to temporarily avoid intense, aversive emotions, including a gymnast balking, a swimmer stopping in the middle of races, a rower stopping in the middle of ergometer tests (on an indoor rowing machine), a long-distance runner chronically stopping in the last quarter mile of a race, and a baseball player unable to play catch. The sport psychology literature describes the psychological and behavioral outcomes of such sport anxiety, including muscle tension; bracing habits (muscles fighting one another); hypervigilance; aggressive overreactivity; the athlete caring too much or too little; disrupted breathing patterns; cold, sweaty hands; and negative self-talk (Weinburg & Gould, 2011). Yet, the current approach is to have athletes change either how they are thinking or what they are focusing on (e.g., Hill et al., 2009), or, conversely, through mindfulness intervention, have them accept what is occurring (e.g., John, Verma, & Khanna, 2011) and commit to performance-valued behaviors (e.g., Chapter 7; Gardner & Moore, 2007). All of these may independently or together help athletes optimize performance.

Yet, more attention needs to be focused on ways to enhance distress tolerance for performers such that they can learn to tolerate the negative emotion in a balanced way and, when relevant, refocus on the task at hand. The idea of emotional tolerance in performance was introduced by Jorome Sashin (1993) when he theorized about the requisite emotional tolerance of Duke Ellington, the jazz musician, who may have had to tolerate acute, difficult emotions while creating live music in front of the audience. Yet, we have much to learn about how best to help performers with distress tolerance.

Mindfulness Intervention: Is Compassion Part of the Training?

Mindfulness interventions have very successfully targeted and ameliorated high-stress responses in medical and clinically based mindfulness interventions (see Keng, Smoski, & Robins, 2011). Mindfulness-Based Stress Reduction (MBSR) serves as the main intervention for many of these studies (Keng et al., 2011) – a time-intensive (2.5 hours per week over eight weeks plus a one full day silent meditation) mindfulness meditation–based intervention, which emphasizes in the *process of teaching* the integration of kindness, acceptance, and warmth for the students (Kabat-Zinn, personal communication, May 24, 2014). Other clinically focused mindfulness interventions (e.g., Linehan's Dialectical Behavior Therapy, 1993) offered individually by clinicians provide individualized support, which may include warmth and unconditional acceptance. Both the MAC approach for sport (i.e., Gardner & Moore, 2007) and Mindful Sport Performance Enhancement (e.g., Kaufman, Glass, & Arnkoff, 2009) offer similar types of individualized support and/or intensive intervention.

However, with the explosion of mindfulness intervention being used in the general public and more recently in the sport and performance realm, there is a growing risk that students, coaches, and sport psychology practitioners are not trained in mindfulness – beyond that which they read in popular media and in skeletal descriptions of mindfulness practices in empirical journal method sections. In turn, performance-based practitioners may not then integrate compassion into mindfulness-based interventions. The overt value and emphasis of compassion within the practice is becoming lost when mindfulness interventions are, for example, boiled down to only a ten minute CD with minimal further instruction. It is possible that the direct focus on and practice of compassion and warmth are lost in such practices. Though there is great benefit from practicing mindfulness – the straightforward practice of present-moment focus and acceptance of experience (e.g., learning to maintain attentional focus) – an integration of compassion is essential to learn to tolerate negative emotions and thoughts as they arise.

When it comes to coping with intense performance anxiety, I contend that a mindfulness practice without a parallel emphasis on self-compassion does not serve the performer optimally. Steven Hayes (2004), thought leader in the value of directly integrating mindfulness and self-compassion in his widely recognized ACT, notes the importance of noticing one's suffering kindly. He states that first we must acknowledge that it is problematic to pretend that the negative thoughts and feelings are not there (suggesting that just being mentally tough may not be the answer). Instead, Hayes contends that we must address the internal, aversive emotional states by noting the problems that arise when we do not. "Deliberate attempts to suppress thoughts and feelings can increase their occurrence and behavioral impact" (p. 650). The goal of ACT practitioners is "to support the client in feeling and thinking what they directly feel and think already, as it *is*, not as what it *says it is*, and to help the client move in a valued direction, *with* all of their history and automatic reactions" (p. 562). Hence, according to ACT the goal is *not to try and change* or *avoid* our uninvited thoughts or difficult emotions and reactions, but to accept them and continue moving toward one's values. And in the sport context, the individual values lead to focusing on the task at hand and optimizing performance while tolerating feelings as they are.

Yet, what is requisite for the performer in that moment of performance dukkha to be empowered to be able to withstand the emotional distress and to move toward value-directed goals? The answer may lie in the athlete cultivating warmth and acceptance of his or her experience when faced with intense aversive emotions. Yet the conversation on how to help the performer bring warmth and soothing to such moments remains an area in our sport and performance research and practice that needs to be expanded. Self-compassion may be the essential missing component.

Self-Compassion

As researchers and practitioners, we have lost sight of compassion in our modern, operationally defined constructs in the empirical research of mindfulness. Within the Buddhist tradition, beyond bare awareness, the purpose of mindfulness is to cultivate compassion toward ourselves and others (Markansky, 2012). Compassion includes sensitivity to the experience of the suffering of self and others, paired with a desire to alleviate that suffering (Neff & Dahm, in press).

Neff and Germer (2013), thought leaders within the realm of *self-compassion,* define self-compassion as "being touched by one's own suffering, generating the desire to alleviate one's suffering and treat oneself with understanding and concern" (p. 28). With self-compassion, the individual, who is suffering, focuses care and concern toward themselves (Neff, 2003). And, within the construct of self-compassion, mindfulness is requisite; mindfulness is essential to offer a balanced awareness of one's suffering before anything can be done to help relieve the suffering itself (we must notice the suffering before we can do anything about it). Mindfulness, as a subdimension of self-compassion, has been conceptualized as the "ability to pay attention to any experience – positive, negative, or neutral – with acceptance and equanimity" (Neff & Germer, 2013, p. 29); and the experience of self-compassion necessarily includes personal suffering, in some way, and on soothing and comforting oneself when faced with distressing experience. Neff and Germer (2013) identify three interdependent dimensions of self-compassion:

1. *Self-kindness* represents being caring and understanding with self, in contrast to giving oneself harsh self-criticism. For example, a dancer

who just made an error during rehearsal could demonstrate kindness to self by treating herself as she would a good friend (Neff & Dahm, in press), by being gentle and encouraging with herself (e.g., noting it is okay to make a mistake and to just go back and enjoy the movement) instead of agreeing with intrusive thoughts of harsh self-criticism. That is not to say she cannot learn to improve, but instead that she wouldn't be fully lost and distracted by the harsh self-evaluation. Neff and Germer (2013) suggest that being self-kind in such a moment would be reflected by intentionally being soothing to self: they state, "When life circumstances are stressful, instead of immediately trying to control or fix the problem, a self-compassionate response might entail pausing first to offer oneself soothing and comfort" (Neff & Germer, 2013, p. 28). Offering oneself unconditional acceptance is contrary to the typical, perfectionistic approach of most high-level performers. Yet learning to be kind to self allows the performer to respond more wisely in the moment (Neff & Germer, 2013). Instead of getting lost in a long, painful lapse in concentration and obsessing over the missed step, the performer could sooth herself enough such that she could refocus on her dancing.

2. A sense of *common humanity* reflects the idea that suffering is a shared human experience. When being self-compassionate, the performer is able to recognize and accept that all human beings are not perfect, that failure and making mistakes are part of being human (Neff & Germer, 2013). Again, such a self-compassionate approach is the antithesis of what high-level achievers are taught or learn from the performance culture. Accepting failure is often perceived as giving up. Yet, without being able to accept failure and cope with such disappointment wisely, the performer is setting himself or herself for continued distracting emotions, such as anxiety, frustration, anger, and humiliation. Canadian sport psychologist Terry Orlick (2000) offers a similar idea when he writes about what it takes to achieve excellence. He emphasizes that athletes must accept the possibility of failure. Orlick (2007) notes that for an athlete to overcome such difficult moments, he or she must focus on what can be controlled in the next moment. He states, "Most seemingly impossible obstacles can be overcome by seeing possibilities, focusing on what is within your control, and taking the first step . . ." (p. 14). Yet, such a refocus is impossible if the performer is lost or tangled in self-recrimination.

3. *Mindfulness* is the last component of self-compassion. Neff and Germer's (2013) conceptualization of mindfulness is aligned with the

Eastern, Buddhist perspective. They note that mindfulness, within the context of personal suffering, "Involves being aware of one's painful experiences in a balanced way" (Neff & Germer, 2013, p. 29). Their Aristotelian approach to mindfulness includes neither an excess nor deficit of attention on the thought, emotion, or physical sensation. In the performance context, the performer would neither be oblivious to nor obsessed with mistakes or failures. The performer's mindful awareness of their personal suffering is requisite such that once aware of their suffering – their anxiety, anger, or disappointment – they can offer themselves kindness and acceptance. In such instances, the performer would need to remain grounded and tolerant of what is occurring to mitigate the habit or temptation to become fully absorbed with what has or might occur. Neff & Germer (2013) state,

> It is necessary to be mindfully aware of personal suffering to be able to extend compassion towards the self. At the same time, it is important to pay attention in a grounded way that prevents being carried away by the storyline driving the suffering (p. 29).

Neff and Germer (2013) offer a list of benefits of self-compassion for the general population, including lower levels of anxiety and less rumination, perfectionism, and fear of failure.

Self-compassion in sport: Can it help?
Predictably, high-level achievers may be wary of self-compassion, thinking it may promote acceptance of poor or substandard performance and undermine their motivation. Going soft or being weak may, at first blush, be what coaches and athletes suspect are the offerings of self-compassion. Yet, in the general population, the findings demonstrate just the opposite. Self-compassion has been found be positively related to less rumination, less perfectionism, lower levels of anxiety, and less fear of failure (Neff & Germer, 2013). Because self-compassionate people do not berate them-selves when they fail, they are less afraid of failure and more able to take on new challenges (Neff, Hsieh, & Dejitterat, 2005). Self-compassionate people are also less likely to suppress unwanted thoughts and thus more willing to acknowledge and value their negative emotions (Neff & Germer, 2013), and self-compassion is positively associated with intrinsic motivation (Neff, Rude, & Kirkpatrick, 2007).

Sport researchers have found links of self-compassion with performance-related factors. Athletes with relatively higher levels of self-compassion perform better and cope more effectively with sport stressors. For example,

female athletes with higher self-compassion levels, in hypothetical and recalled sport scenarios (i.e., being responsible for losing a game and their worst sport experience, respectively), responded in healthier ways, including establishing "behavioral equanimity" and experiencing relatively less catastrophizing thoughts, personalizing thoughts, and negative affect (Reis et al., 2015). In the same study, athletes' self-compassionate reactions to such failure (e.g., bringing to mind positive affirmations) were more helpful than constructive distractions – which we often offer to help athletes to cope with such upset. Athletes with higher self-compassion also have been shown to experience relatively more positivity, more perseverance, less rumination, and more willingness to take responsibility (Ferguson et al., 2014). And finally, athletes with relatively higher self-compassion experienced lower body shame and less body surveillance, fear of failure, fear of negative evaluation, and social physique anxiety (Mosewich et al., 2011).

When athletes are able to offer themselves self-compassion, they are creating enough emotional safety to notice what is actually occurring. With such honest awareness, the athlete is then freed up for possible new ways to interact in the sport environment. When "one is self-compassionate, one is accepting of the self; and this acceptance provides the emotional safety to clearly identify areas for change and growth" (Magnus, Kowalski, & McHugh, 2009, p. 364).

Cultivating wisdom through one's awareness is consistent with the understanding of mindfulness mediation training in general. The initial phase of being mindful is concerned first with simply being aware of what is occurring. The advanced phase includes, through "introspective awareness [that offers a] means to understanding the moment-to-moment workings of adaptive and maladaptive thoughts and feelings" (Chiesa & Malinowski, 2011, p. 409). Thus, with awareness, athletes and performers are able to be mindfully aware of the *sport dukkha* and at once be empowered to address themselves with kindness before they face the challenge at hand. Performers can learn to discern the meaning of both adaptive and maladaptive thoughts (including emotions) and ultimately be able to make wiser choices as they engage in their performance realm.

Current Mindfulness and Self-Compassion Training in Sport

We are just at the beginning of bringing self-compassion directly into the training of athletes. In this next section, I will consider both formal and informal means to bring self-compassion into sport. The following subsections include an example of a sport-based self-compassion intervention used in research and in the integration of self-compassion in a mindfulness-based program for athletes, respectively.

Self-compassion program in sport

Mosvich and colleagues (2013) have led the way in offering a sport-specific self-compassion intervention, basing their self-compassion training on the type of intervention advocated by Leary and colleagues (2007): Leary and colleagues invited participants to respond to three writing prompts, each one based on one of the three components of self-compassion (i.e., kindness to self, common humanity, and mindfulness), with the goal of enhancing self-compassion. Mosevich and colleagues (2013) offered similar writing prompts to female athletes who were pre-identified as self-critical. Athletes were first offered psycho-educational information regarding self-compassion and then were guided to complete five writing exercises over a one-week period. The self-compassion intervention was effective in increasing self-compassion and decreasing self-criticism, rumination, and concern over mistakes.

Mindfulness and compassion training in sport

An mPeak Program *exercise* Steven Hickman is an MBSR teacher, a trainer for the Center of Mindful Self-Compassion, and a director of the University of California, San Diego (UCSD) Center for Mindfulness. He recently has created a three-day mindful self-compassion program for sport entitled *mPeak*. He generously shares of one of his exercises, used in mPeak, entitled *Finding Your Compassionate Inner Coach*. The mPeak program, which focuses on cultivating mindfulness and self-compassion for high-level sport, was developed to help athletes optimize performance (see Haase et al., 2015, for full description of mPeak). The following script was tailored to cyclists.

Finding Your Compassionate Inner Coach

Please take out a piece of paper.

I'd like to lead you through an exercise that I hope will help you find ways to encourage and motivate yourself from a place of care and compassion instead of self-criticism.

1. Think about something about yourself as an athlete that you would like to change – something you often beat yourself up about. It's important that you don't identify a permanent trait like not being tall enough or

having poor vision. Rather, choose a behavior or a tendency that you think is unhelpful, for example:

- "I get hyped up and impatient in the gate."
- "I have intense anxiety before I compete."
- "I don't train hard enough."
- "If I fall behind or make a mistake, I totally lose belief in myself."

Please write down something that you often criticize yourself for (*give few minutes*).

2. Now please write down what you typically say to yourself when this issue comes up. How does your Critical Inner Coach express itself?

3. Now consider how this self-criticism makes you feel and how it has affected you in the past. After a race or competition when you haven't done as well as you wanted, what do you find yourself saying to yourself, and what is the feeling you would associate with that? Write that down.

4. Consider why you criticize yourself for this.

    Is the Critical Inner Coach trying to achieve something or protect you from something in some way, even if it's unproductive? Have you simply taken on board what was told to you as a child, by an earlier coach or mentor? If so, does it serve any purpose to keep that conversation going in your mind?

5. Now we're going to see whether we can build a brand-new inner coach with a compassionate voice.

Please close your eyes and pause for a moment to feel your breath.

Now, recall the words of the Critical Inner Coach. Can you hear the words in your mind?

Please acknowledge what the Critical Inner Coach is doing. "Yes, I see you."

Or, if it's appropriate, "I know you want me to succeed and win. Thanks for trying to help me do my best."

(*Pause.*)

Now let's make room for the Compassionate Inner Coach. This coach accepts you as you are and wants to encourage you to perform at the highest level. If you pause and consider what this coach might look and sound like, you might call to mind the image of a previous coach, mentor, parent, or other supportive figure in your life. Take the time to notice how you felt when that person worked with you to achieve your goals and aspirations.

The motivation of the Compassionate Inner Coach is, "I want you to achieve everything that is possible for you to achieve. You have everything you need to be successful and together we can make that happen." This is the essence of the Compassionate Inner Coach.

Not only is the Compassionate Inner Coach kind and supportive, it is also very wise and sees clearly what is working and not working for you. From this perspective, what new language might you use to *encourage* yourself to do better, make a change, or overcome an obstacle? Talk to yourself from the position of a coach who truly has your best interests at heart and wants you to succeed almost as much as you do.

If you are having trouble finding the words, that's okay too. It takes some time. The important thing is that we set our intention to try to be kinder to ourselves, and eventually new habits will form.

In pairs, take some time to talk about what came up as you did this. Consider the following questions:

- Could you hear the Critical Inner Coach?
- How did it make you feel?
- What is the purpose of your Critical Inner Coach?
- Could you make room for a Compassionate Inner Coach?
- How did that go? How did that feel?

I had the opportunity to share this exercise in a workshop in Sweden. A performance coach of Swedish Cycling, a workshop participant, engaged in the Inner Compassionate Coach exercise. She noted the typical harsh self-criticism that is endemic within the elite cycling culture and her response to potentially shifting her own inner critic as a cyclist:

> The heart is a symbol for loving-kindness. But when performing, the thought of it (the heart) is more like a "pump" bringing necessary energy and oxygen to my muscles. If I were to give loving-kindness to one part of my body before a race, it would be my legs. I know they will soon be hurting. "Shut up, legs," has become a well-used term among many [cyclists], but maybe they [our legs] need a little compassion? I still want them to work, and work even harder, when they are starting to hurt badly. Maybe I could give them extra power by saying, "May you be strong," "May you be valued," and "May you have a great ride." The more I think of it, I will bring these sentences to the test, and also be sure to bring my new "Good coach" to compete with me in Ireland, this weekend (Annie Söderberg, personal communication, March 22, 2015).

Though much of the work in self-compassion in sport is new and needs empirical exploration, the response of this cyclist/performance coach suggests that some coaches and athletes would be responsive to integrating self-compassion into their mental training.

Applied Practice: What Can We Learn from Compassion-Focused Therapy?

Though structured self-compassion–focused programs are just beginning to emerge in sport, we can look to clinical psychology for additional ideas of how to aid athletes and performers to bring self-compassion into their training and competition, with the goal of helping optimize sport performance. Specific strategies can be gleaned from Paul Gilbert's (2009a, 2009b, 2010, 2011) CFT and, in particular, his *Compassion Mind Training (CMT)*. CMT offers a variety of ideas to help individuals learn to soothe themselves by practicing self-compassion. I will first provide a brief overview of CFT, including a brief discussion of the *content* dimension of Gilbert's model of the affect (emotion) system and complete the section with specific ways to translate CMT to sport; CMT offers skills to learn to elicit a soothing response to personal suffering in the most difficult, high-pressure performance moments.

CFT focuses on helping cultivate self-kindness, warmth, and support for self when facing difficult emotions. This aligns with the purposes of self-compassion: "Self-compassion emphasizes soothing and comforting the *self* when distressing experiences arise, remembering that such experiences are part of being human" (Neff & Germer, 2013, p. 29). Gilbert (2009a, 2009b) contends that when individuals tend to be self-critical that it is difficult to generate feelings of contentment, safeness, or warmth, for self and others. Based on my experience as a sport psychologist, performers being harshly self-critical is on the rise, and as sport psychology practitioners we need to find practical ways to help athletes create a sense of safeness or warmth such that they can remain steady (enough) to focus on task-relevant cues to optimize performance.

For performers to be able to cope adaptively with the lonely, dark moments of performance dukkha, some will need to learn to first offer kindness to themselves. From my private practice, I have prompted and witnessed athletes experience such kindness in a variety of forms: *imagining* being filled with courage and face a monster of fear (a thirteen-year-old swimmer who had to stop swimming because she thought she was drowning); *recalling times of great success* (as a source of self-kindness) even when feeling tremendous doubt; *mindfully noticing* it is "normal" to compare oneself to other professional runners and to doubt one's speed (a professional runner). Such anecdotal examples can be buoyed and guided by ideas from Paul Gilbert's Compassionate Mind Training – a practical guide of CFT.

Gilbert developed CFT to offer pathways to help individuals who suffer from high shame or self-criticism. Gilbert offers a model of a three-part affect system, which provides a framework for the importance of offering self-kindness in such difficult moments of shame or harsh self-talk. The first two parts of the affect system are familiar: (1) affect (emotions) related to *Drive*, including emotions of excitement and vitality and (2) affect related to *Threat,* including emotions of fear and anxiety. The third dimension of the affect system, (3) affect related to *Soothing/Contentment,* is not often considered in performance psychology. We focus on motivation to succeed and overcoming myriad fears of failure and threat.

Gilbert highlights and places value on soothing the self in difficult psychological moments: the importance of feeling psychologically safe when confronted with internal dis-ease is core to CFT and aligned with core tenets of self-compassion. Though developed for the clinical population, Gilbert's CFT conceptual and applied ideas map well onto the needs of performers who are riddled with shame or self-criticism about past (e.g., recalling a poorly played game just prior to the start of a game), present (e.g., being pulled from the mound after pitching poorly), and future events in sport (e.g., fear of not being good enough to win).

In Compassionate Mind Training, the goal is to activate the soothing/contentment system such that the individual can develop an internal compassionate relationship with herself, and her thoughts, in place of self-castigation via regulation of her affect system. The following ideas offer a pathway to bring self-compassion when facing performance dukkha. People with high self-criticism, whose "threat affect dominates their inner and out worlds," often find it difficult to shift from perpetual feelings of such threat to *Drive* and *Soothing/Contentment* (Gilbert, 2009a, p. 199). And I contend that shifting from threat to drive via the soothing/contentment affect system may just be the answer to help those suffering with performance dukkha.

CMT offers specific ideas for eliciting self-compassion. The behaviors that Gilbert is recommending call for courage; he notes that compassionate behavior "require[s] courage and direct engagement in exposure to threatening and feared situations, feelings or memories." (Gilbert, 2009a, p. 206). Helping performers face their performance dukkha with courage will ultimately allow them to be freed up to focus on task-relevant cues, essential to best performance. The first step in Compassionate Mind Training (Gilbert, 2009a) is to teach basic tenets of mindfulness and soothing rhythm breathing. Once in a present, balanced state of mind – with the help of grounding in the present moment through the breath – the following skills of compassion can be tailored to activate the individual's soothing/contentment (affect) system.

Compassionate attention

The individual purposefully focuses his attention in a way that helps and supports him. In sport, this could involve remembering times when the athlete performed well, even when he was experiencing low self-confidence. Or an athlete struggling with harsh feedback from a coach could intentionally recall a time when the coach was supportive or to bring to mind something about the coach that the athlete authentically values. "The experience of re-focusing attention needs to be associated with warmth, kindness and support" (Gilbert, 2009a, p. 203). Athletes could also be directed to focus their attention on aspects of training, competition, or simply being part of the competitive environment that they authentically enjoy (e.g., lifting weights; running for an hour at one's own pace).

In my private practice as a sport psychology practitioner, a professional runner reported having the following thought prior to racing: "I can't do it"; "I am afraid I am going to run badly"; and "I am at a dead end – I have no idea what to do." Together we worked with her developing ways to shift her attention compassionately. New ways of intentional compassionate thinking included, "I have worked so hard"; "I dig into the tank when I am in striking distance"; and "I am not giving up." The athlete used cues that at once were soothing and helped with performance cues.

Compassionate reasoning

The individual using alternative thoughts and cognitive restructuring in a way that is "kind, supportive and helpful" (Gilbert, 2009a, p. 204) reflects compassionate reasoning; compassionate thinking is substituted for self-critical thinking and rumination. I worked with a world-class musician who was tormented, highly self-critical, when he was unable to learn a musical score quickly enough. His thoughts would rapidly spiral into a decision that he was inadequate and it was time to stop playing music. After some work together, he created some authentic substitutes for such thinking, which included remembering how much he loved to create music when he was not caught up in a negative emotional spiral regarding his expectations of perfection. A second musician, with intense audition anxiety, brought to mind the thought, "My mom loves me." This alternate thought brought a sense of love and safety as he approached the stage.

Compassionate behavior

When the individual is engaged in compassionate behavior, she is both engaging in difficult behaviors and creating an encouraging, warm tone in her supportive thoughts. This combination of thought and behavior supports the individual in having courage while engaged in difficult behavior. For example, if a world-class runner had a habit of stopping before he completed races, he could both commit to continuing to run (no matter what) and prepare in advance *thoughts* he could bring to mind that would be encouraging and kind. The emphasis is process (i.e., effort) versus outcome, which aligns with an effective approach in performance psychology. Compassionate behavior also includes intentionally creating positive emotion – to help clients learn to savor and enjoy their life. For sport, practitioners could help athletes identify areas in practice and performance that are inherently enjoyable and either bring these to mind intentionally or create such experiences.

Compassionate imagery
Compassionate imagery emphasizes bringing to mind, through imagery, compassionate feelings for oneself. In the clinical setting, this can include creating an ideal image of oneself or another as a compassionate being. Bringing compassionate imagery to sport could begin with an athlete who is devastated (e.g., from losing her position on the starting team and being bombarded with rumination and grave, obsessive thoughts). Such self-criticism and rumination can activate the stress response. In such instances, the athlete could bring to mind an image of being gentle with herself or bring to mind a compassionate other (e.g., a past kind coach) whose image brings a sense of soothing to self.

In my private practice for the past fifteen years, I have been guiding athletes to create *scripts* that align with the framework of CMT. I have helped athletes engage in compassionate imagery particularly when also, concurrently, dealing with aversive, self-derisive thoughts. The following is an example of a professional long-distance runner who often got lost in fear of failure at the thought of not being sure she could win an upcoming race (and subsequently would race poorly):

> I am relaxed. I let myself get pulled along. I see what is going on, I position myself well. I feel smooth. As I start to move, I think, "I want." I am excited to race. I am healthy. I am physically capable.

The athlete has found the compassionate (imagery) scripting to be very helpful as she prepares to race.

CMT is focused on creating *compassionate feeling* for the self as well as from and for others. The many previously mentioned methods – compassionate imagery, behavior, and focused attention – can manifest such compassionate feelings. In addition, when practitioners are working with clients, they seek to explore the physical sensations that are arise in the client's body with compassion, *compassionate sensations*. Ultimately clients are supported to help accept whatever feelings emerge with warmth, kindness, and support (Gilbert, 2009a). One example in my private practice is reflected by a nationally ranked tennis player who experienced terror, which manifested in acute tightening of the stomach prior to matches. When unchecked, such sensations resulted in the athlete literally not being able to take complete strokes. Through helping the athlete explore the physical sensations with compassion, we were able to develop a strategy for the tennis player both recognizing and accepting the fear such that, ultimately, such sensations (though still difficult) were no longer predictive of poor performance on the court. The tennis player was able to interact with herself and compete with her opponents in a fresh, renewed way – no longer controlled by her fear.

Conclusion

Traditional sport psychology interventions are typically geared toward stopping negative thinking and focusing on sport-related tasks. Yet, for some performers at times, it is not possible to change such negative thoughts and feelings when they have low distress tolerance. The performer's attention can remain stuck in his or her fears, self-judgment, unrealistic expectations, performance anxiety, harsh self-criticism, comparison to others, and/or giving into the urge to give up when the athlete realizes that he or she cannot win.

Mindfulness approaches offer an empirically supported pathway to help athletes cope with performance anxiety. And the ability to be mindful is unquestionably linked to performance (Chapter 7; John et al., 2011). Performance psychology has made good strides in adapting empirically supported clinical interventions for the purpose of sport performance, such as the Mindfulness-Acceptance-Commitment (MAC) approach (Chapter 7; Gardner & Moore, 2007), formal mindfulness meditation (John et al., 2011; Kabat-Zinn, Beall, & Rippe, 1985) and *Mindful Sport Performance Enhancement (MSPE)* (Kaufman et al., 2009). We are on the precipice of moving toward designing mindfulness interventions that offer athlete–intervention matching based on specific need and time restraints (Baltzell et al., 2014).

Anecdotally, I have been using aspects of such mindfulness interventions with athletes in my private practice over the past many years – offering both formal mindfulness meditation practices and/or educational information about how it is possible to notice uninvited thoughts and feelings and choose not to believe them (buy into them) and, concurrently, optimize performance. For example, is it possible to have the thought,

"I just don't have the stuff today!" and still choose to go out, compete, and focus on moment-to-moment performance demands? However, over the years I have found that asking athletes to learn to accept intense performance anxiety is one of the most difficult things to ask of them; there is a reason for cognitive avoidance or fusion. I have told some of my clients many times that being mindful of intense performance anxiety and facing the thoughts and feelings in a balanced manner may be the hardest things that they may have to do. Zella Moore (in Chapter 2) refers to mindfulness meditative techniques as a general form of exposure. She notes that mindfulness interventions are not designed, in any way, to cultivate a soothing response. And, as we know, exposure interventions can be provocative, if not painful. And when under great performance pressure, such exposure is particularly hard for competitors to tolerate. That is why as a practicing sport psychologist I have only turned to mindfulness practices as the last resort when the athlete was suffering – experiencing performance dukkha.

Self-compassion may be the missing piece of the puzzle in mindfulness-based interventions. Many athletes do not know how to offer themselves self-compassion *after* becoming aware of their sport-related suffering (performance dukkha) and *prior to* forcing their attention back on personally held values and relevant performance cues. We are just beginning to realize that it will help some athletes to be soothing to themselves in such instances prior to bringing their attention back to performance relevant cues. I contend that helping athletes face and tolerate such thoughts and emotions associated with performance dukkha may offer a pathway to mindfulness interventions that are not as painful. And perhaps as researchers and practitioners in a field of sport psychology, we owe more to athletes and performers than just helping them learn to jump higher or perform better – the quality of their experience matters too.

Self-compassion applied to instances of performance dukkha may do more than just help the performer optimize performance. Practices of self-compassion may also contribute to what makes being human worthwhile. Mihaly Csikszentmihali (1975, 2014) has considered for over four decades what brings human happiness. He is the author of the idea of flow, "a particular kind of experience that is so engrossing and enjoyable that it becomes autotelic, that is, worth doing for its own sake even though it may have no consequence outside itself" (Csikszentmihali, 1999, p. 824). Csikszentmihali has become a thought leader in both positive psychology and within the sport psychology literature. One emphasis of his work is on the actual, lived internal experience of the human being. He reflects on the importance of the internal quality of experience of the human being, in terms of making life worth living:

> It is useful to remember occasionally that life unfolds as a chain of subjective experiences. Whatever else life might be, the only evidence we have of it, the only direct data to which we have access, is the succession of events in consciousness. The quality of these experiences determines whether and to what extent life is worth living.
>
> Optimal experience is the "bottom line" of existence. It is the subjective reality that justifies the actions and events in any life history. Without it there would be little purpose in living and the whole elaborate structure of personality and culture would reveal itself as nothing but an empty shell (Csikszentmihali, 2014, p. 209).

It is possible that self-compassion hand in hand with mindfulness may offer some performers the best chance of performing as closely as they can to optimal experience, and do so in a kind, humane way. Certainly low levels of distress tolerance paired with avoidance and a need to escape result in the antithesis of what we are all looking for in our own lives and that which we are aspiring to share with others. Acceptance and understanding of the performer's internal suffering may be the key for them to be freed up to engage authentically and fully in moment-to-moment experience for best performance and best quality of internal life experience.

REFERENCES

Baltzell, A. L. (in press). Mindfulness & performance: The science of meditation and wellbeing. In I. Ivtzan (Ed.), *Mindfulness in positive psychology: The science of meditation and wellbeing*. Hove, East Essex, UK: Routledge.

Baltzell, A. L., Caraballo, N., Chipman, K., and Hayden, L. (2014). A qualitative study of the Mindfulness Meditation Training for Sport (MMTS): Division I female soccer players' experience. *Journal of Clinical Sport Psychology*, 8, 221–244.

Bandura, A. (1997). *Self-efficacy: The exercise of control*. New York, NY: Freeman.

Chiesa, A., and Malinowski, P. (2011). Mindfulness-based approaches: Are they all the same? *Journal of Clinical Psychology*, 67(4), 404–424. doi: 10.1002/jclp.20776

Csikszentmihalyi, M. (1975). *Beyond boredom and anxiety*. San Francisco, CA: Jossey-Bass.

(1997). *Finding flow: The psychology of engagement with everyday life*. New York, NY: Perseus.

(1999). If we are so rich, why aren't we happy? *American Psychologist*, 54(10), 821–827. doi: http://dx.doi.org/10.1037/0003-066X.54.10.821

(2014). Toward a psychology of optimal experience. In M. Csikszentmihalyi (Ed.), *Flow and the foundations of positive psychology: The collected works of Mihaly Csikszentmihalyi* (pp. 209–226). Netherlands: Springer.

Ferguson, L. J., Kowalski, K. C., Mack, D. E., and Sabiston, C. M. (2014). Exploring self-compassion and eudaimonic well-being in young women athletes. *Journal of Sport and Exercise Psychology*, 36, 203–216. doi: 10.1123/jsep.2013-0096

Gardner, F. L., and Moore, Z. E. (2007). *The psychology of enhancing human performance: The Mindfulness-Acceptance-Commitment (MAC) approach.* New York, NY: Springer.

Gilbert, P. (2009a). Introducing compassion-focused therapy. *Advances in Psychiatric Treatment: Journal of Continuing Professional Development*, 15, 199–208. doi: 10.1192/apt.bp.107.005264

(2009b). The nature and basis for compassion focused therapy. *Hellenic Journal of Psychology*, 6, 273–291.

(2010). *Compassion focused therapy: The distinctive features series.* New York, NY: Routledge.

(2011). Shame in psychotherapy and the role of compassion focused therapy. In R. Dearing and J. Tangney (Eds.), *Shame in therapy hour* (pp. 325–354). Washington, DC: American Psychological Association.

Haase, L., May, A., Falahpour, M., Isakovic, S., Simmons, A., Hickman, S., . . . and Paulus., M. (2015). A pilot study investigating changes in neural processing after mindfulness training in elite athletes. *Frontiers in Behavioral Neuroscience.* 9, 1-12. doi: 10.3389/fnbeh.2015.00229

Hayes, S. C. (2004). Acceptance and commitment therapy, relational frame theory, and the third wave of behavioral and cognitive therapies. *Behavior Therapies*, 35, 639–665. doi:10.1016/S0005-7894(04)80013-3

Hill, D. M., Hanton, S., Fleming, S., and Matthews, N. (2009). A re-examination of choking under pressure. *European Journal of Sport Science*, 9, 203–212. doi: 10.1080/1746139090281827

John, S., Verma, S. K., and Khanna, G. L. (2011). The effect of mindfulness meditation on HPA-Axis in pre-competition stress in sports performance of elite shooters. *National Journal of Integrated Research in Medicine*, 2(3), 15–21.

Kabat-Zinn, J. (2003). Mindfulness-based interventions in context: Past, present, and future. *Clinical Psychology: Science and Practice* 10(2), 144–156. doi: 10.1093/clipsy/bpg016

Kabat-Zinn, J., Beall, B., and Rippe, J. (1985, June). *A systematic mental training program based on mindfulness meditation to optimize performance in collegiate and Olympic rowers.* Poster session presented at the World Congress in Sport Psychology, Copenhagen, Denmark.

Kaufman, K., Glass, C., and Arnkoff, D. (2009). Evaluation of mindful sport performance enhancement (MSPE): A new approach to promote flow in athletes. *Journal of Clinical Sports Psychology*, 4, 334–356.

Keng, S. L., Smoski, M. J., and Robins, C. J. (2011). Effects of mindfulness on psychological health: A review of empirical studies. *Clinical Psychology Review*, 31, 1041–1056. doi:10.1016/j.cpr.2011.04.006

Leary, M. R., Tate, E. B., Adams, C. E., Allen A. B, and Hancock, J. (2007). Self-compassion and reactions to unpleasant self-relevant events: The implications of treating oneself kindly. *Journal of Personality and Social Psychology*, 92(5), 887–904. doi: http://dx.doi.org/10.1037/0022-3514.92.5.887

Leyro, T. M., Zvolensky, M. J., and Bernstein, A. (2010). Distress tolerance and psychopathological symptoms and disorders: A review of the empirical literature among adults. *Psychological Bulletin*, 136(4), 576–600. doi: 10.1037/a0019712

Linehan, M. (1993). *Cognitive-behavioral treatment of borderline personality disorder*. New York, NY: Guilford Press.

Magnus, C. M. R., Kowalski, K. C., and McHugh, T. L. F. (2010). The role of self-compassion in women's self-determined motives to exercise and exercise-related outcomes. *Self and Identity*, 9, 363–382. doi: 10.1080/15298860903135073

Markansky, J. (2012). Compassion in Buddhist psychology chapter. In C. K. Germer and R. D. Siegel (Eds.), *Compassion and wisdom in psychotherapy* (pp. 61–74). New York, NY: Guilford Press.

Mosewich, A. D., Crocker, P. R. E., Kowalski, K. C., and DeLongis, A. (2013). Applying self-compassion in sport: An intervention with women athletes. *Journal of Sport and Exercise Psychology*, 35, 514–524.

Mosewich, A. D., Kowalski, K. C., Sabiston, C. M., Sedgwick, W. A. and Tracy, J. L. (2011) Self-compassion: A potential resource for young women athletes. *Journal of Sport and Exercise Psychology*, 33, 103–123.

Neff, K. D. (2003). The development and validation of a scale to measure self-compassion. *Self and Identity*, 2, 223–250. doi: 10.1080/15298860390209035

Neff, K. D., and Dahm, K. A. (in press). Self-compassion: What it is, what it does, and how it relates to mindfulness. In M. Robinson, B. Meier, and B. Ostafin (Eds.), *Mindfulness and Self-Regulation*. New York, NY: Springer.

Neff, K. D., and Germer, C. K. (2013). A pilot study and randomized controlled trial of the mindful self-compassion program. *Journal of Clinical Psychology*, 69(1), 28–44.

Neff, K.D., Hsieh, Y., and Dejitterat, K. (2005). Self-compassion, achievement goals, and coping with academic failure. *Self and Identity*, 4 263–287. doi: 10.1080/13576500444000317

Neff, K. D., Rude, S. S., and Kirkpatrick, K. L. (2007). An examination of self-compassion in relation to positive psychological functioning and personality traits. *Journal of Research in Personality*, 41(1), 908–916. doi:10.1016/j.jrp.2006.03.004

Orlick, T. (2000). *In pursuit of excellence: How to win in sport and life through mental training* (3rd ed.). Champaign, IL: Human Kinetics.

(2007). *In pursuit of excellence: How to win in sport and life through mental training* (4th ed.). Champaign, IL: Human Kinetics.

Reis, N. A., Kowalski, K. C., Ferguson, L. J., Sabiston, C. M., Sedgwick, W. A., and Crocker, P. R. E. (2015). Self-compassion and women athletes' responses to emotionally difficult sport situations: An evaluation of a brief induction. *Psychology of Sport and Exercise*, 16, 18–25. doi: 10.1016/j.psychsport.2014.08.011

Sashin, J. I. (1993). Duke Ellington: The creative process and the ability to experience and tolerate affect. In S. L. Ablon, D. Brown, E. J. Khantzian, and E. Mackman (Eds.), *Feelings: Explorations in affect development and meaning* (pp. 317–332). Hillsdale, NJ: Analytic Press.

Siegel, R. (2010). *The mindful solution: Everyday practices for everyday problems.* New York, NY: Guilford Press.

Simons, J. S., and Gaher, R. M. (2005). The distress tolerance scale: Development and validation of a self-report measure. *Motivation and Emotion*, 29, 83–102. doi: 10.1007/s11031-005-7955-3

Weinburg, R. S., and Gould, D. (2011). *Foundations of sport and exercise psychology* (5th ed.). Champaign, IL: Human Kinetics.

Zvolensky, M. J., Leyro, T. M., Bernstein, A., and Vujanovic, A. A. (2011). Historical perspectives, theory, and measurement of distress tolerance. In M. J. Zvolensky, A. Bernstein, and A. A. Vujanovic (Eds.), *Distress tolerance: Theory, research and clinical applications* (pp. 3–27). New York, NY: Guilford Press.

CHAPTER 4

Flow and Mindfulness in Performance

Susan Jackson

When in flow, everything comes together and actions follow actions seamlessly, creating high levels of task performance. Flow creates order out of chaos, complexity out of the ordinary, and, most importantly, experiences that are optimal. It is the feeling of being in flow that draws people back to this state. It is what is created when in flow that contributes to the most enjoyable moments of one's life. The flow model also provides a way of understanding an optimal mindset for performance.

Much has been written about flow, its attributes and benefits, and I will summarise some of this work, including some of my research on flow, in this chapter. However, a link that has been receiving growing empirical attention is that between flow and mindfulness. Having worked in both areas in the fields of performance psychology and in yoga/meditation, and having found a synchronicity between the two constructs as an applied practitioner, I would like to share a bit about why I believe flow is important to mindfulness, and mindfulness to flow. Some of the recent research that has been examining relationships between flow and mindfulness will be overviewed and possible directions for future research and applied initiatives outlined.

What Is Flow?

Csikszentmihalyi (1975, 1990) developed the flow concept after investigating the experiences of individuals during times when they were totally involved in what they were doing and when everything came together during their performances. Csikszentmihalyi has operationally defined flow as being a psychological state that can occur when challenges and skills in a situation are both high. More precisely, flow is predicted to occur when an individual is being extended by virtue of performing in a challenging situation and has a skill level that matches the challenge being faced. Flow occurs when the individual moves beyond his or her average experience of challenge and skill in a situation. The results of being in flow are outstanding levels of performance and memorable experiences.

Challenges and skills play a critical role in understanding flow and, more broadly, a variety of psychological experiences. In what have become known as the four and eight quadrant flow models, a range of psychological experiences have been predicted to result from different mixes of challenges and skills, or more precisely, from the *perception* of challenges and skills in a situation. Anxiety, for example, is predicted to occur when perceived challenges are high but perception of skills low. Boredom is predicted to occur when skills are perceived to be high but the challenges in a situation are perceived to be low. Flow occurs between the boundaries of anxiety and of boredom: where challenges are high and extending the individual, but not creating a situation where confidence is called into question. Flow represents those moments when everything comes together to create a special state of absorption and enjoyment in what one is doing (Csikszentmihalyi, 1975, 1990). An example of the four-channel flow model is presented in Figure 4.1. Note that in this model, what was initially termed the boredom quadrant (Csikszentmihalyi, 1975, 1990) has been redefined as 'relaxation-boredom' (e.g., Jackson & Csikszentmihalyi, 1999), due to consistent empirical research indicating this quadrant tends to be perceived more positively than what was initially conceptualised.

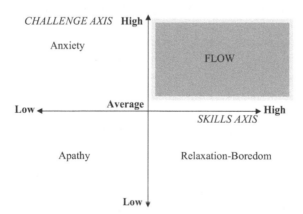

Figure 4.1   Model of the flow state (adapted from Jackson & Csikszentmihalyi, 1999, p. 37).

The Dimensions of Flow

The experience of flow is sufficiently enjoyable so as to be, in itself, a much sought-after and self-rewarding state. Together, the nine dimensions of flow provide a conceptually coherent framework for understanding optimal experience. The nine dimensions of flow include the following:

1. **Challenge-skill.** Csikszentmihalyi (e.g., 1990) conceptualised the flow construct in terms of nine dimensions. The first of these dimensions, challenge–skill balance, is the operational starting point for flow, where challenges and skills in a situation are balanced and extending an individual.

2. **Action–awareness merging.** The action–awareness merging dimension involves a feeling of being at one with the activity being performed. Often used in descriptions by people asked to discuss what it was like being in flow, perceptions of oneness with an activity bring about a sense of peace and harmony to an active engagement with a task.

3. **Clear goals, or clarity of purpose.** Clear goals, or clarity of purpose, occurs on a moment-by-moment basis, keeping a person fully connected to the task and responsive to relevant cues. Closely associated with clear goals is the processing of how performance is progressing in relation to these goals.

4. **Unambiguous feedback.** When in flow, feedback is easy to receive and interpret. The performer receives clear, unambiguous information that he or she processes effortlessly, keeping performance heading in the right direction.

5. **Concentration of the task at hand.** This is one of the clearest indications of being in flow – one is totally focussed in the present on the specific task or activity with which one is engaged. Being totally connected to the task in which one is engaged epitomises the flow state. This connectedness relies on a present-centred focus; flow resides in being in the present moment. A present-centered focus leads to the next dimension of flow.

6. **Sense of control over what one is doing.** Being fully connected to the task or activity in which one is engaged allows a person to perceive a sense of control and confidence in what one is doing. This is an empowering feeling, and one that frees a person from a fear of failure that can creep into performance. The absence of fear of failure enables an individual to engage in the challenges at hand.

7. **Loss of self-consciousness.** The loss of self-consciousness is characterised by a lack of concern about what others may be thinking of

them. A lot of the time, people live their lives surrounded by evaluations of how they are doing. This sense of evaluation can prevent a full focus on the task at hand. Because flow is defined by being totally focussed on the task at hand, it allows for a liberating loss of self-consciousness during engagement in an activity.

8. **Time transformation**. A sense of time passing differently defines the dimension of flow known as time transformation. For some, the experience is that time stops. For others, time seems to slow. Or it may be that time seems to pass more quickly than expected. These sensations come about through the intensity of involvement in flow. Because awareness is tightly focussed during the intense concentration of flow, people can lose track of time, and afterwards can be surprised by the actual passing of time that has occurred during their task involvement.

9. **Autotelic experience**. Autotelic experience is the final flow dimension, and is the culmination of the coming together of the previous eight dimensions. Autotelic experience describes the intrinsically rewarding nature of flow. As described by Csikszentmihalyi (1975), the word is derived from two Greek words that describe doing something for its own sake (i.e., *auto*, which means 'self,' and *telos*, which means 'goal').

Translating these dimensions into how performers in flow describe their experience can help us to understand what the experience is like. The types of phrases used by performers interviewed about what being in flow is like (Jackson, 1996) include descriptors such as 'felt easy', 'complete task focus', 'totally relaxed', 'enjoying experience as it occurs', 'totally absorbed in what I am doing', 'endless supply of energy', 'things happening automatically', 'nothing else enters awareness' and 'leaves you feeling great'. Accompanied by positive experiential characteristics such as these, moments in flow remain etched in our memory, creating a blueprint for our future optimal experiences.

Theoretical Background to Flow

Csikszentmihalyi developed the flow concept in the 1970s after investigating the experiences of individuals during times when everything came together during times of involvement with a chosen activity. The types of activities initially investigated by Csikszentmihalyi (1975) were diverse, including, for example, artists, surgeons, dancers, chess players and rock climbers. Despite diversity in setting, Csikszentmihalyi found considerable consistency of responses regarding what was felt during moments that stood out as being special in some way for the individual.

Csikszentmihalyi and colleagues have continued to examine flow since the early studies in the late 1970s, in settings from daily living (e.g., Csikszentmihalyi, 1997) to reflections on states of mind during major scientific advances (e.g., Csikszentmihalyi, 1996). There has been remarkable consistency in how flow has been described by individuals across diverse settings. When in flow, one feels strong and positive, not worried about self or of failure. Flow can be defined as an experience that stands out as being better than average in some way, where the individual is totally absorbed in what she or he is doing, and where the experience is very rewarding in and of itself. In flow, one is totally involved in the task at hand. Flow can occur at different levels of complexity, but by definition, flow is intrinsically rewarding, regardless of whether it involves a simple task or a complicated and dangerous gymnastics routine. Csikszentmihalyi (1975) categorised the different levels of flow into micro and macro flow experiences. Micro flow experiences were proposed to fit the patterns of everyday life, whereas macro flow was reserved for experiences associated with higher levels of complexity and demand on the participant. These latter experiences are often associated with high levels of performance.

Assessing Flow

Considerable interest in the flow construct led to development of different ways of empirically studying it, and this research effort has made flow a more accessible psychological concept for the applied researcher and also for practitioners interested in flow in their performance settings. Assessing a subjective, experiential phenomenon such as flow presents challenges. I therefore preface this section on empirically assessing flow by endorsing Csikszentmihalyi's (1992) argument that any measure of flow is only a 'partial reflection' of the human experience (Csikszentmihalyi, 1992, p. 183). Secondly, a multimodal approach that incorporates both qualitative and quantitative methods of measurement is likely to yield the greatest gains. A diversity of methodologies will offer the greatest potential to explain the 'what' and 'how' questions posed by the unique phenomenon of the flow experience. The measurement approaches that are described next are tools to tap into the flow experience, and are presented with the understanding that no one empirical tool can fully capture flow.

Qualitative approaches were where Csikszentmihalyi's (1975) early flow research began. Similarly, my initial research of flow in sport (Jackson,

1992, 1995, 1996) used qualitative methods to assess this experience in athletes. Inductive content analyses of elite athletes' descriptions of flow led to identification of factors inherent in their flow experiences. Close correspondence was found between athletes' descriptions of flow and Csikszentmihalyi's nine-dimensional flow model.

Quantitative approaches have enabled flow to be empirically examined in relation to other psychological concepts and life experiences. Csikszentmihalyi (1975) developed his model of flow through the use of experience sampling (Csikszentmihalyi & Larson, 1987), which involves snapshots of individuals' experiences via the use of pagers that randomly beep several times throughout a day. When paged, an experience sampling form is completed by the participant, and responses provide information on the quality of experience individuals have in different activities and settings.

Jackson and colleagues developed a quantitative approach to assessing flow, initially in sport and subsequently with broader application (e.g., Jackson & Eklund, 2002; Jackson & Marsh, 1996; Martin & Jackson, 2008). They developed and validated a suite of self-report scales to suit a diversity of research and applied purposes. In the *Flow Manual*, Jackson, Eklund and Martin (2010) described these scales, which they categorised into three subsets: Long, Short and Core flow scales. One general characteristic of this approach to assessing flow has been to do so at two levels: (a) the *dispositional level*, or frequency of flow experience across time in particular domains (e.g., sport, work, school) and (b) the *state level*, or extent of flow experienced during a particular event or activity (e.g., a race, a work project or a test).

The dispositional and state flow scales are parallel forms, with wording differences reflecting whether the disposition to experience flow, or a specific flow experience, is being assessed. By designing dispositional and state versions of the scales, it is possible to assess both a general tendency to experience flow as well as particular incidence (or nonincidence) of flow characteristics during a particular event. To date, the Long flow scales have had the most empirical support and are probably the most widely known of the flow scales. They are thirty-six-item instruments designed to assess the nine dimensions of flow (Csikszentmihalyi, 1990) and are called Flow State Scale-2 (FSS-2) and the Dispositional Flow Scale-2 (DFS-2). The Short flow scales are nine-item (Dispositional and State) scales, which are abbreviated versions of Long flow. These flow scales provide a brief assessment useful when research or practical constraints prevent use of a longer scale. The Core flow scales are ten-item (Dispositional and State) scales designed to assess the central subjective experience of flow. They complement the dimensional flow assessments provided by the Long and Short flow scales. All versions of the scales have been validated through confirmatory factor analyses, and the scales have demonstrated good psychometric properties (e.g., Jackson & Eklund, 2002; Jackson & Marsh, 1996; Jackson, Martin, & Eklund, 2008; Marsh & Jackson, 1999; Martin & Jackson, 2008).

Understanding the flow experience, including what have been termed the preconditions for flow (Nakamura & Csikszentmihalyi, 2002), being the dimensions of challenge–skill balance, clear goals and unambiguous feedback, has been facilitated through the ability to assess the nine-dimensional flow model via the Long flow scales. Intercorrelations between the flow dimensions have been assessed in several studies (e.g., Jackson et al., 1998; Jackson et al. 2001; Stavrou et al., 2007) and help to provide a more fine-tuned description of what it is like to enter into flow and of what the key components are once in flow.

The pioneering efforts of Csikszentmihalyi (e.g., 1975, 1990, 1997, 2003) have opened a new level of understanding of what is involved when people become totally absorbed in what they are doing. Csikszentmihalyi has examined flow across settings ranging from daily living (e.g., Csikszentmihalyi, 1997) to research endeavour leading to major scientific discoveries (e.g., Csikszentmihalyi, 1996). As was observed in Csikszentmihalyi's (1975) initial investigations, and in the research conducted by Jackson and colleagues (e.g., Jackson, 1996; Jackson et al. 1998; Jackson et al., 2001), remarkable consistency has continued to be encountered across the broadening array of activities and settings examined. The measurement tools thus far developed to help assess flow provide much scope for researchers interested in furthering understanding of flow.

Knowing what is occurring at a neuro-, or psychophysiological level during flow has good potential for furthering understanding of what is happening in the body and mind while in flow. Csikszentmihalyi (Csikszentmihalyi & Csikszentmihalyi, 1988) referred to early neurological studies conducted by Hamilton (e.g., Hamilton, 1976, 1981), where attentional patterns associated with flow were first described. Mental effort, as measured by cortical activation, was shown to decrease in individuals with good ability to concentrate deeply on a task. The challenges of assessing internal, physiological states during a state as elusive as flow have meant that this area of research has moved ahead relatively slowly. Dietrich (2004) provided some evidence for what happens at the neurocognitive level in flow, concluding there is transient hypofrontality, involving suspension of activity in the frontal and medial temporal lobes, allowing well-learned processes to proceed without interference from deliberate thought. In another study, de Manzano and colleagues (2010) examined several psychophysiological parameters and flow state. With piano players as the participants, they found significant associations between flow and heart rate, blood pressure, zygomaticus muscle activity and respiratory depth. With the steady growth in technological advances, new levels of understanding of what happens when in flow will increasingly come to light.

Flow in Sport and Other Performance Domains

Research on sport involvement was a part of Csikszentmihalyi's landmark 1975 book *Beyond Boredom and Anxiety*, wherein the flow construct was initially conceptualised. Investigation of flow and related concepts (e.g., peak experience, peak performance) in sport started to became evident in the literature the 1980s. It was in the late 1980s that I read about flow while pursuing graduate studies in sport psychology. I embarked on what became a program of research on flow in sport and other performance settings and was fortunate to be mentored by Csikszentmihalyi on this path. In 1999, we coauthored, *Flow in Sports: The Keys to Optimal Experiences and Performances.*

I was drawn to the flow concept after reading Csikszentmihalyi's (1975) portrayal of his early investigations into this optimal experience. My early research into flow was, like Csikszentmihalyi's, primarily interview-based. Elite athletes were the initial focus of my research, because of their expected familiarity with optimal performance and flow experiences (Jackson, 1996). More generally, sport has been recognised as an excellent setting in which to examine flow (Csikszentmihalyi, 1990; Jackson & Csikszentmihalyi, 1999).

Sport offers the opportunity to do something better than it has been done before (Csikszentmihalyi, 1990), and so, once having made a choice to engage in a sport activity, a focussed mindset generally results. Further, the experience of sport is generally one of enjoyment – people engage in sport for the quality of experience it provides, as explained by Jackson and Csikszentmihalyi (1999): 'Contrary to what happens in most of life, sport can offer a state of being that is so rewarding one does it for no other reason than to be a part of it' (p. 4). Thus, sport can be considered an autotelic activity, and this also makes it an environment conducive to flow. A third advantage to studying flow in sport is that challenges and skills are built into the domain, are easily observable and can be modified. Thus, in this chapter, the research that has investigated flow in sport, and other performance-based settings, is a focus, to demonstrate what has been learned about flow in these settings.

Research in the performance domain (e.g., Jackson 1996) has demonstrated strong support for Csikszentmihalyi's nine-dimensional flow model. Further, across various quantitative studies, briefly reviewed later in this chapter, positive associations between flow and several important constructs in sport psychology, including task-focussed motivation, perceptions of ability, self-determined forms of motivation, hypnotic susceptibility and use of psychological skills, have been reported. As well, there have been consistent negative relationships between flow and anxiety.

Factors perceived by athletes to influence flow were identified in qualitatively based research (Jackson, 1992, 1995) and served to provide useful understandings of antecedent and disruptive factors. Examples of factors perceived by athletes to influence whether or not flow occurred during their performance included level of motivation towards the performance, physical preparation and readiness, confidence and focus. Jackson and Roberts (1992) examined associations between peak performance and flow with two hundred elite athletes from a wide-ranging sample of sports that included gymnastics, swimming, golf, track and field, cross-country running, tennis and diving. Flow was related to athletes' peak performances. Further, athletes high in orientation towards mastery of the task experienced flow more frequently than athletes low in mastery orientation. An opportunity to interview a subsample of this group of competitive athletes demonstrated clearly that the flow state was not only relevant to athletes – it was a treasured experience. This led Jackson to investigate flow experiences in athletes in greater depth.

Jackson (1992) interviewed U.S. national champion figure skaters to learn about flow in a sport that combines athletic skill with artistry. A close agreement between the skaters' perceptions of flow and the theoretical descriptions of the flow construct (Csikszentmihalyi, 1990) was found. Jackson identified factors perceived as important for attaining flow, and those perceived to prevent flow from occurring. In an extension of this qualitative research of flow, Jackson (1995, 1996) interviewed elite athletes from seven sports to assess whether their descriptive accounts of their optimal sport experiences would also match Csikszentmihalyi's (1990) dimensional model of flow. Results showed a strong consistency in the athletes' flow experience descriptions with Csikszentmihalyi's model and with the figure skating sample from the 1992 study. Antecedent and preventative flow factors were consistent with the skaters' experiences. These factors influencing flow are described in a later section of this chapter.

In a confirmation of the findings of Jackson and Roberts (1992) with regard to flow and task orientation, Kowal and Fortier (1999) found athletes motivated by intrinsic, self-determined reasons experienced flow more readily than those not intrinsically motivated. Their sample of 203 master's level swimmers were described as either being motivated in a self-determined way, by engaging in swimming for their own pleasure, satisfaction or benefit, versus those motivated for more external reasons. They also found that the situational determinants of perceived competence, autonomy and relatedness were positively related to flow experiences.

Jackson and colleagues (1998) examined the flow experience in non-elite, older athletic participants in World Masters Games participants in swimming, triathlon, cycling and track and field. Using an early version of the flow scale (Jackson & Marsh, 1996; Marsh & Jackson, 1999), their findings gave support to Csikszentmihalyi's (1990) concept of an autotelic personality – where participants choose to undertake an activity for its own sake and where the activity provides its own reward. Factors found to be predictive of flow were perceived ability, intrinsic motivation and anxiety (negative relationship).

Interest in flow as a research concept has continued to grow and flourish in the twenty-first century. Concurrent with this growing interest has been an interest in development and application of research tools to investigate what is by nature a somewhat elusive concept. One approach to the assessment of flow for research purposes has been the development of self-report instruments. These developments are described in a subsequent section of this chapter.

Karageorghis, Vlachopoulos and Terry (2000) investigated relationships between subjective feelings of enjoyment and flow in exercise. Using Jackson's flow scale, they found in their sample of 1,231 aerobic dance exercise participants a positive and significant association between levels of flow and the post-exercise feelings of revitalisation, tranquility and positive engagement. This suggested that the experience of flow might also play a role in encouraging adherence to physical activity regimes through the experience of positive post-exercise feelings.

As has been discussed, sport and, more generally, performance-based domains provide ideal contexts in which to research flow. Csikszentmihalyi (1975) initially began investigating flow through interviewing performers in varied domains and was struck by the consistency of the flow experience across domains. Research continues to unfold in different contexts, including various domains of the performing arts (e.g., Jackson & Eklund, 2004; Martin & Cutler, 2002; Moyle, Jackson, & McCloughan, 2014; Wrigley, 2005). For example, Wrigley (2005), using the FSS-2 and his music performance rating scale derived from live evaluations of more than thirty teaching staff, measured the effect of the flow state on the performances of more than two hundred tertiary music students from five instrument families – strings, piano, brass, woodwind and voice – during their live performance examinations. Most of the students experienced flow infrequently during their performance and with a very similar pattern of subscale scores across instrument families. Those that did experience flow achieved significantly higher global and specific performance ratings from their examiners.

Perry (1999) studied creative writers, another activity conducive to flow. Perry's descriptions of the writers' experience of flow provide an in-depth analysis of the experience of writing in flow, as well as suggestions about how to make flow happen while writing. Computer-mediated environments have also been a setting in which flow has been examined, especially Web instruction and design (e.g., Chen, Wigand, & Nilan, 1999; Novak, Hoffman, & Yung, 2000). Novak and colleagues (Novak et al., 2000; Novak, Hoffman, & Duhachek, 2003) found support for their proposition that compelling online experiences are dependent on facilitating flow state. The experience of flow for Web users (Chen et al., 1999) has been found to be similar to flow experiences in other settings.

A performance setting that holds promise for furthering understanding of both mindfulness in action and flow is dance. A recent, and ongoing, field intervention is being conducted in a university dance degree (Moyle et al., 2014) to examine the impact of a systematic mindfulness program on the experience of students studying to be dance performers and/or educators. This program was developed and implemented within the formal university curriculum for the bachelor of fine arts in dance and dance performance in order to provide students with opportunities to develop their psychological skills in conjunction with their physical/somatic skill development. The program is described in detail in Chapter 16 of this volume.

Flow and Mindfulness

Having a present-focussed awareness is key to experiencing flow. Complete involvement in a task at hand – for the sake of the absorbing experience itself – defines flow. Focus and awareness can be developed through the practice of mindfulness. The ever-increasing popularity and use of mindfulness-based approaches to psychology demonstrate the pervasive recognition of the value of present-moment awareness. Mindfulness can be defined as 'paying attention in a particular way: on purpose, in the present moment, nonjudgementally' (Kabat-Zinn, 1994, p. 4).

The present-moment awareness that defines mindfulness also defines the experience of flow. So, the two constructs are highly interrelated. The flow state associated with high-level performance in any endeavour can be one outcome of being mindful in a challenging situation. Interestingly, sport psychologists have been teaching athletes about being mindful (initially perhaps without using the term 'mindfulness') for many years. Take the following quote from 1990 by a leading Canadian sport psychologist, Terry Orlick, where he describes the optimal state for performance:

> The ideal performance focus is total concentration to your performance. Focusing on distracting thoughts (about final placing, others' expectations, the weather) interferes with an effective task focus. Stay in the moment, which is the only one you can influence anyway (Orlick, 1990, p. 16).

Orlick is one of many applied sport psychologists who, in their work with performers, have emphasised the importance of increasing awareness of the present moment as a key factor in peak performance.

Developing an appreciation for bringing present-moment awareness to what one does enhances experience and may lead to performance outcomes that go beyond an individual's prior levels of attainment. Tasks are performed better when the performer is fully focussed on the task, and this concentrated focus may help with the finding of flow in performance. Present-moment awareness is cultivated through mindfulness training, and there are a number of approaches that teach mindfulness, as described elsewhere in this book.

Flow is an optimal state because it involves being totally focussed in the present moment. When in flow, nothing disturbs or detracts from this concentrated state. Neither external nor internal distractions take up mental space. This present-moment focus is congruent with the aims of increasing mindfulness, and thus by helping individuals to be more mindful, psychologists may also be helping create the conditions for flow. There has been some empirical support for the premise that mindfulness enhances propensity to experience flow. For example, Kee and Wang (2008) found an association between propensity for being mindful and self-reported flow in college athletes. Aherne, Moran and Lonsdale (2011) assessed the impact of a mindfulness training program on college athletes' self-reported flow experiences and found the mindfulness training group increased their flow scores on the flow dimensions of Clear Goals and Sense of Control, as assessed by the Flow State Scale-2 (Jackson & Eklund, 2002). Cathcart, McGregor and Groundwater (2014) similarly found associations between self-reported mindfulness and flow, as assessed by the Dispositional Flow Scale-2 (Jackson & Eklund, 2002), in a sample of elite athletes. In line with Kee and Wang (2008), Cathcart and colleagues found no differences in global measures of flow or mindfulness across gender or sport types. Cathcart and colleagues also found global mindfulness and flow scores were negatively correlated with number of illnesses and injuries.

The positive associations that Kee and Wang (2008) and Cathcart and colleagues (2014) found between mindfulness and flow Kaufman, Glass and Arnkoff (2009) also found in a four-week field intervention with a community sample of athletes. These authors developed a mental training program called Mindful Sport Performance Enhancement (MSPE), which they described as a way of extending Mindfulness Based Stress Reduction (MBSR) and Mindfulness-Based Cognitive Therapy (MBCT) to athletes, and which has some similarities with another mindfulness-based performance enhancement approach in sport, the Mindfulness-Acceptance-Commitment (MAC) approach developed by Gardner and Moore (2004). Kaufman and colleagues (2009) found improvements in flow scores, as assessed by the Flow State Scale-2 (Jackson & Eklund, 2002) over the course of the program.

Through using multidimensional measures of both flow (Jackson & Eklund, 2002) and mindfulness (the Five-Facet Mindfulness Question-naire [FFMQ]; Baer et al., 2006), the study by Cathcart and colleagues (2014) was able to examine the association between mindfulness and flow at a more detailed level. Consistent with other research (e.g., Aherne et al., 2011; Swann et al., 2012), the flow dimension of total focus on the task at hand was demonstrated to be key to the association between mindfulness and flow, with correlations found between this flow dimension and several of the FFMQ mindfulness dimensions.

The studies by Kee and Wang (2008) and Cathcart and colleagues (2014) involved creating high and low flow groups, based on responses to the flow scales (Jackson & Eklund, 2002). High flow groups had higher mindfulness scores, leading to conclusions that 'elite athletes with the highest flow propensity also have the highest disposition to mindfulness', and 'propensity to achieve flow states may be enhanced by increasing mindfulness' (Cathcart et al., 2014, p. 137). Directionality of any relationship between flow and mindfulness is an area awaiting further research, but it does seem likely at a conceptual level that the relationship between flow and mindfulness is symbiotic (Kee & Wang, 2008). As Kee and Wang rightly point out, flow can be an elusive state, and therefore developing mindfulness skills as a pathway to flow experiences makes sense from an applied perspective.

Why does flow matter? Because quality of experience in what we do matters, and it is often when we are placed in a challenging situation that we have the opportunity to experience total involvement in what we are doing, as described by Jackson and Csikszentmihalyi (1999):

> What is true for life as a whole is also true in the more limited domain of sport. Winning, getting medals, improving one's time, or beating a record are important to get us motivated in the beginning, but if we take these goals too seriously – so that their pursuit blinds us to the experience along the way – then we miss the main gift that sport can give (p. 163).

Facilitating Flow

A central consideration to facilitating an environment conducive to flow is the presence of a challenging situation. When challenges of an activity are balanced with the skills of an individual, flow can occur. It is a delicate balance, as other relative levels of challenge and skill can bring about quite different experiential states. These relationships among challenge, skill and experience are illustrated in Figure 4.1. When there is a perception that skills match the challenge of a situation, flow can occur. It is the person's *perception* of the level of challenge and degree of skill, and the balance between them, that is essential to flow (Csikszentmihalyi, 1990).

Understanding factors that facilitate flow has been a focus of Jackson's research (e.g., 1992, 1995; Jackson et al., 1998; Jackson et al., 2001), with the goal of developing the knowledge base of what can increase the likelihood of achieving this rewarding optimal experience. In a qualitative study with U.S. national champion figure skaters, Jackson (1992) found that there were certain factors that helped or hindered the achievement of this state. Skaters were more likely to achieve flow when they held a positive mental attitude, experienced positive precompetitive and competitive affect, maintained appropriate focus, felt physically ready and experienced a unity with their skating partner. Skaters' experience of flow was more likely to be prevented or disrupted if they experienced physical problems and made mistakes, had an inability to maintain focus, held a negative attitude or experienced a lack of audience response.

In an extension of her 1992 study, Jackson (1995) considered the factors that facilitated, disrupted and prevented the experience of flow – together with the perceived controllability of flow – with a larger and more diverse range of elite athletes across seven sports. Results showed considerable consistency with results from the earlier study with figure skaters (Jackson, 1992). A set of ten factors were synthesised from the elite athletes' descriptions of what helped or hindered flow from occurring. This set of ten factors included physical, psychological, nutritional and situational variables. Examples of the types of factors athletes cited as being critical to the experience of flow included motivation, planning and preparation, having a positive mental attitude and staying focussed. Support for the multidimensional nature of antecedent and preventive flow factors was provided by these findings. In relation to the question on perceived controllability of flow, there was considerable variability in responses, from little perceived control to considerable perceived control. Interestingly, a large percentage of the factors seen to facilitate or prevent flow were seen as controllable, whereas the factors seen as disrupting flow were largely perceived as being uncontrollable.

Karageorghis and colleagues (2000) made some suggestions to facilitate the flow experience among school students, and these suggestions are equally applicable to other individuals interested in attaining flow. They suggested that students 'set personal goals that are attainable, challenging and well-defined'; 'give pupils a choice from time to time in the activities they engage in', to increase their autotelic experience; and 'use skill-learning techniques' to encourage persistence in mastering the tasks to increase their sense of control (p. 243).

Jackson and colleagues (Jackson, 1995; Jackson & Roberts, 1992; Jackson et al., 1998; Jackson et al., 2001) have found that a high perception of ability was a crucial factor facilitating flow. This led Jackson (Jackson et al., 2001) to suggest that the perceived skills component of the challenge–skill balance that defines flow is a critical aspect in the acquisition of the flow state in sport or other performance-based domains. Perceptions of skill and challenge in a situation, as described in the flow model (see Figure 4.1), also help to explain when the experience of anxiety, rather than flow, is likely to occur. When the challenges are greater than perceived skills, anxiety is the predicted outcome, according to the flow model. Research has consistently demonstrated that anxiety is a factor preventing flow (Jackson, 1995; Jackson & Roberts, 1992; Jackson et al., 1998; Stein et al., 1995; Taylor, 2001). As would be expected, self-determined, intrinsic motivation holds the most potential to facilitate flow. A study by Jackson and colleagues (1998), using a multidimensional measure of intrinsic motivation, showed that only an intrinsic motivation factor demonstrated substantive relationships with flow; the extrinsic factors were unrelated to flow.

There has been some research suggesting that flow may be enhanced by both hypnotic capacity and training in psychological skills. The results of a study by Grove and Lewis (1996) showed that the flow state could be enhanced by the capacity for hypnotic susceptibility. They found that high-susceptibility exercisers had greater increases in flow than low-susceptibility participants. Case studies by Pates and Maynard (2000) and Pates, Cummings and Maynard (2002) found that hypnotic interventions using imagery, relaxation, hypnotic induction, regression and triggers enhanced their experience of, and personal control over, flow. Using an imagery-based intervention in combination with relaxation techniques, Koehn, Morris and Watt (2006) and Koehn (2007) used an imagery script that aimed to increase athletes' confidence and action control in order to facilitate flow state and performance in tennis competition. A small sample of four tennis players increased their service and groundstroke performance, and three participants attained higher flow levels following the intervention phase (Koehn, 2007).

Understanding the factors that facilitate flow has obvious important applied implications. While it is not possible to engineer a flow experience, it is possible to increase its occurrence, as Jackson and Csikszentmihalyi (1999) argued: 'It is not possible to make flow happen at will ... and attempting to do so will only make the state more elusive. However, removing obstacles and providing facilitating conditions will increase its occurrence ...' (p. 138). Learning the skills of mindfulness provides one way to facilitate the occurrence of flow. Future research examining flow and mindfulness holds promise for helping individuals to move from fragmented states of mind to focussed and calm awareness.

Future Directions: Flow and Mindfulness

Researching experiential states of awareness is never easy, and a multi-method approach will yield the most gains in advancing knowledge. Technological advances will increasingly allow for direct measurements of what is happening in the body in flow and when mindful, and there are already promising developments in this area (e.g., Keller et al., 2011; Mansfield et al., 2012). Keller and colleagues (2011) assessed physiological and hormonal aspects of experience and found that in flow there was reduced heart rate variability and relatively high levels of salivary cortisol. Self-reporting of experience will likely continue to be a mainstay of psychological research of subjective experience going forward, although it will be interesting to observe how future research can interweave a mix of methods, including physiological methods, in order to help advance knowledge in this exciting field of subjective experience.

Future research could continue to explore dispositional characteristics that may make it more or less likely that flow will be experienced. Examples of individual difference factors that researchers could explore include such areas as capacity for experiencing enjoyment and fun; personality characteristics, and in particular, the autotelic personality trait; motivational orientations; and cognitive styles and processes, including the capacity to concentrate and immerse oneself in an activity, which has been a focus in this chapter.

In addition to individual difference factors, understanding relevant situational contingencies can help to extend understanding of flow. Social factors, such as the impact of teaching and coaching styles and learning environments, are likely to influence flow and mindfulness. Can programs be designed that help to facilitate flow in learning and performing environments? The wealth of training programs to develop mindfulness offer empirically grounded tools to examine potential to increase flow in these environments. One of the most important research pursuits for the future will be the unravelling of the complex interplay between person and situational variables, to address the question of how certain dispositional characteristics of an individual interact with situational variables to influence the experience of flow, at both the level of mental and of physiological experiencing.

The concepts of mindfulness and flow are different mind states, yet closely related. Both are positive mental experiences that involve a present-centred focus. Both are associated with enhanced performance and emotional wellness, and a state of mindfulness can facilitate an experience of flow. In an interesting recent study by Sheldon, Prentice and Halusic (2015), it was concluded that mindfulness can disrupt a person's ability for flow 'absorption' although being conducive to flow 'control'. Sheldon and colleagues based their argument regarding the experiential incompatibility of flow absorption and mindfulness on the role of self-awareness in both states. The authors argued that self-awareness is antithetical to flow, but that mindfulness involves maintaining self-awareness throughout an activity. The studies conducted by Sheldon and colleagues were innovative and yielded interesting findings on a subject that is intriguing and holds promise to help further understanding of both states of mindfulness and flow.

Further clarification of the concept of self-awareness used to distinguish flow and mindfulness is needed. Mindfulness is certainly about awareness, which is defined by Brown and Ryan (2004) as the 'subjective experience of internal and external phenomena' (p. 242). However, mindfulness does not depend on a focus on 'self'. The freedom of mindfulness is that it is awareness without the evaluation of self (and others) that generally takes up a lot of our attention.

Self-awareness, or more specifically, self-consciousness, is limiting to the ability to experience flow, as Sheldon and colleagues (2015) point out. Csikszentmihalyi (e.g., 1982, 1990, 2014; Csikszentmihalyi & Figurski, 1982) has written extensively about the tenuous relationship between the self and flow:

> The relationship between optimal experiences and the self is fraught with apparent paradox. On the one hand, the self is hidden during a flow experience; it cannot be found in consciousness. On the other hand, the self appears to thrive and grow as a result of such experiences (Csikszentmihalyi, 1982, p. 29).

Csikszentmihalyi has insightfully distinguished between the loss of self-focus *during* a flow state and the growth in complexity of the self *through* flow experiences. As discussed by some researchers interested in the interplay between mindfulness and flow (e.g., Kee & Wang, 2008; Salmon, Hanneman, & Harwood, 2010; Swann et al., 2012), the inhibition of the thinking mind in mindfulness may facilitate a loss of self-consciousness and absorption in the task. This idea was supported for female athletes (but not male athletes) in a study by Cathcart and colleagues (2014). Mindfulness and the loss of self-consciousness dimension of flow in Jackson and Eklund's (2002) flow scales were associated for female athletes (but unrelated for male athletes), in the study by Cathcart and colleagues. The multidimensional structure of the Long flow scales provide opportunity to further empirically examine the associations between the loss of self-consciousness in flow, as well as other flow dimensions, and various aspects of mindfulness.

Conclusion

Flow is the epitome of the positive potential of subjective experience. In the end, how we experience life is what matters most. As Csikszentmihalyi (1982) eloquently expressed many years ago, when arguing that optimal experience is the 'bottom line' of existence, 'It is useful to remember occasionally that life unfolds as a chain of subjective experiences. . . . The quality of these experiences determine whether, and to what extent, life was worth living' (p. 13). Or, as an elite athlete interviewed about the athlete's flow experience described, 'I strive to get to that state of perfection' (S. Jackson, personal communication, 1996). The concept of flow provides researchers and practitioners with a key to understanding those moments in time that make life worth living. Mindfulness, through cultivating present-moment awareness, provides one pathway for developing skills that can help unlock the door to flow.

REFERENCES

Aherne, C., Moran, A., and Lonsdale, C. (2011). The effect of mindfulness training on athletes' flow: An initial investigation. *Sport Psychologist*, 25(2), 177–189.

Baer, R. A., Smith, G. T., Hopkins, J., Krietemeyer, J., and Toney, L. (2006). Using self-report assessment methods to explore facets of mindfulness. *Assessment*, 13(1), 27–45. doi: 10.1177/1073191105283504

Brown, K. W., and Ryan, R. M. (2004). Perils and promise in defining and measuring mindfulness: Observations from experience. *Clinical Psychology: Science and Practice*, 11, 242–248. doi: 10.1093/clipsy.bph078

Cathcart, S., McGregor, M., and Groundwater, E. (2014). Mindfulness and flow in elite athletes. *Journal of Clinical Sport Psychology*, 8(2), 119–141. doi: 10.1123/jcsp.2014-0018

Chen, H., Wigand, R. T., and Nilan, M. S. (1999). Optimal experience of Web activities. *Computers in Human Behavior*, 15, 585–608. doi:10.1016/S0747-5632(99)00038-2

Csikszentmihalyi, M. (1975). *Beyond boredom and anxiety*. San Francisco, CA: Jossey-Bass.

(1982). Towards a psychology of optimal experience. In L. Wheeler (Ed.), *Review of personality and social psychology* (Vol. 2, pp. 13–35). Beverly Hills, CA: Sage.

(1990). *Flow: The psychology of optimal experience*. New York, NY: Harper & Row.

(1992). A response to the Kimiecik & Stein and Jackson papers. *Journal of Applied Sport Psychology*, 4, 181–183. doi: 10.1080/10413209208406460

(1996). *Creativity: Flow and the psychology of discovery and invention*. New York, NY: Harper Collins.

(1997). *Finding flow: The psychology of engagement with everyday life*. New York, NY: Harper Collins.

(2003). *Good business: Leadership, flow, and the making of meaning*. London, UK: Hodder & Stoughton.

(2014). *Flow and the foundations of positive psychology: The collected works of Mihaly Csikszentmihalyi*. Dordrecht, Netherlands: Springer.

Csikszentmihalyi, M., and Csikszentmihalyi, I. (Eds.). (1988). *Optimal experience: Psychological studies of flow in consciousness*. New York, NY: Cambridge University Press.

Csikszentmihalyi, M., and Figurski, T. J. (1982). Self-awareness and aversive experience in everyday life. *Journal of Personality*, 50, 15–28. doi: 10.1111/j.1467-6494.1982.tb00742.x

Csikszentmihalyi, M., and Larson, R. (1987). Validity and reliability of the experience-sampling method. *Journal of Nervous and Mental Disease*, 175, 526–536.

de Manzano, O., Theorell, T., Harmat, L., and Ullen, F. (2010). The psychophysiology of flow during piano playing. *Emotion*, 10, 301–311. doi: http://dx.doi.org/10.1037/a0018432

Dietrich, A. (2004). Neurocognitive mechanisms underlying the experience of flow. *Consciousness and Cognition*, 13, 746–761. doi:10.1016/j.concog.2004.07.002

Gardner, F. L., and Moore, Z. E. (2004). A mindfulness-acceptance-commitment based approach to athletic performance enhancement: Theoretical considerations. *Behavior Therapy*, 35, 707–723. doi: 10.1016/S0005-7894(04)80016-9

Grove, J. R. and Lewis, M. A. E. (1996). Hypnotic susceptibility and the attainment of flow like states during exercise. *Journal of Sport and Exercise Psychology*, 18, 380–391.

Hamilton, J. A. (1976). Attention and intrinsic rewards in the control of psychophysiological states. *Psychotherapy and Psychosomatics*, 27, 54–61.

(1981). Attention, personality, and self-regulation of mood: Absorbing interest and boredom. *Progress in Experimental Personality Research*, 10, 281–315.

Jackson S. A. (1992). Athletes in flow: A qualitative investigation of flow states in elite figure skaters. *Journal of Applied Sport Psychology*, 4, 161–180. doi: 10.1080/10413209208406459

(1995). Factors influencing the occurrence of flow states in elite athletes. *Journal of Applied Sport Psychology*, 7, 135–163. doi: 10.1080/10413209508406962

(1996). Toward a conceptual understanding of the flow experience in elite athletes. *Research Quarterly for Exercise and Sport*, 67, 76–90.

Jackson, S. A., and Csikszentmihalyi, M. (1999). *Flow in sports: The keys to optimal experiences and performances*. Champaign, IL: Human Kinetics.

Jackson, S. A., and Eklund, R. C. (2002). Assessing flow in physical activity: The Flow State Scale-2 and Dispositional Flow Scale-2. *Journal of Sport and Exercise Psychology*, 24, 133–150.

(2004). Relationships between quality of experience and participation in diverse performance settings. Paper presented at the 39th Annual

Conference of the Australian Psychological Society, Sydney, Australia. *Australian Journal of Psychology*, 56, (September Supplement), 193.

Jackson, S. A., Eklund, R. C., and Martin, A. J. (2010). *The FLOW Manual*. Mind Garden, Inc. Retrieved from www.mindgarden.com.

Jackson, S. A., Ford, S. K., Kimiecik, J. C., and Marsh, H. W. (1998). Psychological correlates of flow in sport. *Journal of Sport and Exercise Psychology*, 20, 358–378.

Jackson, S. A., and Marsh, H. W. (1996). Development and validation of a scale to measure optimal experience: The flow state scale. *Journal of Sport and Exercise Psychology*, 18, 17–35.

Jackson, S. A., Martin, A. J., and Eklund, R. C. (2008). Long and short measures of flow: Examining construct validity of the FSS-2, DFS-2, and new brief counterparts. *Journal of Sport and Exercise Psychology*, 30, 561–587.

Jackson S. A., and Roberts, G. C. (1992). Positive performance states of athletes: Toward a conceptual understanding of peak performance. *Sport Psychologist*, 6, 156–171.

Jackson, S. A., Thomas, P. R., Marsh, H. W., and Smethurst, C. J. (2001). Relationships between flow, self-concept, psychological skills, and performance. *Journal of Applied Sport Psychology*, 13, 129–153. doi: 10.1080/10413200175314986S

Kabat-Zinn, J. (1994). *Wherever you go, there you are: Mindfulness meditation in everyday life*. New York, NY: Hyperion.

Karageorghis, C. I., Vlachopoulos, S. P., and Terry, P. C. (2000). Latent variable modelling of the relationship between flow and exercise-induced feelings: An intuitive appraisal perspective. *European Physical Education Review*, 6(3), 230–248.

Kaufman, K., Glass, C., and Arnkoff, D. (2009). Evaluation of mindful sport performance enhancement (MSPE): A new approach to promote flow in athletes. *Journal of Clinical Sports Psychology*, 4, 334–356.

Kee, Y., and Wang, C. (2008). Relationships between mindfulness, flow dispositions and mental skills adoption: A cluster analytic approach. *Psychology of Sport and Exercise*, 9, 393–411. doi:10.1016/j.psychsport. 2007.07.001

Keller, J., Bless, H., Blomann, F., and Kleinbohl, D. (2011). Physiological aspects of flow experiences: Skill-demand-compatibility effects on heart rate variability and salivary cortisol. *Journal of Experimental Social Psychology*, 47, 849–852. doi:10.1016/j.jesp.2011.02.004

Koehn, S., (2007). *Propensity and attainment of flow state*. (Unpublished doctoral thesis). Melbourne, Victoria: Victoria University.

Koehn, S., Morris, T., and Watt, A. P. (2006). Efficacy of an imagery intervention on flow and performance in tennis competitions *Society for Medicine and Science in Tennis*, 11, 12–14.

Kowal, J., and Fortier, M. S. (1999). Motivational determinants of flow: Contributions from self-determination theory. *Journal of Social Psychology*, 139(3), 355–368. doi: 10.1080/00224549909598391

Mansfield, B. E., Oddson, B. E., Turcotte, J., and Couture, R. T. (2012). A possible physiological correlate for mental flow. *Journal of Positive Psychology*, 7, 327–333. doi: 10.1080/17439760.2012.691982

Marsh, H. W., and Jackson, S. A. (1999). Flow experience in sport: Construct validation of multidimensional, hierarchical state and trait responses. *Structural Equation Modelling*, 6, 343–371. doi: 10.1080/10705519909540140

Martin, J. J., and Cutler, K. (2002). An exploratory study of flow and motivation in theater actors. *Journal of Applied Sport Psychology*, 14, 344–352. doi: 10.1080/10413200290103608

Martin, A. J., and Jackson, S. A. (2008). Brief approaches to assessing task absorption and enhanced subjective experience: Examining "short" and "core" flow in diverse performance domains. *Motivation and Emotion*, 32, 141–157. doi: 10.1007/s11031-008-9094-0

Moyle, G., Jackson, S. A., and McCloughan, L. J. (2014). *Mindfulness on the move: The impact of mindfulness training within a university dance program.* Manuscript in preparation.

Nakamura, J., and Csikszentmihalyi, M. (2002). The concept of flow. In C. R. Snyder and S. J. Lopez (Eds.), *Handbook of positive psychology* (pp. 89–105). New York, NY: Oxford University Press.

Novak, T. P., Hoffman, D. L., and Duhachek, A. (2003). The influence of goal-directed and experiential activities on online flow experiences. *Journal of Consumer Psychology*, 13, 3–16. doi:10.1207/S15327663JCP13-1&2_01

Novak, T. P., Hoffman, D. L., and Yung, Y. F. (2000). Measuring the customer experience in online environments: A structural modeling approach. *Marketing Science*, 19, 22–42. doi: http://dx.doi.org/10.1287/mksc.19.1.22.15184

Orlick, T. (1990). *In pursuit of excellence.* Champaign, IL: Human Kinetics.

Pates, J., Cummings, A., and Maynard, I. (2002). Effects of hypnosis on flow states and three-point shooting performance in basketball players. *Sport Psychologist*, 16, 34–47.

Pates, J., and Maynard, I. (2000). Effects of hypnosis on flow states and golf performance. *Perceptual and Motor Skills*, 91, 1057–1075.

Perry, S. K. (1999). *Writing in flow.* Cincinnati, OH: Writer's Digest.

Salmon, P., Hanneman, S., and Harwood, B. (2010). Associative/dissociative cognitive strategies in sustained physical activity: Literature review and proposal for a mindfulness-based conceptual model. *Sport Psychologist*, 24, 127–156.

Sheldon, K. M., Prentice, M., and Halusic, M. (2015). The experiential incompatability of mindfulness and flow absorption. *Social Psychological and Personality Science*, 6, 276–283. doi: 10.1177/1948550614555028

Stavrou, N. A., Jackson, S. A., Zervas, Y., and Karteroliotis, K. (2007). Flow experience and athletes' performance with reference to the orthogonal model of flow. *Sport Psychologist*, 21, 438–457.

Stein, G. L., Kimiecik, J. C., Daniels, J., and Jackson, S. A. (1995). Psychological antecedents of flow in recreational sport. *Personality and Social Psychology Bulletin*, 21, 125–135. doi: 10.1177/0146167295212003

Swann, C., Keegan, R., Piggott, D., and Crust, L. (2012). A systematic review of the experience, occurrence, and controllability of flow states in elite sport. *Psychology of Sport and Exercise*, 13(6), 807–819. doi:10.1016/j.psychsport.2012.05.006

Taylor, M. K. (2001). *The relationships of anxiety intensity and direction of flow in collegiate athletes.* (Unpublished master's thesis). Greensboro, NC: University of North Carolina at Greensboro.

Wrigley, W. J. (2005). *An examination of ecological factors in music performance assessment.* (Unpublished doctoral thesis). Brisbane, Australia: Griffith University.

CHAPTER 5

Peak Performance: Langerian Mindfulness and Flow

Sayyed Mohsen Fatemi, Elizabeth D. Ward, Ellen J. Langer

Performance, including sport performance, appears to transpire in a series of connected and sequentially related moments. The time-oriented context of performance is characterized by the interplay of complex array of behaviors consisting of emotional, cognitive, behavioral, and physiological factors. Some studies have focused on the stress-oriented variables that are embedded within the manifestation of performance configuration (see, for instance, Craft et al., 2003). On the other hand, the analysis of a given performance may suggest that a performance may fall into a low, middle, or high level of excitement. At low levels, performance levels are slow, and at high levels, performance may suffer too since the performance is intensely overwhelmed by the excitement level.

The Yerkes-Dodson Curve (Yerkes & Dudson, 1908) indicates that optimal task performance occurs at the mid-level of excitement or diffuse psychological arousal. In defining a peak performance, scholars have focused on special extraordinary features of a performance, which on the one hand embodies the previously achieved level of competencies and functionality and on the other hand exceeds and supersedes the quality of the past positive experiences in connection with the given task (see Privette 1981, 1983, 1991).

An in-depth exploration of the constituents of a peak performance may highlight the interconnectedness of positive features in the wholeness of a performance, including relaxation, confidence, high energy, present-centered focus, extraordinary awareness, a feeling of being in control, and detachment from distractions (see Cohn, 1991; Garfield & Bennett, 1984). When it comes to sport performance, sport psychology has displayed an interest in exploring the relationship between positive self-talk, emotional regulation, and heightened performance (for instance, see Kornspan, Overby, & Lerner, 2004).

In line with the sport psychology studies, Csikszentmihalyi's (1975, 1979, 1990) conceptualization of flow has inspired the field with continued interest in looking into facilitating factors that can contribute to an enhancement of performance. Flow refers to those experiences in which you become so indulged in an activity that you lose awareness of everything else around you. You feel "in the zone," and time flies. The activity itself becomes a reward in and of itself. Csikszentmihalyi's model of flow, which was earlier called autotelic experiences, originated from his interviews with many people who experienced a full engagement in their activities, such as rock climbers and chess players. Flow describes a state when you can have "the experience of complete absorption in the present moment" (Nakamura & Csikszentmihalyi, 2009, p. 195). Anxiety and boredom may happen when things are not moving in line with the flow: when there is no challenge, there can be boredom; when the task is so overwhelming, there can be anxiety.

Flow is, thus, linked to a performance that is devoid of boredom and anxiety. It is challenging and yet rewarding, it is exhilarating and enlivening, it is empowering and energizing. Studies have found a positive relationship between flow and positive performance. Russell (2001) found that "college athletes appear to have similar experiences of flow states, regardless of gender, or sport type" (p. 83). Other scholars, including Schuler and Brunner (2009), have found a positive relationship between flow and motivation among marathon runners to continue running in the future.

In line with the interest in scrutinizing the research on the optimal experience and peak performance, mindfulness has emerged as a rigorous perspective with multilateral implications (Kabat-Zinn, 1994; Kabat-Zinn, Lipworth, & Burney, 1985; Langer, 1977; Langer & Abelson, 1972; Langer & Imber, 1979). An in-depth analysis of different ramifications of mindfulness demonstrates that mindfulness may be classified into two independently substantive categories with two different directions. One is more attuned to Eastern philosophy and is known as Eastern-based mindfulness, with manifestations in techniques such as mindfulness-based stress reduction and mindfulness-based cognitive therapy. The work by Kabat-Zinn mostly falls into the Eastern category, namely its roots can be traced back to Buddhism. Kabat-Zinn (1994) conceptualizes mindfulness as "paying attention in a particular way: on purpose, in the present moment, and nonjudgmentally" (p. 4). Along similar lines, other forms of mindfulness, including acceptance and commitment therapy, may be ultimately embedded within the first division, with their original roots in the Eastern philosophy of Buddhism. The Eastern practice of mindfulness is inextricably tied to meditation, where meditation serves as a cornerstone in facilitating the process of mindfulness.

In the meantime, a new and a unique form of mindfulness with its roots in empirical and experimental psychology was initiated by Langer around forty years ago. In her work on mindfulness, Langer (2000) defines mindfulness as "a flexible state of mind in which we are actively engaged in the present, noticing new things and sensitive to context" (p. 220). As Crum and Lyddy (2014) succinctly posit, "Eastern mindfulness shines a clear light of unbiased and unattached awareness on existing mindsets whereas Langerian mindfulness involves a continual process or restructuring and creating mindsets anew" (p. 954).

Life is brimming with multiplicity, acceleration, and scattered mental engagements. This is intensified by multitasking and threatens to deprive people of experiencing the moment in its entirety. An occupied mind with previously shaped forms of sporadic directions may not be able to bring to fullness its potential. The result is the loss of the moment and the inability to linger in the present time.

Langerian mindfulness targets the absence in our daily life and presents strategies to enhance connectedness to the moment. This being absent in the moment instead of being present is entrenched within automatically learned behaviors that do not allow the performer to go outside the boxes: "as we blindly follow routines or unwittingly carry out senseless orders, we are acting like automatons, with potentially grace consequences for ourselves and others" (Langer, 1989, p. 4). The key in Langerian mindfulness is to welcome the possibility of a new perspective (Langer, 1997, 2005, 2009).

As soon as we commit ourselves to some established form of information and lock ourselves into a specific mode of thinking, Langerian mindfulness argues, we would deprive ourselves of seeking novel ways or alternative modes of thinking. In Langerian mindfulness, we actively restructure our mindsets through the creation of new categories or distinctions (Langer, 1989, p. 4). Langerian mindfulness presents four interconnected characteristics as the main components of mindfulness: a search for novelty, a phenomenological engagement in the present moment, the creation of new categories of thinking, and flexibility.

One of the main distinctions of Langerian mindfulness from the Buddhist or Eastern form of mindfulness lies in the encouraging propensity of Langerian mindfulness for proactive creation of new categories. Langerian mindfulness within Langerian psychology "examines the hegemony of the context-oriented truth and probes the necessity for looking at the a priori assumptions that act as the driving forces of the psychological analysis" (Fatemi, 2014, p. 135).

Performance can be categorized into two different modes of action: one as something that lies in the array of automatic forms of thinking, and one as something creational that is created by the performer as the creator. The former is mostly associated with activities and undertakings that are subsumed under a category with multiple forms of labels, such as "job," "occupation," "chores," and so on, whereas the latter is born in the heart of a productive form of action known as "work." In other words, the first mode may be done in accordance with the domination of the previously prescriptive modes of thinking in the context of doing something for the sake of its mere implementation. The second is coupled with an act of creation where the performer finds himself or herself as a creator, and the creational relationship between the creation and the creator is a unique one. This relationship is characterized through belonging, love, fervor, and unity. The creator is unified with the creation, and thus wholeness is an emergent state that unfolds itself in the process of the creation.

A wide variety of studies indicate that the flow state is connected to peak performance (Csikszentmihalyi, 1990; Jackson, 2000; Jackson & Csikszentmihalyi, 1999; Jackson & Roberts, 1992; Young & Pain, 1999). Increasingly, there has been interest in the role that mindfulness may play in fostering flow. Research findings also suggest that flow can serve as a central way in which mindfulness training can enhance athletes' performance (Gardner & Moore, 2004; Kaufman, Glass, & Arnkoff, 2009). In their cluster analysis, Kee and Wang (2008) found that university student athletes who scored highest on flow also scored the highest on mindfulness, which was measured using the Mindfulness-Mindlessness Scale (MMS) (Bodner & Langer, 2001).

Research based on Eastern-derived mindfulness has recently begun to focus on the relationship between mindfulness and athletic peak performance. The first documented research that linked mindfulness and sport performance involved college rowers hoping to make the Olympic Rowing Team. In their work with Division I rowers preparing for the Olympics, Kabat-Zinn, Beall, and Rippe (1985) developed a mindfulness meditation program. Based on his Mindfulness-Based Stress Reduction (MBSR) work, the mindfulness meditation program ranged from two weeks to seven months. During this program, the athletes sat in formal meditation individually and with their team. Self-reported benefits included greater relaxation, increased concentration, as well as reduced fatigue and fewer negative thoughts. Furthermore, the Olympic medalists claimed that the program improved their performance (Kabat-Zinn et al., 1985). The Mindfulness-Acceptance-Commitment (MAC) theory of performance enhancement in the body of the Buddhist philosophy also focuses on enhancing athletic performance through mindfulness. It consists of structured sessions and interventions that teach athletes to be mindful (Gardner & Moore, 2004, 2006, 2007).

In the meantime, Langerian mindfulness has provided plenty of empirically and experimentally based examples where mindfulness can give rise to an enhancement of creative performance (see, for instance, Langer, 1997, 2005, 2009). As one becomes proactively involved in the creation of his or her work, he or she notices new things. This search for novelty, which is of particular interest in Langerian mindfulness, posits that knowledge is existentially transformed simultaneously with the radical transformation of the knower being the performer here too. Knowing and being move not only in parallel mode in Langerian mindfulness, but also they become one: knowing is being, and being is knowing. Nonetheless, knowing is not bound by the stability of the previously established frame of reference. In Langerian mindfulness, the intention facilitates the process of focusing on the moment-to-moment response style as it moves in accordance with the foundational component of mindfulness: a search for new perspective.

Langerian Mindfulness and Infinite Possibilities

The mindfulness-based performance is intertwined with fervor and passion on the emotional side and a broadening of perspective on the cognitive side. Recent years' findings of neuroscience demonstrate that our modes of thinking, our forms of actions, and our objects of our attention may change the structure and function of our brains. In Langerian mindfulness, the performer is taught to train his or her attention in view of an enriched understanding of choices.

When one is influenced by anything, two things need to occur: one needs to pay attention to the object of attention and he or she needs to confirm and endorse the emergent propositional implication of the stated implicit or explicit parlance of the attention. For example, a player may fail to operate a successful string of actions during a game, and as he or she fails, the player's attention may highlight the failure and endorses that the so-called failure is an indication that he or she would fail in the second string of action too. As the player corroborates the possibility of failing through reconfirming the failure, he or she will be more prone to fail as the occasion arises. This can happen in a few seconds and can be affected by sundry unconscious factors too. There are evidently numerous signs of automaticity and automatic behaviors within the context of this behavior. In other words, mindlessness can be tied to the dynamics of the failed operation through a recursive pattern of negativity, helplessness, and self-defeating statements.

In Langerian mindfulness, one is trained to become perceptive of the power of his or her choices in paying attention to the wide variety of stimuli. Analogically, when one is watching a TV program with access to a remote control, one can be vigilantly reminded of one's power of changing the channel instead of getting stuck in one channel. Understanding the possibility of the power to change the channel lies at the center of Langerian mindfulness. When one is mindless, he or she is incarcerated within the context of his or her own perspective, namely the channel in this example, and thus the individual cannot undertake any action other than what the already chosen channel or perspective suggests.

The automatic lingering in a single perspective is energy consuming as it is gradually encapsulated within a tedious, monotonous, repetitive, and recursive mode of being. In order to emancipate oneself from the banal and rule-governed behavior and its synchronous fatigue, one is trained to practice shifting attention from one thing to the other in a deliberate and meaningful way. In Langerian mindfulness, therefore, one primarily learns to look at positive and new things in the realm of his or her being. This could be a new look at a friend or even oneself with a positive tone.

Starting everything afresh constitutes one of the main characteristics of Langerian mindfulness. As stale bread tastes dull and disengaging, a stale state of being is frustratingly disengaging too. As one experiences an active state of mind through a meaningful and sagacious search for novelty, the stale state of being is transformed into a delightful state of existentiality through a phenomenological connectedness to Langerian mindfulness.

Langerian mindfulness thus gives rise to a shift of perspective and language. The performer who is cooped up and caged by self-defeating statements learns that he or she is constantly exposed to a series of choices. Thoughts are choices too. As one experiences the power of choice through changing the TV channel, one can experience the power of having a choice through learning to say yay or nay to a string of thoughts. Mindlessly shaped clusters of thoughts inscribe the certitude of apprehending possibility in a fixed form with unchangeable, unalterable, and indubitable layers of reality justified through the recursively unquestionable series of assumptions. Langerian mindfulness targets the fixation and its paramount legitimacy and calls for the possibility of going beyond the stability of the subjective propositional clinging. The fixation is here is meant to encompass the emotional, cognitive, and behavioral domains. So as psychoanalysis, cognitive psychology, and behaviorists concentrate on demonstrating the paralyzing impacts of fixation in their own sphere of interest, Langerian mindfulness helps the performer understand the implications of a premature cognitive and emotional commitment and facilitates the process of reconciling with the emergent possibility of new modes of being.

When one is experiencing the automaticity of a behavior, he or she moves in the path of predetermined pavement of possibility delineated by schemas of the past. The performance in the pathway is enumerated by the kaleidoscopic determined indexes of absolute, possible, and certain steps. If the movement transpires with an abidance by the rule-governed dictum of possibility, the performance turns out to be maximized by virtue of the same identifiers of the operative possibility with the hegemonic context of possibility. This will ultimately produce conceptualization of optimization based on the overall interpretive discourse of a predefined realm of possibility. Hence, performance can flourish or consummate as much as the explication of possibility already determines the depth and width of possible optimization. The points of departure and points of successful landing are already elucidated within the scope of the known possibility. This may be similar to the current manifestation of transportation routes, where the signs already indicate the permissibility or impermissibility of movements (see Chapter 6 in this volume).

Langerian mindfulness changes the whole story here. Possibility is no longer possibility based on the known recursive conceptualization of possibility. In Langerian mindfulness, the known connectedness to the categorization of possibility and impossibility lies in the taxonomy of mindlessness. Langerian notion of possibility goes beyond the cognitive, computational, linear, analytical, and logical mode of possibility (see Fatemi, 2014).

The substantive transformation of the conceptualization of possibility is idiosyncratic to Langerian mindfulness. It starts off with providing the performer with a discernment of a broadening prism of possibility with no finite point of establishment. The performer here learns to realize the imprisoning implications of the finitely translated modes of possibility.

Langerian mindfulness leaps forward through providing the person with the perceptiveness of the creational competencies of one's inner potential. The leaping beyond the established modes of equations would emerge in the heart of the preparatory move of Langerian mindfulness. The subtlety of the cognitive and emotional discernment of the infinite scope of possibility would allow the performer to briskly challenge debilitating mindsets with their psychological and cognitive heftiness. The performer here learns to question and debate the validity and reliability of the existing debilitating mindsets as he or she learns to realize that mindsets can be choices, and that a repeatedly operative mindset is not necessarily the best choice to live with. Choices can be created as affluently as possible when the performer is in touch with three phenomenological states of being: tranquility and calmness, inner intimacy, and inner security. Mindfulness facilitates the possibility of implementing the three aforementioned stages of being: this occurs through developing a nonjudgmental, open, and flexible state of intrapersonal and interpersonal connectedness.

Conclusion

Calmness and tranquility go away when the mind is mindlessly engaged in massiveness, multiplicity, and separation. Mindfulness is empowering as it helps the performer discern the empowering understanding of experiencing the authenticity of one's being. Langerian mindfulness challenges the idea of having a template for peak performance. Relying on a set of determining rules for performance contrasts with the uniqueness of the performer and his or her exclusive sensibility. Langerian mindfulness does not negate the scientific understanding of different domains of performance, which began with an in-depth look into cognition and its wide-ranging operations, including sustained attention, selective attention, conflict monitoring, processing and storing of information, decision making, planning, and problem solving.

Effective utilization of the so-called elite skills is taken into consideration in Langerian analysis of high-level performance. When one finds the possibility of disengaging from the paralyzing compartmentalization of automatic conceptualizations, one would embrace the courage to take upon himself or herself to initiate the first action of creation. The creation espouses the wholeness and the synchronicity of the performer and the performance in that it propounds a synergy between the work and the creator. The creator's psychological connectedness to the object of creation expedites the process of a proactive engagement in the moment. It serves as a preamble for the optimal cognitive preparation too, since it nourishes the performer with a nonjudgmentally based equanimity under pressure, a comprehensive sense of inner intimacy and inner comfort, and an open stage of flexibility with manifestation in response styles.

Mindfulness-based performance is inspired to unlock the cognitive and emotional structures while creating new avenues and alternative ways of exploring possibility. In doing so, the performer is ontologically connected to the experiential process of seeking psychological possibility through the infinitely operative source of possibility. Langerian mindfulness unleashes the possibility of possible examination of creative possibilities in novel cognitive and emotional domains with their behavioral implications.

REFERENCES

Bodner, T., and Langer, E. J. (2001, June). *Individual differences in mindfulness: The Mindfulness/Mindlessness Scale*. Poster presented at the thirteenth annual American Psychology Society Convention, Toronto, Ontario, Canada.

Cohn, P. J. (1991). An exploratory study on peak performance in golf. *Sport Psychologist*, 5(1), 1–14.

Craft, L. L., Magyar, T. M., Becker, B. J., and Feltz, D. L. (2003). The relationship between the Competitive State Anxiety Inventory-2 and sport performance: A meta-analysis. *Journal of Sport and Exercise Psychology*, 25, 44–65.

Crum, A., and Lyddy, C. (2014). De-stressing stress: The power of mindsets and the art of stressing mindfully. In A. N. Ie, C. T. Ngnoumen, and E. J. Langer (Eds.), *The Wiley Blackwell handbook of mindfulness* (1st ed., pp. 948–963). Hoboken, NJ: John Wiley & Sons.

Csikszentmihalyi, M. (1975). *Beyond boredom and anxiety*. San Francisco, CA: Josey-Bass.

 (1979). The concept of flow. In B. Sutton-Smith (Ed.), *Play and learning* (pp. 335–358). New York, NY: Gardner Press.

 (1990). *Flow: The psychology of optimal experience*. New York, NY: Harper & Row.

Fatemi, S. M. (2014). Exemplifying a shift of paradigm: Exploring the psychology of possibility and embracing the instability of knowing the instability of knowing. In A. N. Ie, C. T. Ngnoumen, and E. J. Langer (Eds.), *The Wiley Blackwell handbook of mindfulness* (1st ed., pp. 115–138). Hoboken, NJ: John Wiley & Sons.

Gardner, F. L., and Moore, Z. E. (2004). A Mindfulness-Acceptance-Commitment–based approach to athletic performance enhancement. *Behavior Therapy*, 35, 707–723. doi: 1016/S0005-7894(04)80016-9

 (2006). *Clinical sport psychology*. Champaign, IL: Human Kinetics.

 (2007). *The psychology of enhancing human performance: The Mindfulness-Acceptance-Commitment (MAC) approach*. New York, NY: Springer.

Garfield, C. A., and Bennett, H. Z. (1984). *Peak performance: Mental training techniques of the world's greatest athletes*. Los Angeles, CA: Tarcher.

Jackson, S. A. (2000). Joy, fun, and flow state in sport. In Y. L. Hanin (Ed.), *Emotions in sport* (pp. 135–155). Champaign, IL: Human Kinetics.

Jackson, S. A., and Csikszentmihalyi, M. (1999). *Flow in sports*. Champaign, IL: Human Kinetics.

Jackson, S. A., and Roberts, G. C. (1992). Positive performance states of athletes: Toward a conceptual understanding of peak performance. *Sport Psychologist*, 6, 156–171.

Kabat-Zinn, J. (1994). *Wherever you go, there you are: Mindfulness meditation in everyday life*. New York, NY: Hyperion.

Kabat-Zinn, J., Beall, B., and Rippe, J. (1985, April). *A systematic mental training program based on mindfulness meditation to optimize performance in collegiate and Olympic rowers*. Paper presented at the World Congress in Sport Psychology, Copenhagen, Denmark.

Kabat-Zinn, J., Lipworth, L., and Burney, R. (1985). The clinical use of mindfulness meditation for the self-regulation of chronic pain. *Journal of Behavioral Medicine*, 8, 163–190.

Kaufman, K. A., Glass, C. R., and Arnkoff, D. B. (2009). Evaluation of mindful sport performance enhancement (MSPE): A new approach to promote flow in athletes. *Journal of Clinical Sports Psychology*, 4, 334–356.

Kee, Y. H., and Wang, C. K. J. (2008). Relationships between mindfulness, flow dispositions and mental skills adoption: A cluster analytic approach. *Psychology of Sport and Exercise*, 9, 393–411. doi: 10.1016/j.psychsport.2007.07.001

Kornspan, A. S., Overby, L. Y., and Lerner, B. S. (2004). Analysis and performance of pre-performance imagery and other strategies on a golf putting task. *Journal of Mental Imagery*, 28, 59–74.

Langer, E. J. (1977). The psychology of change. *Journal for the Theory of Social Behavior*, 7, 185–207.

(1989). *Mindfulness*. Reading, MA: Addison-Wesley.

(1997). *The power of mindful learning*. Cambridge, MA: De Capo Press.

(2000). Mindful learning. *Current Directions in Psychological Science*, 9, 220–223. doi: 10.1111/1467-8721.00099

(2005). *On becoming an artist: Reinventing yourself through mindful creativity*. New York, NY: Ballantine.

(2009). *Counterclockwise: Mindful health and the power of possibility*. New York, NY: Ballantine.

Langer, E. J., and Abelson, R. P. (1972). The semantics of asking a favor: How to succeed in getting help without really dying. *Journal of Personality and Social Psychology*, 24, 26–32. doi: http://dx.doi.org/10.1037/h0033379

Langer, E. J., and Imber, L. G. (1979). When practice makes imperfect: The debilitating effects of overlearning. *Journal of Personality and Social Psychology*, 37, 2014–2025. doi: http://dx.doi.org/10.1037/0022-3514.37.11.2014

Nakamura, J., and Csikszentmihalyi, M. (2009). Flow theory and research. In S. J. Lopez and C. R. Snyder (Eds.), *Oxford handbook of positive psychology* (2nd ed., pp. 195–206). New York, NY: Oxford University Press.

Privette, G. (1981). Dynamics of peak performance. *Journal of Humanistic Psychology*, 21, 57–67. doi: 10.1177/002216788102100106

(1983). Peak experience, peak performance, and flow: A comparative analysis of positive human experiences. *Journal of Personality and Social Psychology*, 45, 1361–1368. doi: http://dx.doi.org/10.1037/0022-3514.45.6.1361

Privette, G., and Bundrick, C. M. (1991). Peak experience, peak performance, and flow: Correspondence of personal descriptions and theoretical constructs. *Journal of Social Behavior and Personality*, 6, 169–188.

Russell, W.D. (2001). An examination of flow state occurrence in college athletes. *Journal of Sport Behavior*, 24(1), 83.

Schuler, J., and Brunner, S. (2009). The rewarding effect of flow experience on performance in a marathon race. *Psychology of Sport and Exercise*, 10, 168–174.

Yerkes, R. M., and Dodson, J. D. (1908). The relation of strength of stimulus to rapidity of habit formation. *Journal of Comparative and Neurological Psychology*, 18, 459–482. doi: 10.1002/cne.920180503

Young, J. A., and Pain, M. D. (1999). The zone: Evidence of a universal phenomenon for athletes across sports. *Athletic Insight: The Online Journal of Sport Psychology*, 1(3), 21–30.

CHAPTER 6

Langerian Mindfulness and Liminal Performing Spaces

Sayyed Mohsen Fatemi

One's action or performance in a specific domain may be analyzed by virtue of a wide variety of influencing factors, including social, cultural, physiological, and psychological contexts. Perhaps Lewin's Ecological Model may move in line with the same sort of analysis whereby behavior is considered to be the function of the person and the environment. In looking into the dynamics of the action, one may scrutinize the underlying conscious and unconscious structural components in espousing specific manifestation of a performance.

The hot perspective, which dates back to 1950s and 1960s, was merely interested in the unconscious elements that produced certain types of performance. Thus, any performance, based on the hot perspective, was ultimately embedded within the unconscious interactive process with idiosyncratic emotional, cognitive, and behavioral categories. It was the realization of the clandestine, cryptic, and latently unconscious elements that contributed to the configuration of specific behavioral manifestation (see, for instance, Zajonc, 1984).

An alternative perspective known as the cold approach was inspired by computer-oriented discoveries and focused on the cognitive interplay of the influencing factors of a performance. The focus from the impulsive and unconscious sedimentation of a behavior was here replaced with an interest in the analytical, computational, and serial processing of information and their implications for decision making in a performance. A search for the computational analysis of the performance and its original elements was encouraged in the cold perspective with the intention of identifying the systematic generative constituents of a performance (see, for instance, De Jaegher, Di Paolo, and Gallagher, 2010).

Both perspectives were challenged by critical approaches that indicated how each of the hot and cold outlooks overlooked some of the significant influential factors of a performance. The result was the combination of both perspectives into what was later called the warm look (see, for instance, Sorrentino, 2003; Sorrentino & Higgins, 1986). Dual process theories of social cognition examined two types of information processing that considered both hot and cold perspectives. One led to an effortful and reflective type of thinking, and the other one studied an automatic form of thinking, with each type having implications for behavior and performance (Kruglanski & Orehek, 2007; Petty, 2004).

As much as an in-depth excavation of the multifarious layers of a performance may allow us to detect and acknowledge the interconnectedness of an array of possible variables in shaping the specificity of a performance, one may set out to delve into the implications of agency as the creative force of the performer in giving rise to his or her performance. Agency refers to one's power of having choices and control over life. This may apply to different forms of dual process theories, including the computer model of serial information processing and the neural network model of parallel information processing. The former assumes that only one form of thinking can occur at a certain time, so they rule out the possibility of a simultaneous form of both effortful and effortless thinking, whereas the latter claims the possibility of the simultaneousness of two types of parallel thinking (see Gilovich & Savitsky, 2002; Kahneman & Frederick, 2002). In other words, we may let our analysis concentrate on the status of the performing agent in producing the outcome, namely the performance within a specific domain. This will be ineluctably tied to a perceptive attention to both the process and the outcome as they are mutually linked to the etiological configuration of agency as the cause behind the performance. A rigorous scrutiny of the psychological status of agency may help us notice how agency unfolds itself in the production of a special form of performance. As we reflect on the role of agency in structuring and shaping the quiddity of a performance, we may ponder the significance of such questions as the following:

- Is the agency fully functioning as it facilitates the process of an emerging performance?
- Is an agent behind the power of agency quintessentially connected to the creative process of a performance, or is he or she half-engaged in producing his or her performance?

How can the power of agency enhance the efficacy of a performance? An athlete who believes that he or she can make a difference through his or her movement and considers himself or herself as powerful enough to undertake an action demonstrates his or her power of agency. Are there ways to help an actor behind an agency to increase his or her power of agency?

Such questions would serve as a preamble to lead us toward understanding the significance of mindfulness and its implications for decision making and performance. According to Langer (1989, 2000, 2005, 2009):

> Mindfulness is a flexible state of mind in which we are actively engaged in the present, noticing new things and sensitive to the context. When we are in a state of mindlessness, we act like automatons who have been programmed to act according to the sense our behavior made in the past, rather than the present (Langer, 2000, p. 220).

Focusing on the benefits of mindfulness and the detriments of mindlessness, Langer (1997, 2005, 2009; Langer, Bashner, & Chanowitz, 1985; Langer & Piper, 1987) refers to the experimental research conducted over forty years and mentions an increase in competence; a decrease in accidents; an increase in memory, creativity, and positive affect; a decrease in stress; and an increase in health and longevity as some of the consequences and implications of mindfulness.

Langer (1989, 1997, 2005, 2009; Langer et al., 1985) argues that the majority of teaching and learning approaches harbor mindlessness. As our mindlessness increases, she argues, our creativity and the act of drawing novel distinctions decreases. It is only in mindfulness that we can look into alternative ways and notice new and novel things. It is at the time of mindfulness that we can actively live in the present, situate ourselves in the moment, and think creatively about perspectives and possibilities. On the contrary, it is in the mindlessness that we unquestionably rely on our mindsets and ignore alternative ways of acting. Langer challenges many of our beliefs about learning and argues that these are some of the mindsets that have been mindlessly learned and work to our detriment. She recommends mindful learning and propounds its consequences:

> The result is that we are then able to avert the danger not yet arisen and take advantage of opportunities that may present themselves. Teaching mindfully not only sets students up for these advantages, but has advantages for teachers as well (Langer, 2000, p. 222).

In the meantime, Langer (1997, 2005, 2009; Langer & Piper, 1987; Langer et al., 1985) indicates that "the more mindful we are, the more choices we have and the more creative we become" (Langer, 2005, p. 19). Langer (2000) considers mindfulness as something that liberates us from our limitations and allows us to learn as creatively and openly as possible. On the other hand, she indicates that mindlessness is not only an impediment for novel ideas and distinctions but is also imposing mindsets that have been mindlessly accepted to be true.

Langerian mindfulness offers a special tilt in the experiential and phenomenological process of connectedness to the present moment. The presence is of great significance here as it provides the essence of "being there." The athlete who is "being there" experiences the unifying theme of presence away from multiplicity, absence, and sporadic cognitive and emotional engagements. Langer's revolutionary concept of mindfulness demonstrates that presence is mostly concealed to oblivion through mindless multitasking, incarceration within one perspective, inflexibility in revising one's position of being, and lack of authenticity in the moment-to-moment experiential presentation of self. When mindlessness is rampant, one lives and acts in absentia: he or she is all over the place; he or she fails to experience the panacea of lively connectedness to the present moment, as the occupation of the past or the future would prevent one from an active lingering in the moment. Mindfulness blooms in presence and through presence. It unifies the aptitudes, abilities, competencies, and skills into one and allows the person to experience the wholeness of himself or herself in the interconnectedness of action and the agent. The subjective experience and the objective experience intermingle with one another and the dichotomy of the subject-object relationship ceases to operate. The wholeness within the experiential process of mindfulness is intertwined with the consequential ontological transformation of consciousness where being and mindfulness consummate together.

Mindfulness may transpire in a group of athletes through a promotional prompt of communication where everyone is asked to disengage from the scattered shower of multiplicities and massiveness of mental preoccupations. The tale of the Oxford rowing crew's 1987 race against Cambridge may elucidate the vitality of such moments (Topolski & Robinson, 1989). After losing the race in 1986, the Oxford boat club faced a long year before meeting Cambridge again. Aside from the wounded pride and standard training, those twelve months included an inordinate amount of drama. One of the 1986 Oxford crewmembers, an American named Chris Clarke, returned the following year with several experienced American rowers who had enrolled at Oxford. Their plan was, simply, to put out as strong a team as they could, one that could not possibly lose to Cambridge again.

As often happens in sports, things did not go as planned. The team had little camaraderie, and members even showed outright hostility toward each other and the leaders of the club. The newer rowers did not agree with the established training routines; they felt that the training routines were not necessary to ensure success. Disagreements over training methods resulted in an attempt to oust the club president (who also rowed on the team). When this revolt failed, half of the team members, led by the American contingent, quit the club with just six weeks to go before the boat race. A poorly trained, substandard crew was left to prepare for the race. The team showed no unity, had little confidence in leaders, and was largely disinterested in the race. Training runs and exhibition competitions resulted in poor times, further decreasing team confidence. Team members admitted to each other that they had little chance of winning the race and provided a wide variety of reasons for this impending failure.

However, the team did not fail. Instead, it pulled off a historic upset victory against Cambridge. From a social psychological perspective, one key aspect of this triumph was that, during a final team retreat, the team voted on the lineup for the race with Cambridge, inserting the maligned club president into a key position in the boat. From that point onward, although time was running out, the crew's training performances were excellent (Topolski, as cited in Schneider, Gruman, & Coutts, 2012). This may be further studied in view of the prompt mode of the communication, where one may see the attempt of the coach to disengage the crew from mindless entrapment. Addressing the team, the coach said:

> This is your weather, I told the crew, and out there it's your water – no one can cope with those waves like you guys can, at least of all Cambridge. You have the weight and technique for rough water – and better still, you have the nerve for it. And, I don't think Cambridge has that nerve. If it stays like this, I really think you could pull it off tomorrow (Topolski & Robinson, pp. 274–275, as cited in Schneider et al., 2012).

The preceding story may explicate the importance of influencing one's performance through developing a sense of connectedness to the significance of the present moment and its potential resources. Such connection may be facilitated through a motivational speech as was done in this case. In an individual level too, one may leap beyond the mindlessly accepted self-talk of negativity and helplessness and engage in a productive proactive and positive self-talk.

Langerian mindfulness propounds that thoughts can be taken as a series of choices and that choices are ultimately changeable. The sovereignty of the recursive parade of mindlessly accepted thoughts would impose an unquestionable and indubitable obedience to them. According to Langerian mindfulness, paying attention to a thought is a choice. One can always choose not to choose this choice. Furthermore, one may choose to attend to the thought but choose not to endorse the thought. With an increase of mindfulness and its components, including noticing new things and increasing the experiential and phenomenological presence in the moment, one would be able to ascertain and acknowledge the power of agency namely the power of his or her choices over the context. Mindlessness suggests the availability of no power and no agency. It is equipped with the automatic regurgitation of loss of power and is devoid of agency. Mindlessly driven performance is entrenched within the habitual powerlessness of the tyranny of the past, so in Langerian doctrine, the past overdetermines the present, and there is not presence except the precipitating effects of the past-stricken presence.

Returning to the tale of the Oxford rowing crew's 1987 race against Cambridge, the coach endeavors to bring the focus of the team to the present moment. He then inspires them with the power of choices and hopefulness. Langer's experiments have indicated that with an increase of mindfulness, one would be able to have more influence to empower others. Langer's experiment with the aged people, known as counterclockwise, indicated that an increase of mindfulness would have positive implications for the enhancement of memory, motor tasks, control over decision making, and expressiveness.

It is interesting that mindfulness opens up the way for activating moments of connectedness to both the inner and the external world. On the other hand, social psychologists and researchers who have studied performance indicate that positive messages, an enhancement of conversations among team members between and during plays, expression of emotions, and team cohesion are positively correlated with positive performance (see, Dale & Wrisberg, 1996; Diberardinis et al., 1983; Lausic et al., 2009; Sullivan, 1995; Sullivan & Feltz, 2003; Widmeyer & Williams, 1991). Athletes who receive positive feedback, empathy, understanding, and support would display signs of high performance in their actions. The team members who see themselves connected to one another are able to express themselves more vividly and more comfortably.

Langerian mindfulness highlights the psychological ontology of "being there" as an essential element of a peak performance. The corollary of the psychological ontology purports a perceptive and sagacious distancing from the familiar avenues of being with a search for the unfamiliar. Thus mindfulness ends up being about *the being* itself and not cognition or emotion. When performance and being are mutually tied to the fountains of wholeness in the moment, the performance would intrinsically move in the heart of expansive mindfulness. In other words, mindfulness expands ontologically and experientially, and with the expansion of each moment where the performer experiences the fullness of the link to the presence, his or her performance increases. It is like hiking over a mountain where each step allows you to be more in touch with new horizons of possibilities. According to Langerian mindfulness, these horizons are sequentially and simultaneously giving rise to different stages of mindfulness to the effect that each stage is enriching the scope and breadth of the previous stage and hence liminal spaces are discovered through the expansion of the creative moments. Liminal spaces are spaces unknown to the mindlessly calculated parameters; they are unbeknownst to the logical driven mentality. Yet, they unfold themselves as the process of present-oriented vivacity increases. In doing so, outcome goals, process goals, and performance goals are united in the interactive process of mindfulness and living in the moment.

Langerian mindfulness (see, Langer, 1989, 1997, 2005, 2009; Langer et al., 1985, etc.) would offer the following features in enhancing the richness of a performance:

- The performer experiences a proactive engagement in the moment whereby he or she is consummately engaged in the activity.
- The engagement is associated with noticing new things. The search for novelty occurs at the apogee of the connectedness to the moment.
- Connectedness grows out of the unifying interaction of the performer with the performance.
- The unification provides the performer with an experiential process of wholeness.
- Wholeness and health embrace one another with the activation of multifarious cognitive, emotional, and behavioral components of the performer.
- Multiplicity, massiveness, automaticity, and masquerading of the self are replaced by unification, wholeness, mindfulness, and authenticity. This helps the performer phenomenologically experience the process of "being there."
- With an increase of the scope of mindfulness, one would experience the power of choices through the interactive process of being both an observer and an actor.
- The expansive mode of mindfulness and its ontological implications would allow the performer to realize the distinction between the physiological and the existential presentation of the performance-oriented features: "I feel anger" or "I feel sadness" are different from "I am angry" or "I am sad," where in the first cluster of propositions the performer is separate from the feeling, while in the translation of the second cluster of propositions the performer may existentially

identify with the feeling. Thus the performer may be emotionally, in the language of Goleman, "kidnapped" by the mindlessness of the emotion.

- The power of choices would emerge with an increase of mindfulness whereby the performer comes to realize how his or her choices in the moment can create different types of reality. Understanding the context would help the performer mindfully compose the context through a perspicacious sensitivity toward the context.
- Mindfulness would espouse creativity. A mindful performer is not encapsulated in the templates of the prescribed perspectives. If he or she remains there, he or she would deprive himself or herself of an authentic engagement in the moment. The eyes transfixed in the mirrors of the past would alienate themselves from a genuine indulgence in the windows of the presence. Thus the operative self with a subjugation to the past-stricken sovereignty would end up in a cul de sac of pretentiousness, superciliousness, and bogusness.
- Performance in line with automaticity would eventually give rise to a rupture between the context and the performer, whereas a mindful performance would encourage rapture in the emergent action of mindful engagement.
- Performance in the context of absence-oriented connectedness would impose a sole search for preidentified realms of possibilities.
- Langerian mindfulness activates the search for liminal spaces where the unidentified spaces are incessantly available with their potential horizons of possibilities.
- Mindfulness in its Langerian context would facilitate the process of maximizing one's performance.

Mindfulness and Work–Life Balance

When it comes to work performance, the word "work" often reminds people of something strenuous, stress-oriented, tedious, and monotonous. There tends to be a dichotomy between work-oriented activities and leisure-oriented festivities. Even in a number of psychological models, including Eric Bern's Transactional Analysis, spontaneous ego state is mostly associated with activities that may appear to transpire mostly in out-of-office activities. According to the Transactional Analysis Model, each person has three ego states: parent, child, and adult. Each ego state serves as a source to activate a series of activities and interactions. One of the ego states of a child appears in the child's spontaneous form of action, which may be characterized through displaying the fun side of his or her personality.

The expressions people use to describe "coolness" are largely coupled with enterprises that occur outside the stringently serious realms of one's job. It, thus, may be safe to say that work and life may dramatically move in line in opposite directions if not in contradictory status. This has been historically vociferated in Karl Marx's clamorous contention that works and working conditions impose not only estrangement but also espouse alienation for workers to the extent that they lose their identity. The worker's life is therefore purported to be far from the real taste of life. To dissipate the burden of work from life and to eliminate the alienation of self from work, scholars have often suggested the work–life balance paradigm, where the imbalance caused by the forcible tension of work and life would disappear and a balance be established as a panacea to reconcile both work and personal life situations.

While the balance between life and work has given rise to promising chapters in human interactions and has contributed to facilitating the betterment of life, it intrinsically suggests a clandestine assumption of bipolar categories that potentially stand against one another. The groundbreaking findings of Langer's forty-year-long scholarly research (Langer, 1989, 1997, 2005, 2009) are surprising and present unexpectedly exquisite news on the relationship between work and life. Langerian mindfulness propounds that instead of a work–life balance perspective, work–life integration may lead us to a happier and more prosperous life, with opulently rich results in the realm of our work. When one is at work, he or she is brimming with the vivacity and livelihood that he or she experiences while being with his or her close friends or family members.

Langerian doctrine suggests that the work–life balance perspective, while helpful and valuable in its own context, may develop a split of self in that the self at work may be translated in dramatically different modes than the self at home. This is not meant to be a recapitulation of the split personality, double-bind personality, or multiple personality concept in its clinical term, as you may have seen represented in the movies *Three Faces of Eve* or *Dr. Jekyll and Mr. Hyde*, but it enunciates a drastic connection between two ways of being that may boil down the work–life paradigm to a lack of connectedness to the wholeness of personality.

The work–life integration in Langerian mindfulness is not meant to nullify the manifestation of different roles: it is not expected that a CEO goes home and treats his or her family members in the hierarchical order of organizational chain, nor does one expect that an office worker goes home and by whistling summons up his kids, as you may recall that sort of approach applied in *The Sound of Music*. Langerian doctrine proposes that wholeness and health walk arm in arm: it is interesting to know that etymologically the word "health" and "whole" come from the same root. Once you lose your wholeness, your health becomes jeopardized, and as you stray from being healthy, your wholeness disappears.

Langerian mindfulness argues for a praxis where the integration of work and life conditions can consummate one's way of being. The integration calls for a phenomenological connectedness to the present moment in that one may consciously notice new things and look for novelty whether at home or work. The reason behind fatigue at work or at home, Langerian mindfulness argues, is the sovereignty of mundane, quotidian, banal, and routinized engagements. The work–life integration perspective suggests that one can keep his or her perceptive consciousness alive in the moment and through practicing this liveliness savor pleasure both at work and at home. When one learns to live mindfully and implement mindfulness in both work and home, one would experience the exhilarating joy of both in his or her lived experiences.

Through trends of experimental research, Langerian mindfulness has substantiated the possibility of an experiential change in one's mode of being. Thus, Langerian mindfulness demonstrates that mindfulness can promise a transformation of being: it is not just about cognition; it is about a new mode of being. The novel consummation of work and life experiences would augur the interplay of work and home connectedness in their underlying existential components. One's existence can be mindfully linked to both realms of activities whether at work or home once the existence is nourished through the gift of mindfulness. Langerian mindfulness presents techniques and skills that can enhance the comprehensive interactive process of synergy between work and home. The integrative work and life experiences would give not only a healthier way of being but also produce a more brilliant performance at work. Langerian mindfulness opens up infinite possibilities for discovering liminal spaces in the process of accomplishing presence-oriented performance.

Langerian mindfulness encourages composure, inner security, and inner intimacy as the primordial avenues for achieving higher performance. Through a nonjudgmental view of the self and by virtue of acquiring an authentic way of exploring self-characterization, Langerian mindfulness helps the performer to mindfully look at himself or herself both as an observer and an actor. Embracing ambiguity and openness toward multiple perspectives would provide the person with the possibility of going beyond the rule-governed world of mere prescriptive and proscriptive modes. The mindful performer would feel empowered to look constantly for alternative ways of thinking and incessantly explore the possibility of restructuring and rethinking the assumptions.

Mindfulness facilitates the process of self-actualization as it helps the performer experience the experiential mode of agency in the phenomenological connectedness to the present moment.

REFERENCES

Dale, G. A., and Wrisberg, C. A. (1996). The use of a performance profiling technique in a team setting: Getting athletes and coaches on the "same page." *Sport Psychologist*, 10, 261–277.

De Jaegher, H., Di Paolo, E., and Gallagher, S. (2010). Can social interaction constitute social cognition? *Trends in Cognitive Sciences*, 14, 441–447. doi:10.1016/j.tics.2010.06.009

Diberardinis, J., Barwind, J., Flaningam, R. R., and Jenkins, V. (1983). Enhanced interpersonal relation as predictor of athletic performance. *International Journal of Sport Psychology*, 14, 243–251.

Gilovich, T., and Savitsky, K. (2002). Like goes with like: The role of representativeness in erroneous and pseudo-scientific belies. In T. Gilovich, D. Griffin, and D. Kahneman (Eds.), *Heuristics and biases. The psychology of intuitive judgment* (pp. 617–624). New York, NY: Cambridge University Press.

Kahneman, D., and Frederick, S. (2002). Representativeness revised: Attribute substitution in intuitive judgment. In T. Gilovich, D. Griffin, and D. Kahneman (Eds.), *Heuristic and biases: The psychology of intuitive judgement* (pp. 49–81). New York, NY: Cambridge University Press.

Kruglanski, A. W., and Orehek, E. (2007). Partitioning the domain of social influence: Dual mode and system models and their alternatives. *Annual Review of Psychology*, 58, 291–316. doi: 10.1146/annurev.psych.58.110405.085629

Langer, E. J. (1989). *Mindfulness*. Reading, MA: Addison-Wesley.

(1997). *The power of mindful learning*. Reading, MA: Addison-Wesley.

(2000). Mindful learning. *Journal of the American Psychological Society*, 9, 220–223. doi: 10.1111/1467-8721.00099

(2005). *On becoming an artist: Reinventing yourself through mindful creativity*. New York, NY: Ballantine.

(2009). *Counterclockwise: Mindful health and the power of possibility*. New York, NY: Ballantine.

Langer, E. J., Bashner, R. S., and Chanowitz, B. (1985). Decreasing prejudice by increasing discrimination. *Journal of Personality and Social Psychology*, 49, 113–120. doi: http://dx.doi.org/10.1037/0022-3514.49.1.113

Langer, E. J., and Piper, A. I. (1987). The prevention of mindlessness. *Journal of Personality and Social Psychology*, 53, 280–287.

Lausic, D., Tennebaum, G., Eccles, D., Jeong, A., and Johnson, T. (2009). Intrateam communication and performance in double tennis. *Research Quarterly for Exercise and Sport*, 80, 281–290. doi: 10.1080/02701367.2009.10599563

Petty, R. E. (2004). Multi-process model in social psychology provide a more balanced view of social thought and action. *Behavioral and Brain Sciences*, 27, 353–354.

Schneider, F. W., Gruman, J. A. and Coutts, L. M. (Eds.). (2012). *Applied social psychology, understanding and addressing social and practical problems*. Thousand Oaks, CA: Sage.

Sorrentino, R. M. (2003). Motivated perception and the warm look: Current perspectives and future directions. In S. J. Spencer., S. Fein, M. P. Zanna, and J. M. Olson (Eds.), *Motivated social perception: The Ontario symposium* (Vol. 9., pp. 299–316). Mahwah, NJ: Erlbaum.

Sorrentino, R. M., and Higgins, E. T. (1986). Motivation and cognition: Warming to synergism. In R. M. Sorrentino and E. T. Higgins (Eds.), *The handbook of motivation and cognition: Foundations of social behavior* (pp. 3–19). New York, NY: Guilford Press.

Sullivan, P. J. (1995). *The relationship between communication and cohesion in inter-collegiate rugby players* (Unpublished master's thesis). University of Windsor: Ontario, Canada.

Sullivan, P., and Feltz, D. L. (2003). The preliminary development of the Scale for Effective Communication in Sport Teams (SECTS). *Journal of Applied Social Psychology*, 33, 1693–1715. doi: 10.1111/j.1559-1816.2003.tb01970.x

Topolski, D., and Robinson, P. (1989). *True blue: The Oxford boat race mutiny*. London, UK: Doubleday.

Widmeyer, W. N., and Williams, J. M. (1991). Predicting cohesion in a coaching sport. *Small Group Research*, 22, 548–570. doi: 10.1177/1046496491224007

Zajonc, R. B. (1984). On the primacy of affect. *American Psychologist*, 39, 117–123. doi: http://dx.doi.org/10.1037/0003-066X.39.2.117

Formal Mindfulness Interventions in Sport

Scientific Advancements of Mindfulness- and Acceptance-Based Models in Sport Psychology: A Decade in Time, a Seismic Shift in Philosophy and Practice

Frank L. Gardner

It has been nearly fifteen years since mindfulness- and acceptance-based interventions were formally proposed as an alternative model in sport psychology for the purpose of both enhanced performance and enhanced psychological and general well-being of athletes (Moore & Gardner, 2001). In that time, theoretical insights and empirical advancements have broadened our knowledge base and have shaped these contemporary interventions in exciting ways (Gardner & Moore, 2012). This chapter looks back over the past fifteen years to illustrate how far third-wave thinkers, like all of us, have come, by discussing the formation and use of mindfulness- and acceptance-based models within sport psychology and the current state of the science of associated protocols for the purpose of athletic performance enhancement and overall psychosocial well-being. Herein, I also hope to accentuate the fundamental differences between these procedures and those of traditional cognitive, behaviorally oriented sport psychology practice and address some of the misconceptions often heard about mindfulness- and acceptance-based models and procedures.

Since the first major incorporation of mindfulness- and acceptance-based frameworks into sport psychology occurred over fifteen years ago with the advent of the Mindfulness-Acceptance-Commitment (MAC) approach, the theoretical underpinnings central to traditional models of sport psychology have faced notable challenge. The long-unquestioned traditional psychological skills training (PST) model suggests that internal states (i.e., cognitions, emotions, somatic sensations) need to be modified, reduced, or avoided in order to enhance athletic performance and reach peak performance states. I once believed this. I once incorporated these traditional theories and associated techniques with elite athletes across multiple professional sports. And I once taught and encouraged graduate students to believe this and to take this "tried-and-true" model with them as they embarked upon their own careers.

Yet as new evidence-based developments within clinical psychology emerged, and clinical psychology witnessed the profound and seismic shift in how we conceptualize and approach internal phenomena, I admit that I rightfully started to question my long-held allegiance to traditional forms of sport psychology practice. It was an interesting phenomenon, actually, because as a clinical psychologist, I spent my career at the front of the clinical empirical developments and maintained an unquenched thirst for rigorous scientific advancement. As a clinical psychologist, I was on the top of my game. And while one could assume that I was on the top of my game in the sport psychology world as well, due to extensive experience with the highest levels of elite teams, for a while I actually resisted what I saw as questionable strategies with dubious scientific support and kept plugging along with outdated, theoretically questionable, and empirically unsubstantiated interventions, often hoping for more but doing little about it. But finally it clicked – something so exciting was taking hold in the clinical world, and its relevance to the sport world was nothing short of striking!

The alternative theoretical perspectives that were emerging in clinical psychology were the complementary and typically inextricably connected mindfulness- and acceptance-based models, and these models pushed us to think more deeply and differently about cognition, emotion, and physiology; to conceptualize client cases in a new manner; and to intervene in novel ways that were quickly garnering empirical support for their efficacy. In brief, this exciting new theoretical framework purported that rather than the "control" or "change" approach to internal experiences at the foundation of traditional models of cognitive behavioral therapy (in the clinical psychology world) and PST (in the sport psychology world), mindfulness- and acceptance-based models promote the development of a *modified relationship* with internal states, such as thoughts, emotions, and physiology. So, instead of attempting to change or control the type or frequency of thoughts or emotions, the newer mindfulness- and acceptance-models were seeking to develop the capacity to view all internal experiences as normal, nonthreatening, time-limited, and not in need of elimination or reduction (Gardner & Moore, 2007; Hayes, Strosahl, & Wilson, 1999).

This distinction was clear, and it seemed as though the sport psychology world just *had* to take a chance on seeing whether these theoretical and applied developments that were amassing the coveted empirical support among our clinical cousins could actually do what a deep look into the theories implied it could do – enhance human performance and promote overall psychosocial well-being among our esteemed population of athletes. Contrary to the traditional control-based PST model that was adopted from Donald Meichenbaum's stress-inoculation training model in the late 1970s, which contends that optimal internal states are necessary for the attainment and maintenance of performance excellence, mindfulness- and acceptance-based models of performance take a highly divergent perspective. Specifically, mindfulness- and acceptance-based models posit that purposeful control of internal states is not necessary to attain or maintain optimal performance. Instead, these models assert that optimal performance can be attained and maintained through (1) nonjudgmental, moment-to-moment awareness and acceptance of internal states such as cognitions, emotions, and physiology; (2) an attentional focus on task-relevant cues/stimuli; and (3) an ongoing commitment to actions and behaviors that are based on personal values (i.e., values-driven behavior).

While traditional PST models long adopted by mainstream sport psychology utilize intervention strategies such as goal setting, imagery, precompetitive routines, and self-talk modification, which focus essentially on developing control over cognitions, emotions, and physiological states for the purpose of creating or maintaining an assumed ideal performance state, mindfulness- and acceptance-based models reject such postulations about an "ideal" performance state. Rather, mindfulness- and acceptance-based models utilize meditative and adjunctive experiential exercises to help individuals experience, accept, tolerate, and remain focused on the task at hand while experiencing the vast array of thoughts and emotions shared by all human beings.

Despite this critical difference in purpose, a common misperception is that perhaps mindfulness- and acceptance-based approaches are simply a repackaging of more traditional cognitive behavioral methods for client change. While I will revisit this misconception in greater detail later in this chapter, I should briefly introduce this issue by stating that in response to the mindfulness- and acceptance-based movement and the evidence for its treatment efficacy with a wide range of clientele, traditional cognitive behavioral interventions (that follow from the "cognitive model") are actually shifting *their* focus. A powerful example of this is the changes seen in David Barlow and colleagues' recent uniform treatment of mental disorders (Fairholme et al., 2010). Barlow, a noted clinical scientist and longtime advocate of traditional cognitive behavioral interventions, has substantially reduced his intervention models' emphases on cognitive restructuring in favor of an increasing emphasis on enhanced cognitive and emotional awareness and acceptance.

As might be expected, mindfulness- and acceptance-based models such as MAC propose different mechanisms of change from those thought to operate in traditional cognitive behavioral approaches (Gardner, 2009; Moore, 2007). While rarely mentioned in the extant sport psychology literature, mechanisms of change (sometimes referred to as mechanisms of action) represent the indirect effects that an intervention has on a desired outcome. This, in turn, then describes the *mechanism* by which a given intervention results in a specific end product. As is also described within the clinical psychology professional literature, implicit in the traditional PST model of sport psychology is the assumption that reduction or control of "negative" cognitions, "negative" affect, and/or the development of enhanced self-control skills results in more effective coping strategies to deal with external demands and internal experiences, which in turn are hypothesized to lead to enhanced performance (Hardy, Jones, & Gould, 1996). Despite the fact that this assumptive mechanism of change has long been the norm in sport psychology, to date there remains no empirical evidence to support these assumed mechanisms of change (Gardner & Moore, 2006).

Given that mindfulness- and acceptance-based models of sport psychology have evolved from an empirical foundation, it is not surprising that proponents are committed to determining the efficacy of mindfulness- and acceptance-based interventions in sport, as well as the mechanisms by which positive outcomes may in fact occur. In fact, as will be discussed later in this chapter, to date, the empirical evidence strongly suggests that MAC and similar mindfulness- and acceptance-based interventions are both effective, and work through the precise mechanisms of change predicted by core mindfulness- and acceptance-based theory (Moore, 2009).

Herein, I begin the review of the extant scientific evidence by briefly highlighting important empirical findings in cognitive neuroscience, which illuminates the processes that link mindfulness practice and athletic performance. The discussion then moves on to a review of the efficacy studies of mindfulness- and acceptance-based interventions, including the likely mechanisms of these contemporary sport psychology interventions.

The Cognitive Neuroscience of Mindfulness- and Acceptance-Based Interventions

Using contemporary scanning technologies (i.e., EEG and fMRI), empirical research has clearly detailed some important ways in which regular mindfulness meditation practice, referred to in the neuroscience literature as mental training, modifies basic brain structures and functions (Davidson, 2002). In particular, studies have found that meditative-based mental training promotes cognitive neuroplasticity (i.e., the capacity for neural changes), and that individuals who consistently and regularly meditate experience traitlike differences in their ability to respond to emotion and function in the presence of stress-inducing stimuli (Davidson, 2002). Interestingly, Davidson has suggested that individuals with experience meditating are the functional equivalent to mental athletes, who are able to more effectively and efficiently respond to their cognitive and affective responses to stress. In addition, and importantly, the results of regular meditative training can be seen in overt changes in neural pathways that are both substantial and long term. In fact, Begley (2007) has suggested that through meditative training, "one can sculpt the brain's emotional circuitry as powerfully as one can sculpt one's pectoral muscles" (p. 231).

With obvious relevance to sport psychology, an important empirical investigation attempted to identify the neural correlates of sustained and focused attention. Utilizing the technology of functional magnetic resonance imaging (fMRI), Brefczynski-Lewis and colleagues (2007) compared twelve longtime (i.e., expert) meditators to twelve age-matched novice participants with no previous meditation experience. This study also included a third group of ten novices with no meditation experience who were offered a financial reward if they were among the best participants to activate the neural areas associated with attentional processes. All participants regularly alternated between paying attention to a small dot on a computer screen and a non-active rest time with no attentional demands. Distracting stimuli, including sounds with positive, neutral, and negative associations, were also presented to each participant during both the meditation times and the resting times. Three minutes of meditation and one-and-one-half minutes of rest were alternated and monitored. The results of this study clearly indicated a number of important findings:

1. During the meditation condition, both the novice and experienced meditator groups activated the brain regions known to be associated with attention.
2. Experienced meditators showed significantly greater activation in neural regions associated with attention than novices with no incentive.
3. Interestingly, there were no significant differences in neural activation between experienced meditators and novice meditators with a financial incentive, which suggests that motivation to succeed in meditative training can impact immediate neural activity. However, experienced

meditators are able to sustain attention (and the neural activation associated with that attention) for significantly longer periods of time than either of the novice groups.

This latter result would appear to be of particular importance to sport psychology, as it clearly demonstrates that the skills and neural activation involved in *extended periods* of attentional focus are not simply based on motivation or effort. In fact, while motivation or effort may promote attentional processes in the short term, specific (meditative) training promotes more long-term sustained attention. This conclusion is strengthened by the finding that when looking more closely at the level of experience in meditation, the most experienced meditators, based on total historical hours of meditation (37,000 to 52,000), demonstrated the greatest activation in neural areas associated with attention than somewhat less experienced meditators with half the total meditation hours (10,000 to 24,000). Such findings suggest a pattern of mindfulness development in which early stages of mindfulness skill development would seem to require greater effort, with later stages requiring substantially less overt effort but more total training time. Said in a slightly different way, the skill of sustaining mindful attention can, over time and with regular practice, be systematically trained and automated so that eventually little overt effort is required to reach and maintain the desired enhanced attentional state. Certainly, this has substantial implications for sport psychology practice. Of course, from studies such as the one previously noted, it is reasonable to ask the question: Do mindfulness-based interventions by definition require long periods of training prior to attaining successful skill acquisition? The answer actually appears to be *no*. Slagter and colleagues (2007) found that individuals with a mere three months of meditation training were able to allocate attentional resources much more efficiently than individuals with no mindfulness-focused mental training. Further, a study by Zeidan and colleagues (2010) determined that after only four days of meditative practice, individuals were able to demonstrate significant improvements in visual processing, working memory, and executive functioning when compared to a control condition receiving no meditation training (Zeidan et al., 2010). In addition, Brefczynski-Lewis and colleagues (2007) found that for individuals who were regular meditators, focused and sustained attention required less effort to remain on task, and importantly, competing tasks also requiring attention are performed with fewer demands on one's resources. This capacity for attentional shifting, important in nearly every sporting endeavor, is promoted by meditative training through a more efficient use of attentional resources.

It can reasonably be concluded from these studies that skilled and experienced meditators, who are thus by definition more mindful, are likely to respond to distraction with more efficient autonomic responding. Further, experienced meditators have less need to expend additional effort and cognitive resources to sustain focused attention. Taking this one step further, a summary of studies linking mindfulness, improved cognitive functioning, and general task performance (Slagter, Davidson, & Lutz, 2011) suggests that mindfulness-based mental training is associated with alterations in both brain structure and functionality, as well as enhanced task performance. Readers desiring a more nuanced and comprehensive review of the empirical literature on the relationship among mindfulness, cognitive neuroscience, and sport are directed to a wonderful review article by Marks (2008).

Implications of Cognitive Neuroscience

The evidence from empirical studies in neuroscience (and consistent with the theoretical propositions) suggests that the fundamental mechanism of mindfulness- and acceptance-based interventions is enhanced working memory (i.e., mental efficiency), which comes as a direct result of heightened awareness and acceptance of internal experiences developed through meditative training (see Holzel et al., 2011; Marks, 2008). This has clear and obvious implications for athletic performers and for sport psychologists who work with them! Through the repeated practice of attentional self-regulation in meditation-based mental training, athletes are likely to benefit from an increasingly automated process in which they are able to direct attention onto competitive demands *without* utilizing cognitive resources to detect, reduce, or control other sensory or physiological information.

A common misinterpretation of mindfulness training is that the attentional self-regulation gained through mindfulness practice is relatively similar to the control-based techniques used in traditional cognitive behavioral models, which aim to reduce the assumed distraction caused by cognitions and emotions by using techniques such as relaxation training. Traditional cognitive behavioral methods emphasize enhancing attention by *volitional efforts* at controlling distractions while, in contrast, mindfulness- and acceptance-based interventions emphasize the *complete absence of concerted efforts* at attentional control. Rather, enhanced automated attentional self-regulation, which by definition requires fewer cognitive resources, is a natural result of the emphasis on nonjudging, present-moment acceptance found in meditative training. In fact, cognitive neuroscience appears to support this hypothesis (Brefczynski-Lewis et al., 2007). Crews and Landers (1993) took electroencephalogram (EEG) measurements of thirty-four elite level golfers and found that decreased left-hemispheric cortical activity and increased right-hemispheric cortical activity were strongly associated with golf-putting performance, with alpha-wave activity in left temporal regions (typically correlated with cognitive [i.e., verbal] activity) declining significantly just prior to the putting task. These data imply that within elite golfers (and by extension other elite athletes), verbal/self-instructional activity decreases during competitive performance as kinesthetic memory becomes more salient.

As an alternative to the reduced verbal self-instruction hypothesis just noted, research in the neuroscience of mindfulness has suggested that elite athletes require less activation of the attention centers located in the left temporal and left prefrontal cortex as a result of long-term athletic training than do lower level athletes. In line with this proposition, a review by Hatfield and colleagues (2004) determined that less experienced and/or lower level athletes show higher levels of left-hemisphere (self-instructional) activity when on-task, while more experienced athletes demonstrate more balanced left- and right-hemisphere neural activity. It would seem, then, that elite athletes are more likely to have developed the capacity to utilize neurocognitive resources more efficiently, which happens to also be the outcome of regular and systematic mindfulness training. In turn, it can be concluded that through the process of meditative training intended to direct attentional resources more efficiently and reduce attention to extraneous distraction, athletes can maintain greater awareness of the competitive context and athletic demands while simultaneously engaging in efficient and prolonged task-focused attention.

Consistent with this hypothesis, additional empirical findings in cognitive neuroscience (Jha et al., 2010; Slagter et al., 2011; van den Hurk et al., 2010) suggest that systematic mindfulness training directly promotes the development of a more efficient allocation of cognitive resources. Data also strongly suggest that reducing anxiety and increasing a narrow focus of attention, which were long assumed to be directly related to peak performance (Hatfield & Hillman, 2001), are in fact not prerequisites of optimal performance at all, as both elite competitive athletes and expert meditators are able to experience higher levels of anxiety and broader attention than novices while still maintaining optimal performance states. The automated attentional processes attained by those who engage in regular mindfulness training (with its foundation of nonjudging acceptance) are fundamentally different from efforts at attention training that emphasize control of internal processes such as cognitions and emotions (which typify PST models). In an additional important study with relevance to sport performance, Teper, Segal, and Inzlicht (2013) examined the effects of meditative practice on executive control using encephalography-measured correlates of performance monitoring (i.e., error-related negativity [ERN], a neurophysiological response that transpires within 100 milliseconds of an error). Both the meditation group and the control group took part in a Stroop task, during which ERN amplitudes were measured. Results indicated that meditators demonstrated greater executive control (i.e., fewer errors), a higher ERN, and greater levels of emotional acceptance than the control condition. Mediation analysis indicated that meditation practice resulted in greater executive control, which was in turn accounted for by heightened emotional acceptance and increased brain-based performance monitoring (i.e., attention).

Further adding to this literature, particularly with respect to attentional processes, was a study by Moore and Malinowski (2009), which compared experienced meditators with a "meditation-naïve" control condition on the Stroop interference and d2-concentration and endurance test. Findings demonstrated that attentional performance and cognitive flexibility, which are both necessary cognitive components of athletic performance, were positively correlated with meditation practice and levels of attained mindfulness. The meditator group performed significantly better than the nonmeditator group on all measures of attention, suggesting that mindfulness is strongly associated with improvements in attentional functioning and cognitive flexibility. Finally, further extending the empirical data with respect to meditative practice and attention, Semple (2010) conducted a randomized, controlled trial (RCT) that included three groups: (1) a mindfulness meditation group, (2) a progressive muscle relaxation group (aimed at controlling for the effects of physical relaxation on attentional processes), and (3) a wait-list control group (to control for practice effects associated with repeated measures). Of the fifty-three randomly assigned participants, forty-five fully completed the four-week program that consisted of twice-daily practice. Findings revealed that the meditation group showed significantly greater discriminability on a signal detection task than participants in the other two groups. Importantly, significant improvements in sustained attention were noted following completion of the meditation training, which was not mediated by relaxation or practice effects.

These developments within cognitive neuroscience highlight the fact that mindfulness- and acceptance-based interventions have strong empirical support for the neuroanatomical and neurocognitive changes that are consistent with the theorized mechanisms of mindfulness training. Having an empirically informed foundation from the basic sciences for the effects of a proposed intervention is exceedingly important and provides the foundation for a sound evidence-based practice of sport psychology (Gardner & Moore, 2006). So, with the most relevant findings from neurocognitive research described, let's take a direct look at the application of mindfulness- and acceptance-based models within sport psychology itself.

Mindfulness- and Acceptance-Based Interventions

As noted earlier in this chapter, mindfulness- and acceptance-based approaches view the development of greater awareness and acceptance of internal experiences, such as cognitions, emotions, and physical sensations, as the primary overt mechanism of change. Central to this intervention modality is the construct of *mindfulness,* which can be defined as a "moment-to-moment non-judgmental awareness" (Kabat-Zinn, 2005, p. 24). Only in the last decade or so has a revolutionary change occurred within cognitive behavioral theory and associated practice, in which a wide and voluminous array of studies evaluating and supporting the efficacy of mindfulness- and acceptance-based therapies has found its way into the professional literature. While a full and comprehensive review of the large body of clinical literature is not in the present chapter's scope (see Roemer & Orsillo, 2009, for a comprehensive review), it can be clearly stated that a large number of studies have confirmed the efficacy of mindfulness- and acceptance-based interventions, including the use of these approaches for such diverse problems as substance abuse (e.g., Gifford et al., 2004; Hayes et al., 2004), eating disorders (e.g., Safer, Telch, & Agras, 2001; Telch, Agras, & Linehan, 2001), couples distress (e.g., Christensen et al., 2006; Jacobson et al., 2000), chronic depression (Ma & Teasdale, 2004), anxiety (e.g., Forman et al., 2007), and borderline personality disorder (e.g., Gratz & Gunderson, 2006; Linehan et al., 2007). Further, intensive research has demonstrated that mindfulness- and acceptance-based protocols are empirically supported for the improvement of mood and overall psychological functioning (Teasdale et al., 2002), the enhancement of immune functions (Davidson et al., 2003), and the enhancement of orienting, alertness, and conflict monitoring (Jha, Krompinger, & Baime, 2007). Based on the vast accumulation of empirical data, mindfulness- and acceptance-based interventions have become "empirically supported" interventions for use with a wide variety of clinical and general psychosocial issues, and together, benefits seen in all of these areas have direct implications for our work with athletes above and beyond enhanced competitive performance.

Mindfulness- and Acceptance-Based Interventions in Sport Psychology

The onset of the twenty-first century saw increased emphasis on evidence-based practice and accountability in all disciplines of professional psychology. Bringing sport psychology into this era, Moore (2003) engaged in a comprehensive review of quantitative studies published up to that time in sport psychology that utilized one or more traditional PST procedures, such as goal setting, arousal regulation, imagery, self-talk, and multicomponent interventions that included more than one of the previous strategies, with competitive athlete populations. In her review, Moore utilized long-accepted empirically supported treatment criteria as the comparative standard. In both her initial study (in 2003) and in a later updated version (Gardner & Moore, 2006), it was determined that after more than thirty years of research (now about forty years), none of the PST procedures that were often thought to be the gold standard of sport psychology had attained empirical support sufficient to be classified as "efficacious" for enhancing competitive athletic performance among actual competitive performers. Rather, these procedures were most appropriately assigned the "experimental" level of empirical support (which is the lowest possible level).

Following directly from this comprehensive review, a theoretically and empirically driven alternative to traditional approaches, the MAC protocol for the enhancement of athletic performance, was developed. The evolution of this alternative model was primarily influenced by (1) the near-complete absence of empirical support for the efficacy of PST procedures (Gardner & Moore, 2007; Moore, 2003; Moore & Gardner, 2001) and (2) the tidal wave of change within empirical clinical psychology occurring from mindfulness- and acceptance-based methodologies (Hayes et al., 1999). Based upon the rapid and important advances in both basic and applied research with respect to mindfulness- and acceptance-based interventions, Zella Moore and I first presented the MAC protocol in 2001 as an alternative model with the capacity to positively impact athletic performance as well as the development of overall psychological health and general well-being (Gardner, 2001; Gardner & Moore, 2004; Moore & Gardner, 2001, 2002, 2003).

In fact, the empirical findings published since 2001 strongly indicate that the relationships between mindfulness practice, neural correlates, and cognitive processes can and do facilitate the development of core requirements of optimal athletic performance. These findings have been fully consistent with the theoretical predictions, made fifteen years ago while we were developing MAC, regarding the utility of mindfulness- and acceptance-based procedures for the purpose of promoting performance enhancement (Gardner & Moore, 2004; Moore & Gardner, 2001). In addition, other direct evidence has been accumulated during this time with regard to the strong relationship between mindfulness and high-level athletic performance. For example, as theoretically predicted in the original conference presentation (Moore & Gardner, 2001) and first published paper (Gardner & Moore, 2004) on the MAC approach, data from Kee and Wang's (2008) investigation of 182 student-athletes participating in 23 sports (n = 92 individual sport athletes; n = 90 team sport athletes) clearly demonstrated that "dispositional flow," which is a state that itself has been determined to be correlated with peak athletic performance (Nakamura & Csikszentmihalyi, 2005), was strongly and positively associated with levels of mindfulness. Further, in 2009, Bernier and colleagues also discovered a strong positive correlation between dispositional levels of mindfulness and flow states among ten Olympic-level swimmers. While correlational studies do not demonstrate clear causation, the findings across both of these studies indicating that mindfulness is positively correlated with dispositional flow (which, again, is associated with optimal performance) has been an important step in the natural evolution of mindfulness- and acceptance-based approaches.

In another important study, Gooding and Gardner (2009) sought to investigate the relationship between trait mindfulness and athletic performance by evaluating the relationship between mindfulness, trait-based arousal, preshot routine, and basketball free throw shooting percentage among seventeen NCAA Division I basketball players. Findings revealed that basketball experience, free throw shooting skill level (as measured by previous free throw shooting percentage), and levels of dispositional mindfulness each predicted future competitive (i.e., actual game) free throw shooting percentage. Importantly, level of arousal and preshot routine did not predict actual game free throw shooting. Results indicated that a one standard deviation increase in state mindfulness resulted in a

5.75 percent increase in competitive basketball free throw shooting percentage, a finding with enormous implications for sport (and performance) psychology.

Direct Intervention Studies

Since it was first proposed in 2001, a number of studies have provided support for the MAC program and similar interventions. In brief, the MAC program is a seven-module manualized protocol that emphasizes enhanced attention; greater awareness and acceptance of the entire spectrum of cognitions, emotions, and physiological states; and values-based behavioral commitment; together, these elements enhance attention, awareness, and emotion regulation. The seven flexible modules include (1) psychoeducation; (2) mindfulness and cognitive defusion; (3) values and values-driven behavior; (4) acceptance; (5) commitment; (6) skill consolidation and poise (combining mindfulness, acceptance, and commitment); and (7) maintaining and enhancing mindfulness, acceptance, and commitment. In total, the enhanced cognitive-affective flexibility promoted in the MAC intervention can culminate in enhanced performance and overall psychosocial well-being (readers interested in the comprehensive and manualized presentation of the full MAC protocol are referred to Gardner & Moore, 2007). Highlights from empirical investigations on the MAC and similar interventions include the following (also see Table 7.1):

1. A series of case studies (Gardner & Moore, 2004, 2007; Schwanhausser, 2009) found that improvements in awareness and attention, as well as actual competitive performance, followed the completion of the MAC program with high-level competitive athletes.
2. A MAC open trial with eleven NCAA Division I female volleyball and field hockey collegiate athletes (Wolanin, 2005; Wolanin, Gardner, & Moore, 2003) discovered that MAC training resulted in an increase in ratings of athletic performance, as well as task-focused attention and practice intensity, when compared to a no-intervention control group.
3. Another open trial of the MAC (Hasker, 2010) with nineteen NCAA Division II collegiate athletes from several sports found that compared to athletes receiving a PST intervention (goal setting, imagery, relaxation, positive self-talk, and arousal control), the MAC training resulted in (a) a significant increase in the athletes' capacity to describe and be nonreactive to their internal experiences, (b) an increase in

Table 7.1 *Summary of Direct Sport-related Mindfulness and Acceptance Intervention Studies*

Study	Sample Size	Design	Population	Objectives	Findings
Gardner & Moore (2004)	$N = 2$	Case study	Elite adult weightlifter and Division I university swimmer	Evaluate the utility of MAC	Improved self-report of concentration and experiential acceptance ($d =$ 1.2 to 2.0) and attained personal best competitive performances.
Gross et al., (2015)	$N = 22$	RCT	Division III university athlete	Compare MAC to PST	MAC participants demonstrated significant performance improvements (as measured by coach ratings), MAC > PST intervention in reducing substance use and hostility, and showed significant reductions in anxiety, eating concerns, and general psychological distress.
Schwanhausser (2009)	$N = 1$	Case study	Elite adolescent swimmer	Evaluate the utility of MAC	Increased self-reported mindful awareness, mindful attention, experiential acceptance, flow, and actual competitive diving performance.
Wolanin (2005)	$N = 11$	Open trial	Division I university athletes (women's field hockey and volleyball)	Compare MAC to nonintervention control	MAC = 37% increase in coach ratings of competitive performance. Control group = 14% increase
Hasker (2010)	$N = 19$	Open trial	Division II university athletes (various sports)	Compare MAC to PST	MAC > PST in ability to describe and be nonreactive toward inner experiences, experiential acceptance, and ability to take action toward goals.

Study	N	Design	Population	Comparison	Results
Goodman et al. (2014).	N = 26	Open trial	Division I university athletes (men and women)	Compare MAC + yoga to control	MAC + yoga participants increased goal-directed energy and mindfulness > controls.
Garcia et al. (2004)	N = 16	Nonrandomized matched control	Elite canoeists	Compare sport-adapted ACT to hypnosis intervention	ACT > hypnosis on a canoeing training apparatus performance task.
Bernier et al. (2009)	N = 7	Open trial	Elite adolescent golfers	Compare sport-adapted ACT to PST	4 of 4 sport-adapted ACT participants enhanced national rankings; 2 of 3 in PST group did so. ACT > PST in self-reported mental skills development ($d = 1.72$).
Ahern, Moran, & Lonsdale (2011)	N = 13	RCT	University athletes from various sports	Compare mindfulness intervention to control condition	Mindfulness > control ($d = 1.66$) with regard to Global Flow scores and on Clear Goals, Sense of Control, and Unambiguous Feedback subscales.
Thompson et al., (2011)	N = 57	Open trial	Adult competitive athletes (11 archers, 21 golfers, 25 long-distance runners)	Compare mindfulness intervention to control condition	Mindfulness participants significantly increased ability to act with awareness; increased overall trait mindfulness; increased overall flow; and decreased task-related worries and task-irrelevant thoughts. Runners exhibited significant improvement in race times.
Ruiz & Luciano (2012)	N = 10	Nonrandomized matched control	International chess masters/grandmasters	Compare sport-adapted ACT to control	All ACT participants improved chess performance following protocol completion, and none of the control participants improved chess performance.

Note: MAC = Mindfulness-Acceptance-Commitment (MAC) approach to performance enhancement. PST = psychological skills training (traditional approaches). ACT = Acceptance and Commitment Therapy.

levels of experiential acceptance, and (c) an increased commitment to behaviors aimed at achieving athletic goals and values.

4. In a more recent open trial study (Goodman et al., 2014), an entire NCAA Division I men's athletic team (n =13) received eight ninety-minute group intervention sessions corresponding to the manualized modules of the MAC program, with each session immediately followed by a one-hour Hatha yoga session (intended to incorporate greater physical movement and meditation into the protocol). Results indicated that when compared to a nonrandomized control condition (student athletes from various other sports; n = 13), athlete-participants reported greater mindfulness, greater goal-directed energy, and less perceived stress.

5. A recent RCT compared the effectiveness of the MAC program to a traditional PST package with regard to athletic performance and mental health outcomes in an NCAA collegiate athlete population (Gross et al., 2015). Participants included twenty-two NCAA Division III collegiate athletes from a variety of teams, randomly assigned and assessed at pre-intervention, post-intervention, and a one-month follow-up. Results indicated that only the MAC participants demonstrated significant performance improvements from pre- to post-intervention (as measured by coach ratings), which were also maintained at a one-month follow-up. MAC was also more effective than the PST intervention in reducing substance use and hostility, from pre- to post-test, and these results were also maintained at a one-month follow-up. Additionally, the MAC group showed significant reductions in anxiety, eating concerns, and general psychological distress from pre-intervention to the one-month follow-up. As predicted from mindfulness- and acceptance-based theoretical perspectives, MAC participants also demonstrated increases in adaptive emotion regulation and psychological flexibility from pre-test to the one-month follow-up. Importantly, these results are to our knowledge the first RCT of the MAC protocol with competitive athletes, and this offers further support for MAC as an effective intervention for both athletic performance enhancement and enhanced psychological well-being, as originally hypothesized.

Adding to the studies that have directly assessed the efficacy of the MAC program itself, numerous empirical trials have investigated the use of mindfulness- and acceptance-based interventions that are both theoretically and procedurally connected to, and/or influenced by, the MAC approach.

For instance, Garcia and colleagues (2004) used a sport-adapted version of Acceptance and Commitment Therapy (ACT; Hayes et al., 1999) with sixteen elite canoeists and determined that the sport-modified ACT intervention led to higher levels of performance on a canoeing training apparatus than a matched control group of participants who received an alternative intervention (i.e., hypnosis). Likewise, an investigation by Bernier and colleagues (2009) found that a mindfulness- and acceptance-based intervention developed for elite golfers resulted in improvements in golf performance (determined by increases in national rank) when compared to a control condition that received a traditional PST intervention. An additional study utilized a mindfulness-based intervention with thirteen university student-athletes who were assigned to either an intervention group or a control condition (Ahern, Moran, & Lonsdale, 2011). The intervention group demonstrated increased scores on the flow dimensions of "clear goals" and "sense of control," and demonstrated strong effect size increases ($d = 0.6$–1.6) on flow dimensions of "challenge-skill balance," "concentration," and "loss of self-consciousness."

Adding further to the empirical base, a study by Thompson and colleagues (2011) used a mindfulness-based intervention with twenty-five long-distance runners, golfers, and archers, and results indicated that small but meaningful performance gains occurred from pre-test to follow-up. Interestingly, when considering potential mechanisms of change for their mindfulness intervention, Thompson and colleagues (2011) noted that the athletes in the mindfulness group experienced statistically significant increases in their ability to act with awareness and in their overall levels of trait mindfulness, and experienced statistically significant decreases in task-related worries and task-irrelevant thoughts. Finally, an interesting study compared a brief Acceptance and Commitment Therapy intervention to a no-contact control condition in an effort to improve the competitive performance of international-level chess players (Ruiz & Luciano, 2012). Participants in the sport-adapted ACT condition demonstrated significant reductions in the interference of unpleasant cognitions and emotions during chess competitions and experienced reductions in the frequency of maladaptive reactions to unpleasant thoughts and emotions. Importantly, all participants in the ACT intervention condition improved their chess performance during the seven months following completion of the ACT protocol, and yet none of the control condition participants demonstrated improved chess performance. As would be predicted from theory and empirical findings, changes in the frequency of maladaptive *responses* to internal experiences (and not the frequency of the internal experiences themselves) significantly predicted the effect sizes on chess performance in the ACT condition.

Common Myths/Mischaracterizations about Mindfulness- and Acceptance-Based Theory and Practice

It can certainly be concluded that there is ample empirical support for the proposed mechanisms of change of mindfulness- and acceptance-based interventions in sport psychology, and growing empirical evidence for the efficacy of mindfulness- and acceptance-based interventions such as MAC for the enhancement of athletic performance and overall psychosocial well-being. As such, it is not at all surprising that there has been a recent worldwide surge in sport practitioner interest in mindfulness- and acceptance-based interventions. With the long-accepted connection between science and practice in professional psychology, and given the reality that we are currently in the age of evidence-based practice (Gambrill, 2005) and professional accountability (Gardner, 2009; Moore, 2007), it is not shocking that many – from individual practitioners to large organizations, including national sport psychology governing bodies – are adopting mindfulness- and acceptance-based programming (e.g., MAC) for their athletes (Henriksen, 2015; Si et al., 2014).

Despite, and possibly because of, the rapid growth in interest in mindfulness- and acceptance-based approaches, frequent mischaracterizations and misuses of these interventions still persist. In fact, I hear them all the time – a misguided judgment, a gross mischaracterization, or a myth gone wild. A brief summary of some of the primary mischaracterizations could be particularly useful in a text such as this, as these can have toxic consequences to the discipline as a whole, the professionals within the discipline, and the athletes with whom we work:

Myth 1: Mindfulness/acceptance is Buddhism. Mindfulness certainly has its roots firmly in Eastern contemplative traditions, such as Buddhist philosophy, and in fact it is most often associated with the formal practice of meditation. It is important to note, however, that Buddhist practices are much more than meditation, and mindfulness- and acceptance-based psychological interventions are much more than meditation as well. Mindfulness essentially represents a state of consciousness (to be contrasted with mind*less*ness), which by its nature involves consciously attending to moment-to-moment experiences (Brown & Ryan, 2003). When viewed from this perspective, meditative practice can be used as a training tool to effectively develop the state, or skill, of mindful attention and mindful awareness (Kabat-Zinn, 2005). It is these cognitive and resulting behavioral aspects of mindfulness (nonjudging attention/moment-moment awareness, and task-relevant behavioral engagement) that are the goals of meditative training within mindfulness- and acceptance-based approaches.

Myth 2: Mindfulness/acceptance is "old wine in a new bottle." It has been my experience that more professionals than we would care to think about attempt to dismiss mindfulness- and acceptance-based interventions as "old wine in a new bottle," by suggesting that these new approaches are really the "same" as traditional cognitive behavioral intervention approaches, a view that has sparked intense professional debate (David, 2014; Gardner, Moore, & Marks, 2014). The theoretical and empirical data presented previously in this chapter demonstrates that this attitude could not be further from the truth. Fundamentally, traditional CBT-based PST models are best conceptualized as viewing thoughts, emotions, and physical arousal as variables that in some way must, can, and will change for performance enhancement to occur. In direct contrast, interventions based on mindfulness and acceptance models view thoughts, emotions, and physical arousal as variables to be fully experienced and utilized more effectively (with no need or desire for reduction, control, change, or modification), with a more behaviorally based (i.e., task/performance-related behavior) focus. In essence, a change from the sentence, "I want to perform better, *but* I have these thoughts and emotions," to, "I want to perform better, *and* I have these thoughts and emotions," fully captures the fundamental difference between the two intervention models. This difference is not insignificant, nor does it in any way suggest that the two models are the same.

Myth 3: Mindfulness/acceptance can be readily incorporated into traditional PST. As one can easily surmise from this chapter so far, the fundamental goals and strategies of PST and mindfulness- and acceptance-based approaches are vastly different. Truth be told, the biggest obstacle toward integration of mindfulness- and acceptance-based models and the traditional PST model is the fundamentally contrary nature of each model. One model (PST) holds that internal change and/or self-control must precede and is fully associated with an ideal performance state, with optimal performance to follow. On the contrary, the other model (mindfulness/acceptance) posits that internal experiences are naturally and inevitably fluctuating and passing, and attention and awareness can be trained to remain in the moment and on task regardless of internal events. From this clearly opposite perspective, not all PST techniques can be rationally integrated into mindfulness- and acceptance-based approaches. Goal setting can readily be integrated, and in fact the MAC approach utilizes goal and value identification as a core component. In addition, the appropriate use of stimulus control techniques (i.e., pre-competitive/ performance routines) can easily be integrated into mindfulness- and acceptance-based interventions, especially if the routine includes brief meditative exercises (see Gardner & Moore, 2007, for examples). On the other hand, guided imagery procedures used with an intent to provide "positive" images; self-talk modification procedures used with an intent to change, control, or modify thought processes; and/ or relaxation/arousal control procedures used with an intent to in some way change, control, or modify what we feel and how we respond physiologically – all of these are fully contrary to the foundational premise, goals, and strategies of mindfulness- and acceptance-based interventions (for reasons that by now I hope are clear to readers).

Future Directions

While basic and applied research for mindfulness- and acceptance-based interventions for performance enhancement has and can be expected to continue to grow and evolve, much is yet to be learned. For example, the increasing availability and advancement of brain scan technologies will increasingly allow for further exploration and understanding of the neurocognitive foundations of mindfulness- and acceptance-based interventions. In addition, the practice reality of limited access/time with high-level competitive athletes highlights the importance of developing a greater empirical understanding of how much mindfulness and acceptance training is required to see positive neurocognitive, personal well-being, and competitive performance outcomes. The continued evolution of this knowledge base will ultimately result in more efficient and effective mindfulness- and acceptance-based intervention protocols.

In addition, the professional literature will benefit from further efficacy studies, especially RCT, utilizing (a) larger sample sizes, (b) multiple sports and sport types (e.g., individual vs. team sports), (c) multiple measures of athletic performance, (d) multiple cultural contexts, and (e) multisite investigations. That being said, it is accurate to say that after fifteen years of theoretical development, research, and practice, mindfulness- and acceptance-based interventions for the purpose of enhancing athletic performance and promoting athlete well-being has emerged from being an interesting, albeit controversial, method within sport psychology to a mainstream option for sport psychologists across the globe. I hope that in the course of the next fifteen years, our current iterations of mindfulness- and acceptance-based interventions will continue to evolve in keeping with the fundamental tenets of clinical science.

Conclusion

Since the MAC approach to performance enhancement was first conceived and introduced to the professional community more than fifteen years ago, it has been so gratifying to watch this class of interventions accumulate a strong foundation of a basic scientific and applied empirical base. Empirical findings to date have not only demonstrated efficacious outcomes with respect to athletic performance and personal well-being, but also importantly have supported the theorized mechanisms of change for these interventions, an area of applied research that has been largely absent within sport psychology. While it is certainly expected and in fact anticipated that future empirical research on mindfulness- and acceptance-based interventions (both process and outcome research) will further the evolution of this powerful model, at present, mindfulness- and acceptance-based interventions should be considered viable, empirically informed interventions for the enhancement of athletic performance and the promotion of overall athlete well-being.

REFERENCES

Ahern, C., Moran, A. P., and Lonsdale, C. (2011). The effects of mindfulness training on athletes' flow: An initial investigation. *Sport Psychologist*, 25, 177–189.

Begley, S. (2007). *Train your mind, change your brain: How a new science reveals our extraordinary potential to transform ourselves*. New York, NY: Ballantine.

Bernier, M., Thienot, E., Codron, R., and Fournier, J. F. (2009). A multi-study investigation examining the relationship between mindfulness and acceptance approaches and sport performance. *Journal of Clinical Sport Psychology*, 25, 320–333.

Brefczynski-Lewis, J. A., Lutz, A., Schaefer, H. S., Levinson, D. B., and Davidson, R. J. (2007). Neural correlates of attentional expertise in long-term meditation practitioners. *Proceedings of the National Academy of Sciences of the United States of America*, 104, 11483–11488. doi: 10.1073/pnas.0606552104

Brown, K. W., and Ryan, R. M. (2003). The benefits of being present: Mindfulness and its role in psychological well-being. *Journal of Personality and Social Psychology*, 84(4), 822–830. doi: 10.1037/0022-3514.84.4.822

Christensen, A., Atkins, D. C., Yi, J., Baucom, D. H., and George, W. H. (2006). Couple and individual adjustment for two years following a randomized clinical trial comparing traditional vs. integrative behavioral couple therapy. *Journal of Consulting and Clinical Psychology*, 74, 1180–1191. doi: http://dx.doi.org/10.1037/0022-006X.74.6.1180

Crews, D. J., and Landers, D. M. (1993). Electroencephalographic measures of attentional patterns prior to the golf putt. *Medicine and Science in Sports and Exercise*, 25, 116–126. doi: http://dx.doi.org/10.1249/00005768-199301000-00016

David, D. (2014). Some concerns about the psychological implications of mindfulness: A critical analysis. *Journal of Rational Emotive and Cognitive Behavior Therapy*, 32(4), 310–324.

Davidson, R. J. (2002). Toward a biology of positive affect and compassion. In R. J. Davidson, and A. Harrington (Eds.), *Visions of compassion: Western scientists and Tibetan Buddhists examine human nature* (pp. 107–130). New York, NY: Oxford University Press.

Davidson, R. J., Kabat-Zinn, J., Schumacher, J., Rosenkranz, M., Muller, D., Santorelli, S.,... Sheridan, J. F. (2003). Alterations in brain and immune function produced by mindfulness meditation. *Psychosomatic Medicine*, 65, 564–570. doi: 10.1097/01.PSY.0000077505.67574.E3

Fairholme, C. P., Boisseau, C. L., Ellard, K. K., Ehrenreich, J. T., and Barlow, D. H. (2010). Emotions, emotion regulation, and psychological treatment: A unified perspective. In A. M. Kring, and D. M. Sloan (Eds.), *Emotion regulation and psychopathology* (pp. 283–309). New York, NY: Guilford Press.

Forman, E. M., Herbert, J. D., Moitra, E., Yeomans, P. D., and Geller, P. A. (2007). A randomized controlled effectiveness trial of acceptance and commitment therapy and cognitive therapy for anxiety and depression. *Behavior Modification*, 31, 772–799. doi: 10.1177/0145445507302202

Gambrill, E. (2005). *Critical thinking in clinical practice: Improving the quality of judgments and decisions*. Hoboken, NJ: John Wiley & Sons.

Garcia, R. F., Villa, R. S., Cepeda, N. T., Cueto, E. G., and Montes, J. M. G. (2004). Efecto de la hipnosis y la terapia de aceptcion y compromiso (ACT) en la mejora de la fuerza fisica en piraguistas. *International Journal of Clinical and Health Psychology*, 4, 481–493.

Gardner, F. L. (2001, July). *Principles and practices of acceptance-based sport psychology*. Grand rounds lecture presented at the Department of Psychiatry Grand Rounds at North Shore University Medical Center and Health System, Manhasset, NY.

(2009). Efficacy, mechanisms of change, and the scientific development of sport psychology. *Journal of Clinical Sport Psychology*, 3(2), 139–155.

Gardner, F. L., and Moore, Z. E. (2004). A Mindfulness-Acceptance-Commitment (MAC) based approach to athletic performance enhancement: Theoretical considerations. *Behavior Therapy*, 35, 707–723. doi:10.1016/S0005-7894(04) 80016-9

(2006). *Clinical sport psychology*. Champagne, IL: Human Kinetics.

(2007). *The psychology of human performance: The mindfulness-acceptance-commitment approach*. New York, NY: Springer.

(2012). Mindfulness and acceptance models in sport psychology: A decade of basic and applied scientific advancements. *Canadian Psychology*, 53(4), 309–318. doi: 10.1037/a0030220.

Gardner, F. L., Moore, Z. E., and Marks, D. R. (2014). Rectifying misconceptions: A comprehensive response to "Some concerns about the psychological implications of mindfulness: A critical analysis." *Journal of Rational Emotive and Cognitive Behavior Therapy*, 32 (4), 325–344. doi: 10.1007/s10942-014-0196-1

Gifford, E. V., Kohlenberg, B. S., Hayes, S. C., Antonuccio, D. O., Piasecki, M. M., Rasmussen Hall, M. L., and Palm, K. M. (2004). Acceptance-based treatment for smoking cessation. *Behavior Therapy*, 35, 689–705. doi: 10.1016/S0005-7894(04)80015-7

Gooding, A., and Gardner, F. L. (2009). An empirical investigation on the relationship between mindfulness, pre-shot routine, and basketball free throw percentage. *Journal of Clinical Sport Psychology*, 3, 303–319.

Goodman, F. R., Kashdan, T. B., Mallard, T. T., and Schumann, M. (2014). A brief mindfulness and yoga intervention with an entire NCAA Division I athletic team: An initial investigation. *Psychology of Consciousness: Theory, Research and Practice*, 1(4), 339–351. doi: http://dx.doi.org/10.1037/cns0000022

Gratz, K. L., and Gunderson, J. G. (2006). Preliminary data on an acceptance-based emotion regulation group intervention for deliberate self-harm among women with borderline personality disorder. *Behavior Therapy*, 37, 25–35. doi:10.1016/j.beth.2005.03.002

Gross, M., Moore, Z. E., Gardner, F. L., Wolanin, A. T., Pess, R., and Marks, D. R. (2015). *The Mindfulness-Acceptance-Commitment (MAC) approach: An intervention for the mental health and sport performance of student athletes*. (Unpublished doctoral dissertation, in preparation for submission). Union, NJ: Kean University.

Hardy, L., Jones, G., and Gould, D. (1996). *Understanding psychological preparation for sport: Theory and practice of elite performers*. New York, NY: Wiley.

Hasker, S. M. (2010). *Evaluation of the mindfulness-acceptance-commitment (MAC) approach for enhancing athletic performance* (Doctoral dissertation). Indiana, PA: Indiana University of Pennsylvania. Retrieved from http://dspace.iup .edu/handle/2069/276

Hatfield, B. D., Haufler, A. J., Hung, T., and Spalding, T. W. (2004). Encelphalographic studies of skilled psychomotor performance. *Journal of Clinical Neuropsychology*, 21, 144–156.

Hatfield, B. D., and Hillman, C. H. (2001). The psychophysiology of sport: A mechanistic understanding of the psychology of superior performance. In R. N. Singer, C. H. Hausenblas, and C. M. Janelle (Eds.), *Handbook of sport psychology* (2nd ed., pp. 362–386). New York, NY: Wiley.

Hayes, S. C., Bissett, R., Roget, N., Padilla, M., Kohlenberg, B. S., Fisher, G., . . . Niccolls, R. (2004). The impact of acceptance and commitment training and multicultural training on the stigmatizing attitudes and professional burnout of substance abuse counselors. *Behavior Therapy*, 35, 821–835. doi: 10.1016/j. beth.2005.03.002

Hayes, S. C., Strosahl, K., and Wilson, K. G. (1999). *Acceptance and commitment therapy: An experiential approach to behavior change.* New York, NY: Guilford Press.

Henriksen, K. (2015). Sport psychology at the Olympics: The case of a Danish sailing crew in a head wind. *Journal of Sport and Exercise Psychology*, 13(1), 43–55.

Holzel, B. K., Lazar, S. W., Gard, T., Schuman-Olivier, Z., Vago, D. R., and Ott, U. (2011). How does mindfulness meditation work? Proposing mechanisms of action from a conceptual and neural perspective. *Perspectives on Psychological Science*, 6, 537–559.

Jacobson, N. S., Christensen, A., Prince, S. E., Cordova, J., and Eldridge, K. (2000). Integrative couple therapy: An acceptance-based, promising new treatment for couple discord. *Journal of Consulting and Clinical Psychology*, 68, 351–355. doi: http://dx.doi.org/10.1037/0022-006X.68.2.351

Jha, A. P., Krompinger, J., and Baime, M. J. (2007). Mindfulness training modifies subsystems of attention. *Cognitive, Affective, and Behavioral Neuroscience*, 7, 109–119. doi: 10.3758/CABN.7.2.109

Jha, A. P., Stanley, E. A., Kiyonaga, A., Wong, L., and Gelfand, L. (2010). Examining the protective effects of mindfulness training on working memory capacity and affective experience. *Emotion*, 10, 54–64. doi: http://dx.doi.org/10.1037/a0018438

Kabat-Zinn, J. (2005). *Coming to our senses: Healing ourselves and the world through mindfulness.* New York, NY: Hyperion.

Kee, Y. H., and Wang, C. K. J. (2008). Relationships between mindfulness, flow dispositions, and mental skills adoption: A cluster analytic approach. *Psychology of Sport and Exercise*, 9, 393–411. doi: 10.1016/j.psychsport. 2007.07.001

Linehan, M. M., Comtois, K. A., Murray, A. M., Brown, M. Z., Gallop, R. J., Heard, H. L., . . . Lindenboim, N. (2007). Two-year randomized controlled trial and follow-up of dialectical behavior therapy vs. therapy by experts for suicidal behaviors and borderline personality disorder. *Archives of General Psychiatry*, 63, 757–766. doi: 10.1001/archpsyc.63.7.757

Ma, S. H., and Teasdale, J. D. (2004). Mindfulness-based cognitive therapy for depression: Replication and exploration of differential relapse prevention effects. *Journal of Consulting and Clinical Psychology*, 72, 31–40. doi: http://dx.doi.org/10.1037/0022-006X.72.1.31

Marks, D. R. (2008). The Buddha's extra scoop: Neural correlates of mindfulness and clinical sport psychology. *Journal of Clinical Sport Psychology*, 2, 216–241.

Meichenbaum, D. (1977). *Cognitive behavior modification: An integrative approach*. New York, NY: Plenum.

Moore, A., and Malinowski, P. (2009). Meditation, mindfulness and cognitive flexibility, *Consciousness and Cognition*, 18, 176–186. doi:10.1016/j.concog.2008.12.008

Moore, Z. E. (2003). Toward the development of an evidence based practice of sport psychology: A structured qualitative study of performance enhancement interventions. *Dissertation Abstracts International-B*, 64(10), 5227 (UMI No. 3 3108295).

(2007). Critical thinking and the evidence-based practice of sport psychology. *Journal of Clinical Sport Psychology*, 1, 9–22.

(2009). Theoretical and empirical developments of the Mindfulness-Acceptance-Commitment (MAC) approach to performance enhancement. *Journal of Clinical Sport Psychology*, 3(4), 291–302.

Moore, Z. E., and Gardner, F. L. (2001, October). Taking applied sport psychology from research to practice: Integrating empirically supported interventions into a self-regulatory model of athletic performance. Symposium presented at the meeting of the annual conference of the Association for the Advancement of Applied Sport Psychology, Orlando, FL.

(2002, August). *Psychological skills training for athletic performance enhancement: An evidence-based approach*. Paper presented at the Annual Convention of the American Psychological Association, Chicago, IL.

(2003, August). *A protocol for Mindfulness-Acceptance Commitment (MAC) approach to athletic performance enhancement*. Paper presented at the Annual Conference of the American Psychological Association, Toronto, Canada.

Nakamura, J., and Csikszentmihalyi, M. (2005). The concept of flow. In C. R. Snyder and S. J. Lopez (Eds.), *Handbook of positive psychology* (pp. 89–105). New York, NY: Oxford University Press.

Roemer, L., and Orsillo, S. M. (2009). *Mindfulness and acceptance-based behavioral therapies in practice*. New York, NY: Guilford Press.

Ruiz, F. J., and Luciano, C. (2012). Improving international-level chess players' performance with an acceptance-based protocol: Preliminary findings, *Psychological Record*, 62, 447–462.

Safer, D. L., Telch, C. F., and Agras, W. S. (2001). Dialectical behavior therapy for bulimia nervosa. *American Journal of Psychiatry*, 158, 632–634. doi: http://dx.doi.org/10.1176/appi.ajp.158.4.632

Schwanhausser, L. (2009). Application of the Mindfulness-Acceptance-Commitment (MAC) protocol with an adolescent springboard diver: The case of Steve. *Journal of Clinical Sport Psychology*, 3, 377–396.

Semple, R. J. (2010). Does mindfulness meditation enhance attention: A randomized controlled trial. *Mindfulness*, 1, 121–130. doi: 10.1007/s1267-010-0017-2

Si, G., Duan, Y., Li, H. Y., Zhang, C. Q., and Su, N. (2014). The influence of the Chinese sport system and Chinese cultural characteristics on Olympic sport psychology services. *Psychology of Sport and Exercise*, 17, 56–67. doi: 10.1016/j.psychsport.2014.08.008

Slagter, H. A., Davidson, R. J., and Lutz, A. (2011). Mental training as a tool in the neuroscientific study of brain and cognitive plasticity. *Frontiers of Human Neuroscience*, 5(17). Retrieved from http://www.ncbi.nlm.nih.gov/pmc/articles/PMC3039118/?tool=pubmed

Slagter, H. A., Lutz, A., Greischar, L. L., Francis, A. D., Nieuwenhuis, S., Davis, J. M., and Davidson, R. J. (2007). Mental training affects distribution of limited brain resources. *PLoS Biology*, 5(6), 1228–1235. doi: 10.1371/journal.pbio.0050138

Teasdale, J. D., Moore, R. G., Hayhurst, H., Pope, M., Williams, S., and Segal, Z. V. (2002). Metacognitive awareness and prevention of relapse in depression: Empirical evidence. *Journal of Consulting and Clinical Psychology*, 70, 275–287. doi: http://dx.doi.org/10.1037/0022-006X.70.2.275

Telch, C. F., Agras, W. S., and Linehan, M. M. (2001). Dialectical behavior therapy for binge eating disorder. *Journal of Consulting and Clinical Psychology*, 69, 615–623. doi: http://dx.doi.org/10.1037/0022-006X.69.6.1061

Teper, R., Segal, Z. V., and Inzlicht, M. (2013). Inside the mindful mind: How mindfulness enhances emotion regulation through improvements in executive control. *Current Directions in Psychological Science*, 22, 449–454. doi: 10.1177/0963721413495869

Thompson, R. W., Kaufman, K. A., De Petrillo, L. A., Glass, C. R., and Arnkoff, D. B. (2011). One year follow-up of mindful sport performance enhancement (MSPE) with archers, golfers, and runners. *Journal of Clinical Sport Psychology*, 5, 99–116.

van den Hurk, P. A. M., Giommi, F., Gielen, S. C., Speckens, A. E. M., and Barendregt, H. P. (2010). Greater efficiency in attentional processing related to mindfulness meditation. *Quarterly Journal of Experimental Psychology*, 63, 1168–1180. doi: 10.1080/17470210903249365

Wolanin, A. T. (2005). Mindfulness-Acceptance-Commitment (MAC) based performance enhancement for Division I collegiate athletes: A preliminary investigation. *Dissertation Abstracts International-B*, 65(7), 3735–3794.

Wolanin, A. T., Gardner, F. L., and Moore, Z. E. (2003, August). *A preliminary investigation of Mindfulness-Acceptance Commitment (MAC) based performance enhancement*. Paper presented at the Annual Conference of the American Psychological Association, Toronto, Ontario.

Zeidan, F., Johnson, S. K., Diamond, B. J., and Goolkasian, P. (2010). Mindfulness meditation improves cognition: Evidence of brief mental training. *Consciousness and Cognition*, 19, 597–605. doi: 10.1016/j.concog.2010.03.014

CHAPTER 8

Mindful Sport Performance Enhancement (MSPE)
Development and Applications

Keith A. Kaufman, Carol R. Glass, Timothy R. Pineau

Many traditional mental training strategies for athletes are based on the assumption that negative cognitions need to be altered or stopped in order to optimize performance (Gardner & Moore, 2006). However, attempting to change negative internal states may ironically lead to greater focus on these states, potentially increasing their frequency and interfering with performance (Wegner, 1994; Wenzlaff & Wegner, 2000). Rather than trying to control or eliminate them, athletes may thus benefit more from developing skills in present-moment awareness and nonjudgmental acceptance of negative internal states (Gardner & Moore, 2004, 2007; Kaufman, Glass, & Arnkoff, 2009). This paradigm shift is a central tenet of mindfulness-based interventions, which represent an emerging direction in sport psychology (see Birrer, Röthlin, & Morgan, 2012; Gardner & Moore, 2012).

There are various ways to define mindfulness. One definition, which stems more from Buddhist philosophy, is "paying attention in a particular way: on purpose, in the present moment, and non-judgmentally" (Kabat-Zinn, 1994, p. 4). This view of mindfulness involves maintaining attention on immediate experience while taking an orientation of openness, acceptance, and curiosity (Bishop et al., 2004). Langer (2000) has proposed an alternate conceptualization of mindfulness as "a flexible state of mind in which we are actively engaged in the present, noticing new things and sensitive to context" (p. 220). Her view entails observing the context in which one acts, actively processing new information, and recognizing that stimuli can be seen from multiple perspectives (see also Chapter 5). The former approach to mindfulness has been used more widely to date in psychological research and practice, and is the primary perspective underlying mindfulness-based approaches to sport performance enhancement. For a review of the literature on mindfulness and sport, including relevant studies and associations between sport performance and both conceptualizations of mindfulness, see Pineau, Glass, and Kaufman (2014).

The growing emphasis on mindfulness for athletes derives, at least in part, from an explosion of interest in mindfulness throughout the entire field of psychology and society at large. Due to its rapidly expanding popularity, mindfulness has become a media buzzword. For example, a recent cover story of *TIME Magazine* (Pickert, 2014) dealt with "The Mindful Revolution," and a *Huffington Post* article (Gregoire, 2014) immediately followed, arguing that *TIME* had only hit the tip of the iceberg. This follow-up article boldly claimed that mindfulness is for everyone, regardless of gender, race, age, income, and culture. To date, hundreds of studies have been conducted that support the effectiveness of mindfulness approaches. Systematic reviews and meta-analyses have evidenced that mindfulness-based interventions can significantly improve anxiety, stress, depression, pain, emotionality, and relationship issues (Goyal et al., 2014; Hofmann et al., 2010; Khoury et al., 2013; Piet & Hougaard, 2011; Sedlmeier et al., 2012).

The sport psychology research group at the Catholic University of America has developed one of the two most-studied approaches to bring mindfulness into the domain of sport psychology. Our Mindful Sport Performance Enhancement (MSPE) program (Kaufman & Glass, 2006; Kaufman, Glass, & Pineau, in press) is based on Kabat-Zinn's (1990) Mindfulness-Based Stress Reduction (MBSR). MBSR similarly played a major role in the development of Segal, Williams, and Teasdale's (2002) Mindfulness-Based Cognitive Therapy (MBCT), another primary influence on our work. In this chapter, we will discuss the foundations of MSPE and empirical support. The MSPE protocol is then presented in depth, followed by recommendations for how both MSPE group leaders and participants can maximize their experiences of the training, with the goal of affecting greater change in athletes' mindfulness and performance.

Mindfulness and Sport

The mental skills cultivated through mindfulness training (e.g., enhanced attentional capacity, emotion regulation) seem especially well matched to sport performance enhancement and can also potentially promote wellness in athletes by helping them cope better with stress. News stories focused on the use of mindfulness with athletes have been appearing with increased frequency, suggesting that the word is spreading throughout the sports world about the potential impact of mindfulness on performance. For instance, around the time of their 2014 Super Bowl run, ABC News reported on how Seattle Seahawks head coach Pete Carroll encourages his players to meditate daily with the goal of improving their attention during games (Neoporent, 2014). Also, the *Huffington Post* featured a story ("Athletes Who Meditate," 2013) identifying elite athletes such as Kobe Bryant, Derek Jeter, Ricky Williams, Misty May-Trainor, Kerri Walsh, and the University of Michigan basketball team as practitioners of mindfulness. A *Philadelphia Inquirer* article headlined "Athletes Using Meditation to Improve Performance" (Rush, 2014) described meditation practiced by the Penn State University basketball team and Villanova University football team. Within a recent article in the *Atlantic* (Khazan, 2014), mindfulness is included as one of the seven ways Olympians stay motivated through training, and Jamie Anderson (gold medal winner in slopestyle snowboarding at the 2014 Olympics) talked about trying to "do a little bit of yoga and meditate" the night before competition to cope with pre-performance anxiety. Perhaps the best-known reporting on mindfulness in sport was done by legendary NBA coach Phil Jackson (2006), whose book *Sacred Hoops* describes his philosophy of mindful basketball and the use of meditation sessions with his teams.

Benefits of Mindfulness for Athletes

Mindfulness is gaining traction in athletics because people are realizing that certain mental states crucial to sport performance, such as flow, attention, and relaxation, are positively impacted through mindfulness training. We will now discuss the links between mindfulness and these factors, which in part inspired us to develop MSPE.

Flow and the zone

When reflecting on their sport experiences, successful athletes often speak, almost in a mystified way, about periods of time in which they were able to achieve peak performance, a state commonly referred to as *the zone.* Among the various characteristics attributed to being in the zone are a fusion of body and mind, deep concentration, low self-consciousness, a present-moment focus, feelings of relaxation, and perceptions of effortlessness (Alessi, 1995; Cooper, 1998).

Sport scientists interested in further elucidating the nature of the zone have compared this condition to the psychological state of *flow* (Jackson & Csikszentmihalyi, 1999; Young & Pain, 1999). Flow is a mindset that typically occurs when an individual perceives a balance between the challenges associated with a situation and his or her capabilities to meet those demands, which reflects the sense of effortless action felt when experiencing the best moments in one's life (Csikszentmihalyi, 1990, 1997). Jackson (2000) concluded that there is a clear relationship between the mental characteristics associated with peak sport performance and this conceptualization of flow.

The sport psychology literature has identified characteristics that could promote the occurrence of flow, including elevated confidence, preparation, maintaining constructive thoughts, achieving optimal arousal, appropriate focus, and feeling good during the performance (Jackson, 1995; Russell, 2001), with anxiety elements such as concentration disruption and worry most likely to prevent flow (Jackson et al. 1998). A recent systematic review of the occurrence and experience of flow in elite athletes (Swann et al., 2012) found that the most commonly cited dimensions of flow were concentration on the task at hand and the merging of action and awareness (i.e., moving without having to think about it).

With its emphasis on focusing on the present moment, appreciating the process without judgment, and accepting both internal and external experiences without latching onto the expectations and memories that can foster pressure and doubt, mindfulness training appears to be a logical way to help athletes enter flow states and achieve peak performance. The similarity between characteristics of mindfulness and flow suggests that mindfulness-based interventions for athletes may be helpful in achieving this state, thus leading to optimized performance (Gardner & Moore, 2004; Kaufman et al., 2009).

Research has supported this proposed connection between mindfulness and flow, with a number of studies finding not only a robust relation between measures of these two constructs in athletes (Bernier et al., 2009; Cathcart, McGregor, & Groundwater, 2014; Kaufman et al., 2009; Kee & Wang, 2008; Pineau et al., 2014b), but also significant increases in athletes' levels of flow after receiving mindfulness-based interventions (Aherne, Moran, & Lonsdale, 2011; Kaufman et al., 2009).

Attention

Attention in sport generally includes four components: selective attention, sustained attention, situational awareness or orienting attention, and attentional flexibility or divided attention (Memmert, 2009; Weinberg & Gould, 2011). In other words, athletes must be able to focus on relevant cues while disregarding irrelevant ones, maintain an appropriate level of focus throughout their performance, remain aware of relevant environmental stimuli, and shift attention between stimuli or among multiple stimuli as necessary. The disruption of attention in sport may result from both external distractions, such as crowd noise or weather, and internal distractions, such as fatigue and emotional arousal (Moran, 1996; Smith, 1996). At his peak, Tiger Woods was renowned for his ability to enter a "cocoon of concentration" and maintain focus (Brooks, 2008).

Learning to direct attention consciously is a core feature of mindfulness training (Kabat-Zinn, 1994). Mindfulness practice has been shown to improve attentional abilities (Chiesa, Calati, & Serretti, 2011) and be associated with superior selective attention (van den Hurk et al., 2010), sustained attention (Chambers, Lo, & Allen, 2008), situational awareness (Moore & Malinowski, 2009), and attentional flexibility (Hodgins & Adair, 2010) – in other words, exactly what is required of attention in sport performance. Specific to sport, Moore (2009) has suggested that mindfulness practice may help athletes cultivate their attentional resources. Salmon, Hanneman, and Harwood (2010) have offered a mindfulness-based conceptual model of attention emphasizing both awareness and acceptance of present-moment experience, which may be able to promote a shifting of attentional strategies, depending on the demands of the task, and enhance sport performance. Also, Klinger, Barta, and Glas (1981) found that setbacks can lead to attentional shifts from task-relevant cues to self-evaluative ones that may result in decreased sport performance, something mindfulness training may help guard against.

A common concern we have heard regarding becoming more mindful while participating in sports is that certain uncomfortable sensations (e.g., fatigue, pain, frustration) often associated with athletics may rise in salience. Our feeling on this valid concern is that the discomfort is there regardless, but learning to have a nonreactive attitude toward these sensations can allow for more efficient use of available attentional and physical resources by not getting oneself trapped in distracting, task-irrelevant worries about possible meanings of the discomfort. Mindfulness is not a tool for distracting attention from what is present, even when what is present is difficult to tolerate. Rather, it is a technique that athletes can use to train their attention in a manner that is consistent with optimal sport performance states (i.e., flow, as described previously). While the impact of mindful awareness on perceptions of pain and exhaustion is beyond the scope of this chapter, see Pineau and colleagues (2014) for a detailed discussion.

Relaxation and letting go
Emotions, whether positive or negative, can have a profound impact on athletic performance (Hanin, 2000; Lazarus, 2000). What may be

regarded as the ultimate positive emotion, the experience of intrinsic joy (i.e., autotelic experience), is an integral element of flow (Jackson & Csikszentmihalyi, 1999). In contrast, sport anxiety, often considered a negative emotional experience, has been associated with muscle tension and fatigue (Pijpers et al., 2003), concentration disruption (Hatzigeorgiadis & Biddle, 2001), as well as burnout and loss of confidence (Hackney, Pearman, & Nowacki, 1990).

Evidence with non-athlete populations suggests that mindfulness-based interventions can both enhance positive affect and decrease negative affect (see Woodruff, 2014), although Goyal et al. (2014) found insufficient evidence of meditation programs impacting positive mood based on four randomized controlled trials with clinical populations. Also, mindfulness has been associated with the ability to let go of negative thoughts with greater ease (Frewen et al., 2008). Although not an explicit goal of this practice, increased feelings of relaxation are often reported by people after mindfulness meditation (e.g., Jain et al., 2007). A recent study revealed that meditators (with an average of over eighteen years of meditation experience) indicated having "mindful" thoughts significantly more often than did nonmeditators (Hirschhorn, Glass, & Arnkoff, 2014). Such thoughts (e.g., "This will pass," "It's okay to feel this way," "Let it go") could be useful for athletes during competition, potentially facilitating relaxation, although the benefits of mindfulness for relaxation in sport still need to be explored.

Among athletes, mindfulness has been found to have a significant negative association with sport anxiety (Kaufman, 2008; Pineau, 2014; Pineau et al., 2011) and a significant positive association with sport-related optimism (Pineau, 2014). Additionally, in response to mindfulness- and acceptance-based training programs, athletes have shown significant reductions in aspects of sport anxiety (De Petrillo et al., 2009; Gardner & Moore, 2004) and significant increases in sport optimism (Kaufman et al., 2009).

While change in affect may be an important result of mindfulness training, even greater benefits for sport performance might be produced from enhanced emotion regulation, which may be a primary mechanism of change in mindfulness interventions (see Gratz & Tull, 2010, for a review). The ability of athletes to manage their reactions to the strong emotions that are inevitably produced by competitive sports is a key aspect of the sport psychology literature (e.g., Jones, 2003). Athletes who receive mindfulness-based interventions may thus engage in less experiential avoidance (avoiding thoughts, feelings, and physical sensations) and become more accepting of their current emotional experiences (Gardner & Moore, 2004; Schwanhausser, 2009), whatever they happen to be, potentially freeing up precious resources like attention to devote to performance.

Initial Applications and Current Mindfulness Approaches for Athletes

Jon Kabat-Zinn was a pioneer in developing a systematic treatment that emphasizes meditation practices. His MBSR program consists of two-hour classes that meet over the course of eight weeks and includes instruction in various types of meditations (e.g., mindfulness of the breath, body scan, mindful yoga) and how to incorporate mindfulness into daily life (Kabat-Zinn, 1982, 1990, 1994, 2013). For over three decades, MBSR has been implemented around the world, across age groups, for a wide range of physical and mental disorders, as well as in healthy populations. Meta-analytic reviews have shown MBSR to have significant beneficial effects on depression, anxiety, and psychological distress in adults with chronic medical disease (Bohlmeijer et al., 2010), cancer (Ledesma & Kumano, 2009), breast cancer (Cramer et al., 2012; Zainal, Booth, & Huppert, 2012), and social anxiety disorder (Jazaieri et al., 2012), as well as on quality of life and pain for patients with fibromyalgia (Lauche et al., 2013). Furthermore, MBSR has led to improvement in psychological outcomes in nonclinical settings (Eberth & Sedlmeier, 2012) and in stress reduction for healthy adults (Chiesa & Serretti, 2009). A meta-analysis across a wide range of clinical populations (e.g., heart disease, pain, cancer, anxiety, depression) and stressed nonclinical samples similarly evidenced that MBSR has a significant positive effect on both mental and physical well-being (Grossman et al., 2004).

Shortly after introducing his MBSR approach in 1982, Kabat-Zinn worked with Olympic and college rowing teams to conduct what appears to be the first empirical test of a mindfulness-based intervention for athletes (Kabat-Zinn, Beall, & Rippe, 1985). This study was never published, and the only reference available is for a conference poster. When we contacted Kabat-Zinn inquiring about his work with the rowers, he kindly reconstructed his original poster for us, saying that retyping the text "brought those wonderful days back in a big and very vivid way" (J. Kabat-Zinn, personal communication, January 25, 2006).

This early application of meditation to rowing focused on concentrating, relaxing, letting go of thoughts, noting key associations to stay centered, and experiencing flow and harmony between athletes and the

boat. Following their mindfulness training, Olympic rowers who med-
aled in various events reported that the meditation practice had helped
them to prepare for and achieve optimal performance during their races.
The college rowers performed well above the expectations of their
coach and claimed that the training had enhanced their concentration,
relaxation, and synchronicity of technique while reducing the impact of
their fatigue, pain, and negative thoughts.

Bruce Beall, who coached the college rowing teams that participated in
Kabat-Zinn's study and was also a member of the 1984 U.S. Olympic
rowing team, shed more light on the nature of this pioneering work
(B. Beall, personal communication, March 7, 2006). Beall highlighted
two aspects of how mindfulness was most helpful to him and his teams.
First, he discussed how athletes need to be able to focus when working
on changing aspects of their technique and be totally present with what
they are doing in a given moment. Second, Beall stressed how mindfulness can help in dealing with fatigue and pushing the limits of physical
abilities.

Athletes can learn to recognize their mind wandering toward negative
thoughts about limits during competition (e.g., "I can't sustain this pace"),
but then mindfully label these experiences as "just thoughts," let them go,
and bring attention back to a present-moment anchor like their breathing.
Through this process, athletes can free themselves from judgments that
might unnecessarily determine their limits. Beall paralleled mindfulness
practice to physical practice by saying it is like a "drill for your mind."
He remarked that coaches often tell athletes that sport is 95 percent
mental, but they do not seem to know *how* to train the mind. The benefit
of mindfulness training is that it targets concrete skills in present-moment
awareness and nonjudgmental acceptance that athletes can practice to
benefit their performance.

After the work of Kabat-Zinn and colleagues (1985), it would be nearly
two decades before more rigorous empirical studies of mindfulness-based
interventions for athletes were conducted, and high-quality, controlled
mindfulness research within sport is still in its infancy. Although a few
outcome studies have been conducted by other researchers (Aherne et al.
2011; Baltzell & Akhtar, 2014; Baltzell et al., 2014; Bernier et al., 2009;
John, Verma, & Khanna, 2011), two mindfulness approaches created
specifically for athletes have received the most empirical support: Gardner
and Moore's Mindfulness-Acceptance-Commitment approach (2004, 2006,
2007; see Chapter 6 in this volume) and our own MSPE intervention
(Kaufman et al., 2009; Kaufman et al., in press).

Overview and Empirical Support of MSPE

Based on a mutual interest in mindfulness and a curiosity about the potential applications of mindfulness in sport, Kaufman and Glass developed the initial manual for MSPE in 2006, building upon the innovative work of Kabat-Zinn and colleagues (1985). MSPE was designed to be adaptable to any sport of focus and was originally structured as a four-session program, meeting once weekly for two hours. Although the program was intended for a group format, elements of MSPE can easily be used in work with individual athletes. The updated version of the MSPE manual (Kaufman et al., in press), reflecting an expanded six-session program with meetings occurring once weekly for ninety minutes, will be detailed in this chapter. Having more but shorter sessions was thought to facilitate the development of an ongoing mindfulness routine by providing additional weeks of access to MSPE instructors and fellow participants while also better accommodating the often busy schedules of athletes.

Description of MSPE

The expanded version of MSPE includes original scripts for all mindfulness exercises. Audio recordings of these exercises, as well as line drawings of the yoga poses, are provided to guide the assigned home practice. The goal of MSPE is to teach a variety of mindfulness skills and, through systematic practice, help athletes learn to apply those skills both to their sport performances and their everyday lives. Time is spent at the outset of the training on delineating the rationale behind MSPE. This explanation is adaptable to any sport of focus and should be tailored to include relevant quotations about mindfulness or similar mental states from authors, coaches, and athletes in that sport. Core MSPE exercises are taught in a sequence that progressively moves athletes from sedentary mindfulness practice to mindfulness while in motion (e.g., during yoga poses, when walking), culminating in an applied sport-specific meditation that builds the necessary bridge between cultivating mindfulness skills and applying them during performances.

Empirical Support for MSPE

Three published studies from our sport psychology lab have demonstrated the initial effectiveness of the MSPE program. Using a sample of thirty-two archers and golfers, Kaufman and colleagues (2009) found significant increases in overall trait mindfulness and in optimism (an aspect of sport confidence) for archers, aspects of state and trait mindfulness for golfers, and in state flow for the whole sample of athletes. Additionally, post-workshop feedback suggested that the athletes felt the MSPE workshop had positively impacted their sport performance, especially by improving focus on the task at hand, and that they expected additional benefit in the future. De Petrillo and colleagues (2009) administered MSPE to a community sample of twenty-five long-distance runners and found a significant increase in acting with awareness (a dimension of trait mindfulness) and in state mindfulness, as well as significant decreases in aspects of perfectionism and sport-related anxiety.

Moreover, it appears that athletes who participated in an MSPE intervention continue to experience benefits over time. Specifically, in a one-year follow-up of participants from both studies, the athletes showed significant decreases in task-irrelevant thoughts and task-related worries from pre-test to follow-up, as well as a significant increase in the ability to act with awareness (an aspect of trait mindfulness) and overall trait mindfulness (Thompson et al., 2011). Additionally, both the golfers and runners reported sport performance in the year following the workshop that had significantly improved compared to their best performance in the year prior to the workshop and indicated at least moderate confidence that the MSPE workshop had impacted their sport performance (mean ratings of 5.48 on a scale from 1 [not at all confident] to 10 [very confident]). The runners' performance improvement was associated with increases in mindfulness. Finally, participants reported an increase in general life satisfaction, with several of them indicating enhanced enjoyment of their sport.

Responses to open-ended questions further elucidated how MSPE had influenced these athletes after one year. For example, a number of archers, golfers, and runners described feeling more confident and/or relaxed, greater enthusiasm and enjoyment of their sport, and/or improved ability to focus attention and ignore distractions. They most commonly attributed these changes to the body scan, yoga, and breathing meditation exercises they had learned in MSPE, which helped them better let events go, acknowledge and accept feelings, pay more attention to what was "going on" with their body, and appreciate the process (not just the outcome) of competition.

At follow-up, the majority of athletes (84 percent) reported at least occasional mindfulness practice in the year following the workshop, averaging once or twice a week. Mindful breathing/sitting meditation was the most frequently practiced exercise, but a few also did mindful yoga, the body scan, and the sport-specific meditation. Interestingly, a near-significant trend was found for the correlation between duration of weekly mindfulness practice and improvement in runners' mile times (r = 0.60). Lack of available time and difficulty establishing a practice routine were identified as the biggest obstacles to continued systematic practice of mindfulness skills.

These results suggest that MSPE has promise as an intervention that may contribute to both athlete well-being and sport performance. By sustaining a regular practice of mindfulness skills, athletes are likely to find benefits in and beyond their sport. It should be noted, however, that all of our published studies on MSPE to date have been open trials conducted with participants in the community who were specifically recruited for a research workshop. A trial of MSPE involving two NCAA Division I cross country teams (one served as a control) was recently completed, but as we will discuss later in this chapter, this study unfortunately encountered a variety of unanticipated methodological issues that impacted the validity of the results (see Pineau, 2014 for a complete discussion of these issues). Having learned some valuable lessons, which we will mention later in this chapter when we offer recommendations for using MSPE, we are currently launching an MSPE study that is a true randomized controlled trial with student-athletes on our campus who individually volunteered to participate. This study, conducted in collaboration with the athletic department, adds another dimension to the program. Whereas our previous MSPE research included homogeneous groups of athletes in a specific sport (e.g., archery, running), we are now adapting MSPE for use with groups comprised of athletes from multiple sports (e.g., field hockey, lacrosse, baseball, swimming, tennis, track).

MSPE Protocol

Session 1

In the first session of MSPE, athletes are oriented to understanding mindfulness. They are given a rationale for why awareness and acceptance are important to sport performance and the development of mindfulness skills. At first glance, common features of athletic culture, such as striving, competition, and self-improvement, may seem incompatible with a program that is based on principles of nonstriving and self-acceptance. It is thus important to present an accessible rationale to athlete-participants early on in MSPE, which can help promote openness to a training style that may be entirely novel. In describing the potential clinical benefits of mindfulness, Siegel (2007) spoke to a core component of this rationale: acceptance of one's situation can lessen the internal conflict that may emerge when expectations of how life should be fail to match how life actually is. In sport, athletes are constantly ensnared in this tension between expectations and reality, as they are in a perpetual state of competition, either with opponents or with themselves, in an attempt to improve.

While many athletes believe that this tension drives them to improve, some evidence suggests that the negative self-evaluative thoughts that can be generated from this process actually impede sport performance (e.g., Klinger et al., 1981). Given this potential, MSPE begins presenting mindfulness by introducing the concept of nonjudgment. A sport-specific example of how judgmental, self-evaluative thoughts can interfere with focusing on the task at hand is offered to illustrate the importance of this concept. Depending on the sport(s) of focus, the example chosen may highlight different obstacles to performance (e.g., fatigue, boredom, tension, self-criticism) and the related mindfulness skills that address these obstacles (e.g., interoceptive awareness, focus, relaxation, letting go). A crucial point made here is that getting hung up on a past mistake or worrying about a potential future outcome takes athletes out of their present-moment experience. This is important because it is only in the present that athletes have the opportunity to impact performance.

In addition to enabling athletes to explore the power of nonjudgment, MSPE helps explain the connection between mindfulness and flow. Most athletes have experienced or at least heard of being in flow or the zone, so the possibility that mindfulness training can help facilitate this optimal performance state further supports the rationale for MSPE.

Each MSPE session includes both didactic and experiential components. In this first session, once the rationale for the program has been covered, the athletes are introduced to two basic mindfulness exercises: a mindful eating exercise and a breathing meditation. Similar to MBSR, mindful eating is used at the beginning of MSPE to contrast mindful and nonmindful actions (since eating is often done mindlessly), as well as to provide a metaphor for how mindfulness can be incorporated into daily life (e.g., athletics). A breathing meditation is the next exercise because, as Kabat-Zinn (1990) explained, it is the heart of mindfulness practice. This meditation appears throughout MSPE and is expanded in later sessions. Home practice is also assigned for the days between sessions. Participants receive audio recordings of the exercise scripts to guide their home practice, along with a Daily Mindfulness Log in which to document relevant home practice experiences (adapted from that used in MBCT; Segal et al., 2002). The athletes are asked to do between ten and forty minutes of formal mindfulness practice each day over the course of MSPE, and the amount of home practice starts small and increases as the sessions progress.

Session 1 concludes with a discussion about being on "automatic pilot." This concept of mindlessness implies automatically responding to a situation without awareness of one's behavior. Exploration of this topic reemphasizes the notion that present-moment awareness gives athletes the freedom to choose how they respond to the various stimuli, both internal and external, that can impact their sport performance.

Session 2

Every MSPE session, subsequent to the first, begins with a discussion of the home practice from the previous week. Each of these discussions has a particular focus aimed at addressing typical reactions to beginning mindfulness work. In the second session, the focus is on common obstacles to building a mindfulness practice, including finding available time, experiencing feelings of boredom, having self-critical thoughts about practicing "correctly," and misperceiving what it means to calm the mind. Athletes talk about their own unique reactions to the first week of meditation practice. Regardless of the content of this discussion, or of any other discussion in the program, it is crucial for leaders to model in their responses the mindful qualities of compassion, nonjudgment, nonreactivity, and acceptance.

After processing the athletes' experiences with their home practice, the session transitions to a didactic activity in which applications of MSPE to the sport(s) of focus are more deeply explored, with a focus on how mindfulness can help improve sport performance. Sport-specific examples are used to demonstrate how the skills of concentrating, relaxing, letting go of thoughts, forming key associations (i.e., choosing environmental cues to serve as reminders to stay present focused), and finding harmony and flow (i.e., performing in rhythm with a quiet but focused mind) can facilitate enhanced sport performance.

The first experiential exercise of the second session is the body scan. Given the importance of interoceptive awareness in sports, this meditation is seen as a logical next step in the training. Body scan practice helps athletes become more attuned to the sensations in their bodies while also strengthening attentional flexibility, as they sequentially shift their attentional focus to various regions of the body. This exercise is typically performed while lying down in a quiet setting. Practicing this skill in a stationary position establishes the foundation for more dynamic practice (i.e., during sport participation) later in MSPE. Following the body scan, participants repeat the breathing meditation from the first session. Repeating this exercise throughout the MSPE program creates a relatable analogy for the athletes of mindfulness as a type of "mental workout" requiring reps to attain optimal results.

The second session concludes with the assignment of new home practice, and a discussion delving further into the "mental workout" analogy. After a week of MSPE, athletes are likely familiar with how difficult it can be to maintain mindful attention, even for short periods of time, and may be feeling some related frustrations. This discussion reframes the experience of a wandering mind as not a failure, but an opportunity. Every time the mind wanders and attention is returned to the anchor of that meditation (e.g., the breath), it is the equivalent of doing one more mindfulness rep in a mental workout. Over time, these reps help build a stronger "mindfulness muscle."

Session 3

Session 3 opens with a discussion focused on "I can't" reactions (e.g., "I can't stay focused," "I can't relax") that frequently emerge during the early stages of mindfulness practice. This discussion highlights the presence and potential impact of expectations. Sport tends to be an outcome-oriented domain where internal and external expectations of success are high. While athletes are generally aware of such expectations regarding their sports, group leaders can point out how similar reactions may be playing out in the MSPE training (e.g., identifying how the mindfulness practice itself and/or performance during mindfulness exercises is not meeting some expectation). This exchange can help athletes recognize such omnipresent and potentially interfering expectations. Making this connection also serves as an opportunity to revisit the apparent conflict mentioned in Session 1 between the competitive nature of sport and the nonstriving nature of mindfulness, providing another example of the potential benefits of accepting one's present experience, not by stopping or avoiding certain expectations or self-critical thoughts, but by learning to let them go without overidentifying with or reacting to them.

The first experiential exercise in the third session of MSPE is mindful yoga, which begins the transition from sedentary to motive mindfulness practice. Mindful yoga gives athletes the chance to execute the mindfulness skills they have been developing through the body scan and the breathing meditation (e.g., interoceptive awareness, focused attention) while in motion. Participants are encouraged to be fully aware and present in their bodies during a series of nineteen beginner-level poses while accepting the limitations they may encounter in any given moment. Session 3 also includes a longer breathing meditation, "adding weight to the bar," so to speak, and enhancing sustained attention as the reps are continued.

When the home practice for Session 3 is assigned, the group leader acknowledges that participants are being asked to invest more of their time each week on MSPE exercises outside of sessions. Again, the parallel to physical training is made where the volume and intensity of the workload increases as the program progresses.

Session 3 wraps up with a discussion of how participants can begin to incorporate informal mindfulness practice into their daily lives. By this point in the training, the athletes are familiar with how to use physical sensations as an avenue toward mindful awareness. They are therefore encouraged to expand upon this knowledge by, for example, eating meals or brushing their teeth mindfully. An intention of emphasizing informal practice is to further the process of mindfulness skills becoming more easily accessible during sport performances.

Session 4

The home practice discussion in Session 4 of MSPE is focused on the concept of attachment. After now practicing mindfulness for a handful of weeks, the athletes may have begun to notice some pleasurable benefits of the exercises (e.g., mental calmness, physical relaxation). They may also have started thinking of particular meditation experiences as either "good" or "bad." This discussion can help athletes to see how they can become attached to certain expected outcomes. Whether participants are disappointed if they are not more relaxed following meditation or they continue to have difficulties finding time to practice, there is an attachment to a version of reality that they have created (e.g., that meditation "should" result in relaxation, or that a schedule is entirely inflexible). When people are unaware of their attachments, they often react habitually to experiences, likely robbing them of the opportunity to respond in different, possibly more adaptive ways. Direct parallels are made to sport performance, as automatic, habitual reactions in a given sport scenario can limit athletes' abilities to respond in an optimal way while competing.

Mindful yoga is again practiced in Session 4, giving participants another opportunity to practice the postures with the guidance of MSPE leaders. For this iteration, emphasis is placed on the skill of acceptance. Specifically, athletes are invited to explore their limits of flexibility without judgment. They are also encouraged to think about the "limits" they have previously reached in their sport (e.g., personal bests) and how, over time, these "limits" have changed. In other words, a "limit," much like a thought or a feeling, does not represent an absolute reality, but is only a condition of a given moment. Following the mindful yoga, the walking meditation is introduced. This exercise continues the progression of mindfulness in motion and introduces participants to new present-moment attentional anchors that may more closely resemble the actions involved in their sport. The final experiential piece of this session is a brief breathing meditation, again returning to the core of mindfulness training, this time as a "cool-down" exercise.

Session 4 concludes with the assignment of home practice and a more in-depth discussion of acceptance, which is explained as a mindful reaction to attachments. People who are highly achievement-oriented can sometimes misinterpret acceptance as resignation and fear that accepting the conditions of a present moment will translate into loss of motivation to improve. Thus, time is spent reviewing the differences between these concepts. It is explained that acceptance of certain conditions happens in a particular moment and does not necessarily mean that one is resigned to the continuation of those conditions in future moments. On the contrary, present-moment acceptance allows people to let go of the judgments, expectations, and attachments that often inhibit change, opening them up to the possibility of choosing to act differently.

Session 5

Session 5 begins with a home practice discussion that is again focused on acceptance. In particular, this discussion emphasizes the acceptance-based principle of nonstriving. Athletes are encouraged to notice the distinction between accomplishing true acceptance and attempting to use mindfulness techniques to achieve a desired outcome (e.g., "I notice I am stressed and I can tolerate this experience," versus, "I notice I am stressed so I will meditate to relax"). This discussion directly addresses the paradox inherent in applying mindfulness within a competitive environment and clarifies with sport-specific examples how it is possible to both be mindful and have goals. Specifically, one can be aware of a goal (e.g., setting a personal-best time in a race) without trying to alter circumstances from what they are (e.g., accepting that the course terrain is poor). Fighting "what is" by attempting to wish or force it to be something different can end up pushing one further from a goal being pursued (e.g., worrying excessively about the potential impact of terrain conditions can derail an athlete from achieving a personal-best time).

The experiential portion of Session 5 starts with a breathing meditation that is further expanded from previous practice. Whereas earlier breathing meditations were entirely guided, this version introduces the wrinkle of an extended period of silence. This new element adds yet more load to the core "mental muscles" being built throughout MSPE and the ability to observe and accept thoughts and experiences. Following this extended sit, the athletes get moving with a review of the walking meditation and then an introduction to the most applied meditation in MSPE, the sport-specific meditation. The sport-specific meditation gives participants the opportunity to utilize fundamental movements in their sport as a meditative experience. It is the culmination of practice in motion to this point, an opportunity to develop sport-specific anchors for their attention, and the bridge to full integration of mindfulness into their sport perform-ances. For example, runners perform a "running meditation" involving mindfully attending to various aspects of the running process like breathing and what is occurring with their gaze, shoulders, arms, hands, legs, and feet while jogging and gradually picking up speed. The exercises for this session again conclude with a brief breathing meditation that serves as a cool-down.

Session 5 wraps up with the assignment of home practice and a discus-sion of mindful awareness as a route to choice, specifically with regard to self-care. Awareness of what triggers stress and promotes relaxation can allow people to make mindful activity choices that are more likely to increase well-being. Parallels are again made to sport performance in that reduced overall life stress may protect athletes from detrimental states such as burnout.

Session 6

In the home practice discussion of the final session of MSPE, the athletes are asked to reflect on not only their recent practice, but also their overall experience throughout the training. They are invited to observe any changes that have occurred in their mindfulness skills, their thoughts about mindfulness practice, as well as differences in their sport performance and their lives beyond sport (e.g., academics, work, and social relationships). Building a sustained mindfulness practice routine beyond the MSPE program is also addressed, and how, much like athletes may select a sport or a physical training regimen that feels right to them, mindfulness practice can be tailored to each individual's preferences.

No new exercises are introduced in Session 6. Rather, the sport-specific meditation and the body scan are repeated. Returning to these experiential exercises gives the athletes an opportunity to observe changes in their practice and reactions over the past week (the sport-specific meditation) and since early in the training (the body scan). Other major mindfulness programs such as MBSR and MBCT also bookend training with the body scan. Segal and colleagues (2002) noted that it is not uncommon for people to have a different experience of this exercise at the end of MBCT than they did at the start, so reintroducing the body scan in the final session is a valuable chance to highlight the evolution that has occurred over the course of the training. As in the past few sessions, the experiential portion of the session concludes with a brief breathing meditation.

MSPE ends with an invitation to reflect on the mindfulness training that participants have just completed. This processing allows for a final reminder of how important nonjudgmental acceptance of an experience can be and how fighting certain unpleasant events (such as saying good-bye) can ironically serve to exacerbate these experiences. Finally, tips for continuing a systematic mindfulness practice beyond MSPE are offered. MSPE sessions are framed as just a starting point for athletes to continue to reap benefits both within and beyond sport. Among the tips provided are designating a specific time and place for daily meditation practice, making even small commitments to practice (e.g., daily for two weeks, or even for just five minutes a day), and personalizing a practice routine. The athletes are also asked to consider how they can continue incorporating mindfulness into their sport performances and other aspects of their daily lives.

Getting the Most out of MSPE

Having described the foundations, empirical support, and session-by-session protocol for MSPE, the final segment of this chapter offers specific suggestions for how both MSPE group leaders and athlete-participants can maximize their experiences of the program. These recommendations are based on what we have learned through training various groups of athletes in MSPE and by utilizing elements of the protocol with individual clients. For MSPE leaders, we suggest (1) investing ample time for rapport building and education with participants before beginning the training, (2) developing a personal mindfulness practice that combines both formal and informal elements of mindfulness, and (3) obtaining competence both in delivering interventions to groups and in working with athlete populations. For MSPE participants, we suggest (1) considering how mindfulness practice can find a place in existing training routines, (2) examining daily schedules to see where there is room to pause from the constant stream of activity, and (3) finding patience for the process of learning a new skill set that may be wholly unlike anything else practiced to date. What follows is a detailed exploration of each of these recommendations, along with some examples to illustrate their importance.

Recommendations for MSPE Leaders

Presence and rapport

Our initial studies of MSPE included participants from the community who shared a common sport, but more recent work has sought to extend the program to intact sports teams and athletic programs. In the latter cases, MSPE leaders should first endeavor to establish a presence with the athlete-participants by attending team meetings, practices, or competitions. The reduction in resistance that accompanies athletes being familiar with a sport psychologist prior to engaging in a treatment or consultation relationship has been well documented (e.g., Andersen, Van Raalte, & Brewer, 2001; Stapleton et al., 2010). In fact, Stapleton and colleagues (2010) identified "hanging out" and "face time" as critical skills to effective applied sport psychology. Psychologists working in domains other than athletics might understandably flinch at such skills being labeled as key aspects of a job description. However, the reality is that sports environments tend to be closed-off systems until one earns status as an insider, and referrals to sport psychologists for even traditional psychological skills training like goal setting, self-talk, and visualization still commonly carry a stigma. It is reasonable to expect that this stigma could be magnified with a newer intervention such as MSPE, as athletes may have less familiarity with the concept of mindfulness and may not have previously considered how meditation practice could benefit their sport experiences.

A salient example of how a lack of pre-program rapport building can undermine MSPE occurred when we trained an NCAA Division I cross country team in our area (as part of the study mentioned earlier in this chapter that faced this and other methodological issues). Unlike previous iterations of MSPE, we offered our program to coaches for their teams rather than contacting athletes directly. Although we did meet at length with the coaching staff, we assumed that providing an introduction of ourselves and mindfulness during a preseason camp meeting was sufficient for the athletes. The next time the runners saw us was at Session 1 of the training, and we proceeded to meet with them once a week for ninety minutes until the six sessions were complete. We had no interactions with the runners either between sessions or after a planned follow-up assessment.

While this schedule was efficient for us (traveling from another part of the city) and the coaches (wanting to preserve their team's practice routine), many runners never really warmed to us or the demands we were placing on them through the training. They were reluctant to participate in discussions or to complete the home practice, and, toward the end of the program, there were a few instances of athletes flatly refusing to perform certain meditations. On several assessment measures taken before and after the intervention, there were no changes, and a post-training feedback questionnaire yielded informative explanations. Many of the runners spoke to the time imposition they felt coming from us as outsiders, and there were suggestions that "being more involved with the athletes" or "overseeing more [team] practices" would have been beneficial. In fact, members of the team invited the MSPE group leaders to watch a home race on one occasion, but scheduling conflicts prevented attendance. Maybe this was just a particularly resistant team, but it seems reasonable to suspect that putting in more "face time" before and during the MSPE training could have made a significant difference in the program's effectiveness. This was a valuable learning experience for us and emphasized the importance of rapport building with athletes prior to beginning an MSPE program, perhaps especially in situations where athletes do not clearly self-select for the training.

It is also worthy of mention that cultivating a presence within a team can allow leaders to observe specific performance-related behaviors that could then be addressed during MSPE discussions. Being able to infuse such personalized material can further facilitate athlete engagement with the training and the connectivity that is so crucial to both sport psychology (Andersen et al., 2001) and mindfulness-based interventions (Bowen & Kurz, 2012).

Establishing a personal mindfulness practice
Another recommendation for MSPE leaders is to establish their own routine of mindfulness practice. Segal and colleagues (2002) explained that

the necessity for such a routine is due to the inevitability that participants in mindfulness training will experience difficulties that cannot be addressed with intellectual knowledge alone. Leaders must be able to embody the skills that they are inviting the participants to cultivate. For instance, an MSPE leader needs to be capable of responding mindfully in a group discussion if an athlete shares a judgmental reaction to a particular exercise or meditation performance. It is likely that one needs to have an actual experience of mindfulness practice to achieve the deep level of understanding that can come from a felt sense (Gendlin, 1978) of it, based on bodily awareness beyond verbal expression. MSPE includes training in formal meditation exercises (e.g., body scan, sport meditation) as well as in how to apply the mindfulness skills learned in an informal way during sport performances and everyday life. It is essential that leaders be adept at both formal and informal mindfulness practice, so that they can most effectively serve as guides for the development of skills in awareness and acceptance throughout the training process.

We will use the path traveled by one of this chapter's coauthors to illustrate how this type of mindfulness practice routine can be built. Keith Kaufman began his own practice in graduate school after attending a mindfulness workshop led by Jon Kabat-Zinn. His experimentations over the years have taught him that the best time for his formal practice is at night, in the hour before bedtime that tends to be most quiet and least likely to have interruptions. To keep the routine fresh, Keith uses a mixture of guided and silent meditations. For the guided meditations, he has assembled a catalogue of recordings that contain different exercises as well as voice styles in terms of tone, accent, and gender.

For informal mindfulness practice, Keith has developed certain "key moments" within the flow of his daily life in which he consciously tunes in to his present-moment experiences, such as while brushing his teeth, between client sessions, and after his commute through rush-hour traffic. Keith also practices exercising mindfully. His primary mode of exercise is distance running, and he has found both great joy and benefit to using his "observing mind" to be present with his body while engaged in this activity. A number of fellow runners have wondered how he can run without headphones or conversing, but he finds that such distractions take away from his fulfillment on the trail and limit his control over performance. Keith has entered flow states numerous times when running with mindful awareness.

Having lived many years as a Type-A personality, one of Keith's main challenges in his mindfulness practice has been letting go of any self-criticisms that emerge when deviations from his routine occur. For instance, he has learned to be compassionate toward himself if he misses a formal practice session or fails to check in after a client appointment. Instead, he tries to observe the circumstances as they are and to find gratitude in the renewed opportunity to be mindful in his current moment of life. Keith's path is just one example. It is important for MSPE leaders to consider their own unique schedules and challenges to find a personalized practice routine that works for them.

Competence with groups and athletes

A final recommendation for MSPE leaders is to have competence in administering group interventions and in working specifically with athletes, so that they have an appropriate knowledge base before attempting to run an MSPE program. Segal and colleagues (2002) provide a parallel cautionary statement in their MBCT manual that leaders should have previous training in counseling or psychotherapy, with some proficiency in delivering cognitive and group interventions. Also, Hack (2005) suggests that mental health professionals wishing to do sport psychology work should obtain specialized education and training to properly understand the science and culture of sport, as well as how to apply that knowledge to athletes, coaches, and others in the athletics domain.

Aspiring leaders can develop these underlying competencies through a combination of course work, continuing education, supervision, and consultation. In their article addressing the ethical issues affecting sport psychology practice, Stapleton and colleagues (2010) advise that pursuing each of these learning avenues, not just one, is key to building true competence.

Recommendations for MSPE Participants

Emphasizing mental training

Turning attention to program participants, one very important consideration for athletes involved in MSPE is how to make room for mental practice within their existing sport training routine. It has been our experience that asking a room full of athletes whether mental factors are significant to sport performance brings near-universal agreement. However, then inquiring about what the athletes do on a regular basis to train their minds for sport performance is met largely with silence and blank stares. As Weinberg and Gould (2011) note, athletes and coaches generally know that physical skills need to be practiced and refined through thousands of repetitions, but there seems to be less awareness that psychological skills also need to be practiced systematically. They comment that mental skills, rather than physical skills, are primarily responsible for the day-to-day performance fluctuations that all athletes face, yet many serious athletes devote at least twenty hours weekly to physical practice and little or no time to exclusive mental practice.

As mentioned previously, when we were developing MSPE we consulted with Bruce Beall, the rowing coach and Olympian involved with Kabat-Zinn and colleagues' (1985) early investigation of mindfulness training in sport. Coach Beall (personal communication, March 7, 2006) conceptualized the process of mindfulness training as "mental weightlifting," an analogy we love because it uses language that athletes can easily relate to and captures the sense of dedication that is required for building mindfulness skills. To extend this analogy further, the mind is like any muscle in the human body in that it needs systematic training to increase in strength and coordination. MSPE offers more than many traditional sport psychology interventions because it can essentially function as a step-by-step guide to building mental fitness. A key to its successful use, however, is athletes' willingness to invest in a form of training (i.e., meditation) that likely is wholly different from what they have done for their sport in the past.

To illustrate the effects of "mental weightlifting" within MSPE, we will describe the case of Craig (a pseudonym), a competitive bowler who participated in private sport psychology services. Craig reported feeling that there was a "hole" in his game that he had been unable to plug by engaging in additional physical practice. He was experiencing distraction and bodily tension during his performances, and no amount of technique refinement was making a difference. Craig did not receive the full MSPE protocol as prescribed in the manual, since it is typically delivered in a group format, but certain exercises lent themselves quite well to this individual work.

After building foundational mindfulness skills such as nonjudgmental awareness of breathing and sensations (e.g., sounds, smells, physical sensations), Craig was introduced to the MSPE sport-specific meditation. He identified particular anchors for his attention during his bowling motion, such as the feeling of the ball in his hand during his approach, and then began to systematically practice this meditation, whether he was at training, a recreational league, or a tournament. Craig kept a log of his mental practice and shared his experiences of the meditation in his sport psychology sessions. While he found himself more fatigued initially, trying to maintain that level of concentration during his performances, he slowly noticed his limits changing and observed improvements in his focus, scores, and enjoyment of bowling. Craig had come to treatment recognizing that physical practice alone was insufficient and looking to try something totally new. His openness ultimately allowed him to change his relationship to his sport and to revitalize his performance.

Find time to be mindful

A second recommendation for MSPE participants is to assess their daily schedule to determine when there is space to pause from the constant stream of activity. One of the key points made in the *TIME Magazine* cover story on the "Mindful Revolution" mentioned earlier (Pickert, 2014) is that we live in an era of hyperconnectivity, where it can feel impossible to take breaks or fully inhabit the task at hand, so that there is a perpetual sense of not having enough time. Pickert suggested that mindfulness can provide an antidote, precisely because the practice challenges us to slow down, unplug, and devote time to the kind of focused attention required for optimal experience. Of course, convincing athletes, who often have tightly packed schedules, of the value of "less is more" or investing precious minutes in nonphysical training can be difficult. Weinberg and Gould (2011) listed perceived lack of time as a top reason why athletes neglect mental training, and the post-MSPE feedback we have received from participants consistently pinpoints time restrictions as the major impediment to ongoing mindfulness practice.

Although there is little doubt that many MSPE participants will enter the training already feeling pinched for time, as when learning any new skill, investing time for deliberate practice is necessary to build proficiency and benefit most from the program. K. Anders Ericsson, whose work has famously become associated with the "10,000 hours" or "10 year" rule to the achievement of expertise, wrote that commitment to deliberate practice distinguishes elite performers from the masses of others who struggle to meet their performance demands (Ericsson, Krampe, & Tesch-Romer, 1993). The good news is that, in our experience, careful examination of a schedule often reveals more time available for formal and informal mindfulness practice than is initially thought, even if only for a few minutes at each opportunity. Also encouraging is the common observation regarding time management that people find the time for activities that are important to them, so a belief in the value of mental skills training can lead athletes to make time for this form of practice (Weinberg & Gould, 2011).

Many competitive athletes face time-management challenges, but we have found that these challenges can be particularly daunting in certain sports. For instance, Keith has worked with a number of swimmers whose schedules might look like this: awake at 5 AM for practice before school, then a full day of classes, followed by a second practice in the afternoon, then home in the evening for dinner and school work, and finally to bed for a few hours before starting the cycle all over again. Such athletes might want to participate in a program such as MSPE but feel stumped about how to find any time for mindfulness practice. It is beneficial to identify even a few moments these athletes have to stop and connect with the present, such as in the locker room before swim practice, at study hall, or in the minutes before bed. Once athletes realize that room for mindfulness exists, they can begin to build a more regular practice routine into their schedules. Prioritization exercises – for example, using Blonna's (2007) model of time management – have also been helpful. This technique involves assigning each daily activity a priority status. If athletes label MSPE skills practice as an activity that "must get done," it significantly raises the odds that mindfulness practice will be incorporated into their day.

Be patient
A final recommendation for athletes is to have patience with the process of learning and implementing MSPE skills. We live in an increasingly outcome-focused world, where there can be tremendous pressure to achieve and to do so immediately. Perhaps nowhere is this trend more salient than in the world of sports, where winning or losing can totally overshadow the richer journey of playing. For example, in the wake of the 2014 NCAA men's basketball national championship game, University of Kentucky star Aaron Harrison was asked about his buzzer-beating heroics in three successive games that had propelled his team to the brink of a title. His response was that, with Kentucky's loss in the championship, his clutch shots "don't mean anything now" (Prisbell, 2014). Granted, this quote came in the emotional moments after the game, but they capture the overwhelming value placed on outcome at the expense of a much larger process that could otherwise be incredibly satisfying.

The odds are good that many MSPE participants will not have practiced anything like mindfulness before, and certainly not in the context of training in their sport. It takes time to understand the nature of MSPE skills, how they can aid performance, and ways to include them within an existing sport routine. We have observed how crucial it can be for participants to remain open-minded and willing to tolerate the inevitable struggles that will occur. Mindfulness is ultimately a nonstriving endeavor, which is really outside the box within the realm of sports. Examples of well-documented concerns among new mindfulness participants, not just athletes, include wondering whether a skill is being executed perfectly and what, in the end, will be gained through the practice. Ironically, it is exactly that kind of unexamined striving toward outcome that can detract from the experience of MSPE.

We will illustrate this irony using one of the core MSPE skills, mindfulness of breathing. An important element of this meditation is breathing diaphragmatically, meaning from the abdomen. Striving to perform this skill "correctly" can lead participants to tense up, triggering the body's stress response, which inhibits the ability to breathe in this fashion. We have actually observed participants get so concerned about their inability to breathe diaphragmatically right away that they began to experience intense physical symptoms of anxiety. It can take time to discover the rhythm of abdominal breathing, and those participants who are patient with that process, recognizing and accepting their desire to "do it right," may be the ones who more easily let go of their striving and end up finding success the soonest.

Conclusion

Mindfulness is soaring in popularity, both within psychology and society at large. The word has gotten out in sport as well, and interest in how this paradigm-shifting training approach could benefit athlete performance and wellness is growing. MSPE is among the small group of sport-specific, mindfulness-based interventions that have emerged, and the empirical support thus far for MSPE has been promising. Adapted from and expanding on the traditions of MBSR and MBCT, the MSPE program uses a unique progression of training to help athletes cultivate the "mental muscle" to be able to participate and compete in their sport mindfully and thus maximize performance, flow, and enjoyment. By following the MSPE protocol and recommendations for how to approach this training, participants may access an entirely new level of their potential and rediscover what they love about being an athlete.

REFERENCES

Aherne, C., Moran, A. P., and Lonsdale, C. (2011). The effect of mindfulness training on athletes' flow: An initial investigation. *Sport Psychologist*, 25(2), 177–189.

Alessi, L. E. (1995). "Breakaway into the zone": A phenomenological investigation from the athlete's perspective. *Dissertation Abstracts International*, 56 (20B), 1087.

Andersen, M. B., Van Raalte, J. L., and Brewer, B. W. (2001). Sport psychology service delivery: Staying ethical while keeping loose. *Professional Psychology: Research and Practice*, 32(1), 12–18. doi: 10.1037//0735-7028.32.1.12

Athletes who meditate: Kobe Bryant & other sports stars who practice mindfulness. (2013, May 30). *Huffington Post*. Retrieved from www.huffingtonpost.com/2013/05/30/ athletes-who-meditate-kobe-bryant_n_3347089.html

Baltzell, A. L., and Akhtar, V. L. V. (2014). Mindfulness Meditation Training for Sport (MMTS) intervention: Impact of MMTS with Division I female athletes. *Journal of Happiness and Wellbeing*, 2(2), 160–173.

Baltzell, A. L., Caraballo, N., Chipman, K., and Hayden, L. (2014). A qualitative study of the Mindfulness Meditation Training for Sport (MMTS): Division I female soccer players' experience. *Journal of Clinical Sport Psychology*. 8, 221–244.

Bernier, M., Thienot, E., Codron, R., and Fournier, J. F. (2009). Mindfulness and acceptance approaches in sport performance. *Journal of Clinical Sport Psychology*, 25(4), 320–333.

Birrer, D., Röthlin, P., and Morgan, G. (2012). Mindfulness to enhance athletic performance: Theoretical considerations and possible impact mechanisms. *Mindfulness*, 3(3), 235–246. doi: 10.1007/s12671-012-0109-2

Bishop, S. R., Lau, M., Shapiro, S., Carlson, L., Anderson, N. D., Carmody, J., . . . Devins, G. (2004). Mindfulness: A proposed operational definition. *Clinical Psychology: Science and Practice*, 11(3), 230–241. doi: 10.1093/clipsy. bph077

Blonna, R. (2007). *Coping with stress in a changing world* (4th ed.). New York, NY: McGraw-Hill.

Bohlmeijer, E., Prenger, R., Taal, E., and Cuijpers, P. (2010). The effects of mindfulness-based stress reduction therapy on mental health of adults with a chronic medical disease: A meta-analysis. *Journal of Psychosomatic Research*, 68(6), 539–544. doi: 10.1016/j.jpsychores.2009.10.005

Bowen, S., and Kurz, A. S. (2012). Between-session practice and therapeutic alliance as predictors of mindfulness after mindfulness-based relapse prevention. *Journal of Clinical Psychology*, 68(3), 236–245. doi: 10.1002/jclp.20855

Brooks, D. (2008, June 17). The frozen gaze. *New York Times*. Retrieved from www.nytimes.com

Cathcart, S., McGregor, M., and Groundwater, E. (2014). Mindfulness and flow in elite athletes. *Journal of Clinical Sport Psychology*, 8(2), 119–141. doi: 10.1123/jcsp.2014-0018

Chambers, R., Lo, B. C. Y., and Allen, N. B. (2008). The impact of intensive mindfulness training on attentional control, cognitive style, and affect. *Cognitive Therapy and Research*, 32(3), 303–322. doi: 10.1007/s10608-007-9119-0

Chiesa, A., Calati, R., and Serretti, A. (2011). Does mindfulness training improve cognitive abilities? A systematic review of neuropsychological findings. *Clinical Psychology Review*, 31(3), 449–464. doi: 10.1016/j.cpr.2010.11.003

Chiesa, A., and Serretti, A. (2009). Mindfulness-based stress reduction for stress management in healthy people: A review and meta-analysis. *Journal of Alternative and Complementary Medicine*, 15(5), 593–600. doi:10.1089/acm.2008.0495

Cooper, A. (1998). *Playing in the zone: Exploring the spiritual dimensions of sports.* Boston, MA: Shambhala.

Cramer, H., Lauche, R., Paul, A., and Dobos, G. (2012). Mindfulness-based stress reduction for breast cancer – a systematic review and meta-analysis. *Current Oncology*, 19(5), e343-e352. doi: 10.3747/co.19.1016

Csikszentmihalyi, M. (1990). *Flow: The psychology of optimal experience.* New York, NY: Harper & Row.

(1997). *Finding flow: The psychology of engagement with everyday life.* New York, NY: Harper Collins.

De Petrillo, L. A., Kaufman, K. A., Glass, C. R., and Arnkoff, D. B. (2009). Mindfulness for long-distance runners: An open trial using Mindful Sport Performance Enhancement (MSPE). *Journal of Clinical Sport Psychology*, 3(4), 357–376.

Eberth, J., and Sedlmeier, P. (2012). The effects of mindfulness meditation: A meta-analysis. *Mindfulness*, 3(3), 174–189. doi: 10.1007/s12671-012-0101-x

Ericsson, K. A., Krampe, R. T., and Tesch-Romer, C. (1993). The role of deliberate practice in the acquisition of expert performance. *Psychological Review*, 100(3), 363–406. doi: 10.1037/0033-295X.100.3.363

Frewen, P. A., Evans, E. M., Maraj, N., Dozois, D. J. A., and Partridge, K. (2008). Letting go: Mindfulness and negative automatic thinking. *Cognitive Therapy and Research*, 32(6), 758–774. doi: 10.1007/s10608-007-9142-1

Gardner, F. L., and Moore, Z. E. (2004). A Mindfulness-Acceptance-Commitment-based approach to athletic performance enhancement: Theoretical considerations. *Behavior Therapy*, 35(4), 707–723. doi: 10.1016/S0005-7894(04)80016-9

(2006). *Clinical sport psychology.* Champaign, IL: Human Kinetics.

(2007). *The psychology of enhancing human performance: The Mindfulness-Acceptance-Commitment (MAC) approach.* New York, NY: Springer.

(2012). Mindfulness and acceptance models in sport psychology: A decade of basic and applied scientific advancement. *Canadian Psychology*, 53(4), 309–318. doi: 10.1037/a0030220

Gendlin, E. T. (1978). *Focusing.* New York, NY: Everest House.

Goyal, M., Singh, S., Sibinga, E. M. S., Gould, N. F., Rowland-Seymour, A., Sharma, R., . . . Haythornthwaite, J. A. (2014). Meditation programs for psychological stress and well-being: A systematic review and meta-analysis. *JAMA Internal Medicine*, 174(3), 357–368. doi: 10.1001/jamainternmed.2013.13018

Gratz, K. L., and Tull, M. T. (2010). Emotion regulation as a mechanism of change in acceptance- and mindfulness-based treatments. In R. A. Baer (Ed.), *Assessing mindfulness & acceptance processes in clients: Illuminating the theory & practice of change* (pp. 107–133). Oakland, CA: New Harbinger.

Gregoire, C. (2014, February 4). *Actually TIME, this is what the "mindful revolution" really looks like. Huffington Post.* Retrieved from www.huffingtonpost.com

Grossman, P., Niemann, I., Schmidt, S., and Walach, H. (2004). Mindfulness-based stress reduction and health benefits: A meta-analysis. *Journal of Psychosomatic Research,* 57(1), 35–43. doi: 10.1016/S0022-3999(03)00573-7

Hack, B. (2005). Qualifications: Education and experience. In S. Murphy (Ed.), *The sport psych handbook* (pp. 293–304). Champaign, IL: Human Kinetics.

Hackney, A. C, Pearman, S. N., and Nowacki, J. M. (1990). Physiological profiles of overtrained and stale athletes: A review. *Journal of Applied Sport Psychology,* 2(1), 21–33. doi: 10.1080/10413209008406418

Hanin, Y. L. (2000). *Emotions in sport.* Champaign, IL: Human Kinetics.

Hatzigeorgiadis, A., and Biddle, S. J. H. (2001). Athletes' perceptions of cognitive interference during competition influences concentration and effort. *Anxiety, Stress, and Coping,* 14(4), 411–429. doi: 10.1080/10615800108248364

Hirschhorn, E. W., Glass, C. R., and Arnkoff, D. B. (2014). *Development and validation of the mindful thoughts questionnaire.* (Unpublished manuscript). Department of Psychology, The Catholic University of America, Washington, DC.

Hodgins, H. S., and Adair, K. C. (2010). Attentional processes and meditation. *Consciousness and Cognition: An International Journal,* 19(4), 872–878. doi: 10.1016/j.concog.2010.04.002

Hofmann, S. G., Sawyer, A. T., Witt, A. A., and Oh, D. (2010). The effect of mindfulness-based therapy on anxiety and depression: A meta-analytic review. *Journal of Consulting and Clinical Psychology,* 78(2), 169–183. doi: 10.1037/a0018555

Jackson, P. (2006). *Sacred hoops: Spiritual lessons of a hardwood warrior* (reissue ed.). New York, NY: Hyperion.

Jackson, S. A. (1995). Factors influencing the occurrence of flow state in elite athletes. *Journal of Applied Sport Psychology,* 7(2), 138–166. doi: 10.1080/10413209508406962

— (2000). Joy, fun, and flow state in sport. In Y. L. Hanin (Ed.), *Emotions in sport* (pp. 135–155). Champaign, IL: Human Kinetics.

Jackson, S. A., and Csikszentmihalyi, M. (1999). *Flow in sports.* Champaign, IL: Human Kinetics.

Jackson, S. A., Kimiecik, J. C., Ford, S. K., and Marsh, H. W. (1998). Psychological correlates of flow in sport. *Journal of Sport and Exercise Psychology,* 20(4), 358–378.

Jain, S., Shapiro, S. L., Swanick, S., Roesch, S. C., Mills, P. J., Bell, I., and Schwartz, G. E. R. (2007). A randomized controlled trial of mindfulness meditation versus relaxation training: Effects on distress, positive states of mind, rumination, and distraction. *Annals of Behavioral Medicine*, 33(1), 11–21. doi: 10.1207/s15324796abm3301_2

Jazaieri, H., Goldin, P. R., Werner, K., Ziv, M., and Gross, J. J. (2012). A randomized trial of MBSR versus aerobic exercise for social anxiety disorder. *Journal of Clinical Psychology*, 68(7), 715–731. doi: 10.1002/jclp.21863

John, S., Verma, S. K., and Khanna, G. L. (2011). The effect of mindfulness meditation on HPA-Axis in pre-competition stress in sports performance of elite shooters. *National Journal of Integrated Research in Medicine*, 2(3), 15–21.

Jones, M. V. (2003). Controlling emotions in sport. *Sport Psychologist*, 17(4), 471–486.

Kabat-Zinn, J. (1982). An outpatient program in behavioral medicine for chronic pain patients based on the practice of mindfulness meditation: Theoretical considerations and preliminary results. *General Hospital Psychiatry*, 4(1), 33–47. doi: 10.1016/0163-8343(82)90026-3

(1990). *Full catastrophe living: Using the wisdom of your body and mind to face stress, pain, and illness*. New York, NY: Delta.

(1994). *Wherever you go, there you are: Mindfulness meditation in everyday life*. New York, NY: Hyperion.

(2013). *Full catastrophe living: Using the wisdom of your body and mind to face stress, pain, and illness* (2nd ed.). New York, NY: Bantam.

Kabat-Zinn, J., Beall, B., and Rippe, J. (1985, June). *A systematic mental training program based on mindfulness meditation to optimize performance in collegiate and Olympic rowers*. Poster session presented at the World Congress in Sport Psychology, Copenhagen, Denmark.

Kaufman, K. A. (2008). *Evaluating mindfulness as a new approach to athletic performance enhancement* (Doctoral dissertation). Washington, DC: Catholic University of America. Retrieved from ProQuest (3340661)

Kaufman, K. A., and Glass, C. R. (2006). *Mindful Sport Performance Enhancement: A treatment manual for archers and golfers* (Unpublished manuscript). Department of Psychology, The Catholic University of America, Washington, DC.

Kaufman, K. A., Glass, C. R., and Arnkoff, D. B. (2009). Evaluation of Mindful Sport Performance Enhancement (MSPE): A new approach to promote flow in athletes. *Journal of Clinical Sport Psychology*, 4, 334–356.

Kaufman, K. A., Glass, C. R., and Pineau, T. R. (in press). *Mindful Sport Performance Enhancement (MSPE): A mindfulness-based mental training program for athletes*. Washington, DC: American Psychological Association.

Kee, Y. H., and Wang, C. K. J. (2008). Relationships between mindfulness, flow dispositions and mental skills adoption: A cluster analytic approach. *Psychology of Sport and Exercise*, 9(4), 393–411. doi: 10.1016/j.psychsport.2007.07.001

Khazan, O. (2014, February 7). How Olympians stay motivated. *The Atlantic*. Retrieved from www.theatlantic.com

Khoury, B., Lecomte, T., Fortin, G., Masse, M., Therien, P., Bouchard, V., . . . Hofmann, S. G. (2013). Mindfulness-based therapy: A comprehensive meta-analysis. *Clinical Psychology Review*, 33(6), 763–771. doi: 10.1016/j.cpr.2013.05.005

Klinger, E., Barta, S. G., and Glas, R. A. (1981). Thought content and gap time in basketball. *Cognitive Therapy and Research*, 5(1), 109–114. doi: 10.1007/BF01172331

Langer, E. J. (2000). Mindful learning. *Current Directions in Psychological Science*, 9(6), 220–223. doi: 10.1111/1467-8721.00099

Lauche, R., Cramer, H., Dobos, G., Langhorst, J., and Schmidt, S. (2013). A systematic review and meta-analysis of mindfulness-based stress reduction for the fibromyalgia syndrome. *Journal of Psychosomatic Research*, 73(6), 500–510. doi: 10.1016/j.psychores.2013.10.010

Lazarus, R. S. (2000). How emotions influence performance in competitive sports. *Sport Psychologist*, 14(3), 229–252.

Ledesma, D., and Kumano, H. (2009). Mindfulness-based stress reduction and cancer: A meta-analysis. *Psycho-Oncology*, 18(6), 571–579. doi: 10.1002/pon.1400

Memmert, D. (2009). Pay attention! A review of visual attentional expertise in sport. *International Review of Sport and Exercise Psychology*, 2(2), 119–138. doi: 10.1080/17509840802641372

Moore, A., and Malinowski, P. (2009). Meditation, mindfulness and cognitive flexibility. *Consciousness and Cognition*, 18(1), 176–186. doi: 10.1016/j.concog.2008.12.008

Moore, Z. E. (2009). Theoretical and empirical developments of the Mindfulness-Acceptance-Commitment (MAC) approach to performance enhancement. *Journal of Clinical Sport Psychology*, 3(4), 291–302.

Moran, A. P. (1996). *The psychology of concentration in sport performers: A cognitive analysis*. Hove, UK: Psychology Press.

Neoporent, L. (2014, January 30). Seattle Seahawks will have "ohm" team advantage: Head coach Pete Carroll encourages players to meditate. ABC News. Retrieved from http://abcnews.go.com/Health/seattle-seahawks-ohm-team-advantage/story?id=21614481

Pickert, K. (2014, February 3). The mindful revolution: Finding peace in a stressed-out, digitally dependent culture may just be a matter of thinking differently. *TIME Magazine*, 40–46.

Piet, J., and Hougaard, E. (2011). The effect of mindfulness-based cognitive therapy for prevention of relapse in recurrent major depressive disorder: A systematic review and meta-analysis. *Clinical Psychology Review*, 31(6), 1032–1040. doi: 10.1016/j.cpr.2011.05.002

Pijpers, J. R., Oudejans, R. R. D., Holsheimer, F., and Bakker, F. C. (2003). Anxiety-performance relationships in climbing: A process-oriented approach. *Psychology of Sport and Exercise*, 4(3), 283–304. doi: 10.1016/S1469-0292(02)00010-9

Pineau, T. R. (2014). *Effects of mindful sport performance enhancement (MSPE) on running performance and body image: Does self-compassion make a difference?* (Unpublished doctoral dissertation). Washington, DC: Catholic University of America.

Pineau, T. R., Glass, C. R., and Kaufman, K. A. (2014). Mindfulness in sport performance. In A. Ie, C. T. Ngnoumen, and E. J. Langer (Eds.), *The Wiley Blackwell handbook of mindfulness* (Vol. II, pp. 1004–1033). Chichester, UK: John Wiley & Sons.

Pineau, T. R., Glass, C. R., Kaufman, K. A., and Bernal, D. R. (2011). *Sport anxiety, cognitive interference, and perfectionism: Differential relations with the dimensions of mindfulness.* Poster presented at the meeting of the American Psychological Association, Washington DC.

____ (2014). Self- and team efficacy beliefs of rowers and their relation to mindfulness and flow. *Journal of Clinical Sport Psychology*, 8(2), 142–158. doi: 10.1123/jcsp.2014-0019

Prisbell, E. (2014, April 8). Remembering runner-up Kentucky already a thing of the past. *USA Today*. Retrieved from www.usatoday.com/story/sports/ncaab/2014/ college-basketball-final-four-kentucky-wildcats/7452917/

Rush, I. R. (2014, March 17). Athletes using meditation to improve performance. *Philadelpha Inquirer*. Retrieved from http://articles.philly.com/2014-03-17/news/48269271_1_meditation-jon-kabat-zinn-strength-coach

Russell, W. D. (2001). An examination of flow state occurrence in college athletes. *Journal of Sport Behavior*, 24(1), 83–107.

Salmon, P., Hanneman, S., and Harwood, B. (2010). Associative/dissociative cognitive strategies in sustained physical activity: Literature review and proposal for a mindfulness-based conceptual model. *Sport Psychologist*, 24(2), 127–156.

Schwanhausser, L. (2009). Application of the Mindfulness-Acceptance-Commitment (MAC) protocol with an adolescent springboard diver: The case of Steve. *Journal of Clinical Sport Psychology*, 3(4), 377–395.

Sedlmeier, P., Eberth, J., Schwarz, M., Zimmermann, D., Haarig, F., Jaeger, S., and Kunze, S. (2012). The psychological effects of meditation: A meta-analysis. *Psychological Bulletin*, 138(6), 1139–1171. doi: 10.1037/a0028168

Segal, Z. V., Williams, J. M. G., and Teasdale, J. D. (2002). *Mindfulness-based cognitive therapy for depression: A new approach to preventing relapse.* New York, NY: Guilford Press.

Siegel, D. J. (2007). *The mindful brain: Reflection and attunement in the cultivation of well-being.* New York, NY: W. W. Norton.

Smith, R. E. (1996). Performance anxiety, cognitive interference, and concentration enhancement strategies in sports. In I. G. Sarason, G. R. Pierce, and B. R. Sarason (Eds.), *Cognitive interference: Theories, methods, and findings* (pp. 261–283). Mahwah, NJ: Laurence Erlbaum Associates.

Stapleton, A. B., Hankes, D. M., Hays, K. F., and Parham, W. D. (2010). Ethical dilemmas in sport psychology: A dialogue on the unique aspects impacting practice. *Professional Psychology: Research and Practice*, 41(2), 143–152. doi: 10.1037/a0017976

Swann, C., Keegan, R. J., Piggott, D., and Crust, L. (2012). A systematic review of the experience, occurrence, and controllability of flow states in elite sport. *Psychology of Sport and Exercise*, 13(6), 807–819. doi: 10.1016/j.psychsport.2012.05.006

Thompson, R. W., Kaufman, K. A., De Petrillo, L. A., Glass, C. R., and Arnkoff, D. B. (2011). One year follow-up of mindful sport performance enhancement (MSPE) for archers, golfers, and runners. *Journal of Clinical Sport Psychology*, 5(2), 99–116.

van den Hurk, P. A. M., Giommi, F., Gielen, S. C., Speckens, A. E. M., and Barendregt, H. P. (2010). Greater efficiency in attentional processing related to mindfulness meditation. *Quarterly Journal of Experimental Psychology*, 63(6), 1168–1180. doi: 10.1080/17470210903249365

Wegner, D. M. (1994). Ironic processes of mental control. *Psychological Review*, 101(1), 34–52. doi: 10.1037/0033-295X.101.1.34

Weinberg, R., and Gould, D. (2011). *Foundations of sport and exercise psychology* (5th ed.). Champaign, IL: Human Kinetics.

Wenzlaff, R. M., and Wegner, D. M. (2000). Thought suppression. *Annual Review of Psychology*, 51, 59–91. doi: 10.1146/annurev.psych.51.1.59

Woodruff, S. C. (2014). *The effects of mindfulness and acceptance-based interventions and cognitive-behavioral interventions on positive and negative affect: A meta-analysis* (Unpublished doctoral dissertation). Washington, DC: Catholic University of America.

Young, J. A., and Pain, M. D. (1999). The zone: Evidence of a universal phenomenon for athletes across sports. *Athletic Insight: The Online Journal of Sport Psychology*, 1(3), np. Retrieved from www.athleticinsight.com

Zainal, N. Z., Booth, S., and Huppert, F. A. (2012). The efficacy of mindfulness-based stress reduction on mental health of breast cancer patients: A meta-analysis. *Psycho-Oncology*, 22(7), 1457–1465. doi: 10.1002/pon.3171

CHAPTER 9

Mindfulness Training in Elite Athletes: mPEAK with BMX Cyclists

Lori Haase, Göran Kenttä, Steven Hickman, Amy Baltzell,
Martin Paulus

We introduce the Mindful Performance Enhancement, Awareness and Knowledge (*mPEAK*) program along with the theory and research that contributed to creating mPEAK, which was developed by Haase, Paulus, and Hickman. The mPEAK program is an intervention for peak performance based on the mindfulness approach and inspired by Jon Kabat-Zinn's Mindfulness-Based Stress Reduction (MBSR). The mPEAK intervention is specifically designed to support high-level athletes in becoming more resilient to high demands and pressure in competitive sport and ultimately optimizing sport performance (see Haase et al., 2015). This chapter will provide a brief overview of the theory and research upon which mPEAK was based, including mindfulness, resilience, and the tenets and efficacy of MBSR. Other interventions in sport using mindfulness meditation (MM) will be considered. In addition, each of the four pillars of mPEAK will be reviewed, namely interoception (i.e., sensitivity to body experience); intentional versus default mode of thinking and acting; orientation toward pain and difficulty (versus avoidance); and rejection of perfectionism (acceptance or tolerance of what is). Finally, the mPEAK intervention will be presented, including initial empirical support for the program.

Background

Mindfulness

The mPEAK program's underlying premise is based on the Buddhist conceptualization of mindfulness. The most commonly cited Buddhist-inspired definition of mindfulness comes from Jon Kabat-Zinn (2003). He writes, "An operational working definition of mindfulness is: the awareness that emerges through paying attention on purpose, in the present moment, and nonjudgmentally to the unfolding of experience moment by moment" (p. 145). The mindful approach to sport performance is quite different from the typical cognitive behavioral approach used in sport psychology, which is geared toward changing or suppressing thoughts. Such attempts to ignore or stop unwanted thoughts, feelings, and physical sensations often result in the increase of such unwanted thoughts and potentially a disappointing performance (Gardner & Moore, 2007; Wegner, 1994). In contrast, a mindfulness-based approach facilitates performance via the *acceptance* of physical experience, thoughts, and emotions.

Bishop and colleagues' (2004) two-component definition of mindfulness brings to light the potential benefit that a mindful approach can bring to performance. Mindfulness practices can cultivate attention, enhance engagement, and when necessary also strengthen the individual's tolerance of emotional or physical difficulty. The authors define mindfulness in the following way:

> The first component is the self-regulation of attention so that it is maintained on immediate experience, thereby allowing for increased recognition of mental events in the present moment. The second component involves adopting a particular orientation toward one's experiences in the present moment, an orientation that is characterized by curiosity, openness, and acceptance (Bishop et al., 2004, p. 232).

Bishop and colleague's definition helps clarify the value of cultivating mindfulness in sport. Through the cultivation of mindfulness, athletes can learn how to regulate their attention with a quality of openness and acceptance and thus enhance the ability to sustain a flexible awareness that can be intentionally focused on task-relevant cues. Such an approach is often aligned with optimal performance, flow, engagement, and absorption in an activity (Swann et al., 2012).

MM practice is core to cultivating mindfulness within the Buddhist tradition. This type of practice relies on intentionally examining one's thoughts, emotions, and physical sensations as well as patterns of behavior that create the conditions of one's moment to moment experience. Inherent in the Buddhist tradition is to do no harm, to self or others, through examining one's mind to see how our actions and reactions could be hurtful to self or others, with the development of training one's mind. Kabat-Zinn (2003) reflects,

> This "view" includes a skillful understanding of how unexamined behaviors and what Buddhists would call an untrained mind can significantly contribute directly to human suffering, one's own and that of others. It also includes the potential transmutation of that suffering through meditative practices that calm and clarify the mind, open the heart, and refine attention and action (p. 146).

Haase, Paulus, and Hickman designed the mPEAK program to integrate a mindfulness approach, including MM, into their program. The next section will consider Kabat-Zinn's pioneering work of MBSR, which provides the foundation for mPEAK.

Mindfulness-Based Stress Reduction (MBSR)

The mPeak intervention is, in part, based on MBSR. MBSR is the most empirically researched mindfulness program (e.g., Keng, Smoski, & Robins, 2011). In brief, MBSR is an eight-to-ten-week program that uses mindfulness mediation and other mindfulness approaches to reduce stress, initially designed for chronic pain patients. Moreover, MBSR encourages a mindful approach to one's experience, specifically an accepting, open-hearted awareness of one's experience. MM practices are used to cultivate a mindful approach to living. The practices include formal MM, mindful eating (i.e., the infamous raisin exercise), body scans, yoga postures, self-reflective exercises, and an invitation to engage mindfully in daily living (e.g., walking, eating, meeting).

There is a plethora of benefits reported from this intensive program, including changes in brain structure (i.e., neuroplactistic changes) (Hölzel et al., 2011), reduced levels of anxiety, depression, rumination, general psychological distress, perceived stress, post-traumatic avoidance symptoms, and medical symptoms. Moreover positive benefits and effects include an enhanced sense of spirituality, empathy, cohesion, mindfulness, forgiveness, self-compassion, and overall satisfaction with life and quality of life (Keng et al., 2011). Thus MBSR has offered a consistent, wide-reaching healing and well-being effects on a wide range of research participants. Much of the research on MBSR, however, has been focused on participants with medical or clinical issues. More recently, the efficacy of MBSR with healthy participants (i.e., nonclinical/treatment-seeking participants with an absence of psychological or medical issues) has been explored. A meta-analysis by Chiesa and Serretti (2009) revealed that MBSR participation resulted in stress reduction, enhanced spiritual values, reduced ruminative thinking and trait anxiety, enhanced empathy, and self-compassion. Thus MBSR has proven to offer significant benefit to both treatment-seeking and healthy participants. It would make sense that programs based on MBSR could also contribute to sport performance. The research using mindfulness-based interventions in sport is still relatively sparse. The next section will consider studies that have either used MM, or programs that integrate mindfulness, into their design with the goal of optimizing sport performance.

Mindfulness Meditation Training (without a Sport-Specific Training Component)

There have been a few studies that have used non-sports-specific MM with athletes. John, Verma, and Khanna (2011) conducted an experimental study with Indian pistol shooters. After four weeks of twenty-minute, daily, group MM practice, the pistol shooters increased shooting performance with the mean score of pistol shooting improving for the MM group (p < 0.001) compared to the control group. In addition, precompetitive stress decreased based as evidenced by decreases in salivary cortisol levels. Aherne, Moran, and Lonsdale (2011) also conducted a quasi-experimental mindfulness-based intervention with elite athletes. Participants completed a ten-minute daily MM and a thirty-minute MM exercise once a week for six weeks. The athletes used a MM CD created by Kabat-Zinn and colleagues. The meditation group experienced significantly more flow post-intervention.

Stankovic and Baltzell (2015) conducted an eight-week, double-blind MM study with master's-level female tennis players. The intervention group was instructed to listen to a ten-minute MM audiotape daily, and the control group was told to listen to a benign "tennis coaching tips" audiotape. The intervention group won more games (499 compared to 242 won by the control group) and lost fewer (188 compared to the 428 lost by the control group) over the seven-week period directly following the intervention, with a strong positive relationship between higher levels of mindfulness and winning.

Mindfulness Meditation Training with a Sport-Specific Training Component

Mindfulness meditation interventions

In 1985, Jon Kabat Zinn and colleagues (Kabat-Zinn, Bealle & Rippe, 1985) presented a poster at the International Sports Medicine Congress in Copenhagen, Denmark. Their research at that time was the first to consider the use of MM with athletes. The intervention was named a *mental training intervention*, and the program was based on MM, with limited modifications to make the practice sport-specific. Kabat-Zinn and colleagues' rationale relied on the overlap between reported experiences of peak performance and meditation; when athletes experience calmness, detachment from thoughts, and being in the present moment, they tend to optimize performance. These researchers argued that practicing MM would strengthen the athletes' ability to achieve such "altered states" (p. 2). Participants in the study included both collegiate Harvard lightweight rowers and rowing Olympians.

The intervention included a blend of formal MM and sport-specific prompts for individual practice, guided by two audiotapes. The first tape focused on a standard breathing (mindfulness) meditation practice. The basic guidance included maintaining attention on their breathing while, concurrently, accepting any thoughts, emotions, or physical sensations that might arise throughout the practice time. The second audiotape was more sport-focused and specific to rowing. Rowers were prompted first to stabilize their attention by focusing on their breathing and then, with a sense of the whole body, imagine themselves rowing while "Evok(ing) feelings of harmony, flow, perfect technique and synchrony, and a sense of being part of one organism" (p. 3). In addition to the individualized practice, the groups of athletes were offered group practice times followed by an opportunity to ask questions and reflect on their experience (generally such sessions lasted thirty minutes). The collegiate and Olympic athletes reported benefit from the training.

Also, Baltzell and colleagues designed and implemented a formal MM program, Mindfulness Meditation Training in Sport (MMTS), as a twice-weekly, thirty-minute mindfulness training intervention. Members of the collegiate women's soccer team experienced an increase in mindfulness scores (Baltzell & Ahktar, 2014), and the athletes reported improved emotional regulation and ability to focus on task-relevant cues when competing (Baltzell et al., 2014).

The Mindfulness Acceptance and Commitment (MAC) approach to sport
Gardner and Moore's (2007, 2012) Mindfulness Acceptance and Commitment (MAC) approach to sport is by far the most heavily researched mindfulness-based intervention in sport. The MAC approach is a seven-module manualized protocol (see Gardner & Moore, 2007) heavily based upon Hayes' Acceptance Commitment Therapy (see Hayes, 2004). It has been studied with a range of athletes and sport settings over the past decade. In more than a dozen studies, improved performance and markers of enhanced performance have been consistently reported, such as

increases in concentration, awareness, flow experience, and coach ratings of athlete performance (see Chapter 7 in this text regarding the MAC approach in sport).

Through a mindfulness-focused educational and therapeutic approach (with brief mindfulness mediation practices), the MAC approach is designed to help athletes improve performance via strengthening their ability to pay better attention to sport-relevant cues when performing. Core to the MAC approach is helping athletes learn to *accept* their range of human experience of thought, emotion, and somatic states (e.g., lack of belief in self, fear, physical pain). Once athletes can accept such states without trying to change them, they are freed up to commit more fully to personally held values in sport (e.g., being persistent, being fully engaged) regardless of how they feel in the moment. For example, it is possible to feel low self-confidence and fearful and nevertheless remain fully engaged in training or performing. Specifically, clients learn about mindfulness, the problems associated with cognitive fusion (e.g., believing and being glued to dysfunctional thoughts that thwart performance) and experiential avoidance (e.g., giving up or avoiding situations that are predictably emotionally difficult). Moreover, clients are supported to clarify personal values-driven behavior and committing to these values (regardless of internal experience or states) with the support of the practitioner. In summary, the MAC approach in sport includes an educational component throughout the modules; brief, guided mindfulness exercises; and encouragement for self-reflection to clarify and commit to personal values.

Mindful Sport Performance Enhancement (MSPE)
Keith Kaufman and Carol Glass designed the Mindful Sport Performance Enhancement (MSPE), a mindfulness meditation-training program designed for athletes and, similar to mPEAK, closely modeled after MBSR (e.g., formal sitting meditation, walking mediation, and body scans). In fact, the exercises offered in MSPE are the same as MBSR with the addition of directly discussing how to apply the tenets to the mindfulness practice in the athlete's given sport realm (Kaufman, Glass, & Arnkoff, 2009). Specifically, in the 2.5-hour-session-per-week, four-week program, half the length of MBSR, included a "Discussion of applications of meditation training to the sport of focus" (p. 355). The remainder of the program focused exclusively on formal MM practices. Recently, MSPE has been revised to a six-week, ninety-minutes-per-week format (Kaufman, Glass, & Pineau, in press). Kaufman and colleagues conducted a series of studies using MSPE and reported performance-related benefits

such as increased mindfulness and state flow for archers and reduction in somatic anxiety for golfers (Kaufman et al., 2009). In addition, mindfulness increased and sport-related worries decreased for runners (De Petrillo et al., 2009). For a full description of MSPE, please refer to Chapter 8 in this book.

Pre-mPEAK Program Research

Prior to the development of mPEAK, two of the developers of the mPEAK program (Lori Haase and Martin Paulus) were involved in studying the impact of Mindfulness-Based Mind Fitness Training (MMFT; Stanley, 2014), designed for individuals engaging in extreme stress environments. MMFT, a twenty-hour program, offers training specifically in mindfulness and stress resilience skills. This program is also modeled closely to Kabat-Zinn's MBSR: MMFT offers eight two-hour weekly meetings followed by a day-long silent retreat. MMFT includes mindfulness training (i.e., formal MM practice) to aid in enhanced attentional control and concentration. Under high stress, it is essential to be able to focus on task-relevant cues for survival and optimal performance (e.g., a soldier implementing his or her mission instead of becoming lost in thoughts of fear regarding the risk to his or her life). In addition, MMFT includes *military stress inoculation*. Stress resilience skills are developed via creating extreme challenges that stress the body and mind, and, once the individual is experiencing such distress, MMFT offers education and training such that the individual can learn to recover effectively for physical functioning and improved decision-making skills (Haase et al., 2014). See Stanley (2014) for MMFT details.

The U.S. Marines who participated in the MMFT demonstrated changes in brain response associated with increased resilience (Haase et al., 2014; Johnson et al., 2014). In particular, when the marines who received the MMFT were put under physical and emotional stress, based on fMRI assessment of *interoception* (i.e., the processing of the body's internal state), they showed attenuated right-anterior insula and anterior cingulate cortex activation (Haase et al., 2014). In addition, they were better able to maintain homeostatic balance when faced with external demands and at once better able to maintain goal-directed behavior (Johnson et al., 2014). These studies provide evidence that mindfulness-based training in non–treatment-seeking individuals modulates the brain response to an aversive interceptive stressor, in such a way that the brains of those individuals respond to stress in a more resilient manner.

mPEAK: Mindfulness Training in Sport

The mPEAK program is a new, mindfulness training for sport. The foundation of the program, similarly to MSPE, is based on the highly respected and empirically supported MBSR program (Kabat-Zinn, 1982). In addition, mPEAK also focuses on increasing a resilient response by the athlete when facing significant emotional or physical strain. Thus, the purpose of the mPEAK program is to enhance resilience in high-level sport performers, with the integration of a mindfulness training approach, and to help them concentrate and optimally perform particularly when under performance-related stress. This section will consider research-based mindfulness interventions, present the theoretical and conceptual underpinnings of mPEAK, and provide an overview of the program, including initial empirical support.

Resilience is a complex construct that supports adaptive coping responses to stressful events (Campbell-Sills, Cohan, & Stein, 2006; Sarkar & Fletcher, 2014). In lay terms, we often think of resilience as the ability to bounce back from difficulty. Respected resilience researchers Masten, Best, and Garmezy (1990) define resilience as "[t]he process of, capacity for, or outcome of successful adaptation despite challenging or threatening circumstances" (p. 426). And this is precisely what the mPEAK program is designed to address, offering athletes educational and applied practices to help them become more resilient when facing sport-related threats, such as competitive anxiety, choking, physical discomfort, or fear of failure. When more resilient, an athlete can more adaptively cope with naturally occurring challenges in sport, such as disappointment, failure, and fear. A resilient athlete can become more proactive in his effort to optimize performance versus feeling aversive emotions and mindlessly using maladaptive, habitual coping mechanisms.

Resilience has not typically been the overt focus of sport interventions (Sarkar & Fletcher, 2014). An underlying issue that calls for a resilient response in sport is anxiety, the perception that the demand of the situation outweighs the resources of the individual. Addressing anxiety is of paramount concern in the sport psychology literature. Temporal considerations of anxiety are specifically considered and studied by the field of sport psychology, such as pre-performance anxiety, performance anxiety, and state anxiety in sport. Also, models of performance have been built on the efforts to theoretically understand the impact of anxiety on performance, beginning with the drive theory (a direct, positive relationship between anxiety and performance) to more nuanced considerations, such as Yuri Hanin's Zone of Optimal Functioning (the theory posits that each athlete has a level of anxiety, ranging from low to high, in which he or she optimally performs).

Interventions on how to cope with the range of sport threat, both coping with aversive psychological and physical state, are minimal to date. Interventions in sport psychology are mainly based on a cognitive behavioral control approach (e.g., just shift one's thinking) that may have minimal benefits and may, in fact, thwart performance (Gardner & Moore, 2007). The question remains how to best empower athletes when faced with extreme sport threat and how to help them become more resilient. One pathway is MM training: a plethora of empirical evidence now finds that mindfulness training improves the brain's response to stressful situations and, by extension, one's resilience (Bowen et al., 2006; Carlson et al., 2007; Hofmann et al., 2010; Kabat-Zinn, Lipworth & Burney, 1985). Next we will consider the four pillars of mPEAK, the conceptual framework and the design of the program with the purpose of enhancing sport resilience through mindfulness training.

The Four Pillars of mPEAK

Lori Haase, Martin Paulus, and Steven Hickman at the University of California at San Diego designed the mPEAK program, which was established on neuroscience-based experimental evidence together with research on optimal performance to create performance-focused mindfulness training. The mPEAK "pillars" include (1) *interoception* (noticing and accepting somatic experience in sport training and competition); (2) *intentional versus the default mode* of responding (understanding the universality of the wandering mind; learning to respond the way one chooses, in place of habitual, automatic response to sport threat); (3) *orienting toward pain and difficulty* (learning to acknowledge and accept physical and emotional pain in a balanced manner); and (4) *letting go of perfectionism* (learning to accept nonperfection as a normal, human experience – even in high-level performance – to minimize distractions associated with disappointment, frustration, and failure). This section will briefly explain each pillar of mPEAK.

Interoception
The awareness of body experience is core to the design of the mPEAK program. Part of the goal of mPEAK is to support athletes to become more

aware of body experience and, at once, become more resilient in the face of unpleasant or difficult interoceptive experience. Interoception is the processing and awareness of stimuli arising from the body, which can be sensed as warmth, pressure, tingling, coolness, and tightness. Also important in body awareness is proprioception, the processing and awareness of stimuli arising regarding the body's position, movement, and spatial orientation. The mPEAK training is geared to help athletes learn to more efficiently notice aversive experience, label the experience, and self-regulate through attentional control.

Within the brain, interoceptive information is processed within the insula (Craig, 2003). The insula has reciprocal connections with subcortical, limbic, and executive control brain systems, which integrate body-relevant signals with hedonic evaluation (Craig, 2009; Critchley et al., 2004) – in other words, offering information about the pleasant or unpleasant subjective experience. Research conducted by Paulus and colleagues suggests that efficient interoceptive processing – that is, attenuated insula brain response to aversive interoceptive stimuli – may be the neural marker of optimal performance (Paulus et al., 2009; Paulus et al., 2012). Furthermore, mindfulness-based training has been shown to modulate interoceptive processing in relatively healthy non–treatment-seeking marines in such a way that their brain response is more similar to that of an optimal performer (Haase et al., 2014). Thus mPeak is expected to modulate (i.e., improve) interoceptive processing through mindfulness training.

Intentional versus the default mode
The second pillar of the mPEAK program is devoted to addressing obstacles that athletes encounter with regard to the wandering mind and the identification of one's performance story and subsequent influence on athletic performance. The human mind spends a considerable amount of time wandering; most frequently, our minds do so in an unintentional manner. We often find ourselves unintentionally thinking about the past and future rather than being present to what is actually taking place in the present. Unhappiness can result from such unintentional mind wandering (Killingsworth & Gilbert, 2010).

Over the last decade, neuroscientists have identified what is happening in the brain when such unintentional thinking occurs. Specifically, functional neuroimaging studies have delineated (ie., located in the brain) a medial default mode network (DMN), a frontal control network, and a limbic salience network (Spreng et al., 2013). The DMN is a network of brain regions that are active when the mind is not engaged with the outside world (Raichle et al., 2001). The DMN is thought to play a role in mind wandering (Fox et al., 2015) and in self-related and self-referential aspects of cognitive processing (Brewer & Garrison, 2014; Whitfield-Gabrieli & Ford, 2012).

Brewer and colleagues have conducted a series of studies showing reduced DMN activation in experienced meditators during meditation (Brewer et al., 2011; Garrison et al., 2015). Interestingly, in experienced meditators, when the brain is distracted, there is increased activation in the DMN, in particular, in the posterior cingulate cortex (PCC), and when such meditators are undistracted, activation in the PCC is reduced (Garrison et al., 2013). Moreover, lower connectivty between PCC and ACC during task was found in experienced meditators when compared to novices (Brewer & Garrison, 2014).

Taken together, research suggests that mindfulness training can result in reduced mind wandering and changes in brain function within the DMN. Part of the goal of mPEAK is to support athletes in becoming more aware of the wandering mind and to bring awareness to their "performance story" (e.g., "I can't win today because I don't have the right feeling in my legs"). Training is aimed at helping the athlete see how their uninvited thoughts (i.e., the wandering mind) can offer thoughts or stories that potentially can thwart performance unless the athlete establishes a different relationship with such thoughts.

Orienting toward pain and difficulty
Competitive sport is a culture that values being successful. There is little value put on failure, with failure often associated with humiliation and quiet internal suffering. Unless directed to do otherwise, athletes will often prefer to avoid or ignore thoughts and feelings associated with failure or unpleasant physical sensations. However, attempts to suppress painful experiences can often result in greater distress (Cioffi & Holloway, 1993). Coaches, athletes, and the sport culture in general teach performers that they should not accept failure, to divorce themselves from such feelings. The zero tolerance of failure leaves many athletes and high-level performers quite susceptible to harsh self-criticism. Ironically, their unwillingness to accept their experience of failure makes it more difficult to move beyond. With acceptance of failure, the athlete is freed to learn from it and move on.

Everyone fails. Being willing to face failure as a normal part of the performance experience may be essential for optimal sport performance. The same holds true for being willing to experience unpleasant physical sensations. Such tolerance includes bodily signals related to training at the right level and intensity (and minimize excessive overtraining or damaging the body). Also such tolerance minimizes reactive thoughts that can also thwart performance. Mindfulness training can modulate one's experience of painful physical sensations (Zeidan et al., 2010) and emotions (Zeidan et al., 2014) and change how the brain responds to pain (Zeidan et al., 2011). Part of the goal of mPEAK is to challenge the notion that avoidance is the best strategy when it comes to difficult experiences (pain, fear, stress, failure, etc.). Exercises are focused on working with the body as a way of grounding oneself in the moment of difficulty, as a way to remain present to their performance.

Self-compassion and letting go of perfectionism

One of the pillars of mPEAK is to encourage athletes *not* to be perfectionistic and to introduce self-compassion as an alternative. Perfectionism is a personality disposition or habitual approach to life that is characterized by striving for flawlessness and maintaining extreme performance standards. When perfectionistic, athletes also tend to be harshly self-critical and, often, highly concerned about the evaluation of others (Stoeber, 2012). Perfectionism has long been considered a sign of psychological, if not pathological, maladjustment. When athletes are perfectionistic, they are at risk for being excessively concerned over mistakes; experiencing intense self-doubt; and often, for the younger athletes, having concern with parental perception and expectations (Gould, Dieffenbach, & Moffett, 2002). This intolerance of mistakes becomes particularly noteworthy when athletes face the inevitable failures and losses of an athletic career and makes it particularly difficult to overcome these challenges to persist and improve performance.

Yet, high-level athletes must consistently work toward improvement, from the physical capacity of strength and fitness to the tactical excellence. Success is often measured in differences of split seconds. The vulnerability of becoming perfectionistic is quite tempting for those constantly striving toward improvement and holding high standards. The issue is not the high standards but, instead, how the individual responds to failure to meet those standards. Gould and colleagues (2002) found that when Olympic athletes maintained high standards and had relatively lower concerns about mistakes, that such an approach was positively associated with achievement. Whether such athletes were defined perfectionistic or not, the results are compelling: helping athletes maintain high standards and adaptively cope with performance disappointments helps with optimizing performance and is one of the pillars of the mPEAK design.

We will next emphasize the inclusion of self-compassion directly into the mindfulness training for sport, given that mPEAK is the first training to integrate both MM training and self-compassion, together, in an intervention for sport (although self-compassion is addressed only in the section "mPEAK: Session 2," in the description that follows). Kristin Neff (2003a, 2003b) has led the way in bringing research and applied attention to the Buddhist concept of self-compassion. At first consideration, the concept of kindness to self when suffering seems antithetical to the realm of competitive sport and performance. Yet high self-compassion athletes respond in healthier ways (compared to low self-compassion athletes) to emotional difficulty (Reis et al., 2015). Other benefits of athletes with higher self-compassion include fewer maladaptive issues with the body (e.g., body shame, body surveillance), reduced fear of failure and negative evaluation, and less social physique anxiety (Mosewich et al., 2011).

Neff (2003b) introduces self-compassion in her seminal paper, where she introduces the concept to the academic community. She describes self-compassion in the following way:

> Self-compassion, therefore, involves being touched by and open to one's own suffering, not avoiding or disconnecting from it, generating the desire to alleviate one's suffering and to heal oneself with kindness. Self-compassion also involves offering nonjudgmental understanding to one's pain, inadequacies and failures, so that one's experience is seen as part of the larger human experience (p. 87).

Self-compassion in performance is called for when maladaptive emotions or thoughts arise as a result of perceptions of failure, from feeling inadequate (e.g., compared teammates or opponents) to coping with difficult physical pain (e.g., chronic sport injury). When responding with self-compassion, the athlete learns to *accept* such personal, internal experiences (though the strong preference is to experience something else) and can, in turn, experience enhanced emotional safety. When feeling emotionally safe enough to face and accept such a range of difficulty, the performer is freed up to focus on requisite performance cues.

Self-compassion is comprised of three main components: (1) *self-kindness* reflects intentionally offering kindness and understanding toward oneself (rather than self-harshness), particularly when faced with pain, failure, and disappointment; (2) *common humanity* includes the choice to perceive "one's experiences as part of the larger human experience rather than seeing them as separating and isolating" (Neff, 2003b, p. 85); and (3) *mindfulness*, within the construct of self-compassion, focuses on the self as sufferer and gently remaining aware of painful thoughts and feelings, in balanced manner. One is aware of the pain and neither avoiding nor overidentifying with difficult emotions, thoughts, or physical sensations (Neff, 2003b). To be self-compassionate requires all three components (self-kindness, common humanity, and mindfulness). With self-compassion, in competition, the athletes can choose to experience unpleasant internal experience in a different way such that they can ultimately choose to stay engaged in competition and not psychologically give up, even when the urge is strong to do so. Christopher Germer (2009) emphasizes that often self-compassion develops through a stage process. Developing a different relationship with difficult thoughts, feelings, and physical sensations begins with resisting and avoiding that which is uncomfortable, then moves on to tolerating and ultimately befriending the discomfort and being willing to learn from the difficult experience.

The mPEAK Intervention

The mPEAK intervention is an eight-week (twenty-hour) intensive mindfulness training course that was initially built around four core sessions (three hours per session) with six foundational practice sessions (sixty minutes per session), with practice sessions included to strengthen the skills being taught. One of the goals of mPEAK is to teach and support the ongoing integration of mindfulness practices and responses within the training and competitive environment of high-level sport. The consistent effort to connect the training to sport is novel within the mindfulness training programs in sport. Though MSPE does include a prompt to make the connection of the mindfulness training to the participants' sports, mPEAK includes a consistent focus on supporting the athlete to apply the insights from formal mindfulness practice to the competitive sport arena. All sessions provide educational information, an opportunity to practice mindfulness, and a forum for discussion. Though still early in its development and subject to change, the mPEAK program implements many of the core mindfulness exercises of MBSR. The four core sessions are each described in the following subsections.

mPEAK session 1: inhabiting your body
The first core session introduces the athletes to the concept of mindfulness both from an educational- and activity-based approach (e.g., formal

breathing practice). The individual's experience of the physical body is the primary focus of attention and platform upon which mindfulness unfolds. Session 1 is designed to introduce participants to the experience of mindful awareness of the body, including *interoception* (awareness of stimuli arising from the body that can be sensed as warmth, pressure, tingling, coolness, and tightness) and *proprioception* (awareness of stimuli arising regarding the body's position, movement, and spatial orientation). Through discussion, the athletes consider how such body awareness, while training and competing, could contribute to sport performance. In addition, participants are prompted to consider how our interpretations of body experience (e.g., "My legs feel tired, that means I am going to lose this race") or *stories* we make up about the competitive sport world ("I could never beat him") can thwart performance.

mPEAK session 2: getting out of your own way and letting go

The second core session is devoted to addressing initial challenges encountered by participants between session 1 and 2 when engaged in formal and daily living practice of mindfulness. This session empowers the athlete to experience a changed relationship with thoughts that threaten the athlete's ability to perform. Related, common challenges are addressed, such as the wandering mind and the fruitlessness of trying to stop the mind from wandering. Another aligned pivotal idea in session 2 is the importance of recognizing "the story" and the way in which how we think can influence how we perform (i.e., how we often make up stories like "my coach hates me," which can become quite distracting and get in the way of practice and performance). In addition to mindfulness-based body awareness (including yoga and mindful breathing), participants retrospectively reflect on times when their thinking was inconsistent with outcome (e.g., the thought, "I can't win this one today," followed by a win). The participants, through this process, are offered the opportunity to gain insights regarding the relationship between thoughts and behavior. Athletes can learn to see patterns of thoughts and behaviors and are empowered to let go of unhelpful, untrue thought or strong preferences that get in the way of performance. Participants have an opportunity to see that such ideas are generated from a wandering mind or the stories we tell ourselves.

mPEAK session 3: working with stress, fear, and failure

The third core session is intended to challenge the notion that avoidance is the best strategy when it comes to difficulty arising (pain, fear, stress, failure, etc.) and to use the experience of working with the body as a way of grounding oneself in the moment, in the face of difficulty. Avoidance of difficult thought and feelings is the hallmark approach in traditional sport psychology intervention (Meichenbaum, 1977). The mPEAK approach offers a radically different pathway to optimal performance that aligns with the current challenge of the acceptance commitment therapy (Hayes, 2004). In addition to practicing mindfulness breathing, athletes are also prompted to recall a failure or difficulty in sport and practice maintaining awareness with the associated interoception. The goal, in the competitive sport environment, is not to stop our thinking and feeling but to change our relationship to such experience. Athletes are commonly surprised and relieved when coming to terms with this alternative approach.

mPEAK session 4: the challenges of perfectionism and goals
The fourth and final core session deals specifically with the contradictory nature of some mental approaches and attitudes that athletes may perceive as beneficial, but which in fact become problematic for optimal perform-ance. Athletes may perceive that the drive for optimal training and per-formance is an outgrowth of perfectionism. And athletes may also come to believe that offering themselves harsh self-criticism when they fail can be good motivators. In this session, athletes explore both the benefits of their strengths in sport and, at once, see the problematic nature. For example, if an athlete is determined to be the fittest on their team, they may consist-ently overtrain, ignore their body signals, and manifest sport injury or sport burnout. Athletes are also introduced to the concept of self-compassion paired with an applied exercise. In this session, participants also engage in a range of MBSR-based formal MM practices (e.g., mindful walking, awareness of breathing). A secondary intention of this session is to set the stage for continued regular personal practice of mindfulness through the post-intensive period.

Practice sessions
The four core sessions (presented in two day-long sessions) are followed by six foundational mindfulness and self-compassion practice sessions. These sessions are dedicated to checking in with participants, supporting their ongoing, individual formal meditation practice. The sessions include both formal mindfulness practice and invited inquiry and discussion. Each session also includes a specific relevant topic drawn from the four core sessions, to focus the meeting and reinforce the importance of continued practice. When engaged in the mPEAK intervention, participants are

encouraged to practice mindfulness and self-regulation skills daily, for at least thirty minutes.

The mPEAK Study: MBX Professional Cyclists

Haas and colleagues (2015) conducted a study using mPEAK as the intervention with the U.S. BMX (Bicycle Motocross) Cycling Team, seven members of which participated in the eight-week mPEAK program. The primary aim of the investigation was to examine whether the mPEAK intervention, aimed at improving mindfulness and self-compassion, would modify how the brains of elite athletes processed aversive interoceptive stimuli. In addition, the researchers explored whether this modification would be related to the BMX cyclists' self-reports of being better able to adjust physically and emotionally to extreme conditions. This section briefly considers the design and result of the study. (Refer to Haase et al., 2015, for a full consideration of the design, results, and discussion.)

Based on fMRI pre-mPEAK and post-mPEAK data, the mPEAK training resulted in changes in self-reported interoceptive awareness and sensitization of interoceptively relevant brain structures. Greater body awareness coupled with greater attentional control following mPEAK training may result in more efficient neural processing (in the brain) during the anticipation of and recovery from aversive interoceptive experience. Such findings were supported by the BMX cyclists' self-reports. Following the mPEAK training, the BMX athletes reported significantly less difficulty identifying feelings, reported greater levels of self-regulation and trust, as well as greater levels of being able to describe/label their experience with words (e.g., "this is overwhelming"; "I am exhausted and may not be able to overtake the rider in front of me").

Conclusion

The mPEAK program is a mindfulness-based intervention brought to sport from neuroscientists and expert MBSR mindfulness teachers. The program offers both core concepts from MBSR and the integration of important new scientific ideas to help high-level athletes integrate the core tenets of Buddhist mindfulness into their training, competing, and daily living.

The mPEAK program maintains a consistent focus on helping athletes make the knowledge-based and psychological connection between their sport world and formal mindfulness mediation practice. Helping athletes make this bridge was done by Kabat-Zinn and colleagues (1985) and minimally by Kaufman and colleagues (2009) in the MSPE intervention. Clinical sport psychologists Gardner and Moore (2007), in their more educational, clinical MAC approach, also emphasize how to bring a mindful approach to sport training and competition. We also know that cultivating self-compassion is facilitative to the athletes' ability to cope with difficulty, yet mPEAK is the only formalized training program that overtly integrates self-compassion into the primarily mindfulness-based training in sport. In terms of the efficacy of mPEAK, initial results are promising, particularly with paired fMRI data with qualitative reports of BMX cyclists reporting an enhanced ability to cope with difficult interoceptive experience and an improved ability to be more resilient. The BMX study offers initial evidence that the response of the body and mind to extreme distress can be trained to cope more adaptively, which is experienced as less reactivity to external stress and threat. The development of the mPEAK intervention offers a pathway to help athletes become more resilient to sport-related distress via the integration of formal mindfulness training, expert guidance to help bridge the ideas to the sport context, the inclusion of self-compassion in the training, and an emphasis on interoceptive awareness and tolerance, and certainly makes a significant contribution to our understanding of how mindfulness training can facilitate enhancing performance.

REFERENCES

Ahern, C., Moran, A. P., and Lonsdale, C. (2011). The effects of mindfulness training on athletes' flow: An initial investigation. *Sport Psychologist*, 25, 177–189.

Baltzell, A. L., and Ahktar, V. L. (2014). Mindfulness Meditation Training for Sport (MMTS) intervention: Impact of MMTS with Division I female athletes. *Journal of Happiness and Well-being*, 2(2), 160–173.

Baltzell, A. L., Caraballo, N., Chipman, K., and Hayden, L. (2014). A qualitative study of the Mindfulness Meditation Training for Sport (MMTS): Division I female soccer players' experience. *Journal of Clinical Sport Psychology*, 8, 221–244.

Bishop, S. R., Lau, M., Shapiro, S., Carlson, L., Anderson, N. D., Carmody, J., ... Devins, G. (2004). Mindfulness: A proposed operational definition. *Clinical Psychology: Science and Practice*, 11(3), 230–241. doi: 10.1093/clipsy. bph077

Bowen, S., Witkiewitz, K., Dillworth, T. M., Chawla, N., Simpson, T. L., Ostafin, B. D., ... Marlatt, G. A. (2006). Mindfulness meditation and substance use in an incarcerated population. *Psychology Addictive Behaviors*, 20(3), 343–347. doi: 10.1037/0893-164x.20.3.343

Brewer, J. A., and Garrison, K. A. (2014). The posterior cingulate cortex as a plausible mechanistic target of meditation: Findings from neuroimaging. *Annals of the New York Academy of Sciences*, 1307, 19–27.

Brewer, J. A., Worhunsky, P. D., Gray, J. R., Tang, Y. Y., Weber, J., and Kober, H. (2011). Meditation experience is associated with differences in default mode network activity and connectivity. *Proceedings of the National Academy of Sciences of the United States*, 108(50), 20254–20259. doi: 10.1073/pnas.1112029108

Campbell-Sills, L., Cohan, S. L., and Stein, M. B. (2006). Relationship of resilience to personality, coping, and psychiatric symptoms in young adults. *Behaviour Research and Therapy*, 44(4), 585–599. doi: 10.1016/j.brat.2005.05.001

Carlson, L. E., Speca, M., Faris, P., and Patel, K. D. (2007). One year pre-post intervention follow-up of psychological, immune, endocrine and blood pressure outcomes of Mindfulness-Based Stress Reduction (MBSR) in breast and prostate cancer outpatients. *Brain, Behavior, Immunity*, 21(8), 1038–1049. doi: 10.1016/j.bbi.2007.04.002

Chiesa, A., and Serretti, A. (2009). Mindfulness-Based Stress Reduction for stress management in healthy people: A review and meta-analysis. *Journal of Alternative and Complementary Medicine*, 15(5), 593–600. doi:10.1089/acm.2008.0495

Cioffi, D., and Holloway, J. (1993). Delayed costs of suppressed pain. *Journal of Personality and Social Psychology*, 64(2), 274–282. doi: http://dx.doi.org/10.1037/0022-3514.64.2.274

Craig, A. D. (2003). Interoception: The sense of the physiological condition of the body. *Current Opinion in Neurobiology*, 13(4), 500–505. doi: 10.1016/S0959-4388(03)00090-4

(2009). How do you feel – now? The anterior insula and human awareness. *Nature Reviews Neuroscience*, 10(1), 59–70. doi: 10.1038/nrn2555

Critchley, H. D., Wiens, S., Rotshtein, P., Ohman, A., and Dolan, R.J., 2004. Neural systems supporting interoceptive awareness. *Nature Neuroscience*, 7, 189–195. doi:10.1038/nn1176

De Petrillo, L., Kaufman, K., Glass, C., and Arnkoff, D. (2009). Mindfulness for long-distance runners: An open trial using Mindful Sport Performance Enhancement (MSPE). *Journal of Clinical Sport Psychology*, 3(4), 357–376.

Fox, K. C., Spreng, R. N., Ellamil, M., and Andrews-Hanna, J. R. (2015). The wandering brain: Meta-analysis of functional neuroimaging studies of mind-wandering and related spontaneous thought processes. *Neuroimage*, 111, 611–621. doi: 10.1016/j.neuroimage.2015.02.039

Gardner, F. L., and Moore, Z. E. (2007). *The psychology of enhancing human performance: The Mindfulness-Acceptance-Commitment (MAC) approach*. New York, NY: Springer.

(2012). Mindfulness and acceptance models in sports psychology: A decade of basic and applied scientific advancements. *Canadian Psychology*, 53(4), 309–318. doi: 10.1037/a0030220

Garrison, K. A., Santoyo, J. F., Davis, J. H., and Thornhill, T. A. T. (2013). Effortless awareness: Using real time neurofeedback to investigate correlates of posterior cingulate cortex activity in meditators' self-report. *Frontiers in Human Neuroscience*, 7, 440–449. doi: 10.3389/fnhum.2013.00440

Garrison, K. A., Zeffiro, T. A., Scheinost, D., and Constable, R. T. (2015). Meditation leads to reduced default mode network activity beyond an active task. *Cognitive, Affective, and Behavioral Neuroscience*, 1-9. doi: 10.3758/s13415-015-0358-3

Germer, C. (2009). *The mindful path to self-compassion*. New York, NY: Guilford Press.

Gould, D., Dieffenbach, K., and Moffett, A. (2002). Psychological characteristics and their development in Olympic champions, *Journal of Applied Sport Psychology*, 14, 172–204. doi: 10.1080/10413200290103482

Haase, L., May, A., Falahpour, M., Isakovic, S., Simmons, A., Hickman, S., Liu, T., and Paulus, M. (2015). A pilot study investigating changes in neural processing after mindfulness training in elite athletes. *Frontiers in Behavioral Neuroscience*, 9, 1–12. doi: 0.3389/fnbeh.2015.00229

Haase, L., Thom, N. J., Shukla, A., Davenport, P. W., Simmons, A. N., Paulus, M. P., and Johnson, D. C. (2014). Mindfulness-based training attenuates insula response to an aversive interoceptive challenge. *Social Cognitive and Affective Neuroscience*. 1-9. doi: 10.1093/scan/nsu042

Hayes, S. C. (2004). Acceptance and commitment therapy, relational frame theory, and the third wave of behavioral and cognitive therapies. *Behavior Therapy*, 35, 639–665. doi: 10.1016/S0005-7894(04)80013-3

Hofmann, S. G., Sawyer, A. T., Witt, A. A., and Oh, D. (2010). The effect of mindfulness-based therapy on anxiety and depression: A meta-analytic review. *Journal of Consulting and Clinical Psychology*, 78(2), 169–183. doi: 10.1037/a0018555

Hölzel, B. K., Lazar, S. W., Gard, T., Schuman-Olivier, Z., Vago, D. R., and Ott, U. (2011). How does mindfulness meditation work? Proposing mechanisms of action from a conceptual and neural perspective. *Perspectives on Psychological Science*, 6, 537–559.

John, S., Verma, S. K., and Khanna, G. L. (2011). The effect of mindfulness meditation on HPA-Axis in pre-competition stress in sports performance of elite shooters. *National Journal of Integrated Research in Medicine*, 2(3), 15–21.

Johnson, D. C., Thom, N. J., Stanley, E. A., Haase, L., Simmons, A. N., Shih, P. A., ... Paulus, M. P. (2014). Modifying resilience mechanisms in at-risk individuals: A controlled study of mindfulness training in marines preparing for deployment. *American Journal of Psychiatry*, 171(8), 844–853. doi: 10.1176/appi.ajp.2014.13040502

Kabat-Zinn, J. (1982). An outpatient program in behavioral medicine for chronic pain patients based on the practice of mindfulness meditation: Theoretical considerations and preliminary results. *General Hospital Psychiatry*, 4(1), 33–47. doi: 10.1016/0163-8343(82)90026-3

(2003). Mindfulness-based interventions in context: Past, present, and future. *Clinical Psychology: Science and Practice*, 10(2), 144–156. doi: 10.1093/clipsy/bpg016

Kabat-Zinn, J., Beall, B., and Rippe, J. (1985, June). *A systematic mental training program based on mindfulness meditation to optimize performance in collegiate and Olympic rowers.* Poster presented at the World Congress in Sport Psychology, Copenhagen, Denmark.

Kabat-Zinn, J., Lipworth, L., and Burney, R. (1985). The clinical use of mindfulness meditation for the self-regulation of chronic pain. *Journal of Behavioral Medicine*, 8, 163–190.

Kaufman, K. A., Glass, C. R., and Arnkoff, D. B. (2009). Evaluation of Mindful Sport Performance Enhancement (MSPE): A new approach to promote flow in athletes. *Journal of Clinical Sport Psychology*, 4, 334–356.

Kaufman, K. A., Glass, C. R., and Pineau, T. R. (in press). *Mindful Sport Performance Enhancement (MSPE): A mindfulness-based mental training program for athletes.* Washington, DC: American Psychological Association.

Keng, S. L., Smoski, M. J., and Robins, C. J. (2011). Effects of mindfulness on psychological health: A review of empirical studies. *Clinical Psychology Review*, 31, 1041–1056. doi: 10.1016/j.cpr.2011.04.006

Killingsworth, M. A., and Gilbert, D. T. (2010). A wandering mind is an unhappy mind. *Science*, 330, 932. doi: 10.1126/science.1192439

Masten, A. S., Best, K. M., and Garmezy, N. (1990). Resilience and development: Contributions from the study of children who overcome adversity. *Development and Psychopathology*, 2, 425–444. doi: http://dx.doi.org/10.1017/S0954579400005812

Meichenbaum, D. (1977). *Cognitive behavioral modification: An integrative approach.* New York, NY: Plenum.

Mosewich, A. D., Kowalski, K. C., Sabiston, C. M., Sedgwick, W. A., and Tracy, J. L. (2011) Self-compassion: A potential resource for young women athletes. *Journal of Sport and Exercise Psychology*, 33, 103–123.

Neff, K. D. (2003a). The development and validation of a scale to measure self-compassion. *Self and Identity*, 2, 223–250. doi: 10.1080/15298860390209035

(2003b). Self-compassion: An alternative conceptualization of a healthy attitude toward oneself. *Self and Identity*, 2, 85–101. doi: 10.1080/15298860390129863

Paulus, M. P., Flagan, T., Simmons, A. N., Gillis, K., Kotturi, S., Thom, N., . . . Swain, J. L. (2012). Subjecting elite athletes to inspiratory breathing load reveals behavioral and neural signatures of optimal performers in extreme environments. *PLoS One*, 7, e29394. doi: 10.1371/journal.pone.0029394

Paulus, M. P., Potterat, E. G., Taylor, M. K., Van Orden, K. F., Bauman, J., Momen, N., . . . Swain, J. L. (2009). A neuroscience approach to optimizing brain resources for human performance in extreme environments. *Neuroscience and Biobehavioral Reviews*, 33, 1080–1088. doi: 10.1016/j.neubiorev.2009.05.003

Raichle, M. E., MacLeod, A. M., Snyder, A. Z., and Powers, W. J. (2001). A default mode of brain function. *Proceedings of the National Academy of Sciences of the United States of America*, 98(2), 676–682. doi: 10.1073/pnas.98.2.676

Reis, N. A., Kowalski, K. C., Ferguson, L. J., Sabiston, C. M., Sedgwick, W. A., and Crocker, P. R. E. (2015). Self-compassion and women athletes' responses to emotionally difficult sport situations: An evaluation of a brief induction. *Psychology of Sport and Exercise*, 16, 18–25. doi: 10.1016/j.psychsport.2014.08.011

Sarkar, M., and Fletcher, D. (2014). Psychological resilience in sport performers: A review of stressors and protective factors. *Journal of Sport Sciences*, 32(15), 1419–1434. doi: 10.1080/02640414.2014.901551

Spreng, R. N., Sepulcre, J., Turner, G. R., Stevens, W. D., and Schacter, D. L. (2013). Intrinsic architecture underlying the relations among the default, dorsal attention, and frontoparietal control networks of the human brain. *Journal of Cognitive Neuroscience*, 25(1), 74–86. doi: 10.1162/jocn_a_00281

Stankovic, D., and Baltzell, A. L. (2015). Mindfulness meditation in sport: Improved sport performance of master tennis players. Manuscript in preparation.

Stanley, E. A. (2014) Mindfulness-Based Mind Fitness Training (MMFT): An approach for enhancing performance and building resilience in high stress contexts. In A. Ie, C. T. Ngnoumen and E. J. Langer (Eds.), *The Wiley Blackwell handbook of mindfulness* (pp. 964–985). London, UK: Wiley-Blackwell.

Stoeber, J. (2012). Perfectionism and performance. In S. Murphy (Ed.) *The Oxford handbook of sport and performance psychology* (pp. 294–306). New York, NY: Oxford University Press.

Swann, C., Keegan, R. J., Piggott, D., and Crust, L. (2012). A systematic review of the experience, occurrence, and controllability of flow states in elite sport. *Psychology of Sport and Exercise*, 13(6), 807–819. doi: 10.1016/j.psychsport.2012.05.006

Wegner, D. M. (1994). Ironic processes of mental control. *Psychological Review*, 101(1), 34–52. doi: 10.1037/0033-295X.101.1.34

Whitfield-Gabrieli, S., and Ford, J. M. (2012). Default mode network activity and connectivity in psychopathology. *Annual Review of Clinical Psychology*, 8, 49–76. doi: 10.1146/annurev-clinpsy-032511-143049

Zeidan, F., Gordon, N. S., Merchant, J., and Goolkasian, P. (2010). The effects of brief mindfulness meditation training on experimentally induced pain. *Journal of Pain*, 11(3), 199–209. doi: 10.1016/j.jpain.2009.07.015

Zeidan, F., Martucci, K. T., Kraft, R. A., Gordon, N. S., McHaffie, J. G., and Coghill, R. C. (2011). Brain mechanisms supporting the modulation of pain by mindfulness meditation. *Journal of Neuroscience*, 31(14), 5540–5548. doi: 10.1523/JNEUROSCI.5791-10.2011

Zeidan, F., Martucci, K. T., Kraft, R. A., McHaffie, J. G., and Coghill, R. C. (2014). Neural correlates of mindfulness meditation-related anxiety relief. *Social cognitive and affective neuroscience*, 9(6), 751–759.

Mindfulness: Theory to Practice in Sport and Exercise

CHAPTER 10

Mindfulness and the Olympic Athlete – A Personal Journey

Peter Haberl

Imagine, if you will, standing at the starting blocks at the Olympic Games. Let's say your race will last just under a minute. The margin of victory or defeat will be determined by one-hundredths of a second. You are part of a world-class field, a field consisting of a world record holder, a world champion, and to top it off, an Olympic champion. One of these is you (you can take your pick!). You are superbly fit, and so are your competitors. With the best time of the year, and your track record, you are considered one of the favorites. The emphasis is on "one" of the favorites. The outcome is uncertain. Your goal is to win. A victory today, an Olympic gold medal, may change your world. Anything less than a medal would be considered a disappointment by you and your team. Failure would mean a four-year-long wait for a chance at redemption that you know, full well, may never come again. Indeed, this is a very special moment for you – a moment for which you have trained for what seems like a lifetime. Certainly you have put in the proverbial ten years and the ten thousand plus hours of deliberate practice to get to just this moment and this level of expertise. You will give yourself the best chance to perform optimally if both your mind and your body are ready.

Your body is ready to perform, yet will your mind be ready? What happens to your mind in this moment when it comes time to perform? Will you be aware of what is on your mind, and will you be able to put your mind where you need it to be? Will you be able to direct your attention on the execution of the task at hand and keep it there, or will the pressure, the stress, and the magnitude of the moment constrain your mind, highjack your attention, and derail you from staying in the here and now?

My singular focus as an applied sport psychologist is to work with Olympic hopefuls to navigate the territory that is performance at the Olympic Games. To navigate this territory, these questions of what is on your mind and where you will put your mind are vital. To navigate this territory and address these questions, a map, a guide, and a compass come in handy. It is easy for the mind to lose its way once the finish line of the Olympic Games is in sight. Yes, physiology obviously matters to performance, and your body may be a well-oiled machine, but your mind often is a different story. Your mind may not work like a well-oiled machine but rather more like a moody diva, no matter how much you may have trained your body. Multiple Olympic swimming gold medalist Natalie Coughlin gives us a glimpse of the mind of the Olympian in the starting blocks, from a news article by Williams (2012):

> The pressure at the Olympic Games is really, really, really overwhelming, even if you are incredibly experienced. The feeling of walking onto the pool deck, standing behind the blocks knowing the race that you've prepared for the last four years, or the past decade, [that] everything is going to culminate in that 58 seconds or so, it's quite stressful.

Even the most experienced Olympic athlete can experience pressure and stress. It can be easy for the Olympic athlete to get lost in his or her own mind when it comes time to navigate the territory of performance at the Games. The stress of the Olympic Games challenges the mind of the athlete perhaps like no other competition, like no other athletic performance situation. The Olympic Games happen only every four years and may only happen once in an athlete's prime. It takes years of practice to require the necessary expertise to qualify for the Games and eventually contest for a medal. Yet, the outcome is always uncertain. There are more media representatives than athletes at the Games, and each one of those media members is looking for a story. The media spotlight glares brightly at the athlete, with an almost singular focus on the ability to medal at the Games. Often, athletes perceive the Games as a once in a lifetime opportunity to showcase themselves and their sport and achieve ultimate success and justification for years of dedicated practice. Expectations ("I need to win") are unavoidable. The Olympic territory easily invites thoughts such as "if I don't make it, I have wasted eight (ten, twelve) years of my life." Such thoughts are a hallmark of a stressed mind and are not conducive to optimal performance because the focus then shifts from the process to the outcome.

Mindfulness, as a specific way of paying attention (in the present, on purpose, and with acceptance), offers a map, a guide, and a compass to approach this territory of performance. In this chapter, I will outline why and how mindfulness has become my guiding paradigm in helping athletes successfully navigate the performance stress of the Olympic Games. I will begin with a general as well as a personal history of mindfulness at the Games. What is the historical trajectory of mindfulness at the Games, and how has mindfulness become my guiding paradigm of doing sport psychology in the Olympic Games environment? This historical perspective will be interwoven with a practical, a theoretical, and a research-based rationale for athletes utilizing mindfulness as a guiding framework to work with their minds effectively at the Games. The chapter will finish with a discussion on how mindfulness not only offers a useful conceptual framework for an understanding of how the athlete's mind works in Olympic competition, but also the mind of the sport psychologist. Furthermore, mindfulness can also serve as a framework for how an athlete (and a sport psychologist) can work effectively with his or her mind in life in general.

Mindfulness at the Olympic Games

Jon Kabat-Zinn is credited as the person arguably most responsible for introducing mindfulness to Western medicine and psychology (Kabat-Zinn, 1990; Siegel, 2014). The Mindfulness-Based Stress Reduction program he started at the University of Massachusetts in 1979 was the catalyst that launched the research and application boom in mindfulness in the West. Perhaps less known is the fact that Kabat-Zinn was perhaps also the first person to introduce Western Olympic athletes to mindfulness (Birrer, Röthlin, & Morgan (2012). In 1984, Kabat-Zinn worked with members of the U.S. Men's Olympic rowing team and helped them prepare mentally for the Olympic Games (Kabat-Zinn, Beall, & Rippe, 1985)[1]. Alas, Kabat-Zinn's sojourn into Olympic sport psychology was very brief and limited. His focus, rightfully so, was on a broader realm, namely stress in general. Kabat-Zinn housed the initial Mindfulness-Based Stress Reduction program at the University of Massachusetts Medical School. In his later writings, Kabat-Zinn (2005) refers to hospitals as "dukkha[2] magnets," as places that attract suffering in its broadest sense, and hence the hospital setting was a perfect lab for him to introduce mindfulness to reduce stress and suffering.

---

[1] The story of some of the members of that U.S. Olympic rowing team is captured in Halberstam (1996).

[2] *Dukkha* is a term from Pali, one of the languages in which the oral teachings of the Buddha were codified and transmitted. It is often translated as suffering. However, many writers, including Kabat-Zinn (2005), prefer not to translate the word itself but rather to use the word to capture its broader meaning, that our human experience is inevitably characterized by frustration, dissatisfaction, and dis-ease.

The term "dukkha magnet" may not immediately come to mind when one thinks about the Olympic Games, nor would one associate the Games at first sight with mindfulness. The image of mindfulness is often the act of sitting peacefully on a cushion, eyes closed, with attention centered on breathing, perhaps in the pursuit of the four heavenly abodes of loving kindness, compassion, sympathetic joy, and equanimity and the pursuit of no-self (Kabat-Zinn, 1994; Salzberg & Goldstein, 2001). The image of the Olympic Games, on the other hand, is more often the relentless pursuit of victory, with a winner-takes-all and losers-go-home mentality, in the pursuit of individual glory, national honor, and sporting immortality. Furthermore, the Olympic pursuit requires a certain narrow-minded focus, a focus on individual accomplishment. Not infrequently, this pursuit can come at a high cost. Reaching for the top of the podium can at times become a Faustian bargain, a deal with the devil, for the Olympic athlete.[3] So by any stretch of the imagination, the image of the Olympic Games may be pretty far removed from the four heavenly abodes and from sitting peacefully on a Zafu cushion.

Yet, if mindfulness at the Games is not the image of calm serenity, what would be the proper image and what does mindfulness have to offer the Olympic athlete?[4] No doubt, there is *dukkha* at the Olympic Games, particularly if one uses the more broad definition of *dukkha* as not just suffering, but the wide range of dissatisfaction, stress, and dis-ease that comes with being human (e.g., Kabat-Zinn, 2005; Teasdale, 2009). Athletes are not immune to this type of dissatisfaction. After all, in competition athletes finish fourth, just outside of the medals, last, or anywhere in between. Athletes fail to meet their expectations, get injured, or fail to qualify for the Games altogether. Outside of competition, athletes naturally deal with any of the other misfortunes of life that can befall any and all of us. So this broader definition of *dukkha* as more than simply suffering may surely fit the athlete experience as well. And mindfulness certainly can be a way to approach dissatisfaction and suffering in this specific context of the Olympic Games. But when we think about the Olympic Games from a sport psychology perspective, first and foremost we think about performance.

---

[3] For an illustration of just such a Faustian bargain, the documentary *The Prize of Gold* (http://vimeo .com/51345348) hauntingly recounts the story of a number of Swedish Olympic athletes and the prize they paid on their journey to Olympic immortality.

[4] A trusted friend and colleague, two-time Olympian Cristina Fink, asked me after a presentation on mindfulness at a sport psychology conference why I always use images of calm serenity when I talk about mindfulness at the Olympic Games. She pointed out that this image of serenity and calm, of sitting still, isn't really our world (the world of competitive sport), and she suggested I use a "different," more appropriate image for a discussion of mindfulness in sports. Wise words.

Can mindfulness be a way to approach optimal performance at the Olympic Games? When Kabat-Zinn introduced mindfulness to the Olympic rowers back in 1984, the intent was to facilitate performance at the Games. Kabat-Zinn presented his work to a sport psychology audience at the World Congress in Sport Psychology in Denmark in 1985. The athletes in the study perceived the mindfulness intervention to help their performance.

Yet, after this initial introduction, mindfulness as a psychological approach to optimize performance at the Olympic Games did not spread across the world of applied Olympic sport psychology (Birrer et al., 2012). Rather, mindfulness in this context became dormant again, kind of like Sleeping Beauty in the Grimm fairy tale. The "prince" who metaphorically came and awoke the sleeping beauty of mindfulness in elite sports was Phil Jackson, the legendary basketball coach of the Chicago Bulls and the Los Angeles Lakers. Jackson's teams have won a combined total of eleven NBA championship rings. In his 1995 book *Sacred Hoops*, Jackson wrote about how he views the game of basketball through the lens of Zen and why he introduced mindfulness to the Chicago Bulls:

> Basketball is a complex dance that requires shifting from one objective to another at lightning speed. To excel, you need to act with a clear mind and be totally focused on what *everyone* on the floor is doing. Some athletes describe this quality of mind as a "cocoon of concentration." But this means shutting out the world when what you really need to do is become acutely aware of what's happening right now, *this very moment.*
>
> The secret is *not thinking.* That doesn't mean being stupid; it means quieting the endless jabbering of thoughts so that your body can do instinctively what it's been trained to do without the mind getting in the way. All of us have had flashes of this sense of oneness – making love, creating a work of art – when we're completely immersed in the moment, inseparable from what we're doing. This kind of experience happens all the time on the basketball floor; that's why the game is so intoxicating. But if you are really paying attention, it can also occur while you're performing the most mundane tasks (pp. 115–116; italics in the original text).

In this description, Jackson offered us a vivid image and a clear rationale for mindfulness in sport. In essence, mindfulness is a recipe for optimal performance, a recipe for working effectively with the mind in sport. In sport, the cushion moves, and the challenge is to act with a clear mind to master the "complex dance at lightning speed." We find mindfulness in movement. In order to excel at this dance, when you need to *shift focus from one object to another at lightning speed,* you benefit from an uncluttered mind, with a focus on what everyone is doing.

Two key components of a clear mind emerge here: awareness and attention. When it comes time to execute, is the performer aware of what is on his or her mind, and can the performer put his or her mind where it needs to be? To come back to Natalie Coughlin's quote and the mind of the athlete in the starting block: Are the athletes aware of what is on their mind at this moment? Are the athletes aware of the feeling of stress and the thoughts that come with it? And will they have the ability to accept those feelings and thoughts and then direct attention to the task at hand, to executing the start?

Attention as the Currency of Performance

Full attention on the task at hand is the psychological currency of successful execution at the Games – an attention that is flexible, not rigid, an attention that can quickly move between objects, an attention that doesn't come at the exclusion of the athlete's teammates. Bishop and his colleagues (2004) offer a two-part definition of mindfulness. The first part of their definition discusses mindfulness as the self-regulation of attention. To regulate attention, we need to aim it, sustain it, and regain it the moment it is lost. The second part of their definition emphasizes an open, curious, and accepting orientation toward one's experience in the present moment.

The opponent of immersion in the moment and of clear attention, as Phil Jackson (1995) puts it, is the "endless jabbering of thoughts" (p. 115). Bishop and colleagues (2004) refer to this jabbering of thoughts as "elaborative processing" (p. 4). Elaborative processing is the almost instant story in our head, a near-constant stream of commentary on our moment-to-moment experience to which we can all fall prey. Mindfulness "inhibits secondary elaborative processing of thought" through awareness and the regulation of attention (Bishop et al., 2004, p. 4). The jabbering thoughts (e.g., "I've prepared for this race for the last decade, if I don't medal I will have wasted my time") attempt to highjack attention. The jabbering thoughts (such as "I will let me country down") attempt to draw attention internally. Then focus is not on what is in front of us, focus is not on execution, focus is internal, on thoughts, on the past or the future. We get lost in the story in our head. And when we are lost in the story in our head, the complex dance that is performance becomes complicated, and we lose the way on our journey. And thus, our moment-to-moment requisite full attention is splintered.

An example of elaborate processing at the Olympics

At the 2010 U.S. Olympic Trials for figure skating, Keauna McLaughlin and her partner, Rockne Brubaker, were heavily favored to qualify at trials and be the first U.S. pairs skating team that could contend for a medal at the Olympic Games since 1988. Practice went well all week. Physically, the athletes seemed to be optimally prepared to win their spot on the team. Yet, during the short program, McLaughlin stumbled on a triple Salchow, a jump she hadn't missed in a long time (on this jump, the take-off is from the back inside edge of one foot). The initial error cascaded into further mistakes. The pair finished the trials in fifth place and did not qualify for the Games. In an online *Vanity Fair* article (Hanel, 2010), McLaughlin reflected on what happened and offered an insight into her psyche: "I just let my mind take over. I was thinking, 'I hope I don't mess up, I hope I don't mess up,' and that's absolutely not what you're supposed to think."

Based on her description, McLaughlin's thinking mind took over. The result was cognitive fusion, where you become "hooked" by your own thoughts and subsequently pulled out of the present moment (Harris, 2009). As I will discuss in more detail later in the chapter, the aim of mindfulness is not to prevent such thoughts from arising (a near impossibility), but rather to learn to relate to such thoughts more skillfully by redirecting attention back onto the task at hand. The story in the head – in this case, "don't mess up" – interfered with performance.

McLaughlin became trapped in elaborate processing, which took attention away from the present moment. McLaughlin stated that you are not supposed to think that way as an athlete. Athletes often talk about the need to think like a champion. They talk about the need to have the right thoughts, so to speak, and avoid the wrong thoughts (such as "don't mess up"), yet Phil Jackson says, "the secret is not thinking." The secret to performance for him is a quiet mind that doesn't get in the way of the body doing what it has been trained to do instinctively. Or, to be more precise, the secret is a brain where the motor cortex takes over and is not interrupted by internal commentary that is often in the form of criticism and judgment.

A quiet mind is an ideal state, a mind characterized by undivided attention, rather than performance-interfering thoughts, but the ideal state is often difficult to attain at the Games or, as we saw with McLaughlin, at the Olympic Trials. Thinking does happen, for as Harris (2009) puts it, the mind is a thought-producing factory. It is precisely because thoughts will arise that mindfulness is so helpful. Mindfulness is not about *not* having thoughts, mindfulness is about relating to thoughts more skillfully when they do arise. To this end, it is helpful for athletes to learn to make a distinction between thoughts and attention and learn how mindfulness can be of use when thinking occurs at the Games during performance.

Thinking versus Attention

Thinking and attention are different functions of the human mind. Both are important functions, yet in the moment of execution, attention helps performance, whereas thinking more often than not gets in the way of performance. So it is not so much the wrong thoughts that get athletes such as the figure skater into trouble, but thoughts in general. Even positive thoughts can be a dangerous distraction from being immersed in the moment. Mikaela Shiffrin, an eighteen-year-old skiing sensation, was on her way to a gold medal during her second slalom run in Sochi, at the 2014 Winter Olympic Games (she was in the lead after the first run). Unexpectedly and unplanned, the thought "I will win my first medal" arose in her mind during her run (Abrahamson, 2014). Attention was disrupted, and she almost crashed out of the course. The thought, pleasant and positive as it may have been, was a distraction and almost cost her the race and the medal. Her ability to refocus on the task-relevant cues of skiing, once the mistake jolted her to full awareness, made the difference in her winning her first gold medal. Shiffrin skillfully worked with her mind, she didn't fight her thoughts (e.g., "I shouldn't be thinking this way") but rather was aware of what was on her mind and then successfully redirected her attention onto skiing the right way.

So it is not about not having the right thoughts, as it is about noticing when the thinking mind takes over. Mindfulness practice helps us to understand the difference between thinking and attending. Awareness allows the athlete to notice when the thinking mind gets in the way of attention. Shiffrin's mind noticed, and she came back and focused on her skiing. Michael Phelps, the world's most decorated Olympic Champion, captured this distinction between thoughts and attention and how it relates to performance perfectly when reporters asked him what he thinks about on the starting blocks before the gun goes off. His answer, "Nothing" (Phelps & Abrahamson, 2008, p. 51). He doesn't think about anything at this point in time. Not thinking about anything is not the same as having nothing on your mind, though. His mind at this point in time is characterized by attention. He is fully present with this moment, so he may *see* his lane, *hear* the announcer, *feel* his feet make contact with the blocks, press against them, and then *explode* off the blocks when the gun goes off. And indeed, it bears repeating: it is just such attention on the task at hand, this singular focus, that is the psychological currency of performance at the Games.

Flow

All the theoretical models of optimal performance in sport psychology have attention at the forefront. My preferred model is Csikszentmihalyi's (1990) flow model adapted by Sue Jackson (no relation to Phil Jackson) to sport. As with the original model, an athlete can achieve a flow state in sport when there is a balance between the perceived challenges and skills in the given situation. When challenges and skills are balanced, then action merges with awareness. The athlete is completely focused on the task at hand, goals are clear and self-evident, and feedback is immediate and obvious. The athlete experiences a perceived sense of control and a loss of a sense of self (for the self-critical internal voice completely disappears). The experience itself becomes its own reward (Jackson & Csikszentmihalyi, 1999).

Flow hardly ever happens when it matters the most, such as when a medal is on the line at the Olympic Games. The balance between challenge and skills is a tenuous one at the Games, not because the athletes don't have the skills to meet the challenge, but because the element of world-class competition in the unique Olympic environment introduces an irreducible sense of uncertainty into the equation. The uncertainty of the outcome mixed with the desire to achieve that outcome creates an almost irresistible siren call away from the present moment, away from focusing on the now, to thinking about the future, to the joy of victory or the agony that defeat would serve up.

Equanimity

The uncertainty of the outcome can be a hurricane that blows away any sense of equanimity, any sense of mental calmness and composure. While Michael Phelps has mastered the art of thinking about nothing in the starting blocks, many athletes are not as fortunate as we saw in Natalie Coughlin's description of the mind at the starting blocks. It is very hard for the Olympian not to think in those moments, and it is hard not to have thoughts when so much is on the line. Phil Jackson shares a similar observation about his NBA players: "Many of the players I've worked with tend to lose their equanimity after a certain point as the level of competition rises, because their minds start racing out of control" (Jackson & Delahanty 1995, p. 117). At the Olympic Games, almost by definition, the level of competition rises. The Games come around only every four years, and often only once in the athlete's life. And then the mind can easily start to race out of control. The mind of the athlete can become unruly and hard to tame under the shadow of the five rings. Since thinking can happen so easily, perhaps it is not about not thinking, but rather it is about knowing how the mind works and how to work with it effectively. And mindfulness is precisely about understanding how the mind works and about working with the mind effectively.

The Serbian tennis player and Olympic medalist Novak Djokovic, winner of ten Grand Slam titles, provides a wonderful example of how the mind works and how to work with it effectively in his autobiography (Djokovic, 2013). He practices mindfulness daily, and in his description and definition of mindfulness we can see how he works with his thinking mind: "It's a form of meditation where, instead of trying to silence your mind or find inner peace, you allow and accept your thoughts as they come, objectively, without judging them, while being mindful of the moment in real time" (Djokovic, 2013, p. 86). Djokovic (2013) says he still has "flashes of doubt," but he knows how to work differently with such thoughts after cultivating mindfulness skills. He acknowledges the presence of thoughts, and then lets them go by focusing on the moment, by focusing back on the task-relevant cues.

In my mind, Djokovic provides an example here of how mindfulness can be that precious compass that helps athletes stay on course on the uncertain journey of performance at the Olympic Games. Mindfulness practice trains awareness and attention (Hölzel et al., 2011). Mindfulness offers an understanding of how the mind works not just in general, but specifically in competition. Thoughts, whether positive or negative, will arise in the mind during competition. With mindfulness practice, we can notice such thoughts quickly, acknowledge them nonjudgmentally, and guide our attention back to the present moment, and thus skillfully work with our own mind.

A Personal Journey

The first key turning point toward mindfulness in my own development as a sport psychologist emerged from the confluence of reading *Sacred Hoops*, with its description of mindfulness in elite sports, and Kabat-Zinn's (1990) *Full Catastrophe Living*, with its clearly outlined training plan, along with an elective course in Zen during graduate school. The second key turning point came in 1999, when I had the privilege of a two-year applied fellowship at the Olympic Training Center in Colorado Springs. At that time, one of the resident sports I was assigned to work with was the sport of Olympic weightlifting. An aspiring Olympic hopeful in this sport, Tara Nott, expressed an interest in strengthening her attention as she prepared herself for the Olympic trials and, she hoped, the Olympic Games. Mindfulness, among more traditional sport psychology techniques, seemed to complement everything else we were working on. I made use of Jon Kabat-Zinn's materials from *Full Catastrophe Living* (1990) and introduced her to mindfulness. She was intrigued by the practice, and then practiced diligently in the year leading up to the Olympic trials and subsequently the Olympic Games in 2000. She qualified for the Games with an American record at the Olympic trials and then competed very successfully in Sydney, where she found herself on top of the podium. In the hectic aftermath of the Olympic Games, in the fall of 2000 she was kind enough to speak to a group of resident athletes at the Olympic Training Center about her mental preparation during a public sport psychology session titled *Psyched at Noon* (Nott, 2000).

> I used a lot of things at the Olympics to stay mentally focused. I worked on meditation beforehand, and at first I started out with five minutes and I was opening my eyes and I was like "are we done yet" because it was just so hard to sit there and breathe and relax and allow all the thoughts of expectations of the Olympics to come in and pass through and me and not really judge them or worry about them. Later I got to the point where I could sit for 30 minutes and really relax and deep breathe and focus and I really used that at the Olympics.

Tara's description of her experience with mindfulness is highly informative. In many ways, she understood mindfulness better than myself in those days[5].

Tara Nott's description of her experience with mindfulness matches Bishop's first component of mindfulness. Focus, the self-regulation of attention, was a stated performance objective. In Olympic weightlifting, you have six lifts, three clean and jerks, and three snatches. Often, for your first lift, you start with a weight that is close to your personal best if not your personal best. This is a high-stress moment from a performance perspective: the challenge is high, and the outcome is uncertain. The completion of the lift is a feat of strength, but first and foremost it is a feat of excellent technique and intense attention. As we have seen,

---

[5] Reader beware, understanding mindfulness is an ongoing journey for myself.

attention easily can be disrupted by overengaging with the story in our own head, initiated by self-referential processing: Will I make the first lift? What if I don't? What if I miss the first lift? Will I bomb out? Will I have a chance for a personal best? Will I have a chance to medal? Will I qualify for the Games or will I have wasted the last eight years of my life? Will I disappoint my friends and family? Will I let my coaches down? These are just some of a multitude of thoughts that may possibly arise at this point in time in the mind of the athlete.

Tara experienced such self-referential processing in the form of thoughts about the Olympic Games, specifically thoughts about expectations of winning a medal. In sport psychology, we refer to such thoughts as outcome-based thinking. Sport psychologists always instruct athletes to focus on the process, and outcome-based thinking can get a bad rap. However, outcome-based thinking isn't wrong per se. Such thinking matters from a motivational perspective: if you don't want to win, you most likely won't, and then it is doubtful you will put in the years of work and dedication that are required to hone your skills. So outcome-based thinking has a place in performance. Outcome-based thinking clarifies the destination, where you want to go in the future. It is not just about the process. The outcome does matter, and needs to matter to the athletes. Plus, given how the mind works, outcome-based thoughts will arise whether you want them or not. But outcome-based thinking is highly detrimental from an attentional perspective in the moment of execution, precisely because it takes the mind into the future (or the past), while performance happens in the present.

Tara wanted to be focused on each lift and not get tangled up in thoughts about the future. If you are lifting more than your body weight over your head, it matters to be fully present, it matters to be focused on the here and now. In high-level competition, the lens is narrowed to the essential performance cues. And when the mind wanders (which it often does), it matters to notice and then refocus quickly on those narrowed performance cues, both of which are the work of mindfulness. Again, attention is the psychological currency of performance. As mentioned earlier, Bishop's second part of the definition of mindfulness consists of an attitude of openness, acceptance, and curiosity. You are open to whatever arises in the mindscape; as Kabat-Zinn (2005) puts it, you accept what already is present, regardless of whether it is pleasant, unpleasant, or neutral, and you approach your moment-to-moment experience with an attitude of curiosity and wonder rather than judgment and condemnation.

Tara's short description of her experience with mindfulness reflects this aspect of the definition quite well. Tara "allows" the thoughts of expectations to come and pass through her mind and not judge the thoughts. Tara is open and accepting of what is already present, namely outcome-based thoughts. She does not fight these thoughts. She does not judge herself for having outcome-based thoughts, for having expectations (there is no "I shouldn't be having these thoughts"); instead, she displays an openness and a curiosity about how her mind worked with the idea of winning a medal at the Olympic Games. And because she takes this open and accepting stance to her own experience, the thoughts "pass through" her, the thoughts don't linger any more than necessary. She does not get lost in the thoughts, she does not get carried away, and she does not get entangled in them. The thoughts are simply thoughts, rather than the truth or reality. With awareness and acceptance of these outcome-based thoughts, she is able to refocus on her breathing. When it came time to lift, she was able to let go of thinking and focus on her technique, to focus on execution. With this process focus, she gave herself the best chance to be successful.

Formal mindfulness practice: Not a quick fix

Tara also talks about the difficulty of the practice, particularly early on. To sit still, to do seemingly nothing, to just sit and focus on your breathing, is a lot harder than it sounds. Anybody who has ever practiced mindfulness knows how the thinking mind will raise its hand almost instantly to fill the silence with all kinds of thoughts. Neuroscience refers to this state of mind as the default mode of the human mind (Raichle & Abraham, 2007). This default network is also referred to as the task negative network and stands in contrast to the task positive network, which comes on line when we are focused on a specific task. So when the mind isn't actively engaged in a task, the mind tends to wander and the default network becomes active (Mason et al., 2007). McGonigal (2012) lists four main activities as characteristic of the default state, four mental activities to which the brain defaults. First, there is an almost constant commentary on whatever we are experiencing in the present moment, almost like play-by-play on sports television. Second, the mind defaults to time travel; the mind rehashes the past or predicts the future. Third, the mind can default to self-referential processing, as it tries to decide what a given moment means for one's sense of self. And fourth, the mind engages in social cognition, where we can get caught up in thoughts about social comparison.

Whenever the default mode of the mind kicks in, we are no longer fully engaged in the present moment, and with mindfulness practice we can notice when this switch of attention happens. The thought, "Are we done yet?" arises quickly in the mind of an athlete who tastes mindfulness for the first time in a formal setting, and the thought can be excellent grist for the mill. All-time basketball great and Olympic Gold medalist Michael Jordan had a very similar experience when he was introduced to mindfulness by Phil Jackson: "When we first started meditating during stretching before practice, I thought it was crazy. I'm closing one eye and keeping the other eye open to see what other fool is doing this besides me" (Jordan, 1998, p. 95).

Nott's and Jordan's observations are spot on and insightful when it comes time to introduce mindfulness to Olympic athletes. Mindfulness is not easy for athletes; it is not a quick fix, and it is not a silver bullet (the mind of the Olympian all too often hungers for the illusion of a silver bullet). Rather than approaching mindfulness from the perspective of a cynic or a true believer, Kabat-Zinn (1990) suggests to take the perspective of a skeptic. Be open-minded about it and give it a serious try by actually engaging fully in the practice, just like Michael Jordan did:

> Eventually I became more accepting because I could see everyone making an effort. I opened my mind to meditation and Phil's teachings. My mind still travels a bit, but Phil taught us to concentrate on breathing to bring the mind back to center. There are certain times when I incorporate those thoughts into my daily life, but I certainly haven't mastered the concepts yet (Jordan, 1998, p. 99).

Mindfulness practice leads to three types of changes with regard to the default network (McGonigal, 2012). We recover more quickly from default mode distractions and move back into the experiencing self; we spend less time in the default mode in general; and we strengthen the area that creates the experiencing self, the self that is fully present with this moment. Mindfulness is a skill, and like any other skill, it requires training. Fortunately, training and hard work are concepts athletes can relate to. Yes, we live in a world where we tend to look for the quick and easy fix. Athletes are no different in this regard, and certainly they can fall prey to the allure of the quick fix, such as performance-enhancing drugs. Mindfulness is not a performance-enhancing drug; it doesn't come cheap, precisely because it requires serious training. It is important to communicate to the athletes the skill- and practice-based approach of mindfulness and dispel the illusion of a quick fix.

As Tara said, initially she started with five minutes, then eventually she worked her way up to thirty minutes (daily). So there was a clear training progression, kind of like an athlete would progress in training in general, where you would either increase volume, intensity, or task difficulty over time to get (and to allow) your body to adapt and grow. Tara made mindfulness practice a habit; she engaged in what Jon Kabat-Zinn (1994) called "the slow disciplined work of digging trenches" (p. 111). For only when you patiently dig these trenches will you be able to be mindful in key moments and not become overwhelmed at the big events.

My personal journey continues
Despite this highly positive experience in Sydney, I did not become a mindfulness convert and wholeheartedly begin to introduce every athlete to mindfulness. This hesitancy was partly based on my own inexperience and lack of understanding of mindfulness, and partly based on the assumption that this Eastern approach was still too foreign for Western athletes. I have encountered such attitudes with Olympic athletes. For example, one deeply religious athlete during a first consultation specifically stated not wanting to be exposed to any "Eastern" methods.

The next key turning point in my own development came in 2004 at the Athens Olympic Games. A team I worked with at the time, in a partner sport, was one of the Olympic favorites in the pair's event, along with two traditional powerhouses. The competition consisted of multiple rounds and progressed just as planned, with all three of the favorite teams eventually occupying the number one, two, and three positions with one round to go. Everything was going according to plan. The dogfight the athletes had prepared for was on, meaning three favorites were vying for the gold medal. Yet then something surprising happened. The number one favorite team fell by the wayside with a completely botched execution by one of the two members. And as fate would have it, the number two favorite also suffered a mishap immediately afterward. Now the number two favorite team was out of the medals as well. The coast was clear, only one original favorite was left, and the gold medal was in clear sight. The dogfight to the very end, for which the favorites had prepared, was over and the gold medal was there for the taking.

Sitting in the stands, I sensed my own excitement, and the thought entered, "Wow, we've got this, what a great way to start the competition, this will have a ripple effect for the whole team, this will be so cool," and then also, unbidden and unwelcome, there was the thought, "Just don't screw it up now." I was simply a spectator, yet here was my own "self-referential processing," the mind automatically went to the future and spun a story, the default network in full bloom. And I got tangled up in the story. Imagine what might have gone through the athletes' mind at this point in time. Perhaps it is safe to say that they most likely had to deal with their own self-referential processing. The competition did not end well for the last of the three favorites. The mistakes that had befallen the two other favorite teams proved to be contagious, and they shared the same fate as their fellow competitors who were in the lead with one round to go. All three favorites finished outside of the medals. All of the three favorites were confident, experienced, and mentally tough teams. All were well prepared, and all handled the competition well up to this final stage.

Yet, as far as the athletes I worked with were concerned, there was a key skill missing in their preparation, a skill I had not introduced. I had never talked to the athletes about mindfulness because I thought it was too far out there, too "Eastern" for their worldview. The missing skill in their preparation for performance at the Olympic Games was a particular type of awareness: an awareness of what is on the mind in general and specific-ally in those crucial moments in competition; an understanding of what was on your mind; an acceptance of what was on your mind; and then, with that awareness, understanding and acceptance, the ability then to direct attention back to the task at hand and away from the outcome.

In this moment, for those athletes, with the illusion of the gold medal around their neck, it was next to impossible for them not to have thoughts about that medal. It was next to impossible not to have self-referential processing. Yes, a clear mind would have been ideal. But a clear mind does not mean no thoughts; a clear mind means an awareness of what's on your mind and an ability to work with what's on your mind. Muesse (2011), in his introduction to mindfulness course, offers the metaphor of a bottle of water filled with mud. If you shake the bottle, the mud is everywhere and clouds the water. If you let it settle, the mud settles and the water becomes clear. The mud is still there, but it no longer clouds the water. Similarly, thoughts can (and will) still be there in competition, but they no longer need to cloud the mind if you can let them settle. And you can metaphor-ically let them settle if you understand how the mind works and if you can work with your mind. Athletes are often relieved to hear that mind-fulness is not about not having thoughts but rather about understanding how to work with the mind when thoughts arise. Thoughts will arise in competition; you work with such thoughts by being aware of them, by letting the thoughts settle, so to speak, and then have the clear mind of concentration emerge.

This experience at the 2004 Games convinced me that a different approach was warranted in my own methods for preparing athletes for performance at the Games. To grasp how the mind works was paramount for optimal preparation and this required the training of awareness and the self-regulation of attention. I intended to heed the lesson from 2004. Mindfulness would no longer be "too far out there," too "Eastern," but rather be front and center in my approach to sport psychology.

A Training Camp for the Mind

Committing to mindfulness meant, however, I needed more training. And more training proved to be the next key turning point in my own development. First came a seven-day Mindfulness Based Stress Reduction (MBSR) training retreat led by Jon Kabat-Zinn and Saki Santorelli in Rhinebeck, New York, in 2006. The retreat offered in-depth instruction in MBSR, and a key lesson from this retreat was Kabat-Zinn's admonition: The teaching comes from practice. If you want to teach mindfulness, you better practice yourself! So daily mindfulness practice became a habit. After this initial MBSR training, I started to offer weekly voluntary mindfulness sessions at the Colorado Springs Olympic Training Center. This was practice for the athletes and practice for myself in providing group instruction. To reinforce adherence and understanding, I also wrote a weekly note to all the athletes who participated in the weekly practice, usually a quote from an athlete taken from the media and interpreted through the lens of mindfulness. Earlier in the chapter, I discussed the "practice" aspect of mindfulness.

Kabat-Zinn makes a distinction between formal and informal mindfulness practice. Informal practice really can be any activity to which we bring our full attention and awareness. Formal practice generally consists of mindful sitting or mindful walking. Formal practice provides the foundation and helps to strengthen the notion of informal practice. Dan Siegel (2010) points out that any practice can be used intentionally to practice attention. This insight is important for athletes, particularly for athletes who might be a bit reluctant to engage in formal sitting practice. Any time an athlete trains in his or her sport, the athlete has the opportunity to bring full attention intentionally to the practice of the sport. Any time the athlete practices his or her sport, there is the opportunity to work with the mind; this is the opportunity to practice awareness ("What is on my mind right now?") and cultivate attention ("Where will I put my mind?"). While I strongly encourage athletes to engage in formal practice, the objective is to transfer mindfulness to their training and competition setting.

Ron Siegel (2010) uses the metaphor of physical training to explain the trajectory from informal to formal practice to sitting in retreat. You can get some exercise by taking the stairs, rather than the elevator, or by going for a walk; you can train more deliberately by going to the gym, or by running four times a week, and then you can also go to training camp to get in shape. For Siegel, a ten-day silent retreat would be like going to a training camp for the mind. In 2009, my schedule allowed me to participate in two such training camps for the mind. The ten-day silent retreats were held at Spirit Rock in the Vipassana tradition with strong emphasis on science. The first retreat, titled "Scientists' Meditation Retreat," included presentations by Cliff Saron on the recently completed Shamatha project (S. Boorstein, C. Saron, W. Nisker, T. Goodman, & D. Winston, personal communication, January 11–18, 2009). The Shamatha project attempted to understand the effects of meditation on attention, health, empathy, and emotion by studying sixty randomly assigned retreat participants who participated in two three-month retreats (Saron, 2013).[6] The second retreat, titled "Insight Meditation Retreat for MBSR & MBCT Professionals," was led by Kabat-Zinn, John Teasdale, and Christina Feldman (J. Kabat-Zinn, J. Teasdale, & C. Feldman, personal communication, December 3–12, 2009). These retreats offered formal practice in the spirit of a training camp and consisted of such exercises as sitting, walking, and eating mindfully, as well as doing mindful chores (such as cleaning the toilets) and dharma talks in the evening.[7] Every day started with the first sitting at 6 AM. Training was all day long, for ten days, nine of which were in silence. Indeed, this was a training camp for the mind. Athletes understand the experience of a training camp. Informal practice, formal practice, retreat practice; daily training, a training progression, and training camp – intuitively, mindfulness can fit into the worldview of the Olympic athlete. Mindfulness made sense practically and experientially, with the emphasis on hard-nosed science in both retreats. Mindfulness also made sense scientifically, which proved to be another key turning point in my development.

The Science of Mindfulness

Triggered by Jon Kabat-Zinn's work in Mindfulness-Based Stress Reduction, a plethora of research papers started to populate psychology journals

---

[6] For a first person account of the Shamatha project, see Van Waning (2014).
[7] The journalist Dan Harris (2014) provides an in-depth and highly entertaining description of the experience of a ten-day silent retreat in his book *10 % Happier*.

in the late 1990s and early 2000s, followed by many trade books that brought mindfulness to a lay audience. Slowly but surely, sport psychology also came on board, with research papers and applied texts entering the marketplace. For example, the golf teaching professional Joe Parent, trained in the Shambala Buddhist tradition, wrote a delightful little book titled *Zen Golf*, where he applied the lessons of Zen to teaching golf (Parent, 2002). Gardner and Moore, two sport psychologists, published *The Psychology of Enhancing Human Performance* (Gardner & Moore, 2007) as a follow up to their book *Clinical Sport Psychology* (Garden & Moore, 2006), in which they make a case for mindfulness in sport psychology. In both books, they adopted Acceptance and Commitment Therapy (ACT) for sport psychology and titled it the Mindfulness-Acceptance-Commitment (MAC) approach to sport. ACT, which does not require formal sitting practice, offers a host of mindfulness techniques (e.g., Harris, 2009) that seem very applicable to sport psychology. The plethora of basic research findings spoke to someone trained in a Western science-practitioner model who is convinced that attention is the currency of performance.

Based on a review of the existing research findings, Hölzel and colleagues (2011) proposed a theoretical framework that consists of several impact mechanisms of mindfulness that lead to increased self-regulation: (a) attention regulation, (b) body awareness, (c) emotion regulation, and (d) change in perspective on the self. Birrer and colleagues (2012) offered a similar framework and summarized the still sparse mindfulness research in sport psychology. Without launching an in-depth review of the relevant research, here is one example of how the science of mindfulness fits the psychology of the Olympic Games. One of the papers cited in these two review articles is a study by Jha and colleagues (2010). The study, conducted with predeployment soldiers, examined the protective effects of mindfulness training on working memory capacity and mood. Jha and colleagues (2010) stated that "persistent and intensive demands, such as those experienced during high-stress intervals, may deplete working memory capacity and lead to cognitive failures and emotional disturbances" (p. 54). The research team concluded that sufficient mindfulness practice "may protect against functional impairment associated with high-stress challenges that require a tremendous amount of cognitive control, self-awareness, situational awareness and emotional regulation" (Jha and colleagues, 2010, p. 54).

A high-stress challenge that requires tremendous cognitive control, self-awareness, situational awareness, and emotional regulation seems to be a particularly apt description of the Olympic environment and the challenge athletes face there. And perhaps the epitome of such a high-stress challenge at the Olympic Games may have been Michael Phelps successful attempt to win eight Olympic Gold medals in eight events at the 2008 Beijing Olympic Games. Interestingly enough, and as anecdotal support for Jha's study, his coach, Bob Bowman, said that Phelps's had learned over the years of his development to turn the inevitable fatigue and stress of competing in so many events into sheer focus (Shipley, 2012). Michael Phelps may have never heard of mindfulness, but based on his perform-ance he understood how to work with his mind in competition and trained his mind. The fascinating science of mindfulness was the final nail in the coffin and swept away any final concerns about adopting mindfulness as the guiding paradigm for Olympic sport psychology.

Mindfulness beyond Attention and Stress

John Teasdale (2009), in one of his dharma talks during the silent retreat, pointed out that mindfulness isn't just a way of paying attention; rather, mindfulness is about the dharma, the whole of the Buddha's teaching. The whole of the Buddha's teaching goes far beyond this chapter. But suffice to say, mindfulness isn't just about being focused but about understanding yourself, understanding your own mind, and acting ethically. From an Olympic perspective, this outlook is reminiscent of the admonition over the entrance of the ancient Greek oracle in Delphi: Know thyself. And one aspect that athletes may want to know about themselves, from a Buddhist perspective, is that the source of *dukkha* is craving or attachment to desire. What is it that Olympic athletes desire? They desire to participate in the Games, first and foremost, and once there, almost naturally, they desire an Olympic medal, preferably one with a golden color.

Desire and craving a medal are why the mind of the Olympian can become so unruly. John Teasdale (2009) points out that the Pali word for craving is *Thanha*, best described as an unquenchable thirst, a thirst that can never be satisfied. Yet, desire is natural and normal, and as we have seen when we discussed outcome goals, almost certainly necessary for an Olympic athlete in the pursuit of a medal at the Games. It is the attachment to desire that can become the big stumbling block for athletes rather than desire itself. It is the inability to let go of desire when it comes time to focus solely on the execution that will get the athlete in trouble. An athlete who understands the attentional danger that attachment to desire brings is in a better position to work with his or her mind in the Olympic environment.

Desire, of course, is also present for the sport psychologist in the Olympic setting. You "desire" your athletes to be successful, and you think of the athletes you work with as "your" athletes, and if "your" athletes do well, it reflects well on your work, and if "your" athletes don't do well, it can reflect poorly on "you." Sport psychologists also bring a self to the table, and as Teasdale (2009) put it so wisely, "selfing" can get you in trouble because you fail to see the myriad uncontrollable factors that impact performance. Taking the outcome of performance personally is not a wise approach. My colleague at the U.S. Olympic Committee, Sean McCann offers a helpful antidote to "selfing" at the Games: Take your work very seriously, but don't take yourself too seriously (McCann, 2000).

Conclusion

Mindfulness has become perfect paradigm for me to understand the mind of the athlete (and my own mind) in the context of the Olympic Games. At the outset of this chapter, I used the metaphor of mindfulness as a map, a guide, and a compass. A mindful approach to performance allows me to address what I consider to be three key questions when working with athletes:

Key question #1: What is on your mind right now, in this moment of performance? Are you focused on execution, or are you distracted by your own thoughts? Metaphorically, this question addresses where you are on the "map" of performance.

Key question #2: Where will you put your mind in this moment of performance? Can you as an athlete regulate your attention and put your mind where it needs to be during performance? Metaphorically speaking, can the athlete "guide" his or her attention on the task at hand and keep it there?

Key question #3: Why do you do what you do? This question addresses the individual values that can act like a compass and point the athlete in the right direction no matter the outcome of competition.

With these three questions in mind, mindfulness offers a way to train the mind of the athlete, not only to perform to his or her potential in the sporting arena, but also to perform to the athlete's potential in life. Not too long ago, I attended a ten-year reunion of a medal winning team I had the privilege to work with. I hadn't seen many of these athletes in the ten years that had passed since they won their medal. It was fun to reconnect with all the athletes and see what their post-Olympic life was like. Some were married with children, some worked very successfully in the corporate world, some were coaches, and one became a nurse who now works in a cancer center. She shared a fascinating insight with me at this reunion. She said she loves working at the cancer center, as challenging as it is, because it reminds her of her Olympic journey. Both journeys being an Olympian and being a cancer patient, as different as they are, share some commonalities. Both journeys challenge you mentally and physically, and for both the outcomes are very uncertain. Mindfulness offers the athlete and the sport psychologist a way to prepare mentally for such uncertain journeys in the world of high-performance sport. While we desire a "winning" outcome in sport (and certainly in the battle against cancer), we have little to no control over it. Yet we do control how we prepare and how we engage with the present moment. Phil Jackson (1995) puts it best: "winning is important to me, but what brings me real joy is the experience of being fully engaged in whatever I'm doing" (p. 201). Mindfulness offers the Olympic athlete (and the sport psychologist) a pathway to be fully engaged in whatever he or she is doing in the face of the uncertainty of the outcome and in the face of attachment to desire.

REFERENCES

Abrahamson, A. (2014, February 21). Confidence, skill a golden combination for "young gun" Mikaela Shiffrin. *NBC Olympics*. Retrieved from www.nbcolympics.com/news/confidence-skill-golden-combination-young-gun-mikaela-shiffrin?ctx=golden-moments

Birrer, D., Röthlin, P., and Morgan, G. (2012). Mindfulness to enhance athletic performance: Theoretical considerations and possible impact mechanisms. *Mindfulness*, 3(3), 235–246. doi: 10.1007/s12671-012-0109-2

Bishop, S. R., Lau, M., Shapiro, S., Carlson, L.E., Anderson, N.D., Carmody, J., . . . Devins, G. (2004). Mindfulness: A proposed operational definition. *Clinical Psychology: Science and Practice*, 11(3), 230–241. doi: 10.1093/clipsy.bph077

Csikszentmihalyi, M. (1990). *Flow: The psychology of optimal experience*. New York, NY: Harper & Row.

Djokovic, N. (2013). *Serve to win: The 14-day gluten-free trial plan for physical and mental excellence*. New York, NY: Ballantine.

Gardner, F. L., and Moore, Z. E. (2006). *Clinical sport psychology*. Champaign, IL: Human Kinetics.

(2007). *The psychology of enhancing human performance. The Mindfulness-Acceptance-Commitment (MAC) approach*. New York, NY: Springer.

Halberstam, D. (1996). *The amateurs: the story of four young men and their quest for an Olympic gold medal*. New York, NY: Ballantine.

Hanel, M. (2010, January, 20) Psyched out: Pairs skaters Keauna McLaughlin and Rockne Brubaker's disastrous Olympic trials. *Vanity Fair*. Retrieved from www.vanityfair.com/online/daily/2010/01/psyched-out-pairs-skaters-keauna-mclaughlin-and-rockne-brubakers-diastrous-olympic-trials

Harris, D. (2014). *10 % happier: How I tamed the voice in my head, reduced stress without losing my edge, and found self-help that actually works – a true story* (reprint ed.). New York, NY: Dey Street.

Harris, R. (2009). *ACT made simple. An easy to read primer on Acceptance and Commitment Therapy*. Oakland, CA: New Harbinger.

Hölzel, B. K., Lazar, S. W., Gard, T., Schuman-Olivier, Z., Vago D. R., and Ott, U. (2011). How does mindfulness meditation work? Proposing mechanisms of action from a conceptual and neural perspective. *Perspectives on Psychological Science*, 6(6) 537–559. doi: 10.1177/1745691611419671

Jackson, P., and Delehanty, H. (1995). *Sacred hoops. Spiritual lessons of a hardwood warrior*. New York, NY: Hyperion.

Jackson, S. A., and Csikszentmihalyi, M. (1999). *Flow in sports: The keys to optimal experiences and performances*. Champaign, IL: Human Kinetics.

Jha, A. P., Stanley, E. A., Kiyonaga, A., Wong, L., and Gelfand, L. (2010). Examining the protective effects of mindfulness training on working memory capacity and affective experience. *Emotion*, 10(1), 54–64. doi: 10.1037/a0018438

Jordan, M. (1998). *For the love of the game: My story*. M. Vancil (Ed.). New York, NY: Crown.

Kabat-Zinn, J. (1990). *Full catastrophe living: Using the wisdom of your body and mind to face stress, pain, and illness*. New York, NY: Delta.

(1994). *Wherever you go, there you are: Mindfulness meditation for everyday life*. New York, NY: Hyperion.

(2005). *Coming to our senses: Healing ourselves and the world through mindfulness*. New York, NY: Hyperion.

Kabat-Zinn, J., Beall, B., and Rippe, J. (1985, June). A systematic mental training program based on mindfulness meditation to optimize performance in collegiate and Olympic rowers. Poster session presented at the World Congress in Sport Psychology, Copenhagen, Denmark.

Mason, M. F., Norton, M. I., Van Horn, J. D., Wegner, D. M., Grafton, S. T., and Macrae, C. N. (2007). Wandering minds: The default network and stimulus-independent thought. *Science*, 315, 393–395. doi: 10.1126/science.1131295

McCann, S. (2000). Doing sport psychology at the really big show. In M. Andersen (Ed.), *Doing sport psychology* (pp. 209–222). Champaign, IL: Human Kinetics.

McGonigal, K. (2012). *The neuroscience of change: A compassion-based guide to personal transformation*. Louisville, CO: Sounds True.

Muesse, M. W. (2011). *Practicing mindfulness: An introduction to meditation*. Chantilly, VA: Teaching Company.

Nott, T. (2000, November). Psyched at noon. In P. Haberl (Chair), *Lecture series presented at the Olympic Training Center*. Lecture conducted at Olympic Training Center, Colorado Springs, CO.

Parent, J. (2002). *Zen golf: Mastering the mental game*. New York, NY: Random House.

Phelps, M., and Abrahamson, A. (2008). *No limits: The will to succeed*. New York, NY: Simon & Schuster.

Raichle, M. E., and Abraham, Z. S. (2007). A default mode of brain function: A brief history of an evolving idea. *NeuroImage*, 37(4), 1083–1090. doi: 10.1016/j.neuroimage.2007.02.041

Salzberg, S., and Goldstein, J. (2001) *Insight meditation: A step-by-step course on how to meditate*. Boulder, CO: Sounds True.

Saron, C. (2013). Training the mind: The Shamatha project. In A. Fraser (Ed.), *The healing power of meditation: Leading experts on Buddhism, psychology, and medicine explore the health benefits of contemplative practice*. Boston, MA: Shambala.

Shipley, A. (2012, June 14) Michael Phelps has mastered the psychology of speed. *Washington Post*. Retrieved from www.washingtonpost.com/sports/olympics/michael-phelps-has-mastered-the-psychology-of-speed/2012/06/13/gJQAHiQuZV_story.html

Siegel, D. (2010). Neuroscience & mindfulness: Spirit rock Monday and Wednesday talks. *Spirit Rock*. Retrieved from www.spiritrock.org/Dan Siegel

Siegel, R. D. (2010). *The mindfulness solution: Everyday practices for everyday problems*. New York, NY: Guilford Press.

(2014). *The science of mindfulness: A research-based path to well-being*. Retrieved from www.thegreatcourses.com/courses/the-positive-mind-mindfulness-and-the-science-of-happiness.html

Teasdale, J. (2009, December 3). *Suffering and selfing: The 1st and 2nd noble truth*. Retrieved from www.spiritrock.org/John Teasdale

Van Waning, A. (2014). *The less dust, the more trust: Participating in the Shamatha project, meditation and science*. Washington, DC: Mantra.

Williams, D. (2012, April 17). 100-day-countdown flying by for athletes. *Team USA*. Retrieved from www.teamusa.org/News/2012/April/17/100-Day-Countdown-flying-by-for-athletes

CHAPTER II

Mindfulness Training Program for Chinese Athletes and Its Effectiveness

Gang-yan Si, Karen Lo, Chun-qing Zhang

On August 1, 2012, at the London Olympic Games, Yutong Luo, a Chinese diving athlete, won his first Olympic gold medal in the three-meter springboard synchronized diving men's final. However, prior to this achievement, he had been silent in the Chinese diving "Dream Team" for over twelve years and had failed to qualify to represent China in the previous three Olympic Games. The truth was that he had been highly competitive at every competition, but it seemed *luck* was never on his side.

Eleven months before the London Olympic Games, the first author of this chapter was contacted and invited to work with Yutong. Yutong explained that his major problem over the years had been that he did not know how to deal with the overwhelming anxiety and stress, which had severely sabotaged his performance. By making use of some psychological skills (mainly relaxation techniques) to control his anxiety, he had managed to locate the source of his stressors and change his belief patterns. However, despite this, every time an important competition arrived, he was still unsuccessful in controlling his anxiety and the pressure he felt.

An alternative mindfulness-based training approach, as outlined in this chapter, was introduced to Yutong. This approach highlighted to him the importance of accepting and decentering from his anxieties rather than trying to control or change them. In addition to the formal mindfulness practice, he implemented a three-minute meditation technique to practice during his diving training. Since this mindfulness training, Yutong learned to embrace various experiences, which were also accompanied by positive feedback from his coaches.

A gold medal in hand, Yutong Luo finally realized his Olympic dream in London, resulting from the tough technical, physical, and mental preparation. As demonstrated by this example, mindfulness training is now being used as an alternative approach to enhance athletes' performance and overall well-being (Gardner & Moore, 2004; Moore, 2009), compared to the traditional psychological skill training (PST) programs that are based on cognitive behavioral training models (Meichenbaum, 1977).

Traditional PST has dominated athletes' mental training over the last thirty years (Harmison, 2011). The basic assumption of traditional PST is that athletes need to develop the capacity to control internal states for the purpose of achieving an optimal psychological state (Hardy, Jones, & Gould, 1996). However, to change or control the naturally occurring internal states in PST is at best ineffective and at worst counterproductive (Gardner & Moore, 2004). Besides, there is a lack of empirical support for the efficacy of traditional PST (Gardner & Moore, 2007).

Although PST can help athletes achieve an ideal performance state, the challenging situations that can arise during competition make it difficult to maintain this ideal performance state (Haberl, 2007; Si, 2006). As such, the mindfulness-based approach may have an advantage over PST due to its focus on awareness and acceptance (Gardner & Moore, 2004). Accordingly, a sport-specific mindfulness training program, the Mindfulness-Acceptance-Commitment (MAC) approach (Gardner & Moore, 2004, 2007), has been developed and is the dominant mindfulness-based intervention in sport. This program is based on two widely used and well-developed mindfulness- and acceptance-based therapies, namely, Mindfulness-Based Cognitive Therapy (MBCT; Segal, Williams, & Teasdale, 2002) and acceptance and commitment therapy (ACT; Hayes, Strosahl, & Wilson, 1999).

The MAC is a flexible protocol comprising seven modules, including (a) preparing the client with psychoeducation; (b) introducing mindfulness and cognitive defusion; (c) introducing values and value-driven behavior; (d) introducing acceptance; (e) enhancing commitment; (f) consolidating skills and developing poise; and (g) maintaining and enhancing mindfulness, acceptance, and commitment (see Moore, 2009, for a review). Regarding the goal of intervention and the mechanism of action, the MAC targets acceptance and emotion regulation, including improving acceptance, emotional awareness, clarity, and distress tolerance (Moore, 2009).

In addition, the Mindful Sports Performance Enhancement (MSPE; Kaufman, Glass, & Arnkoff, 2009) has been developed by adapting the mindfulness meditation and mindfulness movements used in MBSR and MBCT. The MSPE is a four-session protocol consisting of (a) introduction, diaphragmatic breathing exercise, body scanning meditation, and mindful breathing practice; (b) diaphragmatic breathing exercise, body scanning meditation, sitting meditation, and mindful yoga; (c) diaphragmatic breathing exercise, sitting meditation, mindful yoga, and walking meditation; and (d) diaphragmatic breathing exercise, body scanning meditation, sitting meditation, and walking meditation. The first three sessions take 2.5 hours, and the last session takes three hours. All sessions include a summary, discussion, and home practice.

Along with the development and application of the mindfulness programs for athletes, the effectiveness of mindfulness-based training on the well-being and performance of athletes has been preliminarily established over the last decade (Gardner & Moore, 2012). Since the pioneering study on the application of mindfulness meditation to collegiate and Olympic rowers was conducted by Kabat-Zinn, Beall, and Rippe in 1985 and the formal introduction of the MAC approach (Gardner & Moore, 2004), real interest in this particular applied research area has only grown. Recent correlational and intervention studies have indicated that mindfulness has a positive association with the flow construct (Aherne, Moran, & Lonsdale, 2011; Kee & Wang, 2008). In line with findings from healthy and clinical populations (e.g., Baer, 2003; Hofmann et al., 2010; Keng, Smoski, & Robins, 2011), performance improvements, positive psychological states, and a decrease in negative psychological states have been reported by several empirical sport studies (e.g., Bernier et al., 2009; Kaufman et al., 2009; Thompson et al., 2011). Despite these positive findings, there is still a lack of high-quality experimental studies using randomized control trial designs in order to make causal inferences regarding the mindfulness–performance and the mindfulness–well-being relationships (Birrer, Röthlin, & Morgan, 2012; Chung, Si, & Zhang, 2013; Gardner & Moore, 2012).

The benefit of applying mindfulness-based training to Chinese athletes has also been acknowledged, given its effectiveness for our Western counterparts (Zhang, Bu, & Si, 2012). However, the direct application of the Western mindfulness-based programs, such as the MAC, into a Chinese context might be somewhat limited. It seems imperative that socioculturally relevant education and training should be integrated into mindfulness training programs for Chinese athletes (Chung et al., 2013). Specifically, the application of mindfulness-based therapy for Chinese athletes should be integrated with Chinese culture and the Chinese sport system (the Whole-Nation system).

In Chinese culture, mindfulness should not be separated from the heart. Kabat-Zinn (2003) declared that mind and heart are the same in Asian languages, and therefore the philosophy of Chinese psychology is based on the concept of heart (Shen, 2009). For example, when asking Chinese people to refocus and become aware of the present moment, an often-asked question is "Where is your heart?" And, individuals from Chinese culture can use heart as an anchor to refocus to the present moment instead of just relying on the breathing.

Given that the Chinese athletes train and compete under the Whole-Nation system, which is a political and administrative mechanism founded by the government, they are required to adapt themselves to two main characteristics of this system: (a) the prioritization of collective interests and (b) an executive-led system that takes charge of professional and technical issues (Si et al., 2011). The process of adaptation to this system can be difficult, and a full understanding of personal values and their relationship with the collective interest in a sport career is bound to play an important role in this adaptation. Under the Whole-Nation sport system, Chinese athletes' values are a dynamic integration of personal values and collective interests. Given that coaches and administrative officials in Chinese sport contexts emphasize the value of collective interests, it is sometimes not easy for Chinese athletes to discover and consistently commit to their personal values. Nonetheless, many elite Chinese athletes continue to thrive in their sport careers by establishing a new understanding of the meaning of their life and their personal values, which we define as "insight" in this chapter. As such, the concept of insight should be incorporated into mindfulness training for Chinese athletes, as it is a distinct component, frequently used by elite Chinese athletes and coaches in Chinese sport culture, to teach the athletes to adjust optimally to training and competition life under the Whole-Nation system.

We developed the Mindfulness-Acceptance-Insight-Commitment (MAIC) program for Chinese athletes, given concerns about the differences between Western and Chinese athletes in the application of mindfulness-based training for performance enhancement and athletes' general well-being. This program integrates the concepts of heart and mind, socially oriented values, insight, and acceptance-based adversity coping (Si, 2006) into the existing, well-developed MAC approach (Gardner & Moore, 2004; 2007). The theoretical origin and key components of the MAIC will be explained, and its effectiveness will be demonstrated through a single-case design study with elite Chinese synchronized swimming athletes.

The Development of the Mindfulness-Acceptance-Insight-Commitment (MAIC) Program for Chinese Athletes

Theoretical Origin of MAIC

Before we introduce the key components of the MAIC, we will explain the theoretical origins of the program. The MAIC was built on the existing MAC protocol (Gardner & Moore, 2007), with the addition of the integration of the concepts of heart and mind, socially oriented values, insight, and acceptance-based adversity coping (Si, 2006). Firstly, we will illustrate the limitations of the application of the MAC to Chinese athletes based on our applied studies and further explain why we have integrated the additional concepts into the MAC to form the MAIC protocol.

The Mindfulness-Acceptance-Commitment (MAC) approach in sport

The third wave of cognitive behavioral therapy typically includes Mindfulness-Based Stress Reduction (MBSR; Kabat-Zinn, 1990, 1994), Mindfulness-Based Cognitive Therapy (MBCT; Segal et al., 2002), Dialectical Behavior Therapy (DBT; Linehan, 1993), and Acceptance and Commitment Therapy (ACT; Hayes et al., 1999). In the sporting domain, the MAC approach (Gardner & Moore, 2004; 2007) was developed based on the ACT and MBCT, aiming to improve sport performance and the general well-being of athletes.

The third wave of cognitive behavioral therapy emphasizes changing the context of the thoughts rather than changing the contents of thoughts (Hayes, Follette, & Linehan, 2004). In other words, it attempts to alter the function of events rather than the actual content. For example, when athletes feel nervous or anxious in competition, the third-wave cognitive behavioral therapy encourages the athlete to embrace the anxiety with an open-minded awareness and in an accepting way rather than trying to control or replace it with a relaxed state. The ultimate goal of third-wave cognitive behavioral therapy is to establish psychological flexibility and effective action (Wilson & Murrell, 2004). The therapy process includes exploring the roots and consequences of one's psychological patterns (e.g., experiential avoidance and the ubiquity of pain), which helps clients to learn acceptance (i.e., of aversive thoughts and feelings) and decentering or cognitive defusion, which is described as individuals cognitively "defusing" or distancing themselves from private thoughts and feelings (Hayes et al., 1999). Clients are encouraged to stay in the present moment with awareness and see all events as a transient phenomenon;

they are then guided to understand their life and performance expectations (i.e., values) before establishing effective actions alongside their goals and values (Wilson & Murrell, 2004). The therapeutic skills include mindfulness, cognitive defusion, acceptance, willingness, value, and commitment (Hayes, 2004).

In the MAC, acceptance and nonjudgmental awareness allow athletes to adopt a constructive way to experience the present moment, by forsaking the desire to control cognitive events by viewing them from a decentered perspective. Decentered awareness, in contrast to the habitual or automatic cognitive behavioral model (i.e., experiential avoidance), helps athletes form an open and accepting attitude.

Value provides the direction and dynamic aspect to an athlete's ideal life and performance by highlighting the elements that athletes value most in their life, and this value is manifested during the process of the pursuit of excellence. For instance, if an athlete's value is to realize his maximum potential during the Olympic Games, he or she will train and fight for this value during the process of its achievement. The MAC approach is designed to help athletes clarify their values and learn how to take action based on their values within the sport realm (Gardner & Moore, 2004, 2007). Commitment can be viewed as an athlete who is regularly and consistently involved in actions that are congruent with his or her goals and values. In doing so, this encourages athletes to execute the most appropriate behaviors consistently and to fulfill his or her personal values. In short, commitment links up an athlete's values with their related short- or long-term goals and promotes the action execution of effective behaviors that are derived from his or her values.

Until now, the MAC has been the most systematically developed, and empirically studied, mindfulness training program in the sport psychology field (Gardner & Moore, 2004; 2012; Schwanhausser, 2009; Wolanin & Schwanhausser, 2010). The concept of value and commitment in the MAC allows athletes to connect their behaviors and actions to their values and provides them with a purpose and direction to facilitate training persistence. Athletes need to commit to specific and concrete value-directed behaviors, rather than emotion-driven behaviors, to achieve performance-related values.

When applying the MAC to Chinese athletes (Bu, 2013; Zhang, 2013) we found, however, that it was difficult for Chinese athletes to apply the concept of personal values to which they could consistently commit. For example, in studies by Bu (2013) and Zhang (2013), free combat (Chinese-style) and Wushu athletes were not able to recognize their own values and therefore needed consultants to help them clarify the "right" values. In addition, although some athletes had clear personal values, they found it hard to commit to these as they could not overcome the effects of the ebb and flow of performance, injuries, and, most importantly, the conflict between values of the individuals and the sport system.

One unique characteristic about the Chinese Whole-Nation sport system is that interpersonal relationships are directed by the value of respecting authoritative figures, meaning athletes should obey and respect both the coaches and the administrative officials (Si et al., 2011). As such, when there is a conflict between athletes' personal values and those of the authoritative figures, athletes need to comply with the authoritative values. Put it another way, the values for Chinese athletes are possibly more socially oriented (e.g., the honor of winning for the country, putting collective interests first) than personally directed. Given the limitation of directly applying the core concept of value to Chinese athletes, especially for those athletes who compete at national and international levels, we included the integration of socially oriented values with personal values in the MAIC for Chinese athletes.

Insight from Eastern Zen Buddhism

Chinese athletes need to be clear about socially oriented values beyond their own personal values. They also need to be able to extricate themselves from interpersonal and environmental obstacles to achieve their goals; as a result, insights from Eastern Zen Buddhism are used to link mindfulness practice with socially oriented values and commitment.

In Eastern Zen Buddhism, obsession is viewed as a concept, which leads to desires and cravings for related behaviors, and thus obsession obstructs one's thinking and behavior. Most people are self-centered, taking the concept of self very seriously and never relinquishing it. Under the influence of this condition, thoughts and behaviors point toward the self and are buried beneath the shadow of the self, which also implies an unconscious expectation that everything in the world must fit one's own principles and understanding. Such self-centeredness is closely related to the self-pride of narcissists or the self-abasement of pessimists. When an individual is self-obsessed, he or she may experience distorted cognitions and negative emotions (Xiong & Yu, 2010). For Chinese athletes, an obsession with excellent performance and related personal goals might cause confusion and distress. In addition, the obsession might cause interpersonal problems among athletes, coaches, and team officials under the Whole-Nation system.

To overcome obsession, the acceptance of suffering and imperfection is advocated by Zen Buddhism, and individuals are encouraged to live in the present moment (the here and now). Zen mindfulness is described as a heart with no distraction, a mind with no fluctuation; ones' mind is focused on a single object, observing it wholeheartedly (Song, 1992). Mindfulness is a specific method of observation that is deliberately in the present moment and nonjudgmental (Lan, 2009). In light of the concepts of Zen Buddhism, we propose that mindfulness is an authentic understanding of one's dynamic physical and mental condition as well as living in, and for, the present moment. As it is all too common to find athletes becoming distracted by perceived threats, varying results, and other distractions, to live in the present moment is crucial for athletes, and such an attitude would improve an athlete's behavioral effectiveness.

Focusing on the here and now (the present moment) with a nonjudgmental attitude is crucial for enhancing the quality of present-moment task behavior (i.e., performance). During mindfulness practice, insight might arise, and discernable different stages of insight may appear, including (a) knowledge of mind and body; (b) knowledge of cause and effect; (c) knowledge of the three characteristics (impermanence, suffering, and not-self); (d) knowledge of arising and passing away; (e) knowledge of suffering (dissolution, fear, misery, disgust, and desire for deliverance); (f) knowledge of suffering: re-observation; (g) knowledge of equanimity towards phenomena; and (h) attainment of fruition (see Grabovac, 2015, for a review).

Insight is defined by Grabovac, Lau, and Willett (2011) as "a direct, non-conceptual understanding achieved through the repeated examination of the three characteristics in the objects of meditation" (p. 159). In a Chinese sport context, we define insight as a new awareness or discovery of life, and its manifestation can be observed when an individual establishes a new understanding of his or her meaning of life and personal values, which strengthens the athlete's ability to face a variety of life issues. The manifestation of insight can be seen as an individual's commitment to, and immersion in, the current task, via detachment, which means detaching oneself from obsession in order to reach nonattachment (a release from mental fixation) and coming to know the authentic heart. When an individual is not self-obsessed, there is no greed, hatred, ignorance, or worry (Xiong & Yu, 2010). Nonattached thinking refers to a release from any mental fixation by repudiating any constant cognitive logic, which includes forsaking the holding onto of any logic, or old thinking patterns, and to become ready to accept any new understandings of life.

Nonattachment demonstrates flexibility with which to understand the world and human values, and this is in line with insight, which is a commonly used concept in Chinese daily life and is also frequently mentioned by elite Chinese athletes and coaches.

For Chinese athletes, their main goal in life is to be successful in their sporting career, and as such, athletes can use insight, a new awareness or discovery in life, to explore their values, through which they can decide on the direction of their behavior, all under the executive-led Whole-Nation system. Only those behaviors that are consistent with individual values and collective interests can effectively enhance athletes' quality of life and behavioral efficiency. The MAIC further encourages athletes to decide upon and persist in those behaviors that are congruent with the integration of personal and socially oriented values and ultimately improve their performance through their commitment.

Returning to the example case introduced at the beginning of this chapter, the Chinese diver had been *obsessed* by the desire of winning Olympic gold so much so that his performance was easily destroyed by overwhelming anxiety caused by such intense pressure. Encouraging him to be more insightful, as part of his mindfulness training, gave him a new understanding of his career such that he was able to reach a non-attached state, which allowed him to stabilize his performance during the competition.

Acceptance-based adversity coping
Compared to the traditional psychological interventions that focus on changing or controlling mental states, acceptance-based adversity coping emphasizes that the relationship between mental states and behavior can vary depending on how successfully athletes are able to accept and coexist with adversities (Si, Lee, & Lonsdale, 2010). Si (2006) emphasized that peak performance is not about performing perfectly, but rather coping with adversities effectively through accepting and learning to coexist with them. According to Si (2006), adversity in competition should be viewed as normal, and athletes' successful performances are closely related to their ability to cope with adverse situations. In other words, even though athletes may not achieve "peak" psychological state during competition, if they are able to cope with adversity reasonably well, they will still be able to consider their performance successful.

As one's attitude toward adversity (i.e., events leading to negative mental states) is a key factor affecting performance, acceptance-based adversity coping advocates training acceptance instead of training athletes to control or change mental states. Acceptance-based adversity coping (Si, 2006) aligns with the principles of Zen Buddhism, which states that suffering is natural and unavoidable. Suffering, much like happiness and fortune, is part of life, and as such, human life is a combination of perfection and imperfection. Translating this into the sporting domain, it is clear that adversity is natural and unavoidable, and both adversity and successful experiences are part of athletes' life throughout their sporting careers. Athletes are encouraged to accept these things as they are.

By applying the concept of accepting and coexisting with adversities into mindfulness-based sport psychology training, the MAIC is designed for Chinese athletes to gain a better understanding of acceptance and become less judgmental. Specifically, this training cultivates the willingness to encounter adversities and embrace various experiences, which is consistent with the perspective from the third wave of cognitive behavior therapy. On the other hand, mindfulness training can also be used to cultivate and improve skills for coping with adversity. Taken together, acceptance-based coping framework can serve as introductory material with which to confirm the importance of mindfulness training for Chinese athletes.

Key Components of MAIC

The MAIC was developed based on several substantial components (e.g., mindfulness, acceptance, cognitive decentering, and value clarification) from the MAC and some new adaptations (e.g., insight, nonattachment, and willingness to encounter adversity) that were specially designed for Chinese athletes. Given the importance of values in athletes' mindfulness-based training, the concept of insight is presented in the introduction to values session as a process of new awareness and discovery in life, or career, and implies flexibility of thinking and nonattachment of cognition. As athletes will inevitably face various difficulties and adversities, they may experience confusion, bewilderment, and doubts in the pursuit and commitment to their values. Insight can help athletes cope more effectively with these issues and enable them to work toward their values more effectively, which, as a result, subsequently is expected to improve performance as well as general well-being. Consistent with the key principles of acceptance-based adversity coping, the MAIC aims at raising athletes' willingness to encounter adversities and advocates that individuals accept the existence of adversity as it is, including any negative emotions, thoughts, and body sensations. The MAIC suggests that adversities are inevitable in life, and athletes are encouraged to divert their attention away from resisting or fighting against adversities, and instead direct their attention towards the behavioral tasks that are required at the present moment, and learn to coexist with the mental events. As a result, essential mental resources are available for allocation to the required task, and as such, behavioral efficiency can be improved (Si, 2006).

The aims, content, practices, and evaluations of seven sessions in the MAIC program for Chinese athletes follow within the overview of each MAIC session.

Session 1: Introduction and psycho-education of the MAIC

The introductory session aims to raise athletes' interest in participating in the whole MAIC program. The MAIC structure is presented to the athletes by briefly introducing the topics of each session. In line with the MAC, the theoretical rationale and specific goals of the program are introduced, such as accepting rather than changing the internal and external experiences during training and competition in order to improve flow, subjective well-being, and performance. Built on the rationale of acceptance-based adversity coping, the concept of the necessity of learning to coexist with sport adversities is also introduced.

A case study of the application of mindfulness training with an athlete well known to the Chinese athletes is introduced and discussed. Self-rated performance is evaluated, and tangible brief mindfulness skill exercises, such as the brief centering exercise (Gardner & Moore, 2007, p. 75), are practiced in this session. Finally, homework is provided to athletes. This requires practice of the brief centering exercise for thirty minutes to one hour each day or at least three times over the following week.

Session 2: Introducing and practicing mindfulness

Mindfulness is viewed as a fundamental concept and is the first concept and skill to be introduced in the MAIC. Mindfulness is described as an authentic understanding of ones' physical and mental condition in the present moment (i.e., seeing it as it is). Two key concepts of present-moment mindfulness are introduced, including "as it is" and "here and now." The "as it is" refers to the state in which one places his or her full attention on the internal experience (i.e., thoughts, emotions, and body sensations) by simply being aware of its existence without any judgment or reaction. The "here and now" refers to attention to the present moment without preoccupation with the past or the future. To be precise, the "here and now" not only describes the direction of ones' attention, but also implies a relaxed and patient state, free from burden and with no specific agenda.

Mindfulness is not only a state of mind, but is also regarded as a skill that can be improved through ongoing practice. During mindfulness practice, athletes focus on their experiences in that moment, remaining constantly alert, and with the readiness and ability to cope with any incident that may potentially arise (Hanh, Mai, & Ho, 1999). It can be observed as an ongoing nonjudgmental and nonresponsive acceptance of all negative and positive experiences, where athletes learn to accept these experiences in order to let them go.

Most of the concepts introduced in this session are similar to the mindfulness in the MAC; however, as described in the following subsections, the mindfulness in the MAIC is introduced in a more acceptable way to Chinese athletes. The concepts of mind and heart in mindfulness are also introduced to the athletes by requiring the athletes to find their heart, as well as settle the heart down and be in the present moment. When mind wanders, athletes are required to refocus to the present moment through locating where their hearts are and then use the heart as an anchor.

Once athletes have been introduced to the concept of mindfulness, they are guided through a practical exercise to experience mindfulness for themselves, and it is recommended that they make use of it in their daily life. Athletes are also encouraged to try continuously to comprehend the meaning of mindfulness within their daily life experiences, by exploring their mind and heart experiences. The exercises introduced in this session include the Zen relaxation body scan (Zong, 2010), drinking in slow motion (Suan, 2012), the mindful fruit eating exercise, the mindful walking exercise, and the mindful breathing exercise (Gardner & Moore, 2007, p. 119). Although many exercises have been included in this session, not all of them are practiced during the session. Finally, mindfulness levels are evaluated using existing self-reported measures, and homework is provided, where the Zen relaxation body scan and mindful breathing are two compulsory exercises that each need to be practiced at least thirty minutes once every two days. The other mindfulness exercises are supplementary, and athletes are encouraged to use them in daily training.

Session 3: Introducing and practicing decentering
Decentering refers to "the ability to observe one's thoughts and feelings as temporary, objective events in the mind, as opposed to reflections of the self that are necessarily true" (Safran & Segal, 1990, p. 117). Decentering can enable athletes to let themselves, or their egos, go. It also assists athletes in breaking away from their own thoughts and focus instead on the present

task. As decentering is strongly related to mindfulness (Carmody et al., 2009), athletes are guided to experience the "here and now," physically and mentally, via a decentered perspective on thoughts and behavioral processes. In addition, athletes are encouraged to immerse themselves in the present-moment task, thus moving from ruminating and self-orientated thoughts to a decentered task orientation, which is an application of the "here and now" in the behavioral or task process. However, it should be noted that in the MAC, the concept is introduced as cognitive defusion. These two concepts can be used interchangeably, although cognitive defusion is viewed as more behaviorally oriented (Gillanders et al., 2014).

Practice recommendations for athletes include adopting mindfulness training in order to let go of oneself and release any lingering distractions (i.e., decentering) and to direct one's attention away from the internal self (e.g., satisfying ego) and external distraction (e.g., expecting fame and gain) and toward the experience of effective performance behaviors. Exercises introduced in this session include the "forgetting the self" behavior exercise (Hanh et al., 1999), the mindful imagery exercise, and the mindful dishwashing exercise (Gardner & Moore, 2007, p. 119). Self-reported measures, such as the Experiential Questionnaire (EQ; Fresco et al., 2007) and Cognitive Fusion Questionnaire (CFQ; Gillanders et al., 2014), can be used to evaluate decentering or cognitive defusion. Homework on formal mindfulness practice is provided, where a mindful breathing exercise and a mindful imagery exercise are two compulsory exercises that each needs to be practiced at least thirty minutes once every two days, and the "forgetting the self" exercise and mindful dishwashing exercise are supplementary exercises that are suggested to athletes for application in their daily training.

Session 4: Introducing and practicing acceptance
Acceptance-based adversity coping (Si, 2006; Si et al., 2011) is introduced at this stage by emphasizing the importance of accepting and coexisting with adversity, given that adversity is unavoidable in sport. While decentering is a manifestation of identifying thoughts and feelings as transitory events in the mind and a clear awareness of "here and now" in behavioral performance, acceptance is viewed a manifestation of "as it is."

The first step is the identification of adversities through present-moment attention and awareness, and the second step is to adopt experiential acceptance to coexist with the given adversities. The emphasis on accepting and being nonjudgmental of adversity serves as an introduction to this session; in addition, acceptance is generalized to all internal experiences, including joy and enjoyment.

Acceptance can be observed when an athlete is aware of things happening around them with an open mind, while staying in the moment, knowing simply that events are taking place, without trying to judge, react, or confront them. The athletes simply attempt to experience thoughts and emotions, as well as body sensations and negative experiences, which are accepted as part of life, while making no attempt to avoid them or to expect negative elements to vanish through this acceptance. The individual simply accepts the existence of these experiences as they are. The acceptance exercises include coexistence exercises I and II (Suan, 2012) and the mindful yoga exercise. The effectiveness of mindfulness training on acceptance can be evaluated by a decrease in experiential avoidance by using the Acceptance and Action Questionnaire–II (AAQ–II) after the appropriate training. Homework on the coexisting exercise and mindfulness practice is provided, where coexistence exercises I and II and the mindful yoga exercise each needs to be practiced at least thirty minutes once every two days.

Session 5: Introducing values and insight

In this session, athletes are guided to explore their behavioral direction, as components ("as it is" and "here and now"), skills (meditation, body scanning, and related practices) and beneficial mindfulness processes (decentering and acceptance) have been illustrated during previous sessions. Values are important beliefs or viewpoints, and for the MAIC values include valued sport behavior (what the athlete is willing to commit to regardless of feelings and thoughts that emerge), which can direct and motivate athletes' behavior. Athletes are first introduced to the concept of personal and socially oriented values and are guided through an exploration of their value system, which is followed by completing the value assessment questionnaire developed by the research team. One sample item is, "I think it is valuable not only because it makes my life better and more meaningful but it also fulfills expectations from my coach."

Secondly, athletes are introduced to the concept of insight, which is defined as a new awareness or discovery of life, and its manifestation can be observed when an individual establishes a new understanding of his or her meaning of life and personal value, which strengthens his or her ability to face a variety of life issues. Two components are included in this operational definition of insight: (a) understanding the career and life from an impermanent (i.e., nonattachment) and nonself perspective and

(b) understanding the relationship between the individual and society (the Chinese sport system) from a holistic and dynamic perspective. This new understanding, or perception, of a philosophy of life and values can facilitate the nonattachment of distracting cognitions. When individuals comprehends nonattached thinking (Sahdra, Shaver, & Brown, 2010), they may develop new understandings or perceptions toward important issues in their life, which can improve cognitive flexibility, the ability to adjust ones' values, and face difficulties in the pursuit of these values.

Beyond the formal mindfulness meditation exercise, a personal mindful exercise on valued sport behavior is practiced in this session where athletes are guided to achieve a new awareness and understanding of the meaning of life and values. In addition, a storytelling and sharing format (scenarios from lived experiences of athletes) is adopted to help athletes develop new understandings of their own sport careers. This storytelling and sharing approach is not conducted in an educational or persuasive way but rather through a mutual discussion and is mostly initiated by the athletes' thinking.

In line with the decentering evaluation method using the Measure of Awareness and Coping in Autobiographical Memory (MACAM; Moore, Hayhurst, & Teasdale, 1996 as cited in Fresco et al., 2007), raters (sport psychology consultants) are trained to rate on a five-point scale (1 = no insight at all; 5 = extremely high insight) the athletes' insight (i.e., new understanding and awareness of meaning of life and values) using different vignettes, which have been adapted from a qualitative study regarding Chinese athletes' insights (Chen, 2014). In addition, the self-reported Nonattachment Scale (Sahdra et al., 2010) can be used to evaluate the improvement of athletes' nonattachment. Most importantly, training and competition behavioral change is used as one of the key indicators, and any changes can be systematically monitored by coaches and supporting staff. Values are evaluated using a self-reported values assessment form (Gardner & Moore, 2007). Homework includes asking athletes to reflect on their personal values and understandings about personal and socially oriented values.

Session 6: Introducing commitment
According to the MAC, commitment is demonstrated when athletes regularly and consistently perform behaviors that are congruent with their values and goals, resulting in more effective behaviors. This is an extension of Session 5 regarding how values provide athletes with the necessary direction and commitment being the behavioral expression of those values. In line with the MAC, athletes are guided to discover effective behaviors that correspond to their values and to explore any potential difficulties

that may occur along the way, as well as how to apply the mindfulness, decentering, and acceptance skills to continue to perform effective behaviors. More importantly, the concept of insight can be used to integrate athletes' personal values with socially oriented values in order to help the athletes commit to value-driven behaviors. Commitment is evaluated with an open-ended self-evaluation form, and homework includes mindfulness meditation and self-reflection of personal commitment.

Session 7: Comprehensive review and consolidation
The summary session aims to provide the athletes with an overall understanding of the MAIC. Given that various interrelated skills and concepts have been covered in the previous sessions, it is important to review and reflect on the athletes' understanding of all previous sessions. This can help athletes to consolidate their understanding of mindfulness and to plan for its application into their training and daily life. Prior to comprehensive practice, athletes are guided in a review of the MAIC content. In addition, athletes are encouraged to practice key exercises (e.g., mindfulness meditation, body scanning, and brief centering exercise) and to commit themselves to continuous MAIC practices.

MAIC Training for Elite Synchronized Swimming Athletes

The MAIC training program was developed by a research team, led by Ganyan Si. In order to examine the effectiveness of this training program, a single-case design study was conducted with the Guangdong provincial synchronized swimming team to assist team members in preparation for the 2013 All-China Games (i.e., the Chinese National Games). Supervised by the whole research team, one of the team members who had three years' experience in mindfulness practice and was also a qualified sport psychology consultant implemented the training. This sport psychology consultant prepared the relevant materials (e.g., PowerPoint, learning materials, and homework) for each training session. Subsequently, other members of the research team collectively discussed the materials and reached consensus on the content and arrangement of training sessions, which included a debriefing meeting after each training session.

The All-China Games is the most important domestic competition in China, occurring once every four years; athletes, coaches, and team officials attach great importance to the All-China Games. The first author of this chapter was contacted by the head coach of the Guangdong provincial synchronized swimming team due to the quite unstable performance of some of the athletes. The main issue was a large fluctuation in the quality of movements and consistency of performance among teammates during training. The coaches and other training supporting staff (e.g., the team doctor, the fitness trainer, the team manager) considered that these fluctuations were closely related to the intense pressure, especially considering that the team's target was a gold medal. The swimmers' symptoms were exemplified by a lack of complete attention during training as well as obvious avoidance behaviors toward difficult and intense training sessions. Based on the initial contact and the first meeting, Si recommended to the head coach the MAIC training program (see Table 11.1) to improve training performance and athletes' attention during training and to decrease the ineffective avoidance behaviors. One week after the completion of the MAIC intervention, the team participated in the qualifying games for the All-China Games.

Efficacy of the MAIC with a Chinese Synchronized Swimming Team

This section presents the empirical method and results regarding the efficacy of the MAIC when implemented with six Chinese athletes. Specifically, the purpose of the study was to explore the effectiveness of the MAIC to enhance mindfulness and training performance and to decrease experiential avoidance among Chinese synchronized swimmers.

Method

Participants
After the Research Ethics Committee at the Hong Kong Sport Institute and the Scientific Training Department at Guangdong Provincial Sport Training Center approved the study, consent forms were collected from six athletes from the Guangdong synchronized swimming team. All six participants were competing at the national level with an average age of 19.33 years old and an average of 10.5 years of training.

Procedure
The study lasted eighteen weeks, from January to May 2013. A multiple-baseline single-case design was employed, including three phases:

1. The Baseline Monitoring phase, in which the self-reported measures (mindfulness, experiential avoidance, training performance, and commitment) were collected from seven data points over a three-week period. MAIC training started immediately after this phase.

Table 11.1 *Summary Outline of the MAIC Treatment Protocol for Chinese Synchronized Swimming Athletes*

Time of Intervention	Theme of Intervention	Content
Week 1	Introduction and Psychoeducation of the MAIC	1. Introduction of the entire structure of the mindfulness training program 2. Theoretical rationale and specific goals of the program 3. Introduction of acceptance-based adversity coping and related concepts 4. A story on the application of mindfulness of an elite athlete 5. The practice of brief centering exercise, followed by group discussion 6. Homework
Week 2	Introducing and Practicing Mindfulness	1. The concept of mindfulness ("as it is" and "here and now") 2. The concepts of mind and heart in mindfulness 3. The practice of exercises of mindfulness breathing, mindfulness walking, and mindfulness fruit eating, followed by group discussion 4. Homework
Week 3	Introducing and Practicing Decentering	1. Introduction to the concept of decentering 2. Ruminated self-orientation to decentered task-orientation 3. Introduction to mindfulness exercises such as the forgetting-self behavior exercise, followed by group discussion 4. Homework
Week 4	Introducing and Practicing Acceptance	1. Strengthening of athletes' understanding of acceptance and avoidance of experiences using acceptance-based adversity coping 2. Emphasis on accepting and nonjudging of adversity 3. Introduction of coexistence exercises I and II, followed by group discussion 4. Homework
Week 5	Introducing Value and Insight	1. Introduction to the concept of value (personal and socially oriented value) 2. The concept of insight 3. Understanding of the relationship between values and insight 4. A format of storytelling and sharing approach to help athletes develop a new understanding of their sports career 5. Homework

Table 11.1 (cont.)

Time of Intervention	Theme of Intervention	Content	
Week 6	Introducing Commitment	1.	Introduction to the concept of commitment
		2.	Understanding of commitment in the face of adversity
		3.	Linking of commitment with insight and value
		4.	Homework
Week 7	Comprehensive Review and Consolidation	1.	Summary of all sessions' aims and an overall understanding of the program
		2.	Practice of key exercises
		3.	Explanation of the requirement for continuous commitment

Note. The duration of each session is from eighty minutes to ninety minutes. Athletes are required to commit to the homework for at least thirty minutes per day every day or at least three days per week.

2. The Intervention phase, during which eleven data points were collected over a seven-week period. The MAIC training was implemented every Sunday afternoon in a counseling room for seven consecutive weeks, with each session lasting approximately eighty to ninety minutes.

3. The Post-intervention phase, which was conducted five weeks after the end of the Intervention phase, with six data points collected over a three-week period.

All the data collections during the three phases were conducted in the training venue or in the counseling room. In addition, in order to assess the social validity of the MAIC training program at the end of the Post-intervention phase, the six athletes and two coaches were invited to complete the Practical Evaluation Questionnaire developed by the research team (see the subsection "Social Validity").

Measures

The Five-Faced Mindfulness Questionnaire (FFMQ)
The FFMQ is a thirty-nine-item self-report questionnaire that measures five facets of mindfulness, including observing, describing, acting with awareness, nonjudging, and nonreacting. Items are rated on a five-point Likert scale ranging from 1 (never or very rarely true) to 5 (very often or

always true) (Baer et al., 2006). Subscale scores for each facet can be calculated, and a high composite score on all facets indicates a high level of mindfulness (Baer et al., 2006). The Chinese version of FFMQ was developed by Deng and colleagues (2011) using a sample of Chinese college students, with internal consistency coefficients for the five facets of the Chinese FFMQ: of α = 0.75 (observing); α = 0.84 (describing); α = 0.79 (act with awareness); α = 0.66 (nonjudging); and α = 0.45 (nonreacting).

The Acceptance and Action Questionnaire-II (AAQ-II)
The AAQ-II is a seven-item single-dimensional self-report questionnaire measuring one's levels of experiential avoidance and psychological inflexibility (the opposite of psychological flexibility) (Bond et al., 2011). Items are rated on a seven-point Likert scale from 1 (never true) to 7 (always true), with low scores indicating a low level of experience avoidance and psychological inflexibility. The Chinese version of the AAQ-II demonstrated a high level of internal consistency and reliability in two samples of Chinese college students (composite reliability: ρ = 0.89 and ρ = 0.88) and a sample of elite Chinese athletes (ρ = 0.85) (Zhang et al., 2014).

Athletes' Training Performance (ATP)
Although synchronized swimming is a team sport, athletes may take sessions of both individual and group training practices during their training. Based on the competition criteria, the ATP was originally developed by the Scientific Training Department (including training experts and coaches) at the Guangdong Provincial Sports Training Center. It had been used to assess the training quality of synchronized swimming athletes during daily training sessions (Wang & Zhang, 2012). The research team adjusted the ATP slightly after consulting with the coaches. The ATP consists of three facets including (a) skill difficulties, in which different combinations of synchronized swimming skills, practiced during the training sessions, can be divided into five levels; (b) movement qualities, which include the position, strength, and pacing of movements; and (c) cooperation among teammates, which contains team formation and consistency of movements. Each of these three dimensions is scored on a ten-point Likert scale ranging from 1 (worst) to 10 (best). The total score of the ATP was acquired by summing the scores of three facets, thus demonstrating the athletes' level of training performance.

The ATP was completed by two coaches separately at the end of a training session. Subsequently, coaches discussed their assessments with each other and reached a consensus if there were any discrepancies between them. In addition, in order to help coaches confirm and maximize the accuracy of their assessments, video clips of certain core sections of the training session were selected and shown to coaches. It should be noted that the recording of videos at each training session is routine and a regular part of their training.

Athletes' Commitment (AC)

The AC was designed by the research team to assess athletes' commitment to their training, which includes (a) commitment to training, which comprises attention to coaches' requests, acceptance of training difficulty, and intensity; (b) attitude to training, which includes preparation and responsibility for the training; and (c) self-requirement in training, which includes initiative and discipline. The training sessions include both in-water and on-land training. Each of the three AC aspects is scored on a ten-point Likert scale from 1 (worst) to 10 (best). The total score is calculated by adding the scores of the three aspects representing athletes' level of commitment. As with the evaluation of the ATP, the AC was assessed by two coaches and the video clips were used to facilitate coaches' assessments.

Social validity

In order to further assess the effectiveness of the MAIC training, a practical evaluation questionnaire was developed to evaluate social validity from the perspectives of both coaches and athletes (Hrycaiko & Martin, 1996). The questionnaire consisted of four questions: (1) "Do you think that the MAIC program was helpful in enhancing your (your athletes') training performance?" (2) "During and after the MAIC training, do you think that the stability of your (your athletes') concentration and emotion has improved?" (3) "Are you (or do you think your athletes are) satisfied with your (their) performance at the qualifying games of the All-China Games?" (4) "Do you think that the relevant facets of MAIC program (the schedule, content, implementation etc.) are acceptable (to your athletes)?" The items of the practical evaluation questionnaire are rated on a five-point Likert scale from 1 (not at all) to 5 (very much so).

Data Analyses

Visual analysis is the traditional assessing method in single-case design, which involves visual examination of data for each participant to evaluate subjectively whether a reliable change in the outcome variable can be observed (Jenny et al., 2014). Based on several suggested criteria

(Barlow & Hersen, 1984), one can have greater confidence in whether performance change following the intervention is positive if (a) baseline performance is stable or in a direction opposite of the anticipated effects of the treatment, (b) there are relatively few overlapping data points between baseline monitoring and intervention phases, (c) changes in performance are observed soon after the introduction of the intervention, and (d) changes in subsequent performance demonstrate consistency within and between participants.

In addition, the Nonoverlap of All Pairs (NAP) was employed in this study to evaluate the magnitude of effect sizes of the intervention. In short, the NAP refers to the percentage of positive pairs out of all pairs between phases A and B (Parker, Vannest, & Davis, 2011). For the method of how to calculate the NAP, refer to Parker and colleagues (Parker & Vannest, 2009; Parker et al., 2011). Typically, NAP ranges between 0.50 and 1.00. However, if NAP lies between 0.00 and 0.499, it indicates that there is deterioration in the intervention phase (Parker & Vannest, 2009). The formula $NAP^{0.00-1.00} = (NAP^{0.50-1.00} / .5) -1$ is used in case that the NAP needs to be adjusted (rescaled) in order to allow it lie within the range between 0.00 and 1.00 for effect size calculation (Parker et al., 2011). Specifically, if the original value of NAP was ≥ 0.50, the NAP will then be converted into a rescaled value. As suggested, the criteria for the magnitude of the effect size of rescaled NAP (Parker & Vannest, 2009) are (a) weak effects (0–0.31), (b) medium effects (0.32–0.84), and (c) large or strong effects (0.85–1.0). As can be seen in the figures, NAP1 denotes a comparative analysis between the Baseline Monitoring and Intervention phases, while NAP2 represents a comparative analysis between the Baseline Monitoring and Post-intervention phases. The area between the two blue lines (indicated as "Overlap Zone1") refers to the overlapping area between the Baseline Monitoring and Intervention phases, while the area between two red-dotted lines (indicated as "Overlap Zone2") refers to the overlapping area between the Baseline Monitoring and Post-Intervention phases. The solid circles refer to the overlapping points of "Baseline Monitoring–Intervention phases," while the circled dots refer to the overlapping points of "Baseline Monitoring–Post-intervention phases."

Results

Variation analysis of mindfulness

Through a visual inspection of Figure 11.1, the change of FFMQ score of participant 1 could be observed in both the Intervention and

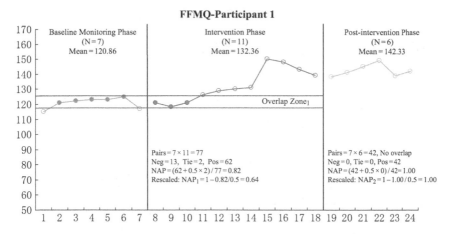

Figure 11.1   *FFMQ score variation plot for participant 1.*

Post-intervention phases compared to that in the Baseline Monitoring phase (the remaining plots of the other five participants are available upon request from the first author of this chapter). For all six participants, the mean scores of FFMQ in the Intervention and Post-intervention phases were obviously higher than that of the Baseline Monitoring phase, implying that the intervention was effective in leading to an overall improvement in mindfulness. More importantly, in the Intervention phase, rescaled NAP1 values of participants 2, 3, 4, 5, and 6 were 0.90, 1.00, 0.98, 0.98, and 0.92, respectively, indicating that intervention had a strong effect, while the rescaled NAP1 value of participant 1 was 0.64, indicating a medium effect. At the Post-intervention phase, the rescaled NAP2 values were all 1.0 for all six participants, indicating that MAIC training still had a large effect on participants five weeks after the end of the Intervention phase. Taken together, MAIC training had a strong effect for five participants and a medium effect for one participant in improving the overall level of mindfulness during the Intervention phase, and the effect of the MAIC training was maintained during the Post-intervention phase.

Variation analysis of experiential avoidance
Through a visual inspection (see Figure 11.2 for the AAQ-II score variation plot of participant 1; the remaining plots of the other five participants are available upon request from the first author of this chapter), the change of AAQ-II scores during the Intervention phase are obvious for participants 2, 3, 4, and 5, but not so obvious for participants 1 and 6, although the change

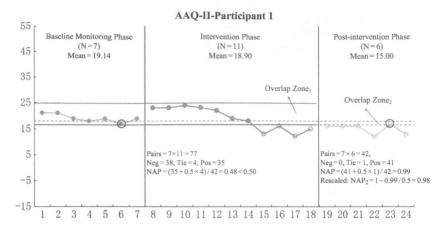

Figure 11.2   *AAQ-II score variation plot for participant 1.*

trend at the Post-intervention phase was quite clear for all six participants, compared to that of the Baseline Monitoring phase. The mean scores of AAQ-II at the Intervention and Post-intervention phases are obviously lower than scores at the Baseline Monitoring phase for all participants except for participant 1 at the Intervention phase. This implies that the MAIC training had an effect, which led to an overall decrease in experiential avoidance (i.e., improvement in athletes' experiential acceptance).

Regarding statistical analysis at the Intervention phase, rescaled NAP1 values for participants 2, 3, 4, 5, and 6 were 0.84, 0.78, 0.74, 0.94, and 0.32, respectively, indicating that the intervention had a medium effect (0.32–0.84) for most participants, while the original NAP value for participant 1 was 0.48 (<0.50), indicating that intervention had no effect for this participant. At the Post-intervention phase, all the rescaled NAP2 values reached a strong effect level, indicating that MAIC training still had a strong effect on the participants five weeks after the end of the Intervention phase. Taken together, the MAIC training had a medium effect for most participants in decreasing experiential avoidance (i.e., improving the level of experiential acceptance) at the Intervention phase, while this training had a strong effect for all participants at the Post-intervention phase.

Variation analysis of Athletes' Training Performance (ATP)
A visual analysis shows that the change of ATP scores at the Intervention phase was quite obvious for participants 1, 3, 4, 5, and 6, but not for participant 2 (see Figure 11.3 for the ATP score variation plot of participant

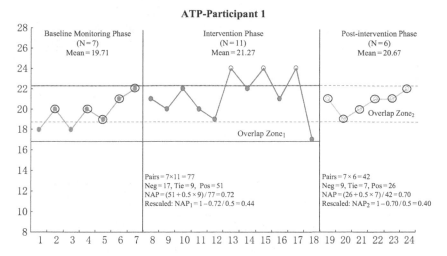

Figure 11.3   *ATP score variation plot for participant 1.*

1; the remaining plots of the other five participants are available upon request from the first author of this chapter). The ATP scores at the Post-intervention phase showed no improvement for any participants except for participant 3 compared to the Baseline Monitoring phase.

An analysis of the magnitude of effect size, at the Intervention phase, showed that rescaled NAP1 values of the participants1, 3, 4, 5, and 6 were 0.44, 0.64, 0.62, 0.78, and 0.64, respectively, indicating that the intervention had a medium effect (0.32–0.84) for these five participants, while the original NAP value of the participant 2 was 0.40 ($<$0.50), indicating that the intervention had no effect for this participant. At the Post-intervention phase, the rescaled NAP2 values of participants 1 and 3 were 0.40 and 0.24, respectively, while the original NAP values for the other four participants were all smaller than 0.50, indicating that intervention had no continuous effect for these four participants five weeks after the end of the Intervention phase. Taken together, the MAIC training had a medium effect for five out of six participants in improving training performance at the Intervention phase, while this training effect did not continue for four out of six participants at the Post-intervention phase.

Variation analysis of Athletes' Commitment (AC)
As indicated by visual inspection (see Figure 11.4 for the AC score variation plot of participant 1; the remaining plots of the other five participants are

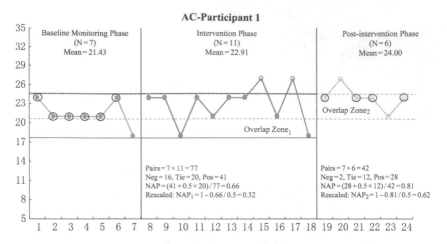

Figure 11.4   *AC score variation plot for participant 1.*

available upon request from the first author of this chapter), change in AC scores was not clearly observed, although the means had increased slightly, at both Intervention and Post-intervention phases, compared to the Baseline Monitoring phase for all six participants. An analysis of the magnitude of effect size showed that all rescaled NAP1 and NAP2 values at the Intervention and Post-intervention phases, from all participants, were within the range of medium effect (0.32–0.84), except for the rescaled NAP1 value for participant 6 at the Intervention phase, which was 0.20, indicating a small effect. Taken together, the MAIC training had a medium effect for five participants and a small effect for one participant in improving the level of commitment at the Intervention phase, and a medium effect of MAIC training, which was maintained at the Post-intervention phase for all participants.

Social validity

Six athletes answered the questionnaire and gave scores of 4, 4, 5, 5, 4, and 4 for the first question, "Do you think that the MAIC program was helpful for enhancing your training performance?" They gave scores of 4, 4, 5, 5, 5, and 4 for the second question, "During and after the MAIC training, do you think that the stability of your concentration and emotion has improved?" They gave scores of 5, 4, 5, 4, 3, and 3 for the third question, "Are you satisfied with your performance at the qualifying games of the All-China Games?" They gave scores of 4, 5, 4, 5, 5, and 5 for the fourth question, "Do you think that the relevant facets of the

MAIC program (the schedule, content, implementation etc.) are acceptable." These scores indicate that the effectiveness of the intervention was well recognized by all the six athletes. Both coaches completed the coach-relevant questions and gave scores of 4 and 5 for the first question, 5 and 4 for the second question, 4 and 5 for the third question, and 5 and 5 for the fourth question, which showed that the effectiveness of the MAIC training was also well recognized by the coaches. However, it is acknowledged that due to the observer-expectancy effect, participants might have bias when rating on the effectiveness of the training.

Discussion

The findings from the current study show that the MAIC training had a strong effect on the individual mindfulness at both the Intervention (with a medium effect for one participant) and Post-intervention phases. It has also been demonstrated that the MAIC training had a medium or strong effect for five out of six participants on decreasing levels of experiential avoidance at the Intervention phase, and a strong effect for all participants at the Post-intervention phase. In addition, the effect size of the MAIC training at the Post-intervention phase seemed higher than at the Intervention phase for both FFMQ and AAQ-II. It should be noted that the athletes participated in the qualifying games of the All-China Games and won the championship, and this happened between the Intervention phase and the Post-intervention phase. Therefore, it is presumed that athletes chose to maintain their mindfulness practice during the Post-intervention phase, as they felt that the MAIC training had helped them in preparation for the All-China Games. Furthermore, this point was supported by the athletes' and coaches' social validity assessments.

Regarding training performance, the findings suggested that MAIC training had a medium effect on five out of six participants on improvement at the Intervention phase, although the MAIC training did not retain this effect for four out of six participants at the Post-intervention phase. One possible explanation is that the synchronized swimming training programs had been significantly altered during the Post-intervention phase. After winning the championship at the qualifying games for the All-China Games, the entire team took a rest for one week and then started an ambitious training program that aimed at winning the final of the All-China Games. Many adjustments were related to the difficulties of skills, quality of movements, and cooperation among teammates. At the time of the Post-intervention phase, some athletes had not yet adapted themselves well to some elements of the new training program. To some degree, this situation may account for the decrease in athletes' training performance at the Post-intervention phase.

One limitation of this study is that we used coaches' subjective evaluation to assess athletes' training performance and commitment. Although synchronized swimming is a subjectively evaluated sport, additional objective indicators are preferable for analysis. Future studies may employ objective measures (e.g., physiological or biomechanical parameters) in order to assess athletes' training performance and use more precise indicators (e.g., behavior observation recordings, qualitative interviews) to assess athletes' commitment. By making use of objective or quantitative measures on athletes' performance (training, competition, or both) and commitment, studies could evaluate the effectiveness of mindfulness training programs in a more robust manner. Nonetheless, the findings of this single-case design study have confirmed the effectiveness of the MAIC training program among elite Chinese synchronized swimming athletes. The results of the visual analysis, NAP analysis, and social validation have revealed positive benefits of the MAIC to athletes with regard to mindfulness, experiential acceptance, commitment, and training performance.

Conclusion

In recent years, sport psychology consultants in China have endeavored to explore sport psychology interventions and identify which are most suitable for the Chinese culture (Si et al., 2011; Zhang & Zhang, 2011). As an alternative to the traditional change and control-oriented psychological skill training approach, the MAIC has integrated the MAC with the Chinese concept of heart, insight from Zen Buddhism, the concept of socially oriented values, and acceptance-based adversity coping. Essentially, this is the result of local experts who have systematically incorporated their cultural understanding with the practical application of mindfulness training specifically for Chinese athletes. In order to demonstrate the effectiveness of the MAIC, we have presented the results of a single-case design study of six elite Chinese synchronized swimming athletes, who all compete at a national level. The findings demonstrate the effectiveness of the MAIC program, among Chinese athletes, on mindfulness, experiential avoidance, commitment, and performance. We welcome more Chinese researchers to adopt the MAIC in their sport psychology practice and research, and we also recommend additional robust, randomized control experimental studies to evaluate the effectiveness of the MAIC program further.

REFERENCES

Aherne, C., Moran, A. P., and Lonsdale, C. (2011). The effect of mindfulness training on athletes' flow: An initial investigation. *Sport Psychologist*, 25(2), 177–189.

Baer, R. A. (2003). Mindfulness training as a clinical intervention: A conceptual and empirical review. *Clinical Psychology: Science and Practice*, 10(2), 125–143. doi: 10.1093/clipsy/bpg015

Baer, R. A., Smith, G. T., Hopkins, J., Krietemeyer, J., and Toney, L. (2006). Using self-report assessment methods to explore facets of mindfulness. *Assessment*, 13(1), 27–45. doi: 10.1177/1073191105283504

Barlow, D. H., and Hersen, M. (1984). *Single-case experimental designs: Strategies for studying behavior change*. Oxford, UK: Pergamon Press.

Bernier, M., Thienot, E., Codron, R., and Fournier, J. F. (2009). Mindfulness and acceptance approaches in sport performance. *Journal of Clinical Sport Psychology*, 25(4), 320–333.

Birrer, D., Röthlin, P., and Morgan, G. (2012). Mindfulness to enhance athletic performance: Theoretical considerations and possible impact mechanisms. *Mindfulness*, 3(3), 235–246. doi: 10.1007/s12671-012-0109-2

Bond, F. W., Hayes, S. C., Baer, R. A., Carpenter, K. M., Guenole, N., Orcutt, H. K., Waltz, T., and Zettle, R. D. (2011). Preliminary psychometric properties of the Acceptance and Action Questionnaire–II: A revised measure of psychological inflexibility and experiential avoidance. *Behavior Therapy*, 42(4), 676–688. doi: 10.1016/j.beth.2011.03.007

Bu, D. R. (2013). *The influence of psychological intervention based on mindfulness-acceptance on the provincial athletes' performance enhancement: A single-case design [以正念接受为基础的心理干预对省级运动员表现提高的影响: 一项单被试实验设计研究]*. (Unpublished master's thesis). Wuhan, P. R. China: Wuhan Institute of Physical Education.

Carmody, J., Baer, R. A., Lykins, E. L. B., and Olendzki, N. (2009). An empirical study of the mechanisms of mindfulness in a mindfulness-based stress reduction program. *Journal of Clinical Psychology*, 65(6), 613–626. doi: 10.1002/jclp.20579

Chen, B. M. (2014). *The grounded theory research of athlete insights in Chinese culture context [中国文化背景下运动员觉悟的扎根理论研究]*. (Unpublished master's thesis). Wuhan, P. R. China: Wuhan Institute of Physical Education.

Chung, P. K., Si, G. Y., and Zhang, C. Q. (2013). A review on the application of mindfulness-based interventions in sport field [正念训练在运动竞技领域应用述评]. *Chinese Journal of Sports Medicine*, 32(1), 65–74.

Deng, Y. Q., Liu, X. H., Rodriguez, M. A., and Xia, C. Y. (2011). The Five Facet Mindfulness Questionnaire: Psychometric properties of the Chinese version. *Mindfulness*, 2(2), 123–128. doi: 10.1007/s12671-011-0050-9

Fresco, D. M., Moore, M. T., van Dulmen, M. H. M., Segal, Z. V., Ma, S. H., Teasdale, J. D., and Williams, J. M. G. (2007). Initial psychometric properties of the Experiences Questionnaire: Validation of a self-report measure of decentering. *Behavior Therapy*, 38, 234–246. doi: 10.1016/j. beth.2006.08.003

Gardner, F. L., and Moore, Z. E. (2004). A Mindfulness-Acceptance-Commitment-based approach to athletic performance enhancement: Theoretical considerations. *Behavior Therapy*, 35(4), 707–723. doi: 10.1016/S0005-7894(04)80016-9

(2007). *The psychology of enhancing human performance: The Mindfulness-Acceptance-Commitment (MAC) approach*. New York, NY: Springer.

(2012). Mindfulness and acceptance models in sport psychology: A decade of basic and applied scientific advancements. *Canadian Psychology*, 53(4), 309–318. doi: 10.1037/a0030220

Gillanders, D. T., Bolderston, H., Bond, F. W., Dempster, M., Flaxman, P. E., Campbell, L., ... and Remington, B. (2014). The development and initial validation of the cognitive fusion questionnaire. *Behavior Therapy*, 45, 83–101. doi: 10.1016/j.beth.2013.09.001

Grabovac, A. (2015). The stages of insight: Clinical relevance for mindfulness-based interventions. *Mindfulness*, 6(3), 589–600. doi: 10.1007/s12671-014-0294-2

Grabovac, A. D., Lau, M. A., and Willett, B. R. (2011). Mechanisms of mindfulness: A Buddhist psychological model. *Mindfulness*, 2(3), 154–166. doi: 10.1007/s12671-011-0054-5

Haberl, P. (2007). The psychology of being an Olympic favorite. *Athletic Insight*, 9(4), 37–49.

Hanh, T. N., Mai, V. D., and Ho, M. (1999). *The miracle of mindfulness: An introduction to the practice of meditation*. Boston, MA: Beacon Press.

Hardy, L., Jones, G., and Gould, D. (1996). *Understanding psychological preparation for sport: Theory and practice of elite performers*. New York, NY: John Wiley & Sons.

Harmison, R. J. (2011). Peak performance in sport: Identifying ideal performance states and developing athletes' psychological skills. *Sport, Exercise, and Performance Psychology*, 1, 3–18. doi: 10.1037/2157-3905.1.S.3

Hayes, S. C. (2004). Acceptance and commitment therapy, relational frame theory, and the third wave of behavioral and cognitive therapies. *Behavior Therapy*, 35, 639–665. doi: 10.1016/S0005-7894(04)80013-3

Hayes, S. C., Follette, V. M., and Linehan, M. (Eds.). (2004). *Mindfulness and acceptance: Expanding the cognitive-behavioral tradition*. New York, NY: Guilford Press.

Hayes, S. C., Strosahl, K. D., and Wilson, K. G. (1999). *Acceptance and commitment therapy: An experiential approach to behaviour change*. New York, NY: Guilford Press.

Hofmann, S. G., Sawyer, A. T., Witt, A. A., and Oh, D. (2010). The effect of mindfulness-based therapy on anxiety and depression: A meta-analytic review. *Journal of Consulting and Clinical Psychology*, 78(2), 169–183. doi: 10.1037/a0018555

Hrycaiko, D., and Martin, G. L. (1996). Applied research studies with single-subject designs: Why so few? *Journal of Applied Sport Psychology*, 8(2), 183–199. doi: 10.1080/10413209608406476

Jenny, O., Munroe-Chandler, K. J., Hall, C. R., and Hall, N. D. (2014). Using motivational general-mastery imagery to improve the self-efficacy of youth squash players. *Journal of Applied Sport Psychology*, 26, 66–81. doi: 10.1080/10413200.2013.778914

Kabat-Zinn, J. (1990). *Full catastrophe living: Using the wisdom of your body and mind to face stress, pain and illness*. New York, NY: Delta.

(1994). *Wherever you go, there you are: Mindfulness meditation in everyday life*. New York, NY: Hyperion.

(2003). Mindfulness-based interventions in context: Past, present, and future. *Clinical Psychology: Science and Practice*, 10(2), 144–156. doi: 10.1093/clipsy. bpg016

Kabat-Zinn, J., Beall, B., and Rippe, J. (1985, June). *A systematic mental training program based on mindfulness meditation to optimize performance in collegiate and Olympic rowers*. Paper presented at the World Congress in Sport Psychology, Copenhagen, Denmark.

Kaufman, K. A., Glass, C. R., and Arnkoff, D. B. (2009). Evaluation of Mindful Sport Performance Enhancement (MSPE): A new approach to promote flow in athletes. *Journal of Clinical Sport Psychology*, 4, 334–356.

Kee, Y. H., and Wang, C. K. J. (2008). Relationships between mindfulness, flow dispositions and mental skills adoption: A cluster analytic approach. *Psychology of Sport and Exercise*, 9(4), 393–411. doi: 10.1016/j.psychsport.2007.07.001

Keng, S.-L., Smoski, M. J., and Robins, C. J. (2011). Effects of mindfulness on psychological health: A review of empirical studies. *Clinical Psychology Review*, 31(6), 1041–1056. doi: 10.1016/j.cpr.2011.04.006

Lan, M. (2009). *The illustration of mindfulness [图解正念]. Shan Xi, P. R.* China: Shaanxi Normal University Press.

Linehan, M. M. (1993). *Cognitive-behavioral treatment of borderline personality disorder*. New York, NY: Guilford Press.

Liu, H. N. (2012). *"Change" or "Acceptance" – Young athletes psychological intervention study of resilience under the guidance of two different concepts [*"接受"与"改变"——两种不同理念指导下的青少年运动员心理韧性干预研究*]* (Unpublished master's thesis). Wuhan, P. R. China: Wuhan Institute of Physical Education.

Meichenbaum, D. (1977). *Cognitive-behavior modification: An integrative approach*. New York, NY: Plenum.

Moore, R. G., Hayhurst, H., and Teasdale, J. D. (1996). *Measure of awareness and coping in autobiographical memory: Instruction for administering and coding*. (Unpublished manuscript.) Cambridge, UK: University of Cambridge.

Moore, Z. E. (2009). Theoretical and empirical developments of the Mindfulness-Acceptance-Commitment (MAC) approach to performance enhancement. *Journal of Clinical Sport Psychology*, 3(4), 291–302.

Parker, R. I., and Vannest, K. J. (2009). An improved effect size for single case research: Nonoverlap of all pairs. *Behavior Therapy*, 40(4), 357–367. doi: 10.1016/j.beth. 2008.10.006

Parker, R. I., Vannest, K. J., and Davis, J. L. (2011). Effect size in single-case research: A review of nine nonoverlap techniques. *Behavior Modification*. 35(4), 302–322. doi: 10.1177/0145445511399147

Safran, J. D., and Segal, Z. V. (1990). *Interpersonal process incognitive therapy*. New York, NY: Basic Books.

Sahdra, B. K., Shaver, P. R., and Brown, K. W. (2010). A scale to measure nonattachment: A Buddhist complement to Western research on attachment and adaptive functioning. *Journal of Personality Assessment*, 92(2), 116–127. doi: 10.1080/00223890903425960

Schwanhausser, L. (2009). Application of the Mindfulness-Acceptance-Commitment (MAC) protocol with an adolescent springboard diver: The case of Steve. *Journal of Clinical Sport Psychology*, 3(4), 377–395.

Segal, Z. V., Williams, J. M. G., and Teasdale, J. D. (2002).*Mindfulness-based cognitive therapy for depression: A new approach to preventing relapse*. New York, NY: Guilford Press.

Shen, H. Y. (2009). *Mind and realm [心灵与境界]*. Zhengzhou, P. R., China: Zhengzhou University Press.

Si, G. (2006). Pursuing "ideal" or emphasizing "coping": The new definition of "peak performance" and transformation of mental training pattern [追求"最佳"还是强调"应对"—对理想竞技表现的重新定义及心理训练范式变革]. *Sport Science*, 26, 43–48.

Si, G., Duan, Y., Li, H. Y., and Jiang, X. (2011). An exploration on social-cultural meridians of Chinese athletes' psychological training. *Journal of Clinical Sport Psychology*, 5(4), 325–338.

Si, G., Lee, H. C., and Lonsdale, C. (2010).Sport psychology research and its application in China. In M. H. Bond, (Ed.), *The Oxford handbook of Chinese psychology* (pp. 641–656). Hong Kong, P. R. China: Oxford University Press.

Song, Z. L. (1992). *The Noble Eightfold Path [/八正道]*. Taibei, P. R., China: Hongtai Press.

Suan, N. (2012). *Eliminate anxiety by slowly drinking: Meditation of slow motion [慢动作冥想法]*. Jiangsu, P. R., China: Jiangsu Wen Yi Press.

Thompson, R. W., Kaufman, K. A., De Petrillo, L. A., Glass, C. R., and Arnkoff, D. B. (2011). One year follow-up of Mindful Sport Performance Enhancement (MSPE) for archers, golfers, and runners. *Journal of Clinical Sport Psychology*, 5(2), 99–116.

Wang, Y., and Zhang, Q. (2012). The influence of the mood management to the provincial swimming athletes' training quality: A single-subject design ["心境管理"对于省级游泳运动员训练质量的影响]. *Chinese Journal of Sports Medicine*, 31, 257–263.

Wilson, K. G., and Murrell, A. R. (2004). Values work in acceptance and commitment therapy: Setting a course for behavioral treatment. In S. C. Hayes, V. M. Follette, and M. M. Linehan (Eds.), *Mindfulness and acceptance: Expanding the cognitive-behavioral tradition* (pp. 120–151). New York, NY: Guilford Press

Wolanin, A. T., and Schwanhausser, L. A. (2010). Psychological functioning as a moderator of the MAC approach to performance enhancement. *Journal of Clinical Sport Psychology*, 4(4), 312–322.

Xiong, W. R. (2011). *The lost and reversion of the theory of human nature of the mindfulness psychotherapy [正念疗法的人性论迷失与复归]* (Unpublished doctoral dissertation). Changchun, P. R. China: Jilin University,.

Xiong, W. R., and Yu, L. (2010). Researching the thought of psychotherapy of the mind-nature theory of Zen *[西方心理学对禅定的功效研究]*. *Psychological Exploration*, 30(2), 7–10.

Zhang, C.-Q., Chung, P.-K., Si, G., and Liu, J. D. (2014). Psychometric properties of the Acceptance and Action Questionnaire–II for Chinese college students and elite Chinese athletes. *Measurement and Evaluation in Counseling and Development*, 47, 256–270. doi: 10.1177/0748175614538064

Zhang, G. Z. (2013). *The effect of psychological intervention of "Mindfulness-Acceptance-Commitment" approach ["正念-接受-投入" 心理干预效果的研究]*. (Unpublished master's thesis). Wuhan, P. R. China: Wuhan Institute of Physical Education.

Zhang, G. Z., Bu, D. R., and Si, G. (2012). Psychological intervention based on Mindfulness-Acceptance-Commitment approach: A mental training paradigm for athletes [以正念接受为基础的心理干预: 一种运动员心理训练的新范式]. *Chinese Journal of Sports Medicine*, 31, 1109–1116.

Zhang, K., and Zhang, L. W. (2011). Doctrine and method: What Chinese culture can contribute to athletes' psychological training and consultation [道与术: 中国文化对运动员心理咨询与训练的启示]. *Journal of Tianjin University of Sport*, 26, 196–199.

Zong, J. (2010). *Body scan of Zen relaxation [全身扫描式禅修]*. Sina. Retrieved from http://blog.sina.com.cn/s/blog_636ea1f70100macl.html

he Mindful AFL Player: Engagement, Mobile Apps, and Well-Being

Jo Mitchell, Craig Hassed

> I was someone who worried a lot about my footy and what everyone thought. I would go home and lie awake at night and having meetings in my head, so now I try to live more day-by-day and be in the present moment.
>
> Brett Kirk, past player and captain, Sydney Swans (Kirk, 2007)

This chapter focuses on mindfulness, well-being, engagement, and smartphone applications in the context of the Australian Football League (AFL). It starts with an introduction to AFL, the role of the AFL Players' Association (AFL Players), and the current state of mind and well-being science in the AFL. We consider mindfulness and well-being research outcomes in nonclinical populations and then explore the use of mobile technology to engage people in the practice of mindfulness. Finally, we describe how AFL Players have approached integrating mindfulness as part of a broader well-being program for players. The mindfulness program implemented at AFL Players was developed by the first author (JM[1]) and informed by the research and applied work of the second author (CH[2]).

The AFL and AFL Players' Association

AFL refers to the elite Australian Rules football competition known as the Australian Football League. The origins of Australian Rules football can be traced back to 1858, when a game was invented in Melbourne to help cricket players remain fit in the winter months. It is a full-contact, free-flowing, and fast game with players passing the ball by foot and hand, and played on a field the size of a cricket oval (450 to 500 feet in diameter).

---

[1] The first author, Jo Mitchell, is employed as Well-Being Manager for the AFL Players Association, as well as Director and Clinical Psychologist at the Mind Room, a Melbourne-based well-being and performance psychology practice.

[2] Craig Hassed, Senior Lecturer and Mindfulness Coordinator at Monash University, is a medical practitioner and author.

The AFL was officially formed in 1997 when the Victorian Football League (VFL) expanded to include a number of interstate clubs. Today it is Australia's premier sporting code in terms of participation and viewing (see Appendix A for a more detailed description).

The AFL Players' Association (originally called the Victorian Football League Players' Association) was created by the players in 1973 to protect and enhance the collective interests of all football players, current and past. There are approximately more than eight hundred players across the league in a season, and more than five thousand past players. Every current AFL player is a member (plus more than 2,500 alumni members) and contributes to the running of the Association, by paying yearly fees and also by directing a portion of the funding allocation under the Collective Bargaining Agreement to the organization. AFL Players provides a range of services directly to players, such as financial services, well-being support, legal advice, and career and education support. It also offers spirited representation of players' views and interests to a wide range of stakeholders within the AFL industry and also in the broader community (see Appendix A for a more detailed description). Importantly, player health and well-being are firmly on AFL Players' agenda. In the next section, we reflect on well-being philosophy and science, and the role of mindfulness as part of this health and well-being strategy.

Beyond Survival to Well-Being

Oscar Wilde (1854–1900) once said, "To live is the rarest thing in the World. Most people exist, that is all." The *art* of living well, moving beyond mere survival in life, has consistently been the subject of philosophers, poets, and artists for many thousands of years. Early philosophers such as Socrates (470–399 BC) and Epicurus (341–270 BC) are attributed with being among the first in Western civilization to argue that happiness was obtainable through human effort. Their respective theories of happiness differed in focus. Epicurus saw pain avoidance and pleasure seeking (*hedonia*) as the source of happiness (Konstan, 2014). In contrast, Socrates talked of transcending pain and pleasure, as well as doing good (e.g., contributing to the well-being of others) and functioning well in society (*eudaimonia*) as essential determinants of personal and collective happiness (Ryff, 1989). For thousands of years, many of the world's great wisdom traditions, such as Buddhism, have described the suffering that comes of desiring and clinging to things that are inherently transient, such as success, fame, and youth (Hassed, 2002). In the famous words of English poet and novelist Rudyard Kipling, also inscribed over the entrance to the centre court at Wimbledon, "If you can meet with triumph and disaster, and treat those two imposters just the same." Kipling's quote alludes to the transient nature of life events, and the path to well-being lies in holding both lightly.

In the modern-day pursuit of well-being, academics have built on the work of early philosophers and added the scientific method of psychology. Psychology has, until recently, been dominated by a search into psycho-pathology and unhappiness. The *science* of living well has a shorter and more potted history. We did not really see a serious scientific exploration of happiness, or well-being, until the work of William James (1842–1910), doctor, philosopher, and psychologist. Then followed a handful of avant-garde scientists who addressed the topic, such as social psychologist Marie Jahoda (1907–2001), who offered the *Theory of Ideal Mental Health* in 1958, and father of humanistic psychology, Abraham Maslow (1908–1970), who is well known for offering the *hierarchy of needs*.

The more recent collective scientific exploration of happiness, or well-being science, has come from two main directions. In the late 1970s, the first research was begun on the health benefits associated with meditative or contemplative practices (Kabat-Zinn, 2003). Secondly, in 1990 the positive psychology movement was established. Since then, there has been burgeoning research on happiness, well-being, and the scientific study of what makes individuals and communities thrive.

The focus in the study of psychology has been biased toward pathology and dysfunction, meaning what is wrong with people and how to fix or treat them. Little consideration has been given to what is right with people and what we can learn about living well and realizing potential, looking beyond merely surviving life. What is now clear is that the absence of illness does not equate to the presence of well-being (Keyes, 2002). This is summarized well by the World Health Organization's definitions of health: *"Health* is a state of complete physical, mental and social well-being and not merely the absence of disease or infirmity" (WHO, 1948):

> *Mental health* is defined as a state of wellbeing in which every individual realizes his or her own potential, can cope with the normal stresses of life, can work productively and fruitfully, and is able to make a contribution to her or his community (WHO, 2014).

Ignoring the insights of those who were preeminent in well-being and functioning has come at a cost for the modern world. Depression is taking over as the number-one burden of disease despite this being a time of unprecedented affluence and material comfort (Mathers & Loncar, 2006).

The Bias Created by Mind–Body Dualism

In the seventeenth century, philosopher Descartes argued for the separation between mind and body as two distinct entities: the nonphysical mind and the physical body. In the modern scientific age, dominated by materialism, this mind–body dualism resulted in highly valuing the body with little scientific attention on the nonphysical mind or even the influence of the mind on the body. The contention that mind and body are separate and distinct entities has doggedly remained with Western culture regarding healing and wellness ever since. One of the consequences of this materialist emphasis on the body within the mind–body dualism has resulted in a slow, begrudging integration of mind sciences or psychology into considerations of healing and well-being. The latest frontier has been the reintegration of mind and body through the study of mind–body medicine.

In contrast to the science around our mental well-being, the physical health sciences are decades ahead in terms of understanding peak physical functioning and performance and having accessible language around what it means to be physically fit – compared with what it means to be mentally fit. The difference is the nuanced understanding of the body, compared to the mind. This difference has created a significant divide in sport, and the community more broadly, between our understanding of and resources given to peak physical functioning versus mental well-being and functioning. Unfortunately, the almost exclusive focus on the body ignores the fact that one cannot function well physically without the mind functioning well, and in the performance realm this means being on task.

Focus on mind and body

A majority of adults know how to look after their physical fitness. When asked what they can do for exercise to enhance their well-being, most can reference a specific exercise routine in which they engage or know that they should engage. Whether they ideally would jog, swim, play a team sport, or just bounce on a trampoline for fun and fitness, there is an acceptance of the importance and knowledge of applying fitness strategies. However, the same is not true when we ask people, "What's your mental health and well-being plan?" Most people think that you are talking about addressing clinical problems such as depression or anxiety, not about what they can do proactively to enhance their mind fitness and well-being.

Some sectors of the population seem to have a better grasp of the relevance of mind to body and vice versa, and sport is one of them.

Though the sport community may understand the mind–body connection 'better,' there remain significant gaps. When we look at AFL teams, the ratio of people caring for players' physical versus mental fitness is significantly skewed (at best 10:1 staff). Approximately three-quarters of the eighteen AFL clubs have a dedicated psychologist, nearly all of whom are part-time and often expected to cover a diverse portfolio. AFL psychologists are expected to help recruit players and offer sport psychology consulting services, from improving on-field performance, enhancing organizational culture, and providing services related to player well-being.

Such varied tasks for the AFL psychologists are quite different from those required for those professionals offering services related to caring for the body. In these days of professional sport, you would not expect a physical conditioning coach to also play the role of physiotherapist, masseuse, midfield coach, and doctor. Mental fitness and well-being are often referred to as an important part of the game. Anecdotally, we often hear players and coaches say things like, "We weren't mentally prepared," or, "My head wasn't in the game." Yet dedicated resources and time in the club schedules to develop players' resilience, well-being, and mental health are still quite limited. When psychological skills sessions are arranged, they are often scheduled for during the players' own time or given low priority, and thus are the first services to get squeezed out of the training program.

Part of the problem may be the culture and bias that comes in male-dominated domains such as football. Like the general male population, male athletes have low rates of seeking help for mental health problems. Seeking support or help is often viewed as admitting weakness rather than building resilience. The major barriers to seeking help include a lack of understanding about mental health and well-being, stigma around mental health problems, help seeking being perceived as a sign of weakness, and the perception that mental health is not linked to performance outcomes (Gulliver, Griffiths, & Christiansen, 2012; NCAA, 2013).

One coach who has emphasized the mental aspect of AFL better than most is Paul Roos. In a recent interview, Roos reflected that, "Coaching is all about psychology. You've got to have an understanding of your staff and your players." (Wilmoth, 2014). After a great playing career at two AFL clubs, Fitzroy and the Sydney Swans, Roos went on to coach the Swans to their first premiership in over seventy years in 2005.

We know that AFL players are no different to their non-AFL peers in terms of susceptibility to mental illness (one in five will struggle in their lifetime) and that the most vulnerable period for the onset of mental illness is fifteen to twenty-five years old (AIHW, 2011). Anxiety and mood disorders are the most common psychological issue encountered in elite athletes (Schaal et al., 2011), similar to the general population. While being physically active is a protective factor for good mental health (Morgan et al., 2013), there are also numerous stressors that elite athletes face that may increase risk for poor mental health. Stressors include the physical and mental demands of training and competition, operating in a high-pressure performance environment, injuries, time commitment to their sport, social difficulties with teammates and/or coaches, and media attention (Gulliver et al., 2012; NCAA, 2013; Schaal et al., 2011).

Two key issues are also particularly relevant to AFL Players. First is the period of vulnerability when they retire or are delisted, a time where they face increased susceptibility to depression and anxiety (Johnson, 1997; Leddy, Lambert, & Ogles, 1994; Reardon & Factor, 2010), and key transition points throughout life. Secondly, players who suffer from multiple concussions during their career (a regular occurrence in AFL) may also be at increased risk of depression (Guskiewicz et al., 2007).

There have been multiple high-profile examples of AFL players who have publicly talked about mental illness (Mitchell & Sale, 2015). We also know that we can help prevent player mental illness and enhance well-being by teaching the basics of how the mind, body, and emotions work together. The added benefit is that these mind basics (e.g., mindfulness practices) are also good for on-field performance as well as other aspects of life, such as study, relationships, and social life.

A Well-Being Strategy

To redress the imbalance in psychological and well-being services, compared to physical body–related services, the AFL Players' Association has devised a clear well-being strategy that provides individual and group support to current and past players. The strategy includes providing individual psychological support directly to players through a national network of psychologists. To maintain confidentiality and player privacy, these sessions are provided at the psychologist's private practice, away from the club environment and the AFL Players' Association offices. The focus of these sessions is on players' mental health, well-being, resilience, and life performance. All AFL Player psychologists are registered and experienced in working across the continuum from mental illness to well-being and optimal performance. Player and team on-field performance remain the responsibility of the clubs, rather than of this service, so the AFL Players' Association predominantly contracts clinical and counseling psychologists with knowledge and experience of high-performance environments rather than sport and performance psychologists, who may have less knowledge or experience with mental illness.

The second part of the AFL Players' well-being strategy delivers proactive health and well-being messages and skills through sixty-minute workshops. The workshops, similarly to the individual sessions, are focused on the holistic development of players as people with on-field and off-field lives. The well-being workshops cover skills and strategies to enhance players' well-being, resilience, and life performance. They are designed using the latest evidence-based research and applied knowledge from Acceptance and Commitment Therapy (ACT; Hayes, Strosahl, & Wilson, 1999) and positive psychology (e.g., Seligman & Csikszentmihalyi, 2000; Sin & Lyubomirsky, 2009) in consultation with industry experts and players. The suite of workshop topics includes, but is not limited to, clarifying your values and strengths; managing stress, thoughts, and emotions; building hope, relationships, and social connection; and mindfulness.

The emphasis in the workshops is on creating an engaging and practical experience for players that plants seeds of how the mind sciences can help them understand themselves and how to maximize their potential in all aspects of life. These workshops are intended to support and educate players and encourage clubs to develop a culture that emphasizes mental and physical health and fitness in a complementary way. The workshops are based on the premise that understanding body and mind and how they work together is the secret to success.

Mindfulness, or the ability to pay attention and notice what is happening in the mind, body, and environment, is a foundation skill for the well-being program. The Ancient Greek aphorism, "Know thyself," encapsulates this. Many athletes prefer to focus on knowing their sporting code and opposition well, rather than the less obvious but more challenging idea of being willing to look within. The skill of mindfulness plays a crucial role in learning to pay attention to what is occurring in the mind, body, and environment. Mindfulness, in our program, is defined as the ability to focus intentionally on our present-moment experience with curiosity and acceptance. Awareness is the generic skill that underpins our ability to understand and learn and is therefore a prerequisite for other well-being skills. For example, apart from being associated with better mental health, mindful awareness is also associated with the following (Hofmann et al., 2010):

- Down-regulating the brain's stress center, the amygdala (Way et al., 2010)
- Better executive functioning (Zeidan et al., 2010)

- Greater mental flexibility in problem solving (Greenberg, Reiner, & Meiran, 2012)
- More emotional intelligence (Baer, Smith, & Allen, 2004)
- Better attention switching and shorter attentional blink (Slagter et al., 2007)

A crucial factor that players and clubs need to appreciate about mindfulness is that it is not primarily a relaxation exercise. It is an exercise in awareness with relaxation being a common side effect. Even if there is anxiety, an athlete can learn to be mindful of it and, rather than trying to *control it,* which only escalates the symptoms, the athlete learns to stand back from it and be less *controlled by it.* This is also useful in the ability to manage emotions such as anger and impulsivity on the field.

One model of the relaxation/stress and performance relationship that is commonly cited is the Yerkes-Dodson stress-performance curve (Yerkes & Dodson, 1908). In this model, performance is said to increase with physiological or mental arousal, but only up to a point. When levels of arousal become too high, performance starts to decrease. The process is represented graphically as a curvilinear, inverted *U*-shaped curve. Relaxation without awareness and engagement is on the far left of the Yerkes-Dodson stress-performance curve, and although it is useful for sleep, it is not useful for imminent sporting performance. For this reason, many players avoid "relaxation" before games or in other performance situations. Higher performance is associated with partial activation of the stress response that lifts the athlete out of apathy and engages him or her with what is about to happen. If the athlete becomes more stressed or anxious, or if the athlete assumes that simply increasing activation will continue to enhance performance further, then he or she will go over the top of the stress performance curve to the far right. Here performance is very poor and the athlete feels terrible. In this situation, the athlete becomes increasingly self-conscious (suffering performance anxiety) and is therefore losing focus from the present-moment activity (poor situational awareness, performance, and decision making).

Unfortunately, most people assume that stress is the only factor that drives performance, but there is another theoretical explanation: the Hassed (2006) mindfulness-based stress-performance curve (see Figure 12.1). As with the Yerkes-Dodson stress-performance curve, stress moves the athlete from apathy toward improving performance: Moving toward the highest level of performance results from relatively higher levels of focus.

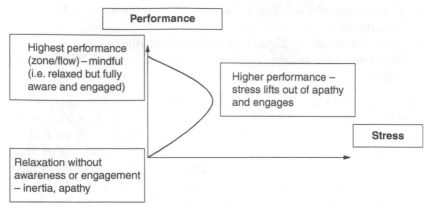

Figure 12.1   The Hassed stress-performance curve.

This means that with the obtainment of complete focus on an activity, the athlete moves into a state of flow where she is neither concentrating on herself or the outcome, but in the fully engaged experience.

A hallmark of zone or flow states is therefore a lack of performance anxiety paired with full focus on the task at hand, which, in turn, is often associated with the highest level of performance (Csikszentmihalyi, 1990). Flow reflects an inner relaxation, an inner calmness, while at once in complete engagement with the moment-to-moment task at hand. In other words, flow is represented by effortlessness, efficacy, and efficiency all in the one state. Athletes who describe their flow often offer exquisite descriptions of what it means to be in such a focused, mindful state including at once awareness, lack of anxiety about the outcome, and enjoyment. Billie Jean King offers a quote that depicts a quintessential state, reflecting mindfulness, during a peak sporting moment:

> It almost seems as though I'm able to transport myself beyond the turmoil on the court to some place of total peace and calm. . . . I appreciate what my opponent is doing in a detached, abstract way. Like an observer in the next room. . . . It is a perfect combination of (intense) action taking place in an atmosphere of total tranquillity. When it happens, I want to stop the match and grab the microphone and shout that's what it's all about, because it is. It is not the big prize I'm going to win at the end of the match or anything else. . . . When I'm in that kind of state . . . I feel that tennis is an art form that's capable of moving both the players and the audience (Harung et al., 2009, p. 881).

The mindful approach to sport competition was also summed up by Australian Murray Rose, one of the greatest swimmers of all time: An athlete who seemed to have perfect composure and rhythm, even in the Olympic finals, Murray also managed to balance international swimming, full-time collegiate studies in the United States, and numerous outside interests (e.g., acting). The following is part of a transcript of an ABC television interview with him in 1962:

MURRAY ROSE.   My philosophy as an athlete is a very broad one. I think first of all it's one of discipline and secondly it's one of concentration. When I'm swimming I like to think and do nothing else but swim.
REPORTER.   Do you have any philosophy on life as an individual?
MURRAY ROSE.   I think it revolves around this perhaps secret of concentration on one thing. When you're eating, you do nothing else but eat. And when you're swimming, you do nothing else but swim, and I think that by doing that you achieve the greatest satisfaction by devoting your whole self, your whole energies, your whole thoughts to just one activity at a time. And I think that perhaps would be the essence of my personal philosophy (ABC, 2013).

Murray's personal philosophy to swimming and life patterns after the core elements of mindfulness, particularly being fully present to moment-to-moment experience through full concentration on the task at hand.

Engagement

Time is one of the biggest challenges faced in engaging AFL players with mindfulness and other well-being practices. Until the AFL clubs and players prioritize the mental side of the sport as much as the physical and support the notion that well-being contributes to the players' on- and off-field performance, then there will be an ongoing struggle to get adequate time to work with the players. Delivery of AFL Players wellbeing programs in clubs starts with building good relationships with players and club staff while, concurrently, emphasizing the value of well-being interventions. Word of mouth of players who have found such interventions useful to engage new athletes is invaluable.

The second challenge to engaging players is attention. While the content of the well-being workshops may be technically correct and based on the best evidence-based science, attention is quickly lost if players view the program as boring or irrelevant. And even if they do participate, the acquisition of well-being knowledge typically depends on giving full attention to the sport psychologists. One of the biggest complaints of

AFL players is the number of club and industry meetings that they have to sit through. So the irony is that in order to teach mindfulness, we first have to create a learning environment that engages their attention.

Since 2013, AFL Players has captured engagement data from players (N = 165) at the end of every workshop by anonymously responding to a questionnaire that asks, "Did you find this workshop engaging or interesting?" and, "Did you find this workshop helpful?" Players responded on a five-point Likert-type scale with the anchors, "Not at all," to, "Very." They also had the option to comment on what they liked or disliked and suggest ways to improve the workshop. This information is used to improve the workshop content and delivery. In 2014, the average response score across all workshops has been 4 out of 5, indicating a high level of engagement and helpful content.

AFL Player engagement strategies include using adult learning principles, and taking what we know about how male adult athletes learn best. We use active learning with short bursts of information or concepts followed by an activity to bring the concept to life in a practical way. For example, some of the mindfulness science is presented on the impact of mindfulness on relationships, followed by a conversation drawing on relevant player experiences, then an activity where players engage in an unmindful and mindful conversation. We contextualize the content and use examples from sport and peers whom they respect. Audio-visual tools, varying content and delivery, and encouraging peer learning and conversation all help maintain engagement. We keep the group size small, with four to ten participants and one facilitator per session. We end the workshop with one or two key messages and a specific task to practice in their everyday lives in order to reinforce and deepen learning.

One additional engagement technique is the use of technology to deliver content and encourage ongoing practice of the skills introduced in the workshops. Since 2013, all first-year players are provided with an iPad from AFL Players during the Player Induction Camp. This camp is an annual two-day event hosted by AFL Players in pre-season for all new club recruits (126 new players in 2014) to orient them to the services provided by AFL Players (e.g., financial, legal, personal brand, and well-being) and some of the rules and regulations of the AFL (e.g., regarding gambling, doping, and respect and responsibility). All current players have a smartphone and/or their own computer or access to a club computer. AFL Players are in the process of creating a digital platform called Players U, so that players can access education modules from across the organization (e.g., finance, career transition, well-being) from anywhere, at any time, and across multiple digital formats (computer, mobile phone, tablet). Currently, the AFL Players mindfulness program "Practical Mindfulness" has been delivered only in a small group format and supported by a number of recommended mobile applications. A description of this program follows.

Practical Mindfulness for AFL Players

The Practical Mindfulness program was developed in 2011 and has been delivered over three sessions of approximately sixty-minutes to players through seasons 2012 through 2014. Given the limited amount of time we were given with the players, we viewed this as an opportunity to plant seeds, raise awareness, and engage the players in a practice that they – or, in some cases, the clubs – would continue to encourage and develop. The focus of the program is on developing mindfulness as a life skill that can enhance players' resilience, well-being, and life performance.

The mindfulness program

In the first two years of delivery, the program was primarily delivered to third- and fourth-year players (aged twenty to twenty-five). However, now the program is open to players at any stage of their career (age range eighteen to thirty-eight years). The emphasis is on making sessions practical, interactive, and a little bit playful. Facilitators to date have all been psychologists trained in mindfulness, who regularly practice mindfulness, and who have an understanding of the AFL industry and player issues. The Practical Mindfulness program (for full description, see Table 12.1) is offered weekly, for three sessions:

- **Session I.** Players are introduced to a definition of mindfulness, the evidence-based benefits, and relevance to them as players. The concepts of mindfulness and being on autopilot are highlighted, and the group completes a five-to-ten-minute mindfulness practice.
- **Session II.** The concept of mindfulness is reviewed, and the concepts of stress and perception are introduced and discussed. Players are prompted to practice a brief formal (body meditation) and also an informal mindfulness practice (mindful conversations) and invited to commit to a five-minute daily practice.
- **Session III.** The intersection between mindfulness and emotions is introduced and discussed. Players practice a brief mindfulness meditation (emotions) and an informal practice (eating). Players are, again, invited to commit to a five-minute daily practice.

Table 12.1 *Description of the AFL Players Practical Mindfulness Program*

Session 1	
Overview	The first session introduces players to what mindfulness is, to identify their own experience of being on autopilot and being mindful, and the benefits of applying these mental skills in their own life. We take a look at who is being mindful in sport (e.g., AFL, NFL, NBA, FIFA, Olympic athletes) and do a brief 5–10 minute formal meditation and informal mindfulness practice. Players are invited to commit to a 5-minute daily practice (formal or informal).
Learning objectives	• To understand mindfulness vs. autopilot; and identify when they are mindful and when they are on autopilot in their own life. • To understand the benefits of developing mindfulness skills. • To understand the mind–body connection. • To understand how mindfulness can be applied to key life domains. • To experience a brief (5–10 minute) mindfulness meditation practice (breathing). • To experience a brief (2-minute) daily practice (stretching). • To explore self-help tools to help them apply these skills (e.g., mobile applications, books, websites).

Session 2	
Overview	Session two starts with a review of what mindfulness is and asks players about their own mindfulness experiences since last sessions. It provides an opportunity to practice a brief formal mindfulness meditation (body) and an informal practice (mindful conversations). The concept of stress and perception is introduced. Players are invited to commit to a 5-minute daily practice (formal or informal).
Learning objectives	• To understand how mindfulness can be applied to key life domains, especially relationships and sleep. • To explore the relationship between stress and perception. • To experience a brief (10–15 minute) mindfulness meditation practice (body). • To experience a brief (2-minute) daily practice (mindful conversations). • To troubleshoot any practice issues. • To encourage use of self-help mindfulness tools for ongoing daily practice.

Session 3	
Overview	Session two starts with a review of what mindfulness is and asks players about their own mindfulness experiences since the last sessions. It provides an opportunity to practice a brief mindfulness meditation (emotions) and an informal practice (eating). The role of emotions is discussed as well as how to have a mindful attitude (acceptance and curiosity). Players are invited to commit to a 5-minute daily practice (formal or informal). Options for continued practice beyond the program are explored.

Table 12.1 (cont.)

Session 3	
Learning objectives	• To understand how mindfulness can be applied to key life domains. • To explore the concept of a mindful attitude and the role of emotions. • To experience a brief (10-minute) mindfulness meditation practice (emotions). • To experience a brief (2-minute) daily practice (mindful eating). • To troubleshoot any practice issues. • To encourage use of self-help mindfulness tools for ongoing daily practice. • To discuss future options to explore or practice mindfulness skills beyond the program.

The mobile technologies: The applications (apps)

Mobile technologies were recommended to the players to support their mindfulness practice A range of apps were recommended such that the players could select an app that most aligned with their lifestyle demands. The apps offer a range of mindfulness meditations prompts and resources, including guided and unguided meditations (some meditations were designed for particular parts of the day), audio, and timed reminders to practice (see Table 12.2 for detailed description of the specific apps offered).

These mobile applications were chosen because they are user-friendly and provided a mix of interactive and engaging ways to practice formal and informal mindfulness skills. They are accessible via a range of digital media (e.g., computer, Android smartphone, iPhone, iPad, and iPod touch). The fact that they are not sport-specific (although Smiling Mind has now produced a sport version for Cricket Australia) was not a concern given the group workshop provided the context and could answer sport-related issues. The Practical Mindfulness program was developed on the premise that mindfulness is a universal skill applicable to all life domains. Players were also encouraged to discover or share alternative mobile applications that they found helpful, especially with a constant stream of new applications entering the market.

Player feedback on the practical mindfulness program

The focus of our evidence-based well-being workshops has been on player engagement rather than health and well-being outcomes. Engagement data (reported earlier in the chapter) and qualitative feedback on the Practical

Table 12.2 *Mindfulness Apps Recommended as Part of the Practical Mindfulness Program*

Name	Cost	Website	Android	iPhone	iPad	iPod Touch	Description
Buddhify² (UK)	$2.99		In development	✔	✔		Buddhify² is the mindfulness app for modern life. It is a practical, playful, and beautifully designed tool. It helps you to practice mindfulness-based meditation on the go: as you walk; while you commute and when you are at the gym, at your desk, online, going to sleep, or at home. Buddhify² gives you a simple but effective way to bring more mindfulness and calm to your busy day. It has over 40 guided audio meditations ranging from 5 to 20 minutes in length. It tracks your progress and provides tips and ideas to help you be more mindful.
Smiling Mind (Australia)	Free	✔	✔	✔	✔		Smiling Mind is meditation made easy. It is a web- and app-based program that provides provide accessible, lifelong tools based in mindfulness meditation. Smiling Mind is a not-for-profit initiative that provides 6 free mindfulness meditation programs designed for specific age groups (7–11 years; 12–15 years; 6–22 years; adults). It has a mix of bite-size and longer meditations as part of a sequential program. It also has sport-specific meditations, developed with Cricket Australia.
Get Some Headspace (UK)	Free version or	✔	✔	✔	✔		Headspace is meditation made simple, a way of treating your head right.

Table 12.2 (cont.)

Name	Cost	Website	Android	iPhone	iPad	iPod Touch	Description
	$12.95 per month or $95 per year						You can start with a free Take10 program that teaches the basics of meditation in just 10 minutes a day over 10 days. Beyond this, you need to subscribe to gain access to hundreds of hours of original meditations, including guided and unguided, ranging from 2 to 60 minutes. It provides a personal progress page, a buddy system, and a community to support your journey, and heaps of information on a range of health and well-being topics.
Mindfulness Daily (U.S.)	$2.49			✓	✓	✓	Mindfulness Daily guides you through 21-day mindfulness audio lessons on topics such as mindful breathing, body awareness, and kindness. It includes a "pause" feature for a 15-second mindfulness break. It maps progress overtime, and has a remix feature to mix up the 21-day program.
The Now (U.S.)	Free			✓	✓		The Now helps you retrain your mind to live more fully in the moment. It does this using a technique called continuous mindfulness training: providing push notifications with an audible chime and a relevant mindful message or quote, to remind you to be fully focused on the present. The mindfulness training runs for a 3 week cycle.

Mindfulness program have been collected. Ideally, future research will look at longitudinal outcomes, including sport performance outcomes and stress reduction, for players who engage in mindfulness training.

Based on the feedback from our four main facilitators (one male and three female psychologists), the majority of AFL players respond well to the practical nature of the Practical Mindfulness program. They report appreciating the opportunity to ask questions and to engage in the practice of mindfulness. There is typically one player in every group (i.e., each group ranges from four to ten players) who is resistant or disengaged. Generally, however, such players are not disruptive to their group. At times, it has been useful to have a discussion about the source of this resistance while also respecting the player's right to not engage with the mindfulness practice. Healthy skepticism can be a catalyst for useful conversation. Unhealthy skepticism, in the form of a closed mind, on the other hand, does not support engagement and learning. Such a player is uninterested in practicing mindfulness and may not ever be willing to try, and an attempt to impose the practice upon such players can have the opposite of the intended effect. Players need to take it at their own pace and be supported to apply it, or not, to their overall training program.

The emergence of mindfulness practices across the AFL has not been systematic, but instead centered around people of influence who value the benefits of formal mindfulness practice. Paul Roos, one notable proponent of mindfulness and meditation practices, is a former player and a senior coach (formerly of the Sydney Swans and currently of the Melbourne Demons). Roos's influence has spread to a number of players, such as past team captain for the Sydney Swans Brett Kirk, who is also an ambassador for the mindfulness program Smiling Mind. Current Sydney Swans player Dan Hanneberry talks about the how Roos and Kirk introduced him to mindfulness:

> So the way it (mindfulness practice) relates to AFL football for me is that it helps me not worry about making a mistake or to dwell on it when you do make one. To concentrate on the job, you need to be present (Hannebery, 2011, para. 8).

A recent article describing the rise of mindfulness in sport and the AFL highlights a number of the players, coaches, and clubs that are the key proponents of mindfulness (Mitchell, 2014). Mitchell (2014) offers examples of Australian elite sportsmen's positive attitudes toward mindfulness. Former Australian cricketer and current West Australian coach Justin Langer, an advocate of mindfulness for years, states,

Without mindfulness success just isn't possible. Whether you are playing cricket as opening batsman at Test level, or running a business, or working in a service industry, the greatest challenge is to understand that, when the game of life is in full swing, you must live for the moment, to concentrate on that ball. When the pressure is turned on, if you are to fulfil your potential then you must focus on the present (Michie, 2011, para. 3).

Mindfulness strategies have also been applied to on-the-field behavioral issues. In the AFL, after a series of suspensions Richmond player Dan Jackson turned to mindfulness to help manage unhelpful emotions and reduce aggression (Mitchell, 2014). He played every game in the following 2013 season and became the Richmond "best and fairest" player (i.e., most valuable player) that year.

Often the most persuasive engagement approach is to show the impact of mindfulness in the lives of people whom players respect. Pete Carroll, coach of the NFL's Seattle Seahawks, a team that set several season records and went undefeated on its home field, attributes mindful meditation as a major factor in their 2013 Super Bowl championship win. Team member Russell Okung stated, "Meditation is as important as lifting weights and being out here on the field for practice" (Puff, 2014, para. 7). Many other athletes have taken to meditative practices to help them perform well under pressure, including Olympic gold medallist Cathy Freeman and Michael Jordan and the Chicago Bulls under the guidance of legendary coach Phil Jackson (Jackson & Delehanty, 2013). Tennis professional Novak Djokovic took on mindfulness in 2011, and by the end of the year was number one in the world; had won three Grand Slam titles; and, importantly, had begun to enjoy tennis (Merz, 2013).

Highly respected AFL player, dual Brownlow Medallist, and 2014 Australian of the Year Adam Goodes offers a clear, direct endorsement of mindful meditation in his own life: "It (mindfulness mediation) is important, I value it, and it has really helped me" (Tugwel, 2014, para. 6). Presenting the commentary and experience of other athletes, coaches, or people of influence in AFL players' lives is an important engagement strategy for what may seem an "airy fairy" or "unproven" skill to some players. If it cannot be explained in a pragmatic, simple, and accessible way then it will not make sense or be an attractive option. The growing evidence base for the resilience, well-being, and performance outcomes of mindfulness practice is another engagement strategy, though sometimes this is more important to psychologists, coaches, and player support staff than to the players themselves.

Mindfulness Theory and Research

To help understand how mindfulness influences behavior change in general, and well-being in particular, Shapiro and colleagues (2006) developed a nonlinear model based on Kabat-Zinn's (1994) definition of mindfulness, "paying attention in a particular way: on purpose, in the present moment, and non-judgmentally" (p. 4). Shapiro and colleagues (2006) identified three building blocks, or axioms, of mindfulness, namely intention ("on purpose"), attention ("paying attention"), and attitude ("in a particular way").

The authors proposed that mindfulness is a moment-to-moment experience during which these three axioms are simultaneously activated. The experience of mindfulness is theorized to result in a shift in perspective called *re-perceiving*, meaning the ability to observe moment-to-moment experiences (e.g., thoughts, feelings, images, sensations) with greater clarity and objectivity (Shapiro et al., 2006). Re-perceiving facilitates a number of mechanisms, including clarification of personal values; exposure to emotions, thoughts, and sensations; and flexibility in cognitive, emotional, and behavioral responses. With re-perceiving, there is also an increased ability to self-regulate and manage behavior in a way that enhances health and well-being by fostering nonattachment to emotions, thoughts, and sensations as they come and go. If there is no intentional awareness in the moment, there will be little choice other than to react in the way that the person habitually does. With awareness and detachment (from habituated ways of responding), there is the possibility of greater discernment and choice of response. Mindfulness has therefore a significant role to play in developing emotional regulation (Chambers et al., 2014).

The research on mindfulness as a health intervention started only in the late 1970s. The initial focus was on clinical or stressed populations, and the primary health outcomes measured illness rather than wellness, including psychological (e.g., depression, anxiety, stress, coping style) and physical measures of health (e.g., medical symptoms, physical impairment, sensory pain, functional disability). There is a body of evidence that mindfulness-based interventions can effectively improve mental and physical health outcomes in a variety of clinical populations (e.g., mood and anxiety disorders, chronic pain, and heart disease) (Brown, Ryan, & Creswell, 2007; Chiesa & Serretti, 2009; Vollestad, Nielsen, & Nielsen, 2012). There is a smaller but growing body of evidence that mindfulness can have positive health outcomes in nonclinical populations (Eberth & Sedlmeier, 2012; Sedlmeier et al., 2012).

The more limited research literature around mindfulness and psychological health and well-being is beginning to highlight a range of beneficial outcomes. Correlational research has identified that mindfulness is associated with well-being outcomes, including increased positive affect, vitality, life satisfaction, self-esteem, resilience to stress, and optimism (Eberth & Sedlmeier, 2012; Keng, Smoski, & Robins, 2011; Sedlmeier et al., 2012). Longitudinal studies have taken direct and indirect measures of well-being (e.g., positive states of mind, self-compassion, empathy, satisfaction with life, quality of life) and reported significant positive change (Shapiro, Astin, & Bishop, 2005; Shapiro, Schwartz, & Bonner, 1998). These preliminary findings indicate that teaching people to be mindful not only can alleviate illness, but can also build and enhance health and well-being.

The best-researched mindfulness-based interventions are Mindfulness-Based Stress Reduction (MBSR; Kabat-Zinn, Lipworth, & Burney, 1985) and Mindfulness-Based Cognitive Therapy (MBCT; Segal, Williams, & Teasdale, 2002). Other mindfulness-based approaches with a developing evidence base (for a review, see Ost, 2008; Vollestadt et al., 2012) include Acceptance and Commitment Therapy (ACT; Luoma, Hayes, & Walser, 2007), Dialectical Behavioral Therapy (DBT; Linehan, 1993), and Person-Based Cognitive Therapy (PBCT; Chadwick, 2006).

One of the limitations of mindfulness research to date is the inconsistency of the intervention themselves: mindfulness meditation (formal practice) is a central component of some interventions, and in other interventions it is only part of a broader stress reduction or cognitive behavioral program. Such varied use of mindfulness meditation in programs makes it difficult to determine which elements of the program are having an effect and to what extent formal mindfulness practice is contributing (Cavanagh et al., 2013; Eberth & Sedlmeier, 2012).

The day-to-day ability to be aware or mindful (the informal practice of mindfulness) is that which the formal practice seeks to foster. The question is how best to help others cultivate this ultimate, informal practice of performing and living. Engaging people new to mindfulness practice may not be best served by the significant effort and time commitment that these approaches require to teach and to participate (e.g., MBSR and MBCT are eight-week group programs with daily mindfulness practice). For those with less motivation and time, brief practices may be very helpful, and we have found this to be true for the elite athlete, the AFL player, in particular.

With empirically supported research providing initial evidence that mindfulness-based approaches can produce effective results in various domains of life, including alleviating stress and illness and enhancing well-being, more specific mindfulness questions can be addressed. For example, can we use technology to deliver mindfulness training as self-help or to augment face-to-face practitioner delivery? What happens when we teach mindfulness skills without the additional content of an MBSR or MBCT program? How much mindfulness practice do we need to make a difference?

Digital mindfulness delivery
Online or digital mindfulness programs have started to be offered in a range of shapes and formats, from video-conferencing to web-based education modules to mobile applications. A small number of the web-based mindfulness interventions have been tested with beneficial outcomes, including reductions in stress, anxiety, and depression (Cavanagh et al., 2013; Glück & Maercker, 2011; Morledge et al., 2013), increases in self-efficacy for coping with pain and positive engagement in relationships (Davis & Zautra, 2013; Gardner-Nix et al., 2008) and increases in mindfulness (Reid, 2013). These online studies all include mindfulness in the context of a broader therapeutic framework.

The early indication from the small pool of online mindfulness studies conducted offer some support for Internet-based mindfulness programs having outcomes similar to face-to-face interventions (Wolever et al., 2012). There seems to be agreement that they are a cost-effective, highly accessible, and efficient method to teach mindfulness (Glück & Maercker 2011; Krusche, Cyhlarova, & Williams, 2013; Reid, 2013). Internet interventions are not only accessible but often sustainable, with the initial website or mobile application development being the major cost. Subsequent maintenance costs are often minimal, unlike a lot of group or individual programs that require intensive ongoing human support (de Graaf et al., 2008; Mihalopoulos, et al., 2005; Tate et al., 2009).

While there is some preliminary evidence to support the efficacy of web-based mindfulness programs, the specific testing of smartphone (e.g., iPhone and Android) mindfulness apps has only just started. A review by the current authors (October 2014) of the smartphone market indicated 248 Android and 466 iPhone mindfulness-related apps were available. These ranged from simple meditation timers to daily mindfulness activity reminders, or mindful meditation audios, to more complex and interactive apps.

An article by Miller (2012), called "The Smartphone Psychology Manifesto," describes the neophyte world of smartphones, including the implications, limitations, and challenges for psychological research and practice. Miller gives a compelling case for smartphones transforming psychology much more than PCs and brain imaging have. At this stage, however, the application far exceeds the research on the efficacy of mobile technologies.

Mobile-based mindfulness applications remain largely unexplored, with no peer-reviewed effectiveness studies (Chittaro & Vianello, 2014; Plaza et al., 2013). The first mindfulness mobile application study conducted used the AEON app (Chittaro & Vianello, 2014). AEON was designed to train a specific aspect of mindfulness, namely *thought distancing*, awareness without reactivity to thoughts. Chittaro and colleagues evaluated AEON with people with no or minimal mediation experience (i.e., naïve meditators) and compared AEON use with two traditional, non–computer-based, and thought-distancing techniques. One of the motivations for the study stemmed from the premise that traditional mindfulness practice can be difficult for people with minimal meditation experience (Kabat-Zinn, 2005; Sega et al. 2002), lowering uptake and ongoing engagement. AEON's developers were looking for an interactive, engaging, and simple way to engage for naïve mindfulness meditators. Compared to users of the two nonmobile, traditional thought-distancing techniques, AEON participants achieved greater mindfulness and engagement with the tool (measured by perceived level of difficulty and degree of pleasantness). The authors concluded that using a mobile mindfulness tool can be an effective approach to mindfulness training and a novel way to engage naïve mediators.

More recently, a waitlist-controlled trial by Howells and colleagues (2014) looked at stress and well-being outcomes for 238 healthy United Kingdom–based employees who used an early version of the Headspace (on-the-go)^TM mindfulness app. The intervention was for forty-five days and encouraged daily ten-to-twenty-minute guided meditation exercises, with participants completing 16.6 sessions on average. The results indicated increases in mindfulness, social support, and well-being and decreases in job strain and systolic blood pressure, with longer mediation practice predicting greater well-being improvements. Only participants who completed a minimum of one hundred minutes or more of the program showed significant improvements compared to the waitlist control group. Results were maintained for up to ten weeks post-intervention. Interestingly, while the intervention was self-guided, participants who attended a pre-intervention introductory face-to-face talk went on to complete more sessions than those who did not. The program used universal mindfulness content and did not frame the mediations in the context of job stress.

These two studies demonstrate the potential of brief mindfulness interventions (compared to face-to-face MBSR and MBCT program delivery) delivered via smartphone apps to enhance mindfulness and well-being and reduce stress. Personal communication in October 2014 between the author (JM) and three of the app providers that we currently recommend in our AFL Players Mindfulness workshop (i.e., Headspace, Smiling Mind, and Buddhify[2]) indicated they all have effectiveness studies under way, and results are expected to be made public in 2015. Additional research is required to support substantively the effectiveness of app-based mindfulness interventions, for whom they work best, and how to best to use them.

How much is enough?

The question of how much mediation is enough to effect positive change has begun to be investigated. A study by Howell and colleagues (2014) reported that a minimum of one hundred minutes over forty-five days was necessary for significant change, with the minimum length of meditation of ten minutes per day. These findings provide the bases of their entry-level Headspace (on-the-go) program – Take 10 – which provides ten minutes of meditation for ten consecutive days.

A randomized controlled trial (RCT) comparing a brief online mindfulness intervention to a waiting-list control group in a student population found reductions in stress, depression, and anxiety symptoms and increases in mindfulness (Cavanagh et al., 2013). The intervention was delivered online over two weeks, with ten minutes daily practice recommended. Participants reported they practiced mindfulness more than once a week (61 percent) or more than once a day (26 percent). The authors noted that effect sizes were smaller than in a four-week intervention, which may have been a dose-response effect. In other words, more mindfulness practice means greater impact, but ten minutes daily was enough to create positive change.

A randomized control trial by Creswell and colleagues (2014) compared a brief online mindfulness intervention to a cognitive training control program, and found twenty-five minutes of mindfulness on three days was enough to reduce self-reported psychological stress reactivity. A wait-list randomized control trial by Mitchell and colleagues (n.d.) found that a three week web-based intervention that asked participants to complete three mindfulness modules of ten-to-twenty-minutes duration over three weeks and to meditate or do a mindfulness activity for five minutes daily was enough to reduce anxiety symptoms for up to three months and increase life satisfaction for a subset of the group with elevated depression symptoms. Initial research results indicate that brief, online mindfulness interventions can make a positive change for people in terms of mindfulness, stress, anxiety, depression, and well-being. There also seems to be a dose-response effect, with more mindfulness practice resulting in better well-being outcomes.

Future Directions

The AFL Players' Association is committed to the ongoing integration of mindfulness strategies in their work with AFL players and the broader AFL industry, viewing mindfulness skills as a core skill necessary to help build players' self-awareness, resilience, well-being, and life performance. There remains great growth potential regarding the understanding and acceptance of an integrated approach to mind–body sciences, with adequate attention and resourcing given to mindfulness training. In the meantime, the AFL Players' Association will continue creatively to weave mindfulness, as part of a broader well-being strategy, into player support through highlighting and working with influential player and coach ambassadors who are willing to talk about their mindfulness practice and subsequent impact on their life and sporting performance. Mobile technology will continue to be used as essential tools to promote ongoing mindfulness training beyond the scope of the face-to-face workshops. Lastly, AFL Players will work with research partners (e.g., the Young and Well Cooperative Research Centre and La Trobe University) to help understand more about mindfulness, player engagement, mobile technology, mental health, well-being, and life performance outcomes.

As this volume is going to print, we have had exciting news of a major grant from the Movember Foundation of $3 million over the next three years to enhance the health and well-being of AFL Players. This will be put toward developing the current face-to-face and planned digital AFL Player well-being curriculum that can be shared with other sport, school, and corporate organizations. At the core of the curriculum will be mindfulness training. It is hoped that the AFL Players well-being curriculum will not only enhance the mental and well-being of AFL Players, but that they, as role models, will influence the health outcomes for the wider Australian community that support, watch, and play Australian Rules football.

Real happiness is always here. It is always now.
– Osho, Philosopher (1931–1990)

REFERENCES

ABC. (2013, October 30). A feeling for the water part 2. Retrieved from www.abc .net.au/austory/content/2012/s3893380.htm

AFL. (2013, October 28). AFL annual report. Retrieved from www.afl.com.au/afl-hq/ annual-reports

AIHW (Australian Institute of Health and Welfare). (2011). *Young Australians: Their health and wellbeing 2011*. Retrieved from www.aihw.gov.au/WorkArea/ DownloadAsset.aspx?id=10737419259

Allen, N. B., Chambers, R., Knight, W., Hassed, C., Blashki, G., Ciechomski, L., . . . Meadows, G. (2006). Mindfulness-based psychotherapies: A review of conceptual foundations, empirical evidence and practical considerations. *Australian and New Zealand Journal of Psychiatrists*, 40(4), 285–294. doi: 10.1080/j.1440-1614.2006.01794.x

Baer, R. A., Smith, G. T., and Allen, K. B. (2004). Assessment of mindfulness by self-report: The Kentucky Inventory of Mindfulness Skills. *Assessment*, 11(3), 191–206. doi: 10.1177/1073191104268029

Brown, K. W., and Ryan, R. M. (2003). The benefits of being present: Mindfulness and its role in psychological well-being. *Journal of Personality and Social Psychology*, 84(4), 822–848. doi: http://dx.doi.org/10.1037/0022-3514.84.4.822

Brown, K. W., Ryan, R. M., and Creswell, J. D. (2007). Mindfulness: Theoretical foundations and evidence for its salutary effects. *Psychological Enquiry*, 18(4), 211–237. doi: 10.1080/10478400701598298

Cavanagh, K., Strauss, C., Cicconi, F., Griffiths, N., Wyper, A., and Jones, F. (2013). A randomised controlled trial of a brief online mindfulness-based intervention. *Behaviour Research and Therapy*, 51(9), 573–578. doi: http://dx. doi.org/10.1016/j.brat.2013.06.003

Chambers, R., Gullone, E., Hassed, C., Knight, W., Garvin, T., and Allen, N. (2014). Mindful emotion regulation predicts recovery in depressed youth. *Mindfulness*, 1-12. doi: 10.1007/s12671-014-0284-4

Chadwick, P. (2006). *Person-Based Cognitive Therapy for distressing psychosis*. Chichester, WS, UK: John Wiley & Sons.

Chang, V. Y., Palesh, O., Caldwell, R., Glasgow, N., Abramson, M., Luskin, F., . . . Koopman, C. (2004). The effects of a mindfulness-based stress reduction program on stress, mindfulness self-efficacy, and positive states of mind. *Stress and Health*, 20(3), 141–147. doi: 10.1002/smi.1011

Chiesa, A., and Serretti, A. (2009). Mindfulness-based stress reduction for stress management in healthy people: A review and meta-analysis. *Journal of Alternative and Complementary Medicine*, 15(5), 593–600. doi: 10.1089/ acm.2008.0495

Chittaro, L., and Vianello, A. (2014). Computer-supported mindfulness: Evaluation of a mobile thought distancing application on naïve mediators. *International Journal of Human-Computer Studies*, 72(3), 337–348. doi: 10.1016/j.ijhcs.2013.11.001

Creswell, J. D., Pacilio, L. E., Lindsay, E. K., and Brown, K. W. (2014). Brief mindfulness meditation training alters psychological and neuroendocrine responses to social evaluative stress. *Psychoneuroendocrineology*, 44, 1–12. doi: 10.1016/j.psyneuen.2014.02.007

Crone, P., Knapp, M., Proudfoot, J., Ryden, C., Cavanagh, K., Shapiro, D. A., ... Tylee, A. (2004). Cost-effectiveness of computerized cognitive-behavioural therapy for anxiety and depression in primary care: Randomised controlled trial. *British Journal of Psychiatry*, 185, 55–62.

Csikszentmihalyi, M. (1990). *Flow: The psychology of optimal experience.* New York, NY: Harper and Row.

Dannahy, L., Hayward, M., Strauss, C., Turton, W., Harding, E., and Chadwick, P. (2011). Group person-based cognitive therapy for distressing voices: Pilot data from nine groups. *Journal of Behavior Therapy and Experimental Psychiatry*, 42(1), 111–116, doi: 10.1016/j.jbtep.2010.07.006

Davis, M. C., and Zautra, A. J. (2013). An online mindfulness intervention targeting socioemotional regulation in fibromyalgia: Results of a randomized controlled trial. *Annals of Behavioral Medicine*, 46(3), 273–284. doi: http://dx.doi.org/10.1007/s12160-013-9513-7

de Graaf, L. E., Gerhards, S. A. H., Evers, S. M., Arntz, A., Riper, H., Severens, J. L., ... Huibers, M. J. H. (2008). Clinical and cost-effectiveness of computerised cognitive behavioural therapy for depression in primary care: Design of a randomised trial. *BMC Public Health*, 8, 224–234. doi: 10.1186/1471-2458-8-224

Eberth, J., and Sedlmeier, P. (2012). The effects of mindfulness meditation: A meta-analysis. *Mindfulness*, 3(3), 174–189. doi: 10.1007/s12671-012-0101-x

Gardner-Nix, J., Backman, S., Barbati, J., and Grummitt, J. (2008). Evaluating distance education of a mindfulness-based meditation programme for chronic pain management. *Journal of Telemedicine and Telecare*, 14(2), 88–92. doi: 10.1258/jtt.2007.070811

Gluck, T. M., and Maercker, A. (2011). A randomized controlled pilot study of a brief web-based mindfulness training. *BMC Psychiatry*, 11, 175. doi: 10.1186/1471-244X-11-175

Greenberg, J., Reiner, K., and Meiran, N. (2012). "Mind the trap": Mindfulness practice reduces cognitive rigidity. *PLoS ONE*, 7(5), e36206. doi: 10.1371/journal.pone.003 6206

Grossman, P., Niemann, I., Schmidt, S., and Walach, H. (2004). Mindfulness-based stress reduction and health benefits. *Journal of Psychosomatic Research*, 57(1), 35–43. doi: http://dx.doi.org/10.1016/S0022-3999(03)00573-7

Gulliver, A., Griffiths, K. M., and Christensen, H. (2012). Barriers and facilitators to mental health help-seeking for young elite athletes: A qualitative study. *BMC Psychiatry*, 12, 157–171. doi: 10.1186/1471-244X-12-157

Guskiewicz, K. M., Marshall, S. W., Bailes, J., McCrea, M., Harding, Jr. H. P., Matthews, A., ... Cantu, R. C. (2007). Recurrent concussion and risk of depression in retired professional football players. *Medicine and Science in Sports and Exercise*, 39(6), 903–909. doi: 10.1249/mss.0b013e3180383da5

Hannebery, D. (2011, March 26). Dans diary – the moment has come. Sydney Swans News. Retrieved from www.sydneyswans.com.au/news/2011-03-26/dans-diary-the-moment-has-come

Harung, H., Travis, F., Blank, W., and Heaton, D. (2009). Higher development, brain integration, and excellence in leadership. *Management Decision*, 47(6), 872–894. doi: http://dx.doi.org/10.1108/00251740910966631

Hassed, C. (2002) *Know thyself: The stress relief programme*. Melbourne, AU: Michelle Anderson.

  (2006). *Mind–body medicine: science, practice and philosophy*. Retrieved from www.lifestyleandculturelectures.org/lectures/mindfulness/MindBody Medicine.pdf

Hassed, C., De Lisle, S., Sullivan, G., and Pier, C. (2008). Enhancing the health of medical students: Outcomes of an integrated mindfulness and lifestyles program. *Advances in Health Sciences Education*, 14(3), 387–398. doi: 10.1007/s10459-008-9125-3

Hayes, S. C., Strosahl, K. D., and Wilson, K. G. (1999). *Acceptance and Commitment Therapy: An experiential approach to behavior change*. New York, NY: Guilford Press.

Hofmann, S. G., Sawyer, A. T., Witt, A. A., and Oh, D. (2010). The effect of mindfulness-based therapy on anxiety and depression: A meta-analytic review. *Journal of Consulting Clinical Psychology*, 78(2), 169–183. doi: http://dx.doi.org/10.1037/a0018555

Howells, A., Ivtzan, I., and Eiroa-Orosa, F. J. (2014). Putting the "app" in happiness: A randomised controlled trial of a smartphone-based mindfulness intervention to enhance wellbeing. *Journal of Happiness Studies*, 1–23. doi: 10.1007/s10902-014-9589-1

Johnson, U. (1997). Coping strategies among long-term injured competitive athletes. A study of 81 men and women in team and individual sports. *Scandinavian Journal of Medicine and Science in Sports*, 7(6), 367–372. doi: 10.1111/j.1600-0838.1997.tb00169.x

Jackson, P., and Delehanty, H. (2013). *Eleven rings: The soul of success*. New York, NY: Penguin.

Kabat-Zinn, J. (1994). *Wherever you go, there you are: Mindfulness meditation in everyday life*. New York, NY: Hyperion.

  (2003). Mindfulness-based interventions in context: Past, present, and future. *Clinical Psychology: Science and Practice*, 10, 144–156. doi: 10.1093/clipsy.bpg016

  (2005). *Coming to our senses: Healing ourselves and the world*. Hachette, UK: Hyperion.

Kabat-Zinn, J., Lipworth, L., and Burney, R. (1985). The clinical use of mindfulness meditation for the self-regulation of chronic pain. *Journal of Behavioural Medicine*, 8(2), 163–190. doi: 10.1007/BF00845519

Keng, S., Smoski, M. J., and Robins, C. J. (2011). Effects of mindfulness on psychological health: A review of empirical studies. *Clinical Psychology Review*, 31(6): 1041–1056. doi: 10.1016/j.cpr.2011.04.006

Keyes, C. L. M. (2002). The mental health continuum: From languishing to flourishing in life. *Journal of Health and Social Behavior*, 43, 207–222.

Kirk, B. (2007, February 10). Kirk find calm before the chaos. *The Australian.* Retrieved from: www.theaustralian.com.au/

Konstan, D. (2014, June 21). The Stanford encyclopedia of philosophy. *Epicurus.* Retrieved from http://plato.stanford.edu/archives/sum2014/entries/epicurus/

Krusche, A., Cyhlarova, E., and Williams, J. M. G. (2013). Mindfulness online: An evaluation of the feasibility of a web-based mindfulness course for stress, anxiety and depression. *British Medical Journal Open*, 3(11), 1–10. doi: 10.1136/bmjopen-2013-003498

Leddy, M. H., Lambert, M. J., and Ogles, B. M. (1994). Psychological consequences of athletic injury among high-level competitors. *Research Quarterly for Exercise and Sport*, 65(4), 347–354. doi: 10.1080/02701367.1994.10607639

Linehan, M. M. (1993). *Cognitive-behavioural treatment of borderline personality disorder.* New York, NY: Guilford Press.

Luoma, J. B., Hayes, S. C., and Walser, R. D. (2007). *Learning ACT: An Acceptance and Commitment Therapy skills-training manual for therapists.* Oakland, CA: New Harbinger.

Mathers, C., and Loncar, D. (2006). Projections of global mortality and burden and disease from 2002–2030. *PLoS medicine*, 3(11), 2011–2030. doi: 10.1371/journal.pmed.0030442

Merz, T. (2013, June 28). Novak Djokovic taps into the power of Buddha for inner peace during Wimbledon 2013. *Telegraph.* Retrieved from www.telegraph.co.uk/sport/tennis/novakdjokovic/10149230/Novak-Djokovic-taps-into-the-power-of-Buddha-for-inner-peace-during-Wimbledon-2013.html?fb

Michie, D. (2011, August 11). Test cricket and mindfulness. *Times of India.* Retrieved from http://timesofindia.indiatimes.com/edit-page/Test-cricket-and-mindfulness/articleshow/9557730.cms

Mihalopoulos, C., Kiropoulos, L., Shih, S. T.-F., Gunn, J., Blashki, G., and Meadows, G. (2005). Exploratory economic analyses of two primary care mental health projects: implications for sustainability. *Medical Journal of Australia*, 183(10), S73–S76. Retrieved from www.ncbi.nlm.nih.gov/pubmed

Miller, G. (2012). The smartphone psychology manifesto. *Perspectives on Psychological Science*, 7(3), 221–237. doi: 10.1177/1745691612441215

Mitchell, J. (2014, August 21). Mindful wave ready to hit AFL. *AFL Players.* Retrieved from www.aflplayers.com.au/article/mindful-wave-ready-to-hit-afl/

Mitchell, J., and Sale, L. (2015, January, 29). Are you a conversation mate? *AFL Players.* Retrieved from www.aflplayers.com.au/article/are-you-a-conversation-mate/

Mitchell, J., Klein, B., Vella-Broderick, D., Meyer, D., Stanimirovic, R., and Odou, N. (n.d.). Mindfulness online: A randomised controlled trial. (Unpublished manuscript).

Morgan, A. J., Parker, A. G., Alvarez-Jimenez, M., and Jorm, A. F. (2013) Exercise and mental health: An Exercise and Sports Science Australia commissioned review. *Journal of Exercise Physiologyonline*, 16, 64–73.

Morledge, T. J., Allexandre, D., Fox, E., Fu, A. Z., Higashi, M. K., Kruzikas, D. T., . . . Reese, P. R. (2013). Feasibility of an online mindfulness program for stress management – a randomized, controlled trial. *Annals of Behavioral Medicine*, 46(2), 137–148. doi: 10.1007/s12160-013-9490-x

NCAA. (2013). *2013–14 NCAA sports medicine handbook*. Retrieved from www.ncaa.org/

Ost, L. (2008). Efficacy of the third wave of behavioural therapies: A systematic review and meta-analysis. *Behaviour Research and Therapy*, 46(3), 296–321. doi: 10.1016/j.brat.2007.12.005

Plaza, I., Demarzo, M. M. P., Herrera-Mercadal, P., and García-Campayo, J. (2013). Mindfulness-based mobile applications: Literature review and analysis of current features. *Journal of Medical Internet Research*, 1(2). Retrieved from http://mhealth.jmir.org/2013/2/e24/

Puff, J. (2014, February, 6). How meditation won the Super Bowl. *Psychology Today*. Retrieved from www.psychologytoday.com/blog/meditation-modern-life/201402/how-meditation-won-the-super-bowl

Reardon, C. L., and Factor, R. M. (2010). Sport psychiatry. *Sports Medicine*, 40 (11), 961–980. doi: 10.2165/11536580-000000000-00000

Reid, D. T. (2013). Teaching mindfulness to occupational therapy students: Pilot evaluation of an online curriculum. *Canadian Journal of Occupational Therapy/Revue Canadienne D'Ergotherapie*, 80(1), 42–48. doi: http://dx.doi.org/10.1177/0008417413475598

Ryan, R. M., and Deci, E. L. (2000). Self-determination theory and the facilitation of intrinsic motivation, social development, and well-being. *American Psychologist*, 55(1), 68–78. doi: 10.1037/0003-066X.55.1.68

Ryff, C. D. (1989). Happiness is everything, or is it? Explorations on the meaning of psychological well-being. *Journal of Personality and Social Psychology*, 57(6), 1069–1081. doi: 10.1037/0022-3514.57.6.1069.

Schaal, K., Tafflet, M., Nassif, H., Thibault, V., Pichard,C., Alcotte, M., … Toussanit, J. (2011). Psychological balance in high level athletes: Gender-based differences and sport-specific patterns. *PLoS ONE*, 6(5), 1–9. doi: 10.1371/journal.pone.0019007

Sedlmeier, P., Eberth, J., Schwarz, M., Zimmermann, D., Frederick, H., Jaeger, S., and Kunze, S. (2012). The psychological effects of meditation: A meta-analysis. *Psychological Bulletin*, 138(6), 1139–171. doi: http://dx.doi.org/10.1037/a0028168

Segal, Z. V., Williams, J. M. G., and Teasdale, J. D. (2002). *Mindfulness-based cognitive therapy for depression: A new approach to preventing relapse.* New York, NY: Guilford Press.

Seligman, M. E. P., and Csikszentmihalyi, M. (2000). Positive psychology: An introduction. *American Psychologist*, 55 (1), 5–14. doi: 10.1037//0003-066X.55.1.5

Shapiro, S. L., Astin, J. A., and Bishop, S. R. (2005). Mindfulness-based stress reduction for health care professionals: Results from a randomized trial. *International Journal of Stress Management*, 12(2), 164–176. doi: http://dx.doi.org/10.1037/1072-5245.12.2.164

Shapiro, S. L., Carlson, L. E., Astin, J. A., and Freedman, B. (2006). Mechanisms of mindfulness. *Journal of Clinical Psychology*, 62(3), 373–386. doi: 10.1002/jclp.20237

Shapiro, S. L., Schwartz, G. E., and Bonner, G. (1998). Effects of mindfulness based stress reduction on medical and premedical students. *Journal of Behavioral Medicine*, 21(6), 581–599. doi: 10.1023/A:1018700829825

Sin, N. L., and Lyubomirsky, S. (2009). Enhancing well-being and alleviating depressive symptoms with positive psychology interventions: A practice-friendly meta-analysis. *Journal of Clinical Psychology*, 65(5), 467–487. doi: 10.1002/jclp.20593

Slagter, H., Lutz, A., Greischar, L. L., Francis, A. D. Nieuwenhuis, S., Davis, J. M., and Davidson, R. J. (2007). Mental training affects distribution of limited brain resources. *PLoS Biology*, 5(6), 1228–1235. doi: 10.1371/journal.pbio.0050138

Tate, D. F., Finkelstein, E. A., Khavjou, O., and Gustafson, A. (2009). Cost effectiveness of Internet interventions: Review and recommendations. *Annals of Behavioral Medicine*, 38(1), 40–45. doi: 10.1007/s12160-009-9131-6

Tugwel, N. (2014, June). Adam Goodes preaches meditation gospel for Swans. *Daily Telegraph*. Retrieved from: www.dailytelegraph.com.au/sport/adam-goodes-preaches-meditation-gospel-for-swans/story-e6frexni-1225720603417

Uhls, Y. T., Michikyan, M., Morris, J., Garcia, D., Small, G. W., Zgourou, E., and Greenfield, P. M. (2014). Five days at an outdoor education campy without screens improves preteen skills with nonverbal emotional cues. *Computers in Human Behaviour*, 39, 387–392. doi: 10.1016/j.chb.2014.05.036

Vollestad, J., Nielsen, M. B., and Nielsen, G. H. (2012). Mindfulness- and acceptance-based interventions for anxiety disorders: A systematic review and meta-analysis. *British Journal of Clinical Psychology*, 51(3), 239–260. doi: 10.1111/j.2044-8260.2011.02024.x

Way, B. M., Creswell, J. D., Eisenberger, N. I., and Lieberman, M. D. (2010). Dispositional mindfulness and depressive symptomatology: Correlations with limbic and self-referential neural activity during rest. *Emotion*, 10(1), 12–24. doi: http://dx.doi.org/10.1037/a0018312

WHO (World Health Organization). (1948, April 7). WHO definition of health. Retrieved from www.who.int/about/definition/en/print.html

WHO (2014, August). Mental health: A state of wellbeing. Retrieved from http://www.who.int/features/factfiles/mental_health/en/

Wilmoth, P. (2014, June, 15). The demon inside. *Weekly Review*. Retrieved from www.theweeklyreview.com.au/well-read/cover-story/9246-the-demon-inside/

Wolever, R. Q., Bobinet, K. J., McCabe, K., Mackenzie, E. R., Fekete, E., Kusnick, C. A., and Baime, M. (2012). Effective and viable mind-body stress reduction in the workplace: A randomized controlled trial. *Journal of Occupational Health Psychology*, 17(2), 246–258. doi: http://dx.doi.org/10.1037/a0027278

Yerkes, R. M., and Dodson, J. D. (1908). The relation of strength of stimulus to rapidity of habit-formation. *Journal of Comparative Neurology and Psychology*, 18, 459–482. doi: 10.1002/cne.920180503

Zeidan, F., Johnson, S. K., Diamond, B. J., David, Z., and Goolkasian, P. (2010). Mindfulness meditation improves cognition: Evidence of brief mental training. *Consciousness and Cognition*, 19(2), 597–605. doi: 10.1016/j.concog.2010.03.014

Full Description of AFL and AFL Players' Association

AFL refers to the elite Australian Rules football competition known as the Australian Football League. The origins of Australian Rules football can be traced back to 1858, when a game was invented in Melbourne to help cricket players remain fit in the winter months. It is a full-contact, free-flowing, and fast game, with players passing the ball by foot and hand, and played on a field the size of a cricket oval (450 to 500 feet in diameter).

The AFL was officially formed in 1997, when the Victorian Football League (VFL) expanded to include a number of interstate clubs. Today it is Australia's premier sporting code in terms of participation and viewing. The AFL had the fourth highest average attendance per game (32,163) during the 2013 Premiership season in all professional sports behind America's NFL (67,358), Bundesliga soccer in Germany (42,609), and Premier League soccer in the United Kingdom (35,931) (AFL Annual Report, 2013). The 2013 Premiership season drew an average national television audience of 4.7 million viewers and the largest weekly online audience for any sports competition in Australia. Across the eighteen AFL club membership in 2013 were 756,717 members (AFL Annual Report, 2013). Total domestic participation in the game at a community level throughout Australia reached 938,069 players, while a further 129,775 players participated in the game in various countries around the world (AFL Annual Report, 2013). Although football has predominantly been a male sport, there is a growing female competition. Women are involved in many aspects of the game: in 2013, the first female AFL club president, Peggy O'Neal, was named at Richmond Football Club, and in 2014 the first female AFL team coach, Peta Searle, was hired by St. Kilda Football Club.

The AFL Players' Association (originally called the Victorian Football League Players' Association) was created by the players in 1973 to protect and enhance the collective interests of all football players, current and past. There are approximately 800+ players across the league in a season, and 5,000+ past players. Every current AFL player is a member (plus 2,500+ alumni members) and contributes to the running of the Association, by paying yearly fees and also by directing a portion of the funding allocation under the Collective Bargaining Agreement to the organization.

AFL Players provides a range of services directly to players, such as financial services, well-being support, legal advice, and career and education support. It also offers spirited representation of players' views and interests to a wide range of stakeholders within the AFL industry and also in the broader community.

AFL Players sees it has a role in promoting something more lasting, human, and broad than merely game day performance and club success. The organization employs approximately twenty-eight full-time staff with experience and expertise in player representation, finance, legal, marketing, communications, commercialization, and importantly, mental health and well-being. Most players associations do not get beyond the basics of contract negotiations, finances, and legal issues. Admirably, AFL Players' unique role in the industry allows the association to consider and implement strategies for players to maximize their time in the game from a professional and personal perspective, and to exit the game with the skills and knowledge to thrive in their next stage of life. Player health and well-being are firmly on the agenda and have strong player and club engagement.

CHAPTER 13

Mindfulness and Exercise

Rebecca Shangraw, Vanessa Loverme Akhtar

American lifestyles are becoming increasingly sedentary. Consequently, diagnoses of health conditions related to sedentary lifestyles are on the rise in the United States. While Americans' participation in physical activity has decreased, gym memberships have recently hit an all-time high (IHRSA, 2014; Ng & Popkin, 2012). How can this contradiction be explained? We hypothesize that while many Americans have good intentions when signing up for gym memberships, they lack the psychological skills needed to overcome physical and psychological blockages that often interfere with establishing consistent, committed behavior change. When used to address psychological blockages associated with the development of exercise habits, mindfulness- and acceptance-based practices can help exercisers establish the consistent, high-quality exercise practices required to experience the health benefits of exercise and physical activity.

Just as air, food, and water are necessary for the well-being of the human body, so too is exercise. The American College of Sports Medicine (ACSM, 2014) has identified many health-related benefits associated with regular exercise, including improved cardiorespiratory endurance, muscular strength, muscular endurance, body composition, and flexibility, as well as decreased cardiovascular disease risk factors, morbidity, anxiety, and depression. Additionally, engagement in regular exercise has been shown to promote and support motor and cognitive development, hormone release and regulation, and generation of neurons in the brain (Ratey, 2008).

Despite the well-documented health benefits of regular exercise, America's growing reliance on comfort- and convenience-oriented technology has dramatically stripped physical activity and exercise from many Americans' daily lives (ACSM, 2014; Ng & Popkin, 2012). In a 2012 study, Ng and Popkin quantified physical activity trends organized in five domains (sleep, leisure, occupation, transportation, and home-based activities[1]). Ng and Popkin (2012) found that Americans' physical activity levels fell dramatically from an estimated 235 MET hours[2] per week in 1965 to an estimated 160 MET hours per week in 2009. Based on these data, Ng and Popkin (2012) predict that Americans' physical activity levels will fall to an estimated 142 MET hours per week in 2020 and an estimated 126 MET hours per week in 2030.

As a result of Americans' decreasing physical activity levels, incidences of health conditions related to sedentary lifestyles have risen dramatically. Health survey data reported by the National Center for Health Statistics (NCHS, 2006, 2014) estimates that American adults' (ages eighteen to seventy-five) body mass indexes (BMI) have steadily increased since 2005. The NCHS estimates that 60 percent of adult Americans were overweight or obese in 2005, 62 percent of adult Americans were overweight or obese in 2008, and 63 percent of adult Americans were overweight or obese in 2012 (NCHS, 2006, 2009, 2014).

Aside from increased BMI, incidences of other health conditions resulting from decreased physical activity levels have risen as well. According to Centers for Disease Control and Prevention (CDC) data, the prevalence of coronary heart disease among American adults has risen from 4.4 percent of the U.S. population in 2002 to 4.8 percent of the U.S. population in 2011 (CDC & Division for Heart Disease and Stroke Prevention, 2013). Similarly, the CDC reports a steadily growing trend in new cases of diagnosed diabetes mellitus among American adults; between 2002 and 2011, new diagnoses of diabetes mellitus increased from 1,304,000 to 1,568,000 (CDC, 2013). Type II diabetes mellitus, a diabetes type closely associated with obesity (Moraes-Vieria et al., 2014), has been estimated to account for 95 percent of all diabetes mellitus diagnoses among U.S. adults (CDC, 2012).

Whereas current NCHS and CDC health survey data suggest that Americans are divesting from physical activity and exercise, a May 2013 International Health, Racquet, and Sportsclub Association (IHRSA) report touted a 10 percent increase in U.S. health club memberships every year since 2008. Additionally, the IHRSA celebrated a 2013 industry milestone with U.S health club use exceeding an estimated 5 billion visits by more than 62.1 million patrons (IHRSA, 2014). If health club

---

[1] Ng and Popkin (2012) alternatively refer to these domains (sleep, leisure, occupation, transportation, and home-based activities) as the SLOTH model.

[2] MET hours reflect metabolic energy expenditure during specific physical activities.

participation in the United States is increasing at record rates, why too are health conditions related to sedentary lifestyles also increasing? We hypothesize that many exercisers' intentions are not translating into the consistent, committed behavior change required to experience health-related benefits of regular exercise.[3] While many Americans may be well intentioned when initiating exercise programs, research suggests that, "within the exercise domain, a relatively large change in intention only results in a small change in behavior" (Banting, Dimmock, & Lay, 2009, p. 80). In other words, intention by itself is not enough when trying to develop regular exercise habits; something else is needed to overcome blockages to consistent behavior change. Blockages to behavior change, the hurdles exercisers cite when discontinuing an exercise program, have myriad physical and psychological originations, including the following:

1. *Physical considerations:*
    Exercisers may experience a reduced ability to cope with injury and/or feelings of physical discomfort that either existed prior to beginning an exercise program or began as a result of an exercise program (Carson & Polman, 2010).
2. *Psychological considerations:*
    a. Exercisers may experience the presence of automatic, self-regulatory judgments that conflict with the intent to exercise, such as judgments that are used to justify missing workouts due to fatigue or bad weather (Buckley & Cameron, 2011).
    b. Exercisers may have low self-efficacy with regard to exercising and/or breaching perceived barriers to exercise (DuCharme & Brawley, 1995). Self-efficacy theory, which "predicts that individuals' appraisals of their ability to complete required behaviors will regulate their subsequent actions," has been hypothesized to effect exercise behavior (DuCharme & Brawley, 1995, p. 480).
    c. Exercisers' schema type may impact how they identify with and relate to exercise (Banting et al. 2009). Schema, or "generalizations about the self, derived from past experience, that organize and guide the processing of self-regulated information," can play a large role in shaping one's perception of themselves as an exerciser (Banting et al., 2009, p. 81).

---

[3] In order to experience health-related benefits associated with regular exercise, the American College of Sports Medicine recommends engaging in moderate exercise five or more days a week or vigorous exercise three or more days a week (ACSM, 2014).

The preceding factors, independently or in combination, can play a detrimental role in developing a habit of regular exercise participation, as well as participating in high-quality exercise that maximizes health benefits related to exercise. As a way to support the development of effective, regular exercise habits, mindfulness- and acceptance-based practices can be incorporated into several important areas of exercisers' psychological skill sets.

Mindfulness and Exercise

Jon Kabat-Zinn (2003a) defines mindfulness as "the awareness that emerges through paying attention on purpose, in the present moment, and non-judgmentally to the unfolding of experience moment by moment" (p. 145). This conceptualization of mindfulness highlights the present-moment awareness of both internal and external stimuli, whereas Ellen Langer's conceptualization of mindfulness focuses primarily on external stimuli (Hart, Ivtzan, & Hart, 2013). Two core tenets of Kabat-Zinn's view of mindfulness are the goal of nonjudgmental present-moment awareness and the realization that thoughts, feelings, and sensations are *transient* rather than *sustained* states (Baer, 2003; Kabat-Zinn, 1982, 2003a). This approach to mindfulness, similar in many concepts to Lazarus and Folkman's (1984) transactional model of stress and coping, provides a way to explore some of the physical and psychological challenges associated with exercise.

Coping versus Mindfulness in the Exercise Setting

Kabat-Zinn's (e.g., 2003a, 2003b) Mindfulness-Based Stress Reduction (MBSR) model, which will be explored in more depth later in this chapter, draws on Kabat-Zinn's conceptualization of mindfulness as outlined previously (Baer, 2003; Kabat-Zinn, 1982, 2003a), as well as Lazarus and Folkman's (1984) transactional model of stress and coping (Ulmer, Stetson, & Salmon, 2010). In particular, MBSR is a mindfulness intervention combining Eastern philosophies of meditation with a Western focus on behavioral interventions, developed as an add-on to traditional treatment models to help patients in clinical populations experience improved physical and psychological well-being (e.g., Hart et al., 2013; Kabat-Zinn, 2003a). This model was originally known as the Stress Reduction and Relaxation Program (Baer, 2003). There are important and inherent links between coping and stress, both of which may shape the experiences of exercisers.

Coping, in relation to physical activity, is the traditional conceptualization of understanding how exercisers face the challenges and stressors associated in beginning or sustaining an exercise commitment. Lazarus and Folkman (1984) define coping as the "constantly changing cognitive and behavioral efforts to manage specific external and/or internal demands that are appraised as taxing or exceeding the resources of the person" (p. 141). Stress is based on an individual's perception of the situation, and the effectiveness of coping strategies is dependent on the appraisal of the situation (Laubmeier, Zakowski, & Bair, 2004). Coping strategies were initially conceptualized as either emotion-focused (i.e., one's emotional response to the situation) or problem-focused (i.e., seeking to change or deal with the cause of the stress) (Laubmeier et al., 2004; Lazarus & Folkman, 1984). While avoidance and/or denial are commonly employed emotion-focused coping mechanisms when exercisers are faced with difficult situations, such as the pain of a sprained ankle or the effort of running up a steep hill, these strategies are considered ineffective because they limit the likelihood of engaging in problem-focused coping (Lazarus & Folkman, 1984).

We propose that mindfulness and acceptance, as outlined by Kabat-Zinn (1982, 2003a), can play a critical role in enabling exercisers to cope appropriately with both the physical and psychological challenges associated with exercise. Just as one goal of MBSR in clinical settings is to help patients respond – versus react – with present awareness to current physical and psychological symptoms (Hart et al., 2013), a mindful and acceptance-based approach to exercise may result in similarly increased levels of physical and psychological well-being when coping with challenges. For example, Ulmer and colleagues (2010) suggest that, "consistent with the transactional model of stress ... mindfulness and acceptance intervene between activity-related cognitions/emotions and overt behavior in a way that facilitates one's ability to respond to rather than react to cognitive, behavioral or emotional threats to physical activity" (p. 807). Salmon, Hanneman, and Harwood (2010) suggest that a mindful approach to exercise and cognitive regulation is ideal because this approach views cognitive focus as flexible and controllable, allowing for present-moment focus as well as fluctuation between focus on physical and cognitive/emotional stimuli, and encourages acceptance of one's current state. Furthermore, exercisers who are more mindful and accepting may be better able, in the present moment, to accept nonjudgmentally the discomfort of exercise and maintain greater psychological and behavioral flexibility, so as to better navigate the challenges of exercise. This increases the likelihood of effective, responsive coping strategies rather than ineffective, reactive strategies that may actually lead to dropping out or inconsistent maintenance of an exercise regimen (Ulmer et al., 2010).

Coping with Physical and Psychological Stress

Physical discomfort and psychological stress that exist prior to initiating new exercise programs, or those stresses that are produced while engaging in exercise, can present significant coping challenges to exercisers. Preexisting injuries are those that are incurred prior to initiating an exercise program and include injuries resulting from trauma, such as sprains or strains to the ankle, knee, or elbow joints (ACSM, 2014). Additionally, chronic conditions such as inflammation associated with arthritis may be present prior to the initiation of an exercise program (ACSM, 2014). Even when healed or managed under a medical doctor's care, these injuries can produce residual feelings of soreness or pain that may lead to unpleasant feelings during exercise.

Exercisers who have been medically prescribed an exercise program following a significant medical event, such as a heart attack or orthopedic surgery, are often challenged with kinesiophobia, a fear of reinjury, as well as pain at their injury or surgical sites. In a 2013 study of 135 patients who underwent anterior cruciate ligament (ACL) reconstruction surgery, 73 patients did not return to pre-injury exercise levels following their surgery (Flanigan et al., 2013). Among the patients who did not return to pre-injury exercise levels, pain or swelling associated with their injured knee (79 percent) and kinesiophobia (52 percent) were the most reported reasons for ceasing exercise programs.

Injuries caused by participation in exercise programs include injuries sustained from trauma, as well as overuse injuries such as tendonitis, plantar fasciitis, and lower back pain (ACSM, 2014). These injuries may make continuing an exercise program routinely painful or uncomfortable and can result in an injured exerciser dismissing exercise programs entirely. Additionally, as physiological reactions to aerobic exercise include feeling out of breath, hot, light-headed, and mildly nauseous and having sore muscles, many novice exercisers perceive the initial feelings that accompany aerobic exertion as unsettling.

Numerous psychological challenges can manifest before or during the undertaking of an exercise program. The presence of automatic, self-regulatory judgments can inhibit exercise-related behaviors by influencing the exerciser to focus on "numerous competing goals (e.g., family and work), and disincentives to exercise (e.g., fatigue and stress)" (Buckley & Cameron, 2011, p. 324). Self-regulatory judgments are often used as justifications that allow the exerciser to avoid stressful or uncomfortable situations associated with exercise. For instance, if a novice exerciser who has been experiencing sore muscles after running begins to stay late at his workplace instead of going for after-work runs, he may have created a stronger sense of responsibility to his job in order to avoid the uncomfortable feeling of sore muscles.

Additionally, low self-efficacy with regard to exercising and/or breaching perceived barriers to exercise can deter exercisers from consistently participating in exercise programs (DuCharme & Brawley, 1995). Self-efficacy, a belief in one's ability to successfully perform a specific task, plays a critical role in predicting behaviors and task outcomes (ACSM, 2014; DuCharme & Brawley, 1995). Research has shown that exercisers with high self-efficacy are more likely to overcome physical and psychological barriers to exercise involvement (e.g., DuCharme & Brawley, 1995; Poag & McAuley, 1992).

Aside from self-regulatory judgments and self-efficacy, schema can encourage or deter exercisers from exercise participation. Banting and colleagues (2009) suggest that exercisers who identify as exerciser schematics "find exercise and exercise-related concepts to be descriptive of themselves" (p. 81), while aschematic exercisers do not relate to descriptions of exercisers and do not connect these descriptions to their self-images. Non–exerciser schematics do not relate to descriptions of exercisers, but do connect these descriptions to their self-images. More than aschematic exercisers and non–exerciser schematics, exerciser schematics show a greater ability to follow through with exercise intentions.

As a result of the coping challenges associated with the aforementioned physical and psychological stressors, as well as many more, exercisers may utilize experiential avoidance and/or suppression as a way to avoid situations that involve seemingly negative feelings or experiences (Tapper et al., 2009; Ulmer et al., 2010). An attempt to evade undesirable feelings experienced within the self, such as negative thoughts or physical pain, experiential avoidance is a frequently used coping mechanism in populations undertaking health-behavior change (Carson & Polman, 2010; Tapper et al., 2009). Similar to experiential avoidance, suppression is a conscious attempt to avert a specific thought, such as those experienced by many exercisers when beginning new exercise regimens (for example, "I'm too out of shape to finish my workout," or, "I look stupid on the exercise bike")(Ulmer et al., 2010).

Experiential avoidance and/or suppression are emotion-focused coping strategies that intend to protect an individual's cognitive well-being (Lazarus & Folkman, 1984). However, in the context of exercise adherence, these strategies are insufficient because they hinder problem-focused coping, in turn heightening the likelihood of ceasing a regular exercise regimen when faced with typical physical discomfort, such as soreness, or psychological discomfort, such as low self-efficacy (Salmon et al., 2010; Ulmer et al., 2010).

As Lazarus and Folkman (1984) outline in the transactional model of stress and coping, effective coping requires both emotion-focused and problem-focused coping strategies. When faced with difficult situations that involve cognitive and/or physical discomfort, whether real or perceived, avoidance is a common yet ineffective coping strategy (Laubmeier et al., 2004; Lazarus & Folkman, 1984). Taking a mindfulness- and acceptance-based approach to exercise, rather than an avoidant approach, allows for both emotion-focused and problem-focused coping when one is faced with the challenges of sustained physical activity. Such an approach may aid exercisers in regulating their response to the stress produced from exercise by allowing them to view any discomfort as transient rather than persistent. Furthermore, a mindful and accepting attitude toward exercise increases cognitive and behavioral flexibility by encouraging a nonjudgmental appraisal of the exercise experience (Salmon et al., 2010; Ulmer et al., 2010).

Mindfulness and Acceptance Models

Mindfulness-Based Stress Reduction (MBSR) programs
The most commonly cited mindfulness intervention (Baer, 2003), MBSR draws on the many concepts of Lazarus and Folkman's (1984) transactional model of stress and coping, as well as its success in supporting improved coping skills for clinical populations (Laubmeier et al., 2004; Ulmer et al., 2010). Kabat-Zinn (1982, 2003a) sought to create a mindfulness program that was digestible for clinical populations and could be used as a complement to traditional treatment plans without losing the core elements of mindfulness, based in Buddhist philosophy. The intention of MBSR programs is to help patient populations become less reactive to physical and psychological symptoms and to better adapt to negative thinking (Hart et al., 2013).

The eight-week MBSR program consists of two-and-a-half-hour group sessions, with time given to body scanning, seated meditation, and Hatha yoga (Kabat-Zinn, 2003a). The instructor walks participants through each of these elements in class and then asks students to practice on their own for forty-five to sixty minutes per day, most days of the week, starting first with the aid of an audiotape and then without assistance. As part of the program, participants are taught two forty-five-minute asana sequences. Yoga is incorporated into the program for a variety of reasons. First, the physical practice helps combat disuse atrophy (i.e., muscle deterioration due to physical inactivity), which is common in clinical populations (Salmon et al., 2009). Second, Hatha yoga, in particular, is low-impact, gentle, and commonly practiced as a component of Western medicine treatment plans. Additionally, yoga, at its core, is focused on the union among mind, body, and spirit. Research has shown that yoga complements mindfulness-based practices because it encourages focus on the present moment; uses breath as an attentional anchor; is based in nonjudgmental experience; allows for the practice of mindfulness in motion; is intentionally simple; increases awareness of inner states; is often more engaging than meditation alone; and rests responsibility within the practitioner (e.g., Briegel-Jones et al., 2013; Brisbon & Lowery, 2011; Curtis, Osadchuk, & Katz, 2011; Salmon et al., 2009). Therefore, yoga is an ideal activity for promoting increased mindfulness as well as physical well-being (Brisbon & Lowery, 2011; Salmon et al., 2009).

MBSR has been used as a component of treatment in a variety of clinical settings and has yielded many positive results. The program has been shown to have lasting positive results over time, including decreases in chronic pain, blood pressure, anxiety, depression, fatigue, insomnia, and stress; better management of Type II diabetes and Axis I disorders; increased skin clearance of psoriasis; and improved well-being, self-awareness, and relaxation (Baer, 2003; Brown & Ryan, 2003; Salmon et al., 2009; Tácon & McComb, 2009; Wall, 2005). Additionally, in nonclinical populations, MBSR participants showed increased activation of the left-side anterior cortical area of the brain, which is associated with positive emotion, and increases in antibody titers post–flu shot compared to a control group (Kabat-Zinn, 2003b). The extensive research done on MBSR has shown that it has strong practical implications for both clinical and nonclinical populations.

MBSR programs applied to exercise
As previously discussed, yoga is a core component of the MBSR program (Kabat-Zinn, 2003a, 2003b; Salmon et al., 2009). The majority of the literature on the effectiveness of MBSR focuses on the program as a whole, making it difficult to identify the specific role that yoga plays in its overall effectiveness for both clinical and nonclinical populations (e.g., Baer, 2003;

Brown & Ryan, 2003; Kabat-Zinn, 2003b). Wall (2005), however, took a unique approach to the MBSR program, combining aspects of MBSR with T'ai Chi for adolescent students in an urban school. Notably, neither MBSR nor T'ai Chi are typically used with such a young population. Wall (2005) adapted the two practices to suit the population, with a focus on using both to help students learn to be more aware of their emotional reactions, in order to increase self-regulation and decrease their reactivity to various emotional triggers. Qualitative data revealed that students experienced improved well-being, increased calm/relaxation, better sleep, better self-care and self-awareness, less reactivity, and an increased sense of interconnectedness with nature (Wall, 2005). This study suggests that other physical activities that focus on a mind–body connection, aside from yoga, can also be combined with MBSR to yield positive outcomes.

While research has investigated the applications of MBSR to athletic performance (e.g., Gooding & Gardner, 2009), athletes' flow states (e.g., Aherne, Moran & Lonsdale, 2011; Kaufman, Glass & Arnkoff, 2009), and sports injury rehabilitation (e.g., Carson & Polman, 2010), more research is needed to empirically explore the hypothesized benefits of MBSR and exercise.

Yoga and mindfulness

Yoga is often used as an intervention to improve athletic performance because of the cognitive and somatic benefits associated with it, which include decreased stress and heart rate and increased focus. Salmon and colleagues (2009) highlight that yoga practice has been shown to have the greatest positive impact on psychological well-being and decreasing psychological symptoms in the context of all components of the MBSR program. While there is little research on the effectiveness of yoga and mindfulness within the specific scope of the MBSR program, other research has highlighted the benefits of yoga and mindfulness.

In a study of elite youth swimmers, researchers found that those athletes who practiced yoga reported improved mindfulness and flow. More specifically, they reported increased awareness of internal sensations (both thoughts and feelings) that the athletes attributed to increased overall awareness and engagement with the activity, improved ability to reframe negative thinking, increased focus and control, decreased worry, and increased motivation (Briegel-Jones et al., 2013). An eight-week yoga intervention was also found to yield positive outcomes with a non-athlete, clinical population. Curtis and colleagues (2011) found that a Hatha yoga program led to both physical and psychological improvements for women suffering from fibromyalgia, a chronic condition commonly characterized by musculoskeletal pain, fatigue, anxiety, depression, and stiffness. Exercise, including yoga, is a commonly recommended treatment for fibromyalgia. When used as an explicit intervention, yoga practice resulted in reduced chronic pain, reduced pain catastrophizing, increases in mindfulness, and increases in acceptance of chronic pain (Curtis et al., 2011). Advanced Hatha yoga practitioners have been shown to have higher levels of mindfulness and lower levels of stress (Brisbon & Lowery, 2011). This suggests that yoga, whether or not explicitly combined with a mindfulness intervention, can increase mindfulness and contribute to favorable cognitive and somatic outcomes.

Acceptance and Commitment Therapy (ACT) programs

Another commonly cited mindfulness intervention, Acceptance and Commitment Therapy (ACT) was developed from Relational Frame Theory (RFT) and more general behavior principles with the intention of offering a more useful clinical model compared to behavior therapy models (Brinkborg et al., 2011; Hayes et al., 2013; Hayes et al., 2006). Extending beyond RFT, which views cognition as a learned behavior that influences other behavior processes and is context-specific, and Cognitive Behavior Therapy (CBT), ACT seeks to help patients not only change their thoughts and behaviors but also their context (Hayes et al., 2006). Furthermore, ACT rests on the notion that attempting to avoid negative thoughts, feelings, or sensations can actually reinforce that negative event. Acceptance is viewed as a more useful alternative to avoidance (Hayes et al., 2013).

Within this overarching goal of embracing acceptance over avoidance, "ACT explicitly teaches clients to abandon attempts to control thoughts and feelings, but instead to observe them non-judgmentally and accept them as they are, while changing their behaviors in constructive ways to improve their lives" (Baer, 2003, p. 128). By shifting toward acceptance (of thoughts and feelings), clients increase their psychological flexibility and are therefore better able to influence positively their own context and behaviors (Brinkborg et al., 2011). ACT is comprised of six core processes that are meant to increase cognitive flexibility:

1. *Acceptance.* The nonjudgmental awareness of events, feelings, thoughts, and actions.
2. *Cognitive defusion.* Changing how one interacts with thoughts in order to detach oneself from private events (e.g., "I'm having the thought that . . .").

3. *Being present.* Nonjudgmental experiencing of the present moment, as events occur.

4. *Self as context.* Viewing oneself within the context of language and perspective, as learned constructs, which in turn increases defusion and acceptance.

5. *Values.* Using the previous four core processes to create a path for leading a values-based life.

6. *Committed action.* A commitment to long-term behavior change, with the ultimate goal of increased psychological flexibility (Hayes et al., 2006).

ACT programs, based on these six core processes and the goal of increasing cognitive flexibility, have shown positive results in clinical and non-clinical populations. An ACT intervention with social workers resulted in decreases in stress and burnout and increased overall mental health, particularly for those social workers with moderate to high levels of stress at baseline (Brinkborg et al., 2011). In clinical populations, ACT has been shown to be effective as a short-duration intervention for decreasing stress and psychological symptoms (Hayes et al., 2006). Additionally, obese participants who participated in a six-hour ACT workshop showed long-term improvements at follow-up in terms of obesity stigma, psychological distress, quality of life, stress tolerance, and BMI (Lillis et al., 2009). Lastly, patients with epilepsy who participated in one individual ACT session and one group ACT session showed decreases in seizures and increases in quality of life at follow-up (Lundgren et al., 2008). In addition to the positive outcomes of mindfulness programs with clinical populations, the effect of MBSR and other mindfulness approaches within the context of physical activity is beginning to be explored more in depth by researchers. While the research on ACT and physical activity is more limited than that for MBSR and other mindfulness approaches, some literature has begun to explore the relationship between exercise and ACT.

ACT programs applied to exercise

Unlike MBSR, ACT does not include an emphasis on physical activity as part of its program. This may account for the lack of research exploring the role of ACT in an exercise context. Some research has been conducted that might suggest, however, that ACT could be combined with physical activity to enhance positive outcomes. Lillis and colleagues (2009) explored the role of mindfulness and acceptance in relation to obesity-related stigma, quality of life, BMI, and psychological distress. Many who are combating obesity struggle with both the physical discomforts of exercise, as highlighted earlier, and psychological discomfort due to stigma. Researchers found that participants in a six-hour ACT workshop, for those who had been involved in a structured weight-loss program, experienced decreased obesity-related stigma, BMI, and psychological distress and increased quality of life at three months post-intervention (Lillis et al., 2009). This suggests that an ACT intervention may be extremely effective when paired with a weight-loss program for obese patients.

Researchers have also compared the effects of ACT and yoga for patients with epilepsy. Patients were divided into two treatment groups. The ACT sessions focused on the core processes of ACT, including understanding one's reactions to events, values, barriers, and increasing acceptance and psychological flexibility. The yoga intervention, on the other hand, was geared toward helping patients respond to internal stimuli in an aware and present way (Lundgren et al., 2008). Lundgren and colleagues (2008) found that both groups experienced decreases in seizures and increases in quality of life. The ACT group experienced greater decreases in seizure activity. However, the two interventions had many similarities, including a focus on mindfulness and acceptance; the inclusion of discussions of challenges; and the participation of significant others. Therefore, it is difficult to assess the core processes that lead to the positive outcomes and whether or not a combined yoga and ACT intervention would have yielded even greater outcomes (Lundgren et al., 2008).

In addition to the research on MBSR programs, yoga, and ACT interventions in the context of physical activity, minimal research has examined the role of mindfulness and physical activity in a more broad sense. Some research suggests that a mindfulness approach to cognitive regulation is most effective for exercisers during sustained physical activity, because it focuses on cognition as flexible, allowing for acceptance of the present-moment physical and emotional state, helping exercisers recognize the transient nature of physical and/or psychological discomfort in the moment (Salmon et al., 2010). Other research suggests that exercisers who are more mindful and accepting have more success in maintaining an exercise regimen (Ulmer et al., 2010). Taken as a whole, the literature suggests that physical activity has the potential to increase mindfulness and, on the other hand, taking a mindful approach to physical activity can lead to positive cognitive and physiological outcomes, for both clinical and nonclinical populations.

Table 13.1 *Mindfulness Components and Psychological Skills Identified in Birrer and Colleagues' 2012 Framework: Mechanisms of Mindfulness Practice for Athletes*

Mindfulness components	Psychological skills
Attention	Personal development and life skills
Attitude	Self-skills
Values clarification	Recovery skills
Self-regulation	Coping skills
Clarity	Motivation skills
Exposure	Volition (pain management skills)
Flexibility	Attentional skills
Nonattachment	Arousal regulation skills
Less rumination	Perceptual cognitive skills
	Motor control skills
	Communication and leadership skills

A Research-Based Model for Exercise and Mindfulness

Based on their synthesis of theoretical mindfulness models applied to athlete performance, Birrer, Röthlin, and Morgan (2012) developed Mechanisms of Mindfulness Practice for Athletes, a framework containing nine components of mindfulness that are proposed to influence athletes' psychological skills. Mindfulness mechanisms and psychological skills identified in Birrer and colleagues' (2012) model are listed in Table 13.1.

While most recreational exercisers do not face the same competitive stressors as athletes, they do experience similar stressors associated with training routines. Additionally, exercisers and athletes often call on similar psychological skills to cope with physical and psychological challenges experienced during training. With this similarity in mind, it is suggested that Birrer and colleagues' (2012) mindfulness framework can be applied to exercisers while still maintaining the integrity of the model. Using the nine components of mindfulness identified by Birrer and colleagues (2012), the following framework has been adapted by this chapter's authors to discuss components of mindfulness in relation to exercise habit and quality.

Mechanisms of Mindfulness Practice for Athletes (Adapted from Birrer et al., 2012)

Attention

Mindfulness practice can help exercisers improve their attentional focus, therefore decreasing inattention and distractibility (Aherne et al., 2011;

De Petrillo et al., 2009). Strengthening attentional skills can allow exercisers to minimize self-regulatory judgments and focus on goal-specific tasks, such as a runner correcting foot strike or a weight lifter focusing on her hip angle during a squat. *Example of a psychological skill associated with attention: attentional skills.*

Attitude

Mindfulness practices can help exercisers experience challenging situations or environments with fewer judgmental, reactive thoughts. Having an accepting inner dialogue can help exercisers more readily accept disappointing or, conversely, outstanding performances. Birrer and colleagues (2012) note that it is important for athletes (or exercisers) "to understand that acceptance does not mean the approval of the present moment condition but the non-judging awareness of the present circumstances or the reaction to it in the form of thoughts and emotions" (p. 243). Though what is occurring may not be their preference, exercisers can ultimately be less reactive with a cultivated nonjudgmental awareness, which may lead to decreased instances of experiential avoidance behaviors and an increased coping ability. *Example of a psychological skill associated with attitude: volition skills.*

Values clarification

Mindfulness practice can help exercisers clarify their values, which can bring to light any "conflicts between their personal values and goals" (Birrer et al., 2012, p. 241). Values clarification can play a significant role in addressing self-regulatory judgments and can increase self-concordance, thus strengthening perception of need satisfaction and motivation (Gardner & Moore, 2004). *Example of a psychological skill associated with values clarification: motivation skills.*

Self-regulation

Self-regulation of thoughts and emotions can be strengthened through mindfulness practice, which can help exercisers cope with feelings of pain, discomfort, fear, and anxiety (Buckley & Cameron, 2011; De Petrillo et al., 2009). Self-regulation can be especially helpful when experiencing judgmental or negative self-talk. Additionally, self-regulation can help exercisers with low self-efficacy shift their perceptions of competence, and aschematic or non–exerciser schematic types transition their exerciser identities. *Example of a psychological skill associated with self-regulation: self-skills.*

Clarity

Through mindfulness practice, exercisers may be able to better understand psychological feelings, especially in the presence of negative affect. Being able to clarify psychological feelings can bring to light any fears and anxieties that have the potential to inhibit exercise quality or participation (Gardner & Moore, 2004). When fears and anxieties are clarified and confronted, instances of avoidant behavior are likely to decrease. *Example of a psychological skill associated with clarity: coping skills.*

Exposure

Exposure, "the willingness to remain in contact with an unpleasant experience," can be greatly increased by mindfulness practice (Birrer et al., 2012, p. 241). With a more practiced ability to endure exposure to negative emotions and physical discomfort, exercisers can better cope with difficult physical and psychological feelings associated with exercise. Because of the initial discomforts associated with new exercise programs, a strong exposure threshold can be especially helpful to novice exercisers or exercisers increasing the difficulty of their typical exercise routine. *Example of a psychological skill associated with exposure: motor control skills.*

Flexibility

Mindfulness practice can help exercisers develop cognitive flexibility skills, which can help them confront and adapt to unforeseen challenges in the workout or environment (Birrer et al., 2012; Ulmer et al., 2010). The strengthening of cognitive flexibility can be especially useful for those exercisers who are prone to skipping workouts due to environmental factors outside their control, such as outside temperature or music volume in a gym. Additionally, cognitive flexibility can help exercisers increase their problem-solving and decision-making skills while decreasing the frequency of avoidance-based thoughts or behaviors. *Example of a psychological skill associated with flexibility: perceptual-cognitive skills.*

Nonattachment

Mindfulness practice can help exercisers strive toward positive outcomes and at once be more accepting when they do not occur, therefore helping exercisers cope and recover from negative (or disappointing) experiences (De Petrillo et al., 2009). Nonattachment can be an important mindfulness component for exercisers recovering from injury or when fitness levels are compromised during the injury recovery process. Detaching from the need to have specific outcomes for one's happiness and satisfaction from exercise performance can help the recovering exerciser maintain motivation during injury rehabilitation. *Example of a psychological skill associated with nonattachment: recovery skills.*

Less rumination
We believe mindfulness practice can lead to less rumination, which can decrease the degree to which exercisers worry about discomfort, failure, and other undesirable thoughts. Being able to reduce rumination levels through mindfulness practice can be a very powerful tool for exercisers who tend to feel concerned about their appearance when exercising or those exercisers who struggle to turn off self-critical thoughts. For exercisers with low self-efficacy, a decrease in ruminating thoughts can be an initial step toward increasing feelings of competence (Birrer et al., 2012). *Example of a psychological skill associated with less rumination: personal development and life skills.*

The mindfulness mechanisms outlined in the preceding model illustrate the role MBSR, or a more general mindfulness approach, can play in helping exercisers recognize physical and psychological barriers to exercise, address barriers to exercise, and focus on the *process* of exercising while also accepting the outcome. When collectively employed, these mechanisms can help exercisers develop regular exercise habits and engage in effective exercise programs.

Conclusion

Anecdotally, many committed health club patrons remark about the dreaded January onslaught of new gym members who invade treadmill and free weight areas shortly after making New Year's resolutions. While tales of annoyance may vary, concluding thoughts usually include, "Oh, well, they'll be gone by next month." This well-known anecdote speaks to the difficulty experienced when beginning an exercise habit, as well as the greater difficulty of sustaining an exercise habit.

Similar to running around a track where hurdles appear at random intervals, barriers to developing an exercise habit include physical and psychological considerations that can appear at any time, for seemingly any reason. These barriers, many including physical pain or intense urges of avoidance, are rarely overcome with intention alone. Amid increasing concerns regarding Americans' sedentary activity levels and decreasing health, it is critical to bring to light any methodologies that may contribute to increasing success rates among novice exercisers, including those methodologies that can help exercisers overcome barriers to the development of regular exercise habits.

We suggest that mindfulness- and acceptance-based practices can help exercisers – novice or seasoned – identify, confront, and work through physical and emotional barriers to exercise, thereby decreasing chances of attrition and potentially increasing exercise effectiveness. Specific mindfulness interventions, such as MBSR and ACT, focus on nonjudgmental, present-moment awareness, which may increase coping skills and cognitive flexibility (e.g., Hayes et al., 2006; Kabat-Zinn, 2003a, 2003b) and can be employed or used to guide the development of less time-intensive interventions for exercisers. Both of these interventions have demonstrated positive outcomes with a variety of clinical and nonclinical populations, including exercisers (e.g., Baer, 2003; Lillis et al., 2009; Salmon et al., 2009; Wall, 2005).

More general views of mindfulness (i.e., those that are not tied specifically to mindfulness or acceptance models such as MBSR or ACT) have also been shown to be effective in helping exercisers achieve more positive outcomes (e.g., Curtis et al., 2011). Additionally, those exercisers who are more mindful tend to be better able to maintain a consistent exercise regimen (Ulmer et al., 2010). This suggests that taking an intentionally mindful and accepting approach to exercise, regardless of the specific framework of this approach, can increase the likelihood of successful coping with the physical and psychological barriers of exercise.

REFERENCES

Aherne, C., Moran, A., and Lonsdale, C. (2011). The effect of mindfulness training on athletes' flow: An initial investigation. *Sport Psychologist*, 25, 177–189.

American College of Sports Medicine (ACSM). (2014). *ACSM's resources for the health fitness specialist*. Philadelphia, PA: Lippincott Williams and Wilkins.

Baer, R. A. (2003). Mindfulness training as a clinical intervention: A conceptual and empirical review. *Clinical Psychology: Science and Practice*, 10(2), 125–143. doi: 10.1093/clipsy/bpg015

Banting, L. K., Dimmock, J. A., and Lay, B. S. (2009). The role of implicit and explicit components of exerciser self-schema in the prediction of exercise behavior. *Psychology of Sport and Exercise*, 10(1), 80–86. doi: 10.1016/j.psychsport.2008.07.007

Birrer, D., Rothlin, P., and Morgan, G. (2012). Mindfulness to enhance athletic performance: Theoretical considerations and possible impact mechanisms. *Mindfulness*, 3(3), 235–246. doi: 10.1007/s12671-012-0109-2

Briegel-Jones, R. M. H., Knowles, Z., Eubank, M. R., Giannoulatos, K., and Elliot, D. (2013). A preliminary investigation into the effect of yoga practice on mindfulness and flow in elite youth swimmers. *Sport Psychologist*, 27(4), 349–359.

Brinkborg, H., Michanek, J., Hesser, H., and Berglund, G. (2011). Acceptance and commitment therapy for the treatment of stress among social workers: A randomized controlled trial. *Behavior Research and Therapy*, 49(6–7), 389–398. doi: 10.1016/jbrat.2011.03.009

Brisbon, N. M., and Lowery, G. A. (2011). Mindfulness and levels of stress: A comparison of beginner and advanced hatha yoga practitioners. *Journal of Religion and Health*, 50(4), 931–941. doi: 10.1007/s10943-009-9305-3

Brown, K. W., and Ryan, R. M. (2003). The benefits of being present: Mindfulness and its role in psychological well-being. *Journal of Personality and Social Psychology*, 84(4), 822–848. doi: 10.1037/0022-3514.84.4.822

Buckley, J., and Cameron, L. D. (2011). Automatic judgments of exerciser self-efficacy and exercise disengagement in adults experienced and inexperienced in exercise self-regulation. *Psychology of Sport and Exercise*, 12, 324–332. doi: 10.1016./j.psychsport.2010.12.003

Carson, F., and Polman, R. C. J. (2010). The facilitative nature of avoidance coping within sports injury rehabilitation. *Scandinavian Journal of Medicine and Science in Sports*, 20(2), 235–240. doi: 10.1111/j.1600-0838.2009.00890.x

Centers for Disease Control and Prevention (CDC). (2012). *Diabetes report card 2012*. Retrieved from www.cdc.gov/diabetes/pubs/pdf/DiabetesReportCard.pdf

CDC. (2013). *Annual number of new cases of diagnosed diabetes among adults aged 17–79 years, United States, 1980–2011*. Retrieved from http://www.cdc.gov/diabetes/statistics/incidence/fig1.htm.

CDC and Division for Heart Disease and Stroke Prevention. (2013). *Data trends & maps Web site*. Atlanta, GA: U.S. Department of Health and Human Services, Centers for Disease Control and Prevention (CDC), National Center for Chronic Disease Prevention and Health Promotion. Available at www.cdc.gov/dhdsp/.

Curtis, K., Osadchuk, A., and Katz, J. (2011). An eight-week yoga intervention is associated with improvements in pain, psychological functioning and mindfulness, and changes in cortisol levels in women with fibromyalgia. *Journal of Pain Research*, 4, 189–201. doi: 10.2147/JPR.S22761

De Petrillo, L., Kaufman, K., Glass, C., and Arnkoff, D. (2009). Mindfulness for long-distance runners: An open trial using mindful sport performance enhancement (MSPE). *Journal of Clinical Sport Psychology*, 4, 357–376.

DuCharme, K. A., and Brawley, L. R. (1995). Predicting the intentions and behavior of exercise initiates using two forms of self-efficacy. *Journal of Behavioral Medicine*, 18(5), 479–497. doi: 10.1007/bf01904775

Flanigan, D. C., Everhart, J. S., Pedroza, A., Smith, T., and Kaeding, C. C. (2013). Fear of reinjury (kinesiophobia) and persistent knee symptoms are common factors for lack of return to sport after anterior cruciate ligament reconstruction. *Arthroscopy: The Journal of Arthroscopic and Related Surgery*, 29(8), 1322–1329. doi: 10.1016/j.arthro.2013.05.015

Gardner, F., and Moore, Z. (2004). A Mindfulness-Acceptance-Commitment–based approach to athletic performance enhancement: Theoretical considerations. *Behavior Therapy*, 35, 707–723. doi: 10.1016/S0005-7894(04)80016-9

Gooding, A., and Gardner, F. (2009). An investigation of the relationship between mindfulness, preshot routine, and basketball free throw percentage. *Journal of Clinical Sports Psychology*, 4, 303–319.

Hart, R., Ivtzan, I., and Hart, D. (2013). Mind the gap in mindfulness research: A comparative account of the leading schools of thought. *Review of General Psychology*, 17(4), 453–466. doi: 10.1037/a0035212

Hayes, S. C., Levin, M. E., Plumb-Vilardaga, J., Villatte, J. L., and Pistorello, J. (2013). Acceptance and Commitment Therapy and contextual behavioral science: Examining the progress of a distinctive model of behavioral and cognitive therapy. *Behavior Therapy*, 44(2), 180–198. doi: 10.1016/j.beth.2009.08.002

Hayes, S. C., Luoma, J. B., Bond, F. W., Masuda, A., and Lillis, J. (2006). Acceptance and Commitment Therapy: Model, processes and outcomes. *Behavior Research and Therapy*, 44(1), 1–25. doi: 10.1016/j.brat.2005.06.006

International Health, Racquet and Sportsclub Association (IHRS). (2013). *58.5 million americans utilize health clubs*. Retrieved from www.ihrsa.org/media-center/2013/5/8/585-million-americans-utilize-health-clubs.html.

IHRS. (2014). *Total health club visits surpass 5 billion for the first time*. Retrieved from www.ihrsa.org/media-center/2014/4/14/total-health-club-visits-surpass-5-billion-for-the-first-tim.html.

Kabat-Zinn, J. (1982). An outpatient program in behavioral medicine for chronic pain patients based on the practice of mindfulness meditation: Theoretical considerations and preliminary results. *General Hospital Psychiatry*, 4(1), 33–47. doi: 10.1016/0163-8343(82)90026-3

(2003a). Mindfulness-based interventions in context: Past, present, and future. *Clinical Psychology: Science and Practice*, 10(2), 144–156. doi: 10.1093/clipsy/bpg016

(2003b). Mindfulness-Based Stress Reduction (MBSR). *Constructivism in the Human Sciences*, 8(2), 73–107.

Kaufman, K., Glass, C., and Arnkoff, D. (2009). Evaluation of Mindful Sport Performance Enhancement (MSPE): A new approach to promote flow in athletes. *Journal of Clinical Sports Psychology*, 4, 334–356.

Laubmeier, K. K., Zakowski, S. G., and Bair, J. P. (2004). The role of spirituality in the psychological adjustment to cancer: A test of the transactional model of stress and coping. *International Journal of Behavioral Medicine*, 11(1), 48–55.

Lazarus, R. S., and Folkman, S. (1984). *Stress, appraisal, and coping*. New York, NY: Springer.

Liguori, G. (2014). *ACSM's resources for the health fitness specialist*. Philadelphia, PA: Lippincott Williams and Wilkins.

Lillis, J., Hayes, S. C., Bunting, K., and Masuda, A. (2009). Teaching acceptance and mindfulness to improve the lives of the obese: A preliminary test of a theoretical model. *Annals of Behavioral Medicine*, 37(1), 58–69. doi: 10.1007/s12160-009-9083-x

Lundgren, T., Dahl, J., Yardi, N., and Melin, L. (2008). Acceptance and Commitment Therapy and yoga for drug-refractory epilepsy: A randomized controlled trial. *Epilepsy and Behavior*, 13(1), 102–108. doi: 10.1016/j/yebeh.2008.02.009

Moraes-Vieira, P. M., Yore, M. M., Dwyer, P. M., Syed, I., Aryal, P., and Kahn, B. B. (2014). RBP4 activates antigen-presenting cells, leading to adipose tissue inflammation and systemic insulin resistance. *Cell Metabolism*, 19(3), 512–526. doi: 10.1016/j.cmet.2014. 01.018

National Center for Health Statistics (NCHS). (2006). Summary health statistics for U.S. adults: National health interview survey, 2005. *Vital Health Statistics*, 10(232), 11.

NCHS. (2009). Summary health statistics for U.S. adults: National health interview survey, 2008. *Vital Health Statistics*, 10(242), 12.

(2014). Summary health statistics for U.S. adults: National health interview survey, 2012. *Vital Health Statistics*, 10(260), 9.

Ng, S. W., and Popkin, B. M. (2012). Time use and physical activity: A shift away from movement across the globe. *Obesity Reviews*, 13(8), 659–680. doi: 10.1111/j.1467-789x.2011.00982.x

Poag, K. G., and McAuley, E. (1992). Goal setting, self-efficacy, and exercise behavior. *Journal of Sport and Exercise Psychology*, 14, 352–360.

Ratey, J. (2008). *Spark: The revolutionary new science of exercise and the brain.* New York, NY: Little, Brown.

Salmon, P., Hanneman, S., and Harwood, B. (2010). Associative/dissociative cognitive strategies in sustained physical activity: Literature review and proposal for a mindfulness-based conceptual model. *Sport Psychologist*, 24 (2), 127–156.

Salmon, P., Lush, E., Jablonski, M., and Sephton, S. E. (2009). Yoga and mindfulness: Clinical aspects of an ancient mind/body practice. *Cognitive and Behavioral Practice*, 16(1), 59–72. doi: 10.1016/j.cbpra.2008.07.002

Tacón, A. M., and McComb, J. (2009). Mindful exercise, quality of life, and survival: A mindfulness-based exercise program for women with breast cancer. *Journal of Alternative and Complementary Medicine*, 15(1), 41–46. doi: 10.1089/acm.2008.0255

Tapper, K., Shaw, C., Ilsley, J., Hill, A. J., Bond, F. W., and Moore, L. (2009). Exploratory randomized controlled trial of a mindfulness-based weight loss intervention for women. *Appetite*, 52(2), 396–404. doi: 10.1016/j.appet. 2008.11.012

Ulmer, C. S., Stetson, B. A., and Salmon, P. G. (2010). Mindfulness and acceptance are associated with exercise maintenance in YMCA exercisers. *Behavior Research and Therapy*, 48(8), 805–809. doi: 10.1016/j.brat.2010.04.009

Wall, R. B. (2005). Tai Chi and Mindfulness-Based Stress Reduction in a Boston public middle school. *Journal of Pediatric Health Care*, 19(4), 230–237. doi: 10.1016/j.pedhc.2005.02. 006

CHAPTER 14

Mindfulness, Eating, Body, and Performance

Jessyca Arthur-Cameselle

We are regularly out of touch with our immediate conscious experiences due to "ignoring our present moments in favor of others" (Kabat-Zinn, 2005, p. 5), a habit of operating on autopilot at the cost of truly engaging with our surroundings. This chapter discusses the ways that such automaticity can, and typically does, extend to eating and body awareness. As detailed in this chapter, mindless eating is commonplace and is linked to poor body image, disordered eating, and obesity. For athletes and performers, training in mindful eating may assist performance and help counter unique body image and eating concerns found in elite sport and performance environments. In the pages that follow, you will find relevant research regarding the relationship between mindfulness and eating behaviors, body image, and performance. In parallel, at the end of the chapter, there are specific suggestions for positively influencing eating behaviors through a mindful approach.

Mindless Eating and Eating Disorders

Making automatic food choices, without awareness of possible environmental and emotional cues, or consuming food while distracted from the physical sensations of eating is deemed *mindless eating* (Wansink & Sobal, 2007). In modern culture, mindless eating is rampant; we eat on couches with minds absorbed in television shows; we eat past the point of fullness with friends, distracted by stimulating conversation. These tendencies divert our attention from fully experiencing meals, predictably leading to increased consumption (Wansink, 2004) because we fail to notice when we are satiated.

How many total decisions have you made about food and beverages in the past twenty-four hours? Wansink and Sobal (2007) asked a similar question to a group of research participants, who estimated that they made a total of fourteen decisions in the previous day. Through detailed follow-up questions, the researchers determined that the 139 adults in the study actually made an average of 227 decisions regarding food and beverages. The participants' gross underestimation indicates that much of food-related behavior is outside of conscious awareness; they failed to accurately assess the multifaceted elements of eating, such as when, where, how much, and with whom they ate.

Mindless eating is also fueled by environmental and cultural factors. For example, Wansink and colleagues have repeatedly shown that food container sizes influence consumption (e.g., Wansink & Kim, 2005). Additional research on cultural factors has shown that samples of American adults, as compared to Japanese, French, and Belgian samples, worry the most about what they eat, yet report the least healthy food choices and least amount of pleasure associated with food (Rozin et al., 1999). The researchers contend that, in general, the French have a different relationship with food because they spend more time mindfully appreciating flavors and culinary activities compared to Americans.

Bays (2009) offers an additional explanation when she states that mindless eating is connected to being "afraid to be empty" (p. 144), and that she believes we have low tolerance for the sensations of hunger and emptiness so we "move quickly to put an end to them" (p. 144). As a result, we neglect the moment and the pleasure of eating, because food is approached as a means to an end; consequently, we are more likely to choose foods that are convenient or packaged because they most quickly meet our needs.

The behavior of binge eating may be similarly explained, as it is often connected with meeting emotional needs immediately. Two of the three clinical eating disorders involve mindless binge eating: bulimia nervosa and binge eating disorder. *Bulimia nervosa* (BN) is characterized by binge eating episodes, defined as eating an amount of food in a short period that is more calorie dense than others would eat. In BN, binges are followed by vomiting, overexercising, or use of laxatives to compensate. This pattern occurs at least once a week for three months (APA, 2013). *Binge eating disorder* (BED) includes binge eating episodes (same definition as BN) at least once per week for three months, without any compensatory behaviors (APA, 2013). In both disorders, sufferers report feeling out of control of their eating, eat until uncomfortably full, and often use food as a way to manage and cope with difficult emotions (Whiteside et al., 2007). In such cases, eating is used to ignore or alter emotions and is not a response to physical hunger cues. This emotion-driven approach to eating leads to guilt, anxiety, and self-loathing.

People with *anorexia nervosa* (AN) have the following symptoms: food restriction that leads to significantly low body weight, fear of gaining weight, and distorted body image (APA, 2013). Those with AN typically avoid experiencing emotions (Wildes, Ringham, & Marcus, 2010) and distract themselves from hunger cues and their body's needs. Indeed, women with AN have poor "interoceptive awareness," a reduced self-knowledge of internal, physiological sensations. For example, studies have shown decreased awareness of hunger and satiety in participants with AN (Matsumoto et al., 2006), which may explain why they continue to restrict food despite having low energy consumption.

Replacing Mindlessness with Mindfulness

Understanding the pull of mindlessness will help you to replace it with *mindfulness*, defined as purposeful awareness and attention to current experiences with "no agenda other than being fully present in each moment" (Kabat-Zinn, 2005, p. 35). The goal of mindfulness is to awaken to the reality of your current state and respond nonjudgmentally (Kabat-Zinn 2005). The desired outcome, then, is insight, which may bring increased connection with one's inner self and improved self-understanding (Hahn & Cheung, 2010). Regarding eating, such insight may offer an understanding of either satiety or hunger.

Mindfulness training is most commonly implemented via an eight-to-ten-week program in Mindfulness-Based Stress Reduction (MBSR), which was first created for chronic pain patients and is conducted in weekly 2.5-hour group workshops (Kabat-Zinn, 1990). MBSR includes a non-judgmental awareness of experience in formal sitting meditation practice, body awareness via body scans, Hatha yoga postures, and engagement in mindfulness during everyday behaviors such as walking. Although MBSR was not initially created for people with issues related to food, mindfulness practice is easily tailored to eating.

To be more specific, *mindful eating* is an approach to food with conscious, nonjudgmental awareness of the physical and emotional sensations aroused by each bite (Framson et al., 2009). Important elements of mindful eating include awareness of all the senses, possible physical and mental distractions, the environmental setting of the meal, portion sizes, and thoughts and feelings about your physical body (Bays, 2009; Hahn & Cheung, 2010; Kristeller, 2003). Mindful eating does not have to be a somber experience. You can "be curious and even playful" (Bays, 2011, p. 177) as you explore, using a "beginner's mind" to appreciate food as if it is your first encounter. When practiced, mindful eating helps to push back against multitasking, which is typically prioritized in modern culture.

So, how do you eat mindfully? The most simple aspect of mindful eating is to give focused attention to all of your senses during a meal: the colors of your foods to appreciate their vibrancy; the texture of foods as your hands and mouth experience their surface; the odor of foods and the pleasure your sense of smell can bring to a meal; and, of course, the taste of foods (Bays, 2011). This means that you (probably) will need to slow down and chew your food more completely; otherwise, you will miss the opportunity to savor your experience. Try the "Raisin Exercise" and "Blind Tasting Exercise" at the end of the chapter to practice slow, mindful eating that incorporates all of your senses.

It is critical to remember that slowness in and of itself is not mindfulness; instead, slowness must be accompanied by attention and redirection back to the present moment should your thoughts wander (Bays, 2011). Therefore, mindful eating also requires stillness (Hahn & Cheung, 2010), eliminating physical or mental multitasking in order to be fully present. Without the distraction of television, books, or phone calls, or getting stuck in the past or worrying about the future, you will sharpen your focus onto the moment and possibly experience gratitude for your meal.

Mindful eating can even begin before you take the first bite, if you cultivate awareness of the setting for meals, choice of foods, as well as the portion sizes served. Improving your awareness of the many daily food choices you make is simpler than it sounds. Take, for example, the participants in Wansink and Sobal's (2007) study, who grossly underestimated their food decisions in one day. Six months later, three of their participants were asked to record each food decision they made in twenty-four hours. Without substantial training, they each recorded over 215 decisions per day, indicating that they were more aware of their eating behaviors. The task of recognizing your daily decisions regarding food consumption is an excellent starting point on a journey to more mindful eating, which you can practice in the "Food Choice Log" exercise at the end of the chapter.

To continue, Somov (2008) writes that mindful eating is "physiologically triggered eating," a response to physical hunger cues with the purpose to provide the body with necessary fuel. By contrast, mindless eating is either "psychologically triggered," as a way to respond to emotional needs, or "environmentally triggered," in response to learned cues (Somov, 2008, pp. 7–8). When we lose touch with physiological drives for eating, we fall victim to "habit energy," a force that leads to multitasking, rushing, serving large portions, and eating automatically, because mindlessness requires less effort (Hahn & Cheung, 2010, p. 15). By contrast, a mindful eater starts a meal when in need of energy and stops when fullness is achieved; therefore, a common side effect of mindful eating is a reduction in overeating and binge eating (e.g., Timmerman & Brown, 2012). Taking breaks between bites and breathing deeply during meals increases awareness of fullness.

It is important to acknowledge the impossibility of eating every meal mindfully. There will certainly be times when you need to work, socialize, or think while eating. However, a mindful approach can provide more awareness of when you do eat mindlessly. Although it may sound counterintuitive, you can make a deliberate mindful decision to eat mindlessly or multitask should it be of necessity (Bays, 2011). Similarly, a mindful eater is keenly aware of emotions and pays attention if anxiety or sadness, rather than hunger, prompts eating (Kristeller, 2003). This awareness allows for an active choice to respond or not to respond to emotional triggers.

Body Awareness and Mindfulness

A related element of mindful eating is being in touch with thoughts about your body, acknowledging that food fuels body function. Additionally, connection with the body means that you bring attention to body form, including body shape and weight, as well as the state of your body, including illnesses, health, or pain. For many, focused attention to the body produces negative emotions, such as shame and disgust. A mindful approach does not make promises to alter these negative states immediately; instead, it encourages nonjudgmental awareness and appreciation of emotions and the body's functions (Kristeller, 2003). For example, bringing focused attention to inhaling and exhaling is a way to foster conscious awareness of your body's vitality (Hahn & Cheung, 2010). Mindful eating can be related to body appreciation; when you make nutritious food choices, in correct portions, you help your body to function fully.

Research on Mindful Eating

A growing body of research examines the relationship between mindful eating and various health factors. It is of note that when exploring mindful eating, researchers and clinicians have identified two additional, but related, constructs: intuitive eating and self-compassion. *Intuitive eating* is comprised of three interconnected practices: permitting oneself unconditionally to eat when there are physical hunger cues; eating for hunger (instead of emotional needs); and determining portion sizes based on internal hunger and fullness cues (Tribole & Resch, 1995). Intuitive eating overlaps with mindful eating, most notably, with food choices guided by physiological needs. *Self-compassion* has ties to Buddhist philosophy and is characterized by being kind to yourself rather than critical in the face of failure or negative occurrences; understanding that you are not alone but rather you share in the general human experience; and maintaining mindful, nonjudgmental awareness of both positive and negative thoughts and emotions (Neff, 2003).

Mindful Eating, Food Enjoyment, and Food Choice

Mindful raisin eating has become a typical starting exercise in mindfulness training. Hong, Lishner, and Han (2014) examined the extent to which participating in mindful raisin eating affects eating enjoyment and willingness to sample new foods. After their participants mindfully ate a raisin, they were more likely to sample a typically disliked food (e.g., wasabi peas) and reported significantly greater enjoyment of food than participants in both a nonmindful raisin eating group and a no-task control group. In other research, higher levels of college students' mindfulness was connected to increased daily intake of fruits and vegetables (Gilbert & Waltz, 2010).

Researchers investigating mindful eating habits regularly use the twenty-eight-question Mindful Eating Questionnaire (MEQ; Framson et al., 2009). The MEQ is a reliable instrument that includes five subscales: *disinhibition* (e.g., "If there's good food at a party, I'll continue eating even after I'm full"); *external cues* (e.g., "I recognize when food advertisements make me want to eat"); *awareness* (e.g., "I notice when there are subtle flavors in the foods I eat"); *emotional response* (e.g., "When I'm sad, I eat to feel better); and *distraction* (e.g., "I think about things I need to do while I'm eating"). Higher scores on the MEQ reflect more mindful eating tendencies. Recent research using the MEQ indicates that mindful eating is related to self-selected portion size. Beshara, Hutchinson, and Wilson (2013) found that adult participants' MEQ scores were significantly negatively correlated to consumption of energy-dense foods (e.g., cakes, cookies, French fries) over the week previous to the study. In particular, scores on the emotional response and disinhibition subscales were the strongest predictors of energy-dense servings. Interestingly, when the researchers controlled for mindful eating behaviors, everyday general mindfulness practices were not significantly correlated to serving sizes, consistent with Kearney and colleagues' (2012) finding that implementation of general MBSR programs did not significantly reduce emotional eating or increase fruit and vegetable intake. By contrast, the success of interventions such as "mindful restaurant eating" training in enhancing weight loss programs (Timmerman & Brown, 2012) indicates that specific mindful eating skills, not just general mindfulness training, are needed for changing mindless eating patterns.

Mindfulness, Body Image, and Eating Disorders

Research on body image and awareness, an aspect of mindful eating, is abundant. Although multiple factors influence body image, experimental findings have reliably shown increases in body dissatisfaction after female participants view images in the media that portray the "thin-ideal" (e.g., Birkeland, Thompson, & Herbozo, 2005). For males, media focus is on leanness combined with muscle mass, which seems to represent the "ideal" male body and explains tendencies for males to feel dissatisfied with the perceived smallness of their muscles (McCabe & Ricciardelli, 2004). Training in "media literacy" appears to mitigate negative influence on body satisfaction, seemingly because the training disrupts mindless consumption of media, replacing it with critical thinking and awareness (Yamamiya et al., 2005). However, media literacy training is usually a one-time event with short-lived effects. Mindfulness training may provide a long-term solution because it offers a holistic shift, bringing awareness to internal emotional states in response to the environment, such as the daily onslaught of media images.

Indeed, dispositional (i.e., trait) mindfulness, self-compassion, and intuitive eating have been targets of recent research on body image. Studies using female participants indicate that higher levels of intuitive eating habits, including relying on physiological drives to determine eating, are related to lower experiences of pressure to be thin, as well as higher levels of self-esteem and life satisfaction (e.g., Tylka & Kroon Van Diest, 2013). Similar findings were observed in a sample of 296 college males; those with higher levels of dispositional mindfulness reported lower drive for muscularity and higher body satisfaction (Lavender, Gratz, & Anderson, 2012).

Regarding specific elements of body image, Avalos and Tylka (2006) reported strong positive correlations between intuitive eating habits and body appreciation as well as emphasis on body function in a sample of 181 college women. As expected, participants who focused on the importance of their bodies' function (instead of appearance) were more likely to eat in response to their physiological hunger cues and felt more positively about their bodies. Oh and colleagues (2012) observed the same pattern in a sample of 160 college female athletes from a variety of sports. Like the results of Tylka and colleagues, their findings indicate that perceived body acceptance by others increased both body appreciation and a focus on body function, which in turn were connected to more intuitive eating behaviors. Overall, these studies provide convincing evidence of a link between trait mindfulness and enhanced body image.

Mindful eating is also connected to lower incidence of clinical eating disorder behaviors. For example, Tylka and Wilcox (2006) found that female college students' scores on measures of intuitive eating were significantly negatively correlated to measures of eating disorder symptomatology. More specifically, students who most often gave themselves unconditional permission to, rather than imposing rigid dieting rules, had lower scores on eating disorder measures. Numerous other studies show significant correlations between greater mindfulness habits and lower reported body dissatisfaction and eating disorder symptoms (e.g., Denny et al., 2013). With regard to gender differences, some studies have indicated that men are more likely to pay attention to internal hunger cues (Tylka & Kroon Van Diest, 2013) and trust their bodies to inform them about how much to eat (Denny et al., 2013), possibly explaining why men are at lower risk for eating disorders (Streigel-Moore et al., 2009).

Mindfulness and Exercise

In the past two decades, research has also emerged on the connection between mindfulness habits and exercise behaviors. Overall, everyday mindfulness behaviors are positively correlated with participation in moderate and vigorous exercise (Gilbert & Waltz, 2010) and maintenance of regular exercise as well as perceived success in meeting exercise goals (Ulmer, Stetson, & Salmon, 2010). However, Moor, Scott, and McIntosh (2013) did not find a connection between mindful eating habits (as measured by the MEQ) and self-reported exercise levels of one hundred college students. In fact, more active participants were significantly more likely to eat in response to negative emotions and less likely to have awareness of food and their sensations during eating. This contradictory finding may be related to differences in the type of exercise participants select, as it has become clear that not all forms of exercise are connected with a mindful approach to living and eating.

For example, Framson and colleagues (2009) found a positive correlation between regular participation in yoga and mindful eating habits in sample of 314 mostly female participants (average age forty-two years), but such a relationship was not evident between other forms of exercise and mindful eating. Other studies have revealed similar relationships between yoga practice and positive health behaviors. For example, in a sample of 571 female fitness center attendees (average age thirty-six years), Prichard and Tiggemann (2008) found that time spent on cardiovascular exercise was significantly positively related to disordered eating symptoms and significantly negatively related to body esteem, likely because the women engaged in this type of exercise specifically to lose weight and improve attractiveness. By contrast, those engaging in yoga had no elevated eating disorder symptoms and were more focused on health than on appearance. Likewise, Martin and colleagues (2013) found that participation in yoga was significantly positively related to body awareness and was significantly negatively related to disordered eating and consumption of take-out food. By contrast, time spent in cardio-based exercise was positively related to disordered eating. Although each of these studies is correlational in nature, taken together, they suggest that cardiovascular exercises, which are typically recommended for weight loss, do not facilitate a healthy relationship with food. By contrast, yoga practice may be best for those at risk for eating disorders, as its tenets are aligned with a mindful approach to eating. See Salmon and colleagues (2009) for a review of the clinical benefits of yoga and a detailed description of the sequence of MBSR Hatha yoga.

Mindfulness, Eating, and Performance

For athletes and performers who already engage in high levels of physical activity, the benefits of mindfulness on weight loss and exercise maintenance are not as necessary. In this population, mindfulness interventions regarding eating may be more effectively used to manage appropriate energy/calorie intake and ensure a diet that is wide in variety of nutrients to support performance needs. Perhaps somewhat surprisingly, many professional athletes exhibit nutritional deficiencies. For example, female national team soccer players' food journals revealed daily deficits in vitamins D and E (Mullinix et al., 2003), and female national team basketball and volleyball players were deficient in overall calorie consumption for their output level, specifically in carbohydrate and protein intake (Papadopoulou et al., 2008). Young professional male soccer players also reported inadequate levels of overall calorie intake (Murphy & Jeanes,

2006), as did 83 percent of a sample of twenty-four Brazilian male and female Olympic weight lifters (Cabral Costa et al., 2006). This body of research indicates that, even at the elite and professional level, athletes need increased attention to providing adequate fuel and varied nutrition for their bodies. Mindful eating practices that emphasize listening to the body's hunger cues might be beneficial for this group, which seems generally to undereat for their output level.

College athletes' eating behaviors are of similar concern as there is evidence that their eating habits are not appreciably better than those of non-athlete students, given that athletes regularly lack in fruit and vegetable servings (Malinauskas et al., 2007). Alarmingly, in a sample of fifty-two female college athletes, only 9 percent met their daily caloric needs, only 27 percent ate breakfast daily, and only 16 percent monitored their hydration levels (Shriver, Betts, & Wollenberg, 2013), which suggests that they are inadequately fueled to perform at their best. Similarly, a sample of twenty-eight college football players reported deficiency in overall energy intake based on the intensity of their activity level (Cole et al., 2005), though other studies have found abdominal obesity and risk of cardiovascular disease to be larger concerns in college football players (Buell et al., 2008). Such patterns in reported energy deficiency indicate that college athletes generally do not meet their bodies' specific needs and most likely do not eat mindfully.

Although college athletes report desires both to eat healthy foods and cook for themselves, time constraints due to training demands affect intentions to eat healthily, often resulting in consumption of packaged foods that minimize preparation time (Pawlak, Malinauskas, & Rivera, 2009). With convenience and time efficiency driving food choice, it is likely that these athletes are eating mindlessly. College athletes also indicate that the developmental transition to college brings a change in eating habits, due to increased focus on eating as a method to enhance performance and looking to older players on their team as models for eating (Smart & Bisogni, 2001). As such, young college students are impressionable and their eating habits are in flux. Mindful eating training at this stage may help them to cope with the transition and develop lifelong healthy eating habits.

Currently, there are no research studies that examine the relationship between mindful eating habits and athletic performance. However, it seems reasonable to expect that if mindful eating can help athletes to achieve the proper energy intake, performance would be enhanced. It is possible too that the relationship between mindful eating and performance would depend on the particular sport in question. For most sports, energy intake appropriate to activity level would be beneficial. However, for weight class sports such as wrestling and crew, it is possible that mindful eating and paying attention to the body's needs would inhibit athletes' ability to cut weight. Although cutting weight is certainly a generally unhealthy practice, in certain sports, it appears to be a normative way to facilitate performance. One could argue that mindful eating could still be employed to help these athletes savor the smaller portions they consume, and might discourage dangerous practices such as purging.

Mindfulness, Body Image Concerns, and Eating Disorders in Athletes and Performers

Athletes and other elite performers may also specifically benefit from mindfulness training as a way to address the unique body image concerns that can accompany their athletic roles. Meta-analyses on athletes' body image have shown some benefits of participating in sport, specifically that athletes report more body satisfaction than non-athletes overall (Hausenblas & Downs, 2001); however, when broken down by level of competition, athletes at higher levels report more body dissatisfaction than athletes at lower levels (Varnes et al., 2013). Survey research indicates that there are unique body pressures experienced by athletes, by way of coach and sport demands regarding weight as well as stress related to appearance and performance, which are not accounted for by general sociocultural pressures (Galli et al., 2014; Reel et al., 2013). Sport-specific triggers were also reported in qualitative research with female collegiate athletes, who reported that performance pressure and injuries that prevented sport participation were factors that contributed to the onset of their eating disorders (Arthur-Cameselle & Quatromoni, 2010). Athlete participants reported that they binged or restricted food intake as a reaction to difficult emotions aroused by their participation in sport.

Sport-specific body pressures appear to play out differently based on the performer's gender. For male athletes, pressures are often related to increasing muscularity while maintaining leanness (Ridgeway & Tylka, 2005). Although females also value muscularity for performance, several studies suggest that a strong build that distinguishes them from non-athletes can create body image concerns about perceived femininity outside of sport contexts (e.g., Krane et al., 2004). Additionally, Blacker and colleagues (2007) reported that all sixty-one of their female college athlete participants, from a variety of sports, selected an "ideal" body image that was less muscular than their own current body. More specifically, volleyball players reported the highest level of body dissatisfaction compared to other athletes in the sample, which may be explained by other studies that have reported a connection between tight-fitting uniforms and increased body dissatisfaction in athletes (Krane et al., 2004). Male swimmers, football players, and wrestlers are also susceptible to anxiety related to revealing uniforms or body weight requirements (Galli & Reel, 2009). Thus, elite athletes and performers experience unique body image concerns that seem exacerbated by mandated performance clothing.

Negative thoughts about body weight, appearance, or clothing fit are possible distractions during competition. A mindful/intuitive approach to eating may be useful then, to increase appreciation of body function with reduced emphasis on body appearance, as was found in non-athlete research (Avalos & Tylka, 2006). Nonjudgmental acceptance of the body may be helpful in reducing athletes' distracting body image thoughts, possibly translating to improved performance. However, research is needed to determine whether this claim is empirically supported.

In more extreme cases, negative body image can contribute to eating disorder behavior. Research findings on the prevalence of eating disorders in athletes compared to their non-athlete peers have been somewhat inconsistent; a recent literature review documented higher prevalence of eating disorders in athletes compared to non-athletes and concluded that between 0 to 19 percent of male and 6 to 45 percent of female athletes have disordered eating (Bratland-Sanda & Sundgot-Borgen, 2013); however, there are studies that document lower rates in more active athlete samples (e.g., DiPasquale & Petrie, 2013). To date, the most consistent finding is that athletes from thin-build sports (i.e., sports that emphasize leanness, such as distance running) or aesthetic sports (i.e., sports that involve judging, such as diving and figure skating) are at higher risk for the development of eating disorders (e.g., Smolak, Murnen, & Ruble, 2000). A recent meta-analysis on prevalence rates confirmed that 12 percent of all types of dancers and 16 percent of ballet dancers met clinical criteria for eating disorders (Arcelus, Witcomb, & Mitchell, 2014). Of the three clinical eating disorders, thin-build athletes and aesthetic performers seem to be particularly susceptible to anorexia (Arcelus et al., 2014). Their restrictive eating is of particular concern because very low body weight is typically accompanied by amenorrhea, making them more vulnerable to skeletal injuries such as stress fractures (Reel et al., 2007). For this group, training in mindful eating, with an emphasis on trusting the body's hunger cues, would likely help increase energy consumption, thereby reducing injury. Spending less time sidelined by injury may be an indirect way that mindful eating can assist achievement of long-term goals for athletes and performers.

Unfortunately, at present, there are no studies on the use of mindfulness in eating disorder or body image treatments for athlete or performer populations. To date, the only study on mindful eating in athlete participants, described earlier, found that in a nonclinical sample of athletes, levels of intuitive eating were essentially equal to non-athlete samples (Oh et al., 2012). The authors stated that intuitive eating was indirectly influenced by the athletes' perceived body acceptance by their coaches, teammates, and other important people in their lives and was directly influenced by their appreciation of their own body. The results suggest that improving nonjudgmental awareness and appreciation of one's body – a target in typical mindful eating interventions – will facilitate healthy eating habits. It is necessary to determine whether mindful eating interventions actually translate to fewer eating disorder symptoms and fewer cases of amenorrhea or skeletal injuries in athletes. It seems prudent to recommend yoga, where there is no emphasis on winning or teammate competition. Past research on non-athletes determined that participation in yoga was connected with increased body acceptance and focus on body function (Prichard & Tiggemann, 2008), which would likely help athletes with eating disorders to decrease their overemphasis on body weight.

Mindfulness in the Treatment of Eating Disorders and Body Image Concerns

In my role as a clinical psychologist, I regularly use mindfulness-based interventions in my work with clients, many of whom are high-level athletes and dancers with poor body image or eating disorders. Increased mindfulness about eating, particularly nonjudgmental awareness of the emotions connected to and driving binge eating or restricting food intake, has been transformative for many of my clients. Eventually, they learn that they can (and should) eat when their body is hungry and that they can trust themselves to make a decision to stop when they are full.

Self-care and nurturance are themes that emerge in my work with performers. We reflect on their tendencies to ignore and suppress emotions with restricting or binging while also punishing themselves with purging or overexercise when they make mistakes. Mindfulness provides an opportunity to observe their negative thoughts and feelings, as well as habitual eating patterns, without an immediate requirement that they change them.

Clients typically find this approach nonthreatening, so they are more willing to follow through with treatment and are more willing later to discuss making changes. During treatment, I regularly employ Linehan's (1993) dialectical approach (described later in this section) when I ask my clients to simultaneously increase both self-acceptance and personal change. I also keep Kabat-Zinn's (2005) teachings in mind, which also emphasize the interplay between self-compassion and transformation.

My positive anecdotal experiences are supported by numerous studies on the effectiveness of mindfulness in clinical settings. One problem in comparing results from the available research on mindfulness interventions is that there are varied techniques used in the studies. For this reason, I will discuss results only regarding studies that implemented clearly defined approaches that incorporate mindfulness in the treatment of body image concerns and eating disorders, including Acceptance and Commitment Therapy, Dialectical Behavioral Therapy, Mindfulness Based Cognitive Therapy, and Mindfulness-Based Eating Awareness Training.

The main objectives in *Acceptance and Commitment Therapy* (ACT), developed by Hayes, Strosahl, and Wilson (1999), are to address clients' ineffective control strategies and tendencies toward emotional avoidance (i.e., attempts to suppress negative emotions). The treatment emphasizes nonjudgmental awareness and acceptance of one's current state. Through dialogue and exploration of metaphors, the client is asked to redirect energy from areas that are uncontrollable to those that are within the client's control. Eating disorder clients redirect focus from thinness toward healthier personal, career, or academic goals. ACT uses mindfulness to increase awareness and acceptance of "bothersome thoughts and feelings" (Heffner et al., 2002, p. 232) that were previously avoided or altered with food. The therapist normalizes the experience of both positive and negative emotions and trains the client to conceptualize emotions as temporary experiences that do not need to be avoided or labeled as "good" or "bad." An example of an ACT intervention, which counters emotional avoidance, is the chessboard metaphor. The client is asked to change perspective from one of the chess pieces participating (and losing) in the battle against "fat thoughts" (i.e., other pieces) to a perspective of the chessboard, a part in the game that never wins or loses but merely observes nonjudgmentally (Heffner et al., 2002).

Though small in number, research studies on the efficacy of ACT for eating disorders are convincing. The chessboard and other metaphors were utilized in a case study of a fifteen-year-old with anorexia, who showed significant decrease in cognitive symptoms and increased weight gain at the end of thirteen sessions of ACT (Heffner et al., 2002). Notably, in a randomized clinical trial, individual ACT was found to be significantly more effective than cognitive therapy in reducing eating pathology for participants with subclinical eating disorders (Juarascio, Forman, & Herbert, 2010). In the most comprehensive study to date, Juarascio and colleagues (2013) found that female inpatients in an ACT group showed greater reduction in overall eating pathology and in weight concern and were twice as likely to have moved into a nonclinical range than those in treatment as usual (TAU). Importantly, at six-month follow-up, those in the ACT group were less likely to be rehospitalized (3.5 percent) than those in TAU (18 percent).

Another effective treatment for eating disorders is *Dialectical Behavioral Therapy* (DBT), which was created by Marsha Linehan (1993) to treat borderline personality disorder and is now regularly used in eating disorder populations. The treatment is based on dialectical theory, which explains that multiple or opposing truths can exist at one time. For example, the therapist models dialectics when communicating acceptance of the client while also simultaneously encouraging the client to change. Standard DBT is delivered in both individual sessions and weekly two-hour manualized group skills sessions. The treatment is designed to address clients' emotion dysregulation and their lack of effective distress tolerance skills (e.g., binge eating to cope with emotions). DBT incorporates cognitive therapy elements such as challenging maladaptive thoughts, behavioral therapy concepts such as chain analysis, and mindfulness skills such as "radical acceptance" of the self and the present moment. Mindfulness is most emphasized in the group sessions, where clients observe urges to binge and gain awareness of impulsive tendencies to use food to blunt negative emotions. An important mindfulness intervention in DBT that employs dialectics is to use one's "Wise Mind," an intersection between one's impulsive "Emotional Mind" with one's intellectual and logical "Reasonable Mind," when faced with decisions or difficult interpersonal situations.

Research on the effectiveness of DBT, including a recent meta-analysis (Lenz et al., 2014), suggests that it is successful in reducing eating disorder symptoms. For example, in a recent randomized controlled study, participants in DBT reported faster reductions in binges than those in the comparison treatment (Safer, Robinson, & Jo, 2010). The use of DBT also appears effective in adolescents with bulimia (BN) and AN (Salbach-Andrae et al. Few studies have assessed the effectiveness of DBT in adult BN and AN populations that do not have other comorbid diagnoses;

currently, most studies also include participants with comorbid borderline personality disorder, which complicates interpretations of findings specific to eating symptoms. However, using participants with BN, Hill, Craighead, and Safer (2011) found fewer binge/purge episodes in adult participants after six weeks of DBT compared to those in a delayed treatment group. At post-treatment, 62 percent no longer met BN diagnostic criteria, and 27 percent had no binge/purge episodes.

Mindfulness Based Cognitive Therapy (MBCT) is another option for eating disorder treatment and is delivered in an eight-week manualized group format. The treatment is based on Kabat-Zinn's MBSR (1990) and has been most commonly used to treat depression. Like ACT and DBT, MBCT places strong emphasis on developing a nonjudgmental reaction to negative thoughts and cultivation of an attitude that such thoughts are temporary and changing and do not define the person (Segal, Williams, & Teasdale, 2002). It is of note that there is less emphasis in MBCT on changing negative thoughts than in typical cognitive therapy. Also, mindfulness training is typically general, with an emphasis on meditation rather than specific mindful eating skills (Baer, Fisher, & Huss, 2005a). MBCT reduced binge-eating episodes as well as concern about eating in both a BED case study (Baer et al., 2005a) and in a sample of ten women with clinical or subclinical BED (Baer, Fisher, & Huss, 2005b). Certainly, more research is needed to determine appropriate application of MBCT in treatment settings, particularly given the lack of research including BN and AN clients; however, initial results are positive.

Finally, the clinical treatment that most emphasizes specific mindful eating skills and directly addresses body shape concern is *Mindfulness-Based Eating Awareness Training* (MB-EAT; Kristeller & Hallett, 1999; Kristeller, & Wolever, 2011). This approach was developed for BED and focuses on increasing one's attention to hunger and satiety cues via eating-related guided meditations (e.g., the raisin exercise). The treatment also encourages awareness of mindless eating, using exercises that require mindful attention to food choices, as well as addresses binge eating with exercises that require eating a typical binge food (e.g., chips or cookies) mindfully or participating in a "potluck-style" meal (Kristeller & Wolever, 2011). The overall aim is to reduce eating driven by environment or social cues, by increasing sensitivity to physiological drives. MB-EAT, which can be implemented in nine to ten group sessions, also emphasizes personal forgiveness and encourages clients to believe that they have the wisdom to make healthy choices (Kristeller & Wolever, 2011).

Though only two studies have examined the efficacy of MB-EAT, initial evidence suggests that it is effective. Using a sample of middle-aged obese women with BED, Kristeller & Hallett (1999) found that after seven sessions of MB-EAT, the participants' average number of binges per week was significantly reduced, from 4 down to 1.6 episodes, and depression levels also decreased. Recently, a randomized clinical trial compared the effectiveness of twelve sessions of MB-EAT to twelve sessions of a psycho-educational cognitive behavioral intervention and a waitlist control for obese or overweight participants, the majority of whom had BED (Kristeller, Wolever, & Sheets, 2014). Remission rates were highest in the MB-EAT group, and 95 percent of those in MB-EAT who had been diagnosed with BED no longer met diagnostic criteria at four-month follow-up. Only 76 percent of those in the cognitive behavioral group were in remission, while only 48 percent of the waitlist control group had achieved remission. As expected, increased mindfulness practice was related to more weight loss for the MB-EAT group.

Overall, the four treatments for eating disorders that incorporate mindfulness show very promising results. It is of note that most of the research has been conducted in samples with binge eating as the primary symptom, with few studies on anorexia, though preliminary results in that population are still positive. Common elements of the four treatments include self-acceptance and nonreactive awareness of negative thoughts and emotions; as such, these elements are likely the most important aspect of mindfulness interventions for eating disorders. At present, we lack information to know how these treatment approaches would affect the eating concerns of elite athletes and performers, though one would expect the results would be positive.

Conclusion

In summary, mindless eating is common, influenced by consumption norms, and fueled by psychological, instead of physiological, factors (Somov, 2008; Wansink, 2004). Moreover, research on elite athletes' diets suggests that athletes lack essential nutrients (e.g., Mullinix et al., 2003) and do not typically eat in accordance with their physiological energy needs (e.g., Murphy & Jeanes, 2006). As such, it appears that athletes would benefit from mindful eating training, which emphasizes responding to hunger cues and has been shown to increase intake of fruits and vegetables (Gilbert & Waltz, 2010) as well as result in greater enjoyment of food (Hong et al., 2014).

In particular, athletes and performers may benefit from mindfulness as a way to address their unique body image concerns. Athletes experience general media pressure on body image, which is known to decrease body satisfaction (e.g., Birkeland et al., 2005), as well as performance pressure, coach pressure, teammate body comparisons, and pressure from revealing uniforms (Blacker et al., 2007; Krane, et al., 2004). These sport-specific pressures warrant attention, as they have been reported to influence the onset of eating disorders (Arthur-Cameselle & Quatromoni, 2010). A mindful or intuitive approach to eating that also cultivates awareness of sport pressures may shift athletes' focus from body shape toward body function, as has been found in non-athletes (Avalos & Tylka, 2006).

As previously described in detail, trait mindfulness and intuitive eating are associated with fewer eating disorder symptoms (e.g., Denny et al., 2013). Therefore, it is important to determine how to increase mindfulness effectively in performers who experience clinical eating disorders. Overall, treatments for eating disorders that incorporate mindfulness are effective for non-athletes. In addition, it appears that specific mindful eating training, rather than general mindfulness, is most useful in reducing overeating (Timmerman & Brown, 2012). Thus, Mindfulness Based-Eating Awareness Training (MB-EAT; Kristeller & Hallett, 1999) may be the best treatment for athletes with bulimia and binge eating disorder. At present, more research on treatments using mindfulness for those with anorexia are needed to determine whether performers and athletes with AN would benefit from their implementation.

It is possible that athletes and performers with body image or eating concerns would be more receptive to mindfulness interventions than typical talk therapy as a way to increase their food intake to meet draining demands or reduce overeating of nonnutritious foods. Most high-level athletes and performers have learned some form of relaxation training and are also aware of the importance of focusing on the present moment to enhance performance. Additionally, most performers have at some point tried yoga, which typically incorporates mindfulness. Thus, mindfulness exercises might serve as a good place to start for a treatment-resistant performer, as mindful eating may seem more familiar, and thus less threatening, than other interventions. Athletes and performers should also be encouraged to practice yoga more regularly, given findings that those who practice yoga report better body image and lower eating disorder symptoms than peers who do cardiovascular exercises (Martin et al., 2013).

Finally, research on mindful eating in elite athlete and performer populations is an additional important area for future exploration. Given the consistent correlations between mindful/intuitive eating and positive psychological functioning in non-athletes (e.g., Tylka & Kroon Van Diest, 2013) it is expected that athletes would similarly benefit from mindful approaches to food. However, studies that specifically target mindful eating are needed in order to substantiate claims that mindfulness can positively influence the eating behaviors, body image, and performance of elite athletes and performers.

Mindful Eating Application Exercises

Application Exercise #1: "The Raisin Exercise" (Adapted from Bays, 2011)

This activity requires that you eat a single raisin mindfully. It is often the first exercise in mindfulness programs such as MBSR because it is helps to reduce anxiety about meditation and counters preconceived notions that meditation is abstract or spiritual.

Start by taking a single raisin and placing it in your hand. Imagine that you are from another planet and have come to Earth for the first time. You have never seen or heard of a raisin. Investigate the raisin with each of your senses, as if it is the first time you have ever encountered one. Carefully appreciate its appearance and color. Slowly examine the texture with your fingers. Then take in the smell. Place it in your mouth and roll it around without chewing. Pay attention to what you notice first. Now you can bite the raisin one time only. Try to fully describe the taste. Continue to chew it slowly and note the changes in texture after several bites. After you swallow it, how long does the taste linger? What other sensations do you notice? How is this experience of mindful raisin eating similar to and different from other times you have eaten a raisin?

Application Exercise #2: Blind Tasting (Adapted from Somov, 2008)

When we look at foods we have tasted before, we automatically know what to expect, and "as soon as we know what to expect, we stop paying attention" (Somov, 2008, p. 81). To increase your mindful awareness, have someone put some foods into a container for you and while blindfolded, then take one out, not knowing what to expect. Notice how the experience of eating is fuller when you have no preconceived notions about flavors. How is this experience similar to or different from the way that you normally eat?

Application Exercise #3: Food Choice Log

For twenty-four hours, record the number of food decisions you make. In addition to what *you eat*, note when, where, *with* whom, *and* how much you eat. *What was your total daily number? What patterns in food choice do you notice? In what settings are you likely to under or over eat?*

Application Exercise #4: Increasing Mindfulness Habits

Now that you have a clear sense of the definition of mindful eating, how many times in the past week have you eaten truly mindfully, slowing down to appreciate all of your senses while focusing on nothing else but the food in front of you? If the answer is "zero," set a goal to eat one meal mindfully per week. If you have started to eat mindfully, set a goal to increase your mindful eating practice.

REFERENCES

American Psychiatric Association (APA). (2013). *Diagnostic and statistical manual of mental disorders* (5th ed.). Arlington, VA: American Psychiatric Publishing.

Arcelus, J., Witcomb, G. L., and Mitchell, A. (2014). Prevalence of eating disorders amongst dancers: A systemic review and meta-analysis. *European Eating Disorders Review*, 22(2), 92–101. doi: 10.1002/erv.2271

Arthur-Cameselle, J. N., and Quatromoni, P. A. (2010). Factors related to the onset of eating disorders reported by female collegiate athletes. *Sport Psychologist*, 25, 1–17.

Avalos, L. C., and Tylka, T. L. (2006). Exploring a model of intuitive eating with college women. *Journal of Counseling Psychology*, 53(4), 486–497. doi: 10.1037/0022-0167.53.4.486

Baer, R. A., Fischer, S., and Huss, D. B. (2005a). Mindfulness-Based Cognitive Therapy applied to binge eating: A case study. *Cognitive and Behavioral Practice*, 12(3), 351–358. doi: 10.1016/S1077-7229(05)80057-4

(2005b). Mindfulness and acceptance in the treatment of disordered eating. *Journal of Rational-Emotive and Cognitive-Behavior Therapy*, 23(4), 281–300. doi: 10.1007/s10942-005-0015-9

Bays, J. C. (2009). *Mindful eating: A guide to rediscovering a healthy and joyful relationship with food*. Boston, MA, US: Shambhala.

(2011). Mindful eating. In B. Boyce (Ed.), *The mindfulness revolution: Leading psychologists, scientists, artists, and meditation teachers on the power of mindfulness in daily life* (pp. 177–184). Boston, MA: Shambhala.

Beshara, M., Hutchinson, A. D., and Wilson, C. (2013). Does mindfulness matter? Everyday mindfulness, mindful eating and self-reported serving size of energy dense foods among a sample of South Australian adults. *Appetite*, 67(1), 25–29. doi: 10.1016/j.appet.2013.03.012

Birkeland, R., Thompson, J. K., Herbozo, S., Roehrig, M., Cafri, G., and van den Berg, P. (2005). Media exposure, mood, and body image dissatisfaction: An experimental test of person versus product priming. *Body Image*, 2(1), 53–61. doi: 10.1016/j.bodyim.2004.11.002

Blacker, K., Drake, R., Reed, A., Almeida, J., and Raudenbush, B. (2007). Body image satisfaction among intercollegiate female athletes using a scale of muscularity. *Appetite*, 49(1), 279. doi: 10.1016/j.appet.2007.03.035

Bratland-Sanda, S., and Sundgot-Borgen, J. (2013). Eating disorders in athletes: Overview of prevalence, risk factors and recommendations for prevention and treatment. *European Journal Of Sport Science*, 13(5), 499–508. doi: 10.1080/17461391.2012.740504

Buell, J. L., Calland, D., Hanks, F., Johnston, B., Pester, B., Sweeney, R., and Thorne, R. (2008). Presence of metabolic syndrome in football linemen. *Journal of Athletic Training*, 43(6), 608–616. doi: 10.4085/1062-6050-43.6.608

Cabral Costa, C. A., Paizao Rosado, G., Osorio Silva, C. H., and Bousas Marins, J. C. (2006). Diagnosis of the nutritional status of the weight lifting permanent Olympic team of the Brazilian Olympic Committee. *Review of Brazilian Sports Medicine*, 12(6), 308e–312e.

Cole, C. R., Salvaterra, G. F., Davis, J. E., Borja, M. E., Powell, L. M., Dubbs, E. C., and Bordi P. L. (2005) Effectiveness of the evaluation of dietary practices of National Collegiate Athletic Association Division I football players. *Journal of Strength Conditioning Research*, 19(3): 490–494. doi: 10.1519/14313.1

Denny, K. N., Loth, K., Eisenberg, M. E., and Neumark-Sztainer, D. (2013). Intuitive eating in young adults: Who is doing it, and how is it related to disordered eating behaviors? *Appetite*, 60(1), 13–19. doi: 10.1016/j.appet.2012.09.029

DiPasquale, L. D., and Petrie, T. A. (2013). Prevalence of disordered eating: A comparison of male and female collegiate athletes and nonathletes. *Journal of Clinical Sport Psychology*, 7(3), 186–197.

Framson, C., Kristal, A. R., Schenk, J. M., Littman, A. J., Zeliadt, S., and Benitez, D. (2009). Development and validation of the Mindful Eating Questionnaire. *Journal of the American Dietetic Association*, 109(8), 1439–1444. doi: 10.1016/j.jada.2009.05.006

Galli, N., Petrie, T. A., Reel, J. J., Chatterton, J. M., and Baghurst, T. M. (2014). Assessing the validity of the Weight Pressures in Sport Scale for male athletes. *Psychology of Men and Masculinity*, 15(2), 170–180. doi: 10.1037/a0031762

Galli, N., and Reel, J. J. (2009). Adonis or Hephaestus? Exploring body image in male athletes. *Psychology of Men and Masculinity*, 10(2), 95–108. doi: 10.1037/a0014005

Gilbert, D., and Waltz, J. (2010). Mindfulness and health behaviors. *Mindfulness*, 1(4), 227–234. doi: 10.1007/s12671-010-0032-3

Hanh, T. N., and Cheung, L. (2010). *Savor: Mindful eating, mindful life.* San Francisco, CA: HarperOne/HarperCollins.

Hausenblas, H. A., and Downs, D. S. (2001). Comparison of body image between athletes and nonathletes: A meta-analytic review. *Journal of Applied Sport Psychology,* 13(3), 323–339. doi: 10.1080/104132001753144437

Hayes, S. C., Strosahl, K. D., and Wilson, K. G. (1999). *Acceptance and Commitment Therapy: An experiential approach to behavior change.* New York, NY: Guilford Press.

Heffner, M., Sperry, J., Eifert, G. H., and Detweiler, M. (2002). Acceptance and Commitment Therapy in the treatment of an adolescent female with anorexia nervosa: A case example. *Cognitive and Behavioral Practice,* 9(3), 232–236. doi: 10.1016/S1077-7229(02)80053-0

Hill, D. M., Craighead, L. W., and Safer, D. L. (2011). Appetite-Focused Dialectical Behavior Therapy for the treatment of binge eating with purging: A preliminary trial. *International Journal of Eating Disorders,* 44(3), 249–261. doi: 10.1002/eat.20812

Hong, P. Y., Lishner, D. A., and Han, K. H. (2014). Mindfulness and eating: An experiment examining the effect of mindful raisin eating on the enjoyment of sampled food. *Mindfulness,* 5(1), 80–87. doi: 10.1007/s12671-012-0154-x

Juarascio, A. S., Forman, E. M., and Herbert, J. D. (2010). Acceptance and Commitment Therapy versus Cognitive Therapy for the treatment of comorbid eating pathology. *Behavior Modification,* 34(2), 175–190. doi: 10.1177/0145445510363472

Juarascio, A. S., Shaw, J., Forman, E. M., Timko, C., Herbert, J. D., Butryn, M., ... Lowe, M. (2013). Acceptance and Commitment Therapy as a novel treatment for eating disorders: An initial test of efficacy and mediation. *Behavior Modification,* 37(4), 459–489. doi: 10.1177/0145445513478633

Kabat-Zinn, J. (1990). *Full catastrophe living: Using the wisdom of your body and mind to face stress, pain, and illness.* New York, NY: Delacorte.

(2005). *Wherever you go, there you are: Mindfulness meditation in everyday life.* New York, NY: Hyperion.

Kearney, D., Milton, M., Malte, C., McDermott, K., Martinew, M., and Simpson, T. (2012). Participation in mindfulness-based stress reduction is not associated with reductions in emotional eating or uncontrolled eating. *Nutrition Research,* 32(6), 413–420. doi: 10.1016/j.nutres.2012.05.008

Krane, V., Choi, P. L., Baird, S. M., Aimar, C. M., and Kauer, K. J. (2004). Living the paradox: Female athletes negotiate femininity and muscularity. *Sex Roles,* 50(5–6), 315–329. doi: 10.1023/B:SERS.0000018888.48437.4f

Kristeller, J. L. (2003). Mindfulness, wisdom, and eating: Applying a multi-domain model of meditation effects. *Constructivism in the Human Sciences,* 8(2), 107–118.

Kristeller, J. L., and Hallett, C. B. (1999). An exploratory study of a meditation-based intervention for binge eating disorder. *Journal of Health Psychology,* 4(3), 357–363. doi: 10.1177/135910539900400305

Kristeller, J. L., and Wolever, R. Q. (2011). Mindfulness-based eating awareness training for treating binge eating disorder: The conceptual foundation. *Eating Disorders: The Journal of Treatment and Prevention*, 19(1), 49–61. doi: 10.1080/10640266.2011.533605

Kristeller, J., Wolever, R. Q., and Sheets, V. (2014). Mindfulness-Based Eating Awareness Training (MB-EAT) for binge eating: A randomized clinical trial. *Mindfulness*, 5(3), 282–297. doi: 10.1007/s12671-012-0179-1

Lavender, J. M., Gratz, K. L., and Anderson, D. A. (2012). Mindfulness, body image, and drive for muscularity in men. *Body Image*, 9(2), 289–292. doi: 10.1016/j.bodyim.2011.12.002

Lenz, A., Taylor, R., Fleming, M., and Serman, N. (2014). Effectiveness of Dialectical Behavior Therapy for treating eating disorders. *Journal of Counseling and Development*, 92(1), 26–35. doi: 10.1002/j.1556-6676.2014.00127.x

Linehan, M. M. (1993). *Cognitive-behavioral treatment of borderline personality disorder*. New York: Guilford Press.

Malinauskas B. M., Overton R. F., Cucchiara A. J., Carpenter, A. B., and Corbett, A. B. (2007). Summer league college baseball players: Do dietary intake and barriers to healthy eating differ between game and non-game days? *Sport Management and Related Topics Journal*, 3(2), 23–34.

Martin, R., Prichard, I., Hutchinson, A. D., and Wilson, C. (2013). The role of body awareness and mindfulness in the relationship between exercise and eating behavior. *Journal of Sport and Exercise Psychology*, 35(6), 655–660.

Martinsen M., and Sundgot-Borgen, J. (2013). Higher prevalence of eating disorders among adolescent elite athletes than controls. *Medicine and Science in Sports and Exercise*, 45(6), 1188–1197. doi: 10.1249/MSS.0b013e318281a939

Matsumoto, R., Kitabayashi, Y., Narumoto, J., Wada, Y., Okamoto, A., Ushijima, Y. . . . Fukui, K. (2006). Regional cerebral blood flow changes associated with interoceptive awareness in the recovery process of anorexia nervosa. *Progress in Neuro-Psychopharmacology and Biological Psychiatry*, 30, 1265–1270. doi: 10.1016/j.pnpbp.2006.03.042

McCabe, M. P., and Ricciardelli, L. A. (2004). Body image dissatisfaction among males across the lifespan: A review of past literature. *Journal of Psychosomatic Research*, 56(6), 675–685. doi: 10.1016/S0022-3999(03)00129-6

Moor, K. R., Scott, A. J., and McIntosh, W. D. (2013). Mindful eating and its relationship to body mass index and physical activity among university students. *Mindfulness*, 4(3), 269–274. doi: 10.1007/s12671-012-0124-3

Mullinix, M. C., Jonnalagadda, S. S., Rosenbloom, C. A., Thompson, W. R., and Kicklighter, J. R. (2003). Dietary intake of female U.S. soccer players. *Nutrition Research*, 23(5), 585–593. doi: 10.1016/S0271-5317(03)00003-4

Murphy, S., and Jeanes, Y. (2006). Nutritional knowledge and dietary intakes of young professional football players. *Nutrition and Food Science*, 36(5), 343–348. doi: 10.1108/00346650610703199

Neff, K. D. (2003). Self-compassion: An alternative conceptualization of a healthy attitude toward oneself. *Self and Identity*, 2(2), 85–101. doi: 10.1080/15298860309032

Oh, K., Wiseman, M. C., Hendrickson, J., Phillips, J. C., and Hayden, E. W. (2012). Testing the acceptance model of intuitive eating with college women athletes. *Psychology Of Women Quarterly*, 36(1), 88–98. doi: 10.1177/0361684311433282

Papadopoulou, S. D., Papadopoulou, S. K., Vamvakoudis, E., and Tsitkaris, G. (2008). Comparison of nutritional intake between volleyball and basketball women athletes of the Olympic national teams. *Gazetta Medica Italiana – Archivio Per Le Scienze Mediche*, 167(4), 147–152.

Pawlak, R., Malinauskas, B., and Rivera, D. (2009). Predicting intentions to eat a healthful diet by college baseball players: Applying the Theory of Planned Behavior. *Journal of Nutrition Education and Behavior*, 41(5), 334–339. doi: 10.1016/j.jneb.2008.09.008

Prichard, I., andTiggemann, M. (2008). Relations among exercise type, self-objectification, and body image in the fitness centre environment: The role of reasons for exercise. *Psychology of Sport and Exercise*, 9(6), 855–866. doi: 10.1016/j.psychsport.2007.10.005

Reel, J. J., Petrie, T. A., SooHoo, S., and Anderson, C. M. (2013). Weight pressures in sport: Examining the factor structure and incremental validity of the weight pressures in sport – females. *Eating Behaviors*, 14(2), 137–144. doi: 10.1016/j.eatbeh.2013.01.003

Reel, J. J., SooHoo, S., Doetsch, H., Carter, J. E., and Petrie, T. A. (2007). The female athlete triad: Is the triad a problem among Division I female athletes? *Journal of Clinical Sport Psychology*, 1(4), 358–370.

Ridgeway, R. T., and Tylka, T. L. (2005). College men's perceptions of ideal body composition and shape. *Psychology of Men and Masculinity*, 6(3), 209–220. doi: 10.1037/1524-9220.6.3.209

Rozin, P., Fischler, C. C., Imada, S. S., Sarubin, A. A., and Wrzesniewski, A. A. (1999). Attitudes to food and the role of food in life in the U.S.A., Japan, Flemish Belgium and France: Possible implications for the diet-health debate. *Appetite*, 33(2), 163–180. doi: 10.1006/appe.1999.0244

Safer, D. L., Robinson, A. H., and Jo, B. (2010). Outcome from a randomized controlled trial of group therapy for BED: Comparing DBT adapted for binge eating to an active comparison group therapy. *Behavior Therapy*, 41(1), 106–120. doi: http://dx.doi.org/10.1016/j.beth.2009.01.006

Salbach-Andrae, H., Bohnekamp, I., Pfeiffer, E., Lehmkuhl, U., and Miller, A. L. (2008). Dialectical behavior therapy of anorexia and bulimia nervosa among adolescents: A case series. *Cognitive and Behavioral Practice*, 15(4), 415–425. doi: 10.1016/j.cbpra.2008.04.001

Salmon, P., Lush, E., Jablonski, M., and Sephton, S. E. (2009). Yoga and mindfulness: Clinical aspects of an ancient mind/body practice. *Cognitive and Behavioral Practice*, 16(1), 59–72. doi: 10.1016/j.cbpra.2008.07.002

Segal, Z. V., Williams, J. G., and Teasdale, J. D. (2002). *Mindfulness-based cognitive therapy for depression: A new approach to preventing relapse.* New York, NY: Guilford Press.

Shriver, L. H., Betts, N. M., and Wollenberg, G. (2013). Dietary intakes and eating habits of college athletes: Are female college athletes following the current sports nutrition standards? *Journal of American College Health*, 61(1), 10–16. doi: 10.1080/07448481.2012.747526

Smart, L., and Bisogni, C. A. (2001). Personal food systems of male college hockey players. *Appetite*, 37(1), 57–70. doi: 10.1006/appc.2001.0408

Smolak, L., Murnen, S. K., and Ruble, A. E. (2000). Female athletes and eating problems: A meta-analysis. *International Journal of Eating Disorders*, 27(4), 371–280.

Somov, P. G. (2008). *Eating the moment: 141 mindful practices to overcome overeating one meal at a time.* Oakland, CA: New Harbinger.

Striegel-Moore, R. H., Rosselli, F., Perrin, N., DeBar, L., Wilson, G. T., May, A., and Kraemer, H. C. (2009). Gender differences in the prevalence of eating disorder symptoms. *International Journal of Eating Disorders*, 42, 471–474. doi: http://dx.doi.org/10.1002/eat.20625

Timmerman, G. M., and Brown, A. (2012). The effect of a mindful restaurant eating intervention on weight management in women. *Journal of Nutrition Education and Behavior*, 44(1), 22–28. doi: 10.1016/j.jneb.2011.03.143

Tribole, E., and Resch, E. (1995). *Intuitive eating: A recovery book for the chronic dieter.* New York, NY: St. Martin's Press.

Tylka, T. L., and Kroon Van Diest, A. M. (2013). The Intuitive Eating Scale–2: Item refinement and psychometric evaluation with college women and men. *Journal of Counseling Psychology*, 60(1), 137–153. doi: 10.1037/a0030893

Tylka, T. L., and Wilcox, J. A. (2006). Are intuitive eating and eating disorder symptomatology opposite poles of the same construct? *Journal of Counseling Psychology*, 53(4), 474–485. doi: 10.1037/0022-0167.53.4.474

Ulmer, C. S., Stetson, B. A., and Salmon, P. G. (2010). Mindfulness and acceptance are associated with exercise maintenance in YMCA exercisers. *Behaviour Research and Therapy*, 48(8), 805–809. doi: 10.1016/j.brat.2010.04.009

Varnes, J. R., Stellefson, M. L., Janelle, C. M., Dorman, S. M., Dodd, V., and Miller, M. D. (2013). A systematic review of studies comparing body image concerns among female college athletes and non-athletes, 1997–2012. *Body Image*, 10(4), 421–432. doi: 10.1016/j.bodyim.2013.06.001

Wansink, B. (2004). Environmental factors that increase the food intake and consumption volume of unknowing consumers. *Annual Review of Nutrition*, 24(1), 455–479. doi: 10.1146/annurev.nutr.24.012003.132140

Wansink, B., and Kim, J. (2005). Bad popcorn in big buckets: Portion size can influence intake as much as taste. *Journal of Nutrition Education and Behavior*, 37(5), 242–245. doi: 10.1016/S1499-4046(06)60278-9

Wansink, B., and Sobal, J. (2007). Mindless eating: The 200 daily food decisions we overlook. *Environment and Behavior*, 39(1), 106–123. doi: 10.1177/0013916506295573

Whiteside, U., Chen, E., Neighbors, C., Hunter, D., Lo, T., and Larimer, M. (2007). Difficulties regulating emotions: Do binge eaters have fewer strategies to modulate and tolerate negative affect? *Eating Behaviors*, 8(2), 162–169. doi: 10.1016/j.eatbeh.2006.04.001

Wildes, J. E., Ringham, R. M., and Marcus, M. D. (2010). Emotion avoidance in patients with anorexia nervosa: Initial test of a functional model. *International Journal of Eating Disorders*, 43(5), 398–404. doi: 10.1002/eat.20730

Yamamiya, Y., Cash, T. F., Melnyk, S. E., Posavac, H. D., and Posavac, S. S. (2005). Women's exposure to thin-and-beautiful media images: Body image effects of media-ideal internalization and impact-reduction interventions. *Body Image*, 2(1), 74–80. doi: 10.1016/j.bodyim.2004.11.001

Mindfulness and the Performing Arts

CHAPTER 15

Langerian Mindfulness and Optimal Performance

Amy L. Baltzell, Trevor A. Cote

What it takes to optimize sport performance remains a mystery. A Langerian mindfulness approach, an untapped approach to facilitating optimal sport performance, may be an answer for the well-trained athlete to perform his or her best in the present (i.e., *moment to moment*) in both practice and competition. Pathways to help athletes optimize performance within the sport psychology literature are predominantly past- and future-based. The majority of such interventions are focused on helping athletes cope with sport-related anxiety, to re-create past best performance states and to replicate precursors to flow (a fully engaged, autotelic experience). Mental skills training (e.g., self-talk cues, imagery) is used to help the athlete practice re-creating past experiences in the hopes of reexperiencing (such optimal past scenarios) in the future performances.

There remains little guidance, within the academic sport psychology literature, in terms of what the athlete should focus on in the moment beyond sport psychologists urging athletes to focus on sport-relevant cues. And such emphasis for athletes, on sport-relevant cues, relies heavily on *what it was like before* in a best performance or a focus on general, static cues (e.g., tennis players keeping their eye on the ball; long-distance runners tuning into the rhythm of running when the pain sets in). Although often effective, that approach seems to be forgetting a fundamental aspect of performance.

The problem, of course, is that each practice and each performance is unique. Athletes are never exactly *now* as they *were*, and, of course, the environment, conditions, expectations, and competitors are never exactly as they *were*. This chapter will provide an understanding of how a Langerian mindfulness approach to sport psychology consulting could augment the typical approach to helping athletes optimize performance and provide a direct pathway to enhancing performance by noticing novelty within sport- and performance-relevant cues to help create flow (fully engaged experiences) and augment concentration in the moment-to-moment experience.

Many years ago, I had the joy of having Gregorio Di Leo, world-class Italian kickboxer, in one of my graduate sport psychology courses. He asked a question once that has remained seared in my memory. After many lectures on talking about what helps an athlete optimize performance, including lectures on goal setting, visualization, arousal regulation, and self-talk (intrapersonal intentional, often scripted self-statements), he passionately asked, "How do I know what my best performance looks or feels like? Maybe I haven't had it yet." I was stumped. I vividly recall the visceral disappointment in my professional self that immediately joined the undeniable truth that I had no answer to his question. How can an athlete visualize a performance that he or she has yet to have? An athlete could guess at what a better performance would look like and feel like. But how would they know if that imaginal experience was the right and best possible pathway to success? My mind rapidly reviewed my mental files of sport psychology theory and research. When no answer emerged, I searched my memories from my own experience as a professional and Olympic athlete. Again, I came up with no answer.

Naively, I expected that a world-class kickboxer would know what his best performance *looked* or *felt* like. And he did. He knew what it looked like, in past tense. But did not know what it should be like at each moment, when considering the many changing external (e.g., sparring partners) and internal (his own optimal ability in any given moment) factors. Honestly, as a neophyte professor, I was looking to him for practical, applied answers. I assumed that given that he *had* so many great experiences that he would know what he would want to experience optimally in the future, based on past experience. Yet, Gregorio was well ahead of me. He was not interested in what occurred in the past. He wanted to know how to create optimal performance, moment-to-moment performance on the kickboxing mat.

Langerian Mindfulness and Musicians

In 2009, Ellen Langer and colleagues (Langer, Russell, & Eisenkraft, 2009) conducted a series of two studies with an orchestra that offers answers on how to create never-before-experienced performances. They also offer initial evidence that creating that which has not been experienced is preferred to re-creating past best performance. Unfortunately, during the time with Gregorio these studies had yet to occur, and therefore the important implications for sport psychology research and practice were not yet available. First, essential to discussion and implication of these studies is Ellen Langer's definition of mindfulness:

> [Mindfulness is] the process of drawing novel distinctions. It does not matter whether what is noticed is important or trivial, as long as it is new to the viewer. Actively drawing these distinctions keeps us situated in the present. It also makes us more aware of the context and perspective of our actions than if we rely upon distinctions and categories drawn in the past (Langer & Moldoveanu, 2000, pp. 1–2).

This definition offers a basic understanding of Langerian mindfulness, being intentionally aware of novelty.

When applying Langerian mindfulness to performance in the orchestra studies, Langer and colleagues (2009) prompted a more specific focus. They asked participants to focus on novelty within the constraints of their performance. In study 1, Langer and colleagues (2009) selected sixty orchestra players, a group of performers who were highly skilled and well practiced at the task. Many of the orchestra musicians had performed the same score of music hundreds of times per year. For the intervention, to prompt a performance-focused Langerian mindfulness approach, the musicians were instructed to notice novelty within the musical expression of Brahms' Symphony No. 1: play in the "finest manner you can, offering subtle new nuances to your performance" (p. 127).

The subtle nuance was focused on the creation of music and thus did not prompt musicians to notice *any* novel stimuli. (This point will be critical when considering the application to Langerian mindfulness to sport performance.) What is of particular importance in the design of these studies was that the orchestra players were prompted to draw of novel distinctions within a *boundaried, task-specific focus*. The musicians were not noticing trivial experience, but novelty that was directly related to creating music.

For the control condition, consistent with what athletes are encouraged to do by well-trained sport psychologists, the musicians were prompted to "think about the finest performance of this piece that you can remember, and try to play it" (p. 127). From a sport psychology perspective, the musicians in the control group would be expected to perform better. The study was conducted in front of an audience for the purposes of exploring which version of Brahms' Symphony No. 1 was preferred, a clever way to assess performance.

The results were not in line with what one trained in sport psychology would expect. The Langerian mindfulness intervention, focusing on subtle nuances in performance compared to re-creating a past best performance, was preferred by the orchestral musicians. The musicians reported more enjoyment performing while intentionally focusing on novel distinctions of their musical piece. In addition, the majority of the 126-person audience also preferred the mindfulness performance.

In the follow-up, study 2, similar results emerged for both a preference of the mindfulness piece for both orchestra musicians and the audience while controlling for practice effects and the order in which the pieces were presented to the listeners/audience. For both studies, focusing on novelty, not re-creating best performance, ultimately resulted in preferred performance in terms of quality of music created and the quality of the musician's experience (enjoyment). Langer referred to the control versions as the uninspired, robotic, preprogrammed approach. Re-creating past, preprogrammed experience may perhaps be just what sport psychology has been encouraging elite and highly skilled athletes to do for the past three decades.

The orchestra study provides evidence that Langerian mindfulness can offer a practical, specific, moment-to-moment, external focus that helps the highly skilled performers be more creative, improve the quality of their internal experience, and manifest enhanced performance. This study highlights a call for highly skilled performers to be open to neoteric, moment-to-moment sport engagement. This call is in contrast to sport psychology interventions that emphasize re-creating specific (robotic) thoughts, feelings, and ways of being in performance. Clearly the musicians were relying on well-learned skills and, at once, creating novelty within their musical performance.

Being well prepared for performance is, of course, important. However, focusing only on what is well learned may at times encourage mindless performance. Such preprogrammed psychological approaches may in fact thwart best performance. Langer (2000) describes a mindless state: when in a mindless state, "We act like automatons who have been programmed to act according to the sense our behavior made in the past, rather than the present" (p. 220). Such mindless preparation may lead to robotic engagement in which the athlete is applying an unwarranted previous mindset to current moment-to-moment sport performance.

When applying a Langerian mindfulness approach to performance the musicians in the orchestra study both performed better and experienced more enjoyment while performing. The musicians enjoying Langerian mindfulness prompted performances is noteworthy. Theory and research based on Barbara Fredrickson's *Broaden and Build Theory of Positive Emotion* (Fredrickson, 2003; Fredrickson et al., 2008) indicate that when people experience positive emotion, they tend to become more engaged, creative, and open-minded and persist longer in their moment-to-moment experience. They are more open to learning, and their intuition and creativity increase. Expansion of individual choice of what to do in the moment-to-moment experience occurs, in terms of novel thought and possible behaviors. Thus, bringing Langerian mindfulness to sport may be a practical way to cultivate enjoyment by helping the athletes have an enhanced inner quality of experience and, concurrently, helping enhance performance.

Background: Focus on "What Was" in Sport Psychology Interventions

In contrast to the Langerian mindfulness approach, focusing on past best performances is precisely what is emphasized in applied sport psychology. Psychological skills (e.g., goal setting, visualization) are used to help athletes re-create past best performances or create performances in their imagination that they think would create never-before experienced optimal performance. The sport psychologists and athletes search cues from the past that they hope will propel a future optimal performance.

Toward this end, Yuri Hanin, internationally respected Russian sport psychologist, brought to bear the notion of idiosyncratic patterns of emotions associated with optimal sport experience. His idea of Individualized Optimal Zone of Functioning (IZOF) hypothesis expanded the ideas within the young field of sport psychology that all athletes needed to be at a moderate level of physical/psychological arousal to optimize performance. Such notions were based on hypothesized two-dimensional relationship between arousal and performance. The first model, which has received little support, was the Drive theory, which represents a linear relationship between arousal and performance. The inverted U hypothesis, the model that was relied upon heavily prior to the inception of the IZOF model, represents an increase in arousal and performance concurrently up to an optimal level of arousal. As arousal levels increased beyond this point, performance was expected to decrease proportionally (Hanton, Millalieu, & Williams, 2015).

Hanin's then–cutting-edge research began with providing evidence that, in fact, there was a range of idiosyncratic state anxiety levels related to optimal sport performance per athlete. More recently, Hanin posits in the IZOF theory that there are clusters, or patterns, of both negatively and positively toned emotions that are associated with optimal sport performance per athlete (Hanin, 2000). Once the sport psychologists help the individual athlete understand the idiosyncratic cluster of emotions, the goal is to help the athlete re-create the unique cluster of negatively and positively toned emotions to help prepare the athlete for best performance. Research indicates that when athletes are within their IZOF, the individualized optimal pattern of emotions, they are more successful than those who are not (e.g., Pellizzari, Bertollo, & Robazza, 2011). Such patterns of optimal emotions are also unique across contexts per athlete. For example, different patterns of optimal emotions emerged for cross-country skiers for racing, endurance training, and technical training (Hanin & Syrja, 2000).

Once the IZOF is identified, through self-reflection and retrospection, sport psychologists prompt and guide athletes to re-create such personally ideal states, reflecting individualized combinations of emotions, through the use of mental skills such as using imagery scripts, listening to selected music to evoke a particular emotional response, or implementing self-talk (intrapersonal) cues to prompt the predetermined emotional patterns. Though such approaches are considered efficacious, it is possible that a focus on what is fresh and new could help some performers perform even better than re-creating past ideal mental, emotional states.

Langerian mindfulness offers a literal fresh approach to interacting with the performance environment. A Langerian approach may be just what is needed in helping expert performers move from rote, well-learned habitual approaches on performance day to an enlivened, fresh, vital approach to well-learned movements, strategies, and competitive approaches. Langerian mindfulness, conceptualized as making novel distinctions, is expected to improve focus, presence, and openness to novelty on the athletic field. Langerian mindfulness integrated with current approaches in sport psychology may be the best route in helping athletes optimize performance.

Integrating Langerian Mindfulness with Traditional Mental Skills Training

One living example of integrating Langerian mindfulness in performance as a framework, with traditional sport psychology skills, is the consulting work of Gregorio Di Leo. Fast-forward ten years – after winning five world championships in kickboxing – he now is an international business and performance-focused consultant who (unknowingly) brings a Langerian approach to his practice. What does he do to help his clients attain peak performance?

"Express at your best" is the goal. Di Leo urges clients to be aware that each day they begin at a different point. The approach calls for a fresh presence to themselves, holistically (e.g., biologically, mentally, and socially), and to bring that same fresh awareness to the specific challenges and opportunities they face each day. The goal is to reach one's best training performance daily. He urges clients to "Go home knowing that you have done your best." How is this achieved? He summarizes (G. Di Leo, personal communication, October 30, 2014):

1. ***"Know your starting point.*** Know how are you *today* physically, mentality, and emotionally. Know teammates or training partners. Be aware of what your coach will ask. Be aware of the environment and contextual conditions."

Di Leo calls for his clients to be willing to see both their internal and external environment for what it is. He encourages them to be open and to adjust to new places of beginning each day (such as from feeling exhausted or irritated to noticing a determination to give full effort).

2. ***"Set SMART goals.*** With this information, set SMART (specific, measurable, adjustable, realistic, and time sensitive) goals. Consider the best you can do that day. Visualize it, that day."

Here Di Leo integrates the basic mental skills. He asks clients to set daily goals that are specific and measurable. For that day, he asks that they set realistic goals. For example, if the runner can typically run a six-minute pace for ten miles but feels particularly sore from the weight lifting session the day before, Di Leo would prompt the athletes to set a slower pace. He would want the athlete to set a realistic goal for the day and know at what time, and for how long, the athlete will engage in a particular task. Such daily, specific goal-achievement strategies help the individual create an intention to be fully focused and stretch his or her capacity for the given day.

3. ***"Adjust and create.*** Adjust and create your best psychological and emotional mindset, social interactions, and physical performance."

In the next phase, Di Leo is calling for a Langerian mindfulness approach. It is not enough to replicate what one thinks is optimal. It is important to be aware, moment to moment, such that subtle changes in factors such as attention, effort, and intention can be adjusted as needed with the goal of optimally practicing and competing.

4. ***"Continuously adjust.*** During each session, continuously adjust all of this."

5. *"Conduct a post-training analysis.* Consider how you performed.
    Where could you do better in the first four steps? Visualize what went
    well and what did not go well. Fix what did not go well in your mind.
    Intentionally, with thinking and imagery, store the 'good stuff'."

In the last step, Di Leo again incorporates a cultivating awareness, a commitment to creating one's best and a willingness to be engaged in ongoing
creation of best performance.

Di Leo's call for *adaptation* is key to his approach. Instead of mindlessly
remaining stuck in trying to do it *like one did*, in one's past best moment,
Di Leo calls both to keep in mind what one wants to achieve and how one
wants to achieve it while constantly making adjustments – which reflects a
Langerian mindful approach to moment-to-moment experience such that
one is fully and optimally engaged with one's performance environment.

Di Leo emphasizes both adapting and getting into one's IZOF (one's
pattern of optimal emotions) for both performance and training. Every day
training and performance is approached in the same way. "Express(ing)
yourself at your best in competition will then be much easier because you
will just adapt and visualize the best you can following the same principles." The essence to his approach is helping clients cultivate a habit of
adaptation to whatever is occurring. This flexibility disallows the client to
rely on what was, "doing it the way I did it," to succeed. Di Leo concludes,
"Great athletes, they train to adapt every day. Not just when they compete.
That's not enough." And with the adaptation, it allows the individual to
experience "a total feeling of presence" and "flow state." Such a state allows
the individual to at once be aligned with past, present, and future all at
once. And as a decorated multiple world champion, he recalls:

> Step on the mat for a World Championship focusing only in the things that
> really matter for what you have to do in the 3 dimensions (past, present, and
> future) is one of the most amazing feelings you can experience in life. I will
> always be grateful to fighting for making me discover there is much more to
> discover. And it just inside myself" (G. Di Leo, personal communication,
> November 2, 2014).

Di Leo points to what happens in performance when he comes to the
performance with readiness to adapt, a readiness to be open moment to
moment to experience while keeping in awareness what was, what is, and
what will be. In many ways, this description points to, and in fact De Leo
identifies, the flow state: the enigmatic experience that all performers
desire, hope for, and trust is aligned with an ever-changing moment-to-
moment experience of optimal sport performance.

Flow

The concept of flow has become a cornerstone to models of happiness and well-being in positive psychology (Compton & Hoffman, 2013) and, at once, closely aligned with optimal performance in sport psychology (Jackson & Csikszentmihalyi, 1999). Mihaly Csikszentmihalyi (1975) first introduces the idea of flow in his book *Beyond Boredom and Anxiety*. After interviewing a wide range of performers, from rock-climbers to chess players, he developed a model of enjoyment entitled the *flow model*. All interviewees reflected on an autotelic experience that offered a unique, particularly extraordinary experience in which they engaged in their selected activity for intrinsic rewards, for the inherent enjoyment of the activity itself. (He initially entitled such experience of full engagement *autotelic*, though he changed the term to *flow* given that some of the activities also, at once, offered extrinsic rewards.)

Flow occurs when challenge meets skills, more specifically when perceived opportunities for action (e.g., the opportunity to race in the finals at an Olympic Games) match the individual's capabilities (e.g., having the physical fitness and tactical experience to be competitive in the given race at the Olympic Games). Csikszentmihalyi (1999) defines flow as "a particular kind of experience that is so engrossing and enjoyable that it becomes autotelic, that is, worth doing for its own sake even though it may have no consequence outside itself" (p. 824). He was most interested in what was enjoyable moment to moment for the individual in highly engaging experiences, in contrast to people (mindlessly) being lost in the past or caught up in future rewards. Flow state represents a particular type of happiness, a state of complete absorption that requires full attention to the task at hand. Requisite to flow is that the skills of the actor are stretched to full capacity.

Full engagement with present-moment experience is a hallmark of flow. Yet how can a well-learned task be challenging (stretch the capacity) of a master chess player playing his one thousandth match or a world-renown artist painting her one thousandth painting? It may be a matter of choice. For the flow state, by definition, the activity at hand is autotelic in nature – meaning the activity is enjoyable to the individual. Given this, it may be much more likely that when engaged in activities one truly enjoys that there is more of a propensity to remain fully engaged simply because the activity is compelling. For example, the runner who loves running looks for the state that supports optimal, rhythmic speed or the tennis player who is fully present to hit and place the ball as well as possible. Full attention and presence are requisite for athletes to play as well as they can.

Primarily precursors to flow and descriptors of the flow experience have emerged from the research on flow within performance settings. Susan Jackson's (1992) study was the first to consider flow specifically in sport. Through a study of figure skaters, Jackson found three generalizable flow antecendents, including having a *positive mental attitude, positive precompetitive and competitive affect*, and *maintaining appropriate focus*. After other studies of flow in sport, Jackson also wrote *Flow in Sport* with Csikszentmihalyi (1999), which provided ample evidence that a wide range of top athletes experience flow states, reported experiences that directly align with Csikszentmihalyi's Flow Model. More recently, Jackson (2012) provided a summary of what it takes to prompt flow in sport, summarizing her two decades of study of flow in sport.

Jackson (2012) presents a laundry list that includes precursors, characteristics, and prompts of the flow experience. From the list, there are some factors that would serve primarily as *precursors to flow*:

- *Being well prepared for the challenge*
- *Having high levels of motivation*
- *Having the right level of energy for the performance*
- *Having a clear plan for the performance*

The list includes other factors that represent experiencing flow:

- *Having a sense that performance was progressing to this plan*
- *Staying focused on the task*
- *Remaining confident*
- *Experiencing good team work*
- *Managing distractions* (Flow and Performance section, para. 4)

Jackson and Csikszentmihalyi's (1999) work is monumental in offering a rich description, a conceptual model, and numerous examples of performers' retrospective accounts of this experience, which can range from almost ordinary to extraordinary. Yet, there remains little guidance in how to achieve such a state.

One important clue to the flow model is that engaging in a flow state requires the actor, in this case the athlete, to stretch his capacity moment to moment. It is not enough to be skilled. The athlete must be willing to opt to focus full attention on the task at hand, such as skiing down difficult terrain on a mountain or shooting an air pistol in Olympic trials. The question must be brought to bear, how does a well-learned task capture the full attention of the individual, to stretch their capacity to such an extent that it triggers a flow state?

Langerian mindfulness may just be the answer. The athlete engaged in a well-learned task must be willing to engage with the environment, constantly being willing and interested in making very small adjustments as their moment-to-moment skills and abilities interact with subtle differences in their environment. If all is held as possibly different and unexpected, the athlete then could be more open to nuances perhaps requisite for moment-to-moment optimal experience and performance.

Consider a rower in a race. Rowing is a relatively simple repetitive motion. How could such a motion require the full attention of the rower? The answer is the wide array of factors that vary subtly, but can have a significant impact on the rhythm and power output. Just a few of the things that can impact the stroke of the rower include the wind, the set of the boat (stable or rocking from side to side), the motion of teammates, the temperature of the water (you go faster when the water is warmer), the water surface, and the speed of your competitors.

Di Leo's call for *adjusting* is what a Langerian mindfulness approach can offer – an essential, practical approach to offering athletes insight into what they can actually do in the moment-to-moment experience of training and competition. Remaining open to novel stimuli that are task-relevant and committing to adjusting and changing subtly throughout engagement with the sport of choice are answers that sport psychology researchers and practitioners need to integrate into research and practice, respectively.

The Langerian mindfulness approach also shares essential elements with principles of *qi*, the Chinese term used for life force, the execution of letting go to the moment-to-moment unfolding of experience. When one is open to novel distinctions, we remain situated in the present moment, which suggests a true contextual awareness and heightened understanding of our actions within the moment. Ying and Chiat (2013) introduced tai chi principles of flow *qi* to piano students with the goal of increasing the probability of the students attaining flow state, to become the action (versus to try to create the music). This is similar to the paradox of control identified as a characteristic of flow, where the performer feels in control *without trying to be* in control (Jackson & Csikszentmihalyi, 1999). Ying and Chiat's (2013) *qi* flow training intervention included focused breathing work aligned with muscular contraction (exhaling) and release (inhaling) and intentional imagery implementation of energy flowing from forehead through fingertips. In this study, such a focus on breathing at the start of each musical piece paired with imagery of the flow of energy while playing the piano was a prompted concentration for the given task at hand that created a flow experience for the pianists. Core to Ying and Chiat's (2013) stance is that "the performer may need to shift from the Western cultural norms of prioritizing control to the Eastern way of 'letting go,' where awareness and openness are the main concepts" (p. 100). Langerian mindfulness is a Western approach that supports this notion of letting go (an automatic way of interacting with the environment) such that the performer can remain aware and open to novelty within the performance realm.

Mindfulness Research in Performance Psychology

The mindfulness research in performance psychology, with the exception of select studies (e.g., Langer et al., 2009), has reflected the Buddhist notion of mindfulness. Popularized by Jon Kabat-Zinn, drawing from a Buddhist understanding, he defines mindfulness as "an open-hearted, moment-to-moment non-judgmental awareness" (Kabat-Zinn, 2005, p. 24). Underlying such awareness requires an acceptance of what is occurring; a non-judgmental awareness; and active acceptance of thoughts, feelings, and bodily sensations (Hayes et al., 2004). With the practice of *allowing*, and not resisting all internal and external experience, the individual can learn to experience a changed relationship to emotions, thoughts, patterns of thoughts, and habitual reactions.

Compared to Langerian mindfulness, the Buddhist mindfulness approach is more passive. The Buddhist approach is more focused on allowing (versus noticing) novelty and has been operationalized primarily as an internally focused approach (i.e., thoughts, feelings, and body sensations) and used to alleviate personally harmful responses to difficult internal experience (e.g., anxiety, rumination). Kabat-Zinn's Mindfulness-Based Stress Reduction (MBSR) has served as the premier intervention for a majority of mindfulness (Buddhist-inspired) studies with a focus on improving medical or psychological disorders and has produced consistently positive results for alleviating stress-related physical and psychological problems (e.g., Keng, Smoski, & Robin, 2011).

Kabat-Zinn, Beall, and Rippe (1985) were the first on record to use mindfulness meditation training with athletes. The intervention included collegiate and Olympic-level rowers practicing mindfulness meditation with an integration of rowing-focused imagery for optimal moment-to-moment performance. Athletes reported performance benefits and an appreciation for the mindfulness meditation practice. Though the Kabat-Zinn and colleagues (1985) intervention was designed to practice acceptance of internal thoughts, feelings, and physical sensations, it also was designed for athletes to practice optimal performance states.

There was a twenty-year gap prior to the emergence of other mindfulness-based approaches in sport. In the twenty-first century, researchers of mindfulness in sport have leaned either directly on Kabat-Zinn's approach to mindfulness intervention using formal mindfulness meditation (e.g., Aherne, Moran, & Lonsdale, 2011; John, Verma, & Khanna, 2011), using the MBSR program and adapting to an athletic population (e.g., Kaufman, Glass, & Arnkoff, 2009) or the Mindfulness-Acceptance-Commitment (MAC) approach in sport, based on Hayes's Acceptance Commitment Training (i.e., Gardner & Moore, 2007, 2012). The MAC approach is designed to help athletes accept internal aversive states such that they can commit to actions that support sport performance–related values.

Current mindfulness training for athletes focuses on mitigating aversive internal sport distractions, primarily performance anxiety and/or negative thoughts and feelings associated with fear of failure (e.g., Baltzell et al., 2014; Gardner & Moore, 2007, 2012). Such interventions have led to improved performance (John et al., 2011), increased flow experience (e.g., Kaufman et al., 2009), and a changed relationship to aversive feelings in response to sport mistakes in competition (Baltzell et al., 2014). Conceptually, *enhanced mental efficiency* is the ultimate performance benefit of mindfulness practices (Gardner & Moore, 2012). The logic assumes that with mindfulness practice, a changed relationship to negative internal experience will develop. By accepting aversive thoughts and feelings, eventually less attention is placed on such aversive emotions (i.e., fears, anxiety, and self-doubt), and attention can then be freed up to be placed on task-relevant cues and/or the task at hand.

The current research in sport, based on Buddhist mindfulness, provides interventions that can help with aversive emotions that to date have not been well served by traditional mental skills training. Essentially, when one tries to stop or change aversive emotions or destructive thoughts, there is a paradoxical outcome: attempts to stop them or change them tend to ironically increases them. The relatively new field of Buddhist-based mindfulness in sport research indicates that acceptance of such thoughts may in fact help athletes tolerate them and, at once, be less controlled or distracted by them (e.g., Baltzell et al., 2014). Leveraging Buddhist mindfulness to help reduce the aversive impact of negative, destructive emotions in both the general clinical setting and within sport has been efficacious. Yet, alleviating suffering in sport is not the only reason to optimize performance.

Other Pathways: Langerian Mindfulness and Concentration

There has been little help for athletes to learn how to concentrate on the task at hand in moment-to-moment performance. "Effective concentration entails attending the right things, at the right time, and in the right way," and occurs when the athlete is able to be totally immersed in moment-to-moment experience (Williams et al., 2015, p. 304). Kee and Wang (2008) argue that present-moment focus is essential to cultivate, yet we have very little understanding of such a state given the difficulty to measure such experience. Kee & Wang (2008) state, "Despite the potential link between present moment focus and peak performance, little is done to examine athletes' present moment focus in relation to their performance in sports" (p. 394).

How do we help athletes with the challenge of boredom or even the anxiety-free athlete? If there is no internal dis-ease to attend to, what does an athlete do to help cultivate optimal performance? An answer may be what was provided in Langer and colleague's (2009) orchestra study: the intentional openness to novel stimuli within the constraints of performance-relevant cues. I did stumble on this answer twenty years ago, at the start of my work in sport psychology consulting. However, without a conceptual framework, the revolutionary insight was temporarily lost.

A Division I collegiate ice hockey player, Marcus (a pseudonym), was referred to me because he was underperforming. He was *riding the bench* (not playing in games) though signed to play professional ice hockey after graduation (which he did). The coach said he was not paying attention and not trying in practice. When I met with Marcus, it became quickly apparent that he was bored in practice. He reported that he had been doing the same warm-ups and drills for about fifteen years. And he was especially bored waiting for the coaches to run drills on defense, as Marcus was an offensive player.

I stumbled on the idea of making the waiting time more interesting, more challenging. So I asked, "What can you do to make the down time more fun, more useful, more energizing for you?" "Have you ever enjoyed the same repetitive practices in the past?" The athlete's eyes lit up. He recalled times in high school when he would "play with" the puck as he approached the net. He would creatively move the puck in unusual ways, in subtly unusual directions. I asked him if he could practice like this again, with his current particularly strict coach. We figured the segments in practice when such fun, novel-focused practice would be acceptable.

Surprisingly to me at the time, the ice hockey player became revitalized in practice by *playing with his puck* and his stance, the bend in his knees as he raced around the rink. He went from being a bench player, to a starter, to captain (and is still playing in the NHL).

Conclusion

Performance anxiety, related to myriad performance blocks (e.g., choking), remains the major problem to address for sport psychology consultants in their effort to help athletes optimize performance. In recent years, researchers and practitioners have turned to Buddhist mindfulness interventions to help with such concerns (Gardner & Moore, 2012); such interventions have been designed to help athletes accept aversive internal states such that the athlete is eventually freed up to focus on task-relevant cues.

When anxiety is not an issue, applied sport psychology practitioners focus on helping athletes mentally re-create optimal performances. When an athlete comes in for sport psychology services, typically part of the intervention includes understanding what the athlete *was* thinking and feeling in best and worst experiences to help tailor strategies to help the athlete optimize performance for future performances. The traditional sport psychology intervention prompts athletes to reference past best performances and from such scenarios use mental skills training (such as goal setting and imagery) to re-create such optimal experiences. The problem, of course, lies in the fact that neither the athlete nor the sport psychologist can predict the myriad ever-changing factors that could thwart the well-laid plan based on past data applied to unknown future constraints. For athletes who are not riddled with performance anxiety, our goal in performance psychology needs to be on helping them be more fully engaged, toward the end state of flow, more often.

A Langerian mindfulness approach, though not a panacea for all sport psychology challenges can become an additional conceptual guide for some needs in sport psychology research and practice. The Langerian approach is needed, particularly, to help those athletes and performers who both are experiencing low anxiety and are engaging in well-learned tasks. Langer and colleagues (2009) offer convincing preliminary evidence that noticing new stimuli can contribute to performance for well-learned, goal-oriented tasks. A Langerian approach to mindfulness is a proactive, externally focused curiosity regarding what is occurring in one's environment. This approach is expected to facilitate interest, vitality, and ultimately enhanced performance within the performance realm.

Langerian mindfulness in sport best supports the well-learned tasks and brings a fresh, new way to integrate with the environment. Truly in sport, very little can be perfectly scripted. Imagine a point guard in basketball dribbling down the court at a full run, calling a play, watching for where his players position themselves, and considering the defense and how it will challenge the player and teammates. Certainly automatic (and perhaps even robotic) responses are called for in terms of offering a frame, a mentally established pathway for how the play can potentially unfold. And then there is the magic; the creativity; and the unexpected moves, passes, starts, stops, and spectacular shots. The athlete must be able to be fully present, noticing novelty in all that is unfolding within the structure of focusing on task-relevant cues that will allow and support optimal, unique performance. Langerian mindfulness is called for to enhance creativity and quality of experience and to prompt flow experience.

REFERENCES

Aherne, C., Moran, A. P., and Lonsdale, C. (2011). The effect of mindfulness training on athletes' flow: An initial investigation. *Sport Psychologist*, 25, 177–189.

Baltzell, A. L., Caraballo, N., Chipman, K., and Hayden, L. (2014). A qualitative study of the Mindfulness Meditation Training for Sport (MMTS): Division I female soccer players' experience. *Journal of Clinical Sport Psychology*, 8, 221–244.

Compton, W. C., and Hoffman, E. (2013). *Positive psychology, the science of happiness and flourishing* (2nd ed.). Belmont, CA: Wadsworth.

Csikszentmihalyi, M. (1975). *Beyond boredom and anxiety*. Washington, DC: Jossey-Bass.

    (1999). If we are so rich, why aren't we happy? *American Psychologist*, 54(10), 821–827. doi: http://dx.doi.org/10.1037/0003-066X.54.10.821

Fredrickson, B. L. (2003). The value of positive emotions: The emerging science of positive psychology is coming to understand why it's good to feel good. *American Scientist*, 91(4), 330–335.

Fredrickson, B. L., Cohn, M. A., Coffey, K. A., Pek, J., and Finkel, S. M. (2008). Open hearts build lives: Positive emotions, induced through loving-kindness meditation, build consequential personal resources. *Journal of Personality and Social Psychology*, 95(5), 1045–1062. doi: 10.1037/a0013262

Gardner, F. L., and Moore, Z. E. (2007). *The psychology of enhancing human performance: The Mindfulness-Acceptance-Commitment (MAC) approach*. New York, NY: Springer.

    (2012). Mindfulness and acceptance models in sport psychology: A decade of basic and applied scientific advancements. *Canadian Psychology*, 53(4), 309–318. doi: 10.1037/a0030220

Hanin, Y. L. (2000). Successful and poor performance and emotions. In Y. L. Hanin (Ed.), *Emotions in sport* (pp. 157–187). Champaign, IL: Human Kinetics.

Hanin, Y. L., and Syrja, P. (2000). Optimal emotions in elite cross-country skiers. In E. Muller, H. Schwameder, E. Kornexl, and C. Raschner (Eds.), *Science and skiing* (pp. 408–419). London, UK: SPON.

Hanton, S., Millalieu, S., and Williams, J. M. (2015). Understanding and managing stress in sport. In J. M. Williams (Ed.), *Applied sport psychology: Personal growth to peak performance* (7th ed., pp. 207–239). Mountain View, CA: Mayfield.

Hayes, S. C., Strosahl, K. D., Bunting, K., Twohig, M., and Wilson, K. G. (2004). What is acceptance and commitment therapy? In S. C. Hayes, and K. D. Strosahl (Eds.), *A practical guide to acceptance and commitment therapy* (pp. 1–30). New York, NY: Springer.

Jackson, S. A. (1992). Athletes in flow: A qualitative investigation of flow states in elite figure skating. *Journal of Applied Sport Psychology*, 4(2), 161–180. doi: 10.10 80/10413209208406459

Jackson, S. A. (2012, December). Flow: The mindful edge in sport and performing arts. *Australian Journal for Sport*. Retrieved from http://www.psychology.org.au/Content.aspx?ID=4988

Jackson, S. A. and Csikszentmihalyi, M. (1999). *Flow in sports: The keys to optimal experiences and performances*, Champaign, IL: Human Kinetics.

John, S., Verma, S. K., and Khanna, G. L. (2011). The effect of mindfulness meditation on HPA-Axis in pre-competition stress in sports performance of elite shooters. *National Journal of Integrated Research in Medicine*, 2(3), 15–21.

Kabat-Zinn, J. (2005). *Coming to our senses: Healing ourselves and the world through mindfulness*. New York, NY: Hyperion.

Kabat-Zinn, J., Beall, B., and Rippe, J. (1985, June). *A systematic mental training program based on mindfulness meditation to optimize performance in collegiate and Olympic rowers*. Poster presented at the World Congress in Sport Psychology, Copenhagen, Denmark.

Kaufman, K. A., Glass, C. R., and Arnkoff, D. B. (2009). Evaluation of Mindful Sport Performance Enhancement (MSPE): A new approach to promote flow in athletes. *Journal of Clinical Sports Psychology*, 4, 334–356.

Kee, Y. H., and Wang, C. K. J. (2008). Relationship between mindfulness, flow dispositions and mental skill adoptions: A cluster analytic approach. *Psychology of Sport and Exercise*, 9(4), 393–411. doi: 10.1016/j.psychsport.2007.07.001

Keng S. L., Smoski, M. J., and Robin, C. J. (2011). Effects of mindfulness on psychological health: A review of empirical studies. *Clinical Psychology Review*, 31(6), 1041–1056. doi: 10.1016/jcpr.2011.04.006

Langer, E. J. (2000). Mindful learning. *Directions in Psychological Science*, 9(6), 220–223.

Langer, E. J., and Moldoveanu, M. C. (2000). The construct of mindfulness. *Journal of Social Issues*, 56(1), 1–9. doi: 10.1111/0022-4537.00148

Langer, E. J., Russell, T., and Eisenkraft, N. (2009). Orchestral performance and the footprint of mindfulness. *Psychology of Music*, 37(2), 125–136. doi: 10.1177/0305735607086053

Pellizzari, M., Bertollo, M., and Robazza, C. (2011). Pre- and post-performance emotions in gymnastics competitions. *International Journal of Sport Psychology*, 42(3), 278–302.

Williams, J. M., Nideffer, R. M., Wilson, V. E., and Sagal, M. S. (2015). Concentration and strategies for controlling it. In J. M. Williams (Ed.), *Applied sport psychology: Personal growth to peak performance* (7th ed., pp. 304–325). Mountain View, CA: Mayfield.

Ying, L. F., and Chiat, L. F. (2013). Tai chi Qi flow in the kinematic process of piano playing: An application of Chinese science. *World Applied Sciences Journal*, 21(1), 98–104. doi: 10.5829/idosi.wasj.2013.21.1.1578

CHAPTER 16

Mindfulness and Dancers

Gene M. Moyle

Within the preceding decade, researchers have gained rapid interest in understanding mindfulness in sport performance. Mindfulness in sport research has included exploring differing conceptual models; understanding the relationship of mindfulness to other factors, such as flow, attention and affect; and providing empirical evidence that supports the implementation of specific mindfulness-based interventions (see Pineau, Glass, & Kaufman, 2014). Similar to sport, the performing arts are another domain of human performance, and as such, parallels are commonly drawn between the two, particularly the physical-based pursuits of sport and dance. This has led to many theoretical and applied practice models from the field of sport psychology being applied directly into the world of dance, with a growing body of research becoming evident that critically highlights the suitability and applicability of such an approach (see Nordin-Bates, 2012). As a result, this chapter aims to provide an overview of the current research and exploration of mindfulness with dancers, with particular focus upon the implementation of a mindfulness meditation (MM)–based program within the curriculum of a university dance training program.

Mindfulness in Performance

Mindfulness has its roots in Eastern meditation, specifically in a contemplative Buddhist practice called *vipassana* (Andersen, 2012; Park-Perin, 2010). Kabat-Zinn's (2005) definition of mindfulness (i.e., nonjudgmental, moment-to-moment awareness) is utilised regularly as the foundation for conceptualising mindfulness within performance domains and incorporates two components: regulation of attention in order to maintain focus within the present moment; and adopting an acceptance- and openness-based approach to personal experiences (Bishop et al., 2004).

Moore and Gardner (2014), and many of their colleagues within a sporting context who implement modern-day approaches to mindfulness, often adopt these Eastern traditions and apply them within the frameworks of Western psychological science. Some of these mindfulness approaches, whether intentionally or not, resulted in implementation of mindfulness that also focuses upon the act of drawing novel distinctions that can be developed without meditative practices (e.g., Langer, 1989). While this Langerian mindfulness approach is viewed as more goal-directed with a focus upon the processing of information that is external to the individual (Pineau et al., 2014), its conceptualisation has also been observed to align with the theoretical underpinnings of Acceptance and Commitment Therapy (ACT) (Hayes & Wilson, 1994) – a clinical therapeutic approach that forms one of the key foundations of the Eastern-influenced Mindfulness-Acceptance-Commitment (MAC) intervention utilised within the sport and performance domains (Gardner & Moore, 2010).

In further comparisons between Eastern- and Western-based mindfulness approaches, Carmody (2014) identifies that while their conceptual constructs can vary, training and interventions utilising both approaches result in improvements in well-being. However, there have reportedly been no interventions based upon Langer's (1989) definition to date within sport (Pineau et al., 2014).

Mindfulness and Sport Performance

When reviewing the literature regarding mindfulness within sport and performance contexts, the adoption of an acceptance-based approach known as MAC is quite prevalent and has been demonstrated to be beneficial for enhancing performance (Bernier et al., 2009; Gardner & Moore, 2004, 2006, 2007, 2010; Moore & Gardner, 2014). While an alternate approach such as the Mindful Sport Performance Enhancement (MSPE) has been employed within a sporting context (Kaufman, Glass, & Arnkoff, 2009; Pineau et al., 2014), MAC appears to be the most commonly employed approach. Furthermore, many studies additionally confirm an existing relationship between mindfulness with health and well-being benefits (Bergomi et al., 2013; Brown & Ryan, 2003; Carmody, 2014; Stanley, 2014). A number of other chapters within this book outline in further detail the further exploration and application of mindfulness in sport performance.

Mindfulness in Dance

Not only is dance considered the most physical of all the performing arts, but dancers continuously work with and on their bodies throughout the duration of their careers – both as students and professionals (Aalten, 2004). Dancers and dance educators alike could argue that certain aspects of mindfulness, such as maintaining focus within the present moment through self-regulated attention and awareness, could be considered to be inherent in the practice of dance, regardless of genre. A dancer is required to maintain a strong mind–body connection across their entire being at all times. This is to ensure the correct recall and execution of movement despite distractions and/or processing of information from both internal and external sources while incorporating additional layers of artistic and creative considerations.

While this unique population spends years undertaking such mind–body awareness training and perfecting its use within their own practice, a review of the current literature looking specifically at mindfulness in dance found relatively sparse material. Despite this, two key lines of enquiry within the existing literature became apparent: (a) mindfulness and dance within therapeutic settings and/or used together or comparatively as a therapeutic intervention (e.g., dance therapy); and (b) mindfulness within somatic education in dance and/or somatic movement-based/dance practices (e.g., Pilates, yoga) utilised in combination with mindfulness. Research exploring mindfulness in dance specifically and solely related to performance enhancement, as is outlined in detail within the sport domain, was not found.

Mindfulness and Dance as Therapeutic Tools or Interventions

Barton (2011) outlines that regular inclusion of other movement-based disciplines, such as tai chi, karate, qi-gong and yoga, have been incorporated into professional practice within dance therapy. Review of the literature within this area additionally provide a few examples where dance, as a movement-based method of mindfulness, has been used to assist with health and well-being issues within a therapeutic context.

An example of this includes the 'Movement and Mindfulness: Skills in Stress Reduction and Relaxation' program that Barton (2011) implemented for ten outpatients within a psychosocial rehabilitation facility. The program aimed to increase skills in stress management, coping, relaxation and communication amongst participants with severe mental illness, and involved a combination of yoga and dance/movement therapy practices. Program evaluation indicated improved relaxation and decreased anxiety levels; improved understanding of self and others; improved awareness of thoughts and feelings; and an overall finding that the combination of mindfulness, dance/movement and Yoga therapy skills strengthen the outcome.

Connected to the realms of dance therapy but described as a 'community' practice not clinical intervention, Marich (2013) developed a concept called 'Dancing Mindfulness'. The applied program developed from this concept is delivered in both a class, for general public participants, and a train-the-trainer format, with a focus on utilising dance as the primary medium for discovering mindful awareness. This approach is Marich's interpretation of *mindfulness in motion*. Classes include MM practices to promote awareness of the body, followed by stretching that progressively includes added rhythm and movement, and finally onto dancing. Research studies have yet to be undertaken on Dancing Mindfulness to determine the existence of any empirical evidence that determines impact of this form of practice on mindfulness, well-being and/or performance.

Within the broader movement-based mindfulness literature, Caldwell and colleagues (2010) focused upon the use of movement-based practices within a college student population of 166 to increase levels of mindfulness, and explored whether increased levels of mindfulness impacted upon self-regulation, self-efficacy, mood, perceived stress and sleep. Results indicated that those students who participated in Pilates (dance-based conditioning), taiji quan (i.e., tai chi) or GYROKINESIS (a practice combining dance, yoga, gymnastics and tai chi developed by Juliu Horvath) classes as part of required courses or academic electives over fifteen weeks of the semester, demonstrated increased levels of mindfulness and positive changes in mood and perceived stress, which partially explained improved sleep quality.

Caldwell and colleagues (2010) recommended the inclusion of mindfulness training as part of the curriculum in physical activity and dance courses, in light of the findings that increased mindfulness during the semester was found to significantly improve mood, reduce perceived stress levels and in turn result in better sleep quality at semester's end. This has implications for university dance training programs, as the end of the semester is a time when students are preparing for their end-of-semester academic and practical exams, in addition to their lengthy rehearsal and performance seasons. Furthermore, the results of Mapel's (2012) study involving university students (N = 49) engaging in five to seven minutes of mindfulness training within their weekly lectures and tutorials additionally supported the notion of the inclusion of mindfulness in education settings to enhance students' learning and manage stressful situations more effectively.

Mindfulness versus dance
Other studies have compared dance to, versus with, MM as an intervention for treating depressive symptomatology or addressing emotional

response coherence (i.e., the extent to which self-reports of emotion physiological changes and simple behaviours predict each other), given dance has been reported to be an effective complementary treatment approach (Koch, Morlinghaus, & Fuchs, 2007). Pinniger and colleagues (2012) explored whether Argentine tango dancing was as effective in reducing symptoms of psychological stress, anxiety and depression, and in promoting well-being. Ninety-seven participants with self-reported stress, anxiety and/or depression completed six-week programs of either tango (using Argentinean close-embrace tradition) or MM, based upon Kabat-Zinn's (2005) approach. Tango classes incorporated differing aspects of the dance each session, including consciousness of walking, awareness of your own and your partner's body, resistance and transference of weight and the close embrace. Findings demonstrated that tango is as effective as MM in reducing levels of self-reported depression and psychological stress, in addition to increasing levels of mindfulness.

A key premise of utilising dance versus a general exercise and/or physical activity–based activities in such scenarios implies that the expressive nature of dance (as an art form) assists individuals to deal with feelings they may otherwise find challenging to accept and/or express. Furthermore, dance can increase levels of mindfulness regarding internal and external contexts, since the art form offers opportunities to both access the inner 'witness' while being completely absorbed in the present moment (Rappaport & Van Dort, 2013; Svoboda, 2007). Furthermore, Sze and colleagues (2010) explored whether training in meditation or dance is associated with greater coherence between subjective and physiological aspects of emotion. A total of twenty-one participants were allocated to each experimental group, including a group skilled in Vipassana meditation, a group skilled in modern dance or ballet and a control group. The authors proposed that while dancers' training is similar to meditators in that it develops body awareness skills, the focus of that awareness is typically more somatic-based and often has to switch purposefully amongst time, music, space and the body versus being continuously focused upon the body as a centrepoint of awareness. Results indicated that body-awareness training is associated with a greater coherence between subjective (i.e., participants readings of their bodily responses) and physiological (i.e., clinically measured) aspects of emotions, and that this was stronger in the meditators (visceral awareness) than the dancers (body-awareness).

Dancers are taught to cultivate increased awareness of proprioceptive sensations from muscles, balance and posture to guide and coordinate complex movements as they move through space (Aalten, 2004). This assimilation of somatics into dance training and associated curricula has become increasingly more evident within academic and vocational dance education programs (Batson & Schwartz, 2007; Fortin, Vieira, & Tremblay, 2009; Kearns, 2010) alongside the introduction of an approach that involves the integration of dance science (i.e., kinesiology) and somatics (Gerber & Wilson, 2010) within dance training.

Somatics and mindfulness

When exploring the meaning of somatics, Fitt (1996) utilised Thomas Hanna's definition that referred to it being the 'art and science of the inter-relational process between awareness, biological function and the environment, with all three factors understood as a synergistic whole' (p. 341). This conceptualisation forms the foundation for a variety of somatic-based practices typically used within the dance context, including yoga, Pilates Method, Bartenieff Fundamentals, ideokinesis, experiential anatomy, Feldenkrais Method and Alexander Technique (see Eddy, 2009; Kearns, 2010). Due to the nature of somatic-based practice and its key focus upon increased mind and body awareness, many somatic practices could be considered as having the ability to develop and/or impact positively on mindfulness. A review of the existing literature again revealed a limited number of empirical studies exploring these factors.

Caldwell and colleagues (2010) compared Pilates Method mat classes (dance/movement-based activity) and recreational exercise across a 15-week semester within 308 undergraduate college students. Pre-, during- and post-program testing was undertaken utilising measures of mindfulness (i.e., the Five Facet Mindfulness Questionnaire) and well-being. Findings indicated that participation in Pilates was associated with increases in mindfulness, and consequently with improvements of well-being – namely enhanced self-regulatory self-efficacy, lower levels of stress and improved mood.

Kearns (2010) undertook a qualitative study that explored potential improvements in university dance student's movement, mindfulness and expressiveness (in the execution of modern dance technique) as a result of the integration of somatic practices into the dance curriculum. Approximately twelve advanced-level junior and senior dance major students participated in a 'Somatics in Action' technique class that included the somatic-based movement practices of Pilates, alignment-based yoga, Bartenieff Fundamentals and ideokinesis. Responses from participating students were gathered through their self-reflection papers submitted as part of the class. Significant improvements were observed (via teacher, peer, self-evaluations and video analysis) in the students' approach and engagement with movement, mindfulness, expressiveness and attitudinal shifts in perception, in addition to the transference of these improvements to other classes and settings (e.g., classroom to rehearsal hall to stage). As Kearns identified, somatic practice can assist dancers to more effectively perform complex movement patterns, combine technical and artistic requirements across multiple dance genres and undertake critical and reflective analysis of their dancing performance, all within often time-limited training and rehearsal periods. In other words, somatic practice can assist the complex challenge facing dance educators in preparing students to be twenty-first century dancers.

Mindfulness in a University Dance Training Program

Upon commencing as the Head of Discipline for Dance at Queensland University of Technology (QUT) in November 2012, the first author undertook a review to determine how the existing training in performance psychology for full-time university dance students enrolled in a bachelor of fine arts (BFA) courses (i.e., BFA Dance or BFA Dance Performance), could be further amplified by complementary and/or additional psychological and physical/somatic practices built into the broader dance training curriculum.

Somatic-based practices that encourage the development of mindfulness skills such as the Pilates Method (Caldwell et al., 2013; Caldwell et al., 2010) and yoga (Barton, 2011; Hewett et al., 2011; Salmon et al., 2009) were already included within the formal dance education program. Additionally, sessional classes in other somatic practices, including Alexander Technique and the Feldenkrais Method (see Eddy, 2009) formed part of the Dance Department's Transitional Training Program (TTP) (Huddy & Roche, 2014). Consequently, consideration was given to the incorporation of MM and tai chi in the following university year. Incorporation of tai chi was due not only to its reported impact upon increasing mindfulness levels in participants (Caldwell et al., 2010; Zahn, 2008), but to provide an alternate 'moving' method of mindfulness practice that assisted in scaffolding the students' learning of mindfulness skills from lying or sitting states in Semester 1 to standing and moving practices in Semester 2.

The overall aim of the incorporation of MM and tai chi within the formal training program was to provide students with the opportunity to engage in both psychological and physical/somatic skill development across various points within their curriculum and training experience to assist in the provision of multiple learning pathways towards embedding these skills within their own embodied practice (i.e., dance). These practices were incorporated as part of a broader approach to performance psychology skills training that formed part of the department's complementary Dance Medicine and Science program.

Performance Psychology Curriculum

The recognition of performance psychology as a separate field within sport psychology, or vice versa, has been debated within the literature (Aoyagi et al., 2012; Hays, 2012; Moyle, 2012, 2014; Terry, 2008). The American Psychological Association's (APA, 2011) 'Division 47, Exercise and Sport Psychology' outlined a definition of performance psychology that forms the philosophical foundation within the current training program – 'Performance psychology is the study and application of psychological principles of human performance to help people consistently perform in the upper range of their capabilities and more thoroughly enjoy the performance process' (p. 9). That is, performance can include 'performing' in any domain, location and/or situation, whether on stage, within daily dance class and training environments, in academic lectures and assessment processes, or in day-to-day non-dance–related life experiences. The adoption of this definition can be viewed as helpful when considering the implementation of the MAC approach in sport-based practices within this dance training context, given their purported effectiveness in enhancing learning, performance and overall psychological well-being (Gardner & Moore, 2007, 2010; Moore & Gardner, 2014).

Performance psychology had been taught over the previous eight consecutive years at the QUT dance program through a variety of delivery methods. These have included primary delivery through the teaching of one module (approximately six to seven lectures and tutorials) within a Professional Skills teaching unit (i.e., subject); as regular guest lectures within two other dance education units; and via group workshops scheduled as part of orientation week, TTP and at key identified times throughout each semester for all students. Key areas covered included a neuroscience-based model of brain functioning as a foundation to better understand the application of psychological/mental skills (Rock, 2009), performance profiling, self-confidence, resilience, performance anxiety, stress and coping, emotional regulation and arousal control, perfectionism, motivation, pre-performance routines, language, effective communication and conflict management, cognitions and self-talk, goal setting, locus of control, the psychology of injury and rehabilitation, concentration, attention and mindfulness, relaxation techniques, imagery and visualisation, overtraining and burnout, mental and physical health and well-being, self-identity and career transition (Moyle, 2007, 2008, 2010). The key conceptual foundations for delivery of these topics included cognitive behavioural therapy (CBT) (Mahoney & Meyers, 1989), ACT (Hayes & Wilson, 1994) and Positive Psychology (PP; e.g., Park-Perin, 2010).

Assessment for the primary unit of performance psychology included weekly journal writing activities that culminate in a written assignment due shortly prior to the graduation performance season at the end of the university year. The essay requires students to reflect upon their experience in the application of one to two performance psychology strategies or techniques to their dance training over the duration of the semester and chart their progress, learning and results. Additional opportunities for reflective practice for students are represented across most units of study in both application and assessment activities, whether practical or theory-based units, and form an integral part of the established pedagogical approach within the Dance Department.

Due to course curriculum limitations, at the time of the review students from only one of the two undergraduate BFA courses (i.e., BFA Dance Performance) had access to enrol in the second-year unit that was comprised of the core module focused upon performance psychology and its application within dance. Therefore, aside from group workshops and guest lectures, in-depth exposure to these strategies was limited for the remaining students who were not able to undertake this unit as part of their course progression (i.e., students in the BFA Dance degree). As a result, an ACT-based MM program was introduced for all students as a weekly scheduled class that formed part of their 'Dance Technique Studies,' 'Dance Practice' and 'Performance in Context' units, which covered all three-year levels in both BFA dance courses in Semester 1 (Moyle & Jackson, 2013).

To assist in evaluating the program, Moyle, Jackson and McCloughan (2014) undertook research on the MM program (i.e., the tai chi program was not included) to determine any potential impacts regarding the understanding of mindfulness practice and potential changes in levels of mindfulness awareness in the dance students. The aim of the overall research study was to assist in informing pedagogical decision making regarding the use of MM classes included within the dance training curriculum, teaching and learning considerations and skill development for dance staff and exploring the application of MM specifically with dance students within a university dance training setting.

Introduction of mindfulness meditation (MM): Year one
Version 1 of the MM program consisted of a nine-week mindfulness-meditation, ACT-based program delivered to 118 students undertaking full-time dance training in either the BFA (Dance) or BFA (Dance Performance) course in Semester 1, 2013. Due to timetabling requirements, the students were divided into three groups of mixed year levels and undertook one-hour classes at the same day and time each week (i.e., Monday or Thursday mornings), with MM being the first 'technique' class for the day. Review of attendance rates indicated that 20 per cent of students attended less than half (i.e., ≥ 4) of the total MM classes (N = 9) conducted over the semester.

The sessions were conducted by qualified sport and exercise psychologists and covered key practices such as mindfulness of body (body awareness, mindfulness of breathing, mindfulness of sounds), mindfulness of images (visualisation, mindfulness of body via integrative restoration [iRest], yoga nidra, body awareness, *sankalpa*), mindfulness of feelings and emotions, open awareness, walking meditation and stillness meditation. The definition of mindfulness provided to the dance students by the primary lecturer was:

> Mindfulness is simply being aware of what is happening right now, without wishing it were different; enjoying the pleasant without holding on when it changes (which it will); being with the unpleasant without fearing that it will always be this way (it won't) (Baraz & Alexander, 2012, Step 2 – Mindfulness: Being Present for Your Life section, p. 32).

Moyle and colleagues (2014) undertook pre- and post-testing utilising the Mindful Attention Awareness Scale (MAAS-15; Brown & Ryan, 2003), a unidimensional measure of mindfulness. The testing consisted of a qualitative self-assessment questionnaire checking the current level of awareness and understanding of mindfulness practice and its application in addition to a brief MM practice survey that asked students to self-report on how mindful they were in each of the practices (post-program only). Students were required to maintain a reflective journal that was utilised at the end of each weekly session, in addition to completing a midsemester reflective debrief with identified staff. Teaching staff additionally attended the weekly sessions and actively linked the mindfulness practice into the students' other technique and practical dance classes (e.g., ballet, contemporary, repertoire rehearsals) and academic theory classes where appropriate.

Results from paired samples (N = 108) demonstrated an upward trend in levels of mindfulness awareness, particularly for the BFA (Dance Performance) students; however, the results were not significant. Qualitative feedback indicated that participation in the MM program and the development of the associated mental skills had resulted in positive performance and personal outcomes (Moyle et al., 2014). Examples of students' responses included: 'At the beginning of the lesson I didn't take it 100% seriously. However now at the end of the semester I can't believe how good it is. I find myself doing it regularly and taking meditation outside of uni'; another student reported, 'Mindfulness not only can help with achieving a relaxed and calm state but also a focused and concentrated mindset'; and a final student stated,

> Helpful in day to day class and before performance to hone in on myself and how I am. . . . Removed some mental talk that became unnecessary . . . (learned) how to focus on my body and relax tension areas, to stay aware and in the moment.

Overall, Moyle and colleagues (2014) reported that both formal and informal student feedback indicated that the incorporation of MM into their training was viewed as very positive, assisted with their performance and general well-being both in and outside of the dance studio and was of value to them.

Introduction of MM: Year two

Following the completion of version 1 of the MM program, including a review of the associated research study results (Moyle et al., 2014), debriefing processes were undertaken with both the MM lecturers and Dance Department teaching staff. Planning was undertaken to revise the MM program and introduce version 2 of the training in Semester 1 of 2014. Primary differences between version 1 and version 2 included reordering of the MM practices across the weekly classes; an increase in the number of walking meditations; running five of the nine MM classes outdoors; shortening the MM classes from one hour to forty-five minutes; and collapsing the three weekly MM classes into one MM class for all students to attend.

Version 2 of the MM program consisted of a nine-week MM, ACT-based program delivered to ninety-six students undertaking full-time dance training in either the BFA (Dance) or BFA (Dance Performance) course. Close to half (48.7 per cent) of these students had participated in the previous year's MM classes. Due to timetabling requirements, all students were allocated to the one weekly forty-five-minute session conducted by the primary sport and exercise psychologist who taught MM the previous year. Due to limited access to indoor spaces to accommodate the total number of students, five of the classes were conducted indoors, with the remaining four classes conducted outdoors on the university's sports oval.

Sessions covered the following key practices: mindfulness of body (body awareness and body sensing), mindfulness of breathing, mindfulness of feelings and emotions, walking meditation I (focus on walking), walking meditation II (focus on body awareness and sensations while walking), mindfulness of sounds, walking meditation III (silent walking meditation and loving-kindness mantra) and mindfulness of thoughts and beliefs. The final class asked students to choose their own MM practice out of the eight practices previously covered.

Reflective journals were again utilised with the students throughout the duration of the program and pre- and post-testing followed the same protocols as the previous study on version 1. Dance staff members additionally participated in the weekly MM sessions, with ongoing team discussions regarding embedding approaches for use within students' other dance technique and practical and academic classes undertaken on occasion at fortnightly team meetings.

Moyle and colleagues (2014) reported that results for paired samples included in the study (N = 82) demonstrated a slight downward trend in levels of mindfulness awareness, although the results were inconclusive. The authors outlined a number of considerations within the study that may have impacted upon the MM program and the resulting students' experience, including decreases in the duration of the classes, timing of the sessions (i.e., 7:30 AM) and the introduction of alternating locations and practices (i.e., walking, outdoor, 'buddy' formats). Furthermore, when reviewing attendance rates, 20.7 per cent of students were reported to have attended less than half (i.e., ≥ 4) of the total MM classes (N = 9) conducted over the semester. Further research is required to confirm such hypotheses.

Despite this, qualitative feedback indicated that participation in the MM program had again yielded positive performance and personal outcomes for some participants. Examples of students' responses included:

> To be honest I didn't really understand the point of mindfulness-meditation at the beginning of the semester but now I feel of great benefit because of it. I now understand the different types of meditation and how powerful the brain can be – just rewording your intentions, how you think about things, or just focusing on a particular aspect helps you become calm and aware.

Other reported comments focused upon dance-specific situations:

> I feel like mindfulness-meditation is a great technique and skill to practice before an exam or performance as it would help hone in your nerves and become one with your body so you're a lot more relaxed rather than tense.
>
> I am more aware of my alignment and I can recognise whether my mind is wandering off or if I am engaged when performing.

Conversely, one student reflected upon its lack of assistance within their academic studies, stating, 'Mindfulness hasn't really helped me a lot with my academic studies, apart from relaxing when I'm stressed'. Yet, upon reflection, it appears that MM was a source of support for this student.

Assessment-related observations

Further verbally reported feedback related to the perceived positive impact of MM on the dancers' personal and performance outcomes was observed by dance teaching staff via an oral assessment presentation process completed by all first-year students across both BFA courses.

Forming 50 per cent of their progressive assessment item for their respective units of Dance Technique Studies 1 and Dance Practice 1 (their key teacher assessed them on the remaining 50 per cent), students were required to present an evidence-based justification for their progression over the semester related to a self-selected criterion within both the ballet and contemporary dance genres. This process involved presenting for five minutes on each dance genre, which included one chosen 'performance standard' taken from the unit's Criterion Referenced Assessment (CRA) items (e.g., safe dance practice, alignment, articulation/strength, freedom/breadth of movement, dynamic variance, musical interpretation, dance communication).

The presentation was in a multimedia format that included video recordings and photos captured via handheld devices, such as mobile phones. The students had organised fellow colleagues to take the recordings and photos of them in dance classes across the duration of the semester. A progressive comparative analysis of video clips and photos was undertaken alongside a reflective discussion of their learning and overall progress regarding the development of their specific performance standard and skill.

Close to 80 per cent of students (N = 43) referenced MM as a practice that they observed assisted them throughout the semester with their progressive development of their chosen dance technique performance standard. Furthermore, they reported that MM in combination with the significant focus on somatic-based practices (e.g., yoga, Pilates, Feldenkrais

Method, Alexander Technique) and their integration into dance technique as introduced and covered within the TTP program (i.e., a periodisation-based training program undertaken within first four weeks of Semester 1 for all first-year students to assist with transition into full-time tertiary dance training [see Huddy & Roche, 2014]) was critical to their perceived increase in knowledge, understanding, application and success with both dance technique and dance performance skill development.

Future Teaching, Learning and Research Considerations

While student feedback responses were generally positive regarding the MM program, there was evidence of some operational and pedagogical barriers to potential learning and development of mindfulness skills. Consideration of these are important in light of implementation of version 3 of the MM program that is planned for Semester 1 of 2015.

Operational Reflections

Scheduling constraints were experienced with both versions of the program as there were no other options but to run sessions starting early in the morning (e.g., 7:30 AM). This was due to timetable constraints with other formal classes, lectures and tutorials that limited available timeslots, since both the full-time dance courses typically run from 8:30 AM to 6:00 PM (or later) Monday to Friday, in addition to allocated pretechnique class warm-up times being available for students in each of the dance studios from 7:30 AM to 8:30 AM daily. Furthermore, to maximise available resources (i.e., teacher availability, sessional teaching funds), it was more time and cost effective within version 2 of the MM program to run one class with all students.

Recognition of these challenges and student feedback has been incorporated into scheduling considerations for version 3 of the MM program (in addition to the tai chi program). Sessions will be scheduled during the weekly two-hour extended lunch break that occurs within the Dance timetable to facilitate staff's ability to attend faculty and university-wide activities. This change in class time will still incorporate all students across both courses in being able to attend and places the MM practice in the middle of the day versus the start of the day, which is also within dance students' key rest period. Therefore, the MM program will be expected to provide a relaxation-related activity to assist with performance recovery and general well-being.

Pedagogical reflections

A range of observations related to pedagogical areas have been made over the duration of the implementation of the MM program to date. These have broader teaching and learning implications related to the inclusion of mindfulness practice as a formal part of the dance education curriculum and include areas that would be helpful to explore further empirically. Consideration of this type of approach would additionally complement the existing research findings and future research plans regarding the MM program as an intervention (Moyle et al., 2014).

Relevance to dance training

Observed and reported levels of students' perceptions regarding the relevance and importance of MM to their dance training were varied amongst the year groups and courses (Moyle et al., 2014). In addition to the timetabling issues, it could be suggested that these areas additionally impacted the inconsistency in attendance rates that were noted throughout both programs. Interestingly, similar issues were observed within the tai chi programs across both years, since these classes replicated each version of the MM program in terms of timetabling at early times of the day. In both situations, inconsistent attendance rates occurred despite the fact that all MM and tai chi classes form part of a formal progressive assessment item that contributes to their overall grade, in the associated unit, of each student.

An incorrect belief often observed to be held by dance students is that the only way in which they can increase their dance skills and performance ability is just by attending dance classes. While daily technique classes are critical to the development of technical skill and artistic ability, they are not sufficient. We know from the application of sports science and medicine principles into the dance domain that cross-training involving physical fitness, strength and conditioning, stretching programs and somatic-based practices, in addition to allied health areas such as massage, physiotherapy, nutrition, recovery and psychology training, are critical to injury prevention, body maintenance, performance enhancement and a sustainable career in a very mentally and physically demanding art form (Barrell & Terry, 2003; Buckroyd, 2000; Hamilton, 1997, 1998, 2008; Nordin-Bates, 2012; Taylor & Taylor, 1995).

Program content

After considering changes in the MM program content from version 1 to version 2, the program's developers increased focus and inclusion of walking meditations. As noted by the sport and exercise psychologist teaching all MM classes within version 2, 'I think it worked out well having some sessions on the field (despite some inclement weather), as doing the walking meditations outside were a good environment to do them in...' (S. A. Jackson, personal communication, April 17, 2014). Of interest, however, is that when students were given a choice of one of the eight MM practices to use, the majority reported choosing a nonwalking practice – mindfulness of breathing (Moyle et al., 2014). Further research would be beneficial in exploring any differences in the preferences of dance students towards lying, sitting, standing and/or walking MM practices in light of their physically taxing training schedules.

Repeat cohorts of students
Current second-year students in both courses will be undertaking the MM program in 2015 for the third year in a row. While the program content has slightly changed each year on the basis of keeping up with teaching and learning considerations, ongoing research may be helpful in exploring any longer-term points of interest regarding the impact of MM classes being incorporated within the dance curriculum. Additionally, undertaking further detailed comparative analysis of their perceptions of the relevance and importance of MM with regards to their dance studies over the duration of their respective three-year courses might be worthwhile.

Integration within formal assessment
Following debriefing amongst the dance staff regarding observations about the progressive assessment process (i.e., oral presentations) for dance technique and practical units introduced in Semester 1 of 2014, it was determined that this process was very effective in highlighting the varying levels of understanding and practical application amongst students – particularly where the formal assessment demonstrated an integration of various teaching content and skills from across multiple units and associated classes.

On the basis of the review, some recommendations by teachers for modifications were made for implementation in Semester 2 of 2014, which included decreasing the assessment amount for the oral to 25 per cent of the overall progressive mark (the remaining 75 per cent was to be determined by the teacher's observations of students in class); and requiring students to prepare oral presentations on their chosen performance standard from both ballet and contemporary; however, on the day of the assessment, students would be randomly assigned to present only one of these (the remaining genre's assessment will be 100 per cent based upon teacher observation of progress within that class).

Furthermore, it was identified that the clear repeated positive references to the MM program and other somatic-based practices (e.g., yoga, Pilates, Feldenkrais Method, Alexander Technique, within TTP and/or weekly classes within dance technique/practice units), and their reported helpful impact upon learning within the dance context, indicated that further research and gathering of empirical data related to these areas were warranted. Consequently, exploration of the potential relationships amongst these practices, interventions and dance education and training will be undertaken in due course.

Dance staff training and engagement

Support for the overall MM program was observed to be very positive within the internal dance teaching staff (N = 7), although participation in all classes diminished amongst most staff (with the exception of the unit coordinators), particularly during version 2 (dropping from 85.7 per cent to 28.6 per cent attendance), due to scheduling conflicts and/or prioritisation of other work tasks. Where scheduling conflicts for staff involvement in future MM programs may continue, it would be helpful to focus upon the introduction of staff-specific professional development workshops. In these sessions, staff could cover the same MM practices as the students, but with added components that focus upon how such practices can be incorporated into technique, practical and academic classes.

This additional layer to the staff MM sessions would be helpful in ensuring consistency amongst the dance teaching team regarding: (a) knowledge and understanding of MM practices; (b) effective translation into 'dance language' for classes and lectures; (c) alignment of such practices with the other somatic-based integration activities occurring within the department (see Huddy & Roche, 2014); and (d) formally forming part of the broader embedding framework around performance psychology, somatics and general health and well-being skills and applications across the whole Dance Department. Furthermore, not only could this approach of staff development, skill acquisition and embedding processes (organisational efforts to embed the learning effectively for longer-term adoption and change to occur) be applied to the tai chi program in its future iterations, incorporation of the Tai Chi program within the ongoing MM research agenda could be warranted. This would assist in being able to compare and contrast the potential impacts from both programs and add another level of enquiry into mindfulness and dancers within a university dance training program.

Recommendations

Future research into the MM program would benefit from the inclusion of a range of activities that build upon the observations and results from the previous investigations. These could include: (a) other somatic-based practices used within the curriculum (e.g., tai chi, yoga, Pilates, Feldenkrais Method, Alexander Technique); (b) additional well-being factors, such as self-efficacy, stress management, sleep quality and resilience; and (c) performance enhancement and dance-specific measures to explore potential relationships between mindfulness and performance in dancers.

Conclusion

In summary, the area of mindfulness and dancers is underresearched and would benefit from the application of findings and future research recommendations taken from the more robust literature within the sport and performance domain. Focus upon the empirical identification of benefits regarding both performance enhancement and general health and well-being factors would be helpful and assist in expanding the literature outside of the clinical field and into performance settings. Additionally, further exploration of mindfulness, somatics and dance training within university and vocational training contexts would assist in contributing to the knowledge of how best to prepare dancers not only for successful sustainable careers but for successful and sustainable lives.

Key Points

- Mindfulness within somatic and dance/movement-based practices primarily originates from the Eastern meditation philosophy of nonjudgmental, moment-to-moment awareness. Such regulation of attention is used in order to maintain focus within the present moment, and an accepting and open approach is adopted towards personal experiences.
- Mindfulness may be helpful for enhancing learning, performance and increasing health and well-being in dancers.
- Integration of mindfulness and somatic movement-based practices within the dance curriculum is helpful in complementing and further supporting the mental, physical, technical and artistic skill development of dance students.
- Embedding mindfulness successfully within dance education and training requires an organisational and systems-theory approach to be effective. Implementation of new practices in isolation, regardless of

their alignment and/or similarities with each other, are unlikely to contribute to significant change.

REFERENCES

Aalten, A. (2004). The moment when it all comes together: Embodied experiences in ballet. *European Journal of Women's Studies*, 11(3), 263–276. doi: 10.1177/1350506804044462

American Psychological Association (APA). (2011). *Defining the practice of sport and performance psychology. Division 47, Exercise and Sport Psychology, Practice Committee.* Retrieved from www.apadivisions.org/division47/about/resources/defining.pdf

Andersen, M. B. (2012). Supervision and mindfulness in sport and performance psychology. In S. Murphy (Ed.), *The Oxford handbook of sport and performance psychology* (pp. 725–737). Oxford, UK: Oxford University Press.

Aoyagi, M. W., Portenga, S. T., Poczwardowski, A., Cohen, A. B., and Statler, T. (2012). Reflections and directions: The profession of sport psychology past, present and future. *Professional Psychology, Research and Practice*, 43(1), 32–38. doi: 10.1037/a0025676

Baraz, J., and Alexander, S. T. (2012). *Awakening joy: 10 steps to happiness.* New York, NY: Parallax Press.

Barrell, G. M., and Terry, P. C. (2003). Trait anxiety and coping strategies among ballet dancers. *Medical Problems of Performing Artists*, 18(2), 59–64.

Barton, E. J. (2011). Movement and mindfulness: A formative evaluation of a dance/movement and yoga therapy program with participants experiencing severe mental illness. *American Journal of Dance Therapy*, 33(2), 157–181. doi: 10.1007/s10465-011-9121-7

Batson, G., and Schwartz, R. E. (2007). Revisiting the value of somatic education in dance training through an inquiry into practice schedules. *Journal of Dance Education*, 7(2), 47–56. doi: 10.1080/15290824.2007.10387334

Bergomi, C., Strohle, G., Michalak, J., Funke, F., and Berking, M. (2013). Facing the dreaded: Does mindfulness facilitate coping with distressing experiences? A moderator analysis. *Cognitive Behaviour Therapy*, 42(1), 21–30. doi: 10.1080/16506073.2012.713391

Bernier, M., Thienot, E., Codron, R., and Fournier, J. F. (2009). Mindfulness and acceptance approaches in sport performance. *Journal of Clinical Sports Psychology*, 25(4), 320–333.

Bishop, S. R., Lau, M., Shapiro, S., Carlson, L., Anderson, N. D., Carmody, J., . . . Devins, G. (2004). Mindfulness: A proposed operational definition. *Clinical Psychology: Science and Practice*, 11(3), 230–241. doi: 10.1093/clipsy.bph077

Brown, K. W., and Ryan, R. M. (2003). The benefits of being present: Mindfulness and its role in psychological well-being. *Journal of Personality and Social Psychology* 84(4), 822–848. doi: 10.1037/0022-3514.84.4.822

Buckroyd, J. (2000). *The student dancer: Emotional aspects of the teaching and learning of dance.* London, UK: Dance.

Caldwell, K., Adams, M., Quin, R. H., Harrison, M., and Greeson, J. (2013). Pilates, mindfulness and somatic education. *Journal of Dance and Somatic Practices*, 5(2), 141–154. doi: 10.1386/jdsp.5.2.141_1

Caldwell, K., Harrison, M., Adams, M., Quin, R. H., and Greeson, J. (2010). Developing mindfulness in college students through movement-based courses: Effects on self-regulatory self-efficacy, mood, stress, and sleep quality. *Journal of American College Health*, 58(5), 433–442. doi: 10.1080/07448480903540581

Carmody, J. (2014). Eastern and Western approaches to mindfulness: Similarities, differences, and clinical implications. In A. Ie, C. T. Ngnoumen, and E. J. Langer (Eds.), *The Wiley Blackwell handbook of mindfulness* (Vol. 1, pp. 48–57). Hoboken, NJ: Wiley-Blackwell.

Eddy, M. (2009). A brief history of somatic practices and dance: Historical development of the field of somatic education and its relationship to dance. *Journal of Dance and Somatic Practices*, 1(1), 5–27. doi: 10.1386/jdsp.1.1.5/1

Fitt, S. S. (1996). *Dance kinesiology* (2nd ed.). New York, NY: Schirmer.

Fortin, S., Vieira, A., and Tremblay, M. (2009). The experience of discourses in dance and somatics. *Journal of Dance and Somatic Practices*, 1(1), 47–64. doi: 10.1386/jdsp.1.1.47/1

Gardner, F. L., and Moore, Z. E. (2004). A Mindfulness-Acceptance-Commitment based approach to performance enhancement: Theoretical considerations. *Behavior Therapy*, 35(4), 707–723. doi: 10.1016/S0005-7894(04)80016-9

(2006). *Clinical sport psychology*. Champaign, IL: Human Kinetics.

(2007). *The psychology of enhancing human performance: The Mindfulness-Acceptance-Commitment (MAC) approach*. New York, NY: Springer.

(2010). Acceptance-based behavioural therapies and sport. In S. J. Hanrahan and M. B. Andersen (Eds.), *Routledge handbook of applied sport psychology: A comprehensive guide for students and practitioners* (pp.186–193). New York, NY: Routledge.

Gerber, P., and Wilson, M. (2010). Teaching at the interface of dance science and somatics. *Journal of Dance Medicine and Science*, 14(2), 50–57.

Hamilton, L. H. (1997). *The person behind the mask: A guide to performing arts psychology*. Greenwich, CT: Ablex.

(1998). *Advice for dancers: Emotional counsel and practical strategies*. New York, NY: Jossey-Bass.

(2008). *The dancer's way: The New York City Ballet guide to mind, body, and nutrition*. New York, NY: St. Martin's Griffin.

Hays, K. F. (2012). The psychology of performance in sport and other domains. In S. Murphy (Ed.), *The Oxford handbook of sport and performance psychology* (pp. 24–45). Oxford, UK: Oxford University Press.

Hayes, S. C., and Wilson, K. G. (1994). Acceptance and commitment therapy: Altering the verbal support for experiential avoidance. *Behavior Analyst*, 17(2), 289–303.

Hewett, Z. L., Ransdell, L. B., Gao, Y., Petlichkoff, L. M., and Lucas, S. (2011). An examination of the effectiveness of an 8-week Bikram yoga program on mindfulness, perceived stress, and physical fitness. *Journal of Exercise Science and Fitness*, 9(2), 87–92. doi: 10.1016/S1728-869X(12)60003-3

Huddy, A., and Roche, J. (2014, July). *Identity and the dance student: Implementing somatic approaches in the transition into tertiary dance education.* Paper presented at Contemporising the Past: Envisaging the Future, World Dance Alliance Global Summit, Angers, France.

Kabat-Zinn, J. (2005). *Coming to our senses: Healing ourselves and the world through mindfulness.* New York, NY: Hyperion.

Kaufman, K. A., Glass, C. R., and Arnkoff, D. B. (2009). Evaluation of Mindful Sport Performance Enhancement (MPSE): A new approach to promote flow in athletes. *Journal of Clinical Sport Psychology*, 25(4), 334–356.

Kearns, L. W. (2010). Somatics in action: How "I feel three-dimensional and real" improves dance education and training. *Journal of Dance Education*, 10(2), 35–40. doi: 10.1080/15290824.2010.10387158

Koch, S. C., Morlinghaus, K., and Fuchs, T. (2007). The joy dance: Specific effects of a single dance intervention on psychiatric patients with depression. *The Arts in Psychotherapy*, 34(4), 340–349. doi: 10.1016/j.aip.2007.07.001

Langer, E. J. (1989). *Mindfulness.* Reading, MA: Addison-Wesley.

Mahoney, M., and Meyers, A. (1989) Anxiety and athletic performance: Traditional and cognitive-behavioural perspectives. In D. Hackfort (Ed.), *Anxiety in sports: An international perspective* (pp. 77–94). Washington, DC: Hemisphere.

Mapel, T. (2012). Mindfulness and education: Student's experience of learning mindfulness in a tertiary classroom. *New Zealand Journal of Educational Studies*, 47(1), 19–32.

Marich, J. (2013). *Creative mindfulness: 20+ strategies for recovery and wellness.* Warren, OH: Mindful Ohio.

Moore, Z. E., and Gardner, F. L. (2014). Mindfulness and performance. In A. Ie, C. T. Ngnoumen, and E. J. Langer (Eds.), *The Wiley Blackwell handbook of mindfulness* (Vol. 1, pp. 986–1003). Hoboken, NJ: Wiley-Blackwell.

Moyle, G. M. (2007, October). *Learnings from the implementation of performance psychology as a subject within a university dance program.* In the 17th Annual Meeting of the International Association of Dance Medicine & Science, Canberra, Australia.

(2008). Performance psychology applied to dance. *Australian Journal of Psychology*, 60(1), 172. doi: 10.1080/00049530802385558

(2010). The art of the positive pas de deux: Putting positive psychology into dance! In V. Mrowinksi, M. Kyrios, and N. Voudouris (Eds.), *Abstracts of the 27th International Congress of Applied Psychology* (pp. 451–454).

(2012). Performance in the spotlight: Exploring psychology in the performing arts. *InPsych*, 34(6), 11–13.

(2014). Dr. Seuss and the "Great Balancing Act": Exploring the ethical places you'll go within Australian sport, exercise, and performance psychology. In J. Gualberto Cremades and L. S. Tashman (Eds.), *Becoming a sport, exercise, and performance psychology professional: A global perspective* (pp. 45–52). New York, NY: Psychology Press.

Moyle, G. M., and Jackson, S. A. (2013, November). *Mindfulness-meditation on the move: Implementation of an ACT-based mindfulness practice intervention and training within a university dance program.* Paper presented at the Australian Society for Performing Arts Healthcare Conference, Brisbane, QLD, Australia.

Moyle, G. M., Jackson, S. A., and McCloughan, L. J. (2014). *Mindfulness on the move: The impact of mindfulness training within a university dance program.* Manuscript in preparation.

Nordin-Bates, S. M. (2012). Performance psychology in the performing arts. In S. Murphy (Ed.), *The Oxford handbook of sport and performance psychology* (pp. 81–114). Oxford, UK: Oxford University Press.

Park-Perin, G. (2010). Positive psychology. In S. J. Hanrahan and M. B. Andersen (Eds.), *Routledge handbook of applied sport psychology: A comprehensive guide for students and practitioners* (pp. 141–149). New York, NY: Routledge.

Pineau, T. R., Glass, C. R., and Kaufman, K. A. (2014). Mindfulness in sport performance. In A. Ie, C. T. Ngnoumen, and E. J. Langer (Eds.), *The Wiley Blackwell handbook of mindfulness.* (Vol. 1, pp. 1004–1033). Hoboken, NJ: Wiley-Blackwell.

Pinniger, R., Brown, R. F., Thorsteinsson, E. B., and McKinley, P. (2012). Argentine tango dance compared to mindfulness meditation and a waiting-list control: A randomized trial for treating depression. *Complementary Therapies in Medicine,* 20(6), 377–384. doi: 10.1016/j.ctim.2012.07.003

Rappaport, L., and Van Dort, C. (2013). *Mindfulness and the arts therapies: Theory and practice.* London, UK: Jessica Kingsley.

Rock, D. (2009). *Your brain at work: Strategies for overcoming distraction, regaining focus, and working smarter all day long.* New York, NY: Harper Collins.

Salmon, P., Lush, E., Jablonski, M., and Sephton, S. E. (2009). Yoga and mindfulness: Clinical aspects of an ancient mind/body practice. *Cognitive and Behavioral Practice,* 16(1), 59–72. doi: 10.1016/j.cbpra.2008.07.002

Stanley, E. A. (2014). Mindfulness-based mind fitness training: An approach for enhancing performance and building resilience in high-stress contexts. In A. Ie, C. T. Ngnoumen, and E. J. Langer (Eds.), *The Wiley Blackwell handbook of mindfulness* (Vol. 1, pp. 964–985). Hoboken, NY: Wiley-Blackwell.

Svoboda, E. (2007). Dance helps you process feelings you may have trouble dealing with in conscious, verbal terms. *Psychology Today,* 40(2), 61–63.

Sze, J. A., Gyurak, A., Yuan, J. W., and Levenson, R. W. (2010). Coherence between emotional experience and physiology: Does body awareness training have an impact? *Emotion,* 10(6), 803–814. doi: 10.1037/a0020146

Taylor, J., and Taylor, C. (1995). *Psychology of dance.* Champaign, IL: Human Kinetics.

Terry, P. C. (2008). Performance psychology: Being the best, the best you can be, or just a little better? *InPsych,* 30(1), pp. 8–11.

Zahn, W. L. (2008). *The effects of tai chi chuan on mindfulness, mood, and quality of life in adolescent girls* (Doctoral dissertation). Retrieved from ProQuest, UMI Dissertations Publishing (3324384).

CHAPTER 17

Attention, Centering, and Being Mindful: Medical Specialties to the Performing Arts

Patsy Tremayne, Ashlee Morgan

My experience is what I agree to attend to.
  William James (cited in Gallagher, 2009, p. 1)

As a performer, the act of mindfulness is a valuable and optimal state of being. One's ability to be mindful can discernibly affect physical performance in a diverse range of contexts; for example, a dancer performing as part of a group, or a doctor answering a question in an oral exam. This chapter explores the notion of mindfulness, with a particular focus on the aligned concepts of attention and centering, among performing artists and medical practitioners. Despite the obvious disparities of challenges and tasks between the performing arts and medical specialties, the relevance of mindfulness proves a distinguishable commonality across the disciplines. Throughout this chapter, case study examples will be drawn upon to illustrate the pertinence of mindfulness for the performer and also the important contextual considerations for the performance psychologist.

Mindfulness is being in touch with the present moment. It also involves paying attention in an engaged way. Deciding what to pay attention to takes work. When the performance psychologist is working with the client, he or she needs to be aware of the sociocultural context in which the performance is embedded. Understanding the social norms of the performance domain and the expectations of important others (e.g., family and/or colleagues) is beneficial when endeavoring to enhance the client's performance. In the case studies that follow, we apply a range of psychological skills within different sociocultural contexts, with the goal of enhancing the mindful approach of the performer. It is essential to understand the context when tailoring mindfulness-based interventions. For example, the anesthetist mixing a cocktail of sleep-inducing drugs prior to an operation has substantially different demands and pressures placed upon her or him than an actor about to walk on stage to a full house on the first night. While the hospital registrar and voice student may share similar performance anxiety in relation to their exams, they have different social norms that create a set of background expectations in which performance is compared. However, one thing they all have in common is the need for mindfulness in what they do, and the effective psychologist encourages adaptation of mindfulness to a variety of different performance domains and deals with numerous factors that inhibit mindful performance.

Mindfulness

Mindfulness has been defined as "paying attention in the present moment" (Jha, Krompinger, & Baime, 2007, p. 109). This incorporates one focusing his or her attention on a moment-to-moment basis (Kristeller & Hallet, 1999). As Kabat-Zinn (2005) discerns, mindfulness is an "open-hearted, moment-to-moment non-judgemental awareness" (p. 24) embodying qualities of attention, including focus, stability, sustainability, filtering, and vividness (Weick & Sutcliffe, 2006). Thus, a mindful individual has both concentrated attention and high-quality awareness of their present experience (Shao & Skarlicki, 2009). In contrast, a person acting mindlessly will be less attentive and easily distracted. Individuals with mindless habits tend to focus on the past or develop anxiety about the future, limiting their ability to focus on the present moment (Brown & Ryan, 2003). Brown and Ryan's (2003) empirical study found that mindfulness is related to levels of openness to experience and internal state awareness, while negatively akin to social anxiety.

Mindfulness is about being aware of what is happening in the present moment. All of us have the capacity to be mindful. By cultivating our ability to pay attention in the present moment, we are able to disengage from mental "clutter" and to have a clear and alert mind. It makes it possible for us to respond rather than react to situations, thus improving our decision making and potential for physical and mental relaxation.

While the foundations of mindfulness stem from Eastern meditational practice (Kristeller & Hallet, 1999), it is increasingly being introduced in Western culture. As discussed throughout this book, mindfulness training is being adopted across a range of disciplines and industries. It is suggested that mindfulness training can improve one's self-regulation of attention (Bishop et al., 2004) and, as such, have positive influences on performance.

Attention

Attention is a subset of mindfulness. Sustained attention is the ability to stay vigilant over time (Posner & Rothbart, 1992), which is the foundation of mindfulness, as vigilance, a state of alertness, is required to maintain focus on the present (Shapiro et al., 2006). Attention can be divided into concentrative attention and receptive attention. Jha and colleagues (2007) define concentrative attention as specific focus, such as focusing on breath. Receptive attention is referred to as "objectless," where attention is maintained in the present moment, without limitation or specific direction (Jha et al., 2007). Empirical studies have found that increasing mindfulness can improve alertness and orienting of attention (Jha et al., 2007) and increase immune functioning as a result of enhanced attention (Davidson et al., 2003). Moreover, Chambers, Chuen Yee Lo, and Allen (2008) found that increased mindfulness can positively influence sustained attention abilities and the capacity to switch attention between stimuli.

Attention is always shifting because of internal and external pressures and demands. By that we mean the changes in the environment and the cognitions, feelings, and behaviors within the individual. The performer needs to be mindful of these shifts in attention in order to maintain optimal performance. How often have you been told to concentrate and focus on a task in the face of distractions? A common problem that many performers share is the inability to focus attention appropriately, especially when under pressure (Nideffer & Sagal, 2006). In fact, the difference between people who perform poorly under stress and those who excel under pressure is often due to how mindful they are of situations where arousal is likely to increase above an optimal level for the task and how well they control this arousal and its subsequent attentional processes.

For instance, an experienced stand-up comedian is aware that he has to shift attention rapidly if he is to maintain audience interest. When he first comes out on stage and is about to start his monologue, he scans his audience carefully. He knows he requires a broad focus of attention, almost a street sense, as to the characteristics or perceived mood of the audience, so he can develop an early rapport with them. However, he also has to be mindful of hecklers and other interruptions during his on stage performance, as any response he makes requires a narrower type of concentration, so that he can focus on an appropriate answer.

For performance to be at the optimal level, in which a performer feels confident, in control, and immersed in the task (Krane & Williams, 2006), the focus of the performer should be on the most relevant task-specific cues, and he or she should be able to shift attention in response to the changing demands of the task (Nideffer, 1976). For example, if, while performing, our comedian notices a well-known person "about town" walk in and take a seat, the comedian is aware that this provides an opportunity to elaborate more on a particular point. When the comedian is feeling confident and in control, he can seamlessly alter his patter slightly and include the local celebrity, which can subsequently lead to much laughter. In such an instance, the comedian has mindfully responded to the changing demands of the situation and has been able to shift his attentional focus accordingly. Valentine and Sweet (1999) suggest that this flexibility of attention may be just as important as selective attention.

Central to this flexibility of attention is awareness. Awareness here is twofold. First, there is external environmental awareness, that is, the comedian is cognizant of changes in the external environment and has the ability to adjust and manipulate the situation appropriately. Second, there is internal awareness and the competence to shift attention triggered by external distraction while remaining aware of one's self. As Bernier and colleagues (2009) highlight, this level of performance awareness involves "identifying one's emotional states, arousal level, cognitions, and attentional focus to adjust them" (p. 330). Awareness skills are taught by performance psychologists as a method to improve the client's focus while developing abilities to adjust in changing circumstances.

Each person has a dominant attentional style, and each performance situation makes different demands on the performer. In most situations, it is easy to move between the different attentional demands of the situation; in fact, one is usually not aware of changing focus if performing under conditions where one is not being evaluated. However, when arousal is above an optimal level for the task (e.g., the task is less than comfortable, a significant person is observing), then the performer may gravitate to his or her more dominant attentional style (Hull, 1951). This can cause problems when the attentional style does not match the demands of the situation, and performance can deteriorate, particularly under increasing pressure.

For example, a voice student, in her second year at the conservatorium, is about to commence her second song in front of the rest of the class. She knows the song and sings it well in front of her classmates. However, as she commences, the door opens and the principal walks in and stands at the back of the room. The singer tenses and feels nervous. The piece she is about to sing has a few high notes that she finds difficult. She starts the song but finds it difficult to maintain attention to each note as she keeps thinking about how bad she must sound. The muscles in her throat tighten, the high notes are forced, and she finishes the song feeling very dissatisfied with her performance.

Attentional Dimensions

Attention varies in its width (broad versus narrow) and direction (internal versus external). At a conceptual level, the intersection of width and direction creates four different attentional dimensions relevant for performance (Nideffer, 1989, 1994). The performer may seamlessly and without awareness move from one attentional dimension to another in his or her day-to-day activities. However, in a high-pressure situation, where the emotion is more intense, there is the likelihood of being unable to shift effectively from one dimension to another. The four dimensions include the following:

Broad external
When you quickly scan the environment, noting a wide variety of cues, then you are using a broad external dimension of attention. For example, think of the comedian who is good at assessing the mood of the audience, or a dancer who is scanning the positions of other dancers on stage and taking into account other external conditions, such as the position of props and lights. Generally, an ideal broad external focus of attention is accompanied by mindfulness of the situation and a well-developed *street sense*.

Broad internal
According to Bicchieri (2006), cues from the environment are compared to information stored in your long-term memory. We use this information to analyze and plan a course of action, whether it is choosing the right chords for a musical interlude or deciding the best approach for introducing oneself at an audition. For example, an actor, developing the character for his or her part in a play, who is thinking back to past potentially useful experiences, is using a broad internal dimension of attention.

Narrow internal
Once the plan has been developed and the information has been analyzed, attention shifts to a narrow internal dimension of attention (e.g., problem solving, a systematic mental rehearsal of the performance). A medical doctor who is listening to a patient's heart beat and thinks there might be a murmur listens carefully to the different sounds she hears. In such an instance, when the doctor is determining the type of heart murmur,

she would be using a narrow internal focus when imagining the blood flowing through the four chambers of the heart

Narrow external

One uses a narrow external dimension when actually performing a task, focused on a specific external factor. For a medical doctor, this might be focusing on finding the vein when preparing to give an injection, or for a singer, it might be responding to the pianist's cue. No matter what the task, if one's attention is focused elsewhere (i.e., task-irrelevant cues), then performance is not mindful and is likely to be suboptimal. Examples of task-irrelevant cues may include physiological arousal indicators (e.g., feeling sweat dripping down the back).

Mindfulness and Attention in Medicine

Under optimal performance conditions (such as carrying out daily clinical duties at the hospital), a senior hospital registrar should have little trouble in adjusting his or her attentional focus from a narrow-internal focus, such as thinking about how to solve a specific problem asked by another registrar, to a narrow-external focus, where the question is answered appropriately. Arousal, however, can mediate mindfulness and attentional focus so that activities that are easy to perform in a stress-free environment become substantially more difficult in a pressure-packed situation (Nideffer, 1989; Nideffer & Sagal, 2006). To illustrate the association of arousal and attentional focus in what an individual perceives to be a stressful situation, we present a case study of a senior hospital registrar participating in final exams.

Case Study

John is a senior hospital registrar (a doctor in training to become a consultant) at a major teaching hospital, is in an accredited training program, and has just failed his Fellowship exams to become a consultant anesthetist. He passed the written exams and was invited to sit the orals. His consultants told him his knowledge was excellent and that there was no reason why he should not pass the oral exams. Everyone was surprised when John failed miserably. This failure was a catalyst for John to make an appointment with a performance psychologist, as he had not previously failed an exam.

Initially with the performance psychologist, John identifies that he is always anxious when being verbally evaluated by senior consultants. John's summary of the situation reflects his performance anxiety: "I always feel a bit stupid, especially when a consultant asks questions." At the time of the exam, he was unable to find the right words or respond appropriately; in reflection, he is aware that he knew the correct answer but was hindered by anxiety.

The performance psychologist could see that John was getting anxious at the thought of again failing the orals. She realized that she needed to teach him the centering breath first, before any other intervention, as this not only reduces arousal but also increases attentional focus. She described to John the relationship between arousal and attention. Fundamental to this intervention approach was the necessity to break John's habit of fearing embarrassment and humiliation stemming from an unsatisfactory answer. The psychologist pointed out, as an example, that if, following an incorrect answer to a consultant during clinical rounds, John was to think about how bad that error was and how humiliated and embarrassed he felt, then a link would be created between the wrong answer and that thought. This link would make it more likely that John would have that thought or a similar one following another wrong answer, until eventually every time John made an error he would think this way. Unfortunately for John, making an error had become linked to subsequent strong feelings of humiliation. It had become a habit.

When the psychologist noted the habit, linking mistakes with humiliation, John nodded vigorously. He stated, "I can certainly relate to that example." The psychologist explained that when we are put under pressure we revert back to old habits. Reverting to old habits can be problematic. Ideally, we want to create new helpful habits, by interrupting the sequence of events that led to the old habit. To change such a habit takes about three weeks of mindfulness training (Covey, 1989). Prior to this, it is evident to the psychologist that John needs to learn how to control his energy and arousal levels.

When arousal or anxiety is too high for a particular task, then it becomes very difficult to attend appropriately to that task. In such a situation, attentional capacity is somewhat decreased. However, in John's case, when he answers questions from junior registrars, no matter how difficult or complex the question, he is able to answer the questions competently. He either had no overt arousal or was not overly conscious of it. As interacting with junior registrars is something done on a daily basis, all of John's attention is focused on providing appropriate and accurate responses. However, when asked a similar question by a senior consultant, John is unable to respond. As John explains,

I can't think straight. Even if it's an easy answer, I think there's probably some catch or trick to it, and I stumble for words. Also I try to get some feedback by watching the consultant's face closely for any signs of approval or disapproval as I respond.

This example highlights an important component of being mindful during performance. The quote from John indicates that his attentional focus is not on providing a response to the question. Instead, he is distracted by task-irrelevant cues and is trying to see what is behind the question or is focused on the consultant's expression. He is possibly intimidated by the seniority of the consultant and wants to impress her with his response. Consequently, this distraction increases the chance of error as crucial parts of the consultant's question or his response may be missed.

Arousal can mediate the effects of attentional focus and may change a mindful performance to a mindless performance. As arousal increases, according to Easterbrook's (1959) cue utilization hypothesis, anxiety results in a narrowing of attention such that, in this case study, John takes in fewer peripheral cues and has an increased internal focus of attention. He is no longer fully mindful of the situation. At the same time, physiological changes are occurring in John's body, such as increased heart rate, sweat gland activity, and muscle tension. These factors lead to feelings of pressure, an inability to attend to task-relevant cues, and muscle tightness – and therefore can lead to performance problems. Evidently John could benefit from mindfulness training to manage his arousal and attentional focus.

Centering technique: Mindful breathing

Scholars have long proposed that mindfulness training and rehearsal can enhance both concentrative and receptive attention (Broww, 1977; Speeth, 1982; Valentine & Sweet, 1999). Formal mindfulness training often commences with focusing attention on one aspect of awareness, such as breathing (Schmertz, Anderson, & Robins, 2009). As attention waivers, the individual is encouraged to observe the distractions and, subsequently, draw attention back to the present state of breathing. To break the downward aversive spiral from anxiety to the incapacity to perform, interventions can be targeted at the narrowing of attention and/or at the physiological changes that co-occur with anxiety. The centering technique of focusing on breathing is a quick way to stop the downward spiral and allows the client to be more mindful and in control of the situation.

The performance psychologist introduced John to the importance of breathing. He was taught how to use his breathing as a centering technique and was instructed to practice this twelve to fifteen times a day. As with any facet of mindfulness training, practice and repetition are critical to improving performance. Every time John checked his watch during the day, he took one centering breath. At the end of each day, John reflected on his breathing technique and, based on quantity and quality, gave himself a score from 1 to 10. By getting John to score his results daily in a diary, first, he is more mindful of doing his homework consistently, and second, research indicates that regular monitoring of one's behavior leads to increased motivation (Kazantzis & Deane, 1999). Also, the performance psychologist hypothesized that if John practiced this breath conscientiously for a week to ten days, at home, at the hospital, or when studying, he would develop increased awareness of the first signs of overarousal and would start to take this breath automatically.

After the next couple of sessions with the performance psychologist, John started to use his centering technique specifically when consultants asked him questions. John felt he had improved: one example was that he was able to listen carefully to a question and give a more measured and structured response. He had accomplished a certain amount of inner stability and control by focusing on the awareness of breathing and the accompanying bodily sensations. He had learned how to quiet his mind. However, mindfulness involves awareness of constantly shifting feelings, images, sensations, and thoughts within the body and mind. John needed to recognize how these shifting patterns of thoughts, feelings, images, and sensations impacted his performance when he responded to questions from people in authority, that is, the consultants and examiners.

Role-playing for mindful awareness

In order for John to be more mindful of how he actually sounded when he responded to questions, the performance psychologist role-played a couple of situations. This activity was electronically recorded. During the role-play, when John responded to the junior registrar his voice was louder, deeper, and more resonant, and there was pace of responses and use of pause at appropriate places. John's voice sounded confident, as though it belonged to someone with authority and knowledge. In the second recording, where John was responding to the same question from a senior consultant, his voice sounded tremulous and softer, and the pitch was monotone, the answer tentative, and the content disorganized. It sounded as though a novice student was making the response.

The difference between the recordings was quite astonishing to John. For the following few weeks, the performance psychologist instructed John to record all consultants' questions and his responses. He was to listen and reflect on his responses at the end of each day. This technique was designed for John to identify lapses in attentional focus and develop new, long-lasting good habits in such situations.

Role-play summary

Research on improving substandard habits indicates that, after pointing out how a habit has caused inconvenience, embarrassment, or disruption to the individual, then increasing awareness and developing a planned, practiced alternate response may be effective (Miltenberger & Fuqua, 1985). Awareness training for John was teaching him to become mindful of his nervous demeanor when responding to questions from people in authority, next consciously take a centering breath to ground himself, and finally respond as though teaching an equal or more junior colleague. John was also encouraged to ask his partner and/or colleagues to help him practice this more authoritative and effective response. According to Azrin and Nunn (1973), involving the assistance of significant others to use the planned response successfully helps to motivate the client to eliminate bad habits.

In John's case, like so many others, his mind when responding to questions was probably operating independently from his body. So, for instance, as he answered a question from a consultant, he was at the same time wondering what the hidden agenda in the question was and why the consultant was frowning. If the consultant interjected with a comment, chances were likely that John would have difficulty in comprehending. Rather than being mindful, John was responding automatically – in other words, mindlessly – and the end result of John's responses was that they lacked passion and engagement and consequently were unsatisfactory. Quite literally, John was not present and in the moment. His mind and body were functioning separately.

John's case study provides some insight into introductory training techniques to improve mindfulness and subsequently enhance performance. In a collaborative effort with clients, performance psychologists use a range of skills to enhance their clients' performance. Typically these skills involve energy regulation, self-talk, goal setting, imagery, and attentional focus (or concentration). These skills come directly from cognitive behavioral therapy (CBT) (Meichenbaum, 1985) and can be most effective if mindfully employed in various ways that suit each individual's performance domain. When using a mindful approach, people can use the CBT skills to learn to accept, rather than try to change, negative thoughts or feelings. When using CBT skills within a mindfulness approach, an individual is using the CBT skills in a nontraditional way.

A number of take-home lessons arise from John's scenario. First, attention varies in terms of its width (broad versus narrow) and direction (internal versus external), which can be conceptualized as four different attentional styles: broad-internal, broad-external, narrow-internal, and narrow-external (Nideffer, 1989, 1994). Second, to perform optimally, the performer's focus should be on the most relevant task-specific cues, and he or she should be able to shift attention in response to the changing demands of the task (Nideffer, 1976). Third, arousal mediates the effects of attentional focus. As arousal increases, there are physiological changes that occur, such as increased muscle tension and heart rate. A narrowing of attention may occur such that the performer takes in fewer peripheral cues and increases his or her internal focus of attention. These factors may impact coordination, ability to attend to task-relevant cues, and muscle relaxation, often affecting performance. Fourth, interventions can be targeted at both the physiological and attentional changes, thus reducing bad habits and increasing mindfulness and a feeling of control over one's intentional thoughts and behavior while accepting or tolerating unhelpful, involuntary thoughts and feelings.

Mindfulness and Attention in the Performing Arts

As discussed previously in this book, it has been recognized for over a decade that mindfulness is key to staying in the present moment and producing peak performance in sport (Ravizza, 2002). While less empirical attention has been given to the performing arts, the premise of mindfulness in athletic performance is arguably transferable across disciplines. Kee and Wang's (2008) investigation found that athletes with higher mindfulness capabilities were more likely to experience the flow state. Similarly, in the performing arts, reaching peak performance requires mental and physical preparation to ensure that attention and centering of focus are maintained throughout the stage performance.

In the next case study, imagery is used to enhance mindfulness of a performing artist by incorporating a familiar scenario and guided imagery aligned with the use of the centering breath. Most imagery studies have been used in the area of sport, with a substantial amount of empirical evidence indicating that mental imagery can enhance sport performance levels significantly (Morris, Spittle, & Perry, 2004; Murphy & Martin, 2002). However, the benefits of imagery are also developing in many other areas outside of sport to promote the achievement of the highest potential in a broad range of disciplines. To illustrate the application of mindfulness and the importance of attention, centering, and imagery in the performing arts, a case study of a stage performer, Linda, is discussed.

Case study
Linda is a performing artist in her late twenties who has been working in the stage, film, and TV industry as a singer, dancer, and actor for more than twenty years. She has always been confident and outgoing, but due to an injury to her knee over a year ago where she collided with another performer as she danced off stage, she now finds it difficult to focus her attention appropriately when dancing or practicing with others.

Linda and the psychologist discussed what happens to her when she loses focus, and how, when she makes a mistake, she begins to worry about the consequences. She worries that any mistake she makes not only will cause a reinjury to her knee, which would mean she might not be able to work, but it will affect the movement patterns of other performers. Linda worries that the director or choreographer will notice and that this will impact Linda's chances of getting any further work with the company.

The performance psychologist explained to Linda that her attention was divided: Linda was worrying about past incidents and worrying about the possible, future consequences, meaning she no longer was in the present or focusing on the task at hand. Linda agreed with this, and indicated that she has always had a tendency to worry, but that since the injury last year this worrying had intensified, particularly when she was working with other artists. Linda passionately asked, "How am I going to change it?" The psychologist pointed out that she had probably had this pattern of behavior for a while, at least since her knee injury and that it had become a maladaptive habit of thinking.

Linda was already familiar with using the centering breath to help her focus more in auditions and practice sessions, but her fear of reinjury was impacting her ability to sustain focus. Linda's confidence had decreased and was starting to affect her work. She explained how stage and film/television sets are more complicated than most people realize and require all cast and crew to be in a certain place, doing a certain thing, at a certain time. Linda explained,

If you are a few seconds out or a few steps off, you can put yourself and other performers/crew in danger (not to mention ruining the show!). I was injured because cues were misread. I came onstage early, and collided with another performer.

Working in coordination with fellow performers is crucial in the performing arts. Langer, Russell, and Eisenkraft (2009) discuss mindlessness in musical performance. Based on their study of orchestra musicians, they state that mindless performances can be static and variation limited, due to preconceived notions of how the performance should sound. Langer and colleagues (2009) contend that those musicians who actively draw on their internal musical instincts while simultaneously interacting with their colleagues have the ability to produce a more dynamic performance. While other studies have focused on performance of individuals (e.g., Langer 2005; Langer & Piper 1987), Langer and colleagues (2009) illustrate that mindfulness can also lead to improved group performances. This is similar to organizational studies that have explored "collective mindfulness" among groups of employees. Weick, Sutcliffe, and Obstfeld (2000) defined collective mindfulness as, "the capacity of groups and individuals to be acutely aware of significant details, to notice errors in the making, and to have the shared expertise and freedom to act on what they notice" (p. 34). In this case study, Linda explains the importance of collective performance and coordination when on stage.

When the psychologist asked for more details about onstage movement and coordination, Linda continued to explain how it was not just spatial awareness. Linda reflected, "It's also blocking or hitting your mark. When working on a show, each performer is assigned a specific track or part." Linda went on to say that as well as learning the choreography/vocals/dialogue for this part, artists are also required to learn exactly where to be and when. Numbers are marked on the front of the stage, with "0" being center. "If you were looking at the numbers from a performer's perspective, they would look like this" (Linda pulls out some paper and starts to draw the following):

[stage left] 10 9 8 7 6 5 4 3 2 1 0 1 2 3 4 5 6 7 8 9 10 [stage right]
[performer]

Linda went on to explain that the amount of numbers varies depending on the width of the stage, and that visual cues are also used to determine how far the artist is upstage (toward the back) or downstage (toward the audience). She summarized:

Some of the visual cues might be being in line with the first wing or the second wing. On smaller shows, or one-night gigs, for instance, only visual markers, such as finding the center of the stage by lining up with the center aisle in the auditorium, would be used.

This explanation by Linda reinforced to the psychologist how mindful a performer needs to be of performing in different venues, even if other aspects of the performance are the same.

The psychologist was puzzled by the term "blocking." Linda described how, if she was working as an actor, part of her blocking might be to be downstage right on number 6 by a certain line. Whereas, as a dancer, she instead would need to be on certain numbers at certain points in the music/choreography to ensure the formations work correctly. And when entering or exiting the stage, the dancers must know where and how they cross paths with the other performers. Linda smiled and said:

> So there are no awkward "Who's going where?" moments, which you see in day-to-day life on busy streets! If a dancer misses their blocking, at best there may be an awkward collision with another performer, like the one I experienced when I hurt my knee. At worst, a dancer could be in danger of falling into a pit, or being hit by a set flying in.

Linda then went on to explain how with bigger shows there was assistance with the blocking. You often have a longer rehearsal period in the studios prior to starting technical and dress runs in the theatre. During these rehearsals, the floor of the studio is often marked with tape to give the performers an idea of where any fixed set pieces and features (such as steps) will be. The numbers are also marked so that performers can practice their blocking. Linda explained:

> Once on the actual stage [for large productions], performers have enough time to run the show with sets, lights, costumes, etc. However, on smaller productions, and particularly one-off gigs, the stage is often still under construction or not accessible during the final rehearsal period.

Mindfulness and imagery
With the detailed explanation of blocking, the psychologist could clearly understand how injuries could easily occur when entering and exiting the stage. The psychologist felt that mindfulness and imagery strategies, along with the centering technique that Linda was already using, would be helpful to sustain attention to her tasks during the performance. Successful imagery uses the body's different senses to create or re-create a successful

image of the experience. In doing so, the successful imagery enhances the performer's self-efficacy. Guided imagery encourages the brain to imagine positive experiences, which helps to develop healthy coping skills and master new behaviors. The teacher articulates that during a session or through an audio recording (Franklin, 1996). As such, this type of imagery is useful for the performing artist, in conjunction with the centering breath, to equip performing artists with strategies to enhance mindfulness to important cues, particularly when things are not going according to plan.

As Linda's attention was sometimes distracted by the busy performing environment in which she worked, the psychologist felt that a simple mindfulness technique that Linda could practice in the dressing room or while waiting in the wings would be useful to maintain her equanimity. That is, Linda would be able to focus on awareness of her thoughts and body sensations and remain unperturbed by external events outside her control. The exercise that Linda was asked to practice, using roughly the same script, is as follows:

> Just look down towards your hands, and focus your attention to your breathing. Try and breathe as normally as possible, following the air as it comes in through your nostrils and goes down to the bottom of your lungs. Then follow it as it goes back out again. Now fix your attention to the triangle formed by the nostrils and the outer edges of your upper lip. Notice the air moving in and out of your nostrils: cooler as it goes in, warmer as it comes out. Keep your attention on this triangle, while noticing the movement in and out of your breath. Whatever feelings, urges, or sensations arise, gently acknowledge them, and let them go. At the same time, maintain a peaceful face – relax your forehead, cheeks, and jaw. From time to time, your attention will become distracted by thoughts or feelings, and you will want to cling to them. Each time it happens, return your focus to the triangle formed by the nostrils and upper lip. Keep breathing in and out, as evenly and normally as possible.

After trying this mindfulness technique with the psychologist, Linda reported at the next session three weeks later that she did indeed feel more relaxed and calm, and she was keen to keep using it. The psychologist advised Linda that if she could practice this mindfulness technique at least three or four times a day for a minute or so each time, her ability to sustain attention would increase, she would be more conscious of the fact that thoughts and sensations did not necessarily have to become actions, and that when distracted by thoughts she could bring her attention back to the breath to maintain her equanimity.

The psychologist then explained to Linda that she would like her to work with imagery given that it is a very powerful tool when used effectively (Nordin & Cummin, 2008). The psychologist wanted to work with guided imagery, where Linda could intentionally use her imagination to change behavior. In particular, the psychologist's voice and her evoked images could take Linda into her own inner experience the way that mindfulness does. The difference was that it could provide a more goal-directed, structured kind of imaginal narrative with a desired end state, such as Linda imagining herself successfully moving around on stage or entering and exiting the stage.

The psychologist recorded, on Linda's smart phone, a scenario based on a situation Linda had previously described in detail where errors were made. This recording provided a verbal framework whereby Linda could imagine herself moving around on stage. Linda was invited to direct her attention to different areas as she was imagining herself moving around the stage; however, there was a balance and pacing between the psychologist's verbal guidance and silence, leaving space for Linda to have her own experience within the framework provided. Linda was asked to focus on the breath and the scanning of different sensations she felt in her body as she imagined her movements. It was suggested to Linda that when she imagined situations where errors had previously been made, she breathe and imagine calmly manipulating her movements to perform to the best of her ability.

Such imagery practice diminishes the chances of repeating the same errors and is a purposeful practice of being accepting of aversive thoughts and feeling while in the performance context and intentionally bringing attention back to task-relevant cues. With such an intervention, the dancer can practice handling the situation mindfully and effectively. This imagery can also be used to think of situations that may possibly arise at the future rehearsals or stage shows where the dancer has some apprehension about the performance not going well. Imagining handling these situations, to the best of one's ability, often leads to an increased feeling of control over one's attentional focus.

Linda was keen to get started. "It sounds good! Imagery also might stop me being so focused about the consequences of making mistakes." At this stage, the imagery was explained in more detail to Linda, including how important it was to use all the senses while imagining a situation. The psychologist then asked Linda to recall the previously described situation where she had made errors. The instructions were to shut her eyes, relax in her seat, and take about fifteen seconds to fully imagine the environment and the particular situation (i.e., the sounds around her, such as voices or music, the feel of her feet on the wooden stage, seeing the stage lights and the costumes of other performers, and feeling the movements and sensations as she moved around the stage).

Linda was asked to listen to the recording of the psychologist's voice and was advised that the psychologist would not be watching her. Clients can be somewhat self-conscious if they think the psychologist is watching when they have their eyes shut. She was then asked to evaluate the effectiveness of her imagery, a score of 1 being very poor, and a score of 10 being excellent. Linda listened to the recording of the voice and repeated the same imagery three times. Each time it was more vivid, particularly when she was reminded to use all her senses. She felt pleased that she could recall the situation and could increasingly manipulate the images so that she felt more in control.

After giving instructions for practicing this scenario each evening before bed and recording the effectiveness of her imagery in her diary, the psychologist asked Linda to recall other situations where, with hindsight, she might have done something differently. Linda grinned and said, "One that springs to mind is just recently. My hair became tangled in my hat, which all the dancers had to remove on cue while on stage. I just couldn't get my hat off, and struggled with it. I tried to hide myself in the back of the chorus line, but I think it was obvious that I was the only dancer still with a hat on her head!"

The psychologist indicated that that was an ideal situation to imagine and manipulate and proceeded to record the situation on Linda's smart phone. Her instructions to Linda were to listen to this recording regularly, imagining the situation vividly for ten to fifteen seconds. Then, as she started to get apprehensive about being unable to untangle her costume and hair, the recording asked her to take a centering breath, focusing attention to the breath rather than the hat tangled in her hair. After completing the breath, she was told to refocus onto the situation and imagine handling this to the best of her ability.

Linda initially listened to this recording four times in the session, endeavoring to focus on all of her senses. As she gained confidence, she was able to manipulate the image to her satisfaction. She grinned at the end of the fourth try. "You know, instead of going to the back of the chorus line, I could have just ducked down behind a set of steps that was on the stage, I would have been hidden from view." She was starting to really feel how this imagery could work for her. She was asked to do an imagery scenario of her choice each night before bed, scoring the effectiveness of the manipulation and recording that score in her diary.

The successful use of mental imagery is often dependent on the nature of the task (Romero & Silvestri, 1990). Tasks with a high degree of cognitive components, such as those required by a barrister in a courtroom, a dancer, or a gymnast, are more affected by imagery than those that involve more basic patterns or strength tasks (Feltz & Landers, 1983). Also, the number of imagery sessions and the length of each session are points of contention among researchers (Morris, Spittle, & Watt, 2005). In their meta-analysis of mental practice and imagery, Feltz and Landers (1983) indicated that the largest effects for mental practice in cognitive tasks occurred in trials less than one minute long. The benefits of brief imagery practice were supported by Hinshaw (1991), who found that trials less than one minute in duration were more effective in increasing performance. Furthermore, six or fewer trials in a session were able to produce large effects on cognitive tasks, whereas motor and strength tasks required more trials and more minutes to produce similar results (Feltz & Landers, 1983; Hinshaw, 1991).

Linda found it was very rewarding to use imagery for short periods of time in various situations where she had either been successful or where she was able to manipulate an image to imagine performing more effectively. Being able to utilize imagery satisfactorily is not always easy, and if a client has difficulty imagining or manipulating an image, the performance psychologist may not want to spend a great deal of time on imagery psycho-education. If clients want performance results in a hurry, or they have a major event coming up within a short period of time, it may be more productive to use other strategies that take less time to implement.

A number of key takeaways can arise from this case study. First, imagery is a polysensory experience. Second, while contentious, there is support that imagery for less than one minute is most effective, with fewer than six repetitions of an imaged scenario in a session. Third, imagery is not just about success; it can be used as a means to plan and strategize when events do not unfold as planned. Fourth, imagery is best when the body is relaxed. Finally, using a mindfulness-based imagery exercise when feeling overwhelmed or distracted can lead to increased calm and clarity of thought, thus reducing distractions and irrelevant thoughts.

Conclusion

With both these case studies, we have highlighted the importance of understanding what "success" means for each client. For the hospital registrar, success referred both to managing his anxiety before oral exams and having a strategy to reduce arousal and thus increase his attentional focus to the task. For the performing artist, success meant minimizing distractions and managing her fear of reinjury. In both cases, being mindful of their thoughts, feelings, and sensations while performing, and focusing on staying in the moment, enhanced their performances.

For each of the individuals in the case studies to cope effectively with distracting thoughts and feelings and focus on the task at hand, they each needed to be able to access their skills and knowledge at a moment's notice. The performance psychologist provided a framework so that the clients could mindfully improve their performance within their usual environment. In a collaborative effort with the client in each of these case studies, the psychologist used a range of skills to increase mindful awareness while performing. These included attentional control strategies, psycho-education, mindfulness, self-monitoring, arousal regulation, and imagery techniques specific to the client's environment.

In order for performance psychologists to apply their skills effectively across each of these different performance domains, they need to have systemic knowledge of the norms and expectations of the environment in which the client's performances are embedded. For instance, the psychologist working with a hospital registrar needs to have knowledge of how public and private hospitals vary in their operation and the overall roles and expectations for junior and senior registrars in these environments. The roles and expectations for registrars also differ according to the medical specialties, which range from oncology, to anesthetics, to general surgery, to emergency medicine, and so on. The psychologist also needs to consider the specific hospital environment in which the registrars work – the cohesion of a particular medical team, the amount of supervision given to the registrar, and how a particular department in a hospital is managed.

Mindful learning is an important approach for psychological intervention in any discipline. As discussed in this chapter, mindfulness is essential in achieving optimal outcomes in the performing arts and medical specialties. We have offered specific mindfulness-based interventions used in a performance psychologist's practice (see Table 17.1). As a practical framework, mindfulness integrates the foundations of Eastern meditational practice, constructs of attention, and focus on task-relevant cues. Mindfulness – paying attention in the present moment – is an important approach in the practice of performance psychology.

Table 17.1 *Mindfulness-Based Interventions*

Intervention	Purpose	Exercise
Centering technique: mindful breathing	To teach basics of diaphragmatic breathing in order to use breath as a centering technique, which has a focus on shifting attention to the breath.	• Clients are to take one centering breath each time they check their watch during the day (12–15 times per day). • At the end of each day, they reflect on their breathing technique and, based on quantity and quality, give two scores from 1 to 10.
Role-playing	To improve mindful awareness of bodily sensations and vocal tension when responding to questions from different people.	• Role-play two scenarios with the client. First, act out a situation in which the client is confident. Second, act out a scenario, which in the past has caused the client heightened anxiety and arousal. • This activity is to be electronically recorded. • Play the recordings back to the client, noting the differences in client responses between the scenarios.
Guided imagery	To reinforce positive behaviors and encourage desired images.	• The client listens to psychologist's voice either in session or on recording describing a scenario needing improvement. • The client imagines the scenario and develops the ability to manipulate the images successfully. • The client scores effectiveness of each imagery scenario from 1 to 10.

REFERENCES

Azrin, N. H., and Nunn, R. G. (1973). Habit reversal: A method of eliminating nervous habits and tics. *Behaviour Research and Therapy*, 11(4), 619–628. doi: 10.1016/0005-7967(73)90119-8

Bernier, M., Thienot, E., Codron, R., and Fournier, J. F. (2009). Mindfulness and acceptance approaches in sport performance. *Journal of Clinical Sports Psychology*, 25(4), 320–333.

Bicchieri, C. (2006). *The grammar of society: The nature and dynamics of social norms.* New York, NY: Cambridge University Press.

Bishop, S. R., Lau, M. A., Shapiro, S. L., Carlson, L. E., Anderson, N. D., Carmody, J., ... Devins, G. (2004). Mindfulness: A proposed operational definition. *Clinical Psychology: Science and Practice*, 11(3), 230–241. doi: 10.1093/clipsy.bph077

Brown, K. W., and Ryan, R. M. (2003). The benefits of being present: Mindfulness and its role in psychological well-being. *Journal of Personality and Social Psychology*, 84(4), 822–848. doi: 10.1037/0022-3514.84.4.822

Broww, D. P. (1977). A model for the levels of concentrative meditation. *International Journal of Clinical and Experimental Hypnosis*, 25(4), 236–273. doi: 10.1080/00207147708415984

Chambers, R., Chuen Yee Lo, B., and Allen, N. B. (2008). The impact of intensive mindfulness training on attentional control, cognitive style, and affect. *Cognitive Therapy and Research*, 32(3), 303–322. doi: 10.1007/s10608-007-9119-0

Covey, S. R. (1989). *The 7 habits of highly effective people.* New York, NY: Simon & Schuster.

Davidson, R. J., Kabat-Zinn, J., Schumacher, J., Rosenkranz, M., Muller, D., Santorelli, S.F., ... Sheridan, J. F. (2003). Alterations in brain and immune function produced by mindfulness meditation. *Psychosomatic Medicine*, 65(4), 564–570. doi: 10.1097/01.PSY.0000077505.67574.E3

Easterbrook, J. A. (1959). The effects of emotion on cue utilization and the organization of behavior. *Psychological Review*, 66(3), 183–201. doi: 10.1037/h0047707

Feltz, D. L., and Landers, D. M. (1983). The effect of mental practice on motor skill learning and performance. *Journal of Sport Psychology*, 42, 764–781.

Franklin, E. (1996). *Dance imagery for technique and performance.* Champaign, IL: Human Kinetics.

Gallagher, W. (2009). *Rapt: Attention and the focused life.* New York, NY: Penguin.

Hinshaw, K. E. (1991). The effect of mental practice on motor skill performance: A critical evaluation and meta-analysis. *Imagination, Cognition and Personality*, 11(1), 3–35. doi: 10.2190/X9BA-KJ68-07AN-QMJ8

Hoffman, S. L., and Hanrahan, S. J. (2012). Mental skills for musicians: Managing music performance anxiety and enhancing performance. *Sport, Exercise and Performance Psychology*, 1(1), 17–28. doi: http://psycnet.apa.org/doi/10.1037/a0025409

Hull, C. L. (1951). *Essentials of behaviour.* New Haven, CT: Yale University Press.

Jha, A. P., Krompinger, J., and Baime, M. J. (2007). Mindfulness training modifies subsystems of attention. *Cognitive, Affective and Behavioral Neuroscience*, 7(2), 109–119.

Kabat-Zinn, J. (2005). *Coming to our senses: Healing ourselves and the world throughmindfulness.* New York, NY: Hyperion.

Kazantzis, N., and Deane, F. P. (1999). Psychologists' use of homework assignments in clinical practice. *Professional Psychology: Research and Practice*, 30(6), 581–585. doi: 10.1037/0735-7028.30.6.581

Kee, Y. H., and Wang, C. K. J. (2008). Relationships between mindfulness, flow dispositions and mental skills adoption: A cluster analytic approach. *Psychology of Sport and Exercise*, 9(4), 393–411. doi: 10.1016/j. psychsport.2007.07.001

Krane, V., and Williams, J. M. (2006). Psychological characteristics of peak performance. In J. M. Williams (Ed.), *Applied sport psychology personal growth to peak performance* (5th ed., pp. 207–227). New York, NY: McGraw-Hill.

Kristeller, J. L., and Hallet, C. B. (1999). An exploratory study of a meditation-based intervention for binge eating disorder. *Journal of Health Psychology*, 4(3), 357–363. doi: 10.1177/135910539900400305

Langer, E. J. (2005). *On becoming an artist: Reinventing yourself through mindful creativity*. New York, NY: Ballantine.

Langer, E. J., and Piper, A. I. (1987). The prevention of mindlessness. *Journal of Personality and Social Psychology*, 53(2), 280–287. doi: 10.1037/0022-3514.53.2.280

Langer, E. J., Russell, T., and Eisenkraft, N. (2009). Orchestral performance and the footprint of mindfulness. *Psychology of Music*, 32(2), 125–136. doi: 10.1177/0305735607086053

Meichenbaum, D. (1985). *Stress inoculation training*. Elmford, NY: Pergamon Press.

Miltenberger, R. G., and Fuqua, R. W. (1985). A comparison of contingent vs non-contingent competing response practice in the treatment of nervous habits. *Journal of Behavior Therapy and Experimental Psychiatrty*, 16(3), 195–200. doi: 10.1016/0005-7916(85)90063-1

Morris, T., Spittle, M., and Perry, C. (2004). Imagery in sport and exercise. In T. Morris & J. Summers (Eds.), *Sport psychology: Theory, applications and issues*. Brisbane, Australia: John Wiley & Sons.

Morris, T., Spittle, M., and Watt, A. P. (2005). *Imagery in sport*. Champaign, IL: Human Kinetics.

Murphy, S. M., and Martin, K. A. (2002). The use of imagery in sport. In T. S. Horn (Ed.), *Advances in sport psychology* (2nd ed., pp. 221–250). Champaign: IL: Human Kinetics.

Nideffer, R. M. (1976). Test of attentional and interpersonal style. *Journal of Personality and Social Psychology*, 34(3), 394–404. doi: 10.1037/0022-3514.34.3.394

(1989). Theoretical and practical relationships between attention, anxiety, and performance in sport. In D. Hackfort and D. Spielberger (Eds.), *Anxiety in sport: An international perspective* (pp. 117–136). New York, NY: Hemisphere.

(1994). *Psyched to win*. Champaign, IL: Leisure Press.

Nideffer, R. M., and Sagal, M. (2006). Concentration and attention control training. In J. M. Williams (Ed.), *Applied sport psychology: Personal growth to peak performance* (5th ed., pp. 382–403). New York, NY: McGraw-Hill.

Nordin, S. A., and Cumming, J. (2008). Types and functions of athletes' imagery: Testing predictions from the applied model of imagery use by examining effectiveness. *International Journal of Sport and Exercise Psychology*, 6, 189–206.

Posner, M. I., and Rothbart, M. K. (1992). Attentional mechanisms and conscious experience. In A. D. Milner and M. E. Rugg (Eds.), *The neuropsychology of consciousness*. (pp. 91–111). San Diego: Academic Press.

Ravizza, K. H. (2002). A philosophical construct: A framework for performance enhancement. *International Journal of Sport Psychology*, 33(1), 4–18.

Romero, K., and Silvestri, L. (1990). The role of mental practice in the acquisition and performance of motor skills. *Journal of Instructional Psychology*, 17(4), 218–221.

Shao, R., and Skarlicki, D. P. (2009). The role of mindfulness in predicting individual performance. *Canadian Journal of Behavioural Science*, 41(4), 195–201. doi: 10:1037/a0015166

Schmertz, S. K., Anderson, P. L., and Robins, D. L. (2009). The relation between self-report mindfulness and performance on tasks of sustained attention. *Journal of Psychopathology and Behavioral Assessment*, 31, 60–66. doi: 10.1007/s10862-008-9086-0

Shapiro, S. L., Carlson, L. E., Astin, J. A., and Freedman, B. (2006). Mechanisms of mindfulness. *Journal of Clinical Psychology*, 62(3), 373–386. doi: 10.1002/jclp.20237

Speeth, K. R. (1982). On psychotherapeutic attention. *Journal of Transpersonal Psychology*, 14(2), 141–160.

Valentine, E. R., and Sweet, P. L. G. (1999). Meditation and attention: A comparison of the effects of concentrative and mindfulness meditation on sustained attention. *Mental Health, Religion and Culture*, 2(1), 59–70. doi: 10.1080/13674679908406332

Vealey, R. S., and Greenleaf, C. A. (2006). Seeing is believing: Understanding and using imagery in sport. In J. M. Williams (Ed.), *Applied sport psychology: Personal growth to peak performance* (5th ed., pp. 306–348). New York, NY: McGraw-Hill.

Weick, K. E., and Sutcliffe, K. M. (2006). Mindfulness and the quality of organizational attention. *Organization Science*, 17(4), 514–524. doi: 10.1287/orsc.1060.0196

Weick, K. E., Sutcliffe, K., and Obstfeld, D. (2000). High reliability: The power of mindfulness. *Leader to Leader*, 17, 33–38.

CHAPTER 18

Mindfulness in Music

Tim Patston

Research about the integration of mindfulness into music teaching and learning is still in its infancy. Much of the writing on music and mindfulness relates to the use of music listening as an external entry point to support focus and facilitate mindfulness (Csikszentmihalyi, 1996; Diaz and Silveira, 2013). People listen to music, in part, to help them to enter a mindfulness state, with mindfulness defined as "paying attention in a particular way: on purpose, in the present moment, and nonjudgementally" (Kabat-Zinn, 1994, p. 4). It is somewhat ironic, however, that an art form that can lead to mindfulness and aid flow of listeners, in those who receive the music, is often a source of great stress and anxiety for those who create the music (Patston, 2014).

This chapter will consider the role of mindfulness in the act of music making itself, from both the perspective of the music teacher and music student. Studio music teachers (instrument and vocal) are not part of traditional, formal student education, with little specific education for studio music teachers within higher education. Music Instruction Non-Deficit (MIND), a new model of musical pedagogy designed for studio teachers, will be presented. My thirty years of professional experience working as a researcher, performer, and educator with studio teachers in a range of fields, from pop to music theater, jazz, and classical, across a broad range of instruments, from schools to universities and professional private studios, has led to the conceptualization of this model. In this chapter, I will present the conceptual support for the model and an overview of the MIND model for studio music teachers. The MIND model is designed to extend the joy of music for both the music studio teacher and music studio students. Mindfulness of what is good and right throughout the teaching and practice of studio music is core to the MIND model.

Music is important to the human experience. There is no human culture on the planet without music, and there is evidence of musical instruments existing for over thirty-five thousand years (Conard, Malina, & Munzel, 2009). The role of music in ritual and storytelling is embedded in our collective consciousness. Recent advances in neuroscience reveal that language and music evolved simultaneously in the human brain (Harvey, 2012) and that music involves virtually all of the cognitive processes (Levitin, 2009). Music is deeply connected to human emotion, in individuals and groups, and there is now ample evidence showing positive music experiences can lead to shifts in well-being (Gutman & Schindler, 2007; Lamont, 2011), as well as improving learning across a range of disciplines (McPherson & Welch, 2012). There is also an increasing body of evidence that mindfulness can impact not only well-being and the sense of emotion, but also cognitive and performing skills (Weare, 2012).

Given the powerful neurological and cultural place of music amongst our species, it is critical that music education does not ignore the centrality of music to the human condition, including the musicians and music teachers themselves. Music is key to human emotional and physical well-being (Blood & Zatorre, 2001). Based upon evidence from the areas of study including mindfulness, positive psychology, flow theory, education, sports psychology, and neuroscience, it is time for a model of mindful music pedagogy to be introduced to the education of instrumental and vocal music teachers. This chapter is a call for incorporating a mindful music pedagogy in studio teaching settings as part of a positive pedagogic framework, with the goal of enhancing the quality and effectiveness of studio teaching.

The current teaching practices in instrumental and vocal music pedagogy are based on a deficit-based teaching model. The MIND model challenges the traditional approach and, instead, offers a mindfulness-based, asset-based pedagogic framework as a working counterpoint to the current deficit-based teaching model. A deficit-based teaching model predominantly focuses on correcting errors, either technical or musical, and offers a predominance of negative feedback over positive feedback. Because teachers focus on negative aspects of the process, students find it increasingly difficult to be aware of positive, or even adequate, aspects of their playing. There is an increasing body of evidence that the current deficit-based teaching model can lead to dysfunctional levels of performance anxiety and perfectionism in musicians at all levels (Patston, 2014; Patston & Osborne, 2015). In contrast, an asset-based pedagogic framework fosters student engagement, better outcomes in practice, higher performance standards, and a lifelong love of music.

Mindfulness in Music Education

The origins of mindfulness practice lie in the spiritual elements of Eastern meditative and Western Christian contemplative traditions (Dimidjian & Linehan, 2003), and current mindfulness meditation practice has its origins as clinical treatment of chronic pain (Kabat-Zinn, 1994). There is, however, a great difference between the practice of mindfulness as a form of meditation or therapeutic intervention and the application of a mindfulness framework to pedagogic practice. Currently literature on mindfulness interventions in the field of music performance is limited (Chang, Midlarsky, & Lin, 2003; Farnsworth-Grodd, 2012; Langer, Russell, & Eisenkraft, 2008), and the author could find no studies extant offering applied mindfulness as a pedagogic approach with studio teachers. Studio teachers do not usually have the time to dedicate to mindfulness as a discrete entity, meaning taking studio time to practice meditation or other exclusive mindfulness practices (e.g., body scan, focus on breathing). There is not time to integrate such formal mindfulness meditation practices into a typical studio teaching framework.

A mindfulness approach, however, can become an integral part of a pedagogic holistic music framework. The essential questions include the following: What aspects of mindfulness are particularly relevant to music education? And, how can we best integrate mindfulness into such holistic music framework? At the core of mindfulness is *attention*, the ability to focus on an aspect of a task as an experience without negative bias and the ability to allow experiences to occur in a nonjudgmental way (Bishop et al., 2004). The importance of giving full attention to "the music" is familiar to many music educators. However, while music teaching is primarily focused on attention to and awareness of physical and mental concepts related to technique and musical knowledge, there is not an emphasis on how to give full attention to the music. Core tenets of mindfulness offer a pathway to full attention on the music: acceptance, as emphasized in the Buddhist approach to mindfulness (Bishop et al., 2004), and focus on novel stimuli, which is core to the Ellen Langer approach to mindfulness (Langer, 2005).

Studies in the field of sport psychology (Baltzell & Akhtar, 2014; Thienot et al., 2014) and school education (Weare, 2012) have articulated the benefits of mindfulness within the sport and academic contexts, respectively. Within the music context, and for studio teaching and practice, mindfulness is critical. The Langerian approach (Langer, 2005) supports the proposition that each experience in a lesson, practice session, rehearsal, or performance should be seen as novel, potentially exciting, and always a new opportunity for new experience. This framework is particularly relevant in studio lessons, where, akin to sports coaching and athlete practice, high levels of repetition are most often necessary to achieve technical development.

The development of the new model of musical pedagogy, the MIND model for studio teaching and learning, is based on an amalgamation of the two main approaches to mindfulness from the literature, Buddhist and Langerian mindfulness, as well as two specific mindfulness models. The two models are the Mindfulness-Acceptance-Commitment (MAC) approach to sport (Gardner & Moore, 2007) and the detached mindfulness model (Wells, 2005). The tripartite MAC approach to sport model includes the importance of awareness and acceptance, particularly of aversive negative thoughts and feelings (e.g., "I will never be able to learn this piece of music") and adds the idea of commitment. Applied to the music context, commitment is represented by helping students remain faithful to values-relevant actions: They are encouraged to focus on thoughts and behaviors related to specific goals that support optimal practice or performance. The detached mindfulness model (Wells, 2005), derived from cognitive behavior therapy (CBT), attempts to manage negative, persistent, and intrusive cognitions through acknowledgment and acceptance (compared to the traditional CBT process, which focuses on changing thoughts).

Both the MAC approach in sport and Wells's detached mindfulness models have potential to be employed in the music education setting, and core ideas are integrated into the MIND model for studio teaching. Prior to presenting a mindfulness model for music teaching, termed an *asset model*, it is important to understand the current philosophies and pedagogies of traditional deficit-based music education. This understanding will help to clarify the need to infuse a mindfulness approach, based both on Langerian and a Buddhist mindfulness, into music education and studio teaching specifically.

The Current State of Music Education

In most developed countries, music is taught as a core curriculum classroom subject, generally from the first years of schooling until the early years of high school (or middle school in some countries), after which study becomes optional. In Australia, classroom teachers in secondary schools are usually educated as specialist music teachers. Graduates from university teacher education programs, who specialized in music education, are aware of contemporary pedagogic theory and practice, in particular the shift toward differentiated teaching and learning in order to meet the unique requirements of individuals (Tomlinson et al., 2003). In junior or elementary schools (where students are ages five through eleven) throughout the world, however, there is a strong history of music being taught by generalist teachers with little, if any, formal education in music (Collins, 2014; Jeanneret & DeGraffenreid, 2012).

The training opportunities for studio music teachers, as defined by private or individual lessons offered independent of an organized school system, are at an even lower level, with very few courses available about how to teach in a studio setting (Carey & Harrison, 2007). There is currently no form of accreditation for studio teachers (Carey & Grant, 2014) in the university sector. The idea that teachers are working daily in studios, offering individualized or semiprivate lessons, without education in any form of pedagogy, has been a concern in the field for many years (Jeanneret, 1994). Studio teachers are often successful musicians who have opted to create a private business by teaching children, adolescents, and adults how to play specific musical instruments or voice. This chapter focuses on instrumental and vocal instruction, which are not part of the proscribed core curriculum but rather discretionary activities that students choose to pursue.

Independent studio teaching was previously the domain of the oral and aural tradition. Formally, studio teaching for nonreligious singing has existed since the late 1600s and in instrumental teaching since the founding of the Paris Conservatoire in 1795 (Campbell, 2011). Music tuition was based on the master–apprentice model of instruction. Method books were also introduced in the eighteenth century, often covering techniques for playing several musical instruments (Sluchin & Lapie, 1997). These books included some musical knowledge and position charts, but like many of today's "instrumental teaching methods" did not acknowledge the teaching and learning styles of the instructor or the student.

Specialist instrumental teaching was a relatively late arrival in schools. Piano instruction began in Australian grammar schools at the end of the nineteenth century, and in government schools in 1913 in the United States (Abeles, Hoffer, & Klotman, 1984). Musical instruction in schools in the United Kingdom, Germany, and France was focused on singing (Cox & Stevens, 2010), and instrumental teaching was conducted in private studios outside schools, primarily using European method books (Schleuter, 1996).

Despite the growth in participation in instrumental music making, however, there has been virtually no formal instruction for instrumental teachers, and education in studio pedagogy did not exist until the late 1990s (Carey & Harrison, 2007; Presland, 2005). As a consequence, studio teachers, through no fault of their own, often teach as they were taught under the conservatory model, which focuses on correcting flaws in technical and musical ability and has essentially remained unchanged since the nineteenth century (Carey & Harrison, 2007). Within this model, which I term the deficit model, teachers almost exclusively focus on correcting the flaws of their music and vocal students.

This Darwinian style of training, the survival of those "naturally selected" by and who respond to the teaching model in the system, is still evident in many conservatoria (Carey & Grant, 2014). It therefore comes as no surprise that musicians arrive to teach in studios with a relatively narrow set of beliefs and practices as teachers (Carey & Grant, 2014; Hewitt, 2006). Many may not even be aware of their particular teaching style (Gaunt, 2011; Young, Burnell, & Pickup, 2003) and lack the resources to analyze and reflect upon their practice. In most schools, studio teachers are judged in four areas: (1) the product their students produce in performance; (2) the marks their students receive in external examinations (e.g., the Associated Board of Royal Schools of Music [ABRSM], the Australian Music Examinations Board [AMEB], and Trinity in Australia); (3) whether their students continue to take lessons; and (4) the maintenance of student enrollment numbers in their studio.

Few if any schools have the time and resources to monitor and observe the process component of education, which occupies most of the time in lessons. Unlike most classroom teachers, who typically work in one school, music studio teachers work across many schools. They work with a broad variety of students of differing levels of interest and ability (Hallam, 2001), teach in the music studio rooms, and have little contact with their professional colleagues in the workplace (Ciorba, 2010).

What then is known about what goes on inside instrumental studios in schools? Unsurprisingly, we know very little (O'Neill, 1999). There is an increasing body of work in the literature regarding studio pedagogic practice in tertiary settings (Duke & Simmons, 2006; Krivenski, 2012). The research confirms the hereditary nature of teaching practice in this sector, with teachers teaching as they were taught (Allsup, 2007) – a deficit model.

A relevant example of the deficit approach to studio teaching is provided by Duke and Simmons (2006), an observational study of twenty-five hours of studio instruction by three teachers identified by the researchers as experts in their field. The teachers clearly understood the technique of playing their respective instruments. The study, however, identified a level of attitudinal inflexibility regarding issues such as *how* the teachers responded to mistakes. When a student made a mistake, the teachers would consistently immediately stop the lesson in order to make a correction. The authors reported a predominance of negative feedback over positive feedback in all three studios. The emphasis in the lessons was teacher-centered and-directed, with little, if any, verbal input from the students. The focus was on the technique of the student playing the instrument rather than meeting the specific psychological needs of the individual musician (e.g., using encouragement, noticing what was going well). Teachers tend to be experts at how to play the instrument, but not in understanding the unique character strengths and psychological assets of their students (Carey & Harrison, 2007). Emphasis in lessons is on what is wrong, with little attention on what is right.

How does this inherited deficit model affect student engagement and learning? It may simply stop engagement and learning. There comes a time when instrumental lessons become a discretionary activity, meaning students *choose* to study their instrument. Therefore, autonomous, authentic engagement is critical. Engagement is the process by which students feel a desire to play their instrument and derive pleasure from the acts of learning, playing, and performing. This engagement is a key factor in the conversion from extrinsic to intrinsic motivation (McPherson & Welch, 2012). Disaffection is the opposite of engagement and may lead to students discontinuing their instrumental studies.

There is increasing evidence that a preponderance of negative feedback, implicit in a deficit model, inhibits student engagement (Csikszentmihalyi & Hunter, 2003; Swinson & Harrop, 2012) and that the deficit model may not be the most effective way of promoting student engagement and learning, in particular during the school-age years (Hattie & Timperley, 2007; Swinson & Harrop, 2012). Conversely, specific process-directed and balanced feedback (on both what is going well and what needs to be changed) creates open-minded, self-disciplined individuals who are keen to learn (Dweck, 2006; Swinson & Harrop, 2012).

A shift from a deficit focus to an asset focus, where students embrace the process of learning an instrument, is a necessary, logical next step to improve both the quality of practice and student experience in studio learning. The key lies in developing a new style of studio teaching that emphasizes a mindfulness approach of both teacher and student, draws on the strengths of the students, and finds ways to form deeper relationships between the teachers and students through an appreciative lens. Mindfulness and other ideas within positive psychology can assist musicians in their music teaching and learning, in practice and performance.

The Music Instruction Non-Deficit Model: Keeping Music in MIND

In this section, the new model, MIND is proposed. The MIND model takes into consideration that learning a musical instrument is a complex process, involving physical and mental processes to play the instrument and musical literacy of pitch, rhythm, dynamics, form, and style to read the notes. Instrumental teachers must also take into account the physiological, psychological, and emotional developmental learning pathways of their students. Instruction on different instruments usually begins at different ages. Piano and violin may begin as young as five or six years of age, guitar and drums at eight years old, and some brass and wind around the age of ten. Formal singing instruction, with the exception of boys learning liturgical music as altos or sopranos, does not begin until late adolescence (McPherson & Welch, 2012).

The proposed MIND model uses the concept of mindfulness and positive psychology to enhance the engagement process at all levels of instrumental and vocal learning. Specifically, the core guiding ideas and constructs for the asset-based pedagogic framework include teaching through signature strengths, having a growth mindset, and utilizing mindfulness strategies with openness, curiosity, and enjoyment. The MIND model seeks to enhance the development and growth of practicing musicians.

Teaching through signature strengths

Signature strengths are defined as "A capacity of feeling, thinking, and behaving in way that allows optimal functioning in the pursuit of valued outcomes" (Snyder & Lopez, 2010, p. 38). Based on Seligman, Park, and Peterson's (2004) Virtues in Action model, there are currently twenty-four signature strengths spread across six virtues, including wisdom and knowledge, courage, humanity, justice, temperance, and transcendence. A focus on strengths is essential to the proposed asset model of musical pedagogy. A musician in a lesson has the potential to deploy a range of psychological strengths, or psychological capital (Luthans et al., 2006) that can assist their learning. For example, a student may have a facility for curiosity.

When employing such a signature strength in practice, the student is compelled to explore the full range of sounds of his or her instrument. Other students may have developed resilience, which, when exercised, offers them the ability to work through difficult sections of music with relatively less frustration. Students enjoy exercising their signature strengths (e.g., humor, determination, or a sense of optimism), which each via different pathways can facilitate engagement with lessons.

A growth mindset

Based on Carol Dweck's conceptualization of mindset, those with a *growth mindset* do not believe that talent is preordained or has a finite quantity. Those with a growth mindset believe that for any normal functioning individual, talent can be nurtured like any other skill (see Dweck, 2006). A growth mindset reflects the idea that students can develop not only their musical and technical facilities but also their attitudinal skills.

It is unfortunate that historically talent has often been assumed to be a fixed quality, which Dweck (2006) would term the *fixed mindset*. Studio teachers commonly hold a fixed mindset regarding musical ability (i.e., you are talented or not). Often studio teachers exemplify this fixed mindset by defining and blaming students for "not being musical" or "having a poor ear" (Sand, 2000). In contrast, if teaching with a growth mindset, a teacher in a lesson has the opportunity to identify assets within each student in order to foster an asset-based growth mindset.

Nurturing a growth mindset is essential for the MIND model, which fuels higher self-efficacy, learning, and engagement. Self-efficacy is a student's set of personal beliefs in her own abilities and how capable that student believes herself to be in achieving her goals. Music students with high self-efficacy usually are more accepting of criticism and have high intrinsic motivation. Students with a growth mindset are also likely to be more persistent and resilient to setbacks (Dweck, 2006).

Utilizing mindfulness and savoring

The MIND model emphasizes the utilization of both mindfulness and savoring. Teachers are encouraged to help their musicians intentionally notice what is working; appreciate (savor) such experience; and, in a balanced way, also note what needs to be improved. Within the MIND model, teachers encourage musicians to intentionally notice (mindfully) and appreciate positive aspects (savoring) of musical activities (Bryant & Veroff, 2007), including lessons, practice, rehearsals, and performances.

Mindfulness can also lead to a sense of "flow." Flow usually occurs when we confront tasks we have a chance of completing (challenge meets skill), upon which we are able to fully concentrate, and which have clear goals and provide immediate feedback (Csikszentmihalyi, Rathunde, & Whalen, 1993). Flow also is characterized by being an intensely rewarding experience, in which one is fully immersed. Flow experiences can occur within lessons and practice. The MIND model is designed to encourage teachers and students to have a greater awareness of the process of learning, which occurs between lessons, rather than the snapshot provided by a lesson each week. Students can discuss with their teachers aspects of their practice that engender flow and those that inhibit full engagement. Such information is invaluable in developing practice and rehearsal strategies. Students can also learn to savor positive experiences, reflecting what went well when playing a phrase or doing a performance, rather than dwelling on errors or memory slips. Savoring has been shown to generate, maintain, or enhance positive affect (Bryant, Chadwick, & Kluwe, 2011).

Mindfulness instruction between each phase in the MIND program is an essential aspect of this model (see Figure 18.1). Awareness and acceptance of the somatic, emotional, and psychological arousal experiences of playing, practicing, and performing at each stage of development are expected to aid students in becoming sensitive and thus more wise and able to create music optimally, by observing and accepting moment by moment. This is preferable to being negatively sensitized to the components of music making, by anticipating errors and then dwelling on them once they have occurred.

The Beginners (Curiosity, Interest, Enjoyment)

Many children have instrumental music lessons. The reality of learning an instrument is that, as in sport, many students begin training and most gradually drop out over time. This chapter is not primarily concerned with the select few who become elite professionals but with all students who study an instrument. It is essential that initial experiences are positive and nurturing. And even when students discontinue their studies, there is no value in students leaving music with a negative mindset about music. The apocryphal stories of students who are told to mime in a junior choir because they "couldn't sing," then carry that sense of rejection and perceived lack of ability in music into adulthood, are a disappointing insight into the power of music teachers over young egos. Such experience may thwart the many well-documented benefits of music listeners.

The Proposed Music Instruction Non-Deficit (MIND) model in Music

Figure 18.1   The MIND model uses the concept of mindfulness and positive psychology to enhance the engagement process at all levels of instrumental and vocal learning.

Similarly, there is evidence from sports psychology that poor coaching can lead to athletes dropping out of sport (Gearity & Murray, 2011).

An increasing body of evidence indicates that mindfulness training benefits young people (Mrazek et al., 2013; Waters et al., 2014; Weare, 2012). In order to bring mindfulness to music students, it is important for music teachers to understand how mindfulness can be applied in the studio setting (Crane et al., 2010).

A key component of mindfulness is being open to experience (Greco, Baer, & Smith, 2011), which directly applies to the physical coordination required to make a sound when studying an instrument, particularly with young children. The very first lesson should include an introduction to the concept of mindfulness, in particular the nature of *acceptance*, which is familiar to children in their sense of play. For young children, a mindful introductory lesson would include experiencing the feel of their instrument, each of its component parts, and how they work together to make a sound. The children can then be encouraged to focus on how the instrument feels in their hands as they play. Students should be encouraged to explore without critically judging the sounds they can make (Bates, 2004). This sense of play and exploration can foster a sense of *curiosity* in the process of musical engagement (see Figure 18.1) and has been reported as assisting neural development (Collins, 2013; Flohr, 2010; Hodges, 2010). *Interest* builds on *curiosity* as students are encouraged to experiment with the sounds of their instrument by using technical information provided by the teacher, either through playing simple pieces or looking for pieces that they would like to play.

It is also appropriate at this stage to introduce the concept of awareness, the ability to allow experiences to occur in a nonjudgmental way (Bishop et al., 2004). It is critical to understand that mindful, positive teaching and learning still aim for improvement and a higher level of skill. In a lesson, this would be the observation and remedying of a mistake by offering contextualized feedback, such as "your fingers were in a good position to make that sound; you now need to have a bigger breath to make a better sound." This is preferable to "the sound wasn't very good because you failed to take a breath" (e.g., the deficit model).

Curiosity and interest then lead to *enjoyment*, with students taking pleasure in their music making, learning, and development. Mindfulness activities – such as focusing on and controlling the breath (Kabat-Zinn, 1994), using creative visualization, and mentally playing through a successful performance, including the depth and length of each breath in the performance (Patston, 2010) – are useful techniques. It has been demonstrated that students who are playing a piece they first mastered, which they enjoy or believe they are good at, not only are more likely to continue having lessons but will often play the piece for enjoyment and enter a state of positive mindful reflection when playing the piece many years later (McPherson, 2006).

There is a great deal of discussion in the literature about the experience of "flow" in children (Csikszentmihalyi et al., 1993; O'Neill, 1999), whether flow is a special state related to skills acquisition through perseverance with a sense of control (Csikszentmihalyi et al., 1993) or merely a rewarding activity involving a lack of self-consciousness undertaken for its own sake (Leibovich, Maglio, & Gimenez, 2013; Sinnamon, Moran, & O'Connell, 2012). McPherson (2000) proposed that students, even as young as seven, bring expectations and values to their first lessons, and

Custodero (2002) suggests that young children become increasingly engaged through problem solving which leads to emergent motivation, but there is little research into children's formative instrumental lesson experiences. It has been suggested (Bakker, 2005; Fullagar, Knight, & Sovern, 2013) that a state of flow can travel from teacher to student in a lesson.

The Adolescent Musician (Engagement, Challenge, Extrinsic Motivation)

As children grow into adolescence, the next phase begins, and mindfulness can play a critical role. *Engagement* develops from curiosity and interest, through the *challenge* phase and then to *extrinsic motivation* (see Figure 18.1), the desire to play and strive to improve based on the feedback and expectations of others (Langer, 2005). It is also at this stage that evaluated performances and examinations are likely to begin. At this stage, students become more aware of the physical, psychological, and emotional arousal associated with the music-making experience. Concurrent with this may be the development of performance anxiety and perfectionism (Kenny, 2011; Patston, 2014).

Teachers should share with students of this age the reasons why they have a love of music making, and the place that mindfulness has in their adult lives. Mindfulness may be explained in Buddhist terms related to being present from a moment-to-moment and accepting basis (i.e., accepting unhelpful negative thoughts or fears), which is necessary when experiencing the arousal associated with performance and examinations for the first time. Mindfulness can also be explained using Langerian terminology, as actively noticing new things, relinquishing preconceived mindsets, and then acting on the new observations. The Langerian approach has its place as musicians develop a bank of positive memories and experiences upon which to draw. Both expressions of mindfulness have their place in music teaching, learning, and performance. Adolescents, with their growing and developing psychology and physiology, should find mindfulness a supportive eye in their emotional hurricane, a place they can return to when they find it necessary and a place to go when striving to optimally perform.

There is a growing body of work on the efficacy of mindfulness in adolescents in the fields of education (Waters et al., 2014; Weare, 2012), sport (Gardner & Moore, 2012; Walker, 2013), and psychology (Greco et al., 2011), but nothing specifically related to studio experiences. Mindfulness interventions for students at this age should concentrate on how to develop a mindful practice regime and how to manage their awareness and strive to cope effectively with the somatic features of arousal associated with performance.

Once students have become engaged with music making and are committed to regular lessons and improvement, they need to be *challenged* in order to develop a higher level of skill. Learning to play any instrument is a complex process that takes time. There are no shortcuts. There is general consensus that practice is boring (Ericsson et al., 2006) and that practice makes perfect. These fixed mindset positions need to be challenged. Skilled and experienced classroom teachers and sports coaches understand that variety and purpose are the keys to enjoyment of repetitive tasks, with such repetitive tasks being requisite for skill development. There is also evidence that "mindless practice" leads to lower levels of performance (Langer & Imber, 1979). When practice consists of *mindless* repetition – without purpose, analysis, or goal setting – it runs the risk of students expending "effort" that reaps limited benefits (Williamon, 2004). For example, an hour of mindless practice may lead to a student feeling tired from physical effort but no further developed in his or her playing skills.

The specifics of practice need to be articulated by studio teachers, not just in terms of content, but time, place, and goal setting, as proposed in the tripartite mindfulness model (MAC) (Gardner & Moore, 2007). Part of this is to be cognizant of the importance of awareness and acceptance, particularly of aversive negative thoughts and feelings (e.g., "I will never be able to learn this piece of music"), allowing these thoughts to pass through without judgment. Of equal importance is the idea of commitment. Commitment is represented by helping students commit to value-relevant actions by focusing on thoughts and behaviors related to specific musical goals. These goals need to be varied from session to session and within each session. A session may include goals related to playing technique, performance technique, physical strengthening for stamina, music reading skills, and the ability to listen to pieces to deepen an understanding of style. If the students value optimal practice and performance, they can commit to such values and specific goals to optimize performance.

Mindful practice may begin with the same exercise used with young children, that of the feeling of the instrument, and this positive connection should be reinforced at all levels of playing. A further reason that each practice session should have specific goals, and a balanced use of challenges and new skills, is that these are the key components of inducing mindfulness and flow (Csikszentmihalyi, 1996; Fullagar et al., 2013). As with younger musicians it has been theorized that a flow state can pass from a music teacher to a student (Bakker, 2005).

Students can be introduced to the concepts of observing their responses to cognitions and emotions, and the idea that excitement and anxiety can share similar feelings (Patston, 2010). They can then learn to act with awareness and accept without judgement (Greco et al., 2011) these thoughts and feelings, as suggested by the detached mindfulness model of Wells (2005). Recent research (Patston & Osborne, in press) has shown that perfectionism and performance anxiety not only have high levels of prevalence in populations of adolescent musicians but show the same developmental trajectory in adolescents. Given the strong influence that teachers have (Gearity & Murray, 2011), preventative pedagogy through mindfulness and acceptance may inhibit the onset of these conditions. Students high in levels of flow have been shown to experience lower levels of performance anxiety (Fullagar et al., 2013), with mindfulness training showing reduced burnout in young sportspeople (Jouper & Gustafsson, 2013; Walker, 2013) and improved levels of resilience (Martin & Marsh, 2006). Research is clearly needed in this area with young musicians.

Adult Musicians (Enjoyment, Engagement, Challenge, Intrinsic Motivation)

For a musician to pursue training after adolescence, motivation will ideally shift from *extrinsic* to *intrinsic*, and musician must have his or her psychological needs met to flourish and thrive (Ryan & Deci, 2000). The amount of time spent practicing alone in order to raise technical and artistic standards requires self-motivation. Intrinsic motivation is part of the virtuous circle described in the MIND model in Figure 18.1. Music lessons begin with a sense of curiosity, and intrinsic motivation involves the seeking of novel experiences that extend one's capacities (Ryan & Deci, 2000), a form of curiosity. In order for motivation to be maintained, environmental factors, such as frequency and type of performance experience, as well as psychological factors, become more critical. Adult musicians should have more knowledge of their instrument's capacities; hence, more advanced technique and effective practice regimes are required. At this stage of development, practice efficacy – the developing and maintaining of a varied, stimulating, positive, efficient, and effective practice regime – is essential. Despite many years of music teaching and performance, the idea of what constitutes useful and effective practice is still being debated in the literature (Ericsson, 1996; Patston, 2014). The proposed MIND model contends that practice will be enhanced through diversity, enjoyment, goal setting, and positive experiences in practice, as it combines mindfulness, a growth mindset, and the conditions for generating flow.

As in many areas of research, most studies of mindfulness have been with adult populations, especially undergraduate populations. There are neuroscience studies on mindfulness and brain structure changes (Allen et al., 2012; Blood & Zatorre, 2001), psychology research on the benefits of mindfulness in improving memory and reducing mind wandering (Mrazek et al., 2013), and studies in the sports psychology literature on the efficacy of mindfulness interventions on performance (Garner & Moore, 2012; Thienot et al., 2014). There are also studies on the flow state in musicians (Fritz & Avsec, 2007; O'Neill, 1999; Wrigley & Emmerson, 2013), but there is little research in mindfulness interventions in musicians with the exception of Farnsworth-Grodd (2012) and Langer and colleagues (2008). The study by Fransworth-Grodd (2012) reported that undergraduate music students who were aware within the present moment, rather than distracted by intrusive negative thoughts, were less likely to experience debilitating performance anxiety. Langer and colleagues (2008) focused on Langerian mindfulness and orchestra performance. They reported that musicians who sought to create novel distinctions between performances rather than re-creating past performances made music that was more enjoyable not only to perform but also to hear from an audience's perspective.

Musicians Playing Together

Though it is beyond actual practice within private studio lessons, consideration needs to be given to the far-reaching impact mindfulness could have on ultimately creating music with others. Given that many musicians play in an ensemble, such as rock bands, choirs, or orchestras, rather than a solo setting, music teachers should also discuss with their students the experience of ensemble music making. There is increasing evidence that group activities can generate a sense of mindfulness and flow greater than that of practice or solo performance (Aube, Brunelle, & Rousseau, 2014; Diaz & Silveira, 2013). These experiences, which involve sublimation of ego, a sense of balance, and cooperation within the group, could be discussed from a mindfulness perspective.

Lastly, performance preparation is a key to successful performance outcomes. Preparation should be a part of every lesson and every practice session, familiarizing one's self with the sensations of performance. It is also necessary to appreciate that the environment before each performance will be different due to external factors, such as venue and timing. The advantage that musicians have over sportspeople is that the content of their performance is the same, the same notes in the same sequence, in lessons and practice. Allowing acceptance of preparation done to flow through the mind, and to accept any changes to preparation, is preferable to the inflexible ritualistic behaviors associated with high levels of performance anxiety (Hefferon & Ollis, 2006; Patston, 2010).

Conclusion

The proposed MIND model for studio teachers and learners offers a mindfulness-based approach to teaching and learning, guided by the values of a growth mindset, savoring and emphasizing virtue-based character strengths. A more mindful approach is promising to change the current state of studio teaching and learning. With such an approach, practices and performances can ultimately shift from being emotional, a demonstration of how the musician is feeling at the time, to emotive, music flowing from and through a musician and having an emotional effect upon his or her audience. Although much of the literature suggests that mindfulness can be achieved only through a course of study or even years of meditative practice (Grossman et al., 2004; Kabat-Zinn, 1994), recent studies (Kawakami, White, & Langer, 2000; Langer et al., 2008) have found that educational approaches can cultivate a mindful state while engaged in performance-based tasks.

There is building evidence from the fields of education, clinical psychology, sports psychology, positive psychology, and neuroscience that mindfulness can lead to not only an improved sense of physical, emotional, and psychological well-being, engagement, and motivation, but also improved levels of skill and execution in performance. Much research is yet to be done in the area of mindfulness in the field of music, from lessons to practice, from rehearsal to performance. The proposed MIND model is a positive beginning to helping students and teachers find joy and authentic meaning in their music.

REFERENCES

Abeles, H. F., Hoffer, C. R., and Klotman, R. H. (1984). *Foundations of music education*. New York, NY: Schirmer.
Allen, M., Dietz, M., Blair, K., Van Beek, M., Rees, G., Vestergaard-Poulsen, P., Lutz, A., and Roepstorff, A. (2012). Cognitive-affective neural plasticity

following active-controlled mindfulness intervention. *Journal of Neuroscience*, 32(44), 15601–15610. doi: 10.1523/JNEUROSCI.2957-12.2012

Allsup, R. E. (2007). Democracy and one hundred years of music education. *Music Educators Journal*, 93(5) 52–57.

Aube, C., Brunelle, E., and Rousseau, V. (2014). Flow experience and team performance: The role of team goal commitment and information exchange. *Motivation and Emotion*, 38(1), 120–130. doi: 10.1007/s11031-013-9365-2.

Bakker, A. B. (2005). Flow among music teachers and their students: The crossover of peak experiences. *Journal of Vocational Behavior*, 66, 26–44. doi: 10.1016/j.jvb.2003.11. 001

Baltzell, A., and Akhtar, V. (2014). Mindfulness Meditation Training for Sport (MMTS) intervention: Impact of MMTS with Division I female athletes. *Journal of Happiness and Well-Being*, 2(2), 160–173.

Bates, R. (2004, September). A socially critical view of public education. Paper presented at the Annual Conference of the European Conference on Educational Research, Crete.

Bishop, S. R., Lau, M., Shapiro, S., Carlson, L., Anderson, N. D., Carmody, J., ... Devins, G. (2004). Mindfulness: A proposed operational definition. *Clinical Psychology: Science and Practice*, 11(3), 230–241. doi: 10.1093/clipsy. bph077

Blood, A. J., and Zatorre, R. J. (2001). Intensely pleasurable responses to music correlate with activity in brain regions implicated with reward and emotion. *Proceedings of the National Academy of Sciences*, 98, 11818–11823. doi: 10.1073/pnas.191355898

Bryant, F. B., and Veroff, J. (2007). *Savoring: A new model of positive experience*. Mahwah, NJ: Lawrence Erlbaum.

Bryant, F. B., Chadwick, E. D., and Kluwe, K. (2011). Understanding the processes that regulate positive emotional experience: Unsolved problems and future directions for theory and research on savoring. *International Journal of Wellbeing*, 1(1), 107–126. doi: 10.5502/ijw.v1i1.18

Campbell, M. (2011). *The great violinists*. London, UK: Faber & Faber.

Carey, G., and Harrison, S. (2007, June). *Music in Australian tertiary institutions: Issues for the 21st century*. Paper presented at the 2007 National Conference of National Council of Tertiary Music Schools (NACTMUS), Brisbane, Australia.

Carey, G., and Grant, C. (2014, July). Teachers of instruments, or teachers as instruments? Moving from transfer to transformative approaches to one-to-one pedagogy. In G. Carruthers (Ed.), *Relevance and reform in the education of professional musicians* (pp. 42–54). Paper presented at the Proceedings of the 20th International Seminar of the ISME Commission on the Education of the Professional Musician (CEPROM), Belo Horizonte, Brazil

Chang J. C., Midlarsky E., and Lin P. (2003). Effects of meditation on music performance anxiety. *Medical Problems of Performing Artists*, 18, 126–130.

Ciorba, C. (2010). Professional self-perceptions of future music educators. In *Proceedings of the Tenth International Symposium* (pp. 65–73). Aarhus,

Denmark: Department of Curriculum Research, Danish School of Education, Aarhus University.

Collins, A. (2013). Neuroscience meets music education: Exploring the implications of neural processing models on music education practice. *International Journal of Music Education*, 31(2), 217–231. doi: 10.1177/0255761413483081

(2014). Neuroscience, music education and the pre-service primary (elementary) generalist teacher. *International Journal of Education and the Arts*, 15(5), 1–21.

Conard, N., Malina, M., and Münzel, S. (2009). New flutes document the earliest musical tradition in southwestern Germany. *Nature*, 460, 737–740. doi: 10.1038/nature08169

Cox, G., and Stevens, R. (2010). *The origins and foundations of music education*. London, UK: Continuum International.

Crane, C., Jandric, D., Barnhofer, T., Mark, J., and Williams, G. (2010). Dispositional mindfulness, meditation, and conditional goal setting. *Mindfulness*, 1, 204–214. doi: 10.1007/s12671-010-0029-y

Csikszentmihalyi, M. (1996). *Creativity: Flow and the psychology of discovery and invention*. New York, NY: Harper/Collins.

Csikszentmihalyi, M., and Hunter, J. (2003). Happiness in everyday life: The uses of experience sampling. *Journal of Happiness Studies*, 4(2), 185–199.

Csikszentmihalyi, M., Rathunde, K., and Whalen, S. (1993). *Talented teenagers: The roots of success and failure*. New York, NY: Cambridge University Press.

Custodero, L. (2002). Seeking challenge, finding skill: Flow experience in music education. *Arts Education and Policy Review*, 103(3), 3–9. doi: 10.1080/10632910209600288

Custodero, L., and Stamou, L. (2006, August). *Engaging classrooms: Flow indicators as tools for pedagogical transformation*. Paper presented at the Proceedings of the 9th International Conference on Music Perception and Cognition, Bologna, Italy.

De Manzano, O., Theorell, T., Harmat, L., and Ullén, F. (2010). The psychophysiology of flow during piano playing. *Emotion*, 10(3), 301–311. doi: http://dx.doi.org/10.1037/a0018432

Diaz, F. M., and Silveira, J. M. (2012). Dimensions of flow in academic and social activities among summer music camp participants. *International Journal of Music Education*, doi: 10.1177/0255761411434455

(2013). Mindfulness, attention, and flow during music listening: An empirical investigation. *Psychology of Music*, 41, 42–58. doi: 10.1177/0305735611415144201313

Dimidjian, S. D., and Linehan, M. M. (2003). Mindfulness practice. In W. O'Donohue, J. Fisher, and S. Hayes (Eds.), *Cognitive behavior therapy: Applying empirically supported techniques in your practice* (pp. 229–237). New York, NY: Wiley.

Duke, R. A., and Simmons, A. L. (2006). The nature of expertise: Narrative descriptions of 19 common elements observed in the lessons of three renowned artist-teachers. *Bulletin of the Council for Research in Music Education*, 170, 1–13.

Dweck, C. S. (2006). *Mindset: The new psychology of success*. New York, NY: Random House.

Ericsson, K. A. (1996). *The road to excellence: The acquisition of expert performance in the arts and sciences, sports and games*. Mahwah, NJ: Lawrence Erlbaum.

Ericsson, K., Charness, N., Feltovich, P., and Hoffman, R. (Eds.). (2006). *The Cambridge handbook of expertise and expert performance*. Cambridge, UK: Cambridge University Press.

Flohr, J. W. (2010). Best practices for young children's music education: Guidance from brain research. *General Music Today*, 23(2), 13–19. doi: 10.1177/1048371309352344

Farnsworth-Grodd, V. A. (2012). *Mindfulness and the self-regulation of music performance anxiety*. (Unpublished doctoral dissertation). Auckland, New Zealand: University of Auckland.

Fritz B. S., and Avsec A. (2007). The experience of flow and subjective well-being of music students. *Horizons Psychology*, 16(2), 5–17.

Fullagar, C. J., Knight P. A., and Sovern H. S. (2013). Challenge/skill balance, flow, and performance anxiety. *Applied Psychology*, 62(2), 236–259. doi: 10.1111/j.1464-0597.2012.00494.x

Gardner, F. L., and Moore, Z. E. (2007). *The psychology of enhancing human performance: The Mindfulness-Acceptance-Commitment (MAC) approach*. New York, NY: Springer.

(2010). Acceptance-based behavioral therapies and sport. In S. Hanrahan and M. Andersen (Eds.), *Handbook of applied sport psychology* (pp. 186–193). New York, NY: Routledge.

(2012). Mindfulness and acceptance models in sport psychology: A decade of basic and applied scientific advancements. *Canadian Psychology*, 53(4), 309–318. doi: 10.1037/a0030220

Gaunt, H (2011). Understanding the one-to-one relationship in instrumental/vocal tuition in higher education: Comparing student and teacher perceptions. *British Journal of Music Education*, 28(2), 159–180. doi: http://dx.doi.org/10.1017/S0265051711000052

Gearity, B. T., and Murray, M. (2011). Athletes' experiences of the psychological effects of poor coaching. *Psychology of Sport and Exercise*, 12(3), 212–221. doi: 10.1016/j.psychsport.2010.11.004

Greco, L. A., Baer, R. A., and Smith, G. T. (2011). Assessing mindfulness in children and adolescents: Development and validation of the child and adolescent mindfulness measure (CAMM). *Psychological Assessment*, 23(3), 606–14. doi: 10.1037/a0022819

Grossman, P., Niemann, L., Schmidt, S., and Walach, H. (2004). Mindfulness-based stress reduction and health benefits: A meta-analysis. *Journal of Psychosomatic Research*, 57(1), 35–43. doi: 10.1016/S0022-3999(03)00573-7

Gutman, S. A., and Schindler, V. P. (2007). The neurological basis of occupation. *Occupational Therapy International*, 14(2), 71–85. doi: 10.1002/oti.225.

Hallam, S. (2001). The development of expertise in young musicians: Strategy use, knowledge acquisition and individual diversity. *Music Education Research*, 3(1), 7–23. doi: 10.1080/14613800020029914

Harvey, A. R. (2012). Evolution, music and neurotherapy. In A. Poiani (Ed.), *Pragmatic evolution: Applications of evolutionary theory* (pp. 150–163). Cambridge, UK: Cambridge University Press.

Hattie, J., and Timperley, H. (2007). The power of feedback. *Review of Educational Research, 77*, 81–112. doi: 10.3102/003465430298487

Hefferon, K. M., and Ollis, S. (2006). "Just clicks": An interpretive phenomenological analysis of flow experiences in professional dancers. *Research in Dance Education, 7*(2), 141–159. doi: 10.1080/14647890601029527

Hewitt, A. (2006). A Q study of music teachers' attitudes towards the significance of individual differences for teaching and learning in music. *Psychology of Music, 34*(1), 63–80. doi: 10.1177/0305735606059105

Hodges, D. A. (2010). Can neuroscience help us do a better job of teaching music? *General Music Today, 23*(2), 3–12. doi: 10.1177/1048371309349569

Jackson, S. A., Martin, A. J., and Eklund, R. C. (2008). Long and short measures of flow: Examining construct validity of the FSS-2, DFS-2 and new brief counterparts. *Journal of Sport and Exercise Psychology, 30*, 561–587.

Jeanneret, N., (1994). *Changing preservice primary teachers' attitudes to music: Implications for music education practice.* Paper presented at Annual conference, Australian Association for Research in Education, Newcastle, Australia.

Jeanneret, N., and DeGraffenreid, G. (2012). Music education in the generalist classroom. In G. McPherson and G. Welch (Eds.), *The Oxford handbook of music education* (Vol. 1, pp. 339–416). New York, NY: Oxford University Press.

Jouper, J., and Gustafsson, H. (2013). Mindful recovery: A case study of a burned-out elite shooter. *Sport Psychologist, 27*, 92–102.

Kabat-Zinn, J. (1994). *Wherever you go, there you are: Mindfulness meditation in everyday life.* New York: Hyperion.

Kamins, M., and Dweck, C. S. (1999). Person vs. process praise and criticism: Implications for contingent self-worth and coping. *Developmental Psychology, 35*, 835–847. doi: 10.1037/0012-1649.35.3.835

Kawakami, C., White, J. B., and Langer, E. J. (2000). Mindful and masculine: Freeing women leaders from the constraints of gender roles. *Journal of Social Issues, 56*(1), 49–63. doi: 10.1111/0022-4537.00151

Kenny, D. (2011). *The psychology of music performance anxiety.* Oxford, UK: Oxford University Press.

Krivenski, M. (2012). *Feeding back in musical performance: Exploring feedback practice in relation to students' and tutors' learning and teaching experience.* York, UK: Higher Education Academy.

Lamont, A. (2011). University students' strong experiences of music: Pleasure, engagement and meaning. *Musicae Scientiae, 15*(2), 229–249. doi: 10.1177/1029864911403368

Langer, E. J. (2005). *On becoming an artist.* New York, NY: Ballantine.

Langer, E. J., and Imber, L. G. (1979). When practice makes imperfect: Debilitating effects of overlearning. *Journal of Personality and Social Psychology, 37*(11), 2014–2024. doi: http://dx.doi.org/10.1037/0022-3514.37.11.2014

Langer, E. J., Russell, T., and Eisenkraft, N. (2008). Orchestral performance and the footprint of mindfulness. *Psychology of Music*, 37, 125–136. doi: 10.1177/035735607086053

Leibovich de Figueroa, N., Maglio, A. L., and Giménez, M. (2013). The experience of flow in adolescence: Its relationship with personality traits and age. *Orientación y Sociedad*, 13, 1–21.

Levitin, D. (2009). The neural correlates of temporal structure in music. *Music and Medicine*, 1(1), 9–13. doi: 10.1177/1943862109338604

Luthans, F., Avolio, B. J., Norman, S. M., and Avey, J. B. (2006). *Psychological capital: Measurement and relationship with performance and satisfaction. Gallup Leadership Institute Working Paper*. Lincoln: University of Nebraska.

Martin, A. J., and Marsh, H. W. (2006). Academic resilience and its psychological and educational correlates: A construct validity approach. *Psychology in the Schools*, 43, 267–281. doi: 10.1002/pits.20149

McPherson, G. E. (2006, September). *The home environment and children's musical practice*. Keynote address presented at Music Teachers National Association Leadership Summit, Cincinnati, OH, USA.

McPherson, G.E., and Welch, G. (Eds.). (2012). *The Oxford handbook of music education* (Vol. 1). New York, NY: Oxford University Press.

Mills, J. (2002). Conservatoire students' perceptions of the characteristics of effective instrumental and vocal tuition. *Bulletin of the Council for Research in Music Education*, 153, 78–82.

Mrazek, M. D., Franklin, M. S., Phillips, D., Baird, B., and Schooler, J. (2013). Mindfulness training improves working memory and GRE performance while reducing mind-wandering. *Psychology of Science*, 24, 776–781. doi: 10.1177/0956797612459659

O'Neill, S. (1999). Flow theory and the development of musical performance skills. *Bulletin of the Council of Research in Music Education*, 141, 129–134.

Patston, T. (2010). *Cognitive mediators of music performance anxiety* (Unpublished doctoral dissertation). Sydney, Australia: University of Sydney.

(2014). Teaching stage fright? Implications for music educators. *British Journal of Music Education*, 31, 85–98. doi: 10.1017/S0265051713000144

Patston, T., and Osborne, M. (in press). The developmental progression of music performance anxiety and perfectionism in adolescent music students. *Performance Enhancement and Health*.

Peifer, C., Schulz, A., Schächinger, H., Baumann, N., and Antoni, C. H. (2014). The relation of flow-experience and physiological arousal under stress – can u shape it? *Journal of Experimental Social Psychology*, 53, 62–69. doi: 10.1016/j.jesp.2014.01.009

Perkins, R. (2013), Learning cultures, creativities and higher music education institutions. In P. Burnard (Ed.), *Developing creativities in higher music education: International perspectives and practices* (pp. 223–233). New York, NY: Routledge.

Peterson, C., and Seligman, M. (2004). *Character strengths and virtues: A handbook and classification.* New York, NY: Oxford University Press.

Presland, C. (2005). Conservatoire student and instrumental professor: The student perspective on a complex relationship. *British Journal of Music Education,* 22(3), 237–248.

Ryan, R. M., and Deci, E. L. (2000). The darker and brighter sides of human existence: Basic psychological needs as a unifying concept. *Psychological Inquiry,* 11, 319–338. doi: 10.1207/S15327965PLI1104_03

Sand, B. L. (2000). *Teaching genius: Dorothy DeLay and the making of a musician.* Portland, OR: Amadeus Press.

Schleuter, S. (1996). *A sound approach to teaching instrumentalists: An application of content and learning sequences.* New York, NY: Schirmer.

Seligman, M. E P., Park, N., and Peterson, C. (2004). The values in action (VIA) classification of character strengths. *Special Positive Psychology,* 27(1), 63–78.

Sinnamon S., Moran A., and O'Connell, M. (2012). Flow among musicians: Measuring peak experiences of student performers. *Bulletin of the Council for Research in Music Education,* 60, 6–25. doi: 10.1177/0022429411434931

Sluchin, B., and Lapie, R. (1997). Slide trombone teaching and method books in France (1794–1960). *Historic Brass Society Journal,* 9, 4–29.

Snyder, C., and Lopez, S. (2010). Positive psychology: The scientific and practical explorations of human strengths (2nd ed.). Thousand Oaks, CA: Sage.

Stoeber, J., and Childs, J. H. (2011). Perfectionism. In R. J. R. Levesque (Ed.), *Encyclopedia of adolescence.* New York, NY: Springer.

Swinson, J., and Harrop, A., (2012). *Positive psychology for teachers.* London, UK: Routledge.

Thienot, E., Jackson, B., Dimmock, J., Grove, R., Bernier, M., and Fournier, J. (2014). Development and preliminary validation of the mindfulness inventory for sport. *Psychology of Sport and Exercise,* 15(1), 72–80. doi: 10.1016/j.psychsport.2013.10.003

Tomlinson, C. A., Brighton, C., Hertberg, H., Callahan, C. M., Moon, T. R., Brimijoin, K., Conover, L. A. and Reynolds, T. (2003). Differentiating instruction in response to student readiness, interest, and learning profile in academically diverse classrooms: A review of literature. *Journal of the Education of the Gifted,* 27, 119–145.

Walker, S. (2013). Mindfulness and burnout among competitive adolescent tennis players *South African Journal of Sports Medicine* 25(4), 105–108. doi: 10.7196/sajsm.498

Waters, L., Barsky, A., Ridd, A., and Allen, K. (2014). Contemplative education: A systematic, evidence-based review of the effect of meditation interventions in schools. *Educational Psychology Review,* 26(1), 1–32. doi: 10.1007/s10648-014-9258-2

Weare, K. (2012). Developing mindfulness with children and young people: A review of the evidence and policy context. *Journal of Children's Services,* 8(2), 141–153.

Wells A. (2005). Detached mindfulness in cognitive therapy: A metacognitive analysis and ten techniques. *Journal of Rational-Emotive and Cognitive Behavior Therapy*, 23(4), 337–355. doi: 10.1007/s10942-005-0018-6

Williamon, A. (2004). *Musical excellence: Strategies and techniques to enhance performance.* Oxford, UK: Oxford University Press.

Wrigley W. J., and Emmerson S. B. (2013). The experience of the flow state in live music performance. *Psychology of Music*, 41, 97–118. doi: 10.1177/0305735611418552

Young, V., Burwell, K., and Pickup, D. (2003). Areas of study and teaching strategies in instrumental teaching: A case study research project. *Music Education Research*, 5(2), 139–155.

Mindfulness for Coaches, Practitioners, and Mentors

Interpersonal Mindfulness for Athletic Coaches and Other Performance Professionals

Joe Mannion, Mark B. Andersen

We love the words "once upon a time." They tweak our brains into receptive and ready modes to take in a story. So we wanted to begin this chapter with a tale, or rather a *teaching*, from the Taoist tradition that speaks to coaching practices and mindfulness. Alutcher (2013) retells the story:

> The Taoists have a famous teaching about an empty boat that rams into your boat in the middle of a river. While you probably wouldn't be angry at an empty boat, you might well become enraged if someone were at its helm. The point of the story is that the parents who didn't see you, the other kids who teased you as a child, [the coach who yelled at you], the driver who aggressively tailgated you yesterday – are all in fact empty, rudderless boats. They were compulsively driven to act as they did by their own unexamined wounds, therefore they did not know what they were doing and had little control over it. Just as an empty boat that rams into us isn't targeting us, so too people who act unkindly are driven along by the unconscious force of their own wounding and pain. Until we realize this, we will remain prisoners of our grievance, our past, and our victim identity, all of which keep us from opening to the more powerful currents of life and love that are always flowing through the present moment (p. 1).

We believe that most sport coaches are good people trying to do their best, but because our brains are hardwired to perceive and remember threat, it is direct or vicarious experiences with abusive coaches that often stick with the athlete. Some coaches, probably because of their past wounds or traumas, behave like rudderless boats. We are sure most readers can quickly come up with examples from their own experiences in which they were wounded in some way by a coach on a psychologically speaking rudderless boat, and perhaps those times that they, themselves, have also behaved in a hurtful and unconscious manner.

The Taoist teaching also contains hope and a way to add a rudder to one's boat: mindful awareness of the "powerful currents of life and love that are always flowing through the present moment." A mindful rudder may help coaches successfully navigate both the calm and turbulent rivers and seascapes of their work with athletes. That is our opening story for now. We will tell some more tales later in the chapter. In this chapter, we present ways in which we can offer coaches a pathway to become more mindful and wise about how they interact with their athletes. With this mindful rudder in mind for sport coaches and other performance professionals, we turn to some background on mindfulness, performance, and coaching.

The fields of psychology, neuroscience, and genetics, among others, have demonstrated increasing convergence and consilience since the turn of the twenty-first century (e.g., Cozolino, 2010). Advances in neuroimaging and genetics, for example, have allowed studies (e.g., Levy-Gigi et al., 2013) to be conducted that examine the effects of talking therapies, not just on behaviors but on brain structures and gene expression as well. This increasing convergence of evidence may also be observed in the mindfulness research and practice literature. Our understanding of the fundamental parts of mindfulness, from operational definitions to neurobiological correlates, has begun to coalesce and allow for multidisciplinary examinations, including its interface with other approaches and novel applications, as in the present volume.

In this chapter, we explore *interpersonal mindfulness*, its connections with attachment theory, and the salient neurobiological correlates and supportive evidence for its beneficial effects. Coach–athlete (or coach–performer) relationships are the primary focus here, but they may also be used as a sort of template, or reference, for other types of coaching-oriented relationships, such as in business management, executive coaching, supervision, artistic direction, mentorship, and apprenticeship.

Mindfulness and Performance: Historical and Cultural Contexts

Mindfulness has made a relatively recent entry onto the performance and sport psychology stage, with Gardner and Moore (2004) often being cited as a seminal, or dialogue-opening, publication. What we have seen most in the literature since that article debuted is performance and sport psychologists teaching athletes, and other performers, mindful practices for the main purpose of improving performance. After over a decade of research in this area, the jury is still out on whether mindful practice leads to improvements in real-world competitive performance. In a recent review,

Gardner and Moore (2012) covered the extant literature, and there were only two studies that measured behaviors, and one of those was an artificial laboratory sport-related task. In the other study (i.e., Thompson et al., 2011) on mindfulness for runners, archers, and golfers, only the runners showed a small performance improvement; the archers and golfers did not. The majority of measurements in the other studies had to do with self-reports and coach reports of perceived improvements, not actual, real, competitive behavior.

In Gardner and Moore (2006, chapter 5), the authors presented evidence that almost all of the performance enhancement literature in sport psychology did not meet evidence for efficacy criteria of psychological skills training (PST) interventions for improving actual, real competitive behavior. Their review of the literature on PST interventions from 1960 to 2004 yielded only a few dozen articles that employed at least one of the major psychological skills techniques (e.g., relaxation, imagery, goal setting) with *real* competitive athletes (not analogue populations), with randomized controlled trials where the dependent variables were real competitive sport performance (not laboratory tasks). Their conclusions were that the experimentally based evidence for PST improving performance actually sits on somewhat thin ice.

Gardner and Moore's (2012) review of mindfulness and performance enhancement currently leads us to a similar conclusion as they made in 2006. When it comes to real athletes and real competitive behavior, there just is not much experimentally based evidence at the time of this publication that mindfulness will help athletes improve performance. So where do we go from here? We take a hopeful stance about performance improvements, but we think there is much more to mindfulness than this rather narrow application and will expound on these possibilities throughout the chapter.

There seem to be heuristic reasons to believe mindfulness-based practices may directly or indirectly improve sports performance. Besides anecdotal evidence, studies in the clinical and health psychology literature have demonstrated support for mindfulness-based improvement of cognitive, affective, behavioral, and interpersonal factors that correlate with, and possibly influence, performance outcomes. Birrer, Rothlin, and Morgan (2012), for example, proposed nine possible mechanisms for how mindfulness may enhance sports performance based on their review, primarily of mindfulness-based psychotherapy literature: (a) attention, (b) attitude, (c) values clarification, (d) self-regulation, (e) clarity, (f) exposure, (g) flexibility, (h) nonattachment, and (i) less rumination. In their review of mindfulness-based sport psychology literature, they, too, found only five intervention studies and reported the effects to be relatively small or not statistically significant. Birrer and colleagues (2012) did note, however, that small effects can be important in competitive sport.

Although there are various reasons to believe mindfulness-based interventions may enhance sports performance, there is currently limited and equivocal evidence in the research base, and more empirical studies are needed. Given these findings, we are surprised how mindfulness is sometimes advertised in an unrestrained fashion as a panacea-like intervention on websites and in anecdotes. We believe ethical consideration and prudence should be exercised in descriptions of mindfulness' efficacy on enhanced sports performance based on current findings, particularly for the welfare of clients.

We (Andersen & Mannion, 2011; Mannion & Andersen, 2015) have also previously commented on the Western appropriation of mindfulness from its original Buddhist context (i.e., from the Fourth Noble Truth as one of the Eight-Fold Paths on the way to diminishing human unhappiness), which in some instances may be antithetical to its original purposes (e.g., the realization of *no-self* and the interdependence and interconnectedness of all things). When mindfulness is used to gain more medals, accrue more material things, and dominate others in the service of building up the self or ego, it is not difficult to see the conflict with the Buddhist foundations of non-clinging, impermanence, and no-self.

Westernized versions of mindfulness for performance improvements have caught the attention of international Buddhist leaders, and we feel it is important to acknowledge these cultural and historical concerns out of respect for the origins of mindfulness. Similar to the increasing number of articles re-examining panacea-like mindfulness claims, there are also articles and books focusing on Westernized forms mindfulness (e.g., Langer, 2014). Buddhist master Chögyam Trungpa (2002) referred to the use of spiritual practices for some sort of material gain or personal accomplishment as *spiritual materialism*.

In a recent interview exploring whether mindfulness had been corrupted for material gain, Buddhist master Thich Nhat Hanh nevertheless remarked that it did not matter whether enhanced performance or profits triggered adoption of the practice, believing that mindfulness would change such a perspective to one more focused on compassion (Confino, 2014). He explicitly cautioned, however, that not having a sense of brotherhood and sisterhood in a particular work endeavor is not mindfulness but rather an *imitation*, adding that we cannot be victims of our happiness (a central Buddhist value) as we can be of our successes. Further exploration of this matter could easily fill another manuscript within this broader context. Our focus is on less culturally controversial uses of mindfulness that are both consistent with Buddhist values and supported by psychological and neurobiological research.

The Mindful Coach: Intrapersonal Mindfulness

If one does a simple Google search with the words "mindful coaching," hundreds of sites pop up. Most of the webpages have to do with business and life coaching and are aimed at teaching businesspeople, the general population, and employees mindful practices so that people become happier and healthier in their work and in their lives.

What we (Mark and Joe) often see in the previously described performance and sport psychology literature, and in these myriad websites, is training in *intrapersonal* mindfulness – that is, teaching the athlete, performer, business manager, or employee to be mindful and to watch their internal states (e.g., cognitive and emotional events, somatic sensations) and their external perceptions rise and fall with nonjudgment, with curiosity, with openness, and not becoming attached or, in an acceptance and commitment therapy type of language, not becoming *fused* with their own thoughts and emotions. And, similar to Thich Nhat Hanh (Confino, 2014), we think that's fine: better to have a little mindfulness than no mindfulness at all.

As therapists with mindful practices, we have broader interests in mindfulness that both subsume and extend beyond the intrapersonal and performance levels. In this chapter, we will focus on the mindfulness of the coach/practitioner, and specifically on the *interpersonal* mindfulness *between* coaches and athletes. We believe that if the practitioner (in the case of this chapter, the coach) has a mindful practice, then the coach will be more likely to connect with the athlete, activate less of the athlete's own past histories of unhappiness, and connect in a deep and meaningful way. When one is *interpersonally mindful*, one is observing oneself *and* the other in the coach/athlete dyad. If the coach is interpersonally mindful, then the coach may observe and take in the internal states of the athlete, more accurately represent and feel what the athlete is feeling, come to know what the athlete is knowing, and better connect with and attune to the athlete. Then the athlete may recognize that the coach has actually taken in the athlete's internal states and understands the athlete, and this exchange is how the athlete or performer feels *felt* and understood by the coach.

There is probably nothing more therapeutic in the world than to have someone else be present, be nonjudgmental, be caring, be sensitive, be empathic, take in one's stories, appreciate them, and hold them in loving care. When that happens, we get what is often referred to as *resonance* between two people, and that resonance in itself is quite therapeutic. We are sure many people who are reading this chapter have had the experience of working with somebody and making an interpretation of something that maybe encapsulates, or sets in a new light, some situation that the performer has been experiencing. The performer, then, lets out a big sigh of relief, and says something like, "Exactly!" That is what we call resonance. That resonating dyad can be one of the outcomes of mindful coaching, but we probably need to back up a bit and cover what researchers and authors have written about concerning coach–athlete relationships.

Past Investigations in Coach–Athlete Relationships

Research into coach–athlete relationships, specifically looking at the dyad rather than at coaching styles and athlete congruence with coaching styles, began in earnest in the early part of the twenty-first century. Researcher Sophia Jowett is responsible for much of the investigation into coach–athlete relationships and, in her early work in this area, developed a model she called the "3 Cs." These Cs were three different factors that were important to examine when looking at coach–athlete relationships: *closeness, complementarity,* and *commitment.* Later in her research with colleagues, they added a fourth C, called *co-orientation.* This model led to the development of the Coach–Athlete Relationship Questionnaire (Rhind & Jowett, 2010) and became known as the "3 + 1 Cs."

Closeness has to do with the interpersonal feelings (the emotions, the bonds) that a coach and an athlete may have for each other. The positive aspects of this *C* may be things such as trust, liking, mutual respect, and appreciation. Closeness may also be something that is *not* within the dyad, and that is the negative aspect of that *C*, that the coach and the athlete do not feel close, do not feel like they are respected by each other, and so forth. The *complementarity* aspect of the 3 + 1 Cs model has to do with the quality of the interpersonal exchanges, such as ease in interpersonal interactions, friendliness, cooperativeness, and so forth. The *commitment* part of the model is about the coach's and the athlete's cognitive attachments, or how they are invested in the relationship they have and in their intentions to maintain that commitment to each other and the work that is being done.

The later added *C*, *co-orientation*, represents two distinct interpersonal perspectives: direct self-perceptions that the athlete has (e.g., "How do I feel about my coach?" "Do I like my coach?" "Do I find my coach really helpful?"), and a sort of metaperspective in which one of the individuals in the dyad has the ability to take the viewpoint of the other. In a rapidly growing area of clinical and counseling psychology literature, this meta-perspective is sometimes referred to as *mentalizing* or *theory of mind*, a term that Premack and Woodruff (1978) first coined. The overall relationship quality in the coach–athlete dyad is the result of the combined interrelationships between both direct self-perceptions and the metaperspectives of taking the other's viewpoint, plus where they are in terms of closeness, complementarity, and commitment. Overall, this model is a highly cognitive one. What seems to be missing from the model has to do with more psychodynamic processes, such as unconscious motivation within the dyad and the transferences and countertransferences that are occurring, maybe on conscious but in many ways on unconscious levels. Jowett and her colleagues (e.g., Davis & Jowett, 2013; Davis, Jowett, & Lafrenière, 2013; Felton & Jowett, 2012) have recently expanded their coach–athlete relationship investigation to include attachment theory, a topic we cover next.

Coaching and Parenting

> Knowing the ways our own narratives may be imprisoning us is a first step toward awakening the mind and stirring us from the slumber of automatic pilot.
>
> (Siegel, 2010, p. xxi)

In the conceptual stages of starting to outline and write this chapter, I (Joe) felt keen about the integration of mindfulness and attachment theory to help optimize coach–athlete relationships. I had, however, a nagging concern it might all sound rather ivory tower-like to our intended audience. At the time, I was teaching an undergraduate sport psychology course to a class with approximately 75 percent student-athletes. During a lecture on the psychology of coaching, I asked them what they thought the roles of the coach should be. Their responses included:

1. To direct behavior, attention, strategy, thoughts and feelings
2. To provide feedback and correction
3. To encourage and support
4. To motivate
5. To model/demonstrate skills
6. To communicate well

Looking at the whiteboard list the students generated, I realized the distance from theory to coaching practice might not be as long as I suspected. If we were playing *Jeopardy*, the answer to the set of behaviors could have been, "What are the roles of parents?" The main role that seemed to be missing was "to love unconditionally." But love's absence here is understandable because people sometimes get a bit twitchy when the *L* word appears, especially in sport, psychotherapy, and the academic environment.

Likewise, during a recent workshop-planning meeting, a collegiate football coach mentioned to me how the dynamics of his team had shifted from the previous season, with some players graduating and another batch of recruits just beginning. Observing the changes in some of his returning players as they interacted with new recruits, he casually commented, "You become who you are in relation to the people around you." I smiled at the succinctness of his statement, considering how many different areas of literature supported the idea and how much I resonated with him (e.g., I strive to harness the power of relationships in my service delivery). The question, then, is whether we can use this interpersonal insight in a deliberate way to initiate positive and meaningful change.

Children, let alone adults, do not enter sport as blank slates. Coaches and athletes (and sport psychologists) have learned about how to relate with other people and to predict what to expect from other people from their previous experiences within important relationships, particularly in the early stages of psychological and neurobiological development. Psychoanalyst and pediatrician Donald Winnicott (1971) described these relational learning processes in accessible terms such as the *holding environment* and *good-enough mothering*. According to his object-relations theory, a holding environment allows for optimal learning and development for a child and exists when the child feels the safe yet unobtrusive presence of the parent(s) or caregiver(s). Feeling psychologically *held* in this presence, the child experiences enough reassurance and safety to explore and develop spontaneously within the environment. When feeling distressed or threatened in this exploration, the child is able to return to a consistently available mother (or father or caretaker; called a *secure base*), who helps the child return to a state of ease, curiosity, and sociability. Over time, this reassurance, security, and coping may be internalized both in the subjective experiences of the child's internal states and in the experience-dependent (i.e., neuroplastic) networks of the child's neurobiology, which we will explore further in a coming section. As this sense of security is further internalized over time and through repeated experiences, it may be psychologically referenced, consciously or unconsciously, without the physical presence of the parent(s) or caregiver(s), offering the child (and later adult) substantial capacity to self-regulate.

According to object-relations theory (Winnicott, 1971), the holding environment does *not* develop when the parent(s) or caregiver(s) is either over- or underinvolved in the child's experience and, consequently, does *not* provide the key sense of a safe and reassuring presence. Overinvolvement may take various forms of intrusion, including verbal, physical, and sexual abuse or more subtle forms such as chronic micromanagement. Underinvolvement may take various forms of absence, including emotional and physical neglect or more subtle forms such as inattention to the child. Just as the experiences of a safe, secure, and consistent presence shape the organization of the mind and neuroplastic areas of the brain, so too do these abusive, intrusive, absent, and inconsistent experiences.

Versions of these overinvolved and underinvolved caretaker experiences also occur within sport, and there are a variety of important findings in this realm. Overinvolved parents, caregivers, and coaches may be seen yelling intrusively from the side lines, staking their own esteem on the play or competitive outcomes, rigidly overscheduling, or offering otherwise performance-contingent acceptance and love of players. Underinvolved coaches may be disorganized, frequently lose control of practices, or be inattentive to player needs. Underinvolved parents and caregivers may be absorbed in electronic devices at games or practices or noticeably absent all together, leaving children at risk for other forms of abuse, in addition to not providing a secure and reassuring presence (particularly for young athletes). Further underscoring the relevance of these considerations, survey research has shown that youth sport athletes (children and adolescents) often report that coaches are more influential in their lives than parents or teachers. Also, a report on educator sexual misconduct that Shakeshaft (2004) prepared for the U.S. Department of Education revealed youth sport coaches to be the second most frequent violators, behind teachers, among nine categories of educational positions.

Attachment: Winnicott and Bowlby

Winnicott's holding environment and good-enough mothering sit beside the work of John Bowlby's (1969, 1988) attachment theory. Bowlby contributed much to our understanding of how children form attachments and the different types of attachment patterns a child can have. The child with a Winnicottian good-enough mother will form a *secure* attachment.

The child trusts that the world is safe and that his secure base will be there if something scary happens. Under these conditions, the child is happy and ventures out into the world. Such attachments are optimal, and the majority of the population seems to have at least one secure attachment (Ainsworth, 1985).

Unfortunately, many people do not have Winnicottian parents. If the parent is inconsistently present and attentive and often goes emotionally missing or even physically absent, then the child may develop an *ambivalent* attachment (or *anxious-ambivalent*) style that mirrors the mixed messages of the sometimes attentive and sometimes neglectful parent. If a child has a parent who cannot be reached (emotionally or physically) for soothing and comfort such as often happens with postnatal depression, the child may also become distant, cut off, isolated, and anxious. This insecure attachment is known as an *avoidant* (or *anxious-avoidant*) attachment style. If there are more extreme conditions than for the two aforementioned insecure attachment styles, in terms of threat and violence, then the child may develop quite disturbed behaviors and may exhibit *freeze* responses and even dissociate along with becoming passive and confused. This pattern is what is known as *disorganized* (or *disorganized-disorientated*) attachment.

Attachment styles do not necessarily determine how someone will form future attachments, but they may well help shape how a person connects to others later in life. Attachment styles are also not destiny. Original, insecure attachments can be replaced with secure ones later in life. We know numerous examples of athletes who had intrusive and abusive parents but found loving and caring coaches to whom they became securely attached. For athletes with secure attachments in their lives, a *good-enough* coach will help reinforce those feelings of security and safety. For athletes with insecure attachments, a loving and caring coach can act in a kind of therapeutic reparenting role.

The Relevance of Relationships

As long ago as the 1930s, Rosenzweig (1936) came to the conclusion that different models of psychotherapy were roughly equivalent in their effectiveness and that outcomes had more to do with the common factors across psychotherapies rather than specific techniques and interventions of individual schools of thought. One of those common factors is the quality of the practitioner–client relationship as perceived by the client. If that relationship is marked by mutual respect, compassion, and loving care, then the chances of positive outcomes are high (see Wampold, 2010). Meta-analyses of counseling outcomes and client–therapist relationships, such as Norcross (2011) and Sexton and Whiston (1994), have also supported the centrality of the therapeutic relationship in psychotherapy. For a synopsis of the meta-analyses in Norcross (2011), see NREPP (n.d.).

Given what we now know about the interpersonal neurobiology of human relationships, it is not a long bow to assume that the quality of the coach–athlete relationship will have a substantial influence on athlete happiness and satisfaction with sport. We do not know whether a mindful, compassionate, holding relationship between a coach and an athlete will improve sport performance, but we are quite confident such relationships will not hurt. In addition to surveys of children's ratings of the relative importance of coaches in their lives, researchers (e.g., Ewing & Seefeldt, 2002; Martens, 2012; Smoll & Smith, 1989) have also concluded that one of the key determinants of the effects of youth sport participation is the coach–athlete relationship.

From Broken Mirrors to Mirror Neurons: Neurobiological Aspects of Coaching Relationships

During a session with a collegiate basketball player, I (Joe) noticed that my client kept *lighting up* with emotion and surprise as I offered her basic, Rogerian-like reflections each time she paused. All I was doing was paraphrasing what she had just told me in an interpersonally mindful (i.e., nonjudgmental, open, accepting, curious, present) manner. Each time, she would produce a big smile and say something like, "Oh wow! That's so simple and makes so much sense!" and often finish with something like, "Gosh, I'm so stupid, how could I not see that?" Again, I was just mindfully reflecting back to her what she was already saying.

It suddenly made sense to me, too. Her parents had both been highly preoccupied with struggles of their own: her mother with alcoholism and narcissism and her father with paranoia. During most of her of childhood, her parents were unable to offer helpful reflections when they communicated with her. They were broken mirrors, frequently reflecting distortions and their chaotic inner experiences. These broken reflections left my client without a clear understanding of her inner (and to some extent, external) world, without knowing which mirror pieces were hers and which were her parents'. Clearly, by her harsh self-criticism, she had taken some of her parents' shards and believed them to be accurate reflections of her identity and worth. Just a few weeks prior, she had told me a story of when she was embarrassed to the point of tears in middle school. After running into the bathroom to hide her face from her classmates, she looked in a mirror and recoiled at her own reflection. It became apparent an important part of my role was to continue deliberate effort at creating a relationship in which she felt safe and supported enough to look again; to have some assistance at sorting through the old pieces; and to offer her reflections that were helpful, healing, and allowed her to discover herself with love and compassion. Interpersonal mindfulness became its own intervention, contributing to an *emotionally corrective experience* (Alexander & French, 1946) while also forming a solid foundation for the delivery of other well-being and performance interventions that were still to come.

Like the basketball player in the preceding story, athletes come to coaches (and coaches come to athletes) with a huge variety of experiences in attachment and interpersonal relationships. The basketball player's insecure attachment seemed to stem from her parents' emotional neglect, their inconsistent messages about her worthiness, and their preoccupations with their own chaotic internal worlds. No wonder she responded well to Joe's consistent and empathic reflections and mirroring. Joe, in many ways, helped with her *reparenting*, but this time the parenting was consistent, loving, and comforting. Many coaches almost intuitively understand that they may be, for some of their athletes, cast into reparenting roles. We have heard coaches say to us about an athlete something similar to the following:

> You know, he has it tough at home. His Dad left a few years ago, and his Mom is just barely holding it all together. I want to make sure practice and games are a good place for him to be.

Those coaches know, either implicitly or explicitly, that past histories of abuse can shape people in ways that lead to sadness and unhappiness, and they also know that they can act as sources of *corrective experiences*, or, to sound less clinical, they can be the new good parents who can help the athletes reconnect with adults in ways that may counteract many of the self-destructive lessons they learned in their first *being-parented* experiences

From Basketball Nets to Neural Nets

As mentioned earlier in the chapter, we do not enter sport as blank slates, whether we are athletes, coaches, parents, or sport psychologists. This statement is, of course, also true for people entering business, the performing arts, and other endeavors. Evidence suggests we do not even enter the world from our mothers' wombs as blank slates. For example, the amygdala, a part of the brain that plays a major role in registering and remembering perceived threats and activating protective fight-flight-freeze responses, reaches a considerable level of development by eight months gestation, allowing a fetus to create a fear association with a stimulus in utero (Ulfig, Setzer, & Bohl, 2003). Additionally, neural circuitry associated with shame begins to come on board around twelve months old, whereas the verbal prefrontal cortex areas of the brain begin to accelerate in development around twenty-four months.

These neurodevelopmental stages have important applied implications. Babies have the subcortical ability to have protective fight-flight reactions via the *sympathetic nervous system* and to have protective freeze and shame responses via the dorsal branch of the *parasympathetic nervous system* (Porges, 2011). Babies, however, lack the higher cortical capacity and associated functions (e.g., language) to down-regulate these threat and distress reactions. For down-regulation, for calming, babies rely on their parents or caregivers to act as their prefrontal cortices. In the first eighteen months of life, the right hemisphere of the brain experiences accelerated growth, priming the infant for social and emotional learning. The ways parents down-regulate the infant (e.g., with loving kindness, with calm attention to infant distress), or don't down-regulate or even further activate the infant (e.g., neglect or yell at the child, use corporal punishment), are encoded in these experience-dependent neural networks, shaping the synaptic connections through neuroplasticity (Schore, 2000).

Without the availability of language-associated cortical centers in the infant, these patterns of down-regulation are neurologically encoded as somatosensory sensations. Reminiscent of my basketball client's experience, it is believed one of the pathways through which these patterns are transmitted and encoded are via *mirror neurons*. Researchers (e.g., Iacoboni et al., 1999) originally discovered this type of neuron fired in response to, and imitation of, other people's motor behaviors. For example, infants are often observed striving to mimic the lip movements of their mothers as they speak to them. More recently, researchers (e.g., Gallese, Morris, & Migone, 2007; Iacoboni, 2008) have come to believe mirror neurons also function to translate the outward behaviors of others as signs of their inner states, relaying the observed signals through innervations of similar, corresponding areas in the observer, from the central nervous system to the body proper and back.

Underscoring these points, an Italian study (Aglioti et al., 2008) on mirror and resonance systems examined the predictive accuracy of professional basketball players, basketball coaches, sports journalists who covered basketball, and students with no basketball experience observing a player taking free throw shots, guessing whether the shot would go in or miss. The athletes were found to be more accurate in their predictions than the other groups and did so faster, specifically before the ball even left the shooter's hands. Using electromyography recording and transcranial magnetic stimulation, Aglioti and colleagues (2008) also found that only the observing athletes had a time-specific motor activation when observing a missed shot. The researchers concluded these results were consistent with the suggestion that professional players were able to make accurate predictions based on the imitation firing (via mirror neuron systems) of their experientially refined somatosensory pathways, particularly given that their accuracy was not based on the trajectory of the ball after leaving the shooter's hands but rather on the shooter's form. In other words, consciously or unconsciously, the athletes were able to make more accurate predictions than others because they could feel the motor patterns of the shooter in their own bodies as they observed and were able to note whether it felt like good form.

Consistent with these findings and the more recently proposed empathic functions of mirror neurons, Damasio and colleagues (2000), even earlier than the aforementioned studies, suggested our bodily experiences are our references for knowing, or guessing, what others are experiencing internally. Like the basketball players in the Italian study, it is believed we make interpersonal predictions, often quickly and unconsciously, about the meaning (e.g., intentions) and potential outcomes of other people's behaviors based on our own experientially refined, often implicitly stored, somatosensory encodings that we learned as infants and children from our interactions with caregivers. Once again, these patterned interpersonal predictions and our patterned responses are frequently referred to as attachment styles. We have, for example, *gut feelings* about others or take courses of action with others based on *intuition*, which may be described as nonverbal, somatosensory sensations, about what we feel (not necessarily accurately) is happening or about to happen.

Interpersonal Mindfulness Neurobiology and Down-Regulation

When parents are emotionally available and provide a predictable, loving presence, infants and children usually encode secure attachment styles and may reference those internalized models as adults for down-regulating fear, distress, and other difficult emotions and for self-regulation in general, on their own and in their relationships with others. When parents are dismissive and rejecting, inconsistent, or frightening, infants and children may encode, respectively, avoidant, anxious/ambivalent, and disorganized attachment styles. These experiences shape the neural architecture, among other structures, of the orbitomedial prefrontal cortex (OMPFC), cingulate cortices, and insula and their pathways to the amygdala, which coordinates various protective responses (Coan, 2008). Stated another way, our attachment styles establish how we act in and use relationships to regulate our fears and distresses (Cozolino, 2014). When the three insecure attachment styles have been neurologically encoded, to varying degrees, there is a bias toward an interpersonally reactive and protective state. *Neuroception* is a subconscious sensory system for detecting and distinguishing threats and safety. It has been proposed that neuroception biased toward false positives (i.e., mistaking safety or neutrality for threat) may underlie a number of psychiatric conditions (Porges, 2004).

Siegel (1999) has offered a useful metaphor for thinking about what may be happening both in intra- and interpersonal experiences of neuroception: *windows of tolerance*. He suggested considering that we have varying tolerances for different perceptions, thoughts, emotions, sensations, and behaviors, whether in our own experiences or our experiences of others. When we are well within our windows of tolerance, we feel safe, curious, social, and capable. This experience is how we often feel in a secure attachment. When our attachment styles are insecure, when our neuroception is biased toward false positives for threat, our windows of tolerance for interpersonal connection and vulnerability are narrow. An inverse relationship has been found between activation in the OMPFC and the amygdala. Whether we are athletes, coaches, or sport psychology practitioners, when our neuroception registers a threat (accompanied by increased activation in the amygdala), our usual higher-order, executive capacities, including learning, curiosity, and prosocial relating, are restricted and diminished (e.g., reduced activation in the OMPFC). When we're not in states of fear, protection, or shame, our natural capacities for growth and connection return to us.

Siegel (2010) has suggested we may move from insecure, protective states into more secure, receptive states in at least two ways: by widening our windows of tolerance (i.e., how much distress it takes before we resort, e.g., to a state of fight-flight-freeze) and by learning how to rein ourselves back within our windows when we find ourselves moving toward or beyond their edges. Using new neuroimaging technology, recent studies (e.g., Hölzel et al., 2011; Tang et al., 2012) have found the practice of intrapersonal mindfulness to increase the myelinization and axon density (i.e., indices of neural health and efficient functioning) in brain regions associated with self-regulation, learning, and perspective taking, including the anterior cingulate cortex and left hippocampus.

When coaches and sport psychologists have their own foundations of intrapersonal mindfulness, they're better able to stay present, connected, and available with the athletes in their care, even and especially when those athletes are at or beyond the edges of their own windows of tolerance. In other words, interpersonally mindful coaches and sport psychologists may better tolerate their athletes' distress or fight-flight-freeze reactions by staying within their own windows and, subsequently, adeptly help the athletes get back within their windows, too. The interpersonal mindfulness of the coach can potentially create corrective experiences that lead to more secure attachments for the athlete.

If we as sport psychology practitioners, coaches, and athletes (or executives, performing artists, or other performers) have insecure attachment styles, intrapersonal mindfulness practices may widen our windows of tolerance. Such intrapersonal mindfulness would allow us, for example, to be aware of when our future catastrophe-prediction patterns are telling us, "If I'm open and vulnerable, if I stay present with this person, if I neither fight nor flee nor freeze, it will surely result in an embarrassing air-ball or an emotional technical foul." Coaches and other leaders can learn to understand there is a possibility that those messages, as in the case of the Italian basketball coaches and sports journalists, are inaccurate and neuroceptively biased toward false positives for threats. With this awareness, we may come to see how our autopilot narratives are imprisoning us and perhaps our teams, and then we may be open to make more freely chosen changes. For example, let's look at the following scenario. It is near the end of a close basketball game. A timeout has been called, and when the game resumes a player will go to the free throw line for two shots. The results of those shots may have an influence on the outcome of the game. The coach notices that she, herself, is becoming agitated with images of the future where the player misses the shots and the game is lost. She recognizes that her mindful presence has gone out the window and realizes that the player, who seems anxious and tense, is probably also hooked into a fantasized future disaster (the coach's interpersonal mindfulness). The coach can use her experience of losing her own intrapersonal mindful presence to communicate to the athlete what is most likely going on (attuning to the athlete's anxious internal state) and then act as a reassuring, comforting model for the athlete to help bring her back to the current moment, pulling her back from the future into her intrapersonal present mindful awareness. She might say to the player:

> I know you're anxious and probably thinking of all the bad things that can happen when you go out onto the court soon, but nothing has happened yet except that you, and I, and the team are getting pulled into the future. What I want you to try to do is come back to right here, right now. There is only you, and the ball, and the rim of the basket. The past is long gone, and the future is unknown. I know when you walk to the line that you can bring yourself back to your job, and that is to shoot the ball. Whatever the outcome, I know you can do your best.

What has happened here is a caring, present-moment reminder to be mindful, based on the coach's own experience of losing intrapersonal mindfulness that may help the athlete begin to down-regulate her amygdala activations and perform to the best of her abilities. Such coach interventions may not initially work well, but if they are repeated over and over again, they may begin, through a process of internalization of the mindful, loving coach, to help the athlete return to the ever-present unfolding moment.

Many, perhaps most, statements about neuroscience could be ended, "but it's actually more complicated than that." The aforementioned illustrations represent highly summarized looks at the interactions of neurobiology and social experience; many other neurobiological structures and pathways play important roles. Examining the intricacies of intra- and interpersonal neurobiology can take up many books, and vast questions still remain. There are some great references for those who wish to pursue a more detailed understanding (e.g., Cozolino, 2010, 2014; Siegel, 1999, 2010).

Bringing It All Together: Mindful Coach–Athlete Relationships in and out of Sport

Selling Mindfulness to Coaches

Coaching in many performance areas is a conservative profession, and coaches often coach how they were coached. Verbal abuse and punishment in sport have not gone away because they appear to work but not for the reasons coaches may think. For an example, when a sport psychology practitioner offers a coach some suggestions for mindfully paying attention to athletes in loving care, the coach might respond with the following sentiment:

> Don't come in here with all your liberal and soft, nicey-nice approach and tell me that punishment doesn't work. When the team plays like shit in

the first half, and then I give them a major spray and go ballistic on them, they often play better the second half. So I have to yell and scream at them to get the job done. That's what my coaches did, and it worked for me.

Of course it "worked," but probably not for the reasons the coach believes. After a well-below-par performance in the first half of a game, the likelihood of playing better in the second half is substantial, not because of the coach going off on the players, but rather because of a universal statistical phenomenon: *regression to the mean*. After a poor first half, the coach could say:

> I can see you guys are really struggling out there, and I know it is frustrating when you are not playing up to what you know you can do. These things happen, so let's see what we can do to get everyone focused on the present moment. If you make a mistake, go ahead and beat yourself up for about two seconds, and then say to yourself, "back to the job" and refocus on what is happening right now. Keep coming back to right now. I know you have it in you to pull out a great second half. Get out there and do your best.

Then the team would still probably regress to the mean, but with a lot less activation of shame circuits in their brains. Daniel Kahneman (2013) related a similar vignette in his book *Thinking Fast and Slow*. It is a tough sell to suggest to coaches there might be a better way to interact with athletes, and one is often not hired to be a consultant to the coach. One might soften the sell by giving the coach a copy of Jackson's and Delehanty's (1995) *Sacred Hoops*, which talks a lot about coaching, mindfulness, Buddhism, and compassion in the world of professional basketball.

Being Mindful of Team Members' Needs

For a coach to be mindful of all team members' needs, wishes, desires, hopes, internal states, and so forth is a potentially gargantuan task. There is only so much attention that a coach can devote to individual players in practice and on game days. One situation that highlights problems with mindfulness and attending to athlete needs involves the coach–athlete interactions on competition days in team sports such as football. For example, a football coach may say:

> I know I need to be mindful of what works best for individual players, but I just don't have the time to attend to all of them. I have some players who have told me that if they play poorly in the first half, then they really want me to yell and scream at them because that motivates them to go out

there and give it their all. They really want a swift kick in the bum, but I can see that when I do that, other players start to shrink into themselves. I am mindful that those other players need something different from me, what can I do?

This problem is a difficult one to address, especially because everyone is together in the locker room during halftime. A good spray at the team will help some, but may activate others in negative ways. A Buddha-like compassionate talk about going out and doing one's best may help some players down-regulate and be able to use their resources better, but for other players such a halftime talk will leave them unmotivated. One coach I (Mark) know has coded gestures he uses both at halftime and on the sidelines when he catches his players' eyes. At halftime, the overt talk in the locker room is similar to the one we described previously as an alternative to the spray. For the players who really want the spray and the bum kick, the coach has developed some gestures that communicate to the players who thrive on such feedback that even though he isn't showing it, he is getting ticked off. One gesture is the classic move when the coach points to his own eyes with two fingers and then points with those same two fingers at the athlete who needs the bum kick. The coach has previously explained to the athlete, "When you see me give you the I-am-watching-you fingers, then you know I am getting ticked off and that you better lift your game, or I am going to haul your ass off the field. You got that?!" The coach also has encouraging gestures for the players who respond better to metaphorical pats on the back. This coach is doing his best to be mindful of the individual needs of his players without demotivating some players or overactivating others.

Phil Jackson, eleven-time NBA Championship basketball coach, has acknowledged some of the barriers to adopting mindfulness faced by many coaches. As Jackson has stated (Begley, 2014), mindfulness can be counterintuitive for coaches (and players) because it is so unlike the usual buzz of activity in sport:

> We're about action; we're about this intense activity that we've got to get after. And this mindfulness is about sitting still and being quiet and controlling your breath and allowing you to be in the moment, and yet it's so vital for a team to have this skill or players to have this skill. To be able to divorce themselves from what just happened that's inherent to them – a referee's bad call, or an issue that goes on individually or against your opponent. You've got to be able to come back to your center and center yourself again (p. 1).

Jackson (Jackson & Delehanty, 1995) has incorporated mindfulness with his teams (as a coach and team president) in a variety of ways, and the following are just a few examples that readers may use or adapt:

1. Formal mindfulness training by an instructor for the coaching staff and team in the off- and preseason and eventual incorporation into game days
2. Books and related reading material that Jackson specifically selected for different players. He also altered normal practice conditions to enhance acuity to the present moment, which fits well with related aspects of the aforementioned neuroscience (i.e., the brain registers that something is different, which stirs it from autopilot and heightens awareness)
3. Dim light practice conditions that helped concentration on present-moment play
4. Silent days (i.e., no talking), leading to enhanced attunement (e.g., nonverbal communication) between players

It is not hard to imagine that Jackson's own centered and highly attuned demeanor fostered secure attachments with and among his diverse championship teams. Underscoring this point, Jackson believed, "Good teams become great ones when the members trust each other enough to surrender the 'me' for the 'we'" (Jackson & Delehanty, 1995, p. 21).

Echoing similar earlier cautions about not treating mindfulness as a panacea, we (Joe and Mark) also encourage sport psychologists and coaches to avoid forcing mindfulness on a team. Jackson exposed and offered his teams a variety of potentially helpful practices, including tai chi and yoga, and mindfulness was what ultimately stuck (Jackson & Delehanty, 1995). This type of flexibility and responsiveness is both mindful and congruent with securely attached parenting. Forcing all players to practice mindfulness may be good for some but may be alienating for others. A coercive approach may result in resentfulness, and as resentment and frustration are not good bedfellows with mindfulness meditation, such an approach may result in the opposite of what we want to happen with such training. It is not like mandating strength and conditioning programs where probably most all athletes, even if they grumble about parts of a weight-training regimen, do understand the benefits of becoming stronger. Mandating mindfulness could result, for some players, in practicing and solidifying mindlessness and resentment.

Most indications are that mindfulness will continue to permeate both popular Western culture and sports and performance domains. Increasing the familiarity of mindfulness with coaches and players may make future incorporation of such practices commonplace and help diminish resistance.

The Mindful Down-Regulating Coach

[T]he greatest [orchestra] *musicians, with the greatest instruments in the world, and they still tune first, to themselves and to each other ... meditation, is in some sense, you could say, it's like tuning your instrument before you take it out on the road.*

Jon Kabat-Zinn (2007) at Google Headquarters

I (Mark) have a taekwondo athlete with whom I have worked for several years. He has a long history of acute and chronic trauma and was treated at one time for post-traumatic stress disorder. He had a coach whom I like to think of as one of my models for what a mindful coach should be. He's no longer the athlete's coach and lives in another part of the country, but my client does visit him at least two or three times a year. I have met the ex-coach only briefly, but I have observed him at tournaments and have heard many stories of him from my client. He is getting on in years now; he is of Samoan heritage, and he has a large Buddha belly. When I see him, there is something about the way he holds himself, the way he pays attention to people when they are talking with him, that emits a sense of kindness. Even at a distance, I get the impression of his core goodness. He is present; he is compassionate; he is nonjudgmental; he is loving. Just looking at him makes me feel comfortable, so I imagine that the effect of him on my client is quite profound. I know it is because of the stories my client tells.

At times when the taekwondo athlete has become impaired and activated by different events that have recently occurred, which have pushed a lot of historical trauma buttons, my client will take off and go see his old coach. I know the coach's presence helps down-regulate most of my client's anxieties and confusions. He comes back from those trips refreshed and focused. Those qualities the coach has are everything we want, and they are also the qualities we find in exemplary helping profession practitioners. I think of him as a coach who Carl Rogers would have loved. I know that when I have seen him, I have had a fantasy of just sitting next to him and leaning my head on his shoulder. He down-regulates me from a distance.

Some Final Thoughts

The process of examining basic neuroscience discoveries and linking them to applied understanding and practice is an illustration of *translational neuroscience* (see Milad & Quirk, 2012). We believe the future holds considerable promise for practitioners and their clients, as the edges of neuroscience and psychology continue to blur, one informing the other, and that it will become much more commonplace for sport psychology practitioners and clinicians to be educated and versed in neuroscience. This convergence and consilience enhances conceptualization, may improve confidence in the selection and effectiveness of current interventions, and may in time lead to novel and more effective interventions. Translating this knowledge in palatable and intuitive forms that coaches can relate to is a task and a skill we need to hone.

There is an old Chinese proverb that goes something like this: "The best time to plant a tree is twenty years ago. The next best time is now." Maybe you're a coach working with athletes who didn't get what they needed twenty years ago or who aren't getting what they need now. Maybe you're a sport psychology practitioner working with a coach who didn't get what he or she needed forty years ago. Maybe you didn't get what you needed ages ago. The next best time to give to ourselves, and each other, what we need is now – right here, right now, in this present moment.

REFERENCES

Aglioti, S. M., Cesari, P., Romani, M., and Urgesi, C. (2008). Action anticipation and motor resonance in elite basketball players. *Nature Neuroscience, 11*, 1109–1116. doi: 10.1038/nn.2182

Ainsworth, M. (1985). Patterns of attachment. *Clinical Psychologist, 38*(1), 27–29.

Alexander, F. G., and French, T. M. (1946). *Psychoanalytic therapy: Principles and applications.* New York, NY: Ronald.

Alutcher, C. A. (2013, April 22). *8 Zen master stories that illustrate important truths.* Retrieved from http://thoughtcatalog.com/claudia-azula-altucher/2013/04/8-zen-master-stories-that-illustrate-important-truths/

Andersen, M. B., and Mannion, J. (2011). If you meet the Buddha on the football field, tackle him! In D. Gilbourne and M. B. Andersen (Eds.), *Critical essays in applied sport psychology* (pp. 173–192). Champaign, IL: Human Kinetics.

Begley, I. (2014, October 14). *Knicks take "mindfulness training."* Retrieved from http://espn.go.com/new-york/nba/story/_/id/11694723/phil-jackson-new-york-knicks-taking-mindfulness-training

Birrer, D., Rothlin, P., and Morgan, G. (2012). Mindfulness to enhance athletic performance: Theoretical considerations and possible impact mechanisms. *Mindfulness*, 3, 235–246. doi: 10.1007/s12671-012-0109-2

Bowlby, J. (1969). *Attachment and loss* (Vol. 1: Attachment). New York, NY: Basic Books.

(1988). *A secure base: Clinical applications of attachment theory*. London, UK: Routledge.

Coan, J. A. (2008). Toward a neuroscience of attachment. In J. Cassidy and P. R. Shaver (Eds.), *The handbook of attachment: Theory, research, and clinical applications* (2nd ed., pp. 241–265). New York, NY: Guilford Press.

Confino, J. (2014, March 28). Thich Nhat Hanh: Is mindfulness being corrupted by business and finance? *The Guardian*. Retrieved from www.theguardian.com/sustainable-business/thich-nhat-hanh-mindfulness-google-tech

Cozolino, L. (2010). *The neuroscience of psychotherapy: Healing the social brain* (2nd ed.). New York, NY: W. W. Norton.

(2014). *The neuroscience of human relationships: Attachment and the developing social brain* (2nd ed.). New York, NY: W. W. Norton.

Damasio, A. R., Grabowski, T. J., Bechara, A., Damasio, H., Ponto, L. L. B., Parvizi, J., and Hichwa, R. D. (2000). Subcortical and cortical brain activity during the feeling of self-generated emotions. *Nature Neuroscience*, 3, 1049–1056. doi: 10.1038/79871

Davis, L., and Jowett, S. (2013). Attachment styles within the coach–athlete dyad: Preliminary investigation and assessment development. *Journal of Clinical Sport Psychology*, 7, 120–145.

Davis, L., Jowett, S., and Lafrenière, M. A. K. (2013). An attachment theory perspective in the examination of relational processes associated with coach–athlete dyads. *Journal of Sport and Exercise Psychology*, 35, 156–167.

Ewing, M. E., and Seefeldt, V. (2002). Patterns of participation in American agency-sponsored youth sports. In F. L. Smoll and R. E. Smith (Eds.), *Children and youth in sport: A biopsychosocial perspective* (2nd ed., pp. 39–56). Dubuque, IA: Kendall/Hunt.

Felton, L., and Jowett, S. (2012). Attachment and well-being: The mediating effects of psychological needs satisfaction within the coach–athlete and parent–athlete relational contexts. *Psychology of Sport and Exercise*, 14, 57–65. doi: 10.1016/j.psychsport.2012.07.006

Gallese, V., Morris, N. E., and Migone, P. (2007). Intentional attunement: Mirror neurons and the neural underpinnings of interpersonal relations. *Journal of the American Psychoanalytic Association*, 55, 131–175. doi: 10.1177/00030651070550010601

Gardner, F. E., and Moore, Z. E. (2004). A Mindfulness-Acceptance-Commitment-based approach to athletic performance enhancement: Theoretical considerations. *Behavior Therapy*, 35, 707–723. doi: 10.1016/S0005-7894(04)80016-9

(2006). *Clinical sport psychology*. Champaign, IL: Human Kinetics.

(2012). Mindfulness and acceptance models in sport psychology: A decade of basic and applied scientific advancements. *Canadian Psychology/Psychologie Canadienne*, 53, 309–318. doi: 10.1038/79871

Hölzel, B. K., Carmody, J., Vangel, M., Congleton, C., Yerramsetti, S. M., Gard, T., and Lazar, S. W. (2011). Mindfulness practice leads to increases in regional brain gray matter density. *Psychiatry Research-Neuroimaging*, 191, 36–43. doi: 10.1016/j.pscychresns.2010.08.006

Iacoboni, M. (2008). *Mirroring people*. New York, NY: Farrar, Straus, & Giroux.

Iacoboni, M., Woods, R. P., Brass, M., Bekkering, H., Mazziotta, J. C., and Rizzolatti, G. (1999). Cortical mechanisms of human imitation. *Science*, 286, 2526–2528. doi: 10.1126/science.286.5449.2526

Jackson, P., and Delehanty, H. (1995). *Sacred hoops: Spiritual lessons of a hardwood warrior*. New York, NY: Hyperion.

Kabat-Zinn, J. (2007). *Mindfulness with Jon Kabat-Zinn* [Video]. Available from www.youtube.com/watch?v=3nwwKbM_vJc (time locator 6:18 minutes)

Kahneman, D. (2013). *Thinking, fast and slow*. New York, NY: Farrar, Straus, & Giroux.

Langer, E. J. (2014). *Mindfulness: 25th anniversary edition*. Boston, MA: Da Capo Lifelong.

Levy-Gigi, E., Szabó, C., Kelemen, O., and Kériemail, S. (2013). Association among clinical response, hippocampal volume, and FKBP5 gene expression in individuals with posttraumatic stress disorder receiving cognitive behavioral therapy. *Biological Psychiatry*, 74, 793–800. doi: 10.1016/j. biopsych.2013.05.017

Mannion, J., and Andersen, M. B. (2015). Mindfulness, therapeutic relationships, and neuroscience in applied exercise psychology. In M. B. Andersen and S. J. Hanrahan (Eds.), *Doing exercise psychology* (pp. 3–18). Champaign, IL: Human Kinetics.

Martens, R. (2012). *Successful coaching* (4th ed.). Champaign, IL: Human Kinetics.

Milad, M. R., and Quirk, G. J. (2012). Fear extinction as a model for translational neuroscience: Ten years of progress. *Annual Review of Psychology*, 63, 129–151. doi: 10.1146/annurev.psych.121208.131631

National Registry of Evidence-Based Programs and Practices (NREPP). (n.d.). *Evidence-based therapy relationships*. Retrieved from www.nrepp.samhsa.gov/ Norcross.aspx.

Norcross, J. C. (Ed.). (2011). *Psychotherapy relationships that work: Evidence-based responsiveness* (2nd ed.). New York, NY: Oxford University Press.

Porges, S. W. (2004). Neuroception: A subconscious system for detecting threats and safety. *Zero to Three*, 24, 19–24. Retrieved from http://lifespanlearn.org/ documents/Porges-Neuroception.pdf

(2011). *The polyvagal theory: Neurophysiological foundations of emotions, attachment, communication, and self-regulation*. New York, NY: W. W. Norton.

Premack, D. G., and Woodruff, G. (1978). Does the chimpanzee have a theory of mind? *Behavioral and Brain Sciences*, 1, 515–526. doi: 10.1017/ S0140525X00076512

Rhind, D. J. A., and Jowett, S. (2010). Initial evidence for the criterion-related and structural validity of the long versions of the Coach–Athlete Relationship Questionnaire. *European Journal of Sport Science*, 10, 359–370. doi: 10.1080/17461391003699047

Rosenzweig, S. (1936). Some implicit common factors in diverse methods of psychotherapy. *American Journal of Orthopsychiatry*, 6, 412–415. doi: 10.1111/j.1939-0025.1936.tb05248.x

Schore, A. (2000). Attachment and the regulation of the right brain. *Attachment and Human Development*, 2, 23–47. doi: 10.1080/146167300361309

Sexton, T. L., and Whiston, S. C. (1994). The status of the counseling relationship: An empirical review, theoretical implications, and research directions. *Counseling Psychologist*, 22, 6–78. doi: 10.1177/0011000094221002

Shakeshaft, C. (2004). *Educator sexual misconduct: A synthesis of existing literature*. Washington, DC: U.S. Department of Education, Office of the Under Secretary. Retrieved from www2.ed.gov/rschstat/research/pubs/misconductreview/report.pdf

Siegel, D. J. (1999). *The developing mind: Toward a neurobiology of interpersonal experience*. New York, NY: Guilford Press.

 (2010). *The mindful therapist: A clinician's guide to mindsight and neural integration*. New York, NY: W. W. Norton.

Smoll, F. L., and Smith, R. E. (1989). Leadership behaviors in sport: A theoretical model and research paradigm. *Journal of Applied Social Psychology*, 19, 1522–1551. doi: 10.1111/j.1559-1816.1989.tb01462.x

Tang, Y., Lu, Q., Fan, M., Yang, Y., and Posner, M. I. (2012). Mechanisms of white matter changes induced by meditation. *Proceedings of the National Academy of Sciences*, 109, 10570–10574. doi: 10.1073/pnas.1207817109

Thompson, R. W., Kaufman, K. A., De Petrillo, L. A., Glass, C. R., and Arnkoff, D. B. (2011). One year follow-up of Mindful Sport Performance Enhancement (MSPE) for archers, golfers, and long-distance runners. *Journal of Clinical Sport Psychology*, 5, 99–116.

Trungpa, C. (2002). *Cutting through spiritual materialism*. Berkeley, CA: Shambhala.

Ulfig, N., Setzer, M., and Bohl, J. (2003). Ontogeny of the human amygdala. *Annals of the New York Academy of Sciences*, 985, 22–33. doi: 10.1111/j.1749-6632.2003.tb07068.x

Wampold, B. E. (2010). *The basics of psychotherapy: An introduction to theory and practice*. Washington, DC: American Psychological Association.

Winnicott, D. W. (1971). *Playing and reality*. London, UK: Routledge.

CHAPTER 20

Utilizing Mindfulness Strategies in Mentoring and Coaching Socially Vulnerable Youth

John M. McCarthy, Laura Hayden

This chapter has a twofold objective: (1) to illustrate the role that mindfulness-based approaches can play in mentoring/coaching socially vulnerable youth and (2) to demonstrate how mindfulness-related concepts can assist mentor/coaches in gaining insight about themselves and maintaining a balanced relationship with such environments, specifically when working with youth. Though the impact of mindfulness-based approaches within various elite performance realms has been thoroughly covered in this book, this chapter offers application to socially vulnerable youth populations. We posit that mindfulness-based approaches and mindfulness-related concepts can be instrumental in shaping the interactions that define the nature of the relationships that develop between mentor/coaches and the youth they serve. Mentor/coaches are conceptualized as those who prioritize and foster the development of an accepting and collaborative relationship between the youth and coach (McCarthy, 2012). According to Karcher and Nukkala (2010), despite the different ways of achieving these relationships, it is these sorts of relationships that have the potential to be transformational. Being a mentor/coach then, is a function of the type of relationship being cultivated with the athlete or participant in a program. So a mentor/coach approach can be applied to working with socially vulnerable youth in a sport-based youth development program, but also such an approach, we argue, can be utilized in a variety of other sport settings.

While it is unlikely that coaches and mentors will suddenly begin to adopt meditative practices in any kind of wholesale or even holistic way, in this chapter we suggest that there is still great potential benefit to be derived from strategies and concepts that come from the Eastern spiritual and philosophical traditions and the more recently acknowledged "science" of mindfulness; throughout this chapter, we will consider how to apply such ideas of mindfulness to the role of mentor/coaches who work with socially vulnerable youth.

While purists might argue that choosing select ideas from an entire spiritual tradition lacks a sincerity and thoroughness, we hold that even small steps toward these approaches offer potential benefits to both youth and the mentor/coaches who attempt to serve them. Ordained Tibetan monk and author Alan Wallace, who studied in the monastery overseen by his holiness, the Dalai Lama, is one of the foremost scholars of translation of Tibetan and other spiritual texts that explore mindfulness. He raised the issue of teaching "basic mindfulness practices that were radically decontextualized from the framework of basic Buddhist theory . . . ." Wallace (2011) points out that his holiness, the Dalai Lama noted, "If following these practices helps people to alleviate stress, even without the framework of ethics, . . . , and the larger worldview, this is a good thing" (p. 94).

While the scope of this chapter will not allow for a deep dive into the long arc of various Buddhist or other spiritual traditions, we will put forth and define the relevant concepts of mindfulness that could be useful to practitioners when working with youth in coaching and mentoring roles. Then we consider the potential application of mindfulness-based concepts in the mentor/coach relationship with youth, providing examples of our extensive direct work with youth. Subsequently, we address how mindfulness has been documented to influence socially vulnerable youth, with a focus specifically upon movement-based mindfulness practices. Finally, we provide recommendations and identify challenges for practitioners working with socially vulnerable youth using a mindfulness-based approach.

Socially Vulnerable Youth

There is a broad need for coaches and mentors who can help young people traverse the minefield of youth and adolescence into a productive adulthood. For young people, for whom society has fewer resources and less social capital to call upon when making these transitions, the need for mentor/coaches is even more urgent. For that reason, we refer to such marginalized young people as "socially vulnerable" (Vettenburg, 1998). Haudenhuyse, Theeboom, and Coalter (2011) explain, "Central in the theory of social vulnerability is the progressive accumulation of negative experiences with institutions of society such as family, school, labor market, healthcare, justice that eventually amount into social disconnectedness" (p. 439). Such processes necessitate the guiding presence of mentor/coaches who can assist youth in overcoming challenges and equip youth with approaches and psychological resources that can combat such pervasive and overwhelming forces.

Mindfulness, Education, and Youth Sport

Wallace (2011) explains that, "mindfulness belongs to a class of methods for cultivating insight" (p. 1) and, "The ability to sustain close mindfulness is a learned skill that offers profound benefits in all situations" (p. xiii). Understanding of such practices has been refined over the millennium, beginning with its initial development in Eastern meditational practices (Marlatt & Kristeller, 1999) to its modern application through the prominent work of Kabat-Zinn (1994) and contemporaries. Mindfulness, defined by Kabat-Zinn (1994) as the nonjudgmental focus of one's attention on the experience occurring in the present moment, promotes an attention on internal experiences (i.e., cognitions, emotions, physiological sensations) rather than seeking to change their frequency or form (Gardner & Moore, 2007). While various theories of mindfulness exist, the roots of mindfulness lie in Eastern meditational practice, with the agenda of using mindfulness to direct attention to the present experience (Marlatt & Kristeller, 1999). Shapiro (2009) considers mindfulness to be the awareness that arises out of intentional attendance in an open, accepting, and discerning manner to the thoughts, feelings, and bodily sensations that arise in the present moment.

Researchers (e.g., Brown & Ryan, 2003) consider mindfulness a form of awareness that can be a predisposition for well-being enhancement. Therefore, engaging in meditation exercises and training programs, which are geared toward focusing on nonjudging awareness of one's internal experiences occurring in the present moment (Baer, 2003; Kabat-Zinn, 1994), have been shown to yield positive mental and physical health outcomes across various populations and contexts (Baer, 2003; Greeson, 2009; Grossman et al., 2004). For example, Slagter and colleagues (2007) found that people who engage in meditative experiences over the course of three months were better able to allocate attentional resources than those without mindfulness training, while Zeidan and colleagues (2010) found that only four days of mindfulness practice yielded significant improvements in visuospatial processing, working memory, and executive functioning compared to a control group. Some potential practitioners may be deterred by the amount of time required to engage in meditative practices (Gardner & Moore, 2007), and unfamiliarity might also be a serious barrier to experiencing the potential benefits of mindfulness-based approaches (Kabat-Zinn, 1994). But researchers have begun to devise intervention approaches that are more appropriate for the time demands and other constraints of athletes and coaches in their work and that expose collegiate coaches to the benefits of mindfulness-based meditation (e.g., Baltzell et al., 2014).

Mindfulness in Education

While there is not extensive literature examining the use of mindfulness in coaching and mentoring underserved youth, there is substantial research that indicates promise when working with youth in schools. Given the host of difficulties facing children living in underserved communities, it is fortunate that there are new ways of considering how to work with children who face stressors that can distract and overwhelm teachers and students alike. Overall, mindfulness interventions have gained traction in schools precisely because they are suggested to help both students and teachers improve their attention and sense of well-being. Meiklejohn and colleagues (2012) have examined how mindfulness impacts teacher training programs and found positive effects on their "sense of personal well-being and teaching self-efficacy, as well as their ability to manage classroom behavior and to establish and maintain supportive relationships with students" (para. 1). In these ways, mindfulness interventions appear to have a positive effect on both the students and the teachers. Weare (2013) noted that recent reviews of the literature on the effects of mindfulness "conclude that mindfulness interventions are promising, generally acceptable, and well liked by the young people and the teachers" (p. 143). The sine qua non of teaching and coaching is attention. If you do not have a young person's attention and engagement, then it is unlikely you will be able to do anything productive with them. Mindfulness approaches are thus expected to help mentor/coaches with their youthful charges learn to be able to exist in the moment and not let other pressing issues overwhelm the moment. Additionally, such approaches assist the mentor/coach to do the same.

Mindfulness Interventions in Youth Sport and Youth Serving Program

Due to the potential benefits of mindfulness to learning, schools are integrating mindfulness concepts into their curriculum and various programs. Engaging in meditation and other spiritual practices as a youth coach who potentially could serve as a mentor/coach to young people may initially seem too far out there. But are there alternative ways of engaging in and benefiting from some aspect of these philosophies and approaches?

What follows explains how we see mindfulness-based approaches providing immediate support to enhance the work of mentoring and coaching youth, particularly socially vulnerable youth.

The role of mindfulness in the mentor/coach relationship with youth

In this chapter, we consider the role of the mentor/coach. While it may not be uncommon for some athletes to consider their coach simultaneously as a mentor, the role of the coach in recent decades has been more narrowly defined as a technical and tactical expert who helps teams win games (Jones, 2006). Working with youth, particularly those who are socially vulnerable, requires an understanding of what works for those youth in mentoring relationships. Building on the work of Morrow and Stiles (1995), Karcher and Nukkala's (2010) Theoretical Evolving Activities in Mentoring (TEAM) framework provides a lens for understanding how coaches and mentors can develop relationships with their young adult charges. This TEAM framework shows that mentoring and coaching have some overlap, and we advocate that the sport coach be seen as a mentor. To that end, coaches need a better understanding of what it means to be a mentor and how they can construct their role to foster relationships with their players/students in a way that can be the most transformational for young people. The efficacy of a sport coach as mentor working with socially vulnerable athletes rests on relational interactions rather than solely goal-directed interactions; this focus on relational interactions is foundational for the coach as mentor work.

When we think of the traditional sport-coaching model, one that is usually based on the model of professional sport (Lombardo, 1987), it conjures a very goal-directed and highly directive style of coaching. Given the emphasis and importance that Karcher & Nukkala (2010) placed upon the ongoing quality of mentor–mentee interactions, it follows that coaches too must pay close attention to how patterns of interactions develop with their players both individually and as a group. For this purpose, using mindfulness-based practices has the potential to help mentor/coaches raise their own awareness about their intentional behavior when cultivating impactful and appropriate relationships with socially vulnerable youth.

In the role of the coach as mentor, then, it is possible, according to Karcher and Nukkala (2010), to have at first an "instrumental" approach to working with young people and then, over time, developing a closer relationship. A second type of relationship that has a positive effect on the young person is what Karcher and Nukkala (2010) call a "relational" style. Using this style, the adult coach as mentor gives the young person room to be himself and focuses on the relational aspects of their interactions. Then, when they know each other well enough, the coach is more able to work with the young person to be more goal-directed. Whether embracing the relational or instrumental approach or even some hybrid of these approaches toward working with youth, the mentor/coach is required to be alert to how the relationship is evolving, which can be aided by certain mindfulness-based dispositions or approaches. In the next section, we will focus on some particular ways of thinking about mindfulness that fuel such a way of working with youth.

Langerian Approaches to Mindfulness

Ellen Langer (e.g., 1997, 2000), who some consider the mother of mindfulness in the West, has approached using mindfulness concepts in her research in a very different way than that of Buddhist mindfulness. She (2000) describes mindfulness in this way:

> Mindfulness is a flexible state of mind in which we are actively engaged in the present, noticing new things and sensitive to context. When we are in a state of mindlessness, we act like automatons who have been programmed to act according to the sense our behavior made in the past, rather than the present. Instead of actively drawing new distinctions, noticing new things, as we do when we are mindful (p. 220).

This fresh and alternate understanding of mindfulness offers guidance in how to work with socially vulnerable youth. Specifically, these youth face many internal and external challenges and such a mindful approach with new ways of noticing, being present, and being aware could be especially useful in such contexts of excessive challenge; mentor/coaches need to be astute to subtle changes occurring in and between youth.

Langer's (2009) integration of mindfulness approaches in developing different ways of approaching work in health care offers insight into how to work with socially vulnerable youth. In particular, Langer brings attention to the asymmetrical power dynamics that can result if people uncritically assume traditional roles and relationships (i.e., doctor and patient), such as the doctor as the so-called expert and the patient as having little knowledge of the condition of his or her own health. Brought into the context of coaching and youth mentoring, this approach could help us understand and examine the relationships that develop between adults and youth. If, for example, coaches and mentors mindlessly allow themselves to fall into a traditional role, they might rely on their power and authority as an adult and as a technical expert to influence the direction of the relationship with the youth they serve. While technical expert may be seen as the acceptable and even necessary role that coaches engage in, mentor/coaches must simultaneously realize that by falling exclusively into this role and relationship, it could discourage them from being mindful of the emerging needs of the youth with whom they are working. As a result, the direction and quality of such relationships are likely to be characterized as *top-down*, and unlikely to fall in the type of relationship that mentees deem most valuable to them (Karcher & Nukkala, 2010).

Central to our thinking are core beliefs that guide our work and are important to declare as we situate ourselves in a social reality of a high-needs setting. In working with socially and educationally vulnerable youth, there can be an overwhelming sense, especially of coaches of urban youth, that *you cannot save them all.* That is to say, you can help only those young people who are willing to engage in a productive relationship. In a typical coaching relationship, a baseline for a productive relationship might mean that players come to practice regularly and on time, are prepared for practices and games, are willing to take corrections, and persist when they encounter difficulties.

Coaching/mentoring youth in socially vulnerable settings does not look like this. Coaches insisting that it does or should may be placing blame on young people for not taking advantage of positive relationships with caring adults. In fact, many such youth have insufficient exposure to adults in their lives that fit with this sort of model. So while we do not propose that youth workers and coaches entertain unrealistic notions of their work because of its limitations, we advocate mindfulness and small acts of kindness when working with youth while promoting the Zen Buddhist notion of the first of the four great vows, that is, "the number of (sentient) beings is numberless, we vow to save them all" (O'Brien, 2015, para. 4).

While "saving them all" seems at first to be a grandiose and untenable position, we argue that any other stance in mentoring and coaching youth would be irresponsible. Otherwise, we would find it convenient to adopt the stance of playing triage. Triage in the medical professions refers to saving the persons most likely to survive. If we work only with the youth who are most likely to succeed and thereby make us and our programs look good, such an approach ends up being largely self-serving. The fact is that we often do not know how we are impacting a young person through our work until years later, if at all. For that reason, we must work with any young person who enters our sphere and give each a chance to benefit from that association with us. Whether that young person is able to take advantage of that relationship is ultimately determined by her; it should not be determined by the coach/mentor or program leader.

Particularly in team sports, this notion of trying to save them all seems counterintuitive. Sport in our society at this time is increasingly elitist in the current, mainstream sport system. That is to say, sport opportunity belongs to those who are the *most ready*. Increasingly, sport belongs to those who have the resources, such as transportation, fees for participation, social connections, and other advantages. Socially vulnerable children are often *not ready* to capitalize on opportunities for countless reasons that are usually beyond their control. Since having some set of obstacles is often the precondition of socially vulnerable students, then, within reason we advocate working just as hard with young people who might not make it, cannot seem to turn it around, or might never get serious. When we say "within reason," we advocate that mentor/coaches continually attempt to work with a young person as long as he or she does not seriously impede the development of the productive group, meaning that he or she damages the possibilities for others in the group to benefit from our coaching and mentoring. In our experience, excluding a student has almost never been necessary.

The Mindful Mentor/Coach

As a director of a youth development program that leverages positive movement experiences (PMEs) (Agans et al., 2013), I (John), along with a team of graduate students, follow the basic framework of Don Hellison's (2011) Responsibility Model to our work at a Title I school in Boston. The structure of the Get Ready: Life Fitness program, the current name of the program, includes the following elements:

a. Relational time – time for the mentor/coaches and student athletes to talk and interact in an informal manner
b. Group time – during which we clarify the goals for the day for the group
c. Activity time – integrating social and emotional learning into the activity (e.g., strength training, boxing)
d. Reflection time – during which we attend to how we did individually and as a group

Hayden and colleagues (2012) found that the program, then entitled Team Support, demonstrated fidelity with Hellison's Responsibility Model, despite our adaptations to this particular setting. In this work with underserved youth over the last eight years, it has become clear that our graduate students learn to assume a coach/mentor role that is infused with some basic mindfulness dispositions and approaches. In Get Ready, we teach graduate students basic dispositions of mindfulness because it helps them to be present-focused and not to be overwhelmed by the conditions and challenges that working with the participants present to them. It is hoped that some of these same mindful approaches can, in turn, benefit program participants by providing opportunities for vicarious learning and modeling. In the following, we present a few of the mindfulness-based strategies we have employed with graduate students to help train them to become mindful mentor/coaches while working with socially vulnerable youth.

Mindful noticing

Sometimes when working with high needs and socially vulnerable adolescents, there can initially be some strong resistance to anyone successfully building even basic rapport. In learning to work with this population, both myself (John) and our graduate students have had to learn to practice a basic disposition of mindfulness by noticing what is new or different about a student. For example, we encourage graduate students simply to acknowledge a new pair of sneakers or affirming the freshness of a new hairstyle. But perhaps even more important is noticing when a student makes a positive change (e.g., tries something new, increases effort, helps another student). Sometimes such changes are fledgling efforts and warrant attention because they are baby steps in a positive direction, but if gone unnoticed, the shift might get drowned out by other seemingly more urgent issues or negative behaviors that can overshadow the good. An example of this is when a student who does not normally speak suddenly shares something with the mentor or even with the group. This is no small change!

On the other hand, it is difficult to acknowledge positive change when it is overshadowed by the other things the student is not doing or negative behaviors in which the student may engage. Given that our program currently commences in the first period of the day, we often have students who arrive late. And graduate students are encouraged to welcome all Get Ready participants, regardless of when they show up. One of the first things we teach the graduate students to acknowledge is what the student is doing positively. Very often, the Get Ready participant will be encouraged to jump right in and get to work even though he or she had a late start. In this way, our graduate students are able to use this mindful noticing of not focusing on what many other adults have already called the participant to task for before he or she even reaches us (i.e., being late), but instead on what the participant is doing right or even partially right (e.g., joining the group workout.)

Acceptance and tolerance of what is
Often in high-needs settings, there are conditions that can be quite demotivating and make it challenging to run any program. It is easy to capitulate and just allow the program to come to a grinding halt. For example, in our first year of the Get Ready program, a few days prior to when we were scheduled to start, I (John) learned from the school custodian that the space we use for our program would be closed for over two months because the facilities management in the district was redoing the ventilation in that part of the building. It was difficult to understand why this was scheduled at a time of the year when it was needed for physical education classes and sport practices and to serve students with special needs. After experiencing a limited period of shock and disbelief, it was clear that *my* expectation that things should be done differently was not going to change anything. For us to spend any more time thinking that the school leaders should have informed us or planned differently no longer mattered. After a quick appraisal of this somewhat untenable situation, my graduate students and I decided to take all the exercise equipment to the front of the school near the flagpole. We invented workouts and activities that we could do outside the building. Fortunately, the weather in that first month was uncharacteristically benign, so we were able to carry on without disruption.

Teaching graduate students this mentality of mindful acceptance and "tolerance of what is" is actually a vital skill for coaching and teaching in underserved situations. In this way, our youth worker "mentor/coaches" are modeling toleration of the emotions that accompany such situations that are not ideal. (That is not to say that we would not also teach them to advocate for change, whenever possible.) Additionally, sometimes we are able to leverage such events in a way that we hoped could strengthen the participants' ability to cope with events that are beyond their control. An example of this disposition came up with one of our students who had improperly held on to a cell phone of a fellow student that he *found.* During our program, the school police and disciplinary dean made it clear that the Get Ready student had to return the phone. He was visibly upset because he had to go home to get the phone, but could not leave until his mother picked him up one hour later. In the meantime, one of our graduate students who worked with him was able to persuade him that, since he would have to wait until his mother showed up, he might as well consider doing a workout and participate in our program to do something productive. The student noted afterward that participating made him feel better. He was learning to "tolerate what is" to free himself up to make better choices for himself within his situation.

Compassion toward self and others

Another key disposition of mindfulness is the ability to be compassionate, meaning to acknowledge pain and to suffer along with the other. Many times, as coaches and mentors, we are unlikely to fully comprehend the difficulty that our students face on a daily basis. One of the counseling techniques that we incorporate is the phrase, "Help me understand . . . ," because we are never fully able to comprehend the subjective experience of another (Maslow, 1968). We actually need the participant in the program to help us understand what his or her reality is. But even when we attempt to bridge this gulf, we must still realize that we may never fully understand.

We search within our own experience to grasp something that will allow us to better understand the young person in front of us (Cottle, 2013). Even then, as close as we may come to allowing them to be heard, we must often be ready as the mentor/coach to assist participants to absolve themselves, especially for circumstances they cannot control. For example, participants very often must work at night to make ends meet and as a result are too tired to work out intensely in our first-period program. Self-compassion is both an essential and different approach to this situation. Sometimes we might find ourselves saying things like, "It's not your fault," or, "Give yourself a break." What we realize is that too often the young person has already condemned himself for things like "being lazy" or "not being smart," and has become mired in his own self-disapproval. We as mentor/coaches can model for them a healthy amount of self-discipline, while making allowance for and adjusting to the very real obstacles that face them. Some high-performance coaches might find this approach as being "too soft" and not having high expectations for the student. While this may make sense with someone who is ready for a high degree of accountability and able to withstand criticism, in working with socially vulnerable youth, we have not found such approaches to be useful.

Not only can coaches and mentors benefit from being aware of the emerging needs of the youth they serve, they can also benefit from paying attention to what occurs with youth in the present moment. As young people are often contemplating change or making subtle shifts in behavior in ways that warrant attention and encouragement, it behooves coaches to be mindful and acknowledge those small changes. In other words, when a coach or mentor has a fixed view of an athlete and her potential, it can yield frustration for both the coach/mentor and the athlete. Since young people are constantly changing, or on the verge of change, it is perilous for coaches and mentors to assume they know any particular youth as a fixed entity.

If you listen to some coaches' statements about their athletes, it can reveal how the coaches approach their coach–athlete relationships. For example, if the name of a certain player comes up, coaches will say things like, "He's a good kid," or, "She is a hard worker." While any appraisal may be based upon a particular coach's experience with a particular youth at a particular point in time, the difficulty with this sort of approach to working with youth is the emergence of a form of labeling that might disadvantage those who are on the cusp of learning what it takes to become "good" or a "hard worker." If the coach or mentor does not cultivate that disposition when it occurs, he might miss the opportunity to foster such dispositions in the same young people he is trying to develop.

Coaches and mentors themselves are often challenged by a host of factors that, if they are not careful, can rob their ability to devote their full attention toward the young people with whom they work. In high-needs settings, coaches often are drawn into serving youth in multiple roles such as surrogate parent, advisor, and academic mentor. Furthermore, mentor/coaches operate in environments that rarely have the administrative and logistical support to help coaches deal with even straightforward aspects of providing a high-quality sporting experience. That is to say, all coaches deal with practical challenges (e.g., the bus does not show up, the officials are late, or even the players themselves find it difficult to get to practices and games). But a coach may experience additional demands due to the nature of the high-needs settings, such as the players being hungry, sleep deprived, or stressed by the material conditions of poverty. Dealing with such urgent matters is likely to take a toll on the mentor/coaches' resources to attend to the quality of the relationships they are cultivating with their players. Young people are quick to realize when adults are not paying close attention to them. What is worse, underserved youth may also be used to lacking basic life needs, which in turn makes them even more socially vulnerable.

Langer, Cohen, and Djikic (2012) established that not only can children between the ages of nine and twelve easily detect when adults are not fully engaged with them, but as a result of an adult's inattentiveness, children might suffer the consequences of not feeling valued by that adult. Youth coaches, particularly those who want to become valued in a mentoring role, would certainly not want to convey to their young charges the feeling that they do not value them. So what can be done to counteract the sometimes overwhelming role of the coach of young people in high-needs situations?

Being fully present to what is occurring at a given moment is both a concept and a meditative practice. This basic intention of awareness is part of all mindfulness training. Given the high demands placed on coaches of participants in sport programs that serve socially vulnerable children and adolescents, it is paramount to leave no participant behind; every participant deserves the opportunity to be heard. Some coaches may wield their authority in hopes of getting their players to perform better and to conform to team rules. However, the consequences of such approaches, if left unexamined, leave coaches and mentors leaning toward a style of interaction that is authoritarian and highly directive. Highly directive approaches to coaching may produce the appearance of compliance and organization and even lead to early success, but some coach educators and coaching scholars have challenged whether such approaches benefit young people in the long run, particularly in areas such as decision making and self-direction (Kidman, 2001; Kidman & Hanrahan, 2004). Furthermore, a coach/mentor who does not allow a player to develop genuine choices and an authentic sense of his or her own voice may undercut the player's cognitive, social, emotional, and ethical growth.

Baltzell, McCarthy, and Greenbaum (2014) wrote about the challenges of *mindlessness* in sport coaching. They described situations (e.g., athlete interactions, parent interactions, working with media) in which coaches become locked in aversive emotions, such as self-doubt, anger, frustration, and fear. Baltzell and colleagues (2014) suggested that participants consider the consequences of "mindless" coaching, such as inflexibility (e.g., not noticing changes of players skills or effort), habituated responses in which coaches fail to incorporate new information about their team into their coaching schema, an external focus that causes them to miss opportunities to respond to new stimuli within their team environment, and worry about certain components of the job due to limited resources to the detriment of other essential in-the-moment components. To this end, addressing mindless aspects of coaching – and becoming more mindful – is expected to drastically affect the relationship between coach/mentor and young participant.

Mindfulness Practice in Socially Vulnerable Youth Development

When exploring the influencing factors on youth's development, it can be helpful to situate youth within their various environmental contexts. Bronfenbrenner's (1979) ecological model emphasizes the effect of the interaction between people and their environment by considering the microsystem (e.g., family, school, peers); mesosystem (e.g., relations between the microsystems); exosystem (e.g., occurrences in influential settings in which people may not be present); macrosystem (e.g., cultural context); and chronosystem (e.g., the dimension of time that reflects changes in the person or environment over time). How a person develops in relation to each of these systems can change over time based on environmental and sociohistorical circumstances. Within each system, norms and roles exist that may influence youth's development and that are important to consider when identifying how best to support youth.

Youth residing in underserved urban communities are at risk for various negative outcomes related to chronic stress (e.g., community violence). These outcomes include emotional self-regulation (West, Denton, & Reaney, 2000), social-emotional difficulties, behavioral problems, poor academic performance (Mendelson et al., 2010), and cognitive and affective regulation (Keenan et al., 1997). Additionally, youth who experience chronic stress and adversity in childhood might have impaired stress response systems given that childhood adversity has been found to trigger neurobiological events that alter brain development (Andersen, 2003; Shonkoff, Boyce, & McEwen, 2009; Teicher et al., 2002).

These stress response systems underlie cognitive and emotion regulatory capacities (Andersen & Teicher, 2009), suggesting that youth who experience chronic stress are at risk for cognitive and emotional regulation difficulties. When couched in terms of Bronfenbrenner's ecological model, this suggests the effect of a macrosystem on youth's emotional, social, and behavioral development. Given the relationship between these various outcomes and overall adjustment (Greenberg, 2006), it may behoove practitioners to explore how to train youth to better modulate their responses to chronic adversity and stressors.

While much existing research focuses on adult populations, researchers have suggested that meditation-based interventions with youth show reduced distress, anxiety, and emotional and behavioral reactivity, and improved self-awareness and sleep among youth (Bootzin & Stevens, 2005; Napoli, Krech, & Holley, 2005; Semple, Reid, & Miller, 2005; Wall, 2005). Researchers (e.g., Galantino, Galbavy, & Quinn, 2008;

Greenberg & Harris, 2011; Mendelson et al., 2010) have suggested that mindfulness-based approaches, including meditation and yoga, might enhance regulatory capacities (including stress management) among chronically stressed youth. Yoga, considered one specific form of mindfulness practice, involves maintained focused attention on breath and body while engaging in movements to improve strength and flexibility, and research indicates that yoga increases attention, self-regulation, and functioning in adults while decreasing stress (Arias et al., 2006).

While minimal research has examined the effectiveness of yoga-based interventions with youth, researchers have found that interventions involving meditation with yoga can reduce distress, anxiety, and emotional and behavioral reactivity, while improving self-awareness and sleep (e.g., Bootzin & Stevens, 2005). For example, in relation to the positive effects of including yoga in mindfulness-based interventions, Mendelson and colleagues (2010) piloted a randomized control trial to explore preliminary outcomes of a school-based mindfulness and yoga intervention and found that the intervention had a positive impact on problematic responses to stress, such as rumination, intrusive thoughts, and emotional arousal. Gould and colleagues (2012) conducted a twelve-week, yoga-inspired, school-based mindfulness intervention for urban fourth and fifth graders and found that the intervention reduced involuntary problematic responses to social stress, including rumination, intrusive thoughts, and emotional arousal, which are linked to oversensitization of the stress response system via early and continued exposure to stress and adversity (Andersen & Teicher, 2009). Additionally, Sibinga and colleagues (2013) explored the effects of a school-based mindfulness-based program for young urban males in seventh and eighth grade. Through gathering psychological functioning data (i.e., sleep and salivary cortisol – a physiologic measure of stress), they found that the boys who received the mindfulness-based training experienced less anxiety and rumination and improved coping compared to boys who did not receive the mindfulness-based training.

In relation to the effects on brain development of childhood adversity and stress, it has been suggested that mindfulness meditation can also alter basic brain structures and functions. For example, it can promote neuroplasticity (i.e., the capacity for neural changes in response to training), and meditators with adequate mindfulness training begin to experience traitlike differences in their ability to respond to emotion and function in the face of stress-inducing stimuli (Davidson, 2002). Furthermore, while the condition has yet to be acknowledged in the new

Diagnostic and Statistical Manual of Mental Disorders (DSM-V), some have referred to a type of trauma that is facing urban youth who might be exposed to crime and gang violence over a prolonged period of time, called complex post-traumatic stress disorder (C-PTSD) (Duncan-Andrade, 2010). Youth in such situations may be confronted by violence and reminded of that trauma daily. To this end, engaging with youth in mindfulness-based strategies, such as the one discussed previously, may facilitate the development of vital coping skills that enable children facing stressors to get on a positive youth development trajectory.

In a review of research and curricula addressing the integration of mindfulness training in K-12 education, Meiklejohn and colleagues (2012) summarized that sustained mindfulness practice can enhance attentional and emotional self-regulation while promoting flexibility. Furthermore, initial findings on mindfulness-based teacher training initiatives indicate that mindfulness skill training can increase teachers' sense of well-being, teaching self-efficacy, and ability to manage classroom behavior and establish and maintain supportive relationships with students. Meiklejohn and colleagues (2012) highlight that since 2005, fourteen studies of mindfulness training programs geared toward students have shown various cognitive, social, and psychological benefits to elementary and high school students. Improvements in working memory, attention, academic skills, social skills, emotional regulation, self-esteem, and mood, coupled with decreased anxiety, stress, and fatigue, have been identified as outcomes in mindfulness training initiatives. While these results are promising, they do not entirely focus on underserved urban youth. Uncovering specific outcomes to mindfulness initiatives relevant to underserved urban youth may prove to be challenging, given the constraints of engaging in applied research in underresourced settings. This challenge is further explored in the "Challenges and Recommendations" section later in this chapter.

Given that coaching is often associated with performance, it is befitting to explore the role of mindfulness in sport and exercise, highlighting this relationship within an urban context. Various researchers have explored the relationships between mindfulness and sport performance (e.g., Gardner & Moore, 2004, 2006), with Jackson and Csikszentmihalyi (1999) suggesting that mindfulness is linked to present-moment focus, which is essentially the foundation of peak performance in sport. For example, Bernier and colleagues (2009) found that optimal performance (i.e., "flow") states are experienced similarly to mindfulness and acceptance states by elite swimmers. That is, elite swimmers identified being mindful and accepting of their bodily sensations. Furthermore, Bernier and colleagues (2009) found that a psychological skills training program that included mindfulness and acceptance among young elite golfers enhanced performance in competition. Specifically, the young golfers improved the efficacy of their routines by incorporating relevant internal and external information.

When using mindfulness strategies in sport and exercise with urban youth, a recent study by Kerrigan and colleagues (2011) found that urban youth who participated in a mindfulness-based stress reduction program self-reported positive benefits and enhanced self-awareness in various ways. For example, participants' self-reported changes ranged from reframing and reducing daily stressors to transformational alterations in life and well-being.

Challenges and Recommendations

Despite the potential benefits of incorporating mindfulness strategies and programs into sport and physical-activity based youth development with socially vulnerable youth, challenges exist that threaten the practicality of incorporating mindfulness approaches into this work. Coaches and mentors of socially vulnerable youth have an important, yet challenging, charge in helping youth work toward achieving their full potential. Knowing that there are constraints to reaching them and engaging in mindfulness-based practices with them, there still is great promise in teaching both dispositions and strategies that use mindfulness as a starting point. In relation to the challenges in reaching youth, coaches and mentors may experience their own limitations in understanding mindfulness-based work. In addition, some mindfulness-based practices are time consuming to execute. With the increasing demands on coaches and mentors' time, incorporating initiatives and programs that are simple and efficient may be more desirable for practitioners. However, we believe, despite all these obstacles, integrating mindfulness-based strategies into currently existing practices can still yield effective results. In order to bring mindfulness approaches and concepts to their settings, coaches and mentors must be willing to seek both new understandings of themselves while also striving to understand and support the youth with whom they are working.

Employing an ecological perspective means understanding that cultures and communities affect youth development. It is imperative that coaches and mentors recognize and understand the environment in which they work and, therefore, create culturally sensitive interventions that are relevant to those they serve. For example, in order to apply a mindfulness approach to working with youth, coaches and mentors must recognize and acknowledge the assumptions and biases they bring to the relationship, coupled with the reality in which those they serve live, and make appropriate accommodations to their programs and initiatives accordingly.

An additional challenge lies in exploring how mindfulness approaches actually benefit socially vulnerable youth cognitively, neurologically, socially, mentally, and behaviorally. While a body of research exists on this topic, scientific study of school-aged children and youth residing in underserved neighborhoods may be impeded by the inherent difficulty of partnering with schools, researchers' ability to provide systematic and consistent programming, and evaluators' ability to collect informed consent and data on this population.

Practical Mindfulness Strategies for Coach–Mentors

Despite these challenges, various coaching and mentoring situations can be aided by mindfulness-based strategies. Mentor/coaches can teach directly to youth some basic techniques that fall within the practice of mindfulness and meditation that can benefit both mentor/coaches and the youth whom they serve. Breathing techniques, for example, have been long shown as centering and establishing a mind–body connection for relaxation. Additionally, yoga, a form of mindfulness, has been successfully implemented in many physical activity settings to center attention and find a feeling of grounding. Second, the mindful approach to daily challenges can be taught in myriad ways that could be raised at key moments but could also be weaved into the general practice or team rituals. For example, as a coach, when you see a group of players getting caught up in a tense competitive situation, you can be taught to bring the players' attention to the present moment. Many great coaches are able to help a player snap out of an anxious moment by asking the player to notice something that would focus his or her attention on something totally in the present (McCarthy, 2004).

In our work with socially vulnerable youth, we have embraced different mindfulness-based approaches because using such approaches involves a deep noticing of program participants' needs and how we interact with them. Here are a few ways we attempt to demonstrate an understanding of the cultural and social dynamics of adult–teenage relationships and pay close attention to what is arising with the youth we encounter:

- First, the *ninja*. Like stealthy martial artists, we move to a place ourselves in a way that does not startle the student but situates us physically alongside the student to be able to interact with him or her with a nonthreatening, friendly closeness. A second approach that can be used in conjunction with the ninja approach is the *whisper.*

- The *whisper* is used especially when we notice that the student is giving off a challenging vibe. But even in normal group situations when we talk to a young person, any interaction with an adult can be seen as a confrontation. In this situation, the whisper enables us to address young people in a gentle way that allows them to process our message to them almost privately. And it diffuses the possibility of having them feel they must make a show of defense for their peers.

- Third, *take a knee.* By lowering one's body position relative to the young person, we are communicating from a vantage point that can have a profoundly disarming effect. We think this is so because it seems to reorganize the power differential that youth may feel when addressed by adults (Langer, 2009). It tends to put the young person at ease or at least a little more open to being spoken to by adults.

- In a similar way, the final strategy that we will offer here is to *ask permission.* Asking permission to give coaching allows young people to check in with themselves and see whether they are ready to be coached. This technique promotes a quality of mindfulness in both the youth and the mentor/coach.

Youth coaches and workers would benefit from understanding some of the basic ideas of how teachers in the Eastern spiritual traditions teach mindfulness. Wallace (2011) suggests that practitioners become mindful of the body by directing our attention to our body and our immediate experience of the physical environment in our lived world. This can be accomplished by centering one's attention on one's breathing and the sensations that accompanying those breaths. Additionally, being aware of our own feelings when working with youth can be a tool to practice mindfulness-based interventions (Wallace, 2011). This can be challenging, as young people can stir up negative emotions of anger, impatience, frustration, and even resentment from their coaches and mentors. Strong negative reactions by adults directed at youth are unlikely to yield positive results, particularly with young people who may have already absorbed more than their fair share of negative emotions. So breathing and focusing on one's breath can help mentor/coaches become more centered and better prepared for their work. We have found, with the participants in our program, that almost always when we have used breathing and focusing attention on our breath as part of what we call our "sport yoga," students have reported how helpful it is to them to manage negative emotions and to feel more energized for the rest of their day.

Until youth coaches and mentors are aware of the source of their own negative feelings, they may struggle to control them. Being able to process these feelings in a way that can still be authentic is of crucial importance for successful relationships. Finally, being aware of ideas, thoughts, mental images, and desires and fears, for example, allows coaches and mentors to be mindful of what is emerging within them when they are working closely with youth (Wallace, 2011). There are countless opportunities to observe such events when working as a coach or a mentor. For example, coaches and mentors may hope the youth with whom they work experience success but also fear that success might be challenging to achieve given outside constraints. By noticing and naming these mental events, coaches and mentors may assist youth with overcoming what may be real obstacles. In the same way, teaching youth to be aware of these thoughts and events and to be able to verbalize them may provide coaches and mentors insight into young people's thought processes and may provide clues as to how to work more productively together.

Conclusion

Despite the very real limitations to engaging in mindfulness-based work with urban youth, we are confident that the time and attention it takes to develop a mindfulness-based approach will serve coaches and mentors as they seek to understand themselves, the urban youth whom they serve, and the relationship between them. Coaches and mentors are under increasing scrutiny and duress to deliver positive youth development outcomes that are frequently negatively impacted by elements of urban and other dysfunctional systems that are far beyond their ability to change. Therefore, by adopting a mindfulness-based lens, we are confident there exist novel approaches that practitioners can employ to develop interventions directly with youth, using them in the communities in which they live, work, and play, potentially with stressed parents, family members, teachers, and other stakeholders and influencers. These mindfulness approaches may also be of real and immediate value to youth coaches and mentors, the practitioners who are likely to be the key adult mentors who can show socially vulnerable youth how to adopt different approaches to handling stress and conflict with ease, balance, and clarity (Wallace, 2011).

REFERENCES

Agans, J. P., Säfvenbom, R., Davis, J. L., Bowers, E. P., and Lerner, R. M. (2013). Activity involvement as an ecological asset: Profiles of participation and youth outcomes. *Journal of Youth and Adolescence*, 43(6), 919–932. doi: 10.1007/s10964-014-0091-1

Andersen, S. L. (2003). Trajectories of brain development: Point of vulnerability or window of opportunity? *Neuroscience and Biobehavioral Reviews*, 27, 3–18. doi: 10.1016/S0149-7634(03)00005-8

Andersen, S. L., and Teicher, M. H. (2009). Desperately driven and no brakes: Developmental stress exposure and subsequent risk for substance use. *Neuroscience and Behavioral Reviews*, 33, 516–524. doi: 10.1016/j.neubiorev.2008.09.009

Arias, A. J., Steinberg, K., Banga, A., and Trestment, R. L. (2006). Systematic review of the efficacy of meditation techniques as treatments for medical illness. *Journal of Alternative and Complementary Medicine*, 12, 817–832. doi: 10.1089/acm.2006.12.817

Baltzell, A., Caraballo, N., Chipman, K., and Hayden, L. (2014). Qualitative study of the Mindfulness Meditation Training Program (MMTS): Division I female soccer players' experience. *Journal of Clinical Sport Psychology*, 8, 221–244. doi: 10.1123/jcsp.2014-0030

Baltzell, A., McCarthy, J., and Greenbaum, T. (2014). Mindfulness strategies: Consulting with coaches and athletes: background and presentation of the 2013 AASP annual convention workshop. *Journal of Sport Psychology in Action*, 00, 1–9. doi: 10.1080/21520704.2014.943916

Baer, R. A. (2003). Mindfulness training as a clinical intervention: A conceptual and empirical review. *Clinical Psychology: Science and Practice*, 10(2), 125–143. doi: 10.1093/clipsy/bpg015

Bernier, M., Thienot, E., Codron, R., and Fournier, J. F. (2009). Mindfulness and acceptance approaches in sport performance. *Journal of Clinical Sport Psychology*, 25(4), 320–333.

Bootzin, R. R., and Stevens, S. J. (2005). Adolescents, substance abuse, and the treatment of insomnia and daytime sleepiness. *Clinical Psychology Review*, 25, 629–644. doi: 10.1016/j.cpr.2005.04.007

Bronfenbrenner, U. (1979). *The ecology of human development: Experiments by nature and design*. Cambridge, MA: Harvard University Press.

Brown, K. W., and Ryan, R. M. (2003). The benefits of being present: Mindfulness and its role in psychological well-being. *Journal of Personality and Social Psychology*, 84(4), 822–848. doi: 10.1037/0022-3514.84.4.822

Cottle, T. J. (2013). *Drawing life: A narrative of sense and self*. Lanham, MD: Hamilton.

Davidson, R. J. (2002). Toward a biology of positive affect and compassion. In R. J. Davidson and A. Harrington (Eds.), *Visions of compassion: Western scientists and Tibetan Buddhists examine human nature* (pp. 107–130). New York, NY: Oxford University Press.

Duncan-Andrade, J. M. R (2010). *What a coach can teach a teacher: Lessons urban schools can learn from a successful sports program*. New York, NY: Peter Lang.

Galantino, M. L., Galbavy, R., and Quinn, L. (2008). Therapeutic effects of yoga for children: A systematic review of the literature. *Pediatric Physical Therapy*, 20, 66–80. doi: 10.1097/PEP.0b013e31815f1208

Gardner, F. L., and Moore, Z. E. (2004). A Mindfulness-Acceptance-Commitment (MAC) based approach to athletic performance enhancement: Theoretical considerations. *Behavior Therapy*, 35(4), 707–723. doi: 10.1016/S0005-7894 (04)80016-9

(2006). *Clinical sport psychology*. Champaign, IL: Human Kinetics.

(2007). *The psychology of human performance: The Mindfulness-Acceptance-Commitment approach*. New York, NY: Springer.

Gould, L. F., Dariotis, J. K., Mendelson, T., and Greenberg, M. T. (2012). A school-based mindfulness intervention for urban youth: Exploring moderators of intervention effects. *Journal of Community Psychology*, 40(8), 968–982. doi: 10.1002/jcop.21505

Greenberg, M. T. (2006). Promoting resilience in children and youth: Preventative interventions and their interface with neuroscience. *Annals of the New York Academy of Science*, 1094, 139–150.

Greenberg, M. T., and Harris, A. R. (2011). Nurturing mindfulness in children and youth: Current state of the research. *Child Development Perspectives*, 6, 161–166. doi: 10.1111/j.1750-8606.2011.00215.x

Greeson J. M. (2009). Mindfulness research update: 2008. *Journal of Evidence-Based Complementary and Alternative Medicine*, 14(1), 10–18. doi: 10.1177/ 1533210108329862

Grossman, P., Niemann, L., Schmidt, S., and Walach, H. (2004). Mindfulness-based stress reduction and health benefits: A meta-analysis. *Journal of Psychosomatic Research*, 57(1), 35–43. doi: 10.1016/S0022-3999 (03)00573-7

Haudenhuyse, R. P., Theeboom, M., and Coalter, F. (2011). The potential of sports-based social interventions for vulnerable youth: Implications for sport coaches and youth workers. *Journal of Youth Studies*, 15, 437–454. doi: 10.1080/13676261.2012.663895

Hayden, L. A., Baltzell, A., Kilty, K., and McCarthy, M. (2012). Developing responsibility using physical activity: A case study of team support. *Agora*, 14 (2), 264–281.

Hellison, D. (2011). *Teaching responsibility through physical activity* (3rd ed.). Champaign, IL: Human Kinetics.

Jackson, S. A., and Csikszentmihalyi, M. (1999). *Flow in sports: The key to optimal experience and performances*. Champaign, IL: Human Kinetics.

Jones, R. (2006). *The sport coach as educator: Reconceptualizing sports coaching*. New York, NY: Routledge.

Kabat-Zinn, J. (1982). An outpatient program in behavioral medicine for chronic pain patients based on the practice of mindfulness meditation: Theoretical considerations and preliminary results. *General Hospital Psychiatry*, 4, 33–42. doi: 10.1016/0163-8343(82)90026-3

(1994). *Wherever you go, there are you: Mindfulness meditation in everyday life*. New York, NY: Hyperion.

Karcher, M. J., and Nakkula, M. J. (2010). Youth mentoring with a balanced focus, a shared purpose, and collaborative interactions. *New Directions for Youth Development*, 2010(126), 13–32. doi: 10.1002/yd.347

Keenan, K., Shaw, D. S., Walsh, B., Delliquadri, E., and Giovannelli, J. (1997). DSM-III-R disorders in pre-school children from low-income families. *Journal of the American Academy of Child and Adolescent Psychiatry*, 36, 620–627. doi: 10.1097/00004583-199705000-00012

Kerrigan, D., Johnson, K., Stewart, M., Magyari, T., Hutton, N., Ellen, J. M., and Sibinga, E. (2011). Perceptions, experiences, and shifts in perspective occurring among urban youth participating in a mindfulness-based stress reduction program. *Complementary Therapies in Clinical Practice*, 17, 96–101. doi: 10.1016/j.ctcp.2010.08.003

Langer, E. J. (1997). *The power of mindful learning*. Reading, MA: Addison-Wesley.
  (2000). Mindful learning. *Current Directions in Psychological Science*, 9(6), 220–223. doi: 10.1111/1467-8721.00099
  (2009). *Counterclockwise: Mindful health and the power of possibility*. New York, NY: Ballantine.

Langer, E. J., Cohen, M., and Djikic, M. (2012). Mindfulness as a psychological attractor: The effect on children. *Journal of Applied Social Psychology*, 42(5), 1114–1122. doi: 10.111/j.1559-1816.2011.00879.x

Langer E. J., and Piper, A. (1987). The prevention of mindlessness. *Journal of Personality and Social Psychology*, 53, 280–287. doi: http://dx.doi.org/10.1037/0022-3514.53.2.280

Kidman, L. (2001). *Developing decision makers: An empowerment approach to coaching*. Christchurch, NZ: Innovative Print Communications.

Kidman, L., and Hanrahan, S. J. (2004). *The coaching process: A practical guide to becoming an effective sports coach*. New York, NY: Dunmore Press.

Lombardo, B. (1987). *The humanistic coach: From theory to practice*. Thomas: Springfield, MA.

Marlatt, G. A., and Kristeller, J. L. (1999). Mindfulness and meditation. In W. R. Miller (Ed.), *Integrating spirituality into treatment: Resources for Practitioners* (pp. 67–84). Washington, DC: American Psychological Association.

Maslow, A. (1968). *Toward a psychology of being*. New York, NY: Van Nostrand.

McCarthy, J. M. (2004). *How do master football coaches develop team confidence? A study of strategies and conceptualizations in the psychology of collective efficacy*. (Unpublished doctoral dissertation). Boston, MA: Boston University.
  (2012, August). *Becoming a mentor-coach*. Invited lecture conducted at the meeting of the National Training Institute for Coach across America, Boston, MA.

Meiklejohn, J., Phillips, C., Freedman, M. L., Griffin, M. L., Biegel, G., Roach, A., ... and Saltzman, A. (2012). Integrating the mindfulness training into K-12 education: Fostering the resilience of teachers and students. *Mindfulness*, 3, 291–307. doi: 10.1007/s12671-012-0094-5

Mendelson, T., Greenberg, M. T., Dariotis, J. K., Gould, L. F., Rhoades, B. L., and Leaf, P. J. (2010). Feasibility and preliminary outcomes of a school-based mindfulness intervention for urban youth. *Journal of Abnormal Child Psychology*, 38(7), 985–994. doi: http://dx.doi.org/10.1007/s10802-010-9418-x

Morrow, K. V., and Styles, M. B. (1995). *Building relationships with youth in program settings: A study of Big Brothers/Big Sisters*. Philadelphia, PA: Public/Private Ventures.

Napoli, M., Krech, P. R., and Holley, L. C. (2005). Mindfulness training for elementary school students: the attention academy. *Journal of Applied School Psychology*, 21, 99–125. doi: 10.1300/J370v21n01_05

O'Brien, B. (2015). Bodhisattva vows: Walking the Bodhisattva path. *About Religion.* Retrieved from http://buddhism.about.com/od/mahayanabuddhism/a/bodhisattva-vows.htm

Semple, R. J., Reid, E. F. G., and Miller, L. (2005). Treating anxiety with mindfulness: An open trial of mindfulness training for anxious children. *Journal of Cognitive Psychotherapy: An International Quarterly*, 19, 379–392. doi: http://dx.doi.org/10.1891/jcop.2005.19.4.379

Shapiro, S. L. (2009). The integration of mindfulness and psychology. *Journal of Clinical Psychology*, 65, 550–560. doi: 10.1002/jclp.20602

Shonkoff, J. P., Boyce, W. T., and McEwen, B. S. (2009). Neuroscience, molecular biology, and the childhood roots of health disparities: Building a new framework for health promotion and disease prevention. *Journal of the American Medical Association*, 301, 2252–2259.

Sibinga, E. M. S., Perry-Parrish, C., Chung, S., Johnson, S. B., Smith, M., and Ellen, J. M. (2013). School-based mindfulness instruction for urban male youth: A small randomized controlled trial. *Preventative Medicine*, 57, 799–801.

Slagter, H. A., Lutz, A., Greischar, L. L., Francis, A. D., Nieuwenhuis, S., Davis, J. M., and Davidson, R. J. (2007). Mental training affects distribution of limited brain resources. *PLoS Biology*, 5, 1228–1235. doi: 10.1371/journal.pbio.0050138

Teicher, M. H., Andersen, S. L., Polcari, A., Anderson, C. M., and Navalta, C. P. (2002). Developmental neurobiology of childhood stress and trauma. *Psychiatric Clinics of North America*, 25, 397–426.

Vettenburg, N. (1998). Juvenile delinquency and the cultural characteristics of the family. *International Journal of Adolescent Medicine and Health*, 10(3), 193–209. doi: 10.1515/IJAMG.1998.10.3.193

Wall, R. B. (2005). Tai chi and mindfulness-based stress reduction in a Boston public middle school. *Jounral of Pediatric Health Care*, 19, 230–237. doi: 10.1016/j.pedhc.2005.02.006

Wallace, A. (2011). *Following closely: The four applications of mindfulness.* Ithaca, NY: Snow Lion.

Weare, K. (2013). Developing mindfulness with children and young people: A review of the evidence and policy context. *Journal of Children's Services*, 8(2), 141–153. doi: 10.1108/JCS-12-2012-0014

West, J., Denton, K., and Reaney, L. (2000). *The kindergarten year: Findings from the Early Childhood Longitudinal Study, kindergarten class of 1998–1999.* National Center for Education Statistics (Report No. PS029–031). Retrieved from http://files.eric.ed.gov/fulltext/ED447933.pdf

Zeidan, F., Johnson, S. K., Diamond, B. J., Daivd, Z., and Goolkasian, P. (2010). Mindfulness meditation improves cognition: Evidence of brief mental training. *Consciousness and Cognition*, 19, 597–605. doi: 10.1016/j.concog.2010.03.014

CHAPTER 21

Awareness, Self-Awareness, and Mindfulness: The Application of Theory to Practice

Burt Giges, Gerald Reid

Learning the art of helping others is a personal journey, requiring a commitment to knowing and understanding yourself.

Mark Young (1998, p. 2).

The purpose of this chapter is to provide educational, didactic, and experiential material to help practitioners increase their awareness of their own thoughts, feelings, wants, and behaviors, to ensure that they are effectively meeting the needs of the client with whom they are working. Specifically, the chapter will identify the ways in which mindfulness can benefit the practice of sport psychology consultants (SPCs) by increasing self-awareness. This can enhance the counseling relationship and working alliance, key parts of effective sport psychology consultation (Andersen & William-Rice, 1996; Petitpas, Giges, & Danish, 1999). Mindfulness can help with the flexibility and tact required to maintain the give and take between themselves and the client. While there is currently a paucity of literature on this topic in the field of sport psychology, research from other fields and supplemental exercises will inform how mindful and self-aware SPCs can be more effective in their practice.

Theoretical Background

Self-awareness can be viewed through a number of theoretical orientations. From psychoanalytic theory (Munroe, 1955, pp. 34–47), we learn that all behavior has meaning; past events and unconscious processes influence present functioning; and the relationship between practitioner and client is critical. Transactional analysis (Berne, 1961, p. 35) describes the child within and its influence on communication and relationships. Gestalt therapy (Perls, 1969) emphasizes the significance of awareness and of present experience, that is, how the client is functioning in the here and now. Cognitive therapy (Beck, 1967, p. 318) adopts the principle that thinking is the major determinant of feelings and behavior. Cognitive behavioral therapies teach that our thoughts (e.g., core beliefs, automatic thoughts, and appraisals), feelings (i.e., emotions and somatic sensations), and behaviors (e.g., adaptive or maladaptive) interact with one another, leading to learned patterns (Barlow et al., 2011, p. 52). No matter how one conceptualizes the origins of thoughts, feelings, and behaviors, perhaps the most important skill SPCs can develop to best serve their clients is *self-awareness*. A recent article by Ridley, Mollen, and Kelly (2011) in the *Counseling Psychologist* explains why this is so. While competencies (e.g., assessment and intervention) and micro-skills (e.g., paraphrasing and summarizing) are fundamental to counseling, it is through metacognitive thought (i.e., mindful self-awareness) that counselors develop the good judgment and critical thinking – the *know-how* – for effectively navigating the complexity of counseling. Similarly, mindful self-awareness can allow SPCs to practice "flexibility within fidelity," meaning they follow guidelines of evidence-based practices while also being client-centered (Kendall et al., 2008, p. 987). As an analogy, competencies and micro-skills are the tools and mindful self-awareness guides SPCs to "use the right tool for the job."

"*Awareness* is the conscious registration of stimuli, including the five physical senses, the kinesthetic senses, and the activities of the mind" (Brown, Ryan, & Creswell, 2007, p. 212). Awareness of the external world includes the use of our senses of sight, hearing, smell, touch, taste, and temperature. Awareness of our internal world, *self-awareness*, which this chapter will focus on, consists of our physical sensations (such as pain, tingling, tightness, vibration, palpitation, itching, or burning) and our psychological experience, including our thoughts, feelings, wants, and needs (although needs are not usually in our everyday awareness). It also includes awareness of our behavior, which is the bridge between our inner and outer worlds, allowing us to observe our actions in response to our thoughts, feelings, or wants.

It is important to describe a primary rationale for practicing mindful self-awareness before introducing the first self-awareness exercise. The practice of mindfulness is defined as "self-regulation of attention so that it is maintained on immediate experience, thereby allowing for increased recognition of mental events in the present moment" and "an orientation that is characterized by curiosity, openness, and acceptance" (Bishop et al., 2004, p. 232). Mindful self-awareness is important because habitual reactions, feelings, and biases in perception, thoughts, or behavior can become learned and automatically activated outside one's awareness – that is reacting on autopilot (see Vago, 2014, for a review). There can be a wide range of automatic reactions elicited in SPCs while working with clients.

For instance, in the scenario of a client expressing an intense anxiety about an upcoming event, one SPC may have the natural disposition to tolerate her client's strong emotion, while another may instantly feel the very anxiety of his client and become uncomfortable himself. Neither reaction is right or wrong; rather, it is whether or not the SPC is aware of his or her reaction and what the SPC does with it that may determine the success of his or her work with the client.

The first step of mindful self-awareness is to recognize the reaction itself, instead of letting it unfold into a habit outside of one's intentional volition or choice. As Brown and colleagues (2007) describe:

> People need to be attentive to their inner states and behavior to pursue reflectively considered goals, and failing to bring sufficient attention to oneself tends to foster habitual, overlearned, or automatized reactions, rather than responses that are self-endorsed and situationally appropriate . . . directing attention to subjective mental, emotional, and physical experience is key to healthy self-regulation. Indeed, the willingness to "look inside" is foundational to the development of self-knowledge from which regulated action proceeds (p. 216).

Let's start by practicing this willingness to "look inside." The first exercise will introduce the focus of awareness. Self-awareness is a long-term process and requires continued practice.

Exercise I: Focus of Awareness to Increase Awareness of Inner Psychological Experience

For this exercise, limit your awareness to your thoughts, feelings, or wants (modified from the gestalt therapy "continuum of awareness"). It is important to note that a willingness to reflect on one's inner psychological experience takes some courage because it requires facing whatever arises. You may want to start with a mental note: "looking inside" is part of the journey to become your best as an SPC. Therefore, viewing it as a challenge instead of a threat may help you feel proud for taking this courageous step.

Part 1: Mindful Self-Awareness

Find a partner. Each of you will have two minutes to report to your partner what you are aware of, narrowing your focus to your thoughts, feelings, or wants in any order or frequency. Repeat the question, "What am I aware of right now?" after each answer. Suspend all judgment about the arising thoughts, feelings, or wants. Instead, nonjudgmentally notice ("neutrally notice") them with "acceptance, curiosity, and openness" to their manifestation in your consciousness; this is mindful self-awareness (Hölzel et al., 2011, p. 549).

Part 2: Notice

Notice which of the three categories (thoughts, feelings, or wants) was most frequent and which was least frequent. Choose the one that was least frequent, and take another two minutes to report only that one to your partner. Then your partner will do the same. Discuss with each other your understanding of your least frequent awareness. If none of the three categories emerge, reflect on your experience with the exercise and consider which is least comfortable to express to others.

Benefits of Self-Awareness

What benefits do we derive from increasing our self-awareness through such exercises? Self-acceptance, intentional action, and the opportunity for change are three benefits of mindful self-awareness, all of which have important implications for consultation. This section outlines the rationale.

Self-Acceptance

First, increased self-awareness allows us to gain a fuller knowledge of ourselves, of our complexity and wholeness, and offers the opportunity for increased self-acceptance. Mindful self-awareness is not just about being more aware of our inner experience; it is doing so with nonjudgment, nonreaction, and a sense of self-compassion. Consider the example of an SPC struggling in a session with an athlete who is expressing anger about the season. The SPC is trying to help the athlete develop a positive reframe of the situation, but the athlete is becoming more irritated and adamant about how frustrated he is. A mindful SPC would be aware that his approach is not going as planned. By mindfully noticing the athlete's internal frustration and self-critical thoughts (e.g., "This is terrible"), the SPC could come to terms with the ineffective intervention with a sense of acceptance, self-compassion, and adaptability. For example, the SPC may understand the client's negative reaction as information to learn from (e.g., right now the client needs validation or time to process her frustration), which informs next steps, instead of viewing the reaction as a failure.

An important construct that has been linked to resiliency in the face of failure and uncomfortable reality is self-compassion (Neff, Kirkpatrick, & Rude, 2007), which is closely tied to mindfulness. Self-compassion can come in the form of objectively acknowledging mistakes as part of the process without overidentifying with the frustration and mistake itself, and bringing attention back to what you can do in the present moment to move forward (Neff, 2003). This can be especially beneficial for SPCs, since work with athletes is not always quick and straightforward. It is often a process that requires the SPC to mindfully accept the inevitable barriers to change. In one study, therapists in training reported that mindfulness practice helped them to "shift from automatic negative self-evaluation to a stance of compassionate witnessing" (Christopher & Maris, 2010, p. 123).

Furthermore, mindful self-awareness may help SPCs acknowledge their limits and prevent them from burnout fatigue. For instance, therapists with mindfulness training reported a greater awareness and "more sensitivity to their body's need for rest, hydration, and movement, noticing what their bodies needed before they became ill, exhausted, parched or stiff" (Christopher & Maris, 2010, p. 117).

Intentional Action

Second, self-awareness provides the opportunity to be more in charge of ourselves and better able to make decisions consistent with our values and plan of action. If we are not aware of our feelings, they can surface and interfere in unexpected or unknown ways. Goleman (1995) wrote, "Emotions that simmer beneath the threshold of awareness can have a powerful impact on how we perceive and react, even though we have no idea they are at work" (p. 55). For example, an SPC may feel anxiety about helping a high profile athlete in consulting sessions and without self-awareness may become overcontrolling (e.g., becoming less collaborative or forcing an intervention) and change his or her approach in an attempt to avoid this anxiety (Barlow et al., 2011, pp. 51, 61). This is analogous to trying to find an external solution to an internal problem (internal discomfort), which often leads to reactive ways of thinking and acting that are ultimately less intentional and counterproductive.

Similarly, unrecognized guilt may lead to defensiveness, and hidden shame may trigger blaming others. For instance, an SPC working with a player referred for causing a lot of team turmoil may realize that this player needs a lot of support to feel better about himself and develop coping skills before the player's troublesome actions change. This leaves the team in turmoil for a period of time, for which the SPC may feel guilty. Without being aware of this guilt, and feeling responsible for the team's functioning, the SPC may end up blaming the athlete and losing patience with his progress. This reaction serves to protect the SPC from feeling responsible for the team's struggle. SPCs can benefit from becoming mindfully aware of uncomfortable emotion and act intentionally toward the goal of helping the client.

Opportunity for Change

Third, awareness also creates the opportunity for change. How such change occurs with mindful self-awareness was first described in an earlier workshop (Giges, 1991), then published (Giges, Petitpas, & Vernacchia, 2004). Here is an excerpt from that article:

> Most often, we become aware of a problem behavior after it occurs. When this happens, we may say "I see that I *did that*." With a commitment to change and repeated awareness of the behavior, awareness begins to occur earlier. When it is present during the behavior, we may say "I see that I *am doing* that right now." With additional time and practice, awareness moves earlier in time, until it is present before the undesired behavior occurs. At this point, we can say "I see that I am *about to* do that." When awareness precedes the behavior, a choice can be made to behave differently. This is an opportunity for change, and is represented by the statement "I can do it differently"(p. 433; emphasis in the original text). The process has been called "the Alphabet of Change" (Giges, 2011).

"When **A**wareness precedes
     Behavior, we have a
     Choice, can make a
     Decision, and apply
     Effort toward a
     Focus to reach a
     Goal" (Giges, 2011).

Furthermore, mindful SPCs can notice when a session has become overly problem-focused and find opportunities to promote clients' hope by making connections and noticing strengths. For example, an SPC may say, "I remember you mentioned how much you love to strategize and figure things out on the field. In our work together, we have similarly been learning how your mind works best and what gets in the way so we can strategize a game plan." Mindful SPCs can also be more cognizant of subtle opportunities to build a positive connection when working with teams by being aware of and offering specific praise for small things that may have gone unnoticed. For example, in passing an SPC may say, "By the way, I noticed how you took the lead and spoke up the other day." Also, mindful SPCs may notice when follow-up questions are needed to get to the heart of an issue, when to provide the client time to digest a new revelation, or when a referral is needed to address an issue outside their competence.

The Gift of Presence

Fourth, being more self-aware can enhance our ability to be more fully "present," meaning less distracted by our own experience, more responsive to others, and more understanding of their experience. Goleman (1998) stated "Self-awareness serves as an inner barometer, gauging whether what we are doing (or are about to do) is, indeed, worthwhile" (pp. 57–58). Often, if we know what we are experiencing, we can sense what others are experiencing. If it turns out we are right, we call that "insight" (meaning we have a relatively accurate sense of what the client is experiencing and how the interaction is unfolding). Of course, if we are wrong, then it may be "projection" (attributing our own experience to others) (Giges, 1991). For example, an SPC may assume a client is anxious to discuss something, which may be based upon the SPC's own discomfort.

The three meanings of the word "present" contain the essence of awareness – to be here, to be in the now, and receive a gift – of aliveness – open and ready. A genuine understanding of clients' perspective, experiences, strengths and weaknesses, stage of motivation, and points of entry for effective intervention and support requires SPCs to pay attention to what their clients say, how they say it, and what they don't say. Qualitative research on therapists in training showed that mindfulness practice led them to become "less preoccupied with themselves" and more "present and sensitive to the client's experience and nonverbal communication" (Christopher & Maris, 2010, p. 122).

Mindful attentiveness to the unfolding of experience (as opposed to entering interactions with a rigid predetermined agenda) is related to greater empathy (Dekeyser et al., 2008), an essential skill for building a relationship with a client in sport psychology consultation (Sharp & Hodge, 2011), and is inversely related to treatment dropout in clinical practice (Norcross & Wampold, 2011).

Barriers to Self-Awareness

What considerations or circumstances might interfere with self-awareness? There are four barriers germane to SPCs, including external distractions, motivation to avoid unpleasant internal experiences, disregard for the value of self-awareness, and fear of judgment. Each is outlined in this section.

First, there are external distractions that may detract one from self-awareness. It takes cognitive effort to look inward and maintain self-awareness. Problems with work, school, home, or relationships can be energy-draining distractions that might draw our attention away from our inner experience. Being overly busy has become the norm (even considered a status symbol) and can detract from self-awareness, a major theme of Edward Hallowell's (2006) book *Crazy Busy* (pp. 90–91). For example, in a qualitative study of recently graduated SPCs, it was stated, "As my caseload has got bigger, and I have got busier, I sometimes notice that I move towards being solution-focused . . . . I have to actually consciously not do that" (Tod, Andersen, & Marchant, 2011, p. 100). This is a clear example of how we SPCs can easily get caught up in our own mental clutter instead of being fully present in the room with the client.

Second, internal experiences may also distract SPCs from self-awareness. If awareness leads to negative feelings such as guilt, fear, anger, sadness, or shame, this might result in not wanting to be aware, in order to avoid the discomfort. Without developing *distress tolerance,* the capacity for tolerating uncomfortable or unpleasant internal states (i.e., thoughts, feelings, physical sensations) (Feldman et al., 2014), one may attempt to avoid uncomfortable feelings and therefore become less self-aware. Mindfulness can improve distress tolerance (Robins et al., 2012) while in pursuit of a goal (Feldman et al., 2014). Therapists have reported that mindfulness training helped them attend to manifestations of stress, anxiety, irritation, and confusion by noticing such experience nonjudgmentally. Their awareness helped ease the tension, instead of viewing the feelings as "bad" with self-judgment that would have intensified the tension (Christopher & Maris, 2010, p. 120). This, they reported, in turn helped their clients do the same (Christopher & Maris, 2010), perhaps by providing a helpful model for their clients.

Third, dismissing the importance of one's internal experience can also be a barrier to self-awareness. If we have been taught that our inner experience is not important, we can eventually become less familiar with our feelings and wants and lose awareness of them. Fourth, if there is an expectation of disapproval, reprimand, criticism, or judgment, awareness might be avoided because of its anticipated unpleasant consequences. It is, therefore, essential that awareness be without criticism, a nonjudgmental observing without reprimand or disapproval ("neutral noticing") (Giges, 1991).

Exercise II: To Increase Your Awareness of Your Inner Critic

You may be well acquainted with your inner critic, whether it comes in the form of ruminating over conflict or chastising yourself ("Why did I say that?") after an interaction or other typical frustrations. And yet, through the following exercise you may be surprised to notice how the inner critic can seep into almost all circumstances. Consider a situation in which you are meeting an athlete for the first time:

- Imagine you have come to the appointment early. Think of a self-criticism for doing that.
- Imagine you have come to the appointment late. Think of a self-criticism for doing that.
- Imagine you have come to the appointment on time. Think of a self-criticism for doing that.

Now, repeat the exercise about coming early, late, or on time, and for each, think of a self-statement that is complimentary or self-supporting. Which came easier: the criticism or the compliment? Are critical or self-supporting thoughts more frequent for you? Self-criticism is not uncommon, especially for SPCs who not only provide a service to athletes and teams, but also have the added pressure of needing to convince others that their work has utility.

Whenever we have a strong internal critic, there can be disapproval of what we are doing, how we are doing it, when we are doing it, or why we are doing it. Any thought, feeling, want, or behavior can be the subject of the criticism. Imagine an old man standing at a busy intersection waiting for help to cross the road. You decide to help him, and he expresses his appreciation. As you're walking away, the critic in you says, "You only did that to make yourself feel better!" While helping others is a source of good feelings about ourselves, we can also have a genuine desire to help other people. The critic in us ignores the latter consideration.

When people say, "I'm so stupid," they are not only expressing disapproval of themselves, they are also contributing to feeling worse about themselves. And the internal critic is seen as an expert. To loosen the grip the critic has on us, the question can be asked, "Is all of you stupid? Is the part of you that's calling you stupid also stupid?" This question usually attracts some attention. *The Wizard of Oz* may serve as a useful metaphor. What appears to be wisdom from an expert is nothing more than someone playing a recording. And that is how the internal critic can be understood – an old recording that keeps repeating. The loudest, most critical voice is not always the wisest voice, but rather a habit of the mind. Positive psychology teaches the value of noticing the good (Seligman & Csikszent-mihalyi, 2000) and of practicing self-compassion (Gilbert, 2009; Neff et al., 2007), which can be antidotes to such habitual self-criticism.

Critiquing one's evolving practice as an SPC is part of growing as a practitioner. Research suggests that healthy perfectionism – which is conceptualized as one who has high personal standards that are self-oriented (not socially referenced) and low levels of judgment for mistakes, fear of failure to live up to expectations, and self-criticism – is actually adaptive. It is associated with greater success, less distress, relatively good adjustment, and better performance, compared to unhealthy perfection-ism, defined by the opposite characteristics of healthy perfectionism (see Stoeber & Otto, 2006, for a review). Healthy perfectionism is in line with Carol Dweck's research on the value of a "growth-mindset," where one seeks out useful feedback and challenges and strives for self-referenced improvement (Dweck, 2006, p. 110). This is important for SPCs, as they can embrace a healthy process of growth with humility by learning and making adjustments along the way instead of getting derailed by an unhealthy self-critic. In summary, a balanced approach of mindfully noticing and toning down the distracting and unhealthy self-critic, while also being attuned to healthy and constructive feedback for growth, fosters self-awareness and more effective SPC consultation.

Fifth, another barrier to self-awareness is an automatic compliance or defiance, with no time to reflect about your inner experience. If you are thirsty and going for a glass of water, and a parent harshly said, "You're not drinking enough! I told you to drink more!" you might be distracted by an automatic defiance and walk away thinking, "Nobody's going to tell me what to do," a thought driven by rebellious feelings. The problem is that, in the absence of self-awareness, one can very quickly become over-whelmed and react so quickly that the initial thoughts and feelings that drove the behavior in the first place (e.g., "I feel less in control and weak when I'm told what to do") may go unnoticed. Similarly, the Mindfulness-Acceptance-Commitment (MAC) approach (Gardner & Moore, 2007, p. 104) teaches us that habitual, automatic reactions easily manifest when we do not access clarified personal values that provide wise perspective (e.g., "They are trying to help me, not control me").

Internal Psychological Experiences

Thoughts

Included in the category of thoughts are ideas, beliefs, opinions, reasons, judgments, appraisals, speculations, decisions, expectations, attitudes, and memories. Awareness of our thoughts also includes how attached to them we are and how much they influence us. From cognitive therapy, we accept the principle that our thoughts are the basis for most of our feelings and behavior. The meaning that we give to situations and appraisals of them influences our experience. For example, if a situation is seen as a threat, we may feel anxiety; if it is seen as a challenge, we may feel excitement (Jones et al., 2009).

Thoughts are the link between others' behavior and our feelings. An example would be of a relay runner who felt hurt and disappointed when the coach asked him to change from running anchor leg (last) to running second. The anchor leg is usually given to the fastest runner on the relay team. In this example, the relay runner might have thought that the change meant that his coach lost confidence in him. However, when the coach explained that another team was running their fastest runner in the second position in an attempt to get far ahead of the other teams, the runner's thoughts changed: he became pleased that he was chosen to prevent that from happening.

Thoughts are also the link between others' behavior and our behavior. Consider a crowded team bus, with standing room only. The bus suddenly lurches and one athlete steps on another's foot. Think of a dozen different ways the person stepped on might behave. When you see that there are numerous possibilities for action, it shows that another person's behavior is the stimulus but not the explanation for what we do. Our inner experience determines what we decide to do. The ability to adapt one's thinking approach to understand a new condition is a significant skill for SPCs because an important task is to understand where their client is coming from and find ways to tailor interventions to fit their client's personality and context. Mindfulness can help with this; mindfulness has been shown to be related to cognitive flexibility (Moore & Malinowski, 2009). Furthermore, Ellen Langer's definition of mindfulness is one's ability to be mindfully open to the unfolding present experience as opposed to mindlessly viewing one's current experience through rigid cognitive biases of the past (Langer & Moldoveanu, 2000). In conceptualizing a case, it is important for SPCs not only to consider the accumulated data gathered through assessment, but to also consider the question, *"How am I thinking about this client?"* in order to avoid an overreliance on preconceived notions or biases that interfere with progress.

Negative Thinking

Negative thinking is an anticipation or prediction of undesirable consequences and usually involves an exaggeration or overgeneralization, where an error or mistake becomes a calamity. It can pertain to a task, person, or situation and can be applied to the past, present, or future. While thoughts focused on the negative can be accurate and adaptive (e.g., problem solving), maladaptive negative thinking can be inflexible and inaccurate (Beck 1967, pp. 318–325). Negative thinking can manifest in different ways (Giges, 1991):

a. **Present to permanent** – now to always – if something bad happens once, it will continue to happen. For example, when a batter strikes out, the negative thought is that striking out will keep happening.
b. **Particular to pervasive** – here to everywhere – if a problem is here, it will be everywhere. Consider a student who does poorly in one subject and therefore believes that poor performance will affect all subjects.
c. **Possible to probable** – maybe to likely – if it might go wrong, it will go wrong. For example, if a relay team drops a baton in an important race, the members think they will probably drop the baton in other races. In his book, *Learned Optimism*, Martin Seligman (2006) describes the "possible to probable" style as pessimism (p. 76).

Uncertainty is part of the human experience, and so most importantly is one's reaction to uncertainty, which is often a source of worry and anxiety. When adaptive, worried uncertainty and pessimism prompt us to work harder, become more prepared, and think critically, which allows us to pursue excellence (Seligman, 2006, pp. 107–108). Conversely, at its extreme, an inability to tolerate uncertainty can contribute to dysregulated anxiety (Boswell et al., 2013). At any level, uncertainty can have a significant impact on how we cope with situations and make decisions. It is important for SPCs to be aware of their uncertainties (e.g., how a session will go) and to develop strategies to cope with them. To remain effective in their practice, consultants need to avoid maladaptive rumination and attempts to control the uncontrollable or excessively seek out reassurance (e.g., trying too hard, overpreparing, or constantly seeking approval). To do so may reduce the discomfort of uncertainty in the short term, but undermine an SPC's practice tolerating uncertainty, belief in her plan, and trust in her ability to adapt to the unexpected (Barlow et al., 2011, pp. 62, 98–103). It may also interfere with an SPC from coming across as personable, self-assured, and clear in communication, all of which are identified by athletes as desirable SPC characteristics (Anderson et al., 2004).

Exercise III: To Increase Your Awareness of Your Uncertainties

Get in a comfortable position and close your eyes. Observe your breathing. Increase the rate and volume of breathing by inhaling and exhaling deeply and rapidly for three or four breaths. Now return to normal breathing.

Imagine that you are out in a field at the foot of a mountain. The sun is shining, and there is a gentle breeze. You decide to begin ascending the mountain, being careful to avoid any logs or stones. Step over a small brook and continue to climb. There is a path you can follow without too much obstruction. As you climb, you notice there is a plateau just ahead. As you reach the plateau and look around, you see a small shack. As you approach the shack, you see a wise old person sitting outside. When you reach the shack, the old person greets you and asks what your question is. Choose a question that involves uncertainty and is of some importance to you in your life. Wait for the answer. Then express your thanks and slowly make your way back down the mountain and back to your starting point.

Find a partner. Describe the experience, including the question, the answer, and particularly your reaction to the answer. Are you left with other questions? Will you seek any answers?

Feelings

In this section, feelings pertain to psychological emotions, not sensations or intuition. The word "feel" or "feeling" can be used with other meanings than emotion: "I feel that" can mean I think, believe, suspect, imagine, or predict. "It is my feeling" can refer to my impression, judgment, understanding, belief, or suspicion. In this section, the word "feeling" is limited to meaning emotion.

Awareness of emotions can be increased by having clarity and understanding of the different types of emotion and appreciating the meaning and intensity of them. The types of emotion described in the following are basic, learned, complex, and general. With each category, the specific emotions are listed, along with the range or meaning of each emotion.

Basic Emotions

There are four basic emotions: joy, sadness, fear, and anger. They occur early in life and have a range of language to describe them. They are usually accompanied by strong physical sensations and vary in intensity from mild to moderate to severe. Here are some examples of the four basic emotions.

Joy. From pleased, content, satisfied, happy, to delighted and ecstatic

Sadness. From disappointed, discouraged, unhappy, to dejected and despairing

Fear. From uneasy, insecure, apprehensive, worried, to panicky and terrified

Anger. From irritated, annoyed, resentful, angry, mad, to enraged and furious

Learned Emotions

Learned emotions are almost basic, have physical sensations, but do not occur as early in life and have little range of language. Some authors consider shame a basic emotion. The meaning of each is as follows:

Guilt. "I did something wrong."

Shame. "I am a bad person."

Embarrassment. "I've been exposed."

Hurt. "I'm not as worthwhile or important."

Complex Emotions

Complex emotions contain one or more basic emotions plus one or more thoughts. They are called complex because they contain more than emotions. They each have some thought or thoughts associated with the emotions.

Envious. Resentment plus, "I wish I had or did that."

Jealous. Fear, resentment, plus, "Someone else is loved more than I am."

Helpless. Fear, sadness, anger, plus, "I can't do anything."

Confused. Fear, anger, plus, "I don't know what's going on."

Inadequate. Fear, sadness, anger, plus, "I'm not good enough."

Bored. Uneasiness, anger, disappointment, plus, "I'm not interested."

General Emotions

General emotions can be understood as those that are not specific enough to help one understand the individual's actual experience. The words "upset," "uncomfortable," "strange," "funny," and "peculiar" can represent several thoughts and feelings. They need to be clarified. Questions to help clarify general emotions can be followed up with questions such as, "What type of upset?" or, "Strange in what way?" Such follow-up prompts by the SPC may help to identify the specific thoughts and feelings contained in the general emotions category. Usually, several thoughts and feelings are associated with each general emotion.

For practicing SPCs, interactions in sessions may spark strong emotions within the SPCs themselves. For instance, a client may initially express resistance to receiving help, which may lead the consultant to feel discouraged, frustrated, or angry and result in unproductive behavior (e.g., giving up or arguing). Dialectical Behavior Therapy, which is rooted in mindfulness, teaches that one may perceive interpersonal struggle as unacceptable (e.g., "This is not fair!"), push one's own agenda (e.g., "They're just not listening!"), or give up (e.g., "This is not going to be effective!") instead of "doing what works" by taking steps to work with what we are presented with instead of fighting against it (Brodsky & Stanley, 2013, p. 203). An effective motivational interviewing strategy is to respond to client resistance by becoming aware of the client's feelings and current stage of change (e.g., contemplative), "rolling with their resistance" to the idea of change, and working with the client's viewpoint (Miller & Rollnick, 2002, p. 40). To argue with the client about his or her stance would increase resistance. Mindful awareness of positive emotions may also be helpful for SPCs who are searching for a creative solution in their work. Positive emotion has been linked to a broadening of attention and creativity (Fredrickson, 2001), which may help SPCs and their clients discover effective and innovative approaches for intervention. For instance, SPCs may mindfully be aware of how grateful (a positive emotion) they feel for being able to work in their profession, which may help them find ways to connect with a more challenging client. They may also laugh with their client or notice a positive quality in them, which could open the possibility of having new insights.

Exercise IV: To Increase Awareness of the Past You Inside the Present You

Get in a comfortable position and close your eyes. Observe your breathing. Increase the rate and volume of breathing by inhaling and exhaling deeply and rapidly for three or four breaths. Then return to normal breathing.

Imagine you are out on a grassy plain, with nothing to see all around except a path in front of you. As you are walking on this path, off in the distance, you can see a small child coming toward you. At first, you cannot determine who it is, and then you realize it is yourself as a small child, about four to five years old. When you meet, ask the child what he or she would like. After the child answers, imagine the child asks you what you would like. Then ask what the child is feeling right now. After the answer, have the child ask you the same question. Finally, you ask the child what's important to him or her. After the answer, the child asks you the same question. Then you do an activity together that both of you would enjoy. After playing, you ask the child whether you can pick him or her up in your arms; then ask whether the child will return with you. If the answer is yes, allow the child to merge inside you as you return. If the response is no, say goodbye and ask whether he or she would like to meet again.

Find a partner. Describe the experience, including the questions, the answers, and your reaction to the child's answers. Increased awareness of the child within can heighten one's self-understanding and perhaps self-acceptance.

Wants

Wants are the specifics to help us meet our underlying needs. According to Regulatory Focus Theory, people have two different regulatory systems related to motivation (Higgins, 1997): Promotion-Focus to pursue an opportunity or a gain, which leads to pleasure and cheerful emotions (e.g., happiness, joy, excitement); and Prevention-Focus to avoid a loss and maintain security and safety, which leads to the avoidance of negative emotions (guilt, fear, embarrassment, shame) and low-energy positive emotions (e.g., calmness, contentment, relief) (Halvorson & Higgins, 2013, p. 5). Both motivations for pursuing a gain and avoiding a loss are *wants*.

Everything we do is connected to something we want. Many times, what we want is expressed as a complaint. For example, "It's too hot in here" contains the want to be cooler or to avoid the discomfort of the heat. Other times, a want is expressed as a "have to" or a "can't." Consider the student who has the choice of going to a party or studying for an exam. He or she may say, "I want to party, but I *have to* study." What is the want contained in "I have to study"? Although partying may be a stronger want than studying, doing well on an exam is more important than partying; hence the choice to study. This is called a "priority of wants." Sometimes, thinking "I should do this" conceals the want to avoid the discomfort of not doing it. Also, "I can't" avoids taking responsibility for the decision expressed by "I won't." An important component of self-awareness is to notice the different ways of indirectly expressing wants and understanding why one is chosen over the other.

If we don't get what we need, we may "want" (lack) a lot. Eric Hoffer (1952) wrote that "we can never get enough of that which we really do not want" (p. 4). In other words, substitute gratification will never fully satisfy an unmet need (Hoffer, 1952, p. 4; outlined in the next section). Take for instance the issue of professional relationship boundaries while traveling with a team, not an uncommon scenario (Stapleton et al., 2010). An SPC may feel socially disconnected in his or her own personal life and subsequently be tempted to accept the offer of their client to hang out informally one of the evenings. The "want" for building the informal relationship may in fact function to fulfill the SPC's need for feeling socially connected, as opposed to the SPC thinking critically about the context of the relationship. Mindful self-awareness of "wants" can help SPCs make prudent and wise ethical decisions.

Understanding "wants" can also be helpful for SPCs to understand why they make the decisions they make, which may come in the form of pursuing a gain/opportunity or preventing a loss/pain. For instance, an SPC working with a client may cautiously avoid an issue when in fact their client would benefit from discussing it more directly. The SPC's decision to avoid may be driven by his or her "wanting" to prevent some discomfort (e.g., addressing potential issues for which the SPC lacks competence). Conversely, an SPC may be overbearing in his or her interactions with clients due to the SPC "wanting" to be perceived as helpful. It is important for SPCs to look inward to recognize how their behaviors and choices are driven by underlying "wants" and whether or not these behaviors are serving their clients.

Exercise V: To Increase Awareness of Your Past Experience of Wanting

Close your eyes. Think of a recent decision you've made – perhaps a decision you made while working with a client. Think about the implications and consequences of that decision. What did you get out of the decision, how did the decision affect the client, and what was required of you by the decision?

Now think back to the decision-making process. What were the "wants" that led you to make the decision? Explore the "wants" in detail. What made the "wants" important to you? Were the "wants" facilitative to making a wise decision for the long term or more of a distraction for short-term gratification? Were the "wants" masking underlying unmet needs? Mindfulness is an especially helpful way to objectively notice emerging "wants" and consider whether or not they are facilitative or distracting.

Needs

Needs consist of the basic elements of psychological growth and are not usually in our everyday awareness (Maslow, 1943). They are long range, broad, and enduring. Mindful self-awareness is not a need. It is, rather, a skill to help people get what they need. Carol Ryff endorses the following psychological needs for well-being: autonomy, environmental mastery, personal growth, positive relations with others, purpose in life, and self-acceptance (Ryff, 2014). Additionally, Abraham Maslow has described physiological needs (e.g., food, water, sleep) and safety needs (e.g., security, shelter); love/belonging needs (e.g., friendship); esteem needs (e.g., self-esteem, achievement); and self-actualization needs (e.g., creativity, personal growth, problem solving) (Maslow, 1943). Two additional needs theorized by Martin Seligman are positive emotion and engagement/absorption in one's activities while frequently using one's personal strengths (Seligman, 2011, p. 24). In addition to basic needs, there is another group of "needs" that we have called "acquired needs" (Giges, 1991). Although the word "needs" is used, they are not actually necessary for growth. Rather, they represent attempts to cope with unmet needs and become problems in themselves (Watzlawick, Weakland, & Fisch, 1974, pp. 31–39). Here are some examples of what may happen if basic psychological needs are not met.

If the needs for security and safety (Maslow, 1943) are not satisfied, individuals may develop the "need" to control their environment or dominate other people in their attempt to provide some sense of safety or security. These are not real needs; they are attempts to achieve external solutions to internal problems. Some individuals may seek an opposite solution and develop the "need" to depend on others to provide the sense of safety or security. Either of these "acquired needs" can be problematic for SPCs, such as becoming overly controlling in the consultant–client relationship or depending too much on others (e.g., supervisor/consultation) to make simple decisions.

For those who lack a sense of self-worth (a basic need) (Ryff, 2014), their attempt to compensate for this deficiency might lead to the "need" to please (an acquired "need") or constantly seek approval. Similarly, when individuals have a strong internal critic, the need for self-acceptance may not be satisfied. Ineffective attempts to cope with this unmet need might lead to the "need" to criticize, judge, or disapprove of oneself and/or others.

Another important basic need is the need for autonomy, with its associated sense of mastery (Ryff, 2014). If not met, the acquired "need" to be dependent might develop, leading one to follow someone else's lead (e.g., being overly client-centered and not directive enough). An opposite coping mechanism would be the "need" to be defiant or rebellious, acting as if you are making an independent decision by doing the opposite of what is expected in a given situation.

When the basic need for relationship and intimacy (Maslow, 1943) is not met, an individual may avoid involvement with others and become completely absorbed in work and become what is called a "workaholic." Alternatively, some may become involved with others as "objects," attempting to compensate for the deficiency with repetitive superficial relationships. Issues of countertransference may manifest in the counselor/client relationship if relationship needs are being met through their professional counseling relationships.

Related to the need for relationships is the need to belong (Maslow, 1943). Usually, the need to belong can be satisfied by becoming part of a group, small or large. For those who are unable to make these connections, they may have a "need" to withdraw. For SPCs working with a team that welcomes them as "part of the team," an inability to fulfill the need to belong may interfere with their ability to build connections with the team. On the other extreme, an SPC may overidentify with the team to fulfill a need to belong, such as becoming preoccupied with the outward success of the team, which can distract the SPC them from knowing his or her place and role on the team.

Finally, the need for meaning and purpose, eloquently described by Frankl's (2006) book *Man's Search for Meaning*, has more recently come into prominence, as changes in family and social roles become more frequent. Without a sense of meaning and purpose in life, individuals have a "need" to escape and may drift into some form of addiction. Alternatively, they may develop a hedonistic lifestyle in which nothing has meaning unless it is pleasurable. A foundational meaning or purpose in life can be energizing and provide balance that can allow SPCs to do their best work.

Exercise VI: Part 1

The following questions are intended to stimulate self-reflection and to heighten awareness of thoughts, feelings, and wants in everyday experience (this exercise was adapted from Giges, 1991). Each question should be followed by a moment's pause to allow for some response other than the first thing that comes to mind. For each question, write down something that will help you reflect on your response at a later time.

- What is your main source of enjoyment or satisfaction?
- What gives you good feelings about yourself?
- What do you want most that you don't have?
- What do you have that you don't want?
- What type of situation upsets you? What type of upset is most common?
- How do you usually react when you get upset?
- What might give you bad feelings about yourself?
- What would lead to your feeling guilty? Hurt?
- What might lead to your feeling embarrassed? Ashamed?
- What do you fear?
- What do you pretend?
- Which questions were more difficult or uncomfortable to answer?

Exercise VI: Part 2

The purpose of this two-part exercise is to reflect on a past problem and on a present one. The exercise helps us to learn about an identified problem and also our relationship to the problem itself, which is important for developing awareness of how we react to problems. As we teach our clients to learn from experience, we can do the same.

Review of the Past Problem

Think of something you did and would do differently if you had a chance to do it over. Please select a past problem you might have regrets about, or be bothered by when you think about it. Please consider the following questions:

1. What was the behavior?
2. What was your reaction afterward (what were you thinking, feeling, or wanting)?
3. What was your major concern?
   - What would be its impact on your job or your relationships?
   - What would be its effect on others?
   - How you would be judged?

4. What were the actual consequences?
5. How did that compare with your concern?
6. How would you do it differently now?
7. What different consequences do you imagine?
8. How do you view it now, as you look back on it?

Observation of Current Problem

Think of a current problem (i.e., a situation or person presently causing you difficulty or upset). Attempt to identify the external and internal components (i.e., separate the problem into the situation and your inner experience). The problem can be conceptualized by the following formula: *Problem = External Situation + Internal Experience*. You may need assistance in making the separation.

An illustration of this process would be an athlete who has a problem with his or her coach who demands on-time adherence to a schedule. The external situation is a coach who is very strict about time. The internal experience for the athlete is that when being told what to do, a feeling of being controlled emerges and a strong urge to resist complying interferes with accepting the rules. Hence, the situation becomes a problem. Awareness of the internal experience may help the athlete accept the external situation and cope with it more effectively. And knowing about your own internal experience may help you see what makes a situation a problem for you.

Reflection

In this workshop, consider the following:

1. What was important for you?
2. What was uncomfortable?
3. What was difficult?
4. What was enjoyable?
5. What was satisfying?
6. What, if anything, did you learn about yourself?

These questions are intended to increase your knowledge of your inner psychological experience. In addition, the discussion and exercises about thoughts, feelings, wants, and needs highlight the particular areas involved in heightening your awareness and understanding of your motivation and behavior. With this knowledge, more effective functioning as a consultant can occur.

Conclusion: Learn from Experience

In learning to live with less self-awareness, we also diminish those distinctively human possibilities for freedom, creativity, caring, and ethical insight which are based on that awareness.

Edward Cell (1984, p. 9)

In summary, mindful self-awareness has myriad benefits for applied SPCs. Mindful self-awareness allows SPCs to foster self-acceptance instead of criticism, act with intention instead of habit, and embrace the gift of full presence in working with clients. There are many barriers to self-awareness, including external distractions, such as being overly busy; and internal distractions, such as an inability to tolerate uncomfortable thoughts and feelings, dismissing one's internal experience, self-criticizing, and failing to acknowledge one's thoughts, feelings, wants, and needs. Mindful strategies to foster self-awareness include developing a more extensive vocabulary of emotions, practicing distress tolerance, nonjudgmentally noticing internal states, acting with awareness to make wise decisions, and making sure basic psychological needs are met in order ensure they do not lead to compensating "acquired needs."

REFERENCES

Andersen, M. B., and Williams-Rice, B. T. (1996). Supervision in the education and training of sport psychology service providers. *Sport Psychologist*, 10, 278–290.

Anderson, A., Miles, A., Robinson, P., and Mahoney, C. (2004). Evaluating the athlete's perception of the sport psychologist's effectiveness: What should we be assessing? *Psychology of Sport and Exercise*, 5(3), 255–277. doi: 10.1016/S1469-0292(03)00005-0

Barlow, D. H., Ellard, K. K., Fairholme, C. P., Farchione, T. J., Boisseau, C. L., Allen, L. B., and Ehrenreich-May, J. T. (2011). *The unified protocol for transdiagnostic treatment of emotional disorders*. New York, NY: Oxford University Press.

Beck, A. (1967). *Depression: Clinical, experimental, and theoretical aspects*. New York, NY: Hoeber.

Berne, E. (1961). *Transactional analysis in psychotherapy*. New York, NY: Grove Press.

Bishop, S. R., Lau, M., Shapiro, S., Carlson, L., Anderson, N. D., Carmody, J., ... and Devins, G. (2004). Mindfulness: A proposed operational definition. *Clinical Psychology: Science and Practice*, 11(3), 230–241. doi: 10.1093/clipsy.bph077

Boswell, J. F., Thompson-Hollands, J., Farchione, T. J., and Barlow, D. H. (2013). Intolerance of uncertainty: A common factor in the treatment of emotional disorders. *Journal of Clinical Psychology*, 69(6), 630–645. doi: 10.1002/jclp.21965

Brodsky, B., and Stanley, B. (2013). *The Dialectical Behavior Therapy Primer: How DBT can inform clinical practice*. Somerset, NJ: John Wiley & Sons.

Brown, K. W., Ryan, R. M., and Creswell, J. D. (2007). Mindfulness: Theoretical foundations and evidence for its salutary effects. *Psychological Inquiry*, 18(4), 211–237. doi: 10.1080/10478400701598298

Cell, E. (1984) *Learning to learn from experience*. Albany, NY: State University of New York Press.

Christopher, J. C., and Maris, J. A. (2010). Integrating mindfulness as self-care into counselling and psychotherapy training. *Counselling and Psychotherapy Research*, 10(2), 114–125. doi: 10.1080/14733141003750285

Dekeyser, M., Raes, F., Leijssen, M., Leysen, S., and Dewulf, D. (2008). Mindfulness skills and interpersonal behaviour. *Personality and Individual Differences*, 44(5), 1235–1245. doi: 10.1016/j.paid.2007.11.018

Dweck, C. (2006). *Mindset: The new psychology of success*. New York, NY: Ballantine.

Feldman, G., Dunn, E., Stemke, C., Bell, K., and Greeson, J. (2014). Mindfulness and rumination as predictors of persistence with a distress tolerance task. *Personality and Individual Differences*, 56, 154–158. doi: 10.1016/j.paid.2013.08.040

Frankl, V. E. (2006). *Man's search for meaning: An introduction to logotherapy*. Boston, MA: Beacon Press.

Fredrickson, B. L. (2001). The role of positive emotions in positive psychology: The broaden-and-build theory of positive emotions. *American Psychologist*, 56(3), 218–226. doi:10.1037/003-066X.56.3.218

Gardner, F., and Moore, Z. (2007). *The psychology of enhancing human performance: The Mindfulness-Acceptance-Commitment (MAC) approach*. New York, NY: Springer.

Giges, B. (1991). *Self-awareness for sport psychologists*. Paper presented at the Second Annual Sport Psychology Symposium. Salt Lake City, UT: University of Utah.

(2011). *Self-awareness in sport psychology consulting*. DVD. Wilbraham, MA: Virtual Brands.

Giges, B., Petitpas, A. J., and Vernacchia, R. A. (2004). Helping coaches meet their own needs: Challenges for the sport psychology consultant. *Sport Psychologist*, 18(4), 430–444.

Gilbert, P. (2009). Introducing compassion-focused therapy. *Advances in Psychiatric Treatment*, 15, 199–208. doi: 10.1192/apt/bp.107.005264

Goleman, D. (1995). *Emotional intelligence*. New York, NY: Bantam.

(1998). *Working with emotional intelligence*. New York, NY: Bantam.

Hallowell, E. M. (2006). *Crazy busy: Overstretched, overbooked, and about to snap*. New York, NY: Ballantine.

Halvorson, H. G., and Higgins, E. T. (2013). *Focus: Use different ways of seeing the world for success and influence*. New York, NY: Penguin Group.

Higgins, E. T. (1997). Beyond pleasure and pain. *American Psychologist*, 52(12), 1280–1300. doi: http://dx.doi.org.ezproxy.bu.edu/10.1037/0003-066X.52.12.1280

Hoffer, E. (1952). *The ordeal of change*. New York, NY: Harper & Row.

Hölzel, B. K., Lazar, S. W., Gard, T., Schuman-Olivier, Z., Vago, D. R., and Ott, U. (2011). How does mindfulness meditation work? Proposing mechanisms of action from a conceptual and neural perspective. *Perspectives on Psychological Science*, 6(6), 537–559. doi: 10.1177/1745691611419671

Jones, M., Meijen, C., McCarthy, P., and Sheffield, D. (2009). A theory of challenge and threat states in athletes. *International Review of Sport and Exercise Psychology*, 2(2), 161–180. doi: 10.1080/17509840902829331

Kendall, P. C., Gosch, E., Furr, J. M., and Sood, E. (2008). Flexibility within fidelity. *Journal of the American Academy of Child and Adolescent Psychiatry*, 47(9), 987–993. doi: 10.1097/CHI.0b013e31817eed2f

Langer, E. J., and Moldoveanu, M. (2000). The construct of mindfulness. *Journal of Social Issues*, 56(1), 1–9. doi: 10.1111/0022-4537.00148

Maslow, A. H. (1943). A theory of human motivation. *Psychological Review*, 50(4), 370–396. doi: 10.1037/h0054346

Miller, W. R., and Rollnick, S. (2002). *Motivational interviewing: Preparing people for change* (2nd ed.). New York, NY: Guilford Press.

Moore, A., and Malinowski, P. (2009). Meditation, mindfulness and cognitive flexibility. *Consciousness and Cognition*, 18(1), 176–186. doi: 10.1016/j.concog.2008.12.008

Munroe, R. L. (1955). *Schools of psychoanalytic thought*. New York, NY: Dryden Press.

Neff, K. D. (2003). The development and validation of a scale to measure self-compassion. *Self and Identity*, 2(3), 223–250. doi: 10.1080/15298860309027

Neff, K. D., Kirkpatrick, K. L., and Rude, S. S. (2007). Self-compassion and adaptive psychological functioning. *Journal of Research in Personality*, 41(1), 139–154. doi: 10.1016/j.jrp.2006.03.004

Norcross, J. C., and Wampold, B. E. (2011). Evidence-based therapy relationships: Research conclusions and clinical practices. *Psychotherapy*, 48(1), 98–102. doi: 10.1037/a0022161

Perls, F. S. (1969). *Gestalt therapy verbatim*. Lafayette, CA: Real People Press.

Petitpas, A. J., Giges, B., and Danish, S. J. (1999). The sport psychologist-athlete relationship: Implications for training. *Sport Psychologist*, 13(3), 344–357.

Ridely, C. R., Mollen, D., and Kelly, S. M. (2011). Beyond microskills: Toward a model of counseling competence. *Counseling Psychologist*, 39(6), 825–864. doi: 10.1177/0011000010378440

Robins, C. J., Keng, S.-L., Ekblad, A. G., and Brantley, J. G. (2012). Effects of mindfulness-based stress reduction on emotional experience and expression: A randomized controlled trial. *Journal of Clinical Psychology*, 68(1), 117–131. doi: 10.1002/jclp.20857

Ryff, C. D. (2014). Psychological well-being revisited: Advances in the science and practice of eudaimonia. *Psychotherapy and Psychosomatics*, 83(1), 10–28.

Seligman, M. E. P. (2006). *Learned optimism: How to change your mind and your life*. New York, NY: Vintage.

(2011). *Flourish: A visionary new understanding of happiness and well-being*. New York, NY: Free Press.

Seligman, M. E. P., and Csikszentmihalyi, M. (2000). Positive psychology: An introduction. *American Psychologist*, 55(1), 5–14. doi: 10.1037/0003-066X.55.1.5

Sharp, L.-A., and Hodge, K. (2011). Sport psychology consulting effectiveness: The sport psychology consultant's perspective. *Journal of Applied Sport Psychology*, 23(3), 360–376. doi: 10.1080/10413200.2011.583619

Stapleton, A. B., Hankes, D. M., Hays, K. F., and Parham, W. D. (2010). Ethical dilemmas in sport psychology: A dialogue on the unique aspects impacting practice. *Professional Psychology: Research and Practice*, 41(2), 143–152. doi: 10.1037/a0017976

Stoeber, J., and Otto, K. (2006). Positive conceptions of perfectionism: Approaches, evidence, challenges. *Personality and Social Psychology Review*, 10(4), 295–319. doi: 10.1207/s15327957pspr1004_2

Tod, D., Andersen, M. B., and Marchant, D. B. (2011). Six years up: Applied sport psychologists surviving (and thriving) after graduation. *Journal of Applied Sport Psychology*, 23(1), 93–109. doi: 10.1080/10413200.2010.534543

Vago, D. R. (2014). Mapping modalities of self-awareness in mindfulness practice: A potential mechanism for clarifying habits of mind. *Annals of the New York Academy of Sciences*, 1307(1), 28–42. doi: 10.1111/nyas.12270

Young, M. E. (1998). *Learning the art of helping. Building blocks and techniques*. Columbus, OH: Merrill Prentice Hall.

Watzlawick, P., Weakland, J. H., and Fisch, R. (1974). *Change: Principles of problem formation and problem resolution*. New York, NY: W. W. Norton.

SECTION VI

Future Directions

CHAPTER 22

The Future of Mindfulness and Performance across Disciplines

Amy L. Baltzell, Joshua Summers

Mindfulness, as commonly practiced, refers to a type of awareness that is both tolerant of and interested in the many experiences – both habitual and novel – that make up the human condition. Such awareness allows one to see how past choices influence current and future experiences. In this volume of chapters, we have shared the benefits of mindfulness in the pragmatic, secular realm of performance. With the increasing pressure on performers and the aligned emotional challenges – from significant fears, to harsh self-judgment, to boredom – we believe strengthening our research base and continuing to create clear mindfulness-based pathways supported by solid empirical, evidence-based interventions is essential. In this quest, we must also create nuanced interventions to meet the needs of a range of performers, from the novice to professional – from dancers, singers, athletes, as well as coaches, mindfully oriented clinicians, mindfulness coaches, and sport psychology practitioners – and in such tailored interventions address the many unique demands of performance.

Mindfulness promotes a particular type of presence – a presence that is intentionally aware of and interested in what is occurring moment to moment. Contrary to mainstream assumptions, mindfulness does not necessarily include a quiet, stress-free experience. In fact, mindfulness includes the full spectrum of human experience, from intense fear and anxiety to moments of joy. Mindfulness includes the ability and willingness to engage in the present moment, whether it is fascinating, joyful, or riddled with physical, emotional, or social pain. The high value of being mindful in the performance realm is retaining the ability to focus on task-relevant cues – to concentrate – and to interact mostly wisely moment to moment with one's environment. When performing with mindfulness, one is able to tolerate distractions, such as fear, threat, or boredom such that the given distraction does not derail the performer from being present to opportunities (internal and external) for optimal performance.

A Brief Definition of Mindfulness: Buddhist and Langerian Mindfulness

Attributed to the pioneering work of Jon Kabat-Zinn, the dominant approach to mindfulness in North America within the clinical setting, both medical and psychological, has its roots in Buddhism. Kabat-Zinn defines mindfulness as, "Paying attention in a particular way: on purpose, in the present moment, and nonjudgmentally" (Kabat-Zinn, 1994, p. 4). Kabat-Zinn created Mindfulness-Based Stress Reduction (MBSR), which is an intensive mindfulness training designed to help individuals relate to their physical (i.e., medical) or psychological distress (e.g., anxiety, anger) with acceptance and nonjudgment (Kabat-Zinn, 2014). Such distress, when left unattended, can lead to maladaptive coping responses of avoiding, suppressing, or overengagement with the given distressing thoughts and emotions (Hayes & Feldman, 2004; Kabat-Zinn, 1990).

The impact of the formal practice of mindfulness meditation has been empirically supported with a wide range of medical and psychological disorders (Keng, Smoski, & Robins, 2011), with much of the research contingent on Kabat-Zinn's MBSR. Highlighted in this research is the phenomenon of brain plasticity, or the process whereby the brain remodels itself in response to stimulation and behavior. Practicing mindfulness meditation changes the brain in ways that are correlated with significant decreased anxiety and depression, enhanced overall well-being, and pain reduction (Hölzel et al., 2011).

With a different emphasis, Langerian mindfulness has been applied in the educational and creative settings. Ellen Langer emphasizes the value of intentionally paying attention to new, external stimuli. "Being mindful...," Langer (2000) writes, "is the simple act of drawing novel distinctions" (p. 220). Langerian mindfulness is characterized by an active engagement with the environment compared to the more passive approach of Kabat-Zinn's. Baer (2003) defines Langerian mindfulness as "alertness to distinctions, context, and multiple perspectives, openness to novelty, and orientation in the present" (p. 126). Most typically via Langer's mindfulness intervention, the individual or group is focused on the external terrain of human existence, generally with some goal-oriented focus (Langer, 1989), such as noticing new ways to play music (Langer, Russell, & Eisenkraft, 2009) or the process of giving feedback to children (Langer, Cohen, & Djikic, 2012).

These two approaches to mindfulness are both defined and operationalized very differently in research and in the practice. Together they offer a solid conceptual foundation for bringing mindfulness to the nonclinical, secular population for enhancing both performance and the quality of lives in training and performance and in the private lives of the performers. How so? Both approaches to mindfulness emphasize the importance of noticing what actually is actually emerging moment to moment, which leads to the actor casting off habitual ways of thinking, seeing, noticing, and responding freshly to just what is actually occurring. The future of mindfulness and performance lies within a wide range of applications while informed from an open-hearted acceptance of what is occurring to a willingness to see beyond *robotic, habitual* ways of viewing the world.

As we consider both definitions and applications of mindfulness within the performance realm, from a bird's-eye view, both understandings of mindfulness share similar elements, with an intentional noticing and accepting of what is occurring. Whether drawn from Eastern or Western tools, mindfulness practices range from narrow, internal points of focus (e.g., the breath) to an openness to all external experience (e.g., choiceless awareness and Langerian inspired engagement). Regardless of the disparity of definitions and operational conceptualizations of mindfulness, which lead to divergent interventions, mindfulness-based interventions have celebrated an efficacious impact.

Sport Interventions: Formal Mindfulness Meditation in Sport

Kabat-Zinn, Beall, and Rippe (1985) were the first on record to use mindfulness meditation training within the sport and performance realm. Kabat-Zinn and colleagues offered weekly in-person mindfulness mediation training sessions for both collegiate competitors and rowers preparing for the Olympics: both categories of athletes were also provided guided mindfulness meditation for daily use, and the Olympians were offered guided daily practice at the Olympic Games. The U.S. Olympic team rowers noted that the formal mindfulness meditation aided them in Olympic-level racing (Kabat-Zinn et al., 1985). The audiotapes, offered by Kabat-Zinn for the athletes to use independently, also included a segment in which the athletes were prompted to visualize themselves rowing with harmony and optimal technique. More recently, other studies have also employed the use of formal mindfulness meditation that resulted in increased performance of Indian pistol shooters (John, Verma, & Khanna, 2011); more game and match wins of tennis players (Stankovic & Baltzell, in preparation); increased flow (Aherne, Moran, & Lonsdale, 2011); and collegiate soccer players reporting an empowered, changed relationship to negative emotions when competing (Baltzell et al., 2014).

Frank Gardner and Zella Moore (2004, 2007, 2012), together, have led the way in bringing mindfulness to the performance realm via their eight-module, theoretically sound Mindfulness-Acceptance-Commitment (MAC) approach in sport. Informed by Acceptance Commitment Therapy (ACT; Hayes et al., 2004), the MAC approach helps the performer learn the concepts underlying mindfulness, offers brief formal and informal mindfulness practices, and pairs these components with helping athletes commit to actions that align with their values versus their sport-related emotions. The MAC approach is designed to deliver mindfulness training to one athlete at a time via a clinical sport psychologist.

Keith Kaufman, Carol Glass, and colleagues have also worked to modify Kabat-Zinn's MBSR for a recreational and competitive athlete population via their Mindful Sport Performance Enhancement (MSPE) intervention. Kaufman and colleagues (e.g., Kaufman, Glass, & Arnkoff, 2009; Pineau, Glass, & Kaufman, 2014) have offered the intervention in varying formats, from four to six weeks, in an effort to make the formal mindfulness mediation practices more conducive to the lives of recreational and competitive athletes. They have reported a range of benefits to recreational athletes engaging in MSPE, including enhanced dispositional mindfulness for archers and reduction in somatic anxiety and mindfulness for golfers (Kaufman et al., 2009); also they have shown that mindfulness increased and sport-related worries decreased for runners (De Petrillo et al., 2009).

Dose and Duration of Mindfulness Training in Performance

These researchers have offered mindfulness meditation and clinically driven tools to help performers. These tools have been remarkably impactful given the time intensity of each program and the unwillingness of high-level performers to devote significant time toward an endeavor that is not transparently going to directly impact sport performance. For example, most twenty-year-old Division I ice hockey players would not elect to meditate forty-five to sixty minutes per day or attend many one-on-one sessions (eight to ten for the MAC approach) with a clinical sport psychologist. As a practicing sport psychologist for over fifteen years, I (Baltzell) have found it hard to inspire many athlete-clients simply to bring to mind a visualization of a successful last leg of a race or their perfect tennis serve, even when they have experience and knowledge that such simple exercises can have profound, direct impact on performance. Meditating for long periods of time or going to see a psychologist for many sessions, for mindfulness training specifically, seems unlikely for the majority of athletes or performers who are not contending with clinical challenges.

We have much to learn about dose, intervention design, and intervention-performance demand match when considering the application of mindfulness within the performance realm. Mindfulness-based interventions in sport vary in terms of focus, dose, and duration, from brief clinical interventions that are cognitive and nonmeditative-based (e.g., Langer et al., 2009) and heavily emphasized formal mindfulness mediation practices (Kabat-Zinn et al., 1985), to clinical cognitive behavioral psychology mindfulness (nonmeditation)–based interventions (e.g., MB-EAT; Kristeller et al., 2006) for primarily clinical issues.

In terms of formal mindfulness meditation, noted leader Jon Kabat-Zinn and colleagues (1985) spearheaded the use of mindfulness meditation as intervention in sport with their study of Harvard and collegiate rowers. They offered thirty-minute weekly group sessions paired with a recommendation to listen to one of two audio files that were fifteen minutes in duration. Their intervention, which primarily used formal mindfulness meditation, has continued to be a go-to intervention for researchers exploring how best to bring mindfulness interventions into sport. Yet the presentation and dosage of practice has varied (see Table 22.1).

In nonperformance samples, brief bouts of mindfulness practices (e.g., three days, twenty-five minutes per day) have resulted in benefits. But, we do not know what the right amount is for the athletes to experience performance benefits. And we at once know that time constraints in daily

Table 22.1 *Formal Mindfulness Meditation in Sport Studies: Examples of Practice Dosage*

Intervention	Minutes per day of formal meditation practice	Study
MPSE	45 minutes per day (2.5 weekly group sessions)	Kaufman et al. (2009)
Formal Mindfulness Meditation	20 minutes per day	John et al. (2011)
Formal Mindfulness Meditation	10–30 minutes per day	Aherne et al. (2011)
Formal Mindfulness Meditation	10–15 minutes per day	Stankovic & Baltzell (in preparation)
Mindfulness Meditaton Training in Sport (MMTS)	5 minutes per day (twice weekly 30 minute group sessions)	Baltzell et al. (2014)

life are quite real for the typical high-level performer – from the collegiate basketball player to a professional dancer. Such high-level performers may tend to be less willing to seek any support, much less invest significant amount of time (i.e., forty-five minutes of meditation practice) to their typically rigorous training regimes.

Lessons from Mindfulness-Based Clinical Interventions for Performance

In sport, whether in informal or formal mindfulness practice, we can cull invaluable lessons from well-established clinically based mindfulness interventions for the performance realm. Though Dialectical Behavior Therapy (DBT) was designed for borderline personality disorder (for those with unstable moods, behavior, and relationships with others), the core tenet of the intervention is the *acceptance* of oneself just as one is and, concurrently, willingness to pursue making *positive changes* in one's life regarding mood, behavior, and relationships with others (Baer, 2003). The synthesis of this seeming contradiction, acceptance and change, is just what mindfulness can offer the performer, particularly when coping with intense negative emotions such as performance anxiety, self-doubt, or harsh self-judgment: the performer can learn to accept his or her feelings just as they are and then change habitual patterns of behavior (i.e., instead of the athlete burying her face in her hands crying, she can instead choose to accept the aversive feelings and focus back on the game in play). And it may be that integrating self-compassion into such acute, aversive emotional experience may also help the athlete cultivate the courage to face the situation and refocus on the task at hand (Neff & Germer, 2013).

Mindfulness-Based Cognitive Therapy (MBCT) was designed to mitigate depressive relapse through helping clients nonjudgmentally observe their thoughts and feelings. Clients are taught to view thoughts as mental events that pass through the mind in contrast to accurate aspects of the individual or valid representation of reality. For example, one skill in MBCT is to practice bringing to mind, "I am not my thoughts," when the individual is being flooded with fear and self-criticism. This relational change to thoughts and emotions is a core insight that can be gained from MBCT and formal practice, and this can translate to sport and performance contexts. This change of relationship to thoughts and emotions is precisely what is called for when the athlete is overwhelmed with harsh self-criticism or pre-performance anxiety. This *decentered approach* – defined as "the ability to observe one's thoughts and feelings as temporary, objective events in the mind, as opposed to reflections of the self that are necessarily true" (Fresco et al., 2007, p. 234) – can help free the performer to focus away from the thoughts and feelings onto performance-relevant cues (e.g., Baltzell et al., 2014).

In my (Baltzell) practice, I have found that many elite athletes, who struggle with intense performance-disrupting emotions, are not willing to engage in formal meditation practice yet are very open to the insights that come from a formal mindfulness practice such as *I am not my thoughts*. For example, I worked with an elite runner who was consumed with debilitating pre-performance anxiety. If he had uninvited thoughts like, "I can't win today," or, "I can't grind it out and make it this time," such thoughts would predict a slower race than normal (though he was still one of the fastest runners in the country). The following are a few key questions I asked him that seemed to free him from this negative cycle:

1. Have you ever run your best even with thoughts like, "I can't win this time"?
2. Have you ever run your best even when you thought that your body felt off, that you didn't "have it" that day?

The runner answered yes to both questions. Through brief psycho-education and discussion, he realized that his thoughts did not have to predict how he ran; this insight was radically freeing for this runner. It did not take formal meditation practice; it took a change in awareness that was authentic to the athlete that his thoughts were not always true. His beliefs were not always true. Thus he was able to experience some *decentering* from these thoughts and focus back on racing well.

Performance Benefits of Mindfulness Practices

Empirically demonstrated benefits from mindfulness interventions in sport and performance have focused both on outcome and performance-related factors. Only a few experimental studies have been conducted exploring the mindfulness–performance relationship: John and colleagues (2011) reported significant changes in Indian pistol shooter performance; Stankovic and Baltzell (in preparation) report significant changes in winning games and matches of masters-level female tennis players; and with the MAC approach, coaches reported and athletes self-reported enhanced athletic performance (e.g., Lutkenhouse, 2007; Schwanhausser, 2009) See Gardner & Moore (2012) for overview of performance benefits from implementing the MAC approach with athletes.

Emotional Regulation

Implementing a cognitive decentered approach offers a potential benefit of equanimity that can be translated into improved performance via mindfulness-based interventions. Empirical data from such mindfulness-based clinical interventions, which emphasize the decentered approach, often result in a changed relationship of the client with his or her aversive thoughts, feelings, and body sensations. Translated to sport interventions, the performer would be empowered to better tolerate aversive performance-related emotions. In a study of collegiate women soccer players who engaged in a mindfulness-based intervention, athletes reported an enhanced ability to accept and experience a different relationship with their emotions both on and off the field (Baltzell et al., 2014). Such reports were related to moments on the sport field, such as missing a shot on goal or being beaten to the ball by an opponent.

Attentional Control

One of the claimed benefits of mindfulness practices, based on the Buddhist tradition, is the enhanced ability to control one's attention (Hodgins & Adair, 2010; Moore & Malinowski, 2009). Certainly, from the sport and performance psychology perspective, strong attentional control is golden. When the performer is able to place full focus on appropriate performance cues moment to moment, she gives herself the best chance to optimize performance (Gardner & Moore, 2007) and to achieve flow state (Jackson & Csikszentmihalyi, 1999). Hanson and Mendius (2009) capture the impact of mindfulness practices on attention when they summarize the concentrations benefits from a mindfulness practice: "Having good control over your attention: You can place your attention wherever you want and it stays there and when you want to shift it to something else, you can" (p. 177). Formal mindfulness practice helps the individual anchor her attention where she chooses to place it and purposefully switch from one point of experience to another (Keng et al., 2011).

Ability to Reduce and Let Go of Negative Thoughts

A mindfulness meditator's perceived ability to reduce and let go of negative thoughts is a capacity (Frewen et al., 2008) that would greatly contribute to sport and other performance endeavors. Uninvited disruptive thoughts, such as harsh self-criticism and judgment, are often the culprits that disallow the performer from focusing on the task at hand. Albert Bandura (e.g., 1997), champion of self-efficacy (the belief in your ability to complete the task at hand successfully), contends that:

> Self-efficacious athletes do not exacerbate the performance problems by disruptive emotional reactions and interfering thought patterns. Rather they dissociate each new attempt from how they performed before and approach it anew, with a task-oriented focus … such cognitive restructuring shifts attention away from cumulative failure to effective strategies for current performance (p. 392).

With the learned ability to focus one's attention, through the mindfulness practice, performers are better equipped as Bandura notes to freshly place their attention on current task-relevant cues to optimize performance. This ability to let go of negative thoughts may be linked to the ability to accept mistakes more quickly. Such acceptance (or tolerance) is not resigning or being passive, but simply accepting the fact that something has just occurred that is not one's preference. And with such acceptance the performer is then more empowered to use his or her mind to focus on task-relevant cues (versus becoming lost in negative thoughts). Unfortunately, sometimes the difficulty of letting go of negative thoughts may also be due to suppressing or avoiding thoughts, which can ultimately be problematic (Hayes et al., 2004) – hence the importance of a mindful approach

Mindfulness: A Primer for Flow

Being mindful shares many core features with flow, namely being fully present and interested in moment-to-moment experience. Mihaly Csikszentmihalyi (1990), who coined the term "flow" (1975), describes flow as "a particular kind of experience that is so engrossing and enjoyable that it becomes autotelic, that is, worth doing for its own sake even though it may have no consequence outside itself" (p. 824). A positive relationship between mindfulness and flow in sport has been supported (Kaufman et al., 2009; Kee & Wang, 2008). Aherne and colleagues (2011) found, in their experimental study, that athletes who practiced mindfulness mediation reported more frequently experiencing flow. Bernier and colleagues (2009), based on interviews with ten French national training center swimmers, contended that the experience of flow and being mindful (on a focused performance) is synonymous with optimal performance experience itself. There is initial evidence that mindfulness approaches that cultivate an open acceptance of moment-to-moment experience may help performers cultivate being more mindful, which, in turn, facilitates both pre-performance and performance relationship to thoughts, feelings, and somatic cues for prompting flow and at once enhanced performance in sport.

The Future of Mindfulness Practice and Research in Performance

Operationalizing Mindfulness Revisited

In surveying the applications of mindfulness-based interventions that are being conducted today, it is fair to say that most of these interventions derive their conceptual framework from the definition of mindfulness from the pioneering work of Jon Kabat-Zinn. Whether it be Kabat-Zinn's MBSR or MBCT, Google's Search Inside Yourself, or the U.S. military's Mindfulness-Based Mind Fitness Training, all of these training programs are predicated on Kabat-Zinn's (1994) definition of mindfulness: "Mindfulness means paying attention in a particular way: on purpose, in the present moment, and non-judgmentally" (p. 4). And without question, the evidence in support of interventions based on this definition is empirically strong.

But, as we look ahead toward emerging applications and evolving practices, it may be time to question some of the implemented operative assumptions. And the reason for opening a dialogue around how mindfulness is operationalized is, at least, twofold: (1) particularly for performers, elements of Kabat-Zinn's definition are implemented in a way that may create unintended resistance to mindfulness practice; and (2) exploring newer and possibly broader understandings of mindfulness could lead to novel training methodologies (discussed later in this chapter) as well as more effective applications.

In a deconstructed form, Kabat-Zinn's definition of mindfulness is delineated by three basic clauses: mindfulness is a kind of attention that is (a) on purpose, (b) in the present moment, and (c) without judgment. Volitional intent – that is, a goal sought "on purpose" – appears as central to Kabat-Zinn's definition. Typically, in both research and application, practitioners are prompted to direct their attention deliberately (e.g., on the breath or body sensations). Yet there are times whereby awareness naturally and spontaneously alights upon the basic conditions of the present moment, seemingly by itself. Such spontaneous moments of clear awareness are *actually* the implicit *goal* – that is, to increase the number of moments when present-moment awareness spontaneously arises on its own. And yet such experiences are not explicitly reflected in the typical understanding of Kabat-Zinn's definition and thus not considered in operational definitions and, subsequently, applications.

Performers seek such spontaneous moments of heightened focus on the moment-to-moment experience. In fact, such an inner quiet mind is often aligned with both optimal performance and the experience of flow. And flow by definition is characterized by a loss of self-referential agency. Therefore, it is likely that practicing mindfulness with the explicit intention of doing it "on purpose" could establish a mindset that reinforces greater self-agency and creates a potential obstacle to flow and optimal performance.

In actual mindfulness training, it is likely that the skilled mindfulness instructor or coach would council against striving for particular experiences, against "doing" much of anything, or against trying to control one's experience in formal meditation practice, and these corrective cues could mitigate mental *tightening* that seizes up around *getting it right* by practicing *on purpose*. And, such formal practice could translate into enhanced performance – being fully present and more accepting of whatever arises. But in the absence of such direct coaching, it makes sense to consider expanding how we conceptualize mindfulness to include both intentional and *spontaneous* manifestations of mindful awareness in order to better meet the needs of performance objectives.

The next aspect of the definition, "in the present moment," seems at first, clear enough. Often, the present moment is defined by the experiences that are immediately impinging upon consciousness, that is, bodily sensations, sounds, images, smells, and tastes. Thoughts, emotions, and especially rumination about the future or past are considered "nonpresent," or "mindless." Such focus on immediate task-focused experience is valued in much of performance psychology, including within the MAC approach (i.e., Gardner & Moore, 2007). In fact, many teachers relegate such focus on past and future as *mindless* states. So from this definition, the practitioner, while formally training, is instructed with typical phrases such as "notice when the mind is lost in thought, to let it go, and patiently, nonjudgmentally return to something within the present, such as the breath or a body sensation."

For many, this approach to practice will produce positive benefits, but for others, however, it can also lead to unintended internal conflict whenever the meditator becomes aware of thinking. Even though a competent mindfulness coach might encourage a client to "allow patterns of thought with acceptance" as a way to diminish this conflict, the tendency for a client to infer that thoughts are somehow antithetical to mindfulness is all too common in our coaching experience. This is not to mention the fact that from the perspective of optimal performance, there are times when intentional thinking is absolutely essential and unintentional thinking is extremely common.

Another way in which the "in the present moment" aspect of the definition is potentially problematic appears when we consider the temporal location of thoughts about the future and past. An individual's thoughts about the future and the past appear only within the evolving experience of the present moment. In fact, there is, subjectively, no other moment than this one. Leaving aside the slippery reality of the time it takes for impulses of the "present moment" to be neurologically constructed within the brain, we can operate from an agreed sense of subjectivity that the "now" is all that we ever truly experience.

At present, the consensual model of mindfulness training, based on the Kabat-Zinn line, posits that we simply want to "become aware of thoughts," and "not be lost in thoughts." These cues are well intentioned, but in actual practice a more accurate representation of what occurs for a client is closer to something like this: they intend to be with their "present moment" experience, such as the breath; their mind wanders into thought (which they don't see happening); they spontaneously realize that they have "wandered" from the breath; they proceed to judge, if not, chastise, themselves for having wandered from the breath; and they return to the breath with a strategy to "double down" the effort. As a result, the practitioner inadvertently reinforces aversion to thoughts and more subtly doesn't really learn much about the phenomenological nature of thinking itself. In most cases, particularly outside of long-term retreat environments, practitioners will recognize thoughts *only* after the fact, in hindsight, in what we call "rear-view mirror" recognition. A common practice that is often deployed is to label the awareness of thinking as "thinking" and then return to the breath. In this instance, the noticing of thoughts and the method of labeling both occur *after* the actual experience of thought.

One of the explicit goals of mindfulness training for performers is to increase tolerance of, acceptance of, and capacity to be with thinking, including negative affect and cognitions. Thus, it seems necessary to explore an expanded operationalization of mindfulness, one that explicitly dismantles the inevitable tension many practitioners face if they adopt the narrow, commonly held view of present-moment experience *only* as sensory experience. We contend that, in addition to sensate experience, mindfulness must explicitly include acceptance of thinking in both formal and informal practice. Specifically, we must also value intentional use of one's mind to help make decisions in both the moment-to-moment experience and for the future, such as when strategizing for success.

Finally, the aspect of the definition that emphasizes paying attention "without judgment," as understood, is also potentially problematic as mindfulness is applied to performance. In its more benign form, this aspect of the definition attempts to infuse the practitioner's attitude toward experience with qualities of acceptance and nonresistance. But for many, this aspect of the definition inadvertently builds an internal agenda to become "nonjudgmental" and perhaps not caring, which could easily lead to giving up.

Since mindfulness practice as a mental training discipline emerged from the Buddha's teaching, it may be of interest to consider that the idea of *nonjudgmental awareness* was never mentioned by the Buddha. In traditional Buddhist contexts, mindfulness – a bare awareness of the contents of consciousness – serves a broader mission to facilitate the development of wise discernment (*panna* in Pali, *prajna* in Sanskrit) for the purposes of mitigating personal and interpersonal suffering. In Kabat-Zinn's effort to bring the ancient idea to modern Western medicine, the broader understanding of mindfulness has garnered less attention.

Within the application of mindfulness to performance, the development of wise discernment is both missing and relevant. The practice, as encouraged by the Buddha, entails developing greater objectivity of the contents of awareness to support better life choices (and in this context, performance decisions); this process of practicing mindfulness is ultimately predicated on cultivating good judgment, not lack of judgment. Emphasizing "nonjudging" as an aspect of mindfulness training runs contrary to the explicit goals of the application of mindfulness as put forth by the Buddha.

So, what might an expanded understanding of mindfulness look like? The following is a possible candidate: "Mindfulness is a quality of awareness that objectifies the contents of experience, internally and externally, promoting greater tolerance, interest, and clarity towards that content." In building upon Jon Kabat Zinn's definition, we believe that the qualifier of being done "on purpose" needs to include *spontaneous* expressions of mindfulness; additionally, by expanding our understanding of what constitutes "the present moment" (such as emotions, thoughts, intentional thinking and wise future planning), and by reformulating the emphasis of "without judgment" to "with wise discernment," we believe performers will be better served.

Methodological Upgrade

From a reconsideration of how Kabat-Zinn's standard definition has been operationalized by practitioners and researchers, it naturally makes sense to reconsider training methodology. The MBSR approach is explicitly geared toward reducing stress and has garnered staggering empirical support for the efficacy of the program (Keng et al., 2011). But what is required to reduce stress for medical and clinical populations may not be germane to the needs or the objectives of performers. Mindfulness practice (primarily based on using MBSR as the intervention) leads to neuroplastic changes (Hölzel et al., 2011), just as physical training leads to changes in physical strength and conditioning. However, just as it would seem absurdly inadequate if all coaches were to instruct athletes to train their bodies by following something as vague as "strength-based body-training," the great majority of current mindfulness interventions also suffer from generality and lack of application specificity.

For example, some modern teachers advocate for what Kenneth Folk refers to as "Contemplative Fitness Training." Drawing from a broad spectrum of meditative approaches, these mindfulness coaches create a mental training protocol to meet specific needs of the performer in ways that are both unique to that performer and to the given type of performance. For example, the attentional demands and relevant capacities of an elite golfer are qualitatively very different from that of the professional basketball player or jazz musician. Performance demands vary widely and may require self-regulation (e.g., boxers), concentrated focus (e.g., pistol shooters), panoramic awareness (e.g., football quarterbacks), or kinesthetic sensitivity (e.g., ballet dancers). Given the wide range of performance needs, the current methodology of mindfulness training falls short of meeting such nuanced demands.

Similar to sport coaches' drills in sport that emphasize different physical capacities, mindfulness interventions can leverage similar training principles for different attentional capacities. Rather than issue an open-ended instruction simply to train the mind to be aware of what is arising, moment to moment, as is used in formal mindfulness meditation training, interventions instead can segment a training period into specific contemplative drills that directly apply to the performer's needs. For example, one performer might wrestle with negative affect and have a need to keep her mind from wandering when under performance pressure. A tailored mindfulness approach might have the performer train in two contemplative intervals: three minutes focusing on the breath, three minutes labeling mind states, alternating back and forth for three to six rounds. Conversely, another performer might require the ability to take in a panoramic perspective (e.g., a soccer goalie) and be sensitive to subtle changes in the visual field (e.g., the forward's systematic movement approaching the goal). This performer might be better suited to a meditation training that has him meditate with eyes open, alternating between intervals of "noticing space" (e.g., noticing space between objects) and "labeling shapes and colors" (e.g., labeling the couch as *rectangular*, the shoe as *red*).

The various contemplative practices of the world's wisdom traditions contain an enormous spectrum of potential tools to draw from. Just as mindfulness itself has been decontextualized from its original quasireligious context and made into a secular practice in recent decades, it would seem that one of the next logical steps in the evolving integration of its practice would be to cull, from these various wisdom traditions, other time-tested techniques. The following is a short list of time-tested techniques that could be incorporated, wisely, into a performance context to meet specific performer and context needs:

- *Body-based awareness practices* (including yoga): for increasing kinesthetic sensitivity.
- *Breath-awareness concentration*: for deepening focus and promoting calmness.
- *Concentration with visual objects* (i.e., candle flame or colored discs [*kasina*]): for enhancing visual concentration.
- *Mindfulness of mind states*: for decentering, disidentifying from mental content.
- *Metta/Karuna* (loving kindness and compassion): for improving care and warmth for self and others.
- *Dzogchen* (Tibetan technique): for explicitly developing a wider lens of awareness, a panoramic sky-like mind.
- *Choiceless awareness*: for stabilizing the mind within a vast multitude of changing phenomena.

As one example, the Burmese Mahasi Method of mindfulness training emphasizes "noting" or "labeling" moment-to-moment experience, whereby the practitioner silently or audibly labels the salient element of his or her experience at a rate of roughly one note per second. When using this technique, many practitioners report a much greater reduction of mind-wandering when compared to less technical styles of mindfulness training. This may or may not be advantageous depending on the explicit goals of the given performer (i.e., athlete to musician). Researchers and practitioners (meditation coaches for the performance realm) have much to learn regarding the efficacy of the range of tailored mindfulness interventions. Empirical investigation of the relative strengths and weaknesses of such techniques is needed.

Mindfulness Meditation Training in Sport: Collegiate Soccer

In a study using a mindfulness meditation with collegiate soccer players (Baltzell & LoVerme, 2014; Baltzell et al., 2014), the second author (Summers) designed Mindfulness Meditation in Sport (MMTS), in which he aligned practices from other contemplative methods. MMTS was implemented in a six-week, twelve-session, and thirty-minutes-per-session format. In addition to presenting formal mindfulness meditation, the athletes and their coaches were also introduced to various meditative training intervals (two-to-five-minute segments) that were joined together in series to form a contemplative "workout." The program included intervals of concentrated breath awareness, open awareness, "group mantra" practice (i.e., *metta*), and negative mind–state fire drills.

Description of MMTS program

MMTS is a mindfulness meditation program for sport. According to Sedlmeier and colleagues (2012), typical tools used to teach new mindfulness meditators include "observing one's breathing, counting breaths, and engaging in labeling (labeling the current thought experience as, for instance, 'emotion,' 'pain,' 'planning,' or 'judgment'" (p. 1141). All of these tools were included in the MMTS program as a point of focus while practicing. The core of the MMTS program involved basic mindfulness practices with specific innovations to engage the players and better serve their performance needs.

The primary goal of the MMTS program was to train participants to increase their levels of mindfulness, to practice acceptance and tolerance of thoughts, feelings, and sensations as a means to optimize performance. For this MMTS intervention, the head coach allocated thirty minutes for each group session. Twenty minutes of each session were devoted to educating the participants on various aspects of mindfulness and to prepare them to practice formal meditation. The facilitator also allowed time for questions in each session, consistently offering ten minutes of mindfulness meditation practice.

There were four main areas of the MMTS intervention, including the following;

1. *Concentration exercises:* For this aspect of the training, awareness of breathing was the primary focus. The players were instructed to sustain their attention on their breathing, acknowledge when their attention had wandered, and gently bring their attention back. They were recommended to intrapersonally note, "rising, rising," for the in-breath and "falling, falling," for the out-breath, as in the Mahasi Method of Vipassana.

The facilitator noticed that the soccer players were dozing during the breathing exercise and, in response, implemented a counting technique mentioned by the Sri Lankan monk Bhante Gunaratana in his book *Mindfulness in Plain English*. Players were told to count their breaths, on the exhalation, from one to ten, and then back down to one. At that point, they would repeat the exercise, but on the second round, count from one to nine and then back down. The next round would be from one to eight, and so on, until they got to one. The facilitator called this "Breathing Ladders" and observed the players to be much more engaged with the implementation of this approach. It seemed to add a competitive dimension, which the players themselves acknowledged to be "more fun." Practicing this technique for five minutes was the first contemplative interval in their workout.

2. *Open awareness capacity:* After warming up with the concentration Breathing Ladders, the players were instructed to open their minds like an "open spider's web." In Thailand, Burma, and other parts of Asia, Vipassana meditators are instructed to imagine their minds like a spider's web. The meditators are like the spider in the web, and the center of the web is their breath. This analogy was used in the training. The players were instructed to note, by silently labeling, any occurrence that appeared in their awareness other than the breath. Further, the players were instructed that while noting each occurrence to observe what happened to the occurrence/experience while it was being observed (did it get stronger, more intense, less obvious, fade away?). During this exercise, if nothing special was occurring the players were told to bring their attention to the breath, with the primary emphasis on allowing their awareness to remain open to anything arising and not to give breathing preferential attention. This methodology is based on the Mahasi Method of Vipassana. In this exercise, they were told that they could now observe "thinking," "hearing," "dreaming," and a multitude of physical sensations such as "pressure," "itching," "tension," "tingling," "hot," or "cold."

As with the first exercise, the facilitator (Summers) noticed that the players weren't especially engaged. When he asked what they were noticing, their responses were vague. Recognizing this, the facilitator adjusted the method slightly and included an emphasis from meditation teacher Joseph Goldstein called Noticings per Breath (NPBs). The players were asked to see how many things they could notice, inside themselves and outside themselves, during an out-breath. The players were then told to reset their attention during the in-breath, and then again see how many things they could notice during the out-breath, and so on. The athletes made it clear that intentionally seeing more things was desirable. And again, this slight modification, adding a quantitative and competitive element, dramatically improved the players' engagement. In reports after the exercise, the players described noticing many things, from obvious sounds outside the room to subtle sensations in their body. They reported that their perceptual accuracy and clarity improved. This exercise was practiced for five to ten minutes.

3. *Group mantra (metta)* (caring thoughts for self and teammates): Traditional *metta* practice or loving-kindness meditation involves thinking and sending thoughts of good will and kindness first to oneself and then to different categories of people and beings in one's life. Traditional phrases are used, such as, "May I be peaceful," and, "May I be happy." These sentiments did not reflect the needs of the collegiate female athletes. Rather than working with these traditional phrases, the facilitator led the team through a group process to identify key qualities of mind that the team felt were most essential for their success. After brainstorming many qualities of mind, the team agreed upon "calm" and "resiliency" as being the two most valuable qualities. The athletes were then asked to identify what kind of person, animal, or figure they imagined being "calm" and "resilient." The team unanimously chose the term "beast." And this became their team mantra, "I am a calm, resilient beast."

As with traditional loving-kindness practice, the players were first told to repeat this mantra to themselves in the first person, "I am a calm, resilient beast." After a few rounds, they were then told to "pump up" their favorite teammate with this mantra: "You are a calm, resilient beast." Additional instructions were also given to imagine that teammate absorbing the impact of the statement. How would she look and feel? From the favorite teammate, the players were then told to send the mantra to someone on the team with whom they weren't that close. From this category, the players were instructed to "pump up" someone on the team that they didn't particularly like (the difficult person category in *metta* meditation). And finally, the players were instructed to "pump up" the entire team in the first-person plural: "We are calm, resilient beasts." This exercise would last for five minutes, and it represents an adaptation of traditional loving-kindness meditation to a performance-enhancing context, designed explicitly to align the players, both intrapersonally and interpersonally, with their core values that they themselves established that were based on caring for one another and, at once, for personal sport and team success.

4. *Practicing acceptance of negative mind states*: Participants were prompted to think about past negative performance events that involved a negative feeling, such as frustration, embarrassment, or anger (Siegel, 2010). Once recalled, participants were encouraged to become aware of emotions associated with what they were recalling. Next, participants were asked to observe the pattern of sensations that were present in their bodies with those emotions and thoughts. For instance, participants were asked to notice and accept "frustration" and then to direct their attention in their bodies and identify the somatic correlate to that feeling of frustration, such as tension in the throat and chest, with (for example) some awareness of a faster heart rate.

This exercise was intended to help participants to become more accepting of negative mind and emotional states, to develop a different relationship to such internal experience in sport. With the emphasis on finding the negative mind state or emotion in the body, the players were instructed that it is often easier to deal with the direct sensations of the emotion than the actual thoughts associated with the emotion. And this is why the exercise was described as a fire drill. A fire drill is a rehearsal for what to do in the event of an actual fire. By following a drill of identifying the negative mind state and then finding the expression of that mind state in the body, the players were given a pragmatic tool that could be used in the heat of the game to bring them more easily, ultimately, back to a task-relevant focus. After each session of mindfulness training exercises, there was subsequent discussion about how such practice in the training could be directly transferred to the field, in practice and/or competition. This exercise was practiced for five to ten minutes.

With each exercise, the team practiced the exercise in isolation until the facilitator felt the team members had achieved competency. At that point, the drills were connected into a twenty-minute workout: five minutes of Breathing Ladders, five minutes of open awareness emphasizing NPBs, five minutes of negative mind–state fire drill, and five minutes of group mantra. MMTS is just one example of how mindfulness practices can be adapted to the needs of a specific athlete or team.

Future Research: Mindfulness and Performance

Performance Contexts: Expanding the Scope of Application

In addition to developing greater nuance toward *how* mindfulness itself is practiced, we would also like to begin a discussion of how mindfulness may be a useful skill for different aspects of performance. We imagine the application of mindfulness toward a specific temporal context as a way of optimizing not just in-the-moment performance but as an integral capacity in a performer's life that facilitates growth and development in all areas. Until now, this discussion has primarily been focused on task-specific issues, whether that be self-regulating (emotional) during performances, focusing on task-specific actions (attentional), or being receptive to emergent opportunities while performing. Building on this initial discourse, we would like to recommend that mindfulness practice also holds positive potential within three broad temporal considerations: (1) the stage of skill acquisition (training); (2) the stage before performance, including self-management just prior to the start of performance, and during performance, including self-management throughout the performance itself; and (3) the stage of post-performance review.

1. *Skill acquisition.* At the stage of skill acquisition, much has been written recently on the importance of proper practice, what Dan Coyle (2009) refers to as "deep practice." Deep practice is not a mindless repetition of familiar drills and patterning successes; rather, in deep practice the aim is to focus explicitly on what *isn't* working, to highlight sticky spots (e.g., repeating a play in basketball, practicing a kick turn for the swimmer) and to drill those particular movements or skills slowly and patiently (and correctly) until the problems are worked out such that the athlete can perform the skill at full speed under pressure. Such deep practice is neither fun nor rewarding and can be quite draining. The experts agree that it is this type of practice that leads to mastery, excellence, and an increase in talent or skill. The idea of deep practice is consistent with Ericsson's concept of *deliberate practice* (Ericsson, Krampe, & Tesch-Romer, 1993), which contends that it takes ten years or ten thousand hours of practicing well to become an expert performer. Using mindfulness to help performers tolerate mistakes with

equanimity would help them continue slowly and deliberately to practice aspects of performance that are *not* working – which many performers tend to avoid.

2. *Before and during performance: failure tolerance and growth mindset.* As a vital precondition for effectively coping with thoughts and emotions prior to and during performance, it is essential to develop failure tolerance and a growth mindset. Without the ability to tolerate or embrace mistakes and areas of weakness before or during performance, the performer may stop a performer from fully engaging or trying. In my practice as a sport psychologist, I (Baltzell) have witnessed many athletes be debilitated from performance anxiety or self-critical thoughts. The ability to observe, accept, and tolerate such experience is essential to be able to fully engage. I recall one NBA hopeful who if he missed two shots at the start of the game would literally quit taking shots and accept that it was just "one of those games." He had low failure tolerance and it impacted his internal experience as well as the scoreboard.

We contend that mindfulness training, through its ability to develop a less centralized sense of self whereby the self is not defined nor determined by the contents of experience, can be a vehicle to help the individual establish the requisite failure tolerance and growth mindset that allows the performer to flourish, even in the face of mistakes or failure. Moreover, mindfulness practice could establish the necessary focus and attention to detail that supports best performance. For example, collegiate soccer players who engaged in the MMTS program reported that the program helped them tolerate aversive emotions on the field such that they could more quickly shift from the negativity to the task at hand (Baltzell et al., 2014)

3. *Post-performance review: mindfulness practices.* Researchers have focused primarily on the relevance of mindfulness for in-the-moment performance contexts, but little has been suggested for the application of mindfulness in the post-performance context. Similar to the pre-performance context, in the post-performance context it is recommended that performers go through a review phase, within a formal practice, with the specific intention to learn again from mistakes and grow from difficulties. For a performer who is defined by outcomes, such a practice can be either ignored or challenging to the ego. However, a wise, mindful post-performance review can offer essential lessons for improved performance.

Expanding the Exploration of the Mindfulness Impact: Coachability and Teams

We contend that it is important for future research to also look into coaches' perception of the *coachability* of players and performers. How open are the athletes to coach feedback, and does mindfulness play a role in such coachability? Coaches often seem to see such requisite traits for coachability – such as open-mindedness, distress tolerance, persistence – as inherent to the athlete personality: "That athlete is just a winner." But with the plasticity of the brain (e.g., Hölzel et al., 2011) comes plasticity of many such strengths of character when effort is applied to cultivating such strengths (Lyubomirsky, Sheldon & Schkade, 2005; Peterson, 2007); It would be fascinating to evaluate coaches' perception of their players receptivity to coaching based on mindfulness training for sport intervention.

Another avenue of interest for future exploration is the influence of mindfulness on interpersonal dynamics in group performance contexts. As noted, much has been written and researched on the individual self-regulatory benefits of mindfulness practice. But what happens when groups of individuals all increase their own levels of mindfulness and self-regulation? We cannot assume that the same positive benefits that accrue to the individual as a result of greater mindfulness would confer to the group as a whole; there is a need for empirical research on this topic. Massachusetts Institute of Technology (MIT) business management professor Otto Scharmer has written on the positive effects when individuals and groups shift their consciousness from an "egocentric mode" to an "eco-centric mode" in which the individuals and groups are more attuned to what Scharmer calls the "emergent whole." During the recent World Cup, Scharmer (2014) theorized on the success of Germany's team:

> So what is driving the success of the German team? It's a philosophy that requires all players to operate from a *shared awareness of the evolving whole.* Everyone is required to be aware of what's happening everywhere on the field – the changing positions, the emerging spaces among their own team members and their opponents, to keep the ball moving. It's that shared awareness of the evolving whole that allows them to pass the ball faster than the opposing team at times can comprehend, or react to . . . .

Firing the coach or replacing players cannot fix responding to that style of soccer. It requires starting at a deeper level: in the quality of our thinking, or our sensing, of our awareness of the whole. Scharmer is describing another often-described effect of consistent mindfulness practice. We would like to see greater discussion and research on the effects of mindfulness through the lens of interpersonal (sport teams and performance groups) change, functioning, and development within the performance context.

Conclusion

The body of knowledge on the range of mindfulness approaches, including formal mindfulness practice, on performance processes and outcomes has made good strides over the past decade (e.g. Gardner & Moore, 2012). Performance benefits are expected to continue to emerge from mindfulness practices as the interventions are matched with needs of the performer and context. Ellen Langer (1989) has written on how we can become more "mindful and aware of our mindsets, mental maps and narratives . . . . Just as mindlessness is the rigid reliance on old categories," she says, "mindfulness means the continual creation of new ones" (p. 62). This broader awareness of how the mind frames experience then allows one to recognize the implications of their actions for the longer term, which ultimately prevents them from slipping into a life that pulls them away from their values. The question is how do we best help performers become more mindful and more authentically engaged with their moment-to-moment experience and performance? It would be a mistake to assume that all mindfulness training is beneficial, or that all will lead to similar outcomes, simply because it's named "mindfulness training."

For some athletes, formal meditation practice, MPSE, or MAC approach intervention will help with myriad performance-related factors and in some instances performance directly. Yet we need a wider range of interventions, and some brief interventions, to match performers' specific needs. We need more options to help the range of performers both be exposed to and understand the value of *being present* to what is occurring in their moment-to-moment experience in a way that is productive. Athletes and other performers, though maybe high functioning, are challenged by the pull of past experiences, the demands of internal and external experience, expectations for internal experience from their performance culture (we all should be *mentally tough*), and anticipated future expectation of success or failure. Such pressures can lead to mindless responses before, during, and after a performance, which, at worst, can lead to choking, quitting, and a stifled ability to learn and improve.

Even with the burgeoning, or perhaps explosion, of focus on mindfulness in general research, clinical practice, and the mass media, there is a dearth of nuanced understanding of how to match mindfulness interventions for performances purposes. Moreover, it is a mistake to assume that all mindfulness training is beneficial or that it will lead to similar outcomes simply because it's named "mindfulness training." There is much for researchers and mindfulness innovators to do in the quest to offer information that can best help practitioners skillfully apply the tenants and practices of mindfulness within fast-paced, high-demand environments, from sport and music to the dance world. For many performers there sometimes is a great need for changed relationship to unhelpful, intense emotions, ranging from fear to boredom. There remains a great need to better understand how best to inspire the wisdom of the sages to the twenty-first-century athlete, musician, actor, dancer, and even the practitioners themselves (from mediation teacher to mindfulness-based clinical psychologist).

REFERENCES

Aherne, C., Moran, A. P., and Lonsdale, C. (2011). The effect of mindfulness training on athletes' flow: An initial investigation. *Sport Psychologist*, 25, 177–189.

Baer, R. A. (2003). Mindfulness training as a clinical intervention: A conceptual and empirical review. *Clinical Psychology: Science and Practice*, 10(2), 125–143. doi: 10.1093/clipsy/bpg015

Baltzell, A. L., Caraballo, N., Chipman, K., and Hayden, L. (2014). A qualitative study of the Mindfulness Meditation Training for Sport (MMTS): Division I female soccer players' experience. *Journal of Clinical Sport Psychology*, 8, 221–244. doi: http://dx.doi.org/10.1123/jcsp.2014-0030

Baltzell, A. L., and LoVerme-Ahktar, V. (2014). Mindfulness Meditation Training for Sport (MMTS) intervention: Impact of MMTS with Division I female athletes. *Journal of Happiness and Well-Being*, 2(2), 160–173.

Bandura, A. (1997). *Self-efficacy: The exercise of control.* New York, NY: Freeman.

Bernier, M., Thienot, E., Codron, R., and Fournier, J. F. (2009). Mindfulness and acceptance approaches in sport performance. *Journal of Clinical Sport Psychology*, 25(4), 320–333.

Coyle, D. (2009). *The talent code: Greatness isn't born. It's grown. Here's how.* New York, NY: Bantam.

Csikszentmihalyi, M. (1975). *Beyond boredom and anxiety.* San Francisco, CA: Jossey-Bass.

　　(1990). *Flow: The psychology of optimal experience.* New York, NY: Harper & Row.

De Petrillo, L., Kaufman, K., Glass, C., and Arnkoff, D. (2009). Mindfulness for long-distance runners: An open trial using Mindful Sport Performance Enhancement (MSPE). *Journal of Clinical Sport Psychology*, 4, 357–376.

Ericsson, K. A., Krampe, R. T., and Tesch-Romer, C. (1993). The role of deliberate practice in the acquisition of expert performance. *Psychological Review*, 100(3), 363–406. doi: 10.1037/0033-295X.100.3.363

Fresco, D. M., Moore, M. T., van Dulmen, M., Segal, Z. V., Ma, S. H., Teasdale, J. D., and Williams, J. M. (2007). Initial psychometric properties of the experiences questionnaire: Validation of a self-report measure of decentering. *Behavior Therapy*, 38(3) 234–246. doi: 10.1016/j.beth.2006.08.003

Frewen, P., Evans, E., Maraj, N., Dozois, D., and Partridge, K. (2008). Letting go: Mindfulness and negative automatic thinking. *Cognitive Therapy Research*, 32(6), 758–774. doi: 10.1007/s10608-007-9142-1

Gardner, F. L., and Moore, Z. E. (2004). A Mindfulness-Acceptance-Commitment (MAC) based approach to athletic performance enhancement: Theoretical considerations. *Behavior Therapy*, 35(4), 707–723. doi: 10.1016/S0005-7894(04)80016-9

(2007). *The psychology of enhancing human performance: The Mindfulness-Acceptance-Commitment (MAC) approach.* New York, NY: Springer.

(2012). Mindfulness and acceptance models in sport psychology: A decade of basic and applied scientific advancements. *Canadian Psychology*, 53(4), 309–318. doi: 10.1037/a0030220

Hanson, R., and Mendius, R. (2009). *Buddha's brain: The practical neuroscience of happiness, love & wisdom.* Oakland, CA: New Harbinger.

Hayes, A. M., and Feldman, G. (2004). Clarifying the construct of mindfulness in the context of emotion regulation and the process of change in therapy. *Clinical Psychology: Science and Practice*, 11 (3), 255–262. doi: 10.1093/clipsy.bpho80

Hayes, S. C., Strosahl, K. D., Bunting, K., Twohig, M., and Wilson, K. G. (2004). What is acceptance and commitment therapy? In S. C. Hayes and K. D. Strosahl (Eds.), *A practical guide to acceptance and commitment therapy* (pp. 1–30). New York, NY: Springer.

Hodgins, H. S., and Adair, K. C. (2010). Attentional processes and meditation. *Consciousness and Cognition: An International Journal*, 19(4), 872–878. doi: 10.1016/j.concog.2010.04.002

Hölzel, B. K., Carmody J., Vangel, M., Congleton, C., Yerramsetti, S. M., Gard, T., and Lazar, S. W. (2011). Mindfulness practice leads to increases in regional brain gray matter density *Psychiatry Research: Neuroimaging*, 191(1), 36–43. doi: 10.1016/jpsychresns.2010.08.006

Jackson, S., and Csikszentmihalyi, M. (1999). *Flow in sports: The keys to optimal experiences and performances.* Champaign, IL: Human Kinetics.

John, S., Verma, S. K., and Khanna, G. L. (2011). The effect of mindfulness meditation on HPA-Axis in pre-competition stress in sports performance of elite shooters. *National Journal of Integrated Research in Medicine*, 2(3), 15–21.

Kabat-Zinn, J. (1990). *Full catastrophe living: Using the wisdom of your body and mind to face stress, pain and illness.* New York: Delacorte

(1994). *Wherever you go, there you are: Mindfulness meditation in everyday life.* New York, NY: Hyperion.

(2014, May). Keynote address presented at the MIT Rethinking Mindfulness Conference, Cambridge, MA.

Kabat-Zinn, J., Beall, B., and Rippe, J. (1985, June). *A systematic mental training program based on mindfulness meditation to optimize performance in collegiate and Olympic rowers.* Poster presented at the World Congress in Sport Psychology, Copenhagen, Denmark.

Kaufman, K. A., Glass, C. R., and Arnkoff, D. B. (2009). Evaluation of Mindful Sport Performance Enhancement (MSPE): A new approach to promote flow in athletes. *Journal of Clinical Sports Psychology, 4,* 334–356.

Kee, Y. H., and Wang, C. K. J. (2008). Relationships between mindfulness, flow dispositions and mental skills adoption: A cluster analytic approach. *Psychology of Sport and Exercise,* 9(4), 393–411. doi: 10.1016/j.psychsport.2007.07.001

Keng, S. L., Smoski, M. J., and Robins, C. J. (2011). Effects of mindfulness on psychological health: A review of empirical studies. *Clinical Psychology Review,* 31, 1041–1056. doi: 10.1016/j.cpr.2011.04.006

Kristeller, J. L., Baer, R. A., and Quillian-Wolever, R. (2006). Mindfulness-based approaches to eating disorders. In R. A. Baer (Ed.), *Mindfulness-based treatment approaches: Clinician's guide to evidence base and applications* (pp. 75–91). San Diego, CA: Elsevier Academic Press.

Langer, E. J. (1989) *Mindfulness.* Addison-Wesley/Addison Wesley Longman: Reading, MA

(2000). Mindful learning. *Current Directions in Psychological Science,* 9(6), 220–223.

Langer, E. J., Cohen, M., and Djikic, M. (2012). Mindfulness as a psychological attractor: The effect on children. *Journal of Applied Social Psychology,* 42(5), 1114–1122. doi: 10.1111/j.1559-1816.2011.00879.x

Langer, E. J., Russell, T., and Eisenkraft, N. (2009). Orchestral performance and the footprint of mindfulness. *Psychology of Music,* 37(2), 125–136. doi: 10.1177/0305735607086053

Lutkenhouse, J. M. (2007). The case of Jenny: A freshman collegiate athlete experiencing performance dysfunction. *Journal of Clinical Sport Psychology,* 1, 166–180.

Lyubomirsky, S., Sheldon, K., and Schkade, D. (2005). Pursuing happiness: The architecture of sustainable change. *Review of General Psychology,* 9 (2), 111–131.

Moore, A., and Malinowski, P. (2009). Meditation, mindfulness and cognitive flexibility. *Consciousness and Cognition,* 18(1),176–186. doi: 10.1016/j.concog.2008.12.008

Neff, K. D., and Germer, C. K. (2013). A pilot study and randomized controlled trial of the mindful self-compassion program. *Journal of Clinical Psychology,* 69(1), 28–44.

Peterson, C., Ruch, W., Beermann, U., Park, N., and Seligman, M. E. P. (2007). Strengths of character, orientations to happiness, and life satisfaction.

Journal of Positive Psychology, July 2007; 2(3): 149–156. doi: 10.1080/17439760701228938

Pineau, T. R., Glass, C. R., and Kaufman, K. A. (2014). Mindfulness in sport performance. In A. Ie, C. T. Ngnoumen, and E. J. Langer (Eds.), *The Wiley Blackwell handbook of mindfulness* (Vol. II, pp. 1004–1033). Chichester, UK: John Wiley & Sons.

Scharmer, O. (2014, July 12). Beijing, Brazil, 7–1: Awareness shift in soccer, society. Retrieved from www.huffingtonpost.com/otto-scharmer/beijing-brazil-7-1-world-cup_b_5579976.html

Schwanhausser, L. (2009). Application of the Mindfulness-Acceptance-Commitment (MAC) protocol with an adolescent springboard diver: The case of Steve. *Journal of Clinical Sport Psychology,* 3, 377–395.

Sedlmeier, P., Eberth, J., Schwarz, M., Zimmermann, D., Haarig, F., Jaeger, S., and Kunze, S. (2012). The psychological effects of meditation: A meta-analysis. *Psychological Bulletin,* 138, (6), 1139–1171.

Siegel, R. D. (2010). *The mindful solution: Everyday practices for everyday problems.* New York, NY: Guilford Press.

Stankovic, D. & Baltzell, A.L. (in preparation). *Mindfulness meditation in sport: Improved sport performance of masters tennis players.*

Index